CONSTRUCTING
LITERACIES

A Harcourt Reader for College Writers

CONSTRUCTING LITERACIES

A Harcourt Reader for College Writers

SUSAN BELASCO
University of Nebraska

HEINLE & HEINLE

THOMSON LEARNING

Australia Canada Mexico Singapore Spain United Kingdom United States

HEINLE & HEINLE

THOMSON LEARNING

Constructing Literacies
A Harcourt Reader for College Writers
Susan Belasco

Publisher: Earl McPeek
Acquisitions Editor: Julie McBurney
Market Strategist: John Meyers
Developmental Editor: Camille Adkins
Project Editor: Rebecca Dodson
Art Director: Van Mua
Production Manager: Lois West

Cover credit: "Fog Horns" by Arthur Dove

Printed in the United States of America

2 3 4 6 7 8 9 10 06 05 04 03 02

For more information contact Heinle & Heinle, 25 Thomson Place, Boston, MA 02210 USA, or you can visit our Internet site at http://www.heinle.com

For permission to use material from this text or product contact us:

Tel:	1-800-730-2214
Fax:	1-800-730-2215
Web:	www.thomsonrights.com

ISBN: 0-15-507474-1

Library of Congress Catalog Card Number:
26095

FOR THE JOHNSON BOYS

Preface For Instructors

ABOUT *CONSTRUCTING LITERACIES: A HARCOURT READER FOR COLLEGE WRITERS*

Several years ago, a student came into my office at the community college where I was teaching to meet with me about an essay she had written for her first-year English class. The shy young woman who had grown up in a small central Texas town was struggling in my class for reasons that did not seem to have much to do with her obvious intellectual ability. As we talked about the problems she was having in clarifying the thesis of her essay, she suddenly exclaimed: "The real problem I'm having is that I know why I came to college—my parents said I had to come—but I don't know what I'm supposed to do now that I'm here." The idea for this book, *Constructing Literacies: A Harcourt Reader for College Writers*, began on that day. Throughout my teaching career—at a large community college, a small private liberal arts college, a large state university, and a private research-oriented university—I have encountered first-year students with the same perplexed concern about their educations.

Designed for students in college writing courses and first-year seminars, *Constructing Literacies* is a collection of readings, reviews, and reports on the nature, purpose, and significance of formal education in America today. The thematic focus is on cultures of learning—the multiple literacies that students need not only for negotiating the world of higher education but also for fully participating in an increasingly diverse world. The lively and engaging readings collected here invite students to consider some fundamental questions about their own immediate experience as college students: Why am I here? What is expected of me? What am I supposed to learn? What can I expect from college?

Building on the combination of ideas, skills, attitudes, and values that students bring to college, the readings challenge students to consider and revise their preconceptions as they gain curricular and extracurricular experience in the academic world. The readings are collected from a variety of sources: contemporary memoirs and historical autobiographies, popular magazines and

vii

newspapers, government reports and foundation surveys, academic journals and current books on higher education. The writers whose works are anthologized represent many facets of American society—some are recent college graduates, some are journalists, some are college professors, and some are novelists and poets. While some of the readings provide a historical perspective on American education, most of the readings appeared in the last twenty years and reflect contemporary concerns and issues. A few have been published on the Internet and are presented here in print for the first time. There are selections by both men and women, and the writers come from a variety of ethnic, racial, educational, and religious backgrounds. The readings have been selected for their accessibility and for the ways in which they invite readers—especially students—to connect their own experiences with those of the writer.

THE PLAN OF *CONSTRUCTING LITERACIES: A HARCOURT READER FOR COLLEGE WRITERS*

As Mike Rose first suggested in *Lives on the Boundary*, students have to learn how to "enter the conversation" of the academic world in order to succeed in college. Every student arrives at a campus with a history of educational experience and with practice in the literacy skills expected within the communities of home and school. Many students find that while they are skilled in those literacies and have been educated in a variety of ways, college is not one but many new communities and requires expanded sets of reading, writing, speaking, listening, and behavioral skills. This is especially important as colleges and universities enroll increasingly diverse student populations, and all students must learn to cope with experiences that may be very different from those in their homes and schools. Cultural diversity is, therefore, at the heart of this text. The readings in *Literacies* help students enter the many conversations on their campuses through reading, thinking, and writing about the various literacies of the academic world.

Constructing Literacies is divided into five sections of readings, moving from personal narratives to increasingly the complex genres of research reports, articles, and essays:

*Section I: Literacy narratives by a variety of writers about their individual relationships with language and the impact of informal and formal education on the development of their literacy.

*Section II: Efforts to define what sets of skills and knowledge students should learn in college and what the various purposes of an education should be.

*Section III: Explorations of the differing notions of the relationship between the cultural pluralism of American society and the college curriculum.

*Section IV: Commentaries on the impact of computers and new technology offering perspectives on how "cyberliteracy" is changing our conceptions of reading, writing, and knowing.

*Section V: Investigations into how students can shape their own educations through curricular and extracurricular activities—the multiple literacies within a single campus.

TEACHING STRATEGIES

Constructing Literacies is informed throughout by a pedagogy based on three key assumptions.

First, all writers write best when they are engaged by and involved in their tasks. By focusing on the central issues of culture, literacies, and education, the collection encourages students to consider their past experiences in secondary school and current experiences in college. Through their reading, they are invited to join a central debate in contemporary America about the place and purpose of higher education. The essays, articles, and reports invite students to acknowledge their own stake in the debate and assist them in taking part as informed participants.

Second, writing is best undertaken as a process with many opportunities for discussion of ideas, writing, and revising drafts, consulting with peers and instructors, and producing well-edited final drafts. Writing as a process is integrated into this text in two ways. The general Introduction to *Constructing Literacies* provides commentary and suggestions on how students might proceed with essay assignments. Within the sections themselves, each reading is prefaced by a headnote that explains the immediate context of the reading and offers information about the initial publication and the author. The *Questions for Reading,* given at the end of each headnote, are designed to help students prepare for reading the selection by considering how the title may or may not contribute to an understanding of the text, by defining terms that may be unfamiliar, or by offering a suggestion about something in a student's own experience that may help connect the reading more concretely. Each reading is followed by classroom-tested *Questions for Reaction and Discussion, Writing,* and *Further Explorations,* designed to stimulate conversations, foster e-mail exchanges, facilitate classroom and electronic discussions, and prompt ideas for writing drafts and final essays. Finally, a list of print and electronic resources is given at the end of the text to guide students in further investigation. Reading and writing are related activities; throughout the collection students are encouraged to read carefully, to test assumptions and preconceptions, and to respond critically to the works they are reading.

Third, students need to learn how to access and use sources of information to be effective readers and writers in the academic world. Although students have always needed guidance and assistance in effectively using sources of information for their writing, electronic resources offer new challenges for evaluating and using information. Throughout *Constructing Literacies*, suggestions are offered for locating and using both electronic and print resources, along with specific suggestions for navigating databases and specific Web sites. The general Introduction provides advice to instructors and students on evaluating resources. The *List of Additional Readings and Resources* at the end of the text includes a list of both guides, available in print and on the Internet.

INSTRUCTOR'S MANUAL

The Instructor's Manual accompanying *Constructing Literacies: A Harcourt Reader for College Writers* includes suggestions for using the text in writing courses, first-year seminars, and college orientation courses, sample quarter and semester syllabi, as well as discussions of the specific readings and suggestions for developing the reading, writing, and thinking activities outlined in the text. A section for writing program administrators includes advice for using this text in programs with graduate teaching assistants and programs that include adjuncts and faculty members from a variety of different departments. In addition, a list of print and Internet resources is provided for instructors.

WEB SITE

An accompanying Web site for *Constructing Literacies: A Harcourt Reader for College Writers* is maintained at the Harcourt College main Web site. The site includes suggestions for teaching, a bulletin board for teachers and students, information for writing program administrators, sample syllabi, updated hot links to online resources of information, and additional advice about readings to use in the classroom.

Acknowledgments

Throughout my career as a teacher of writing and literature, I have been helped enormously by a variety of outstanding educators, students, and friends. I have been fortunate to have had excellent training in rhetoric and composition from Gwendolyn Gong, formerly of Texas A&M University; Tim Crucius, Southern Methodist University; Erika Lindemann, the University of North Carolina, Chapel Hill; and Art Young, Clemson University. In significant ways, this text has been shaped by shared experiences with several of my valued colleagues at the colleges and universities where I have taught. I am especially thankful to Lissette Carpenter, formerly of McLennan Community College, for her many years of firm friendship and warm support. I also want to thank Cheryl Bohde, McLennan Community College; Judy Francis and Randy Waller, Baylor University; Bethany Reynders, Brian Rosenberg, and Lloyd Michaels, of Allegheny College; Douglas Lanier, the University of New Hampshire; Carl Selkin, Alfred Bendixen, Virginia Crane, and Marilyn Elkins, of California State University, Los Angeles; and Rebecca Damron and James G. Watson of the University of Tulsa. I am grateful to the graduate teaching assistants at the University of Tulsa, with whom I have worked closely in thinking about the difficult issues of teaching first-year students, especially T. Allen Culpepper (now of Rogers State University). Other current and former students at Tulsa who have provided good conversation and stimulating discussion include David Farley, Chris Kelsey, Sue Hosterman, Elin Dowdican, Shirley Sutliff, John Bury, Allen Bauman, Nancy Bunker, Nainsi Houston, Cristina Dascalu, Mike Gorman, Joann Allen, Maureen Curtin (now of SUNY, Oswego), and Blake Westerlund (now of the University of Wisconsin, Eau Clare). I deeply appreciate the many colleagues who reviewed and commented on this text in varying stages of preparation:

Carol Lea Clark, University of Texas at El Paso
Elizabeth Curtin, Salisbury State University
Robert Donahoo, Sam Houston State University
Jane Dugan, Cleveland State University

Deborah H. Holdstein, Governors State University

Michael A. Miller, Longview Community College

Debbie Jay Williams, Abilene Christian University

My colleagues and editors at Harcourt College Publishers, Felix Frazier, Ben Whitney, Julie McBurney, and Camille Adkins, are models of professionalism and offered me excellent guidance throughout the development of this text.

Pamela Stockton, my friend from my own undergraduate days, has been listening to me and offering sound advice—both legal and academic—for nearly thirty years. My mother, Peggy Bell Belasco, taught me early lessons about the many cultures of a university when she bravely completed her own undergraduate education as one of the first nontraditional students at Louisiana State University at New Orleans (now the University of New Orleans) in the mid-1960s. She and my siblings, Janet Belasco Jenkins and Bill Belasco, have always been enthusiastic supporters of my projects. The memory of my father, Eugene J. Belasco, is an ongoing source of inspiration and encouragement.

I have saved the best for last. My greatest debts are to my husband, Linck Johnson, and my stepson, Max Johnson. They have been my first and most vital audience, providing lively discussion and spirited debate about educational issues both great and small. This book is dedicated to them—the Johnson boys—with love and laughter.

CONTENTS
GENERAL INTRODUCTION

III LITERACIES FOR A DIVERSE WORLD

IV CYBERLITERACY

V AN EDUCATION OF ONE'S OWN

GENERAL INTRODUCTION

STUDENTS AND CONSTRUCTING LITERACIES: A HARCOURT READER FOR COLLEGE WRITERS

At the beginning of his book *Lives on the Boundary*, Mike Rose describes the campus where he teaches, the University of California at Los Angeles:

> It hits you most forcefully at lunchtime: the affluence of the place, the attention to dress and carriage, but the size, too—vast and impersonal, a labyrinth of corridors and classrooms and libraries; you're also struck by the wild intersection of cultures, spectacular diversity, compressed by a thousand social forces. . . . Students are rushing to food lines or dormitories or sororities, running for elevators or taking stairs two at a time. Others "blow it off" and relax, mingling in twos and threes. Fifties fashion is everywhere: baggy pants, thin ties, crew cuts, retro ponytails—but so are incipient Yuppiedom and cautious punk, and this month's incarnation of the *nuevo wavo*. Palm trees sway on the backs of countless cotton shirts. A fellow who looks Pakistani zooms by on a skateboard. A Korean boy whose accent is still very strong introduces himself as Skip. Two Middle Eastern girls walk by in miniskirts and heels.

While your campus may not be as large or as culturally diverse as UCLA, take a moment at your next opportunity to sit in a central location and observe your own campus at lunchtime. How would you describe your campus scene? Who are your fellow students? Why are they attending this college? Why are *you* attending this college? What do you want to learn during your life as a college student? What does an education mean to you?

Constructing Literacies: A Harcourt Reader for College Writers is a collection of readings, reviews, and reports on the nature, purpose, and significance of education in America today designed to serve as a means for you to develop the thinking, reading, and writing skills you will need for success in college. The thematic focus of the book is on the many cultures that shape what and how we learn—the multiple literacies that students need not only for negotiating the world of college but also for participating in the increasingly diverse global environment—the larger world in which we live, work, and participate as citizens. If you are accustomed to thinking about "literacy" as primarily functional—the technical ability to read and write—my emphasis on litera*cies* in the plural may

I

surprise you. In this text, "literacies" means the many different sets of reading, writing, thinking, listening, and behavioral skills that make up the numerous communities of the academic world and beyond. In other words, there are multiple literacies that students must learn to negotiate in order to succeed in college and to participate fully in the world. Think of dodging the Pakistani student on the skateboard, meeting the Korean student named Skip, chatting with the Middle Eastern women in miniskirts, or, for that matter, talking with Professor Mike Rose in his office at UCLA. What are the implications of these encounters for you as a college student? What experiences can you draw on to negotiate these encounters? What do you have to learn from these encounters? What do these encounters have to do with your own college education?

The readings in *Constructing Literacies* invite you, as a college student, to explore issues of immediate concern to you: the process through which individuals in our society achieve full membership in the communities of home, school, and work; the myriad purposes of a college education, what a college curriculum reflects about the cultural diversity of America; how new technologies are altering our assumptions about higher education; and what responsibilities students have in developing their own educational goals. These are the various literacies that you will investigate throughout the readings in this text.

ENTERING THE CONVERSATIONS OF THE ACADEMIC WORLD

All college students enter a campus with long experience in schooling—both formal and informal. While the majority of American students have attended public, coeducational secondary schools, students come from many different educational backgrounds—at private schools, boarding schools, single-sex schools, charter schools, church or synagogue schools, and even home schools. Whatever your own experience has been, you know a great deal about your own educational background as an elementary and secondary school student. You know the curriculum you have followed and the subjects you have taken. You have a sense of the skills you have acquired and those that need more practice. You know a great deal about what it takes for a teacher to be successful or unsuccessful, and you know something about the classrooms that provide opportunities for learning and those that don't. You know at least a little about your own abilities and interests. You also know a great deal about what it means to succeed academically; you wouldn't be a college student now if you had not earned the appropriate grades and scored sufficiently high on standardized tests to meet admissions requirements. The readings in this book invite you to build on your own precollege background as you contemplate new experiences in higher education and as you enter the many conversations of the academic world.

Entering the conversation of the academic world requires learning new sets of literacy skills. For some students—like Mary Antin and Richard Rodriguez, whose literacy narratives are selections in this collection—learning a new set of literacy skills literally means learning a second language. But native speakers of English don't necessarily have an edge on non-native speakers of English when it comes to negotiating the academic world. The literacy skills necessary for success in American colleges require a flexible, inquiring mind as well as an ability to think critically and analytically—skills over and beyond proficiency in the English language. These skills are complex and not achieved in a single semester or in a single course. How could they be? There are a variety of literacies for college students to learn. For most students, the first encounter with an academic literacy is simply learning to grasp the traditions and culture of a particular college campus. Think of your initial experience on your campus. How did you feel when you arrived on the campus for the first time? Did you know where to go? Did you talk with anyone? Did you get lost or confused? On the simplest level, what the building devoted to student activities (the Student Union or Student Center) is called on your campus often signals the first vocabulary words in developing this new literacy. There are codes of conduct to learn (like what to call a professor) and ways of dressing (think of Mike Rose's allusion to "cautious punk").

But learning to look, talk, and act like a student at your college is simply a first step in the process of negotiating academic literacies. Students soon realize that academic disciplines have their own sets of language practices and literacy requirements. These skills are much more difficult to acquire and maintain than getting a grip on the customs and rituals of an individual college campus. A good first step is to *understand* that your task as a college student involves learning new sets of skills in reading, writing, listening, speaking, and behavior. As you read the articles by E. D. Hirsch, Mark Edmundson, Carlos Cortés, and Martha Nussbaum, and others in this text, you will see how different writers define those sets of skills. And as Lisa Schmeiser suggests in "Do Geeks Need to Go to College?" navigating the various literacies of the academic world can prepare you for the wider literacies of the world.

CRITICAL READING AND CRITICAL THINKING

All students arrive at a college campus with a set of rudimentary reading skills in place: you know how to read for information, for access to new ideas, for instructions on how to do or make something, for directions on where to go, and for pleasure and entertainment. Reading—and thinking about what you read—in college courses requires considerably more sophisticated skills. You will need to read to discover relationships between your own ideas and those of others, to develop a body of information about topics that you can discuss inside and outside of the classroom, and to understand difficult concepts, often on your own. These skills are essential to developing the writing skills that you will need to succeed in your college courses. In this text, the selections have been chosen for their lively, provocative nature, and you are invited to read them and to think carefully about them. In this way, you can begin to learn the essential skills of critical reading and critical thinking that are fundamental to all academic disciplines and will also enhance all of the reading that you do in your life.

Critical reading involves two strategies.

First, students are encouraged to read "with" the writer. Follow the argument and the evidence that the writer offers and make sure that you understand the terms, definitions, and thesis of the selection at hand. Without a thorough familiarity with the selection you have been assigned, you won't be able to weigh the comments of the writer or claim a right to participate in a discussion. If it helps you to make notes as you read or mark up the text, you should do so. Many college students develop the habit of summarizing what they read by making notes to themselves in the margins of the text or by keeping reading notes about each selection in a notebook or in a file on a computer. Such recording of impressions and ideas helps students absorb the ideas of the writer and provides good notes for easy reference during class discussions or as materials to draw on for writing assignments related to the reading.

Second, students are encouraged to read "against" the writer. Reading "against" the writer is often difficult, especially if you agree with the opinion that the writer has expressed. Meeting the challenge of reading against the writer, however, is crucial to critical reading. Use the selections in this text to test your preconceptions and assumptions. Try constructing arguments against what the writer has written, even if you agree with her or him. Make notes to yourself about what evidence you find convincing and what you don't. Write questions in the margins of the reading or in your reading notes. In the process, you may find yourself disagreeing with what you thought you agreed with. At the same time, even if you finally do agree, you may find additional evidence that would strengthen your own position. In any case, you will know that you have tested the argument thoroughly.

Critical thinking is closely related to critical reading. In this textbook, "critical thinking" is used to mean the abilities to consider, analyze, and challenge what you see, hear, and read. These are difficult skills and require considerable practice. Students are encouraged to question the opinions they read in this text as well as the opinions offered in class discussions. One reason that students often find critical thinking difficult is that it may seem impolite or even combative to question the opinions of others. While you certainly do not want to offend a classmate or your instructor, it is important to remember that fruitful discussion depends on airing conflicting views and finding appropriate ways to resolve the contradictions that inevitably emerge in a serious discussion. Furthermore, the issues about education raised by the writers in this text are at the heart of your immediate experience as a college student. You will naturally have strong responses, both positive and negative. Questioning what you read and the comments of others on these issues offers a rich context for critical thinking.

THE ARRANGEMENT OF THE SELECTIONS IN THIS TEXT

The structure of *Constructing Literacies* is designed to help you develop the skills of critical reading and thinking that will promote your active engagement through discussion and writing about the major issues facing American higher education. Beginning with narratives of personal experience with language and literacy, the sections include a variety of genres, including essays, research reports, articles from newspapers and popular magazines, articles from Internet sites, articles from academic journals, chapters from books, and in one case, a speech.

SECTION I: LITERACY NARRATIVES

The selections in this section are literacy narratives by a variety of writers describing how different people, in both formal and informal educational situations, achieved an awareness of the power of language, despite barriers of race, class, poverty, gender, physical impairment, and sometimes even physical danger. This section begins with Mike Rose's account of his experience of being erroneously placed in the vocational track of his high school and the numbing mind-set he encountered. Some of the other voices represented here are historical ones, such as Frederick Douglass, who learned to read despite his experience as a slave in antebellum America; other narratives describe the experiences of a native American who was sent to an "assimilation school" and those of Malcolm X, who learned to read in prison. The section concludes with George Steiner's memoir of his childhood as a Jew in Nazi Germany. The purpose of this section is to permit you to read about a wide variety of literacy and schooling experiences, thereby helping you consider your own literacy development and assumptions about the purposes of education.

SECTION II: THE PURPOSE OF A COLLEGE EDUCATION

Selections in this section include efforts to define what sets of skills and knowledge students should learn in college and what the various purposes of an education should be. The section begins with the *Reports on the Course of Yale College* in 1828, which reveals a surprisingly spirited debate on what students of the 1828s were expected to learn in college. One reading is a research report on public perceptions of the importance of the liberal arts by a college president, Richard Hersh. Other readings examine such issues as how universities define their purposes, what constitutes "general education," what students think constitutes a "liberal arts" education, and how former students, at least at one college, fought to maintain a traditional "core" curriculum. The section concludes with an account of the debate about whether a college education should be "professional" or "liberal" in nature, an article from the Internet magazine *Salon* about whether "geeks" need to go to college, and an essay on how both students and faculty members "invent" their universities.

SECTION III: LITERACIES FOR A DIVERSE WORLD

Readings in this section are explorations of the differing notions of the relationship between the cultural pluralism of American society and the college curriculum. The section begins with an extract from E. D. Hirsch's *Cultural Literacy*, a book that moved the debate about what constitutes essential cultural knowledge for students out of school and university curriculum committees and into public and political arenas. In Hirsch's view, "cultural literacy" means the basic information needed to thrive in the modern world. In the ten years since the appearance of this book, a number of responses have appeared, such as those of Henry Louis Gates, Clara Sue Kidwell, Carlos Cortés and others represented here. A range of viewpoints on the definition of cultural literacy is presented here, in the context of the changing demographics of American society.

SECTION IV: CYBERLITERACY

The purpose of this section is to provide a series of commentaries on the impact of computers and new technology that offer perspectives on what I'm calling cyberliteracy and how it is changing our conceptions of reading, writing, and knowing. Readings (from both print and electronic sources) include a chapter from Janet H. Murray's book *Hamlet on the Holodeck* about how hypertext alters narrative. Other writers offer reflections on the ways in which new technologies and the Internet are changing our educational lives and challenging assumptions about literacy (especially about the role of the printed book), how men and women respond to computer technology, the ways in which we learn, and how educational institutions are coping with changes. Ranging from some accessible theoretical considerations to some distinctly pragmatic essays such as how universities go about providing computer access to large student bodies and how to control plagiarism online, the purpose of this section is to help students consider the ways in which electronic technology at once contributes to and shapes contemporary college experience.

SECTION V: AN EDUCATION OF ONE'S OWN

The final section offers investigations into how students can shape their own educations through both the curriculum and extracurricular activities. Beginning with an extensive survey of freshman attitudes, opinions, and demographic data, this section is designed to help students reflect critically about their own educations. Readings are from a variety of sources: an account of one university's efforts to change the social climate on campus; a college president's strong statement about the negative effects of "big-time" college sports on student athletes; sections from a controversial American Association of University Women report on how women students are short-changed; a lawyer's assessment of how a college major contributes to a career path; and a professor's thoughtful meditation on how a classroom both restricts and fosters student learning.

READING AND DISCUSSING THE SELECTIONS IN THIS TEXT

Each of the five sections begins with a short introduction. The introduction provides some contextual information about the topic of the section as well as a set of questions that students can use for doing some preliminary thinking about the readings. The questions are intended to guide but not direct your thinking.

Each reading selection is introduced by a headnote, which provides contextual background about the writer, information about where the article, report, or essay was originally published, and suggestions on how the reading relates to others in the section. The headnote is followed by a short list of *Questions for Reading*, devised to help you make connections between your own experience and what you are about to read. The *Questions for Reading* ask you to think about the title of the selection, prompt you to look up a term or two that might be unfamiliar, encourage you to remember something from your own experience that might help you connect the reading to your own life, or suggest an idea or two to keep in mind as you read.

Following each reading are three sets of questions.

The *Questions for Reaction and Discussion* are intended to prompt electronic or classroom discussion about the text. Some of the questions are designed to ensure that you have closely read and understood the text; in some cases, questions will refer you to particular paragraphs and ask about your comprehension of a point that the writer is making. Some questions ask you to consider the rhetorical power of the essay—the structure, organization, style, tone, and thesis. Other questions are more open-ended and are intended to provoke commentary and response about what you have read.

The *Questions for Writing* suggest possible writing assignments based on the readings. In many questions, you are invited to draw on your own experiences as well as your reading in order to construct a response to a particular selection. Sometimes questions ask you to consider the reading in relation to others in the textbook. In each case, the *Questions for Writing* are intended as departure points for writing assignments. Your instructor may wish to modify and expand the questions, in accordance with the goals of the course.

The *Questions for Further Exploration* invite students to move beyond the readings in the text and investigate both print and online resources available on a particular topic. The questions often advise you about using sources for further information on a topic connected with the reading. Often students are referred to specific Web sites. For example, following the selection from Helen Keller's autobiography, a question refers students to the Deaf World Web, which provides resources and information about education for the hearing impaired; following the selection from Sven Birkerts's book, *The Gutenberg Elegies*, students are referred to an online conference hosted by the *Atlantic Monthly Online*, which includes an interview with Birkerts; and following an essay by Kathleen Green, "Traditional Degrees, Nontraditional Jobs: A Degree Is Not a Life Sentence," you are encouraged to visit the United States Department of Labor Web site to read the current employment outlook for careers you might be considering. As with the *Questions for Writing*, your instructor may modify and revise these according to the goals of the course.

Following each section is a list of *Suggestions for Further Reading, Thinking, and Writing*. Designed to connect readings and provide students a chance to compare and contrast the differing viewpoints they have read within a section, the questions sometimes suggest writing activities, but they also suggest group and individual projects of a variety of kinds.

EVALUATING AND USING PRINT AND ONLINE RESOURCES

At the end of *Constructing Literacies* is a list of print and online resources for further information, arranged according to the topics of this book. These are included to provide suggestions for additional reading and writing. Throughout the sections, the *Questions for Writing*, the *Questions for Further Exploration*, and the *Suggestions for Further Reading, Thinking, and Writing* encourage you to investigate other resources beyond those selected for inclusion in this text. While you may not always use other sources in the papers that you write for the class in which you are using this text, academic writing almost always involves situating yourself in the midst of an ongoing conversation. It's very important to know how to find out about those conversations and to give appropriate credit to the other participants.

A wide variety of handbooks are available that will help you find and locate information and teach you how to document it accurately. Grammar handbooks always have sections on using outside resources, and there are a number of special handbooks such as the *MLA Guide* or the *Chicago Manual of Style*. In addition, many handbooks are now available online; some of the best are listed in *List of Additional Readings and Resources* at the end of *Constructing Literacies*. Finally, the main page or the library page of your campus Web site may direct you to databases, Internet resources, and even online handbooks.

The Internet, while an increasingly useful tool for accessing information and conducting research, presents some special problems for students. Every computer user has had the experience of typing in a phrase in a search engine and finding thousands of possibly relevant and possibly irrelevant resources. The latest statistics show that over 320 million Web pages now exist on the Internet, and more are added every hour. The vastness of the electronic world is mind-boggling, and educators have been struggling for some time now to help students find ways to find and evaluate resources.

The best way to begin to learn how to find information on the Internet is on your own campus. Visit your campus Web site and learn what resources are available online; sometimes these are available through the library homepage and sometimes through the offices of information technology or academic computing. Find out whether your campus provides orientation classes on electronic resources; these are definitely sessions to attend. Learning how to use your campus Web site can save you hours of work; for example, many campuses provide direct links to *Education Abstracts*, the *Reader's Guide to Periodical Literature*, and specific periodicals such as *The New York Times*. In a matter of seconds, you can access recent articles on the influence on American higher education by Paulo Friere, an educational reformer whose work is included in this textbook.

Finding resources, however, is only one part of the challenge that students face on the Internet. Evaluating what you find can be very complicated. It has always been important to evaluate print resources carefully, but the task is somewhat easier there because college and university libraries are careful about purchases. Students can be generally certain that the standards of reliability and relevance have been checked long before a book or periodical is placed on a shelf. There are no such screening procedures for the Internet, and virtually anyone can create a Web site. Typing "Walt Whitman" into the Infoseek search engine is as likely to bring up an anonymous high school student's overly broad and poorly proofread term paper on "Walt Whitman's Life and Work" as it is to bring up the Walt Whitman Hypertext Archive project of the Institute for Advanced Technology in the Humanities at the University of Virginia. Because of its democratic, nonhierarchical nature, the Internet creates the impression that every site is of equal value and importance. Many Web sites are full of erroneous and misleading information. Students must be especially careful to learn how to evaluate what they see on a site.

There are several excellent guides designed to help both students and instructors, and these are listed in the *List of Additional Readings and Resources* at the end of this textbook. Your college or university may have produced its own guide through the library or information technology homepage. Generally speaking, however, students should ask the following questions about the authority, purpose, content, bias, currency, organization, and reliability of a Web site:

- Who is the author or creator of the site?
- What information is provided about the author's background?
- Is there a sponsoring organization, institution, agency or business with an established reputation of good work behind this site?
- What is the purpose of the site? Is it clearly stated?

- How is the content of the site reviewed and edited?
- Is the text of the site well written and free of errors in spelling, punctuation, and usage?
- Are there working links to other sites?
- Is there a political, social, or personal agenda represented in the site? What is it?
- Is contact information provided for users with questions?
- Have permissions and copyright declarations been listed?
- Is there a site map?
- Is the site easy to use?
- How frequently is the site updated?

Finally, it is always important, whether you are evaluating a print or an electronic resource, to keep your skills of critical reading firmly in play. Don't assume that just because a source has been published in a book or on the Internet that the source is authoritative.

WRITING, REWRITING, AND EDITING

Anyone who writes—in school, on the job, or as a full-time occupation—will tell you that writers write best when they are engaged and involved in their topics. The lively and engaging readings collected in *Constructing Literacies* invite you to consider some fundamental questions about your own current experience as a college student: What is expected of me? What am I supposed to learn? What can I expect from college? How am I being taught? By focusing on the topic of education, *Constructing Literacies* provides topics for thinking, reading, and writing of immediate concern to you.

Developing good writing skills is essential to you as a student, and these skills are directly connected with your ability to think and read critically. An underlying assumption in this textbook is that writing is a *recursive* process; that is, the act of writing does not generally occur in a simple three-step sequence in which a student prewrites, writes, and revises. Rather, the approach to writing in this text is that writing occurs through a series of steps that may be continuously repeated as necessary. For instance, writers often discover a new direction in the process of revising an essay and may return to the earlier stage of prewriting and reading in order to think over the new idea or direction. How would you describe the process of composition that you currently use? What problems do you often encounter in writing an assignment for a class? What kinds of writing instruction did you have in your secondary-school experience? As you consider the suggestions about the writing process given in the next pages, keep your past experiences in mind and think about the ways in which you might wish to learn new strategies and modify old ones.

DEFINITIONS TO KEEP IN MIND

A number of terms are used in *Constructing Literacies* to describe the various genres of the reading selections themselves and are also used in the suggested writing assignments. You may want to raise these questions about these terms in class and ask your fellow students and your instructor about a collective sense of the following:

Argument—a set of reasons and evidence in support of a thesis, designed to persuade readers to accept the writer's position.

Article—a generally formal statement of a writer's opinion, observations, and research findings, often published in a periodical, such as a magazine, newspaper or journal.

Discussion List—an electronic bulletin board to which anyone with an e-mail account can post questions or comments and receive responses.

E-mail—electronic exchanges that are usually informal and conversational that can be sent to an individual, a group of students, an entire class, a campus, or anyone on the Internet.

Essay—an analytical, reflective, or interpretive composition that reflects the writer's outlook; generally an essay is less formal than an article.

Hypertext—a composition that is accessible electronically with links to related items, including images, other texts, and sounds.

Journal—a periodical publication, generally published by a scholarly or professional organization or association.

Letter to an editor—a short statement of opinion addressed to the editor of a periodical, generally in response to an item published in the periodical or of general interest to the audience of the periodical.

Listserv—an electronic bulletin board for e-mail exchange, closed to all except subscribers belonging to a particular group, class, or organization.

Magazine—a periodical publication published for a general audience of nonspecialist readers.

Position paper—a formal statement of the writer's attitude or stand on a particular topic, which includes reasons.

Speech—a persuasive, analytic, or interpretative composition that is designed primarily to be presented to an audience.

Summary—the presentation of the substance and general ideas of another's work in a condensed and brief form.

Report—a summary of an investigation, which often includes conclusions reached and/or recommendations for action.

Review—a brief summary of the work of another, which includes an evaluation or assessment of that work.

PREWRITING STRATEGIES

In *Constructing Literacies*, the questions in the introductions to each section and the *Questions for Reading* and the *Questions for Reaction and Discussion* accompanying each individual selection are intended to provide a stimulus for beginning the work of thinking through a topic for a writing assignment. Making notes in response to the questions for reading, writing summaries, marginal comments, and questions of your own in your text, as well as participating fully in electronic and classroom discussions are important ways of generating ideas and materials that you can use in a writing assignment.

While your instructor may give you general guidelines about an assignment, your task as a college writer is to explore your topic on your own and determine your own thesis and support. A common technique used to explore a topic is brainstorming or making a timed list of ideas. Brainstorming simply means taking ten to fifteen minutes and writing down everything you can think of connected with the topic you have been assigned—without worrying about whether you are listing words, phrases, or parts of sentences. For example, assume that you are writing an essay in response to one of the readings in the "Cyberliteracy" section. An article by Kevin Hunt published in an Internet magazine develops the thesis that "Books still carry an authority and sense of permanence that Web sites do not." Do you agree or disagree? Why? You might begin your exploration of this topic by writing a list of all the ideas this topic immediately brings to your mind. When you are finished, look over your list and pull out the ideas that seem related and worth pursuing.

Another prewriting technique is freewriting, which your instructor may use at the beginning of a class discussion of a reading, in order to stimulate thinking and focus conversation. Freewriting is a good exercise to do on your own as well. To return to the example of the writing assignment in response to the Kevin Hunt article, you might simply sit at your computer or use your notebook to write nonstop for fifteen minutes in response to Hunt's notion that books still retain a cultural currency that Web sites do not. Write down everything that occurs to you as you are sitting and thinking about this topic. When you are finished, read over what you have written and read it critically. What ideas there are worth developing? What ideas led you nowhere? Do you have the beginnings of a thesis idea?

The advantage of both brainstorming and freewriting is that you have made a start on writing a paper and are no longer staring at a blinking cursor or a blank page. Most students find that they must use some technique for getting started; over time, you will develop ways of generating your own ideas more efficiently. Some students prefer to use formal outlines. Grammar handbooks often provide detailed suggestions for how to organize your thoughts in this way. Other students prefer to plunge into a first draft, with just a rough thesis and a list of ideas in front of them. Whatever method you finally use, it is important to remember that writers inevitably return to prewriting to rethink a point, find a new direction, or generate new ideas. Does your college or university have a writing center or a writing lab? If so, find out what tutorial services are available to you for further help with getting started on writing assignments.

WRITING A ROUGH DRAFT

Once you have generated some ideas, organized your reading notes, thought about your class or electronic discussion, you can begin to plan a draft. Generally speaking, it is best to allow yourself a good block of time for writing; if you only have twenty minutes before your next class, that time might be better spent reviewing your notes for that class, chatting with a friend, or taking a walk rather than attempting to start a draft that will have to be abandoned so quickly. Writing has a way of building its own momentum, and you will want to have enough time to allow that to happen.

Before you begin to write, decide on the form that your writing will take. Is your assignment an essay, an article, a report, a review? Following that, what is the purpose of your writing assignment? What are you planning to accomplish through your writing? Who is your audience for your writing? If your assignment is to write a letter to the editor of your college newspaper, that will require some different planning than an assignment that asks you to write a report that you will share with your immediate classmates.

As you write your draft, remember that you are writing a *first* draft—one that will be revised and edited at a later date. Most writers write more freely if they avoid trying to polish their work at this stage. As you write, think about the most effective ways to support the points you wish to make. Use examples, illustrations, definitions, comparisons, contrasts, and brief narratives whenever possible. Don't hesitate to try out an example or an anecdote even if you think it may not finally work. The important work in a first draft is getting as many of your ideas as possible on a screen or on paper.

REWRITING AND REVISION

One of the best writers I know says that he is not a good writer but is, in fact, a very good rewriter. Despite what many college students think, writing is hard work and a skill that takes practice—talent has very little to do with how successful a writer may be. Almost no writer, even those who write professionally, can produce a first draft that is a final draft. Students sometimes think that it is inefficient to rewrite and revise—that there must be a way to get it right the first time. Because writing is such a complicated process that constantly prompts rethinking positions, refining meanings, and reconceptualizing ideas, it isn't even desirable to get it right the first time.

After you have completed a first draft of your writing assignment, take some time to look it over carefully and critically. Use the critical reading techniques you have been practicing on the selections in this text to read your own work. Some good questions to consider are:

1. What is the thesis of this essay? Is it clearly presented?
2. What are the major supporting points? Is each one carefully developed and well supported?
3. Do you need additional details, examples, or more information? Where? What kind? Have you used quotations or material from secondary sources appropriately and accurately?
4. Does any part of your essay seem irrelevant or out-of-order?
5. Have you followed your assignment?
6. If this essay was the work of a classmate, what do you think you would say in response to it?
7. Do some sections of the essay seem stronger than others? Why?
8. Is your essay interesting and readable? Why or why not?
9. Does the introduction to your essay prompt a reader to read on? Why or why not? How could you improve it?
10. Do you conclude your essay effectively? How could you improve it?

Use your responses to the questions listed above to work on rewriting and revising sections of your essay that need additional work.

PEER REVIEW

Many instructors encourage classmates to read each other's work. Peer review can be an excellent way to receive constructive feedback on your writing. After all, your classmates thoroughly understand the particular set of skills of reading, writing, and thinking that are in play in your course and can help you learn the conventions of this particular academic community. But you and your classmates will need some guidance and preparation in learning how to be effective peer reviewers. In general, remember that you are there to give your constructive view of the essay—not the student who wrote it. Read the draft that you are presented carefully and critically, making sure that you fully understand the purpose of the essay, the thesis idea, and the major supporting points. Read *with* and *against* the draft, in the same way that you read with and against the selections in this text. If you disagree with the opinions expressed, look for ways to suggest why the opinions are not convincing—not just that you disagree. Avoid comments like this is a "good" paper or that it "flows well." Remember that constructive, specific suggestions will help you and your classmates write better papers.

If you are involved in peer review sessions, be prepared to ask questions of the reviewers of your own work. Never hesitate to ask a fellow classmate for clarification or to ask whether a classmate sees a problem with a particular section of your essay. Sometimes it is especially useful to point out a section that has given you special problems. Above all, take the comments of your classmates seriously, at least until you have had time to think them over carefully. When you return to revising your essay and preparing a final draft, weigh carefully the comments that you have received.

EDITING YOUR WORK

After you have thoroughly revised your essay, according to your own ideas about improving it, and if applicable, according to the comments of your classmates, edit your essay carefully. Use a spellchecker but also check the paper for spelling errors that won't be caught by a checker—such as "there" when you mean "their." Proofread for usage and punctuation; consult handbooks if you are uncertain about a possible error. If you have used quoted material in your work, check it carefully against the original and make sure that any secondary sources are accurately documented. Many writers find it useful to read their work aloud in order to catch awkward phrases or sentences. Finally, make sure that your work looks professional and finished—not as though you slept on it before you turned it in. Follow the guidelines or style manual that you have been given for presentation of finished work.

SELF-EVALUATION

Keep track of your progress as you write essays in response to the selections in *Constructing Literacies*. When you receive assignments back from your instructor, read carefully the comments and notations that are given to you. Make an appointment with your instructor and ask questions if you need clarification about the evaluation of your essay. Notice any recurring problems that you are having. Do you always seem to receive a comment about problems with the organization of your essays? Are there usage and punctuation problems that remain unsolved? How do you evaluate your own work? What can you do to improve the quality of your writing? Be sure to investigate online writing labs; many colleges and universities have writing centers that provide online assistance to students in the form of tutorials or bulletin boards for quick answers to questions.

A FINAL WORD

Constructing Literacies is a book designed to help you focus on the central issues and questions relating to the various literacies that you need for negotiation in the academic world and the world beyond: the process through which individuals in our society achieve literacies; how colleges and universities determine the purposes of education for students; the nature of the relationship between the cultural pluralism of American society and the college curriculum; how new technologies are altering our assumptions about literacy and higher education; and what responsibilities students have in developing their own multicultural literacy. Through the readings in this text, you are invited to participate in the central debates in American education today and investigate a series of questions such as: What is the purpose of a college education today? How do we learn to read and write effectively in the academic community?

What are the responsibilities of educators, parents, and community members in fostering a positive climate for education? How do universities decide on a curriculum? How are computers and emerging technologies changing education? How can students participate in their own educational programs?

In the process of investigating these and other questions, *Constructing Literacies* is also a book designed to foster the skills of critical thinking, reading, and writing. You will be asked to think and read carefully and critically, to ask questions, and to formulate answers. In the process, you will be encouraged to put your ideas and thoughts in writing whenever possible—in the service of helping you develop a flexible writing style. You will be encouraged to learn techniques for writing clearly and directly; to form coherent, logical arguments aimed at a well-defined audience; to conduct research and use Internet and library resources fairly and responsibly; and to develop a writing process, including revision, meeting the expectations and demands of college writing assignments.

Constructing Literacies gathers together contemporary essays, reports, and articles on multiple literacies and the function of higher education at the present time. This collection provides students in first-year writing courses and seminars a basis for challenging reading and writing assignments about a topic of immediate relevance. Indeed, *Constructing Literacies: A Harcourt Reader for College Writers* is designed to raise and help you grapple with questions that are powerfully shaping your education, all too often without your knowledge or understanding of the issues involved. I invite you to participate in the debates, articulate your position, and find your own place in this ongoing conversation.

I

LITERACY NARRATIVES

INTRODUCTION

Autobiography and memoir—the stories and memories of one's own life—are among the most popular books of the day. Visit the best-seller section at Borders or Barnes and Noble, or access an online bookstore like <http://www.amazon.com>, and you will find a lengthy selection of books written by actors, academics, politicians, sports figures, and even by relative unknowns. The popularity of the genre is not hard to understand; we are absorbed with ourselves and our own relationships to the rest of the world. And this self-absorption is not new. In the middle of the nineteenth century, Emily Dickinson wittily wrote a poem about it:

No Romance sold unto
Could so enthrall a Man
As the perusal of
His Individual One—
'Tis Fiction's—to dilute to Plausibility
Our Novel—when 'tis small enough
To credit—'Tisn't true!

In this section of the text, we will read and study a specific kind of "perusal" of the "individual one." Literacy narratives, accounts of an individual's experience in acquiring language and understanding the importance of that experience, are integral to autobiography and memoir. An individual person achieves literacy—both the technical skills of reading and writing and the more complex skills of literacy within a particular community—through a variety of ways. In this section, you will find essays that describe how many different people, in both formal and informal educational situations, achieved an awareness of the power of language, despite barriers of race, class, gender, physical impairment, and sometimes even physical danger.

Some of the questions that writers explore through their writing about their own lives in this section are:

- How does a person learn the fundamental skills of a language?
- How does language shape our interpretation of the world?
- How does institutionalized education alter our relationships with our families and home cultures?
- How do schools and teachers form our characters?
- What is the role of books and reading on a person's educational development?
- What are the differing definitions of literacy in our society?
- Is it a myth or reality that the achievement of literacy leads to improved social and economic status or to liberation from the confines of a repressive culture?

The writers in this section explore these and related questions in a variety of ways. The section begins with Mike Rose's contemporary account of his experience of being erroneously placed in the vocational track of his high school and the numbing mind-set he encountered. From this departure point, the readings are arranged in roughly chronological order and represent a variety of different experiences. Frederick Douglass learned to read despite his enslavement in the American South of the 1840s, while Helen Keller struggled with the physical limitations of blindness and deafness. Zitkala Sa was a native American who was sent to an assimilation school at the beginning of the twentieth century. Mary Antin, a Russian Jewish immigrant, struggled to learn not only a new language but a new culture. Malcolm X learned to read and write in prison, and the Old Order Amish maintain strict restraints on what their children learn and read in their homes. Lisa Montoya and Richard Rodriguez, both American citizens with rich heritages from other cultures, examine how such differences affected their experiences in schools. The section concludes with George Steiner's memoir of his childhood as a Jew in Nazi Germany and a single book that made a singular difference to him in his development. As you read these accounts of diverse experiences, consider your own literacy development and assumptions about the purposes of education.

I

"I Just Wanna Be Average"

Mike Rose is a professor of social research methodology in the Graduate School of Education and Information Studies at UCLA. GSEIS, as it is called at UCLA, has a twofold purpose: to conduct primary research in education and information studies and train teachers, administrators, and librarians in effective methodologies. Rose, who for several years was the director of Writing Programs at UCLA, is the coauthor (with Malcolm Kiniry) of a new textbook for college studies, Critical Strategies for Academic Thinking and Writing; A Text with Readings *(1998), the coeditor (with Barry Kroll) of a collection of essays on the history of literacy and major issues in literacy education today,* Perspectives on Literacy *(1988), and the author of* Possible Lives: The Promise of Public Education in America *(1996), the result of a four-year survey of secondary schools across the country. His* Lives on the Boundary *(1989) is a best-selling account of Rose's own experience as the son of Italian immigrants growing up in an economically disadvantaged section of south Los Angeles. In this book, Rose tells the story of how he was erroneously assigned into a vocational education track in his secondary school and emerged from that experience to go on to college and then to graduate school at UCLA. His personal experience is blended with a vivid narrative of the more general problem of underprepared students in American schools and the programs that are designed for them. As he says in the Preface of his book, "This is a hopeful book about those who fail."* Lives on the Boundary *concerns language and human connection, literacy, and culture, and it focuses on those who have trouble reading and writing in the school and the workplace. It is a book about the abilities hidden by class and cultural barriers. And it is a book about movement: about what happens as people who have failed begin to participate in the educational system that has seemed so harsh and distant to them. "I Just Wanna be Average" is taken from the second chapter of* Lives on the Boundary.

QUESTIONS FOR READING

1. What does the title of Rose's book, *Lives on the Boundary,* suggest to you?
2. Rose begins his chapter with a brief history lesson about the numbers of immigrants who came to the United States at the turn of the nineteenth century into the twentieth century. What do you know about immigration movements and how immigrants learned English? Although Rose doesn't specifically use "assimilation," what is your understanding of this term in the context of immigration?
3. As you read this essay, think about your own experiences in school. Did your school have a system for placing students into different educational tracks?

MIKE ROSE

"I JUST WANNA BE AVERAGE"

Lives on the Boundary (New York: Penguin, 1989)

Between 1880 and 1920, well over four million Southern Italian peasants immigrated to America. Their poverty was extreme and hopeless—twelve hours of farm labor would get you one lira, about twenty cents—so increasing numbers of desperate people booked passage for the United States, the country where, the steamship companies claimed, prosperity was a way of life. My father left Naples before the turn of the century; my mother came with her mother from Calabria in 1921. They met in Altoona, Pennsylvania, at the lunch counter of Tom and Joe's, a steamy diner with twangy-voiced waitresses and graveyard stew.

For my mother, life in America was not what the promoters had told her father it would be. She grew up very poor. She slept with her parents and brothers and sisters in one room. She had to quit school in the seventh grade to care for her sickly younger brothers. When her father lost his leg in a railroad accident, she began working in a garment factory where women sat crowded at their stations, solitary as penitents in a cloister. She stayed there until her marriage. My father had found a freer route. He was closemouthed about his past, but I know that he had been a salesman, a tailor, and a gambler; he knew people in the mob and had, my uncles whisper, done time in Chicago. He went through a year or two of Italian elementary school and could write a few words—those necessary to scribble measurements for a suit—and over the years developed a quiet urbanity, a persistence, and a slowly debilitating arteriosclerosis.

When my father proposed to my mother, he decided to open a spaghetti house, a venture that lasted through the war and my early years. The restaurant collapsed in bankruptcy in 1951 when Altoona's major industry, the Pennsylvania Railroad, had to shut down its shops. My parents managed to salvage seven hundred dollars and, on the advice of the family doctor, headed to California, where the winters would be mild and where I, their seven-year-old son, would have the possibility of a brighter future.

At first we lived in a seedy hotel on Spring Street in downtown Los Angeles, but my mother soon found an ad in the *Times* for cheap property on the south side of town. My parents contacted a woman named Mrs. Jolly, used my mother's engagement ring as a down payment, and moved to 9116 South Vermont Avenue, a house about one and one-half miles northwest of Watts. The neighborhood was poor, and it was in transition. Some old white folks had lived there for decades and were retired. Younger black families were moving up from Watts and settling by working-class white families newly arrived from the South and the Midwest. Immigrant Mexican families were coming in from Baja. Any such demographic mix is potentially volatile, and as the fifties wore on, the neighborhood would be marked by outbursts of violence.

I have many particular memories of this time, but in general these early years seem a peculiar mix of physical warmth and barrenness: a gnarled lemon tree, thin rugs, a dirt alley, concrete in the sun. My uncles visited a few times, and we went to the beach or to orange groves. The return home, however, left the waves and spray, the thick leaves and split pulp far in the distance. I was aware of my parents watching their money and got the sense from their conversations that things could quickly take a turn for the worse. I started taping pennies to the bottom of a shelf in the kitchen.

My father's health was bad, and he had few readily marketable skills. Poker and pinochle brought in a little money, and he tried out an idea that had worked in Altoona during the war: He started a "suit club." The few customers he could scare up would pay two dollars a week on a tailor-made suit. He would take the measurements and send them to a shop back East and hope for the best. My mother took a job at a café in downtown Los Angeles, a split shift 9:00 to 12:00 and 5:00 to 9:00, but her tips were totaling sixty cents a day, so she quit for a night shift at Coffee Dan's. This got her to the bus stop at one in the morning, waiting on the same street where drunks were urinating and hookers were catching the last of the bar crowd. She made friends with a Filipino cook who would scare off the advances of old men aflame with the closeness of taxi dancers. In a couple of years, Coffee Dan's would award her a day job at the counter. Once every few weeks, my father and I would take a bus downtown and visit with her, sitting at stools by the window, watching the animated but silent mix of faces beyond the glass.

My father had moved to California with faint hopes about health and a belief in his child's future, drawn by that far edge of America where the sun descends into green water. What he found was a city that was warm, verdant, vast, and indifferent as a starlet in a sports car. Altoona receded quickly, and my parents must have felt isolated and deceived. They had fallen into the abyss of paradise—two more poor settlers trying to make a go of it in the City of the Angels.

Let me tell you about our house. If you entered the front door and turned right you'd see a small living room with a couch along the east wall and one along the west wall—one couch was purple, the other tan, both bought used and both well worn. A television set was placed at the end of the purple couch, right at arm level. An old Philco radio sat next to the TV, its speaker covered with gold lamé. There was a small coffee table in the center of the room on which sat a murky fishbowl occupied by two listless guppies. If, on entering, you turned left you would see a green Formica dinner table with four chairs, a cedar chest given as a wedding present to my mother by her mother, a painted statue of the Blessed Virgin Mary, and a black trunk. I also had a plastic chaise lounge between the door and the table. I would lie on this and watch television.

A short hallway leading to the bathroom opened on one side to the kitchen and, on the other, to the bedroom. The bedroom had two beds, one for me and one for my parents, a bureau with a mirror, and a chest of drawers on which we piled old shirt boxes and stacks of folded clothes. The kitchen held a refrigerator and a stove, small older models that we got when our earlier (and newer) models were repossessed by two silent men. There was one white wooden chair in the corner beneath wall cabinets. You could walk in and through a tiny pantry to the backyard and to four one-room rentals. My father got most of our furniture from a secondhand store on the next block; he would tend the store two or three hours a day as payment on our account.

As I remember it, the house was pretty dark. My mother kept the blinds in the bedroom drawn—there were no curtains there—and the venetian blinds in the living room were, often as not, left closed. The walls were bare except for a faded picture of Jesus and a calendar from the *Altoona Mirror*. Some paper carnations bent out of a white vase on the television. There was a window on the north side of the kitchen that had no blinds or curtains, so the sink got good light. My father would methodically roll up his sleeves and show me how to prepare a sweet potato or avocado seed so it would sprout. We kept a row of them on the sill above the sink, their shoots and vines rising and curling in the morning sun.

The house was on a piece of land that rose about four feet up from heavily trafficked Vermont Avenue. The yard sloped down to the street, and three steps and a short walkway led up the middle of the grass to our front door. There was a similar house immediately to the south of us. Next to it was Carmen's Barber Shop. Carmen was a short, quiet Italian who, rumor had it, had committed his first wife to the crazy house to get her money. In the afternoons, Carmen could be found in the lot behind his shop playing solitary catch, flinging a tennis ball high into the air and running under it. One day the police arrested Carmen on charges of child molesting. He was released but became furtive and suspicious. I never saw him in the lot again. Next to Carmen's was a junk store where, one summer, I made a little money polishing brass and rewiring old lamps. Then came a dilapidated real estate office, a Mexican restaurant, an empty lot, and an appliance store owned by the father of Keith Grateful, the streetwise, chubby boy who would become my best friend.

Right to the north of us was a record shop, a barber shop presided over by old Mr. Graff, Walt's Malts, a shoe repair shop with a big Cat's Paw decal in the window, a third barber shop, and a brake shop. It's as I write this that I realize for the first time that three gray men could have had a go at your hair before you left our street.

Behind our house was an unpaved alley that passed, just to the north, a power plant the length of a city block. Massive coils atop the building hissed and cracked through the day, but the doors never opened. I used to think it was abandoned—feeding itself on its own wild arcs—until one sweltering afternoon a man was electrocuted on the roof. The air was thick and still as two firemen—the only men present—brought down a charred and limp body without saying a word.

The north and south traffic on Vermont was separated by tracks for the old yellow trolley cars, long since defunct. Across the street was a huge garage, a tiny hot dog stand run by a myopic and reclusive man named Freddie, and my dreamland, the Vermont Bowl. Distant and distorted behind thick lenses, Freddie's eyes never met yours; he would look down when he took your order and give you your change with a mumble. Freddie slept on a cot in the back of his grill and died there one night, leaving tens of thousands of dollars stuffed in the mattress.

My father would buy me a chili dog at Freddie's, and then we would walk over to the bowling alley where Dad would sit at the lunch counter and drink coffee while I had a great time with pinball machines, electric shooting galleries, and an ill-kept dispenser of cheese corn. There was a small, dark bar abutting the lanes, and it called to me. I would devise reasons to walk through it: " 'Scuse me, is the bathroom in here?" or "Anyone see my dad?" though I can never remember my father having a drink. It was dark and people were drinking and I figured all sorts of mysterious things were being whispered. Next to the Vermont Bowl was a large vacant lot overgrown with foxtails and dotted with car parts, bottles, and rotting cardboard. One day Keith heard that the police had found a human head in the brush. After that we explored the lot periodically, coming home with stickers all the way up to our waists. But we didn't find a thing. Not even a kneecap.

When I wasn't with Keith or in school, I would spend most of my day with my father or with the men who were renting the one-room apartments behind our house. Dad and I whiled away the hours in the bowling alley, watching TV, or planting a vegetable garden that never seemed to take. When he was still mobile, he would walk the four blocks down to St. Regina's Grammar School to take me home to my favorite lunch of boiled wieners and chocolate milk. There I'd sit, dunking my hot dog in a jar of mayonnaise and drinking my milk while Sheriff John tuned up the calliope music on his "Lunch Brigade."

Though he never complained to me, I could sense that my father's health was failing, and I began devising child's ways to make him better. We had a box of rolled cotton in the bathroom, and I would go in and peel off a long strip and tape it around my jaw. Then I'd rummage through the closet, find a sweater of my father's, put on one of his hats—and sneak around to the back door. I'd knock loudly and wait. It would take him a while to get there. Finally, he'd open the door, look down, and quietly say, "Yes, Michael?" I was disappointed. Every time. Somehow I thought I could fool him. And, I guess, if he had been fooled, I would have succeeded in redefining things: I would have been the old one, he much younger, more agile, with strength in his legs.

The men who lived in the back were either retired or didn't work that much, so one of them was usually around. They proved to be, over the years, an unusual set of companions for a young boy. Ed Gionotti was the youngest of the lot, a handsome man whose wife had run off and who spoke softly and never smiled. Bud Hall and Lee McGuire were two out-of-work plumbers who lived in adjacent units and who weekly drank themselves silly, proclaiming in front of God and everyone their undying friendship or their unequivocal hatred. Old Cheech was a lame Italian who used to hobble along grabbing his testicles and rolling his eyes while he talked about the women he claimed to have on a string. There was Lester, the toothless cabbie, who several times made overtures to me and who, when he moved, left behind a drawer full of syringes and burnt spoons. Mr. Smith was a rambunctious retiree who lost his nose to an untended skin cancer. And there was Mr. Berryman, a sweet and gentle man who eventually left for a retirement hotel only to be burned alive in an electrical fire.

Except for Keith, there were no children on my block and only one or two on the immediate side streets. Most of the people I saw day to day were over fifty. People in their twenties and thirties working in the shoe shop or the garages didn't say a lot; their work and much of what they were working for drained their spirits. There were gang members who sauntered up from Hoover Avenue, three blocks to the east, and occasionally I would get shoved around, but they had little interest in me either as member or victim. I was a skinny, bespectacled kid and had neither the coloring nor the style of dress or carriage that marked me as a rival. On the whole, the days were quiet, lazy, lonely. The heat shimmering over the asphalt had no snap to it; time drifted by. I would lie on the couch at night and listen to the music from the record store or from Walt's Malts. It was new and quick paced, exciting, a little dangerous (the church had condemned Buddy Knox's "Party Doll"), and I heard in it a deep rhythmic need to be made whole with love, or marked as special, or released in some rebellious way. Even the songs about lost love—and there were plenty of them—lifted me right out of my socks with their melodious longing:

Came the dawn,
   and my heart and her love and the night
   were gone.

But I know I'll never forget
  her kiss in the moonlight Oooo . . .
  such a kiss Oooo Oooo such a night . . .

In the midst of the heat and slow time the music brought the promise of its origins, a promise of deliverance, a promise that, if only for a moment, life could be stirring and dreamy.

But the anger and frustration of South Vermont could prove too strong for music's illusion; then it was violence that provided deliverance of a different order. One night I watched as a guy sprinted from Walt's to toss something on our lawn. The police were right behind, and a cop tackled him, smashing his face into the sidewalk. I ducked out to find the packet: a dozen glassine bags of heroin. Another night, one August midnight, an argument outside the record store ended with a man being shot to death. And the occasional gang forays brought with them some fated kid who would fumble his moves and catch a knife.

It's popular these days to claim you grew up on the streets. Men tell violent tales and romanticize the lessons violence brings. But, though it was occasionally violent, it wasn't the violence in South L.A. that marked me, for sometimes you can shake that ugliness off. What finally affected me was subtler, but more pervasive: I cannot recall a young person who was crazy in love or lost in work or one old person who was passionate about a cause or an idea. I'm not talking about an absence of energy—the street toughs and, for that fact, old Cheech had energy. And I'm not talking about an absence of decency, for my father was a thoughtful man. The people I grew up with were retired from jobs that rub away the heart or were working hard at jobs to keep their lives from caving in or were anchorless and in between jobs and spouses or were diving headlong into a barren tomorrow: junkies, alcoholics, and mean kids walking along Vermont looking to throw a punch. I developed a picture of human existence that rendered it short and brutish or sad and aimless or long and quiet with rewards like afternoon naps, the evening newspaper, walks around the block, occasional letters from children in other states. When, years later, I was introduced to humanistic psychologists like Abraham Maslow and Carl Rogers, with their visions of self-actualization, or even Freud with his sober dictum about love and work, it all sounded like a glorious fairy tale, a magical account of a world full of possibility, full of hope and empowerment. Sindbad and Cinderella couldn't have been more fanciful.

Some people who manage to write their way out of the working class describe the classroom as an oasis of possibility. It became their intellectual playground, their competitive arena. Given the richness of my memories of this time, it's funny how scant are my recollections of school. I remember the red brick building of St. Regina's itself, and the topography of the playground: the swings and basketball courts and peeling benches. There are images of a few students: Erwin Petschaur, a muscular German boy with a strong accent; Dave Sanchez, who was good in math; and Sheila Wilkes, everyone's curly-haired heartthrob. And there are two nuns: Sister Monica, the third-grade teacher with beautiful hands for whom I carried a candle and who, to my dismay, had wedded herself to Christ; and Sister Beatrice, a woman truly crazed, who would sweep into class, eyes wide, to tell us about the Apocalypse.

All the hours in class tend to blend into one long, vague stretch of time. What I remember best, strangely enough, are the two things I couldn't understand and over the years grew to hate: grammar lessons and mathematics. I would sit there watching a teacher draw her long horizontal line and her short, oblique lines and break up sentences and put adjectives here and adverbs there and just not get it, couldn't see the reason for it, turned off to it. I would hide by slumping down in my seat and page through my reader, carried along by the flow of sentences in a story. She would test us, and I would dread that, for I always got Cs and Ds. Mathematics was a bit different. For whatever reasons, I didn't learn early math very well, so when it came time for more complicated operations, I couldn't keep up and started daydreaming to avoid my inadequacy. This was a strategy I would rely on as I grew older. I fell further and further behind. A memory: The teacher is faceless and seems very far away. The voice is faint and is discussing an equation written on the board. It is raining, and I am watching the streams of water form patterns on the windows.

I realize now how consistently I defended myself against the lessons I couldn't understand and the people and events of South L.A. that were too strange to view head-on. I got very good at watching a blackboard with minimum awareness. And I drifted more and more into a variety of protective fantasies. I was lucky in that although my parents didn't read or write very much and had no more than a few books around the house, they never debunked my pursuits. And when they could, they bought me what I needed to spin my web.

One early Christmas they got me a small chemistry set. My father brought home an old card table from the secondhand store, and on that table I spread out my test tubes, my beaker, my Erlenmeyer flask, and my gas-generating apparatus. The set came equipped with chemicals, minerals, and various treated papers—all in little square bottles. You could send away to someplace in Maryland for more, and I did, saving pennies and nickels to get the substances that were too exotic for my set, the Junior Chem-craft: Congo red paper, azurite, glycerine, chrome alum, cochineal—this from female insects!—tartaric acid, chameleon paper, logwood. I would sit before my laboratory and play for hours. My father rested on the purple couch in front of me watching wrestling or *Gunsmoke* while I measured powders or heated crystals or blew into solutions that my breath would turn red or pink. I was taken by the blends of names and by the colors that swirled through the beaker. My equations were visual and phonetic. I would hold a flask up to the hall light, imagining the veils of a million atoms dancing. Sulfur and alcohol hung in the air. I wanted to shake down the house.

One day my mother came home from Coffee Dan's with an awful story. The teenage brother of one of her waitress friends was in the hospital. He had been fooling around with explosives in his garage "where his mother couldn't see him," and something happened, and "he blew away part of his throat. For God's sake, be careful," my mother said. "Remember poor Ada's brother." Wow! I thought. How neat! Why couldn't my experiments be that dangerous? I really lost heart when I realized that you could probably eat the chemicals spread across my table.

I knew what I had to do. I saved my money for a week and then walked with firm resolve past Walt's Malts, past the brake shop, across Ninetieth Street, and into Palazolla's market. I bought a little bottle of Alka-Seltzer and ran home. I chipped up the wafers and mixed them into a jar of white crystals. When my mother came home, dog tired, and sat down on the edge of my couch to tell me and Dad about her day, I gravely poured my concoction into a beaker of water, cried something about the unexpected, and ran out from behind my table. The beaker foamed ominously. My father swore in Italian. The second time I tried it, I got something milder—in English. And by my third near-miss with death, my parents were calling my behavior cute. Cute! Who wanted cute? I wanted to toy with the disaster that befell Ada Pendleton's brother. I wanted all those wonderful colors to collide in ways that could blow your voice box right off.

But I was limited by the real. The best I could do was create a toxic antacid. I loved my chemistry set—its glassware and its intriguing labels—but it wouldn't allow me to do the things I wanted to do. St. Regina's had an all-purpose room, one wall of which was lined with old books—and one of those shelves held a row of plastic-covered space novels. The sheen of their covers was gone, and their futuristic portraits were dotted with erasures and grease spots like a meteor shower of the everyday. I remember the rockets best. Long cylinders outfitted at the base with three slick fins, tapering at the other end to a perfect conical point, ready to pierce out of the stratosphere and into my imagination: X-fifteens and Mach 1, the dark side of the moon, the Red Planet, Jupiter's Great Red Spot, Saturn's rings—and beyond the solar system to swirling wisps of galaxies, to stardust.

I would check out my books two at a time and take them home to curl up with a blanket on my chaise lounge, reading, sometimes, through the weekend, my back aching, my thoughts lost between galaxies. I became the hero of a thousand adventures, all with intricate plots and the triumph of good over evil, all many dimensions removed from the dim walls of the living room. We were given time to draw in school, so, before long, all this worked itself onto paper. The stories I was reading were reshaping themselves into pictures. My father got me some butcher paper from Palazolla's, and I continued to draw at home. My collected works rendered the Horsehead Nebula, goofy space cruisers, robots, and Saturn. Each had its crayon, a particular waxy pencil with mood and meaning: rust and burnt sienna for Mars, yellow for the Sun, lime and rose for Saturn's rings, and bright red for the Jovian spot. I had a little sharpener to keep the points just right. I didn't write any stories; I just read and drew. I wouldn't care much about writing until late in high school.

The summer before the sixth grade, I got a couple of jobs. The first was at a pet store a block or so away from my house. Since I was still small, I could maneuver around in breeder cages, scraping the heaps of parakeet crap from the tin floor, cleaning the water troughs and seed trays. It was pretty awful. I would go home after work and fill the tub and soak until all the fleas and bird mites came floating to the surface, little Xs in their multiple eyes. When I heard about a job selling strawberries door-to-door, I jumped at it. I went to work for a white-haired Chicano named Frank. He would carry four or five kids and dozens of crates of strawberries in his ramshackle truck up and down the avenues of the better neighborhoods: houses with mowed lawns and petunia beds. We'd work all day for seventy-five cents, Frank dropping pairs of us off with two crates each, then picking us up at preassigned corners. We spent lots of time together, bouncing around on the truck bed redolent with strawberries or sitting on a corner, cold, listening for the sputter of Frank's muffler. I started telling the other kids about my books, and soon it was my job to fill up that time with stories.

Reading opened up the world. There I was, a skinny bookworm drawing the attention of street kids who, in any other circumstances, would have had me for breakfast. Like an epic tale-teller, I developed the stories as I went along, relying on a flexible plot line and a repository of heroic events. I had a great time. I sketched out trajectories with my finger on Frank's dusty truck bed. And I stretched out each story's climax, creating cliffhangers like the ones I saw in the Saturday serials. These stories created for me a temporary community.

It was around this time that fiction started leading me circuitously to a child's version of science. In addition to the space novels, St. Regina's library also had half a dozen books on astronomy—*The Golden Book of Planets* and stuff like that—so I checked out a few of them. I liked what I read and wheedled enough change out of my father to enable me to take the bus to the public library. I discovered star maps, maps of lunar seas, charts upon charts of the solar system and the planetary moons: Rhea, Europa, Callisto, Miranda, Io. I didn't know that most of these moons were named for women—I didn't know classical mythology—but I would say their names to myself as though they had a woman's power to protect: Europa, Miranda, Io . . . The distances between stars fascinated me, as did the sizes of the big telescopes. I sent away for catalogs. Then prices fascinated me too. I wanted to drape my arm over a thousand-dollar scope and hear its motor drive whirr. I conjured a twelve-year-old's life of the astronomer: sitting up all night with potato chips and the stars, tracking the sky for supernovas, humming "Earth Angel" with the Penguins. What was my mother to do but save her tips and buy me a telescope?!

It was a little reflecting job, and I solemnly used to carry it out to the front of the house on warm summer nights, to find Venus or Alpha Centauri or trace the stars in Orion or lock onto the moon. I would lay out my star maps on the concrete, more for their magic than anything else, for I had trouble figuring them out. I was no geometer of the constellations; I was their balladeer. Those nights were very peaceful. I was far enough away from the front door and up enough from the sidewalk to make it seem as if I rested on a mound of dark silence, a mountain in Arizona, perhaps, watching the sky alive with points of light. Poor Freddie, toothless Lester whispering promises about making me feel good, the flat days, the gang fights—all this receded, for it was now me, the star child, lost in an eyepiece focused on a reflecting mirror that cradled, in its center, a shimmering moon.

The loneliness in Los Angeles fosters strange arrangements. Lou Minton was a wiry man with gaunt, chiseled features and prematurely gray hair, combed straight back. He had gone to college in the South for a year or two and kicked around the country for many more before settling in L.A. He lived in a small downtown apartment with a single window and met my mother at the counter of Coffee Dan's. He had been alone too long and eventually came to our house and became part of the family. Lou repaired washing machines, and he had a car, and he would take me to the vast, echoing library just west of Pershing Square and to the Museum of Science and Industry in Exposition Park. He bought me astronomy books, taught me how to use tools, and helped me build model airplanes from balsa wood and rice paper. As my father's health got worse, Lou took care of him.

My rhapsodic and prescientific astronomy carried me into my teens, consumed me right up till high school, losing out finally, and only, to the siren call of pubescence—that endocrine hoodoo that transmogrifies nice boys into gawky flesh fiends. My mother used to bring home *Confidential* magazine, a peep-show rag specializing in the sins of the stars, and it beckoned me mercilessly: Jayne Mansfield's cleavage, Gina Lollobrigida's eyes, innuendos about deviant sexuality, ads for Frederick's of Hollywood—spiked heels, lacy brassieres, the epiphany of silk panties on a mannequin's hips. Along with Phil Everly, I was through with counting the stars above.

Budding manhood. Only adults talk about adolescence budding. Kids have no choice but to talk in extremes; they're being wrenched and buffeted, rabbit-punched from inside by systemic thugs. Nothing sweet and pastoral here. Kids become ridiculous and touching at one and the same time: passionate about the trivial, fixed before the mirror, yet traversing one of the most important rites of passage in their lives—liminal people, silly and profoundly human. Given my own expertise, I fantasized about concocting the fail-safe aphrodisiac that would bring Marianne Bilpusch, the cloakroom monitor, rushing into my arms or about commanding a squadron of bosomy, linguistically mysterious astronauts like Zsa Zsa Gabor. My parents used to say that their son would have the best education they could afford. Maybe I would be a doctor. There was a public school in our neighborhood and several Catholic schools to the west. They had heard that quality schooling meant private, Catholic schooling, so they somehow got the money together to send me to Our Lady of Mercy, fifteen or so miles southwest of Ninety-first and Vermont. So much for my fantasies. Most Catholic secondary schools then were separated by gender.

It took two buses to get to Our Lady of Mercy. The first started deep in South Los Angeles and caught me at midpoint. The second drifted through neighborhoods with trees, parks, big lawns, and lots of flowers. The rides were long but were livened up by a group of South L.A. veterans whose parents also thought that Hope had set up shop in the west end of the county. There was Christy Biggars, who, at sixteen, was dealing and was, according to rumor, a pimp as well. There were Bill Cobb and Johnny Gonzales, grease-pencil artists extraordinaire, who left Nembutal-enhanced swirls of "Cobb" and "Johnny" on the corrugated walls of the bus. And then there was Tyrrell Wilson. Tyrrell was the coolest kid I knew. He ran the dozens like a metric halfback, laid down a rap that outrhymed and outpointed Cobb, whose rap was good but not great—the curse of a moderately soulful kid trapped in white skin. But it was Cobb who would sneak a radio onto the bus, and thus underwrote his patter with Little Richard, Fats Domino, Chuck Berry, the Coasters, and Ernie K. Doe's mother-in-law, an awful woman who was "sent from down below." And so it was that Christy and Cobb and Johnny G. and Tyrrell and I and assorted others picked up along the way passed our days in the back of the bus, a funny mix brought together by geography and parental desire.

Entrance to school brings with it forms and releases and assessments. Mercy relied on a series of tests, mostly the Stanford-Binet, for placement, and somehow the results of my tests got confused with those of another student named Rose. The other Rose apparently didn't do very well, for I was placed in the vocational track, a euphemism for the bottom level. Neither I nor my parents realized what this meant. We had no sense that Business Math, Typing, and English–Level D were dead ends. The current spate of reports on the schools criticizes parents for not involving themselves in the education of their children. But how would someone like Tommy Rose, with his two years of Italian schooling, know what to ask? And what sort of pressure could an exhausted waitress apply? The error went undetected, and I remained in the vocational track for two years. What a place.

My homeroom was supervised by Brother Dill, a troubled and unstable man who also taught freshman English. When his class drifted away from him, which was often, his voice would rise in paranoid accusations, and occasionally he would lose control and shake or smack us. I hadn't been there two months when one of his brisk, face-turning slaps had my glasses sliding down the aisle. Physical education was also pretty harsh. Our teacher was a stubby ex-lineman who had played old-time pro ball in the Midwest. He routinely had us grabbing our ankles to receive his stinging paddle across our butts. He did that, he said, to make men of us. "Rose," he bellowed on our first encounter; me standing geeky in line in my baggy shorts. "'Rose'? What the hell kind of name is that?"

"Italian, sir," I squeaked.

"Italian! Ho. Rose, do you know the sound a bag of shit makes when it hits the wall?"

"No, sir."

"Wop!"

Sophomore English was taught by Mr. Mitropetros. He was a large, be-jeweled man who managed the parking lot at the Shrine Auditorium. He would crow and preen and list for us the stars he'd brushed against. We'd ask questions and glance knowingly and snicker, and all that fueled the poor guy to brag some more. Parking cars was his night job. He had little training in English, so his lesson plan for his day work had us reading the district's required text, *Julius Caesar,* aloud for the semester. We'd finish the play way before the twenty weeks was up, so he'd have us switch parts again and again and start again: Dave Snyder, the fastest guy at Mercy, muscling through Caesar to the breathless squeals of Calpurnia, as interpreted by Steve Fusco, a surfer who owned the school's most envied paneled wagon. Week ten and Dave and Steve would take on new roles, as would we all, and render a water-logged Cassius and a Brutus that are beyond my powers of description.

Spanish I—taken in the second year—fell into the hands of a new recruit. Mr. Montez was a tiny man, slight, five foot six at the most, soft-spoken and delicate. Spanish was a particularly rowdy class, and Mr. Montez was as prepared for it as a doily maker at a hammer throw. He would tap his pencil to a room in which Steve Fusco was propelling spitballs from his heavy lips, in which Mike Dweetz was taunting Billy Hawk, a half-Indian, half-Spanish, reed-thin, quietly explosive boy. The vocational track at Our Lady of Mercy mixed kids traveling in from South L.A. with South Bay surfers and a few Slavs and Chicanos from the harbors of San Pedro. This was a dangerous miscellany: surfers and hodads and South-Central blacks all ablaze to the metronomic tapping of Hector Montez's pencil.

One day Billy lost it. Out of the corner of my eye I saw him strike out with his right arm and catch Dweetz across the neck. Quick as a spasm, Dweetz was out of his seat, scattering desks, cracking Billy on the side of the head, right behind the eye. Snyder and Fusco and others broke it up, but the room felt hot and close and naked. Mr. Montez's tenuous authority was finally ripped to shreds, and I think everyone felt a little strange about that. That charade was over, and when it came down to it, I don't think any of the kids really wanted it to end this way. They had pushed and pushed and bullied their way into a freedom that both scared and embarrassed them.

───────

Students will float to the mark you set. I and the others in the vocational classes were bobbing in pretty shallow water. Vocational education has aimed at increasing the economic opportunities of students who do not do well in our schools. Some serious programs succeed in doing that, and through exceptional teachers—like Mr. Gross[1] in *Horace's Compromise*—students learn to develop hypotheses and troubleshoot, reason through a problem, and communicate effectively—the true job skills. The vocational track, however, is most often a place for those who are just not making it, a dumping group for the dis-affected. There were a few teachers who worked hard at education; young

Brother Slattery, for example, combined a stern voice with weekly quizzes to try to pass along to us a skeletal outline of world history. But mostly the teachers had no idea of how to engage the imaginations of us kids who were scuttling along at the bottom of the pond.

And the teachers would have needed some inventiveness, for none of us was groomed for the classroom. It wasn't just that I didn't know things—didn't know how to simplify algebraic fractions, couldn't identify different kinds of clauses, bungled Spanish translations—but that I had developed various faulty and inadequate ways of doing algebra and making sense of Spanish. Worse yet, the years of defensive tuning out in elementary school had given me a way to escape quickly while seeming at least half alert. During my time in Voc. Ed., I developed further into a mediocre student and a somnambulant problem solver, and that affected the subjects I did have the wherewithal to handle: I detested Shakespeare; I got bored with history. My attention flitted here and there. I fooled around in class and read my books indifferently—the intellectual equivalent of playing with your food. I did what I had to do to get by, and I did it with half a mind.

But I did learn things about people and eventually came into my own socially. I liked the guys in Voc. Ed. Growing up where I did, I understood and admired physical prowess, and there was an abundance of muscle here. There was Dave Snyder, a sprinter and halfback of true quality. Dave's ability and his quick wit gave him a natural appeal, and he was welcome in any clique, though he always kept a little independent. He enjoyed acting the fool and could care less about studies, but he possessed a certain maturity and never caused the faculty much trouble. It was a testament to his independence that he included me among his friends—I eventually went out for track, but I was no jock. Owing to the Latin alphabet and a dearth of *R*s and *S*s, Snyder sat behind Rose and we started exchanging one-liners and became friends.

There was Ted Richard, a much-touted Little League pitcher. He was chunky and had a baby face and came to our Lady of Mercy as a seasoned street fighter. Ted was quick to laugh and he had a loud, jolly laugh, but when he got angry he'd smile a little smile, the kind that simply raises the corner of the mouth a quarter of an inch. For those who knew, it was an eerie signal. Those who didn't found themselves in big trouble, for Ted was very quick. He loved to carry on what we would come to call philosophical discussions: What is courage? Does God exist? He also loved words, enjoyed picking up big ones like *salubrious* and *equivocal* and using them in our conversations—laughing at himself as the word hit a chuckhole rolling off his tongue. Ted didn't do all that well in school—baseball and parties and testing the courage he'd speculated about took up his time. His textbooks were *Argosy* and *Field and Stream*, whatever newspapers he'd find on the bus stop—from *the Daily Worker* to pornography—conversations with uncles or hobos or businessmen he'd meet in a coffee shop, *The Old Man and the Sea*. With hindsight, I can see that Ted was developing into one of those rough-hewn intellectuals whose sources are a mix of the learned and the apocryphal, whose discussions are both assured and sad.

And then there was Ken Harvey. Ken was good-looking in a puffy way and had a full and oily ducktail and was a car enthusiast . . . a hodad. One day in religion class, he said the sentence that turned out to be one of the most memorable of the hundreds of thousands I heard in those Voc. Ed. years. We were talking about the parable of the talents, about achievement, working hard, doing the best you can do, blah-blah-blah, when the teacher called on the restive Ken Harvey for an opinion. Ken thought about it, but just for a second, and said (with studied, minimal affect), "I just wanna be average." That woke me up. Average?! Who wants to be average? Then the athletes chimed in with the clichés that make you want to laryngectomize them, and the exchange became a platitudinous melee. At the time, I thought Ken's assertion was stupid, and I wrote him off. But his sentence has stayed with me all these years, and I think I am finally coming to understand it.

Ken Harvey was gasping for air. School can be a tremendously disorienting place. No matter how bad the school, you're going to encounter notions that don't fit with the assumptions and beliefs that you grew up with—maybe you'll hear these dissonant notions from teachers, maybe from the other students, and maybe you'll read them. You'll also be thrown in with all kinds of kids from all kinds of backgrounds, and that can be unsettling—this is especially true in places of rich ethnic and linguistic mix, like the L.A. basin. You'll see a handful of students far excel you in courses that sound exotic and that are only in the curriculum of the elite: French, physics, trigonometry. And all this is happening while you're trying to shape an identity; your body is changing, and your emotions are running wild. If you're a working-class kid in the vocational track, the options you'll have to deal with this will be constrained in certain ways: You're defined by your school as "slow"; you're placed in a curriculum that isn't designed to liberate you but to occupy you, or, if you're lucky, train you, though the training is for work the society does not esteem; other students are picking up the cues from your school and your curriculum and interacting with you in particular ways. If you're a kid like Ted Richard, you turn your back on all this and let your mind roam where it may. But youngsters like Ted are rare. What Ken and so many others do is protect themselves from such suffocating madness by taking on with a vengeance the identity implied in the vocational track. Reject the confusion and frustration by openly defining yourself as the Common Joe. Champion the average. Rely on your own good sense. F--- this bull----. Bull----, of course, is everything you—and the others—fear is beyond you: books, essays, tests, academic scrambling, complexity, scientific reasoning, philosophical inquiry.

The tragedy is that you have to twist the knife in your own gray matter to make this defense work. You'll have to shut down, have to reject intellectual stimuli or diffuse them with sarcasm, have to cultivate stupidity, have to convert boredom from a malady into a way of confronting the world. Keep your vocabulary simple, act stoned when you're not or act more stoned than you are, flaunt ignorance, materialize your dreams. It is a powerful and effective defense—it neutralizes the insult and the frustration of being a vocational kid and, when perfected, it drives teachers up the wall, a delightful secondary effect. But like all strong magic, it exacts a price.

My own deliverance from the Voc. Ed. world began with sophomore biology. Every student, college prep to vocational, had to take biology, and unlike the other courses, the same person taught all sections. When teaching the vocational group, Brother Clint probably slowed down a bit or omitted a little of the fundamental biochemistry, but he used the same book and more or less the same syllabus across the board. If one class got tough, he could get tougher. He was young and powerful and very handsome, and looks and physical strength were high currency. No one gave him any trouble.

I was pretty bad at the dissecting table, but the lectures and the textbook were interesting: plastic overlays that, with each turned page, peeled away skin, then veins and muscle, then organs, down to the very bones that Brother Clint, pointer in hand, would tap out on our hanging skeleton. Dave Snyder was in big trouble, for the study of life—versus the living of it—was sticking in his craw. We worked out a code for our multiple-choice exams. He'd poke me in the back: once for the answer under *A*, twice for *B*, and so on; and when he'd hit the right one, I'd look up to the ceiling as though I were lost in thought. Poke: cytoplasm. Poke, poke: methane. Poke, poke, poke: William Harvey. Poke, poke, poke, poke: islets of Langerhans. This didn't work out perfectly, but Dave passed the course, and I mastered the dreamy look of a guy on a record jacket. And something else happened. Brother Clint puzzled over this Voc. Ed. kid who was racking up 98s and 99s on his tests. He checked the school's records and discovered the error. He recommended that I begin my junior year in the College Prep program. According to all I've read since, such a shift, as one report put it, is virtually impossible. Kids at that level rarely cross tracks. The telling thing is how chancy both my placement into and exit from Voc. Ed. was; neither I nor my parents had anything to do with it. I lived in one world during spring semester, and when I came back to school in the fall, I was living in another.

Switching to College Prep was a mixed blessing. I was an erratic student. I was undisciplined. And I hadn't caught onto the rules of the game: Why work hard in a class that didn't grab my fancy? I was also hopelessly behind in math. Chemistry was hard; toying with my chemistry set years before hadn't prepared me for the chemist's equations. Fortunately, the priest who taught both chemistry and second-year algebra was also the school's athletic director. Membership on the track team covered me; I knew I wouldn't get lower than a C. U.S. history was taught pretty well, and I did okay. But civics was taken over by a football coach who had trouble reading the textbook aloud—and reading aloud was the centerpiece of his pedagogy. College Prep at Mercy was certainly an improvement over the vocational program—at least it carried some status—but the social science curriculum was weak, and the mathematics and physical sciences were simply beyond me. I had a miserable quantitative background and ended up copying some assignments and finessing the rest as best I could. Let me try to explain how it feels to see again and again material you should once have learned but didn't.

You are given a problem. It requires you to simplify algebraic fractions or to multiply expressions containing square roots. You know this is pretty basic material because you've seen it for years. Once a teacher took some time with you, and you learned how to carry out these operations. Simple versions, anyway. But that was a year or two or more in the past, and these are more complex versions, and now you're not sure. And this, you keep telling yourself, is ninth- or even eighth-grade stuff.

Next it's a word problem. This is also old hat. The basic elements are as familiar as story characters: trains speeding so many miles per hour or shadows of buildings angling so many degrees. Maybe you know enough, have sat through enough explanations, to be able to begin setting up the problem: "If one train is going this fast . . ." or "This shadow is really one line of a triangle . . ." Then: "Let's see . . ." "How did Jones do this?" "Hmmmm." "No." "No, that won't work." Your attention wavers. You wonder about other things: a football game, a dance, that cute new checker at the market. You try to focus on the problem again. You scribble on paper for a while, but the tension wins out and your attention flits elsewhere. You crumple the paper and begin daydreaming to ease the frustration.

The particulars will vary, but in essence this is what a number of students go through, especially those in so-called remedial classes. They open their textbooks and see once again the familiar and impenetrable formulas and diagrams and terms that have stumped them for years. There is no excitement here. *No excitement.* Regardless of what the teacher says, this is not a new challenge. There is, rather, embarrassment and frustration and, not surprisingly, some anger in being reminded once again of long-standing inadequacies. No wonder so many students finally attribute their difficulties to something inborn, organic: "That part of my brain just doesn't work." Given the troubling histories many of these students have, it's miraculous that any of them can lift the shroud of hopelessness sufficiently to make deliverance from these classes possible.

Through this entire period, my father's health was deteriorating with cruel momentum. His arteriosclerosis progressed to the point where a simple nick on his shin wouldn't heal. Eventually it ulcerated and widened. Lou Minton would come by daily to change the dressing. We tried renting an oscillating bed—which we placed in the front room—to force blood through the constricted arteries in my father's legs. The bed hummed through the night, moving in place to ward off the inevitable. The ulcer continued to spread, and the doctors finally had to amputate. My grandfather had lost his leg in a stockyard accident. Now my father too was crippled. His convalescence was slow but steady, and the doctors placed him in the Santa Monica Rehabilitation Center, a sun-bleached building that opened out onto the warm spray of the Pacific. The place gave him some strength and some color and some training in walking with an artificial leg. He did pretty well for a year or so until he slipped and broke his hip. He was confined to a wheelchair after that, and the confinement contributed to the diminishing of his body and spirit.

I am holding a picture of him. He is sitting in his wheelchair and smiling at the camera. The smile appears forced, unsteady, seems to quaver, though it is frozen in silver nitrate. He is in his mid-sixties and looks eighty. Late in my junior year, he had a stroke and never came out of the resulting coma. After that, I would see him only in dreams, and to this day that is how I join him. Sometimes the dreams are sad and grisly and primal: my father lying in a bed soaked with his suppuration, holding me, rocking me. But sometimes the dreams bring him back to me healthy: him talking to me on an empty street, or buying some pictures to decorate our old house, or transformed somehow into someone strong and adept with tools and the physical.

Jack MacFarland couldn't have come into my life at a better time. My father was dead, and I had logged up too many years of scholastic indifference. Mr. MacFarland had a master's degree from Columbia and decided, at twenty-six, to find a little school and teach his heart out. He never took any credentialing courses, couldn't bear to, he said, so he had to find employment in a private system. He ended up at Our Lady of Mercy teaching five sections of senior English. He was a beatnik who was born too late. His teeth were stained, he tucked his sorry tie in between the third and fourth buttons on his shirt, and his pants were chronically wrinkled. At first, we couldn't believe this guy, thought he slept in his car. But within no time, he had us so startled with work that we didn't much worry about where he slept or if he slept at all. We wrote three or four essays a month. We read a book every two to three weeks, starting with the *Iliad* and ending up with Hemingway. He gave us a quiz on the reading every other day. He brought a prep school curriculum to Mercy High.

MacFarland's lectures were crafted, and as he delivered them he would pace the room jiggling a piece of chalk in his cupped hand, using it to scribble on the board the names of all the writers and philosophers and plays and novels he was weaving into his discussion. He asked questions often, raised everything from Zeno's paradox to the repeated last line of Frost's "Stopping by Woods on a Snowy Evening." He slowly and carefully built up our knowledge of Western intellectual history—with facts, with connections, with speculations. We learned about Greek philosophy, about Dante, the Elizabethan world view, the Age of Reason, existentialism. He analyzed poems with us, had us reading sections from John Ciardi's *How Does a Poem Mean?*, making a potentially difficult book accessible with his own explanations. We gave oral reports on poems Ciardi didn't cover. We imitated the styles of Conrad, Hemingway, and *Time* magazine. We wrote and talked, wrote and talked. The man immersed us in language.

Even MacFarland's barbs were literary. If Jim Fitzsimmons, hung over and irritable, tried to smart-ass him, he'd rejoin with a flourish that would spark the indomitable Skip Madison—who'd lost his front teeth in a hapless tackle—to flick his tongue through the gap and opine, "good chop," drawing out the single "o" in stinging indictment. Jack MacFarland, this tobacco-stained intellectual, brandished linguistic weapons of a kind I hadn't encountered before. Here was this *egghead,* for God's sake, keeping some pretty difficult people in line. And from what I heard, Mike Dweetz and Steve Fusco and all the notorious Voc. Ed. crowd settled down as well when MacFarland took the podium.

Though a lot of guys groused in the schoolyard, it just seemed that giving trouble to this particular teacher was a silly thing to do. Tomfoolery, not to mention assault, had no place in the world he was trying to create for us, and instinctively everyone knew that. If nothing else, we all recognized MacFarland's considerable intelligence and respected the hours he put into his work. It came to this: The troublemaker would look foolish rather than daring. Even Jim Fitzsimmons was reading *On the Road* and turning his incipient alcoholism to literary ends.

There were some lives that were already beyond Jack MacFarland's ministrations, but mine was not. I started reading again as I hadn't since elementary school. I would go into our gloomy little bedroom or sit at the dinner table while, on the television, Danny McShane was paralyzing Mr. Moto with the atomic drop, and work slowly back through *Heart of Darkness,* trying to catch the words in Conrad's sentences. I certainly was not MacFarland's best student; most of the other guys in College Prep, even my fellow slackers, had better backgrounds than I did. But I worked very hard, for MacFarland had hooked me. He tapped my old interest in reading and creating stories. He gave me a way to feel special by using my mind. And he provided a role model that wasn't shaped on physical prowess alone, and something inside me that I wasn't quite aware of responded to that. Jack MacFarland established a literacy club, to borrow a phrase of Frank Smith's, and invited me—invited all of us—to join.[2]

There's been a good deal of research and speculation suggesting that the acknowledgment of school performance with extrinsic rewards—smiling faces, stars, numbers, grades—diminishes the intrinsic satisfaction children experience by engaging in reading or writing or problem solving. While it's certainly true that we've created an educational system that encourages our best and brightest to become cynical grade collectors and, in general, have developed an obsession with evaluation and assessment, I must tell you that venal though it may have been, I loved getting good grades from MacFarland. I now know how subjective grades can be, but then they came tucked in the back of essays like bits of scientific data, some sort of spectroscopic readout that said, objectively and publicly, that I had made something of value. I suppose I'd been mediocre for too long and enjoyed a public redefinition. And I suppose the workings of my mind, such as they were, had been private for too long. My linguistic play moved into the world; like the intergalactic stories I told years before on Frank's berry-splattered truck bed, these papers with their circled, red B-pluses and A-minuses linked my mind to something outside it. I carried them around like a club emblem.

One day in the December of my senior year, Mr. MacFarland asked me where I was going to go to college. I hadn't thought much about it. Many of the students I teach today spent their last year in high school with a physics text in one hand and the Stanford catalog in the other, but I wasn't even aware of what "entrance requirements" were. My folks would say that they wanted me to go to college and be a doctor, but I don't know how seriously I ever took that; it seemed a sweet thing to say, a bit of supportive family chatter, like telling a gangly daughter she's graceful. The reality of higher education wasn't in my scheme of things: No one in the family had gone to college; only two of my uncles had completed high school. I figured I'd get a night job and go to the local junior college because I knew that Snyder and Company were going there to play ball. But I hadn't even prepared for that. When I finally said, "I don't know," MacFarland looked down at me—I was seated in his office—and said, "Listen, you can write."

My grades stank. I had A's in biology and a handful of B's in a few English and social science classes. All the rest were Cs—or worse. MacFarland said I would do well in his class and laid down the law about doing well in the others. Still, the record for my first three years wouldn't have been acceptable to any four-year school. To nobody's surprise, I was turned down flat by USC and UCLA. But Jack MacFarland was on the case. He had received his bachelor's degree from Loyola University, so he made calls to old professors and talked to somebody in admissions and wrote me a strong letter. Loyola finally accepted me as a probationary student. I would be on trial for the first year, and if I did okay, I would be granted regular status. MacFarland also intervened to get me a loan, for I could never have afforded a private college without it. Four more years of religion classes and four more years of boys at one school, girls at another. But at least I was going to college. Amazing.

In my last semester of high school, I elected a special English course fashioned by Mr. MacFarland, and it was through this elective that there arose at Mercy a fledgling literati. Art Mitz, the editor of the school newspaper and a very smart guy, was the kingpin. He was joined by me and by Mark Dever, a quiet boy who wrote beautifully and who would die before he was forty. MacFarland occasionally invited us to his apartment, and those visits became the high point of our apprenticeship: We'd clamp on our training wheels and drive to his salon.

He lived in a cramped and cluttered place near the airport, tucked away in the kind of building that architectural critic Reyner Banham calls a *dingbat*. Books were all over: stacked, piled, tossed, and crated, underlined and dog eared, well worn and new. Cigarette ashes crusted with coffee in saucers or spilled over the sides of motel ashtrays. The little bedroom had, along two of its walls, bricks and boards loaded with notes, magazines, and oversized books. The kitchen joined the living room, and there was a stack of German newspapers under the sink. I had never seen anything like it: a great flophouse of language furnished by City Lights and Café le Metro. I read every title. I flipped through paperbacks and scanned jackets and memorized names: Gogal, *Finnegan's Wake*, Djuna Barnes, Jackson Pollock, *A Coney Island of the Mind*, F.O. Matthiessen's *American Renaissance*, all sorts of Freud, *Troubled Sleep*, Man Ray, *The Education of Henry Adam*, Richard Wright, *Film as Art*, William Butler Yeats, Marguerite Duras, *Redburn, A Season in Hell, Kapital*. On the cover of Alain-Fournier's *The Wanderer* was an Edward Gorey drawing of a young man on a road winding into dark trees. By the hotplate sat a strange Kafka novel called *Amerika*, in which an adolescent hero crosses the Atlantic to find the Nature Theater of Oklahoma. Art and Mark would be talking about a movie or the school newspaper, and I would be consuming my English teacher's library. It was heady stuff. I felt like a Pop Warner athlete on steroids.

Art, Mark, and I would buy stogies and triangulate from MacFarland's apartment to the Cinema, which now shows X-rated films but was then L.A.'s premiere art theater, and then to the musty Cherokee Bookstore in Hollywood to hobnob with beatnik homosexuals—smoking, drinking bourbon and coffee, and trying out awkward phrases we'd gleaned from our mentor's bookshelves. I was happy and precocious and a little scared as well, for Hollywood Boulevard was thick with a kind of decadence that was foreign to the South Side. After the Cherokee, we would head back to the security of MacFarland's apartment, slaphappy with hipness.

Let me be the first to admit that there was a good deal of adolescent passion in this embrace of the avant-garde: self-absorption, sexually charged pedantry, an elevation of the odd and abandoned. Still it was a time during which I absorbed an awful lot of information: long lists of titles, images from expressionist paintings, new wave shibboleths, snippets of philosophy, and names that read like Steve Fusco's misspellings—Goethe, Nietzsche, Kierkegaard. Now this is hardly the stuff of deep understanding. But it was an introduction, a phrase book, a Baedeker to a vocabulary of ideas, and it felt good at the time to know all these words. With hindsight I realize how layered and important that knowledge was.

It enabled me to do things in the world. I could browse bohemian bookstores in far-off, mysterious Hollywood; I could go to the Cinema and see events through the lenses of European directors; and, most of all, I could share an evening, talk that talk, with Jack MacFarland, the man I most admired at the time. Knowledge was becoming a bonding agent. Within a year or two, the persona of the disaffected hipster would prove too cynical, too alienated to last. But for a time it was new and exciting: It provided a critical perspective on society, and it allowed me to act as though I were living beyond the limiting boundaries of South Vermont.

NOTES

1. Mr. Gross is described in Theodore Sizer, *Horace's Compromise* (Boston: Houghton Mifflin, 1985), pp. 146-148.
2. Frank Smith, *Joining the Literacy Club: Further Essays into Education* (Portsmouth, N.H.: Heinemann Educational Books, 1988).

QUESTIONS FOR REACTION AND DISCUSSION

1. Rose speaks specifically about his experience as the son of Italian immigrants. How do his experiences compare and contrast with other immigrant groups represented by the members of your class? What do you know about your own background?

2. In the opening paragraphs of this selection, Rose provides numerous details to provide a full context for the life he lived on Vermont Avenue. How effective are these paragraphs? What details strike you as particularly vivid?
3. Describe the kind of student Rose became at his elementary school, St. Regina's. How did he spend his time outside of school?
4. Rose's parents were eager to send him to the best schools, so they chose Our Lady of Mercy, a Catholic secondary school, a considerable distance from their home. Describe Our Lady of Mercy and explain what you learn about the curriculum of the school. What is the Voc. Ed. track and how does Rose end up there? How does he emerge from it?
5. How did Jack MacFarland change Rose's life at school?

QUESTIONS FOR WRITING

1. Mike Rose uses arresting examples from his own experiences to provide evidence for the points he wants to make about American education. In an essay, discuss the implications of Rose's example of the student (Ken Harvey in the Voc. Ed. religion class) who just wants to be "average." Consider whether just wanting to be "average" is an inevitable circumstance in which some American students find themselves. Use Rose's example as a departure point and discuss this example from your own educational experience or other experiences you may have had in school with tracking or placement of students according to a perceived ability level.
2. Rose says that he is not using his own life as an emblem—that he does not see himself as a "representative man." Why, then, does he use his own life story as an example in a book about educational problems in America? Write an essay in which you discuss the advantages and disadvantages of using one's own personal experiences to write about larger educational problems.
3. In a striking statement, Rose says, "Students will float to the mark you set." What does your experience tell you about the truth of this statement? Write an essay in which you use this statement as a departure point for an argument about the importance of maintaining high intellectual standards in education.
4. Throughout this essay, Rose talks about teachers—both effective and ineffective. In an essay, define the characteristics of a successful teacher, according to what you abstract from Rose's portrayals. Give examples from his essay and from your own experiences, commenting fully on the characteristics you describe. Do you agree or disagree with Rose on all the characteristics?

Questions for Further Exploration

1. Rose alludes to a number of books and authors that made a difference to him in his educational development, especially toward the end of this essay when he became the student of Jack MacFarland. Take one of the paragraphs in which he refers to several writers or books, and annotate it by providing an explanatory note about each reference.

2. Both Rose's elementary and secondary school experiences were at private, Catholic schools. What are the major differences between a private, religiously affiliated school and a public school? What can you find out about differing standards? The curriculum?

3. The failure of American high schools—both public and private—has been the topic of many reports from the early 1980s through the present time. Among the most provocative and famous is a 1982 report of the National Commission on Excellence in Education, "A Nation at Risk," by David Gardner. Locate a copy of this report at your library and write an essay in which you compare the criticisms that Rose makes of the schools with the findings of this commission.

4. Access the Web site of the United States Department of Education <http://www.ed.gov>. Follow the links to the online educational resources offered there. What information can you find about how schools are expected to deal with underprepared students? What information can you find out about standards for schools?

2

CHAPTER VII

Frederick Douglass (1818–1895) was born into slavery on Edward Lloyd's plantation on the Eastern Shore of Maryland. As a young boy, he was separated from his mother and sent to the Hugh Auld family in Baltimore, where he learned to read and write, first through some instruction by his mistress and later by watching and listening to the white boys in the neighborhood. At the age of fifteen, he was returned to the Eastern Shore as a plantation slave and because he was considered unruly and uncooperative, he was sent to an even more difficult situation on a farm owned by Edward Covey. As an older teenager, he was sent back to Baltimore to work as a slave in the shipyards and after one unsuccessful attempt at escape, he managed to disguise himself as a sailor and escape slavery by going to New York in 1838. Within a few years, he became active in anti-slavery activities in Massachusetts and earned a reputation as a spirited speaker and eloquent orator. His speeches and his articulate speaking style were so impressive that many doubted he had once been a slave; in part to convince his audiences and also to demonstrate the horrors of slavery, Douglass wrote his autobiography, and the Boston Anti-Slavery Society published The Narrative of the Life of Frederick Douglass *in May 1845. The first edition of the book sold out within the first five months of publication, and Douglass earned an even broader audience. In the years after the publication of the* Narrative, *Douglass became a successful newspaper editor; revised and published two more versions of his autobiography (*My Bondage and My Freedom *in 1855 and* The Life and Times of Frederick Douglass *in 1881); served as the first American consul to Haiti; and occupied an important and influential position as a reform leader throughout the second half of the nineteenth century. The reading printed here is Chapter 7 of* The Narrative of the Life of Frederick Douglass.

QUESTIONS FOR READING

1. *The Narrative of the Life of Frederick Douglass* is usually categorized as a "slave narrative." What is your understanding of that genre?
2. What do you know about slavery in the 1840s and the laws about literacy for slaves?
3. A term that Douglass comments on in this section of his *Narrative* is "abolition." What was the abolition movement in the nineteenth century?

FREDERICK   DOUGLASS

CHAPTER VII

Narrative of the Life of Frederick Douglass, *an American Slave, Written by Himself*
(New York: Penguin, 1986)

I lived in Master Hugh's family about seven years. During this time, I succeeded in learning to read and write. In accomplishing this, I was compelled to resort to various stratagems. I had no regular teacher. My mistress, who had kindly commenced to instruct me, had, in compliance with the advice and direction of her husband, not only ceased to instruct, but had set her face against my being instructed by any one else. It is due, however, to my mistress to say of her, that she did not adopt this course of treatment immediately. She at first lacked the depravity indispensable to shutting me up in mental darkness. It was at least necessary for her to have some training in the exercise of irresponsible power, to make her equal to the task of treating me as though I were a brute.

My mistress was, as I have said, a kind and tender-hearted woman; and in the simplicity of her soul she commenced, when I first went to live with her, to treat me as she supposed one human being ought to treat another. In entering upon the duties of a slaveholder, she did not seem to perceive that I sustained to her the relation of a mere chattel, and that for her to treat me as a human being was not only wrong, but dangerously so. Slavery proved as injurious to her as it did to me. When I went there, she was a pious, warm, and tender-hearted woman. There was no sorrow or suffering for which she had not a tear. She had bread for the hungry, clothes for the naked, and comfort for every mourner that came within her reach. Slavery soon proved its ability to divest her of these heavenly qualities. Under its influence, the tender heart became stone, and the lamblike disposition gave way to one of tiger-like fierceness. The first step in her downward course was in her ceasing to instruct me. She now commenced to practise her husband's precepts. She finally became even more violent in her opposition than her husband himself. She was not satisfied with simply doing as well as he had commanded; she seemed anxious to do better. Nothing seemed to make her more angry than to see me with a newspaper. She seemed to think that here lay the danger. I have had her rush at me with a face made all up of fury, and snatch from me a newspaper, in a manner that fully revealed her apprehension. She was an apt woman; and a little experience soon demonstrated, to her satisfaction, that education and slavery were incompatible with each other.

From this time I was most narrowly watched. If I was in a separate room any considerable length of time, I was sure to be suspected of having a book, and was at once called to give an account of myself. All this, however, was too late. The first step had been taken. Mistress, in teaching me the alphabet, had given me the *inch*, and no precaution could prevent me from taking the *ell*.

The plan which I adopted, and the one by which I was most successful, was that of making friends of all the little white boys whom I met in the street. As many of these as I could, I converted into teachers. With their kindly aid, obtained at different times and in different places, I finally succeeded in learning to read. When I was sent of errands, I always took my book with me, and by going one part of my errand quickly, I found time to get a lesson before my return. I used also to carry bread with me, enough of which was always in the house, and to which I was always welcome; for I was much better off in this regard than many of the poor white children in our neighborhood. This bread I used to bestow upon the hungry little urchins, who, in return, would give me that more valuable bread of knowledge. I am strongly tempted to give the names of two or three of those little boys, as a testimonial of the gratitude and affection I bear them; but prudence forbids;—not that it would injure me, but it might embarrass them; for it is almost an unpardonable offence to teach slaves to read in this Christian country. It is enough to say of the dear little fellows, that they lived on Philpot Street, very near Durgin and Bailey's ship-yard. I used to talk this matter of slavery over with them. I would sometimes say to them, I wished I could be as free as they would be when they got to be men. "You will be free as soon as you are twenty-one, *but I am a slave for life!* Have not I as good a right to be free as you have?" These words used to trouble them; they would express for me the liveliest sympathy, and console me with the hope that something would occur by which I might be free.

I was now about twelve years old, and the thought of being a *slave for life* began to bear heavily upon my heart. Just about this time, I got hold of a book entitled "The Columbian Orator." Every opportunity I got, I used to read this book. Among much of other interesting matter, I found in it a dialogue between a master and his slave. The slave was represented as having run away from his master three times. The dialogue represented the conversation which took place between them, when the slave was retaken the third time. In this dialogue, the whole argument in behalf of slavery was brought forward by the master, all of which was disposed of by the slave. The slave was made to say some very smart as well as impressive things in reply to his master—things which had the desired though unexpected effect; for the conversation resulted in the voluntary emancipation of the slave on the part of the master.

In the same book, I met with one of Sheridan's mighty speeches on and in behalf of Catholic emancipation. These were choice documents to me. I read them over and over again with unabated interest. They gave tongue to interesting thoughts of my own soul, which had frequently flashed through my mind, and died away for want of utterance. The moral which I gained from the dialogue was the power of truth over the conscience of even a slaveholder. What I got from Sheridan was a bold denunciation of slavery, and a powerful vindication of human rights. The reading of these documents enabled me to utter my thoughts, and to meet the arguments brought forward to sustain slavery; but while they relieved me of one difficulty, they brought on another even more painful than the one of which I was relieved. The more I read, the more I was led to abhor and detest my enslavers. I could regard them in no other light than a band of successful robbers, who had left their homes, and gone to Africa, and stolen us from our homes, and in a strange land reduced us to slavery. I loathed them as being the meanest as well as the most wicked of men. As I read and contemplated the subject, behold! that very discontentment which Master Hugh had predicted would follow my learning to read had already come, to torment and sting my soul to unutterable anguish. As I writhed under it, I would at times feel that learning to read had been a curse rather than a blessing. It had given me a view of my wretched condition, without the remedy. It opened my eyes to the horrible pit, but to no ladder upon which to get out. In moments of agony, I envied my fellow-slaves for their stupidity. I have often wished myself a beast. I preferred the condition of the meanest reptile to my own. Any thing, no matter what, to get rid of thinking! It was this everlasting thinking of my condition that tormented me. There was no getting rid of it. It was pressed upon me by every object within sight or hearing, animate or inanimate. The silver trump of freedom had roused my soul to eternal wakefulness. Freedom now appeared, to disappear no more forever. It was heard in every sound, and seen in every thing. It was ever present to torment me with a sense of my wretched condition. I saw nothing without seeing it, I heard nothing without hearing it, and felt nothing without feeling it. It looked from every star, it smiled in every calm, breathed in every wind, and moved in every storm.

I often found myself regretting my own existence, and wished myself dead; and but for the hope of being free, I have no doubt but that I should have killed myself, or done something for which I should have been killed. While in this state of mind, I was eager to hear any one speak of slavery. I was a ready listener. Every little while, I could hear something about the abolitionists. It was some time before I found what the word meant. It was always used in such connections as to make it an interesting word to me. If a slave ran away and succeeded in getting clear, or if a slave killed his master, set fire to a barn, or did any thing very wrong in the mind of a slaveholder, it was spoken of as the fruit of *abolition.* Hearing the word in this connection very often, I set about learning what it meant. The dictionary afforded me little or no help. I found it was "the act of abolishing;" but then I did not know what was to be abolished. Here I was perplexed. I did not dare to ask any one about its meaning, for I was satisfied that it was something they wanted me to know very little about. After a patient waiting, I got one of our city papers, containing an account of the number of petitions from the north, praying for the abolition of slavery in the District of Columbia, and of the slave trade between the States. From this time I understood the words *abolition* and *abolitionist,* and always drew near when that word was spoken, expecting to hear something of importance to myself and fellow-slaves. The light broke in upon me by degrees. I went one day down on the wharf of Mr. Waters; and seeing two Irishmen unloading a scow of stone, I went, unasked, and helped them. When we had finished, one of them came to me and asked me if I were a slave. I told him I was. He asked, "Are ye a slave for life?" I told him that I was. The good Irishman seemed to be deeply affected by the statement. He said to the other that it was a pity so fine a little fellow as myself should be a slave for life. He said it was a shame to hold me. They both advised me to run away to the north; that I should find friends there, and that I should be free. I pretended not to be interested in what they said, and treated them as if I did not understand them; for I feared they might be treacherous. White men have been known to encourage slaves to escape, and then, to get the reward, catch them and return them to their masters. I was afraid that these seemingly good men might use me so; but I nevertheless remembered their advice, and from that time I resolved to run away. I looked forward to a time at which it would be safe for me to escape. I was too young to think of doing so immediately; besides, I wished to learn how to write, as I might have occasion to write my own pass. I consoled myself with the hope that I should one day find a good chance. Meanwhile, I would learn to write.

The idea as to how I might learn to write was suggested to me by being in Durgin and Bailey's ship-yard, and frequently seeing the ship carpenters, after hewing, and getting a piece of timber ready for use, write on the timber the name of that part of the ship for which it was intended. When a piece of timber was intended for the larboard side, it would be marked thus—"L." When a piece was for the starboard side, it would be marked thus—"S." A piece for the larboard side forward, would be marked thus—"L.F." When a piece was for starboard side forward, it would be marked thus—"S.F." For larboard aft, it would be marked thus—"L.A." For starboard aft, it would be marked thus—"S.A." I soon learned the names of these letters, and for what they were intended when placed upon a piece of timber in the ship-yard. I immediately

commenced copying them, and in a short time was able to make the four letters named. After that, when I met with any boy who I knew could write, I
would tell him I could write as well as he. The next word would be, "I don't
believe you. Let me see you try it." I would then make the letters which I had
been so fortunate as to learn, and ask him to beat that. In this way I got a good
many lessons in writing, which it is quite possible I should never have gotten in
any other way. During this time, my copy-book was the board fence, brick
wall, and pavement; my pen and ink was a lump of chalk. With these, I learned
mainly how to write. I then commenced and continued copying the Italics in
Webster's Spelling Book, until I could make them all without looking on the
book. By this time, my little Master Thomas had gone to school, and learned
how to write, and had written over a number of copy-books. These had been
brought home, and shown to some of our near neighbors, and then laid aside.
My mistress used to go to class meeting at the Wilk Street meeting-house every
Monday afternoon, and leave me to take care of the house. When left thus, I
used to spend the time in writing in the spaces left in Master Thomas's copy-
book, copying what he had written. I continued to do this until I could write a
hand very similar to that of Master Thomas. Thus, after a long, tedious effort
for years, I finally succeeded in learning how to write.

QUESTIONS FOR REACTION AND DISCUSSION

1. What does Douglass suggest about the negative effects of slavery on
   masters and mistresses?
2. Why does Mistress Hugh stop teaching Douglass to read?
3. What is the impact of reading the selections in *The Columbian Orator*
   on Douglass's thinking about slavery?
4. Why does Douglass feel that learning to read has made his situation as
   a slave more difficult?
5. How does Douglass learn to write?

QUESTIONS FOR WRITING

1. What is the relationship between literacy and Douglass's quest for freedom? Write an essay in which you discuss the importance of learning
   to read and write to Douglass's determination to escape from slavery.
2. How does Douglass learn to read and write? Write an essay in which
   you explain the methods used to teach himself. Contrast these methods with what you can recall from your own experiences. How are
   they alike and different?
3. Douglass says that "The more I read, the more I was led to abhor and
   detest my enslavers." What are the implications of this statement?

What has Douglass learned through reading that he did not know before? Write an essay in which you explore the *power* of reading. Use examples from this essay, your own experiences, and other readings in this section.

4. Douglass's narrative is a powerful, first-person expression of his experiences—and not presented as an argument. And yet Douglass offers powerful arguments against slave-holding throughout his work. What is the difference in the power of a first-person narrative and an abstract argument? Write an essay in which you discuss the ways in which a narrative of personal experience can be more powerful than an argument. Use specific examples from Douglass's narrative to support your main ideas.

QUESTIONS FOR FURTHER EXPLORATION

1. Douglass mentions that he managed to obtain a copy of *The Columbian Orator*, one of the most popular school textbooks of the day. Compiled by Caleb Bingham in 1787 and used throughout the nineteenth century, *The Columbian Orator* served as a primer for white school boys learning the art of persuasive discourse and included speeches, dialogues, and sermons from both ancient and contemporary sources. Locate a copy of *The Columbian Orator* and read the "Dialogue between a Master and a Slave" or Sheridan's "Speech in the British Parliament." Write a report for your class in which you compare your reading of either the dialogue or the speech with Douglass's comments in this section of his *Narrative*.

2. Access The Frederick Douglass Museum and Cultural Center Web site <http://www.ggw.org/freenet/f/fdm> or The Frederick Douglass National Historic Site <http://www.nps.gov/frdo/freddoug.html> and examine the illustrations, chronologies, and other resources available about Douglass's life and work. What can you find out about Douglass's efforts to ensure that African-American children learned to read and write following the emancipation of slaves? Follow links to other sites and prepare a list of Internet resources on Douglass's efforts to reform education after he was a free man.

3

The Day Language Came into My Life

Helen Keller (1880–1968) was born in Tuscumbia, Alabama. Born with normal hearing and sight, she was stricken with a high fever at eighteen months of age, and when she recovered, she was deaf and blind. Although she had begun to talk before her illness, she quickly became mute as well. Braille, the system of writing and reading for blind persons through patterns of raised dots on a page, had been developed in 1826, and methods for teaching the blind and the deaf had been developed in Scotland in 1793. But the Kellers had few resources immediately available to them in a small town. Furthermore, blind and deaf persons were considered idiots in the 1880s. However, the Kellers were determined that their daughter should learn to read and write and sought advice from their influential friend, Alexander Graham Bell, who helped them locate a teacher through the Perkins Institute for the Deaf and Blind in Boston. Anne Sullivan, a young Irish immigrant, was sent to Alabama to teach Helen. A remarkably patient and gifted instructor, Sullivan was able to teach Keller the crucial concept that everything has a name, and, within two years, Keller was reading and writing Braille fluently. With Sullivan at her side to assist her, she was able to go to school and attended the Wright-Humason School for the Deaf in New York, the Cambridge School for Young Ladies, and eventually graduated from Radcliffe College in 1904 with honors. Keller began a career as a writer and a public speaker, dedicating herself to improving education and quality of life for deaf and blind people. With Anne Sullivan, she traveled all over the world and became a celebrity with a wide circle of influential friends, including all of the American presidents in office during her lifetime. Keller was the author of several books: Optimism, or My Key to Life *(1903);* The World I Live In *(1908);* Out of the Dark *(1913);* Midstream *(1929);* Let Us Have Faith *(1940); and* Teacher: Anne Sullivan Macy *(1955). Her first book,* The Story of My Life *(1903), recounts her experiences as she learned to read and write with Anne Sullivan. The reading printed here is from Chapter 4 of this book.*

QUESTIONS FOR READING

1. What do you know about the details of Helen Keller's life? In what ways does she remain a national figure?
2. How does your conception of what it means to be blind and deaf shape your reading of this selection?
3. How familiar are you with techniques and methods for teaching visually and hearing impaired students today?

HELEN KELLER

THE DAY LANGUAGE CAME INTO MY LIFE

The Story of My Life *(New York: Doubleday, Page, & Co., 1907)*

The most important day I remember in all my life is the one on which my teacher, Anne Mansfield Sullivan, came to me. I am filled with wonder when I consider the immeasurable contrast between the two lives which it connects. It was the third of March, 1887, three months before I was seven years old.

On the afternoon of that eventful day, I stood on the porch, dumb, expectant. I guessed vaguely from my mother's signs and from the hurrying to and fro in the house that something unusual was about to happen, so I went to the door and waited on the steps. The afternoon sun penetrated the mass of honeysuckle that covered the porch, and fell on my upturned face. My fingers lingered almost unconsciously on the familiar leaves and blossoms which had just come forth to greet the sweet southern spring. I did not know what the future held of marvel or surprise for me. Anger and bitterness had preyed upon me continually for weeks and a deep languor had succeeded this passionate struggle.

Have you ever been at sea in a dense fog, when it seemed as if a tangible white darkness shut you in, and the great ship, tense and anxious, groped her way toward the shore with plummet and sounding-line, and you waited with beating heart for something to happen? I was like that ship before my education began, only I was without compass or sounding-line, and had no way of knowing how near the harbour was. "Light! give me light!" was the wordless cry of my soul, and the light of love shone on me in that very hour.

I felt approaching footsteps. I stretched out my hand as I supposed to my mother. Some one took it, and I was caught up and held close in the arms of her who had come to reveal all things to me, and, more than all things else, to love me.

The morning after my teacher came she led me into her room and gave me a doll. The little blind children at the Perkins Institution had sent it and Laura Bridgman had dressed it; but I did not know this until afterward. When I had played with it a little while, Miss Sullivan slowly spelled into my hand the word "d-o-l-l." I was at once interested in this finger play and tried to imitate it. When I finally succeeded in making the letters correctly I was flushed with childish pleasure and pride. Running downstairs to my mother I held up my hand and made the letters for doll. I did not know that I was spelling a word or even that words existed; I was simply making my fingers go in monkey-like imitation. In the days that followed I learned to spell in this uncomprehending way a great many words, among them *pin, hat, cup* and a few verbs like *sit, stand* and *walk*. But my teacher had been with me several weeks before I understood that everything has a name.

One day, while I was playing with my new doll, Miss Sullivan put my big rag doll into my lap also, spelled "d-o-l-l" and tried to make me understand that "d-o-l-l" applied to both. Earlier in the day we had had a tussle over the words "m-u-g" and "w-a-t-e-r." Miss Sullivan had tried to impress it upon me that "m-u-g" is *mug* and that "w-a-t-e-r" is *water*, but I persisted in confounding the two. In despair she had dropped the subject for the time, only to renew it at the first opportunity. I became impatient at her repeated attempts and, seizing the new doll, I dashed it upon the floor. I was keenly delighted when I felt the fragments of the broken doll at my feet. Neither sorrow nor regret followed my passionate outburst. I had not loved the doll. In the still, dark world in which I lived there was no strong sentiment or tenderness. I felt my teacher sweep the fragments to one side of the hearth, and I had a sense of satisfaction that the cause of my discomfort was removed. She brought me my hat, and I knew I was going out into the warm sunshine. This thought, if a wordless sensation may be called a thought, made me hop and skip with pleasure.

We walked down the path to the well-house, attracted by the fragrance of the honeysuckle with which it was covered. Some one was drawing water and my teacher placed my hand under the spout. As the cool stream gushed over one hand she spelled into the other the word *water*, first slowly, then rapidly. I stood still, my whole attention fixed upon the motions of her fingers. Suddenly I felt a misty consciousness as of something forgotten—a thrill of returning thought; and somehow the mystery of language was revealed to me. I knew then that "w-a-t-e-r" meant the wonderful cool something that was flowing over my hand. That living word awakened my soul, gave it light, hope, joy, set it free! There were barriers still, it is true, but barriers that could in time be swept away.

I left the well-house eager to learn. Everything had a name, and each name gave birth to a new thought. As we returned to the house every object which I touched seemed to quiver with life. That was because I saw everything with the strange, new sight that had come to me. On entering the door I remembered the doll I had broken. I felt my way to the hearth and picked up the pieces. I tried vainly to put them together. Then my eyes filled with tears; for I realized what I had done, and for the first time I felt repentance and sorrow.

I learned a great many new words that day. I do not remember what they all were; but I do know that *mother, father, sister, teacher* were among them— words that were to make the world blossom for me, "like Aaron's rod, with flowers." It would have been difficult to find a happier child than I was as I lay in my crib at the close of that eventful day and lived over the joys it had brought me, and for the first time longed for a new day to come.

QUESTIONS FOR REACTION AND DISCUSSION

1. Keller opens this chapter with a vivid description of herself before she was able to communicate clearly with others. How effective is the simile of a ship in a dense fog and herself in a dark world? What other figurative language does Keller use in this chapter?
2. How does Sullivan help Keller understand the concept of water? Why is this a breakthrough moment in Keller's life?
3. *The Story of My Life* is Keller's autobiographical recollection of the events of her childhood, written when she was twenty-three. How accurate do you think her memories are? What details strike you as being particularly indicative of her powers of memory?

QUESTIONS FOR WRITING

1. Compare and contrast Keller's recognition of the power of language with that of Frederick Douglass. What are the similarities and differences? Write an essay in which you explore the experiences in achieving literacy of Keller as a disabled woman and Douglass as an enslaved man.
2. In 1960, William Gibson's play about Keller and her teacher, *The Miracle Worker,* won a Pulitzer Prize. Read the play or view the movie version made in 1962 with Anne Bancroft and Patty Duke, and write an essay in which you discuss how the dramatic adaptation of Keller's discovery of words contrasts with her written account.
3. What resources are available for visually and hearing impaired students on your campus? What is the campus policy governing services for assisting students with a variety of disabilities? Write a report designed to orient new students to the services obtainable on your campus and be specific about where students can find and receive help.

QUESTIONS FOR FURTHER EXPLORATION

1. Helen Keller was born at Ivy Green, a house that is preserved today as a center of information about Keller and is listed in the National Register of Historic Places. Access Ivy Green <http://www.bham.net/keller/home.html> and locate information about what programs and events the Helen Keller Property Board sponsors. Write an e-mail message to your classmates in which you report on the circumstances of the house and what biographical information you can learn about Keller by visiting this Web site.

2. Helen Keller was honored after her death by induction into the National Women's Hall of Fame. Access Deaf WorldWeb <http://dww.deafworldweb.org> and follow the links to locate information about Helen Keller. What do you learn about Keller and the National Women's Hall of Fame? What other useful information can you find on this site?

3. Use Infoseek or Excite to search the Internet for resources for blind and deaf persons. One excellent resource is the Blindness Resource Center of New York Institute for Special Education <http://www.nyise.org/blind.htm>. Follow the links there to the Deaf-Blind/Hearing Disability Resources page <http://www.nyise.org/deaf.htm>. Prepare a report for the members of your class on resources available in your area and on the Internet, focusing on a particular topic, such as American Sign Language, Braille literacy, schools for hearing or visually impaired persons, or foundations and organizations that provide resources and/or special services.

4. Research the history of American Sign Language or Braille by using *The Humanities Index* and print resources at your library. Write a brief account of the development of these communication tools for persons who are not hearing or visually impaired, explaining why they might wish to know about them.

4

IMPRESSIONS OF AN INDIAN CHILDHOOD AND THE SCHOOL DAYS OF AN INDIAN GIRL

Zitkala-Ša (1876–1938) was born Gertrude Simmons to a white father and a Dakota mother at the Yankton Sioux Agency in South Dakota. In the aftermath of the Battle of Little Big Horn in 1876, the Sioux had been driven into reservations of increasingly smaller sizes, and native Americans across the United States were finding their tribal cultures eradicated by increasingly repressive laws and policies. Like many Indian children, Zitkala-Ša was recruited for a missionary school, designed to assimilate native children into white culture. In 1884, Zitkala-Ša left her mother and attended White's Manual Institute, a Quaker boarding school in Wabash, Indiana. She attended the school for six years and then studied at Earlham College in Richmond, Indiana, from 1895 to 1897. She later accepted a teaching position at Carlisle Indian Industrial School in western Pennsylvania. An accomplished musician, she also studied at the Boston Conservatory of Music and later in her life wrote an opera about Indian life, The Sun Dance *(1913), with William Hanson. While teaching at Carlisle, Zitkala-Ša began to write and speak about her heritage as a Sioux and in 1900, the prestigious literary magazine, the* Atlantic Monthly, *published "Impressions of an Indian Childhood" and "The School Days of an Indian Girl" under the Sioux name of Zitkala-Ša, which means Red Bird. The next year she published a collection of Sioux myths and legends for children,* Old Indian Legends *(1902), and continued to publish essays in the* Atlantic Monthly *and other magazines. She later published a collection of her essays,* American Indian Stories *(1921), and with Charles H. Fabens and Matthew K. Sniffen, she wrote an account of abuses of Indian tribes in Oklahoma,* Oklahoma's Poor Rich Indians: An Orgy of Graft and Exploitation of the Five Civilized Tribes— Legalized Robbery *(1924). She married a Sioux who worked for the Bureau of Indian Affairs, Raymond T. Bonnin, in 1902, and with him she lived on the Uintah and Ouray Reservation in Utah for many years and later in Washington, D.C. Zitkala-Ša became an activist for Indian rights and was deeply involved in Indian organizations, including the Society of the American Indian; she briefly edited its journal, the* American Indian Magazine. *In 1926, she founded her own organization, the National Council of American Indians, and served as its president until her death in 1938. The selections printed here are from her autobiographical essays published in 1900 in the* Atlantic Monthly, *written when she was twenty-three years old.*

QUESTIONS FOR READING

1. What do you know about missionaries and the establishment of schools for native Americans during the nineteenth century? Make a list of questions for research as you read.
2. Zitkala-Ša schooling and subsequent entry into the literate society of white America was made at the cost of alienating her family. As you read, think of the ways in which family values can come in conflict with the values of formal schooling.

ZITKALA-ŠA (GERTRUDE BONNIN)

IMPRESSIONS OF AN INDIAN CHILDHOOD

Atlantic Monthly, *January and February 1900, 189-192*

The first turning away from the easy, natural flow of my life occurred in an early spring. It was in my eighth year; in the month of March, I afterward learned. At this age I knew but one language, and that was my mother's native tongue.

From some of my playmates I heard that two paleface missionaries were in our village. They were from that class of white men who wore big hats and carried large hearts, they said. Running direct to my mother, I began to question her why these two strangers were among us. She told me, after I had teased much, that they had come to take away Indian boys and girls to the East. My mother did not seem to want me to talk about them. But in a day or two, I gleaned many wonderful stories from my playfellows concerning the strangers.

"Mother, my friend Judéwin is going home with the missionaries. She is going to a more beautiful country than ours; the palefaces told her so!" I said wistfully, wishing in my heart that I too might go.

Mother sat in a chair, and I was hanging on her knee. Within the last two seasons my big brother Dawée had returned from a three years' education in the East, and his coming back influenced my mother to take a farther step from her native way of living. First it was a change from the buffalo skin to the white man's canvas that covered our wigwam. Now she had given up her wigwam of slender poles, to live, a foreigner, in a home of clumsy logs.

"Yes, my child, several others besides Judéwin are going away with the palefaces. Your brother said the missionaries had inquired about his little sister," she said, watching my face very closely.

My heart thumped so hard against my breast, I wondered if she could hear it.

"Did he tell them to take me, mother?" I asked, fearing lest Dawée had forbidden the palefaces to see me, and that my hope of going to the Wonderland would be entirely blighted.

With a sad, slow smile, she answered: "There! I knew you were wishing to go, because Judéwin has filled your ears with the white men's lies. Don't believe a word they say! Their words are sweet, but, my child, their deeds are bitter. You will cry for me, but they will not even soothe you. Stay with me, my little one! Your brother Dawée says that going East, away from your mother, is too hard an experience for his baby sister."

Thus my mother discouraged my curiosity about the lands beyond our eastern horizon; for it was not yet an ambition for Letters that was stirring me. But on the following day the missionaries did come to our very house. I spied them coming up the footpath leading to our cottage. A third man was with them, but he was not my brother Dawée. It was another, a young interpreter, a paleface who had a smattering of the Indian language. I was ready to run out to meet them, but I did not dare to displease my mother. With great glee, I jumped up and down on our ground floor. I begged my mother to open the door, that they would be sure to come to us. Alas! They came, they saw, and they conquered!

Judéwin had told me of the great tree where grew red, red apples; and how we could reach out our hands and pick all the red apples we could eat. I had never seen apple trees. I had never tasted more than a dozen red apples in my life; and when I heard of the orchards of the East, I was eager to roam among them. The missionaries smiled into my eyes, and patted my head. I wondered how mother could say such hard words against them.

"Mother, ask them if little girls may have all the red apples they want, when they go East," I whispered aloud, in my excitement.

The interpreter heard me, and answered: "Yes, little girl, the nice red apples are for those who pick them; and you will have a ride on the iron horse if you go with these good people."

I had never seen a train, and he knew it.

"Mother, I'm going East! I like big red apples, and I want to ride on the iron horse! Mother, say yes!" I pleaded.

My mother said nothing. The missionaries waited in silence; and my eyes began to blur with tears, though I struggled to choke them back. The corners of my mouth twitched, and my mother saw me.

"I am not ready to give you any word," she said to them. "Tomorrow I shall send you my answer by my son."

With this they left us. Alone with my mother, I yielded to my tears, and cried aloud, shaking my head so as not to hear what she was saying to me. This was the first time I had ever been so unwilling to give up my own desire that I refused to hearken to my mother's voice.

There was a solemn silence in our home that night. Before I went to bed I begged the Great Spirit to make my mother willing I should go with the missionaries.

The next morning came, and my mother called me to her side, "My daughter, do you still persist in wishing to leave your mother?" she asked.

"Oh, mother, it is not that I wish to leave you, but I want to see the wonderful Eastern land," I answered.

My dear old aunt came to our house that morning, and I heard her say, "Let her try it."

I hoped that, as usual, my aunt was pleading on my side. My brother Dawée came for mother's decision. I dropped my play, and crept close to my aunt.

"Yes, Dawée, my daughter, though she does not understand what it all means, is anxious to go. She will need an education when she is grown, for then there will be fewer real Dakotas, and many more palefaces. This tearing her away, so young, from her mother is necessary, if I would have her an educated woman. The palefaces, who owe us a large debt for stolen lands, have begun to pay a tardy justice in offering some education to our children. But I know my daughter must suffer keenly in this experiment. For her sake, I dread to tell you my reply to the missionaries. Go, tell them that they may take my little daughter, and that the Great Spirit shall not fail to reward them according to their hearts."

Wrapped in my heavy blanket, I walked with my mother to the carriage that was soon to take us to the iron horse. I was happy. I met my playmates, who were also wearing their best thick blankets. We showed one another our new beaded moccasins, and the width of the belts that girdled our new dresses. Soon we were being drawn rapidly away by the white man's horses. When I saw the lonely figure of my mother vanish in the distance, a sense of regret settled heavily upon me. I felt suddenly weak, as if I might fall limp to the ground. I was in the hands of strangers whom my mother did not fully trust. I no longer felt free to be myself, or to voice my own feelings. The tears trickled down my cheeks, and I buried my face in the folds of my blanket. Now the first step, parting me from my mother, was taken, and all my belated tears availed nothing

Having driven thirty miles to the ferryboat, we crossed the Missouri in the evening. Then riding again a few miles eastward, we stopped before a massive brick building. I looked at it in amazement, and with a vague misgiving, for in our village I had never seen so large a house. Trembling with fear and distrust of the palefaces, my teeth chattering from the chilly ride, I crept noiselessly in my soft moccasins along the narrow hall, keeping very close to the bare wall. I was as frightened and bewildered as the captured young of a wild creature.

THE SCHOOL DAYS
OF AN INDIAN GIRL

I. THE LAND OF RED APPLES

There were eight in our party of bronzed children who were going East with the missionaries. Among us were three young braves, two tall girls, and we three little ones, Judéwin, Thowin, and I.

We had been very impatient to start on our journey to the Red Apple Country, which, we were told, lay a little beyond the great circular horizon of the Western prairie. Under a sky of rosy apples we dreamt of roaming as freely and happily as we had chased the cloud shadows on the Dakota plains. We had anticipated much pleasure from a ride on the iron horse, but the throngs of staring palefaces disturbed and troubled us.

On the train, fair women, with tottering babies on each arm, stopped their haste and scrutinized the children of absent mothers. Large men, with heavy bundles in their hands, halted near by, and riveted their glassy blue eyes upon us.

I sank deep into the corner of my seat, for I resented being watched. Directly in front of me, children who were no larger than I hung themselves upon the backs of their seats, with their bold white faces toward me. Sometimes they took their forefingers out of their mouths and pointed at my moccasined feet. Their mothers, instead of reproving such rude curiosity, looked closely at me, and attracted their children's further notice to my blanket. This embarrassed me, and kept me constantly on the verge of tears.

I sat perfectly still, with my eyes downcast, daring only now and then to shoot long glances around me. Chancing to turn to the window at my side, I was quite breathless upon seeing one familiar object. It was the telegraph pole which strode by at short paces. Very near my mother's dwelling, along the edge of a road thickly bordered with wild sunflowers, some poles like these had been planted by white men. Often I had stopped, on my way down the road, to hold my ear against the pole, and, hearing its low moaning, I used to wonder what the paleface had done to hurt it. Now I sat watching for each pole that glided by to be the last one.

In this way I had forgotten my uncomfortable surroundings, when I heard one of my comrades call out my name. I saw the missionary standing very near, tossing candies and gums into our midst. This amused us all, and we tried to see who could catch the most of the sweetmeats. The missionary's generous distribution of candies was impressed upon my memory by a disastrous result which followed. I had caught more than my share of candies and gums, and soon after our arrival at the school I had a chance to disgrace myself, which, I am ashamed to say, I did.

Though we rode several days inside of the iron horse, I do not recall a single thing about our luncheons.

It was night when we reached the school grounds. The lights from the windows of the large buildings fell upon some of the icicled trees that stood beneath them. We were led toward an open door, where the brightness of the lights within flooded out over the heads of the excited palefaces who blocked the way. My body trembled more from fear than from the snow I trod upon.

Entering the house, I stood close against the wall. The strong glaring light in the large whitewashed room dazzled my eyes. The noisy hurrying of hard shoes upon a bare wooden floor increased the whirring in my ears. My only safety seemed to be in keeping next to the wall. As I was wondering in which direction to escape from all this confusion, two warm hands grasped me firmly, and in the same moment I was tossed high in midair. A rosy-cheeked paleface woman caught me in her arms. I was both frightened and insulted by such trifling. I stared into her eyes, wishing her to let me stand on my own feet, but she jumped me up and down with increasing enthusiasm. My mother had never made a plaything of her wee daughter. Remembering this I began to cry aloud.

They misunderstood the cause of my tears, and placed me at a white table loaded with food. There our party were united again. As I did not hush my crying, one of the older ones whispered to me, "Wait until you are alone in the night."

It was very little I could swallow besides my sobs, that evening.

"Oh, I want my mother and my brother Dawée! I want to go to my aunt!" I pleaded; but the ears of the palefaces could not hear me.

From the table we were taken along an upward incline of wooden boxes, which I learned afterward to call a stairway. At the top was a quiet hall, dimly lighted. Many narrow beds were in one straight line down the entire length of the wall. In them lay sleeping brown faces, which peeped just out of the coverings. I was tucked into bed with one of the tall girls, because she talked to me in my mother tongue and seemed to soothe me.

I had arrived in the wonderful land of rosy skies, but I was not happy, as I had thought I should be. My long travel and the bewildering sights had exhausted me. I fell asleep, heaving deep, tired sobs. My tears were left to dry themselves in streaks, because neither my aunt nor my mother was near to wipe them away.

II. THE CUTTING OF MY LONG HAIR

The first day in the land of apples was a bitter-cold one; for the snow still covered the ground, and the trees were bare. A large bell rang for breakfast, its loud metallic voice crashing through the belfry overhead and into our sensitive ears. The annoying clatter of shoes on bare floors gave us no peace. The constant clash of harsh noises, with an undercurrent of many voices murmuring an unknown tongue, made a bedlam within which I was securely tied. And though my spirit tore itself in struggling for its lost freedom, all was useless.

A paleface woman, with white hair, came up after us. We were placed in a line of girls who were marching into the dining room. These were Indian girls, in stiff shoes and closely clinging dresses. The small girls wore sleeved aprons and shingled[1] hair. As I walked noiselessly in my soft moccasins, I felt like sinking to the floor, for my blanket had been stripped from my shoulders. I looked hard at the Indian girls, who seemed not to care that they were even more immodestly dressed than I, in their tightly fitting clothes. While we marched in, the boys entered at an opposite door. I watched for the three young braves who came in our party. I spied them in the rear ranks, looking as uncomfortable as I felt.

A small bell was tapped, and each of the pupils drew a chair from under the table. Supposing this act meant they were to be seated, I pulled out mine and at once slipped into it from one side. But when I turned my head, I saw that I was the only one seated, and all the rest at our table remained standing. Just as I began to rise, looking shyly around to see how chairs were to be used, a second bell was sounded. All were seated at last, and I had to crawl back into my chair again. I heard a man's voice at one end of the hall, and I looked around to see him. But all the others hung their heads over their plates. As I glanced at the long chain of tables, I caught the eyes of a paleface woman upon me. Immediately I dropped my eyes, wondering why I was so keenly watched by the strange woman. The man ceased his mutterings, and then a third bell was tapped. Every one picked up his knife and fork and began eating. I began crying instead, for by this time I was afraid to venture anything more.

But this eating by formula was not the hardest trial in that first day. Late in the morning, my friend Judéwin gave me a terrible warning. Judéwin knew a few words of English; and she had overheard the paleface woman talk about cutting our long, heavy hair. Our mothers had taught us that only unskilled warriors who were captured had their hair shingled by the enemy. Among our people, short hair was worn by mourners, and shingled hair by cowards!

We discussed our fate some moments, and when Judéwin said, "We have to submit, because they are strong," I rebelled.

"No, I will not submit! I will struggle first!" I answered.

I watched my chance, and when no one noticed I disappeared. I crept up the stairs as quietly as I could in my squeaking shoes,—my moccasins had been exchanged for shoes. Along the hall I passed, without knowing whither I was going. Turning aside to an open door, I found a large room with three white beds in it. The windows were covered with dark green curtains, which made the room very dim. Thankful that no one was there, I directed my steps toward the corner farthest from the door. On my hands and knees I crawled under the bed, and cuddled myself in the dark corner.

From my hiding place I peered out, shuddering with fear whenever I heard footsteps near by. Though in the hall loud voices were calling my name, and I knew that even Judéwin was searching for me, I did not open my mouth to answer. Then the steps were quickened and the voices became excited. The sounds came nearer and nearer. Women and girls entered the room. I held my breath, and watched them open closet doors and peep behind large trunks. Someone threw up the curtains, and the room was filled with sudden light. What caused them to stoop and look under the bed I do not know. I remember being dragged out, though I resisted by kicking and scratching wildly. In spite of myself, I was carried downstairs and tied fast in a chair.

I cried aloud, shaking my head all the while until I felt the cold blades of the scissors against my neck, and heard them gnaw off one of my thick braids. Then I lost my spirit. Since the day I was taken from my mother I had suffered extreme indignities. People had stared at me. I had been tossed about in the air like a wooden puppet. And now my long hair was shingled like a coward's! In my anguish I moaned for my mother, but no one came to comfort me. Not a soul reasoned quietly with me, as my own mother used to do; for now I was only one of many little animals driven by a herder.

III. THE SNOW EPISODE

A short time after our arrival we three Dakotas were playing in the snowdrifts. We were all still deaf to the English language, excepting Judéwin, who always heard such puzzling things. One morning we learned through her ears that we were forbidden to fall lengthwise in the snow, as we had been doing, to see our own impressions. However, before many hours we had forgotten the order, and were having great sport in the snow, when a shrill voice called us. Looking up, we saw an imperative hand beckoning us into the house. We shook the snow off ourselves, and started toward the woman as slowly as we dared.

Judéwin said: "Now the paleface is angry with us. She is going to punish us for falling into the snow. If she looks straight into your eyes and talks loudly, you must wait until she stops. Then, after a tiny pause, say, 'No.'" The rest of the way we practiced upon the little word "no."

As it happened, Thowin was summoned to judgment first. The door shut behind her with a click.

Judéwin and I stood silently listening at the keyhole. The paleface woman talked in very severe tones. Her words fell from her lips like crackling embers, and her inflection ran up like the small end of a switch! I understood her voice better than the things she was saying, I was certain we had made her very impatient with us. Judéwin heard enough of the words to realize all too late that she had taught us the wrong reply.

"Oh, poor Thowin!" she gasped, as she put both hands over her ears.

Just then I heard Thowin's tremulous answer, "No."

With an angry exclamation, the woman gave her a hard spanking. Then she stopped to say something. Judéwin said it was this: "Are you going to obey my word the next time?"

Thowin answered again with the only word at her command, "No."

This time the woman meant her blows to smart, for the poor frightened girl shrieked at the top of her voice. In the midst of the whipping the blows ceased abruptly, and the woman asked another question: "Are you going to fall in the snow again?"

Thowin gave her bad password another trial. We heard her say feebly, "No! No!"

With this the woman hid away her half-worn slipper, and led the child out, stroking her black shorn head. Perhaps it occurred to her that brute force is not the solution for such a problem. She did nothing to Judéwin nor to me. She only returned to us our unhappy comrade, and left us alone in the room.

During the first two or three seasons misunderstandings as ridiculous as this one of the snow episode frequently took place, bringing unjustifiable frights and punishments into our little lives.

Within a year I was able to express myself somewhat in broken English. As soon as I comprehended a part of what was said and done, a mischievous spirit of revenge possessed me. One day I was called in from my play for some mis-conduct. I had disregarded a rule which seemed to me very needlessly binding. I was sent into the kitchen to mash the turnips for dinner. It was noon, and steaming dishes were hastily carried into the dining room. I hated turnips, and their odor which came from the brown jar was offensive to me. With fire in my heart, I took the wooden tool that the paleface woman held out to me. I stood upon a step, and, grasping the handle with both hands, I bent in hot rage over the turnips. I worked my vengeance upon them. All were so busily occupied that no one noticed me. I saw that the turnips were in a pulp, and that further beating could not improve them; but the order was, "Mash these turnips," and mash them I would! I renewed my energy; and as I sent the masher into the bottom of the jar, I felt a satisfying sensation that the weight of my body had gone into it.

Just here a paleface woman came up to my table. As she looked into the jar, she shoved my hands roughly aside. I stood fearless and angry. She placed her red hands upon the rim of the jar. Then she gave one lift and a stride away from the table. But lo! The pulpy contents fell through the crumbled bottom to the floor! She spared me no scolding phrases that I had earned. I did not heed them. I felt triumphant in my revenge, though deep within me I was a wee bit sorry to have broken the jar.

As I sat eating my dinner, and saw that no turnips were served, I whooped in my heart for having once asserted the rebellion within me.

IV. THE DEVIL

Among the legends the old warriors used to tell me were many stories of evil spirits. But I was taught to fear them no more than those who stalked about in material guise. I never knew there was an insolent chieftain among the bad spirits, who dared to array his forces against the Great Spirit, until I heard this white man's legend from a paleface woman.

Out of a large book she showed me a picture of the white man's devil. I looked in horror upon the strong claws that grew out of his fur-covered fingers. His feet were like his hands. Trailing at his heels was a scaly tail tipped with a serpent's open jaws. His face was a patchwork: he had bearded cheeks, like some I had seen palefaces wear; his nose was an eagle's bill, and his sharp-pointed ears were pricked up like those of a sly fox. Above them a pair of cow's horns curved upward. I trembled with awe, and my heart throbbed in my throat, as I looked at the king of evil spirits. Then I heard the paleface woman say that this terrible creature roamed loose in the world, and that little girls who disobeyed school regulations were to be tortured by him.

That night I dreamt about this evil divinity. Once again I seemed to be in my mother's cottage. An Indian woman had come to visit my mother. On opposite sides of the kitchen stove, which stood in the center of the small house, my mother and her guest were seated in straight-backed chairs. I played with a train of empty spools hitched together on a string. It was night, and the wick burned feebly. Suddenly I heard someone turn our door-knob from without.

My mother and the woman hushed their talk, and both looked toward the door. It opened gradually. I waited behind the stove. The hinges squeaked as the door was slowly, very slowly pushed inward.

Then in rushed the devil! He was tall! He looked exactly like the picture I had seen of him in the white man's papers. He did not speak to my mother, because he did not know the Indian language, but his glittering yellow eyes were fastened upon me. He took long strides around the stove, passing behind the woman's chair. I threw down my spools, and ran to my mother. He did not fear her, but followed closely after me. Then I ran round and round the stove, crying aloud for help. But my mother and the woman seemed not to know my danger. They sat still, looking quietly upon the devil's chase after me. At last I grew dizzy. My head revolved as on a hidden pivot. My knees became numb, and doubled under my weight like a pair of knife blades without a spring. Beside my mother's chair I fell in a heap. Just as the devil stooped over me with outstretched claws my mother awoke from her quiet indifference, and lifted me on her lap. Whereupon the devil vanished, and I was awake.

On the following morning I took my revenge upon the devil. Stealing into the room where a wall of shelves was filled with books, I drew forth The Stories of the Bible. With a broken slate pencil I carried in my apron pocket, I began by scratching out his wicked eyes. A few moments later, when I was ready to leave the room, there was a ragged hole in the page where the picture of the devil had once been.

V. IRON ROUTINE

A loud-clamoring bell awakened us at half past six in the cold winter mornings. From happy dreams of Western rolling lands and unlassoed freedom we tumbled out upon chilly bare floors back again into a paleface day. We had short time to jump into our shoes and clothes, and wet our eyes with icy water, before a small hand bell was vigorously run for roll call.

There were too many drowsy children and too numerous orders for the day to waste a moment in any apology to nature for giving her children such a shock in the early morning. We rushed downstairs, bounding over two high steps at a time, to land in the assembly room.

A paleface woman, with a yellowcovered roll book open on her arm and a gnawed pencil in her hand, appeared at the door. Her small, tired face was coldly lighted with a pair of large gray eyes.

She stood still in a halo of authority, while over the rim of her spectacles her eyes pried nervously about the room. Having glanced at her long list of names and called out the first one, she tossed up her chin and peered through the crystals of her spectacles to make sure of the answer "Here."

Relentlessly her pencil black-marked our daily records if we were not present to respond to our names, and no chum of ours had done it successfully for us. No matter if a dull headache or the painful cough of slow consumption[2] had delayed the absentee, there was only time enough to mark the tardiness. It was next to impossible to leave the iron routine after the civilizing machine had once begun its day's buzzing; and as it was inbred in me to suffer in silence rather than to appeal to the ears of one whose open eyes could not see my pain, I have many times trudged in the day's harness heavy-footed, like a dumb sick brute.

Once I lost a dear classmate. I remember well how she used to mope along at my side, until one morning she could not raise her head from her pillow. At her deathbed I stood weeping, as the paleface woman sat near her moistening the dry lips. Among the folds of the bedclothes I saw the open pages of the white man's Bible. The dying Indian girl talked disconnectedly of Jesus the Christ and the paleface who was cooling her swollen hands and feet.

I grew bitter, and censured the woman for cruel neglect of our physical ills. I despised the pencils that moved automatically, and the one teaspoon which dealt out, from a large bottle, healing to a row of variously ailing Indian children. I blamed the hard-working, well-meaning, ignorant woman who was inculcating in our hearts her superstitious ideas. Though I was sullen in all my little troubles, as soon as I felt better I was ready again to smile upon the cruel woman. Within a week I was again actively testing the chains which tightly bound my individuality like a mummy for burial.

The melancholy of those black days has left so long a shadow that it darkens the path of years that have since gone by. These sad memories rise above those of smoothly grinding school days. Perhaps my Indian nature is the moaning wind which stirs them now for their present record. But, however tempestuous this is within me, it comes out as the low voice of a curiously colored seashell, which is only for those ears that are bent with compassion to hear it.

VI. FOUR STRANGE SUMMERS

After my first three years of school, I roamed again in the Western country through four strange summers.

During this time I seemed to hang in the heart of chaos, beyond the touch or voice of human aid. My brother, being almost ten years my senior, did not quite understand my feelings. My mother had never gone inside of a schoolhouse, and so she was not capable of comforting her daughter who could read and write. Even nature seemed to have no place for me. I was neither a wee girl nor a tall one; neither a wild Indian nor a tame one. This deplorable situation was the effect of my brief course in the East, and the unsatisfactory "teenth" in a girl's years.

It was under these trying conditions that, one bright afternoon, as I sat restless and unhappy in my mother's cabin, I caught the sound of the spirited step of my brother's pony on the road which passed by our dwelling. Soon I heard the wheels of a light buckboard[3] and Dawée's familiar "Ho!" to his pony. He alighted upon the bare ground in front of our house. Tying his pony to one of the projecting corner logs of the low-roofed cottage, he stepped upon the wooden doorstep.

I met him there with a hurried greeting, and, as I passed by, he looked a quiet "What?" into my eyes.

When he began talking with my mother, I slipped the rope from the pony's bridle. Seizing the reins and bracing my feet against the dashboard, I wheeled around in an instant. The pony was ever ready to try his speed. Looking backward, I saw Dawée waving his hand to me. I turned with the curve in the road and disappeared. I followed the winding road which crawled upward between the bases of little hillocks. Deep water-worn ditches ran parallel on either side. A strong wind blew against my cheeks and fluttered my sleeves. The pony reached the top of the highest hill, and began an even race on the level lands. There was nothing moving within that great circular horizon of the Dakota prairies save the tall grasses, over which the wind blew and rolled off in long, shadowy waves.

Within this vast wigwam of blue and green I rode reckless and insignificant. It satisfied my small consciousness to see the white foam fly from the pony's mouth.

Suddenly, out of the earth a coyote came forth at a swinging trot that was taking the cunning thief toward the hills and the village beyond. Upon the moment's impulse, I gave him a long chase and a wholesome fright. As I turned away to go back to the village, the wolf sank down upon his haunches for rest, for it was a hot summer day; and as I drove slowly homeward, I saw his sharp nose pointed at me, until I vanished below the margin of the hilltops.

In a little while I came in sight of my mother's house. Dawée stood in the yard, laughing at an old warrior who was pointing his forefinger, and again waving his whole hand, toward the hills. With his blanket drawn over one shoulder, he talked and motioned excitedly. Dawée turned the old man by the shoulder and pointed me out to him.

"Oh han!" (Oh yes) the warrior muttered, and went his way. He had climbed the top of his favorite barren hill to survey the surrounding prairies, when he spied my chase after the coyote. His keen eyes recognized the pony and driver. At once uneasy for my safety, he had come running to my mother's cabin to give her warning. I did not appreciate his kindly interest, for there was an unrest gnawing at my heart.

As soon as he went away, I asked Dawée about something else.

"No, my baby sister, I cannot take you with me to the party tonight," he replied. Though I was not far from fifteen, and I felt that before long I should enjoy all the privileges of my tall cousin, Dawée persisted in calling me his baby sister.

That moonlight night, I cried in my mother's presence when I heard the jolly young people pass by our cottage. They were no more young braves in blankets and eagle plumes, nor Indian maids with prettily painted cheeks. They had gone three years to school in the East, and had become civilized. The young men wore the white man's coat and trousers, with bright neckties. The girls wore tight muslin dresses; with ribbons at neck and waist. At these gatherings they talked English. I could speak English almost as well as my brother, but I was not properly dressed to be taken along. I had no hat, no ribbons, and no close-fitting gown. Since my return from school I had thrown away my shoes, and wore again the soft moccasins.

While Dawée was busily preparing to go I controlled my tears. But when I heard him bounding away on his pony, I buried my face in my arms and cried hot tears.

My mother was troubled by my unhappiness. Coming to my side, she offered me the only printed matter we had in our home. It was an Indian Bible, given her some years ago by a missionary. She tried to console me. "Here, my child, are the white man's papers. Read a little from them," she said most piously.

I took it from her hand, for her sake; but my enraged spirit felt more like burning the book, which afforded me no help, and was a perfect delusion to my mother. I did not read it, but laid it unopened on the floor, where I sat on my feet. The dim yellow light of the braided muslin burning in a small vessel[4] of oil flickered and sizzled in the awful silent storm which followed my rejection of the Bible.

Now my wrath against the fates consumed my tears before they reached my eyes. I sat stony, with a bowed head. My mother threw a shawl over her head and shoulders, and stepped out into the night.

After an uncertain solitude, I was suddenly aroused by a loud cry piercing the night. It was my mother's voice wailing among the barren hills which held the bones of buried warriors. She called aloud for her brothers' spirits to support her in her helpless misery. My fingers grew icy cold, as I realized that my unrestrained tears had betrayed my suffering to her, and she was grieving for me.

Before she returned, though I knew she was on her way, for she had ceased her weeping, I extinguished the light, and leaned my head on the window sill.

Many schemes of running away from my surroundings hovered about in my mind. A few more moons of such a turmoil drove me away to the Eastern school. I rode on the white man's iron steed, thinking it would bring me back to my mother in a few winters, when I should be grown tall, and there would be congenial friends awaiting me.

VII. INCURRING MY MOTHER'S DISPLEASURE

In the second journey to the East I had not come without some precautions. I had a secret interview with one of our best medicine men, and when I left his wigwam I carried securely in my sleeve a tiny bunch of magic roots. This possession assured me of friends wherever I should go. So absolutely did I believe in its charms that I wore it through all the school routine for more than a year. Then, before I lost my faith in the dead roots, I lost the little buckskin bag containing all my good luck.

At the close of this second term of three years I was the proud owner of my first diploma. The following autumn I ventured upon a college career against my mother's will.

I had written for her approval, but in her reply I found no encouragement. She called my notice to her neighbors' children, who had completed their education in three years. They had returned to their homes, and were then talking English with the frontier settlers. Her few words hinted that I had better give up my slow attempt to learn the white man's ways, and be content to roam over the prairies and find my living upon wild roots. I silenced her by deliberate disobedience.

Thus, homeless and heavy-hearted, I began anew my life among strangers.

As I hid myself in my little room in the college dormitory, away from the scornful and yet curious eyes of the students, I pined for sympathy. Often I wept in secret, wishing I had gone West, to be nourished by my mother's love, instead of remaining among a cold race whose hearts were frozen hard with prejudice.

During the fall and winter seasons I scarcely had a real friend, though by that time several of my classmates were courteous to me at a safe distance.

My mother had not yet forgiven my rudeness to her, and I had no moment for letter-writing. By daylight and lamplight, I spun with reeds and thistles, until my hands were tired from their weaving, the magic design which promised me the white man's respect.

At length, in the spring term, I entered an oratorical contest among the various classes. As the day of competition approached, it did not seem possible that the event was so near at hand, but it came. In the chapel the classes assembled together, with their invited guests. The high platform was carpeted, and gayly festooned with college colors. A bright white light illumined the room, and outlined clearly the great polished beams that arched the domed ceiling. The assembled crowds filled the air with pulsating murmurs. When the hour for speaking arrived all were hushed. But on the wall the old clock which pointed out the trying moment ticked calmly on.

One after another I saw and heard the orators. Still, I could not realize that they longed for the favorable decision of the judges as much as I did. Each contestant received a loud burst of applause, and some were cheered heartily. Too soon my turn came, and I paused a moment behind the curtains for a deep breath. After my concluding words, I heard the same applause that the others had called out.

Upon my retreating steps, I was astounded to receive from my fellow students a large bouquet of roses tied with flowing ribbons. With the lovely flowers I fled from the stage. This friendly token was a rebuke to me for the hard feelings I had borne them.

Later, the decision of the judges awarded me the first place. Then there was a mad uproar in the hall, where my classmates sang and shouted my name at the top of their lungs; and the disappointed students howled and brayed in fearfully dissonant tin trumpets. In this excitement, happy students rushed forward to offer their congratulations. And I could not conceal a smile when they wished to escort me in a procession to the students' parlor, where all were going to calm themselves. Thanking them for the kind spirit which prompted them to make such a proposition, I walked alone with the night to my own little room.

A few weeks afterward, I appeared as the college representative in another contest. This time the competition was among orators from different colleges in our state. It was held at the state capital, in one of the largest opera houses.

Here again was a strong prejudice against my people. In the evening, as the great audience filled the house, the student bodies began warring among themselves. Fortunately, I was spared witnessing any of the noisy wrangling before the contest began. The slurs against the Indian that stained the lips of our opponents were already burning like a dry fever within my breast.

But after the orations were delivered a deeper burn awaited me. There, before that vast ocean of eyes, some college rowdies threw out a large white flag, with a drawing of a most forlorn Indian girl on it. Under this they had printed in bold black letters words that ridiculed the college which was represented by a "squaw." Such worse than barbarian rudeness embittered me. While we waited for the verdict of the judges, I gleamed fiercely upon the throngs of palefaces. My teeth were hard set, as I saw the white flag still floating insolently in the air.

Then anxiously we watched the man carry toward the stage the envelope containing the final decision.

There were two prizes given, that night, and one of them was mine!

The evil spirit laughed within me when the white flag dropped out of sight, and the hands which furled it hung limp in defeat.

Leaving the crowd as quickly as possible, I was soon in my room. The rest of the night I sat in an armchair and gazed into the crackling fire. I laughed no more in triumph when thus alone. The little taste of victory did not satisfy a hunger in my heart. In my mind I saw my mother far away on the Western plains, and she was holding a charge against me.

NOTES

1. Bobbed, cut short.
2. Old term for tuberculosis.
3. A four-wheeled open carriage.
4. An oil lamp with a wick made of braided cotton.

QUESTIONS FOR REACTION AND DISCUSSION

1. How do the missionaries convince Indian families to send their children to school? How is the enticement of the "land of red apples" similar to marketing strategies used by educational institutions today?
2. Why was the cutting of Zitkala-Ša's hair so traumatic to her? What were the cultural implications for "shingled" hair?
3. How is language instruction in English handled at the school? What misunderstandings and mistakes arise from the methods?
4. What is the effect of the "white man's devil" on Zitkala-Ša? How do you read her dream?
5. What is the cumulative effect of the mission school on Zitkala-Ša? What would you say that she and her classmates learned through this experience?
6. Why does Zitkala-Ša decide to go to college against her mother's wishes?

QUESTIONS FOR WRITING

1. Unlike many of the other writers represented in this textbook, Zitkala-Ša was literally schooled into a literacy that was very remote

from her own native experience. English, the language she learned to read and write, carried with it a very different set of cultural assumptions from her native Sioux, the only language she knew before she went to the missionary school. Later, when she wrote the selections that appear here, she was fluent in English and had inevitably been influenced by the cultural assumptions inherent in this language. Write an essay in which you explore the cultural assumptions that Zitkala-Ša inherits from her use of the English language.

2. At the same time that Zitkala-Ša criticizes the harsh methods used by the teachers at the mission school to educate Indian students, she also reveals her own complicated feelings of being estranged and alienated from her Sioux culture. Write an essay in which you analyze the methods the Indian school uses to assimilate Indian students into white culture and speculate on the confusion and problems this educational system imposed on students for the future. As you think about this assignment, give careful consideration to the final scene in this reading in which Zitkala-Ša wins a prize at the oratorical contest.

QUESTIONS FOR FURTHER EXPLORATION

1. Visit the South Dakota Guide to the Great Sioux Nation Web site <http://www.state.sd.us/state/executive/tourism/sioux/sioux.htm> and read about the Yankton Sioux Tribe today. What are current living conditions like? What are the current educational opportunities?

2. "Impressions of an Indian Childhood" and "The School Days of an Indian Girl" were published in the *Atlantic Monthly* in January and February 1900. Locate copies of the magazine from this time (either on the shelves of your library in bound copies or on microfilm) and examine the Table of Contents closely. What other author's works appeared along with Zitkala-Ša's? Research the editorship and editorial policies of the magazine at this time by consulting histories and reference works on periodicals in the United States. Consult the Web site for the *Atlantic Monthly* <http://www.theatlantic.com> and learn what you can about the history of the magazine. Write a profile of the *Atlantic Monthly* during 1900 in which you describe the nature of the magazine and how Zitkala-Ša's works are a part of the mission of the periodical at this time.

3. Zitkala-Ša published an essay in 1902 in the *Atlantic Monthly*, "Why I Am a Pagan," in which she rejected the Christianity she had been taught at the mission school and outlines her belief in her native American religion. Locate this essay and analyze her objections to Christianity and her support of her tribal religion.

5

THE PROMISED LAND AND INITIATION

Mary Antin (1881–1949) was born a Jew in czarist Russia at a time when Jews were a despised minority. Beginning in the mid-nineteenth century with the reign of Alexander II and continuing under the reigns of Alexander III and Nicolas II, discriminatory laws were passed against Jews, designed to limit access to education and to establish strict residential restrictions. Anti-Jewish riots, "pogroms," were common and the government made little effort to control anti-Jewish sentiment. Hundreds of thousands of Jews emigrated to western Europe and to the United States. Antin's hometown, Polotzk, was within the "Pale of Settlement" in Russia, a restricted area reserved for Jews, according to the Czar's edict. Even there, however, Jews were subjected to continual harassment, attacks, as well as forced induction of young Jewish boys into the Russian army. Mary Antin and her family immigrated to the United States in 1894, joining her father in Boston. Like many Jewish men, Antin's father had gone before his family to find work and a place to live. Antin's father, who had been trained in Russia to be a rabbi, was ill suited to the various jobs available to immigrants in the United States, and Antin's best-selling autobiography The Promised Land *(1912) recounts the various ways in which her family tried to make a living in Boston and her early life as an immigrant. Education was very important to the Antin family, and Antin was well educated at the Boston Girl's Latin School and later attended (but did not finish) Columbia Teacher's College in New York City. Antin married a geologist and paleontologist, Amadeus William Grabau (1870–1946); during the first quarter of the twentieth century, she enjoyed a career as a successful writer and public lecturer. She contributed articles on immigration to the* Atlantic Monthly *and in addition to* The Promised Land, *she published two other books,* From Polotzk to Boston *(1899) and* They Who Knock at Our Gates, A Complete Gospel of Immigration *(1914). She toured the United States, giving lectures about the subject of immigration and her own personal experiences. This reading is from two chapters of* The Promised Land, *"The Promised Land" and "Initiation," in which Antin recounts her first experiences in Boston and in school.*

QUESTIONS FOR READING

1. Antin immigrated to the United States from Russia, at a time when Jews were harshly treated. What do you know about the history of Jewish persecution in late nineteenth-century Russia? As you read, make notes about places and events that you might research.
2. Like several of the selections in this section of the text, Antin remembers her experiences as a child in coming to live in a new country. What do the titles of the chapters reprinted here, "The Promised Land" and "Initiation," suggest about Antin's attitudes toward her experiences?

MARY ANTIN

THE PROMISED LAND

The Promised Land *(Boston: Houghton Mifflin, 1912)*

Having made such good time across the ocean, I ought to be able to proceed no less rapidly on *terra firma*, where, after all, I am more at home. And yet here is where I falter. Not that I hesitated, even for the space of a breath, in my first steps in America. There was no time to hesitate. The most ignorant immigrant, on landing, proceeds to give and receive greetings, to eat, sleep, and rise, after the manner of his own country; wherein he is corrected, admonished, and laughed at, whether by interested friends or the most indifferent strangers; and his American experience is thus begun. The process is spontaneous on all sides, like the education of the child by the family circle. But while the most stupid nursery maid is able to contribute her part toward the result, we do not expect an analysis of the family, least of all by the engaging infant. The philosophical maiden aunt alone, or some other witness equally psychological and aloof, is able to trace the myriad efforts by which the little Johnnie or Nellie acquires a secure hold on the disjointed parts of the huge plaything, life.

Now I was not exactly an infant when I was set down, on a May day some fifteen years ago, in this pleasant nursery of America. I had long since acquired the use of my faculties, and had collected some bits of experience, practical and emotional, and had even learned to give an account of them. Still, I had very little perspective, and my observations and comparisons were superficial. I was too much carried away to analyze the forces that were moving me. My Polotzk

I knew well before I began to judge it and experiment with it. America was bewilderingly strange, unimaginably complex, delightfully unexplored. I rushed impetuously out of the cage of my provincialism and looked eagerly about the brilliant universe. My question was, What have we here?—not, What does this mean? That query came much later. When I now become retrospectively introspective, I fall into the predicament of the centipede in the rhyme, who got along very smoothly until he was asked which leg came after which, whereupon he became so rattled that he couldn't take a step. I know I have come on a thousand feet, on wings, winds, and American machines,—I have leaped and run and climbed and crawled,—but to tell which step came after which I find a puzzling matter. Plenty of maiden aunts were present during my second infancy, in the guise of immigrant officials, school-teachers, settlement workers, and sundry other unprejudiced and critical observers. Their statistics I might properly borrow to fill the gaps in my recollections, but I am prevented by my sense of harmony. The individual, we know, is a creature unknown to the statistician, whereas I undertook to give the personal view of everything. So I am bound to unravel, as well as I can, the tangle of events, outer and inner, which made up the first breathless years of my American life.

During his three years of probation, my father had made a number of false starts in business. His history for that period is the history of thousands who come to America, like him, with pockets empty, hands untrained to the use of tools, minds cramped by centuries of repression in their native land. Dozens of these men pass under your eyes every day, my American friend, too absorbed in their honest affairs to notice the looks of suspicion which you cast at them, the repugnance with which you shrink from their touch. You see them shuffle from door to door with a basket of spools and buttons, or bending over the sizzling irons in a basement tailor shop, or rummaging in your ash can, or moving a pushcart from curb to curb, at the command of the burly policeman. "The Jew peddler!" you say, and dismiss him from your premises and from your thoughts, never dreaming that the sordid drama of his days may have a moral that concerns you. What if the creature with the untidy beard carries in his bosom his citizenship papers? What if the cross-legged tailor is supporting a boy in college who is one day going to mend your state constitution for you? What if the ragpicker's daughters are hastening over the ocean to teach your children in the public schools? Think, every time you pass the greasy alien on the street, that he was born thousands of years before the oldest native American; and he may have something to communicate to you, when you two shall have learned a common language. Remember that his very physiognomy is a cipher the key to which it behooves you to search for most diligently.

By the time we joined my father, he had surveyed many avenues of approach toward the coveted citadel of fortune. One of these, heretofore untried, he now proposed to essay, armed with new courage, and cheered on by the presence of his family. In partnership with an energetic little man who had an English chapter in his history, he prepared to set up a refreshment booth on

Crescent Beach. But while he was completing arrangements at the beach we remained in town, where we enjoyed the educational advantages of a thickly populated neighborhood; namely, Wall Street, in the West End of Boston.

Anybody who knows Boston knows that the West and North Ends are the wrong ends of that city. They form the tenement district, or, in the newer phrase, the slums of Boston. Anybody who is acquainted with the slums of any American metropolis knows that that is the quarter where poor immigrants foregather, to live, for the most part, as unkempt, half-washed, toiling, unaspiring foreigners; pitiful in the eyes of social missionaries, the despair of boards of health, the hope of ward politicians, the touchstone of American democracy. The well-versed metropolitan knows the slums as a sort of house of detention for poor aliens, where they live on probation till they can show a certificate of good citizenship.

He may know all this and yet not guess how Wall Street, in the West End, appears in the eyes of a little immigrant from Polotzk. What would the sophisticated sight-seer say about Union Place, off Wall Street, where my new home waited for me? He would say that it is no place at all, but a short box of an alley. Two rows of three-story tenements are its sides, a stingy strip of sky is its lid, a littered pavement is the floor, and a narrow mouth its exit.

But I saw a very different picture on my introduction to Union Place. I saw two imposing rows of brick buildings, loftier than any dwelling I had ever lived in. Brick was even on the ground for me to tread on, instead of common earth or boards. Many friendly windows stood open, filled with uncovered heads of women and children. I thought the people were interested in us, which was very neighborly. I looked up to the topmost row of windows, and my eyes were filled with the May blue of an American sky!

In our days of affluence in Russia we had been accustomed to upholstered parlors, embroidered linen, silver spoons and candlesticks, goblets of gold, kitchen shelves shining with copper and brass. We had featherbeds heaped halfway to the ceiling; we had clothes presses dusky with velvet and silk and fine woollen. The three small rooms into which my father now ushered us, up one flight of stairs, contained only the necessary beds, with lean mattresses; a few wooden chairs; a table or two; a mysterious iron structure, which later turned out to be a stove; a couple of unornamental kerosene lamps; and a scanty array of cooking-utensils and crockery. And yet we were all impressed with our new home and its furniture. It was not only because we had just passed through our seven lean years, cooking in earthen vessels, eating black bread on holidays and wearing cotton; it was chiefly because these wooden chairs and tin pans were American chairs and pans that they shone glorious in our eyes. And if there was anything lacking for comfort or decoration we expected it to be presently supplied—at least, we children did. Perhaps my mother alone, of us newcomers, appreciated the shabbiness of the little apartment, and realized that for her there was as yet no laying down of the burden of poverty.

Our initiation into American ways began with the first step on the new soil. My father found occasion to instruct or correct us even on the way from the pier to Wall Street, which journey we made crowded together in a rickety cab. He told us not to lean out of the windows, not to point, and explained the word "greenhorn." We did not want to be "greenhorns," and gave the strictest attention to my father's instructions. I do not know when my parents found opportunity to review together the history of Polotzk in the three years past, for we children had no patience with the subject; my mother's narrative was constantly interrupted by irrelevant questions, interjections, and explanations.

The first meal was an object lesson of much variety. My father produced several kinds of food, ready to eat, without any cooking, from little tin cans that had printing all over them. He attempted to introduce us to a queer, slippery kind of fruit, which he called "banana," but had to give it up for the time being. After the meal, he had better luck with a curious piece of furniture on runners, which he called "rocking-chair." There were five of us newcomers, and we found five different ways of getting into the American machine of perpetual motion, and as many ways of getting out of it. One born and bred to the use of a rocking-chair cannot imagine how ludicrous people can make themselves when attempting to use it for the first time. We laughed immoderately over our various experiments with the novelty, which was a wholesome way of letting off steam after the unusual excitement of the day.

In our flat we did not think of such a thing as storing the coal in the bathtub. There was no bathtub. So in the evening of the first day my father conducted us to the public baths. As we moved along in a little procession, I was delighted with the illumination of the streets. So many lamps, and they burned until morning, my father said, and so people did not need to carry lanterns. In America, then, everything was free, as we had heard in Russia. Light was free; the streets were as bright as a synagogue on a holy day. Music was free; we had been serenaded, to our gaping delight by a brass band of many pieces, soon after our installation on Union Place.

Education was free. That subject my father had written about repeatedly, as comprising his chief hope for us children, the essence of American opportunity, the treasure that no thief could touch, not even misfortune or poverty. It was the one thing that he was able to promise us when he sent for us; surer, safer than bread or shelter. On our second day I was thrilled with the realization of what this freedom of education meant. A little girl from across the alley came and offered to conduct us to school. My father was out, but we five between us had a few words of English by this time. We knew the word school. We understood. This child, who had never seen us till yesterday, who could not pronounce our names, who was not much better dressed than we, was able to offer us the freedom of the schools of Boston! No application made, no questions asked, no examinations, rulings, exclusions; no machinations, no fees. The doors stood open for every one of us. The smallest child could show us the way.

This incident impressed me more than anything I had heard in advance of the freedom of education in America. It was a concrete proof—almost the thing itself. One had to experience it to understand it.

It was a great disappointment to be told by my father that we were not to enter upon our school career at once. It was too near the end of the term, he said, and we were going to move to Crescent Beach in a week or so. We had to wait until the opening of the schools in September. What a loss of precious time—from May till September!

Not that the time was really lost. Even the interval on Union Place was crowded with lessons and experiences. We had to visit the stores and be dressed from head to foot in American clothing; we had to learn the mysteries of the iron stove, the washboard, and the speaking-tube; we had to learn to trade with the fruit peddler through the window, and not to be afraid of the policeman; and, above all, we had to learn English.

The kind people who assisted us in these important matters form a group by themselves in the gallery of my friends. If I had never seen them from those early days till now, I should still have remembered them with gratitude. When I enumerate the long list of my American teachers, I must begin with those who came to us on Wall Street and taught us our first steps. To my mother, in her perplexity over the cookstove, the woman who showed her how to make the fire was an angel of deliverance. A fairy godmother to us children was she who led us to a wonderful country called "uptown," where, in a dazzlingly beautiful palace called a "department store," we exchanged our hateful homemade European costumes, which pointed us out as "greenhorns" to the children on the street, for real American machine-made garments, and issued forth glorified in each other's eyes.

With our despised immigrant clothing we shed also our impossible Hebrew names. A committee of our friends, several years ahead of us in American experience, put their heads together and concocted American names for us all. Those of our real names that had no pleasing American equivalents they ruthlessly discarded, content if they retained the initials. My mother, possessing a name that was not easily translatable, was punished with the undignified nickname of Annie. Fetchke, Joseph, and Deborah issued as Frieda, Joseph, and Dora, respectively. As for poor me, I was simply cheated. The name they gave me was hardly new. My Hebrew name being Maryashe in full, Mashke for short, Russianized into Marya (Mar-ya), my friends said that it would hold good in English as Mary; which was very disappointing, as I longed to possess a strange-sounding American name like the others.

I am forgetting the consolation I had, in this matter of names, from the use of my surname, which I have had no occasion to mention until now. I found on my arrival that my father was "Mr. Antin" on the slightest provocation, and not, as in Polotzk, on state occasions alone. And so I was "Mary Antin," and I felt very important to answer to such a dignified title. It was just like America that even plain people should wear their surnames on week days.

As a family we were so diligent under instruction, so adaptable, and so clever in hiding our deficiencies, that when we made the journey to Crescent Beach, in the wake of our small wagon-load of household goods, my father had very little occasion to admonish us on the way, and I am sure he was not ashamed of us. So much we had achieved toward our Americanization during the two weeks since our landing.

Father himself conducted us to school. He would not have delegated that mission to the President of the United States. He had awaited the day with impatience equal to mine, and the visions he saw as he hurried us over the sun-flecked pavements transcended all my dreams. Almost his first act on landing on American soil, three years before, had been his application for naturalization. He had taken the remaining steps in the process with eager promptness, and at the earliest moment allowed by the law, he became a citizen of the United States. It is true that he had left home in search of bread for his hungry family, but he went blessing the necessity that drove him to America. The boasted freedom of the New World meant to him far more than the right to reside, travel, and work wherever he pleased; it meant the freedom to speak his thoughts, to throw off the shackles of superstition, to test his own fate, unhindered by political or religious tyranny. He was only a young man when he landed—thirty-two; and most of his life he had been held in leading-strings. He was hungry for his untasted manhood.

Three years passed in sordid struggle and disappointment. He was not prepared to make a living even in America, where the day laborer eats wheat instead of rye. Apparently the American flag could not protect him against the pursuing Nemesis of his limitations; he must expiate the sins of his fathers who slept across the seas. He had been endowed at birth with a poor constitution, a nervous, restless temperament, and an abundance of hindering prejudices. In his boyhood his body was starved, that his mind might be stuffed with useless learning. In his youth this dearly gotten learning was sold, and the price was the bread and salt which he had not been trained to earn for himself. Under the wedding canopy he was bound for life to a girl whose features were still strange to him; and he was bidden to multiply himself, that sacred learning might be perpetuated in his sons, to the glory of the God of his fathers. All this while he had been led about as a creature without a will, a chattel, an instrument. In his maturity he awoke, and found himself poor in health, poor in purse, poor in useful knowledge, and hampered on all sides. At the first nod of opportunity he broke away from his prison, and strove to atone for his wasted youth by a life of useful labor; while at the same time he sought to lighten the gloom of his narrow scholarship by freely partaking of modern ideas. But his utmost endeavor still left him far from his goal. In business, nothing prospered with him. Some fault of hand or mind or temperament led him to failure where other men found success. Wherever the blame for his disabilities be placed, he reaped their bitter fruit. "Give me bread!" he cried to America. "What will you do to earn it?" the challenge came back. And he found that he was master of no art, of no trade; that even his precious learning was of no avail, because he had only the most antiquated methods of communicating it.

So in his primary quest he had failed. There was left him the compensation of intellectual freedom. That he sought to realize in every possible way. He had very little opportunity to prosecute his education, which, in truth, had never been begun. His struggle for a bare living left him no time to take advantage of the public evening school; but he lost nothing of what was to be learned through reading, through attendance at public meetings, through exercising the rights of citizenship. Even here he was hindered by a natural inability to acquire the English language. In time, indeed, he learned to read, to follow a conversation or lecture; but he never learned to write correctly, and his pronunciation remains extremely foreign to this day.

If education, culture, the higher life were shining things to be worshipped from afar, he had still a means left whereby he could draw one step nearer to them. He could send his children to school, to learn all those things that he knew by fame to be desirable. The common school, at least, perhaps high school; for one or two, perhaps even college! His children should be students, should fill his house with books and intellectual company; and thus he would walk by proxy in the Elysian Fields of liberal learning. As for the children themselves, he knew no surer way to their advancement and happiness.

So it was with a heart full of longing and hope that my father led us to school on that first day. He took long strides in his eagerness, the rest of us running and hopping to keep up.

At last the four of us stood around the teacher's desk; and my father, in his impossible English, gave us over in her charge, with some broken word of his hopes for us that his swelling heart could no longer contain. I venture to say that Miss Nixon was struck by something uncommon in the group we made, something outside of Semitic features and the abashed manner of the alien. My little sister was as pretty as a doll, with her clear pink-and-white face, short golden curls, and eyes like blue violets when you caught them looking up. My brother might have been a girl, too, with his cherubic contours of face, rich red color, glossy black hair, and fine eyebrows. Whatever secret fears were in his heart, remembering his former teachers, who had taught with the rod, he stood up straight and uncringing before the American teacher, his cap respectfully doffed. Next to him stood a starved-looking girl with eyes ready to pop out, and short dark curls that would not have made much of a wig for a Jewish bride.

All three children carried themselves rather better than the common run of "green" pupils that were brought to Miss Nixon. But the figure that challenged attention to the group was the tall, straight father, with his earnest face and fine forehead, nervous hands eloquent in gesture, and a voice full of feeling. This foreigner, who brought his children to school as if it were an act of consecration, who regarded the teacher of the primer class with reverence, who spoke of visions, like a man inspired, in a common schoolroom, was not like other aliens, who brought their children in dull obedience to the law; was not like the native fathers, who brought their unmanageable boys, glad to be relieved of their care. I think Miss Nixon guessed what my father's best English could not convey. I think she divined that by the simple act of delivering our school certificates to her he took possession of America.

INITIATION

It is not worth while to refer to voluminous school statistics to see just how many "green" pupils entered school last September, not knowing the days of the week in English, who next February will be declaiming patriotic verses in honor of George Washington and Abraham Lincoln, with a foreign accent, indeed, but with plenty of enthusiasm. It is enough to know that this hundred-fold miracle is common to the schools in every part of the United States where immigrants are received. And if I was one of Chelsea's hundred in 1894, it was only to be expected, since I was one of the older of the "green" children, and had had a start in my irregular schooling in Russia, and was carried along by a tremendous desire to learn, and had my family to cheer me on.

I was not a bit too large for my little chair and desk in the baby class, but my mind, of course, was too mature by six or seven years for the work. So as soon as I could understand what the teacher said in class, I was advanced to the second grade. This was within a week after Miss Nixon took me in hand. But I do not mean to give my dear teacher all the credit for my rapid progress, nor even half the credit. I shall divide it with her on behalf of my race and my family. I was Jew enough to have an aptitude for language in general, and to bend my mind earnestly to my task; I was Antin enough to read each lesson with my heart, which gave me an inkling of what was coming next, and so carried me along by leaps and bounds. As for the teacher, she could best explain what theory she followed in teaching us foreigners to read. I can only describe the method, which was so simple that I wish holiness could be taught in the same way.

There were about half a dozen of us beginners in English, in age from six to fifteen. Miss Nixon made a special class of us, and aided us so skilfully and earnestly in our endeavors to "see-a-cat," and "hear-a-dog-bark," and "look-at-the-hen," that we turned over page after page of the ravishing history, eager to find out how the common world looked, smelled, and tasted in the strange speech. The teacher knew just when to let us help each other out with a word in our own tongue,—it happened that we were all Jews,—and so, working all together, we actually covered more ground in a lesson than the native classes, composed entirely of the little tots.

But we stuck—stuck fast—at the definite article; and sometimes the lesson resolved itself into a species of lingual gymnastics, in which we all looked as if we meant to bite our tongues off. Miss Nixon was pretty, and she must have looked well with her white teeth showing in the act; but at the time I was too solemnly occupied to admire her looks. I did take great pleasure in her smile of approval, whenever I pronounced well; and her patience and perseverance in struggling with us over that thick little word are becoming to her even now, after fifteen years. It is not her fault if any of us today give a buzzing sound to the dreadful English *th*.

I shall never have a better opportunity to make public declaration of my love for the English language. I am glad that American history runs, chapter for chapter, the way it does; for thus America came to be the country I love so dearly. I am glad, most of all, that the Americans began by being Englishmen, for thus did I come to inherit this beautiful language in which I think. It seems to me that in any other language happiness is not so sweet, logic is not so clear. I am not sure that I could believe in my neighbors as I do if I thought about them in un-English words. I could almost say that my conviction of immortality is bound up with the English of its promise. And as I am attached to my prejudices, I must love the English language!

Whenever the teachers did anything special to help me over my private difficulties, my gratitude went out to them, silently. It meant so much to me that they halted the lesson to give me a lift, that I needs must love them for it. Dear Miss Carol, of the second grade, would be amazed to hear what small things I remember, all because I was so impressed at the time with her readiness and sweetness in taking notice of my difficulties.

Says Miss Carol, looking straight at me:—

"If Johnnie has three marbles, and Charlie has twice as many, how many marbles has Charlie?"

I raise my hand for permission to speak.

"Teacher, I don't know vhat is tvice."

Teacher beckons me to her, and whispers to me the meaning of the strange word, and I am able to write the sum correctly. It's all in the day's work with her; with me, it is a special act of kindness and efficiency.

She whom I found in the next grade became so dear a friend that I can hardly name her with the rest, though I mention none of them lightly. Her approval was always dear to me, first because she was "Teacher," and afterwards, as long as she lived, because she was my Miss Dillingham. Great was my grief, therefore, when, shortly after my admission to her class, I incurred discipline, the first, and next to the last, time in my school career.

The class was repeating in chorus the Lord's prayer, heads bowed on desks. I was doing my best to keep up by the sound; my mind could not go beyond the word "hallowed," for which I had not found the meaning. In the middle of the prayer a Jewish boy across the aisle trod on my foot to get my attention. "You must not say that," he admonished in a solemn whisper; "it's Christian." I whispered back that it wasn't, and went on to the "Amen." I did not know but what he was right, but the name of Christ was not in the prayer, and I was bound to do everything that the class did. If I had any Jewish scruples, they were lagging away behind my interest in school affairs. How American this was: two pupils side by side in the schoolroom, each holding to his own opinion, but both submitting to the common law; for the boy at least bowed his head as the teacher ordered.

But all Miss Dillingham knew of it was that two of her pupils whispered during morning prayer, and she must discipline them. So I was degraded from the honor row to the lowest row, and it was many a day before I forgave that young missionary; it was not enough for my vengeance that he suffered punishment with me. Teacher, of course, heard us both defend ourselves, but there was a time and a place for religious arguments, and she meant to help us remember that point.

I remember to this day what a struggle we had over the word "water," Miss Dillingham and I. It seemed as if I could not give the sound of *w*; I said "vater" every time. Patiently my teacher worked with me, inventing mouth exercises for me, to get my stubborn lips to produce that *w*; and when at last I could say "village" and "water" in rapid alternation, without misplacing the two initials, that memorable word was sweet on my lips. For we had conquered, and Teacher was pleased.

Getting a language in this way, word by word, has a charm that may be set against the disadvantages. It is like gathering a posy blossom by blossom. Bring the bouquet into your chamber, and these nasturtiums stand for the whole flaming carnival of them tumbling over the fence out there; these yellow pansies recall the velvet crescent of color glowing under the bay window; this spray of honeysuckle smells like the wind-tossed masses of it on the porch, ripe and bee-laden; the whole garden in a glass tumbler. So it is with one who gathers words, loving them. Particular words remain associated with important occasions in the learner's mind. I could thus write a history of my English vocabulary that should be at the same time an account of my comings and goings, my mistakes and my triumphs, during the years of my initiation.

If I was eager and diligent, my teachers did not sleep. As fast as my knowledge of English allowed, they advanced me from grade to grade, without reference to the usual schedule of promotions. My father was right, when he often said, in discussing my prospects, that ability would be promptly recognized in the public schools. Rapid as was my progress, on account of the advantages with which I started, some of the other "green" pupils were not far behind me; within a grade or two, by the end of the year. My brother, whose childhood had been one hideous nightmare, what with the stupid rebbe, the cruel whip, and the general repression of life in the Pale, surprised my father by the progress he made under intelligent, sympathetic guidance. Indeed, he soon had a reputation in the school that the American boys envied; and all through the school course he more than held his own with pupils of his age. So much for the right and wrong way of doing things.

There is a record of my early progress in English much better than my recollections, however accurate and definite these may be. I have several reasons for introducing it here. First, it shows what the Russian Jew can do with an adopted language; next, it proves that vigilance of our public-school teachers of which I spoke; and last, I am proud of it! That is an unnecessary confession, but I could not be satisfied to insert the record here, with my vanity unavowed.

This is the document, copied from an educational journal, a tattered copy of which lies in my lap as I write—treasured for fifteen years, you see, by my vanity.

Editor "Primary Education":—

This is the uncorrected paper of a Russian child twelve years old, who had studied English only four months. She had never, until September, been to school even in her own country and has heard English spoken *only* at school. I shall be glad if the paper of my pupil and the above explanation may appear in your paper.

Chelsea, Mass.   M. S. Dillingham.

SNOW

Snow is frozen moisture which comes from the clouds. Now the snow is coming down in feather-flakes, which makes nice snow-balls. But there is still one kind of snow more. This kind of snow is called snow-crystals, for it comes down in little curly balls. These snow-crystals aren't quite as good for snow-balls as feather-flakes, for they (the snow-crystals) are dry: so they can't keep together as feather-flakes do.

The snow is dear to some children for they like sleighing.

As I said at the top—the snow comes from the clouds.

Now the trees are bare, and no flowers are to see in the fields and gardens, (we all know why) and the whole world seems like asleep without the happy birds songs which left us till spring. But the snow which drove away all these pretty and happy things, try, (as I think) not to make us at all unhappy; they covered up the branches of the trees, the fields, the gardens and houses, and the whole world looks like dressed in a beautiful white—instead of green—dress, with the sky looking down on it with a pale face.

And so the people can find some joy in it, too, without the happy summer.

MARY ANTIN.

And now that it stands there, with *her* name over it, I am ashamed of my flippant talk about vanity. More to me than all the praise I could hope to win by the conquest of fifty languages is the association of this dear friend with my earliest efforts at writing; and it pleases me to remember that to her I owe my very first appearance in print. Vanity is the least part of it, when I remember how she called me to her desk, one day after school was out, and showed me my composition—my own words, that I had written out of my own head—printed out, clear black and white, with my name at the end! Nothing so wonderful had ever happened to me before. My whole consciousness was suddenly transformed. I suppose that was the moment when I became a writer. I always loved to write,—I wrote letters whenever I had an excuse,—yet it had never occurred to me to sit down and write my thoughts for no person in particular, merely to put the word on paper. But now, as I read my own words, in a delicious confusion, the idea was born. I stared at my name: MARY ANTIN. Was that really I? The printed characters composing it seemed strange to me all of a sudden. If that was my name, and those were the words out of my own head, what relation did it all have to *me*, who was alone there with Miss Dillingham, and the printed page between us? Why, it meant that I could write again, and see my writing printed for people to read! I could write many, many, many things: I could write a book! The idea was so huge, so bewildering, that my mind scarcely could accommodate it.

I do not know what my teacher said to me; probably very little. It was her way to say only a little, and look at me, and trust me to understand. Once she had occasion to lecture me about living a shut-up life; she wanted me to go outdoors. I had been repeatedly scolded and reproved on that score by other people, but I had only laughed, saying that I was too happy to change my ways. But when Miss Dillingham spoke to me, I saw that it was a serious matter; and yet she only said a few words, and looked at me with that smile of hers that was only half a smile, and the rest a meaning. Another time she had a great question to ask me, touching my life to the quick. She merely put her question, and was silent; but I knew what answer she expected, and not being able to give it then, I went away sad and reproved. Years later I had my triumphant answer, but she was no longer there to receive it; and so her eyes look at me, from the picture on the mantel there, with a reproach I no longer merit.

I ought to go back and strike out all that talk about vanity. What reason have I to be vain, when I reflect how at every step I was petted, nursed, and encouraged? I did not even discover my own talent. It was discovered first by my father in Russia, and next by my friend in America. What did I ever do but write when they told me to write? I suppose my grandfather who drove a spavined horse through lonely country lanes sat in the shade of crisp-leaved oaks to refresh himself with a bit of black bread; and an acorn falling beside him, in the immense stillness, shook his heart with the echo, and left him wondering. I suppose my father stole away from the synagogue one long festival day, and stretched himself out in the sun-warmed grass, and lost himself in dreams that made the world of men unreal when he returned to them. And so what is there left for me to do, who do not have to drive a horse nor interpret ancient lore, but put my grandfather's question into words and set to music my father's dream? The tongue am I of those who lived before me, as those that are to come will be the voice of my unspoken thoughts. And so who shall be applauded if the song be sweet, if the prophecy be true?

I never heard of any one who was so watched and coaxed, so passed along from hand to helping hand, as was I. I always had friends. They sprang up everywhere, as if they had stood waiting for me to come. So here was my teacher, the moment she saw that I could give a good paraphrase of her talk on "Snow," bent on finding out what more I could do. One day she asked me if I had ever written poetry. I had not, but I went home and tried. I believe it was more snow, and I know it was wretched. I wish I could produce a copy of that early effusion; it would prove that my judgment is not severe. Wretched it was,—worse, a great deal, than reams of poetry that is written by children about whom there is no fuss made. But Miss Dillingham was not discouraged. She saw that I had no idea of metre, so she proceeded to teach me. We repeated miles of poetry together, smooth lines that sang themselves, mostly out of Longfellow. Then I would go home and write—oh, about the snow in our back yard!—but when Miss Dillingham came to read my verses, they limped and they lagged and they dragged, and there was no tune that would fit them.

At last came the moment of illumination: I saw where my trouble lay. I had supposed that my lines matched when they had an equal number of syllables, taking no account of accent. Now I knew better; now I could write poetry! The everlasting snow melted at last, and the mud puddles dried in the spring sun, and the grass on the common was green, and still I wrote poetry! Again I wish I had some example of my springtime rhapsodies, the veriest rubbish of the sort that ever a child perpetrated. Lizzie McDee, who had red hair and freckles, and a Sunday-school manner on weekdays, and was below me in the class, did a great deal better. We used to compare verses; and while I do not remember that I ever had the grace to own that she was the better poet, I do know that I secretly wondered why the teachers did not invite her to stay after school and study poetry, while they took so much pains with me. But so it was always with me: somebody did something for me all the time.

Making fair allowance for my youth, retarded education, and strangeness to the language, it must still be admitted that I never wrote good verse. But I loved to read it. My half-hours with Miss Dillingham were full of delight for me, quite apart from my new-born ambition to become a writer. What, then, was my joy, when Miss Dillingham, just before locking up her desk one evening, presented me with a volume of Longfellow's poems! It was a thin volume of selections, but to me it was a bottomless treasure. I had never owned a book before. The sense of possession alone was a source of bliss, and this book I already knew and loved. And so Miss Dillingham, who was my first American friend, and who first put my name in print, was also the one to start my library. Deep is my regret when I consider that she was gone before I had given much of an account of all her gifts of love and service to me.

About the middle of the year I was promoted to the grammar school. Then it was that I walked on air. For I said to myself that I was a *student* now, in earnest, not merely a school-girl learning to spell and cipher. I was going to learn out-of-the-way things, things that had nothing to do with ordinary life—things to *know*. When I walked home afternoons, with the great big geography book under my arm, it seemed to me that the earth was conscious of my step. Sometimes I carried home half the books in my desk, not because I should need them, but because I loved to hold them; and also because I loved to be seen carrying books. It was a badge of scholarship, and I was proud of it. I remembered the days in Vitebsk when I used to watch my cousin Hirshel start for school in the morning, every thread of his student's uniform, every worn copybook in his satchel, glorified in my envious eyes. And now I was myself as he: aye, greater than he; for I knew English, and I could write poetry.

If my head was not turned at this time it was because I was so busy from morning till night. My father did his best to make me vain and silly. He made much of me to every chance caller, boasting of my progress at school, and of my exalted friends, the teachers. For a school-teacher was no ordinary mortal in his eyes; she was a superior being, set above the common run of men by her erudition and devotion to higher things. That a school-teacher could be shallow or petty, or greedy for pay, was a thing that he could not have been brought to believe, at this time. And he was right, if he could only have stuck to it in later years, when a new-born pessimism, fathered by his perception that in America, too, some things needed mending, threw him to the opposite extreme of opinion, crying that nothing in the American scheme of society or government was worth tinkering.

He surely was right in his first appraisal of the teacher. The mean sort of teachers are not teachers at all; they are self-seekers who take up teaching as a business, to support themselves and keep their hands white. These same persons, did they keep store or drive a milk wagon or wash babies for a living, would be respectable. As trespassers on a noble profession, they are worth no more than the books and slates and desks over which they preside; so much furniture, to be had by the gross. They do not love their work. They contribute nothing to the higher development of their pupils. They busy themselves, not with research into the science of teaching, but with organizing political demonstrations to advance the cause of selfish candidates for public office, who promise them rewards. The true teachers are of another strain. Apostles all of an ideal, they go to their work in a spirit of love and inquiry, seeking not comfort, not position, not old-age pensions, but truth that is the soul of wisdom, the joy of big-eyed children, the food of hungry youth.

They were true teachers who used to come to me on Arlington Street, so my father had reason to boast of the distinction brought upon his house. For the schoolteacher in her trim, unostentatious dress was an uncommon visitor in our neighborhood; and the talk that passed in the bare little "parlor" over the grocery store would not have been entirely comprehensible to our next-door neighbor.

In the grammar school I had as good teaching as I had had in the primary. It seems to me in retrospect that it was as good, on the whole, as the public school ideals of the time made possible. When I recall how I was taught geography, I see, indeed, that there was room for improvement occasionally both in the substance and in the method of instruction. But I know of at least one teacher of Chelsea who realized this; for I met her, eight years later, at a great metropolitan university that holds a summer session for the benefit of schoolteachers who want to keep up with the advance in their science. Very likely they no longer teach geography entirely within doors, and by rote, as I was taught. Fifteen years is plenty of time for progress.

When I joined the first grammar grade, the class had had a half-year's start of me, but it was not long before I found my place near the head. In all branches except geography it was genuine progress. I overtook the youngsters in their study of numbers, spelling, reading, and composition. In geography I merely made a bluff, but I did not know it. Neither did my teacher. I came up to such tests as she put me.

The lesson was on Chelsea, which was right: geography, like charity, should begin at home. Our text ran on for a paragraph or so on the location, boundaries, natural features, and industries of the town, with a bit of local history thrown in. We were to learn all these interesting facts, and be prepared to write them out from memory the next day. I went home and learned—learned every word of the text, every comma, every footnote. When the teacher had read my paper she marked it "EE." "E" was for "excellent," but my paper was absolutely perfect, and must be put in a class by itself. The teacher exhibited my paper before the class, with some remarks about the diligence that could overtake in a week pupils who had had half a year's start. I took it all as modestly as I could, never doubting that I was indeed a very bright little girl,

and getting to be very learned to boot. I was "perfect" in geography, a most
erudite subject.

But what was the truth? The words that I repeated so accurately on my paper had about as much meaning to me as the words of the Psalms I used to
chant in Hebrew. I got an idea that the city of Chelsea, and the world in general, was laid out flat, like the common, and shaved off at the ends, to allow
the north, south, east, and west to snuggle up close, like the frame around a
picture. If I looked at the map, I was utterly bewildered; I could find no correspondence between the picture and the verbal explanations. With words I was
safe; I could learn any number of words by heart, and sometime or other they
would pop out of the medley, clothed with meaning. Chelsea, I read, was
bounded on all sides—"bounded" appealed to my imagination—by various
things that I had never identified, much as I had roamed about the town. I immediately pictured these remote boundaries as a six-foot fence in a good state
of preservation, with the Mystic River, the towns of Everett and Revere, and
East Boston Creek, rejoicing, on the south, west, north, and east of it, respectively, that they had got inside; while the rest of the world peeped in enviously
through a knot hole. In the middle of this cherished area piano factories—or
was it shoe factories?—proudly reared their chimneys, while the population
promenaded on a *rope walk,* saluted at every turn by the benevolent inmates of
the Soldiers' Home on the top of Powderhorn Hill.

Perhaps the fault was partly mine, because I always would reduce everything to a picture. Partly it may have been because I had not had time to digest
the general definitions and explanations at the beginning of the book. Still, I
can take but little of the blame, when I consider how I fared through my geography, right to the end of the grammar-school course. I did in time disentangle
the symbolism of the orange revolving on a knitting-needle from the astro-
nomical facts in the case, but it took years of training under a master of the
subject to rid me of my distrust of the map as a representation of the earth. To
this day I sometimes blunder back to my early impression that any given portion of the earth's surface is constructed upon a skeleton consisting of two
crossed bars, terminating in arrowheads which pin the cardinal points into
place; and if I want to find any desired point of the compass, I am inclined to
throw myself flat on my nose, my head due north, and my outstretched arms
seeking the east and west respectively.

For in the schoolroom, as far as the study of the map went, we began with
the symbol and stuck to the symbol. No teacher of geography I ever had, except the master I referred to, took the pains to ascertain whether I had any
sense of the facts for which the symbols stood. Outside the study of maps,
geography consisted of statistics: tables of population, imports and exports,
manufactures, and degrees of temperature; dimensions of rivers, mountains,
and political states; with lists of minerals, plants, and plagues native to any
given part of the globe. The only part of the whole subject that meant anything
to me was the description of the aspect of foreign lands, and the manners and
customs of their peoples. The relation of physiography to human history—

what might be called the moral of geography—was not taught at all, or was touched upon in an unimpressive manner. The prevalence of this defect in the teaching of school geography is borne out by the surprise of the college freshman, who remarked to the professor of geology that it was curious to note how all the big rivers and harbors on the Atlantic coastal plain occurred in the neighborhood of large cities! A little instruction in the elements of chartography—a little practice in the use of the compass and the spirit level, a topographical map of the town common, an excursion with a road map—would have given me a fat round earth in place of my paper ghost; would have illumined the one dark alley in my school life.

QUESTIONS FOR REACTION AND DISCUSSION

1. How does Antin describe her feelings of what it means to be an "immigrant" in the United States?
2. What are the areas of Boston where the Antin family lives? What are the novelties of American life for Antin? How does Boston contrast with Polotzk?
3. Why do the Antin family members adopt American names? On what basis do they select them?
4. Antin continually describes the United States as a "garden." Find examples of this comparison and participate in a class discussion about Antin's presentation of America as a kind of garden of Eden. What is the effect of this on the members of your class?
5. What was the most important event of Antin's new life in America? Why?
6. How is Antin taught to speak and write English? What is your opinion of the teaching methods used in classrooms of this period?

QUESTIONS FOR WRITING

1. Antin ironically observes about her family's life in Boston that "Anybody who is acquainted with the slums of any American metropolis knows that is the quarter where poor immigrants foregather, to live, for the most part, as unkempt, half-washed, toiling, unaspiring foreigners; pitiful in the eyes of social missionaries, the despair of boards of health, the hope of ward politicians, the touchstone of American democracy." How does Antin develop the contrast between herself as an immigrant and herself as an aspiring citizen? What are the barriers in American society for an immigrant? Write an essay in which you explore how the immigrant experience is "the touchstone of American democracy."

2. Mary Antin is not unlike other immigrants of her day—assimilation into American culture was the greatly desired object. In what ways did she work hard to learn the English language and American modes and manners as taught to her in school? What of her own culture and language does she give up? Write an essay in which you defend or reject the assertion that for Antin literacy meant assimilation. Consider how Antin's position contrasts with the views of other writers in this section.

3. Although Antin is generally very enthusiastic about her teachers and about her education, she also offers some criticism of the subjects she was taught, especially geography. Write an essay in which you discuss the curriculum and the teachers that Antin describes and the limitations that she finds. Consider the following questions: What are the assumptions underlying her criticism? What improvements does she implicitly suggest?

QUESTIONS FOR FURTHER EXPLORATION

1. Like Zitkala-Ša's "Impressions of an Indian Childhood" and "The School Days of an Indian Girl," *The Promised Land* was published in the *Atlantic Monthly*. Antin's book appeared in serialized form throughout 1911–12. Locate copies of the magazine from this time (either on the shelves of your library in bound copies or on microfilm) and examine the Table of Contents closely. What other author's works appeared along with Antin's? Research the editorship and editorial policies of the magazine at this time by consulting histories and reference works on periodicals in the United States. Consult the Web site for the *Atlantic Monthly* <http://www.theatlantic.com> and learn what you can about the history of the magazine. Write a profile of the *Atlantic Monthly* during 1911–12 in which you describe the nature of the magazine and how Antin's works are a part of the mission of the periodical at this time.

2. Arrange to conduct an interview with a family member, relative, classmate, or friend who came to the United States as an immigrant child. Keeping in mind the experiences that Antin had in a school where she barely spoke the language and was a member of a religious minority, construct a set of questions designed to ellicit the educational experiences of a person new to this country. Ask about curriculum, teaching methods, tolerance for the individual's customs and native experiences, as well as for recollections of both positive and negative experiences. Be sure to obtain information about the person's birthplace and time of arrival in the United States. Record or make notes as you conduct your interview and write a report of your interview for your class.

6

BECOMING LITERATE: A LESSON FROM THE AMISH

Andrea Fishman (1947–) is a professor in the English Department at West Chester University in Pennsylvania and is the Director of the Pennsylvania Writing and Literature Project, a major regional site of the National Writing Project <http://www-gse.berkeley.edu/Research/NWP/nwp.html>, which provides resources and sponsors programs and workshops for teachers engaged in teaching writing at all educational levels. The Pennsylvania Writing and Literature Project <http://pawp.home.pipeline.com/home.html> offers summer and school-year courses in a wide variety of topics for teachers, including teaching writing and literature, assessing student writers, and computers and writing. Fishman has studied Amish education and culture intensively and actually lived on an Amish farm in Pennsylvania while she conducted research for her book, Amish Literacy: What and How It Means *(1988), coauthored with Glenda L. Bissex. In this study, Fishman examined the ways in which students are taught to read and write, as well as what the roles of reading and writing are in Amish culture, a closely knit monocultural society with limited contact with other cultures. Based in part on her experience in working with the Amish, Fishman has published many articles and reviews on the diversity within public schools and the problems that arise for teachers and students. This essay was written for a collection of essays,* The Right to Literacy, *published by the Modern Language Association as the result of a national Right to Literacy Conference, held at Ohio State University in 1988. The purpose of the conference was to move discussions beyond college and university faculty members and to examine how those in higher education could involve schools and communities in ways to broaden access to literacy for more citizens and not just the privileged few. This essay, "Becoming Literate: A Lesson from the Amish," is a case study of a particular Old Order Amish family and their attitudes toward literacy.*

QUESTIONS FOR READING

1. Who are the Amish? Where do they live? What are their major beliefs? Before you read, take a few minutes to do some preliminary
   research.
2. What do you know about Amish attitudes toward education? Make a
   list of some of your presuppositions before you read this essay.

ANDREA R. FISHMAN

BECOMING LITERATE:
A LESSON FROM THE AMISH

The Right to Literacy, ed. Andrea A. Lunsford, Helene Moglen, and James Slevin
(New York: Modern Language Association, 1990)

One clear, frost-edged January Sunday night, two families gathered for supper
and an evening's entertainment. One family—mine—consisted of a lawyer, a
teacher, and their twelve-year-old son; the other family—the Fishers—consisted
of Eli and Anna, a dairy farmer and his wife, and their five children, ranging in
age from six to seventeen. After supper in the Fisher's large farm kitchen—
warmed by a wood stove and redolent of the fragrances of chicken corn soup,
homemade bread, and freshly baked apples—the table was cleared and an additional smaller one set up to accommodate games of Scrabble, double Dutch
solitaire, and dominoes. As most of us began to play, adults and children randomly mixed, Eli Fisher, Sr., settled into his brown leather recliner with the
newspaper, while six-year-old Eli, Jr., plopped on the corner of the couch nearest his father with a book.

Fifteen or twenty minutes later, I heard Eli, Sr., ask his son, "Where are
your new books?" referring to a set of outgrown Walt Disney books we had
brought for little Eli and his seven-year-old brother, Amos. Eli, Jr., pointed to a
stack of brightly colored volumes on the floor, from which his father chose
Lambert, the Sheepish Lion. As Eli, Jr., climbed onto the arm of the recliner
and snuggled against his father, Eli, Sr., began reading the book out loud in a
voice so commandingly dramatic that soon everyone was listening to the story,
instead of playing their separate games. Broadly portraying the roles of both
Lambert and his lioness mother and laughing heartily at the antics of the cub
who preferred cavorting with the sheep to stalking with the lions, Eli held his
enlarged audience throughout the rest of the story.

As most of us returned to our games when he finished reading, Eli, Sr.,
asked of anyone and everyone, "Where's the *Dairy?*" Daniel, the Fishers'
teenage son, left his game and walked toward his father. "It's in here," he said,
rummaging through the newspapers and magazines in the rack beside the

couch until he found a thick newsletter called *Dairy World,* published by the Independent Buyers Association, to which Eli belonged.

Eli leafed through the publication, standing and walking toward the wood stove as he did. Leaning against the wall, he began reading aloud without preface. All conversation stopped as everyone once again attended to Eli's loudly expressive reading voice, which said:

> A farmer was driving his wagon down the road. On the back was a sign which read: "Experimental Vehicle. Runs on oats and hay. Do not step in exhaust."

Everyone laughed, including Eli, Sr., who then read the remaining jokes on the humor page to his attentive audience. All our games forgotten, we shared the best and the worst riddles and jokes we could remember until it was time for bed.

Occasions like this one occur in many homes and have recently attracted the interest of family literacy researchers (Heath; Taylor; Wells). The scene at the Fishers could have been the scene in any home where parents value reading and writing and want their children to value them as well. It would not be surprising if Eli and Anna, like other literacy-oriented parents, read bedtime stories to their children, helped with their homework, and encouraged them to attain high school diplomas, if not college degrees. But Eli and Anna do none of these things; they read no bedtime stories, they are annoyed if their children bring schoolwork home, and they expect their children to go only as far in school as they did themselves, as far as the eighth grade.

So, although Eli and Anna appeared on that Sunday night to be ideal pro-literacy parents, they may not be, according to commonly described standards, and one significant factor may account for their variations from the supposed ideal: Eli and Anna are not mainstream Americans but are Old Order Amish, raising their family according to Old Order tradition and belief. The Sunday night gathering I just described took place by the light of gas lamps in a house without radio, stereo, television, or any other electrical contrivance. Bedtime in that house is more often marked by singing or silence than by reading. Schoolwork rarely enters there because household, field, and barn chores matter more. And the Fisher children's studying is done in a one-room, eight-grade Old Order school taught by an Old Order woman who attended the same kind of school herself. So while Eli, Jr., like his siblings, is learning the necessity and the value of literacy, what literacy means to him and the ways in which he learns it may differ in both obvious and subtle ways from what it means and how it's transmitted to many mainstream children, just as Eli's world differs from theirs, both obviously and subtly.

As suggested earlier, Eli, Jr., lives in a house replete with print, from the kitchen bulletin board to the built-in bookcases in the playroom to the tables and magazine rack in the living room. There are children's classics and children's magazines. There are local newspapers, shoppers' guides, and other adult periodicals. And there are books of children's Bible stories, copies of the King James Version of the Bible, and other inspirational volumes, none of which mark the Fisher's home as notably different from that of many other Christian Americans.

Yet there are differences, easily overlooked by a casual observer but central to the life of the family and to their definition of literacy. One almost invisible difference is the sources of these materials. Eli and Anna attempt to carefully control the reading material that enters their home. Anna buy books primarily from a local Christian bookstore and from an Amish-operated dry goods store, both of which she trusts not to stock objectionable material. When she sees potentially interesting books in other places—in the drugstore, in the book and card ship, or at a yard sale—she uses the publisher's name as a guide to acceptable content. Relatives and friends close to the family also supply appropriate titles both as gifts and as recommendations, which Anna trusts and often chooses to follow up.

Another, slightly more visible difference comes in the form of books and periodicals around the Fisher house that would not be found in many mainstream, farm, or Christian homes. Along with the local newspaper in the rack beside the couch are issues of *Die Botschaft,* which describes itself as "A Weekly Newspaper Serving Old Order Amish Communities Everywhere." On the desk is a copy of *The Amish Directory,* which alphabetically lists all the Amish living in Pennsylvania and Maryland by nuclear family groups, giving crucial address and other information, along with maps of the eighty-seven church districts included.

On top of the breakfront in the sitting area are copies of songbooks, all in German: some for children, some for adults, and one—the *Ausbund*—for everyone, for this is the church hymnal, a collection of hymns written by tortured and imprisoned sixteenth-century Anabaptists about their experiences and their faith. Kept with these songbooks is a German edition of the Bible and a copy of the *Martyrs Mirror,* an oversized, weighty tome full of graphic descriptions in English of the tortured deaths of early Anabaptists, each illustrated by a black-and-white woodcut print.

Despite what may seem to be the esoteric nature of these texts, none remain in their special places gathering dust, for all are used regularly, each reinforcing in a characteristic way the Amish definition of literacy and each facilitating the image Eli, Jr., has of himself as literate.

Because singing is central to Amish religious observance and expression, the songbooks are used frequently by all members of the family. Because singing requires knowing what is in the text and because Amish singing, which is unaccompanied and highly stylized, requires knowing how to interpret the text exactly as everyone else does, the songbooks represent a kind of reading particularly important to the community, a kind that must be mastered to be considered literate. Yet because singing may mean holding the text and following the words as they appear or it may mean holding the text and following the words from memory or from others' rendition, children Eli's age and younger all participate, appearing and feeling as literate as anyone else.

Functioning similarly are the German Bible and the *Martyrs Mirror*. Though only the older Fishers read that Bible, they do so regularly and then share what they've read with their children. It is the older Fishers, too, who read the *Martyrs Mirror*, but that text Eli, Sr., usually reads aloud during family devotions, so that Anna and all the children, regardless of age, participate similarly through his oral presentations.

While it may seem easier to accept such variant definitions of reading in shared communal situations like these, the participation of Eli, Jr., was equally welcome and equally effective in shared individual reading. When individual oral reading was clearly text-bound, as it is during family devotions, Eli was always enabled to participate in ways similar to his brothers' and sisters', making him a reader like them. When all the Fishers took turns reading the Bible aloud, for example, someone would read Eli's verse aloud slowly, pausing every few words, so that he could repeat what was said and thereby take his turn in the rotation.

When the older children were assigned Bible verses or *Ausbund* hymn stanzas to memorize, Eli was assigned the same one as Amos, the sibling closest in age. Their assignment would be shorter and contain less complex vocabulary than the one the older children got, yet Amos and Eli would also practice their verse together, as the older children did, and would take their turns reciting, as the older children did, making Eli again able to participate along with everyone else.

Because oral reading as modeled by Eli, Sr., is often imitated by the others, Eli, Jr., always shared his books by telling what he saw or knew about them. No one ever told him that telling isn't the same as reading, even though they may look alike, so Eli always seemed like a reader to the others and felt like a reader himself. When everyone else sat reading or playing reading-involved games in the living room after supper or on Sunday afternoons, Eli did the same, to no one's surprise, to everyone's delight, and with universal, though often tacit, welcome and approval. When the other children received books as birthday and Christmas presents, Eli received them too. And when he realized at age six that both of his brothers had magazine subscriptions of their own, Eli asked for and got one as well. Eli never saw his own reading as anything other than real; he did not see it as make-believe or bogus, and neither did anyone else. So, despite the fact that before he went to school Eli., Jr., could not read according to some definitions, he always could according to his family's and his own.

Just as all the Fishers read, so they all write, and just as Eli was enabled to define reading in a way that made him an Amish reader, so he could define writing in a way that made him an Amish writer. Letter writing has always been a primary family activity and one central to the Amish community. Anna writes weekly to *Die Botschaft*, acting as the scribe from her district. She, Eli, Sr., and sixteen-year-old Sarah all participate in circle letters, and the next three children all write with some regularity to cousins in other Amish settlements.

Yet, no matter who is writing to whom, their letters follow the same consistently modeled Amish format, beginning with "Greetings . . . ," moving to recent weather conditions, then to family and community news of note, and ending with a good-bye and often a philosophical or religious thought. I've never seen anyone in the community instructed to write this way, but in the Fisher family, letters received and even letters written are often read out loud, and though this oral sharing is done for informative rather than instructive purposes, it provides an implicit model for everyone to follow.

With all the other family members writing letters, reading them out loud, and orally sharing those they have received, Eli, Jr., wanted to write and receive letters, too, and no one said he couldn't. When he was very young, he dictated his messages to Sarah and drew pictures to accompany what she wrote down for him. Then, even before he started school, Eli began copying the dictated messages Sarah recorded, so that the letters would be in his own hand, as the drawings were.

Other forms of writing also occur in the Fisher household for everyone to see and use. Greeting cards, grocery lists, bulletin board reminders, and bedtime notes from children to absent parents were all part of Eli's life to some extent, and his preschool writing and drawings always adorned the refrigerator, along with the school papers of his brothers and sisters.

In addition, the Fishers played writing-involved games—including Scrabble and Boggle—in which everyone participated, as the family revised the rules to suit their cooperative social model and their definition of literacy. In any games at the Fishers, the oldest person or persons playing may assist the younger ones. No question of fairness arises unless only some players go unaided. Older players, too, may receive help from other players or from onlookers. Score is always kept, and, while some moves are ruled illegal, age or aid received neither bars nor assures a winner. Eli, Jr., therefore, has always played these games as well as anyone else.

Obviously, Eli, Jr., learned a great deal about literacy from all these preschool experiences but what he learned went far beyond academic readiness lessons. More important, Eli learned that literacy is a force in the world—his world—and it is a force that imparts power to all who wield it. He could see for himself that reading and writing enable people as old as his parents and as young as his siblings to fully participate in the world in which they live. In fact, it might have seemed to him that, to be an Amish man, one must read and write, and to be a Fisher, one must read and write as well.

So, even before the age of six, Eli began to recognize and acquire the power of literacy, using it to affiliate himself with the larger Amish world and to identify himself as Amish, a Fisher, a boy, and Eli Fisher, Jr. However, what enabled Eli to recognize all these ways of defining and asserting himself through literacy was neither direct instruction nor insistence from someone else. Rather, it was the ability that all children have long before they can read and write print text, the ability, as Freire puts it, "to read the world." "It is possible," Friere asserts, "to view objects and experiences as texts, words, and letters, and to see the growing awareness of the world as a kind of reading, through which the self learns and changes."[1] Eli, Jr., clearly illustrates this understanding of how children perceive and comprehend the seemingly invisible text of their lives. What he came to understand and accept this way were the definition and the role of print literacy as his society and culture both consciously and tacitly transmit them.

When Eli, Jr., began school, therefore, he was both academically and socially ready to begin. To smooth the transition from home to school, Eli's teacher—like most in Old Order schools—held a "preschool day" in the spring preceding his entry to first grade. On that day, Eli and Mary, the two prospective first-graders in Meadow Brook School, came to be initiated as "scholars." Verna, their teacher, had moved the two current first-graders to other seats, clearing the two desks immediately in front of hers for the newcomers; all that day Mary and Eli sat in the first-grade seats, had "classes," and did seatwork like all the other children. They seemed to know they were expected to follow the rules, to do what they saw others doing, to practice being "scholars," and Verna reinforced that notion, treating those two almost as she would anyone else.

To begin one lesson, for example, "Let's talk about bunnies," she instructed, nodding her head toward the two littlest children, indicating that they should stand beside her desk. She then showed them pictures of rabbits, with the word *bunnies* and the number depicted indicated in word and numeral on each picture. After going through the pictures, saying, "three bunnies," "four bunnies," and having the children repeat after her, Verna asked three questions and got three choral answers.

"Do bunnies like carrots?" she asked.
"Yes," the two children answered together.
"Do they like lettuce?"
"Yes."
"Do they sometimes get in Mother's garden?"
"Yes."

Were it not for some enthusiastic head nodding, Eli, Jr., and Mary could have been fully matriculated students.

When she was ready to assign seatwork, Verna gave the preschoolers pictures of bunnies to color and asked, "What do we do first? Color or write our names?"

"Write our names," the pair chorused, having practiced that skill earlier in the day.

"Yes, we always write our names first. Go back to your desk, write your name, then color the picture. Do nothing on the back of the paper." And the children did exactly that, doing "what we do" precisely "the way we do it."

Verna also conducted what she called a reading class for the two preschoolers, during which they sat, and she held an open picture book facing them. Talking about the pictures, Verna made simple statements identifying different aspects of and actions in the illustrations. After each statement Verna paused, and the children repeated exactly what she had said. The oral text accompanying one picture said:

> Sally is eating chips and watching TV.
> Sally has a red fish.
> Sally has spilled the chips.

After "reading" the text this way, the children answered questions about it.

> "What does Sally have?" Verna asked.
> "A fish," they replied.
> "What color is her fish?"
> "Red."
> "Did Sally spill the chips?"
> "Yes."
> "Did the cat eat the chips?"
> "Yes."

While the content of this lesson seems incongruous, I know, its form and conduct fit the Meadow Brook model perfectly. Precise recall and yeses are all that the questions demand. Even the last question, while not covered in the "reading," requires recognition of only what happens in the picture.

What happened in Meadow Brook School that day—and what would happen in the eight school years to follow—reinforced, extended, and rarely contradicted what Eli already knew about literacy. Reading and writing at school allowed him to further affiliate and identify himself with and within his social group. While his teacher occasionally gave direct instructions, those instructions tended to be for activities never before seen or experienced; otherwise, Eli and Mary knew to follow the behavioral and attitudinal lead of the older children and to look to them for assistance and support, just as they looked to the teacher. In other words, reading the school world came as naturally to these children as reading the world anywhere else, and the message in both texts was emphatically the same.

Most important here, however, may be the remarkable substantive coherence that Meadow Brook School provided, a coherence that precluded any conflict over what, how, or even whether to read and write. Eli's experience as a Fisher had taught him that reading comes in many forms—secular and religious, silent and oral, individual and communal—and they all count. Through his at-home experience, Eli had also learned which other, more specific, less obvious abilities count as reading in his world. He had learned to value at least four significant abilities: (1) the ability to select and manage texts, to be able to find his mother's letter in *Die Botschaft* or to find a particular verse in the Bible; (2) the ability to empathize with people in texts and to discern the implicit lessons their experiences teach: to empathize with Lambert the lion, who taught the possibility of peaceful coexistence, and to empathize with the Anabaptist martyrs, who taught the rightness of dying for one's faith; (3) the ability to accurately recall what was read, to remember stories, riddles, and jokes or to memorize Bible and hymn verses; and (4) the ability to synthesize what is read in a single text with what is already known or to synthesize information across texts in Amish-appropriate ways.

When Eli got to school, he found a similar definition of reading in operation. He and Mary were helped to select and manage text. Their attention was directed toward what mattered in the text and away from what did not. They were helped to discover the single right answer to every question. They had only to recall information without interpreting or extending it in any significant way. And they were expected to empathize with the people in Verna's lunchtime oral reading without questioning or hypothesizing about what had happened or what would happen next.

Similarly, before Eli went to school, he knew what counted as writing in his world, just as he knew what counted as reading. He learned at home that being able to write means being able to encode, to copy, to follow format, to choose content, and to list. And, when he arrived at school, this same definition, these same abilities, were all that mattered there, too.

While the dimensions of reading and writing that count at Meadow Brook and elsewhere in Eli's life seem little different from those that count in mainstream situations—a terrifying fact, I would suggest—it is important to recognize that several mainstream-valued skills are completely absent from the Amish world as I've experienced it. Critical reading—individual analysis and interpretation—of the sort considered particularly important by most people who are mainstream-educated or mainstream educators is not valued by the Amish because of its potentially divisive, counterproductive power.

Literary appreciation, too, is both irrelevant and absent because the study of text-as-object is moot. How a writer enables a reader to empathize with his characters doesn't matter; only the ability to empathize matters. Text, whether biblical or secular, is perceived not as an object but as a force acting in the world, and it is the impact of that force that counts.

When it comes to writing, the existing Amish definition also differs in what is absent, rather than what is present. While grammar, spelling, and punctuation do count for the Old Order, they do so only to the extent that word order, words, and punctuation must allow readers to read—that is, to recognize and make sense of their reading. If a reader readily understands the intention of an adjective used as an adverb, a singular verb following a plural noun, a sentence fragment, or a compound verb containing a misplaced comma, the Amish do not see these as errors warranting attention, despite the fact that an outside reader may.

Equally irrelevant in Old Order schools is the third-person formal essay—the ominous five-paragraph theme—so prevalent in mainstream classrooms. Amish children never learn to write this kind of composition, not because they are not college-bound but because the third-person-singular point of view assumed by an individual writer is foreign to this first-person-plural society; thesis statements, topic sentences, and concepts like coherence, unity, and emphasis are similarly alien.

One final distinction separates the Amish definition of literacy from that of many mainstream definitions: the absence of originality as a desirable feature. Not only do community constraints limit the number of appropriate topics and forms an Amish writer may use, but original approaches to or applications of those topics and forms is implicitly discouraged by the similarity of models and assignments and by the absence of fiction as an appropriate personal genre. All aspects of community life reward uniformity; while writing provides an outlet for individual expression and identification, singular creativity stays within community norms.

For Eli Fisher, Jr., then, the definition of literacy he learned at home was consistent with the one he found at school, though it differed in several important ways from those of most MLA members, for example. Yet for Eli, as for Friere, "deciphering the word flowed naturally from reading the immediate world."[2] From reading his world, this six-year-old derived a complete implicit definition that told him what literacy is and whether literacy matters. I can't help but wonder, however, what would have happened had Eli gone to school and been told, explicitly or through more powerful behaviors, that he really didn't know what counted as reading and writing, that his reading and writing were not real but other unknown or alien varieties were. What would have happened had his quiet imitative behavior made him invisible in the classroom or, worse yet, made his teacher assume that he was withdrawn, problematic, or less than bright? What if his work were devalued because it was obviously copied or just unoriginal? What if he had been called on to perform individually in front of the class, to stand up and stand out? Or what if he had been asked to discuss private issues in public? Or to evaluate what he read?

Had any of these things happened, I suspect that Eli would have had to make some difficult choices that would have amounted to choosing between what he had learned and learned to value at home and what he seemed expected to learn at school. To conform to his teacher's demands and values, he would have had to devalue or disavow those of his parents—a demand that public schools seem to make frequently of children from cultural or socioeconomic groups differing from those of their teachers or their schools, a demand that seems unfair, uncalled for, and unnecessary, not to mention counterproductive and destructive.

Eli Fisher's experience suggests, therefore, that those of us who deal with children unlike ourselves need to see our classrooms and our students differently from the way we may have seen them in the past. We need to realize that students, even first-graders, have been reading the world—if not the word—for at least five, six, or seven years; they come to school not devoid of knowledge and values but with a clear sense of what their world demands and requires, including what, whether, and how to read and write, though their understandings may differ significantly from our own. We need to realize that our role may not be to prepare our students to enter mainstream society but, rather, to help them see what mainstream society offers and what it takes away, what they may gain by assimilating and what they may lose in that process. Through understanding their worlds, their definitions of literacy, and their dilemmas, not only will we better help them make important literacy-related decisions, but we will better help ourselves to do the same.

NOTES

1. Freire, Paulo. "The Importance of the Act of Reading." *Journal of Education* (Winter 1983): 5–10.
2. Freire 5–10.

QUESTIONS FOR REACTION AND DISCUSSION

1. Describe the opening scene of this case study in your own words. How is it like or unlike family situations that you know?
2. What is the distinction that Fishman makes between mainstream Americans and Old Order Amish? What does it mean to be "Old Order" in the Amish world?
3. What texts do Amish families read and learn?
4. What is the value of oral reading in Amish culture?
5. What are the occasions for writing in Amish culture?
6. How do Amish school classrooms reinforce the notion of literacy children learn at home?

QUESTIONS FOR WRITING

1. What is the concept of Amish literacy that emerges in this study? Define "Amish literacy," summarize its central characteristics, and give examples from Fishman's study.
2. An important point that Fishman makes in this essay is that "several mainstream-valued skills are completely absent from the Amish world as I've experienced it. Critical reading—individual analysis and interpretation—of the sort considered particularly important by most people who are mainstream-educated or mainstream educators is not valued by the Amish because of its potentially divisive, counterproductive power." Write an essay in which you contrast the mainstream literacy skills that Fishman describes with the skills that the Amish value. Fishman's conclusion is that teachers should not merely work to inculate mainstream literacy skills into their students but rather instruct them in what is gained and lost through assimilation. Is that your conclusion? Why or why not?

3. Investigate the many books that Fishman mentions in use at the Fisher house. How widely available are these texts? Prepare an annotated bibliography for distribution to your class.

QUESTIONS FOR FURTHER EXPLORATION

1. View the 1985 movie, *Witness,* starring Harrison Ford and Kelly McGillis and directed by Peter Weir. Write an essay in which you compare and contrast the portrayal of the Amish in Fishman's case study and the movie. Locate some reviews of the movie when it first appeared. What comments did viewers make about Amish society? What judgment can you make of the accuracy of the presentation, based on your reading of Fishman's essay and other materials about the Amish that you read?
2. Investigate the Web site for The National Writing Project <http://www-gse.berkeley.edu/Research/NWP/nwp.html>. What resources are available there for research and study about literacy? Write a report for your class on the goals, purposes, and mission of the NWP. Include a list of resources that classmates might use to investigate the topic of literacy.
3. Investigate Old Order Amish using *The Humanities Index* on the Internet and in print resources at your library. Write a report for your class in which you provide information on the following: geographic location of major settlements, population figures, occupations, religious beliefs, current educational practices, and the extent to which the Amish are involved with the non-Amish.

7

ARIA: A MEMOIR OF A
BILINGUAL CHILDHOOD

Richard Rodriguez (1944–) was born in San Francisco, California, the son of Mexican immigrants. Well educated in Catholic schools in Sacramento, Rodriguez graduated from Stanford University in 1967 and earned an M.S. in English from Columbia University in New York City in 1969; he also did graduate work at the University of California, Berkeley. The recipient of prestigious fellowships, he is the author of two books, Hunger of Memory: The Education of Richard Rodriguez *(1981), his intellectual autobiography; and* Days of Obligation: An Argument with My Mexican Father *(1992), a collection of essays about the complicated moral and spiritual relationship between Mexico and the United States and the impact of that heritage for Mexican Americans. Rodriguez, among the best-known Mexican-American writers of today, uses language as the departure point for an exploration of his experiences of growing up and assimilating in a white world. He has taken controversial stands on affirmative action and bilingual education, both of which he opposes. Rodriguez is a full-time writer whose works appear in a variety of periodicals, and he currently serves as the editor of the Pacific News Service of "The News Hour with Jim Lehrer." Many of his essays and dialogues are available on the Online Newshour <http://www1.pbs.org/newshour>. Although "Aria: A Memoir of a Bilingual Childhood" is the first chapter of* Hunger of Memory, *it first appeared in 1980 as an essay in* The American Scholar, *the journal of Phi Beta Kappa, the nation's oldest and most prestigious undergraduate society.*

QUESTIONS FOR READING

1. What is an "aria" and what does that term and the whole title suggest to you about the essay?
2. What does it mean to be "bilingual"?
3. What do you know about the state of bilingual education in this country?

RICHARD RODRIGUEZ

ARIA: A MEMOIR OF A BILINGUAL CHILDHOOD

The American Scholar 50 (Winter 80/81): 25–42

I remember, to start with, that day in Sacramento, in a California now nearly thirty years past, when I first entered a classroom—able to understand about fifty stray English words. The third of four children, I had been preceded by my older brother and sister to a neighborhood Roman Catholic school. But neither of them had revealed very much about their classroom experiences. They left each morning and returned each afternoon, always together speaking Spanish as they climbed the five steps to the porch. And their mysterious books, wrapped in brown shopping-bag paper, remained on the table next to the door, closed firmly behind them.

An accident of geography sent me to a school where all my classmates were white and many were the children of doctors and lawyers and business executives. On that first day of school, my classmates must certainly have been uneasy to find themselves apart from their families, in the first institution of their lives. But I was astonished. I was fated to be the "problem student" in class.

The nun said, in a friendly but oddly impersonal voice: "Boys and girls, this is Richard Rodriguez." (I heard her sound it out: *Rich-heard Road-ree-guess.*) It was the first time I had heard anyone say my name in English. "Richard," the nun repeated more slowly, writing my name down in her book. Quickly I turned to see my mother's face dissolve in a watery blur behind the pebbled-glass door.

━━━━━━

Now, many years later, I hear of something called "bilingual education"— a scheme proposed in the late 1960s by Hispanic-American social activists, later endorsed by a congressional vote. It is a program that seeks to permit non-English-speaking children (many from lower class homes) to use their "family language" as the language of school. Such, at least, is the aim its supporters announce. I hear them, and am forced to say no: It is not possible for a child, any child, ever to use his family's language in school. Not to understand this is to misunderstand the public use of schooling and to trivialize the nature of intimate life.

Memory teaches me what I know of these matters. The boy reminds the adult. I was a bilingual child, but of a certain kind: "socially disadvantaged," the son of working-class parents, both Mexican immigrants.

In the early years of my boyhood, my parents coped very well in America. My father had steady work. My mother managed at home. They were nobody's victims. When we moved to a house many blocks from the

Mexican-American section of town, they were not intimidated by those two or three neighbors who initially tried to make us unwelcome. ("Keep your brats away from my sidewalk!") But despite all they achieved, or perhaps because they had so much to achieve, they lacked any deep feeling of ease, of belonging in public. They regarded the people at work or in crowds as being very distant from us. Those were the others, *los gringos*. That term was interchangeable in their speech with another, even more telling: *los americanos*.

I grew up in a house where the only regular guests were my relations. On a certain day, enormous families of relatives would visit us, and there would be so many people that the noise and the bodies would spill out to the backyard and onto the front porch. Then for weeks no one would come. (If the doorbell rang, it was usually a salesman.) Our house stood apart—gaudy yellow in a row of white bungalows. We were the people with the noisy dog, the people who raised chickens. We were the foreigners on the block. A few neighbors would smile and wave at us. We waved back. But until I was seven years old, I did not know the name of the old couple living next door or the names of the kids living across the street.

In public, my father and mother spoke a hesitant, accented, and not always grammatical English. And then they would have to strain, their bodies tense, to catch the sense of what was rapidly said by *los gringos*. At home, they returned to Spanish. The language of their Mexican past sounded in counterpoint to the English spoken in public. The words would come quickly, with ease. Conveyed through those sounds was the pleasing, soothing, consoling reminder that one was at home.

During those years when I was first learning to speak, my mother and father addressed me only in Spanish; in Spanish I learned to reply. By contrast, English (*inglés*) was the language I came to associate with gringos, rarely heard in the house. I learned my first words of English overhearing my parents speaking to strangers. At six years of age, I knew just enough words for my mother to trust me on errands to stores one block away—but no more.

I was then a listening child, careful to hear the very different sound of Spanish and English. Wide-eyed with hearing, I'd listen to sounds more than words. First, there were English (gringo) sounds. So many words still were unknown to me that when the butcher or lady at the drugstore said something, exotic polysyllabic sound would bloom in the midst of their sentences. Often the speech of people in public seemed to me very loud, booming with confidence. The man behind the counter would literally ask, "What can I do for you?" But by being so firm and clear, the sound of his voice said that he was a gringo; he belonged in public society. There were also the high, nasal notes of middle-class American speech—which I rarely am conscious of hearing today because I hear them so often, but could not stop hearing when I was a boy. Crowds at Safeway or at bus stops were noisy with the birdlike sounds of *los gringos*. I'd move away from them all—all the chirping chatter above me.

My own sounds I was unable to hear, but I knew that I spoke English poorly. My words could not extend to form complete thoughts. And the words

I did speak I didn't know well enough to make distinct sounds. (Listeners would usually lower their heads to hear better what I was trying to say.) But it was one thing for *me* to speak English with difficulty; it was more troubling to hear my parents speaking in public: their high-whining vowels and guttural consonants; their sentences that got stuck with "eh" and "ah" sounds; the confused syntax; the hesitant rhythm of sounds so different from the way gringos spoke. I'd notice, moreover, that my parents' voices were softer than those gringos we would meet.

I am tempted to say now that none of this mattered. (In adulthood I am embarrassed by childhood fears.) And, in a way, it didn't matter very much that my parents could not speak English with ease. Their linguistic difficulties had no serious consequences. My mother and father made themselves understood at the county hospital clinic and at government offices. And yet, in another way, it mattered very much. It was unsettling to hear my parents struggle with English. Hearing them, I'd grow nervous, and my clutching trust in their protection and power would be weakened.

There were many times like the night at a brightly lit gasoline station (a blaring white memory) when I stood uneasily hearing my father talk to a teenage attendant. I do not recall what they were saying, but I cannot forget the sounds my father made as he spoke. At one point his words slid together to form one long word—sounds as confused as the threads of blue and green oil in the puddle next to my shoes. His voice rushed through what he had left to say. Toward the end, he reached falsetto notes, appealing to his listener's understanding. I looked away at the lights of passing automobiles. I tried not to hear any more. But I heard only too well the attendant's reply, his calm, easy tones. Shortly afterward, headed for home, I shivered when my father put his hand on my shoulder. The very first chance that I got, I evaded his grasp and ran on ahead into the dark, skipping with feigned boyish exuberance.

But then there was Spanish: *español,* the language rarely heard away from the house; *español,* the language which seemed to me therefore a private language, my family's language. To hear its sounds was to feel myself specially recognized as one of the family, apart from *los otros.* A simple remark, an inconsequential comment could convey that assurance. My parents would say something to me and I would feel embraced by the sounds of their words. Those sounds said: *I am speaking with ease in Spanish. I am addressing you in words I never use with* los gringos. *I recognize you as someone special, close, like no one outside. You belong with us. In the family. Ricardo.*

At the age of six, well past the time when most middle-class children no longer notice the difference between sounds uttered at home and words spoken in public, I had a different experience. I lived in a world compounded of sounds. I was a child longer than most. I lived in a magical world, surrounded by sounds both pleasing and fearful. I shared with my family a language enchantingly private—different from that used in the city around us.

Just opening or closing the screen door behind me was an important experience. I'd rarely leave home all alone or without feeling reluctance. Walking down the sidewalk, under the canopy of tall trees, I'd warily notice the (suddenly) silent neighborhood kids who stood warily watching me. Nervously, I'd arrive at the grocery store to hear there the sounds of the gringo, reminding me that in this so-big world I was a foreigner. But if leaving home was never routine, neither was coming back. Walking toward our house, climbing the steps from the sidewalk, in summer when the front door was open, I'd hear voices beyond the screen door talking in Spanish. For a second or two I'd stay, linger there listening. Smiling, I'd hear my mother call out, saying in Spanish, "Is that you, Richard?" Those were her words, but all the while her sounds would assure me: *You are home now. Come closer inside. With us.* "Sí" I'd reply.

Once more inside the house, I would resume my place in the family. The sounds would grow harder to hear. Once more at home, I would grow less conscious of them. It required, however, no more than the blurt of the doorbell to alert me all over again to listen to sounds. The house would turn instantly quiet while my mother went to the door. I'd hear her hard English sounds. I'd wait to hear her voice turn to soft-sounding Spanish, which assured me, as surely as did the clicking tongue of the lock on the door, that the stranger was gone.

Plainly it is not healthy to hear such sounds so often. It is not healthy to distinguish public from private sounds so easily. I remained cloistered by sounds, timid and shy in public, too dependent on the voices at home. And yet I was a very happy child when I was at home. I remember many nights when my father would come back from work, and I'd hear him call out to my mother in Spanish, sounding relieved. In Spanish, his voice would sound the light and free notes that he never could manage in English. Some nights I'd jump up just hearing his voice. My brother and I would come running into the room where he was with our mother. Our laughing (so deep was the pleasure!) became screaming. Like other who feel the pain of public alienation, we transformed the knowledge of our public separateness into a consoling reminder of our intimacy. Excited, our voices joined in a celebration of sounds. *We are speaking now the way we never speak out in public—we are together,* the sounds told me. Some nights no one seemed willing to loosen the hold that sounds had on us. At dinner we invented new words that sounded Spanish, but made sense only to us. We pieced together new words by taking, say, an English verb and giving it Spanish endings. My mother's instructions at bedtime would be lacquered with mock-urgent tones. Or a word like *sí*, sounded in several notes, would convey added measures of feeling. Tongues lingered around the edges of words, especially fat vowels. And we happily sounded that military drum roll, the twirling roar of the Spanish *r*. Family language, my family's sounds: the voices of my parents and sisters and brother. Their voices insisting: *You belong here. We are family members. Related. Special to one another. Listen!* Voices singing and sighing, rising and straining, then surging, teeming with pleasure which burst syllables into fragments of laughter. At times it seemed there was steady quiet only when, from another room, the rustling whispers of my parents faded and I edged closer to sleep.

Supporters of bilingual education imply today that students like me miss a great deal by not being taught in their family's language. What they seem not to recognize is that, as a socially disadvantaged child, I regarded Spanish as a private language. It was a ghetto language that deepened and strengthened my feeling of public separateness. What I needed to learn in school was that I had the right, and the obligation, to speak the public language. The odd truth is that my first-grade classmates could have become bilingual, in the conventional sense of the word, more easily than I. Had they been taught early (as upper middle-class children often are taught) a "second language" like Spanish or French, they could have regarded it simply as another public language. In my case, such bilingualism could not have been so quickly achieved. What I did not believe was that I could speak a single public language.

Without question, it would have pleased me to have heard my teachers address me in Spanish when I entered the classroom. I would have felt much less afraid. I would have imagined that my instructors were somehow "related" to me; I would indeed have heard their Spanish as my family's language. I would have trusted them and responded with ease. But I would have delayed—postponed for how long?—having to learn the language of public society. I would have evaded—and for how long?—learning the great lesson of school: that I had a public identity.

Fortunately, my teachers were unsentimental about their responsibility. What they understood was that I needed to speak public English. So their voices would search me out, asking me questions. Each time I heard them I'd look up in surprise to see a nun's face frowning at me. I'd mumble, not really meaning to answer. The nun would persist. "Richard, stand up. Don't look at the floor. Speak up. Speak to the entire class, not just to me!" But I couldn't believe English could be my language to use. (In part, I did not want to believe it.) I continued to mumble. I resisted the teacher's demands. (Did I somehow suspect that once I learned this public language my family life would be changed?) Silent, waiting for the bell to sound, I remained dazed, diffident, afraid.

Because I wrongly imagined that English was intrinsically a public language and Spanish was intrinsically private, I easily noted the difference between classroom language and the language of home. At school, words were directed to a general audience of listeners. ("Boys and girls . . .") Words were meaningfully ordered. And the point was not self-expression alone, but to make oneself understood by many others. The teacher quizzed: "Boys and girls, why do we use that word in this sentence? Could we think of a better word to use there? Would the sentence change its meaning if the words were differently arranged? Isn't there a better way of saying much the same thing?" (I couldn't say. I wouldn't try to say.)

Three months passed. Five. A half year. Unsmiling, ever watchful, my teachers noted my silence. They began to connect my behavior with the slow progress my brother and sisters were making. Until, one Saturday morning, three nuns arrived at the house to talk to our parents. Stiffly they sat on the blue living-room sofa. From the doorway of another room, spying on the visitors, I noted the incongruity, the clash of two worlds, the faces and voices of school intruding upon the familiar setting of home. I overheard one voice gently wondering, "Do your children speak only Spanish at home, Mrs. Rodriguez?" While another voice added, "That Richard especially seems so timid and shy."

That Rich-heard!

With great tact, the visitors continued, "Is it possible for you and your husband to encourage your children to practice their English when they are home?" Of course my parents complied. What would they not do for their children's well-being? And how could they question the Church's authority which those women represented? In an instant they agreed to give up the language (the sounds) which had revealed and accentuated our family's closeness. The moment after the visitors left, the change was observed. *"Ahora,* speak to us only *en inglés,"* my father and mother told us.

At first, it seemed a kind of game. After dinner each night, the family gathered together to practice "our" English. It was still then *inglés,* a language foreign to us, so we felt drawn to it as strangers. Laughing, we would try to define words we could not pronounce. We played with strange English sounds, often over-anglicizing our pronunciations. And we filled the smiling gaps of our sentences with familiar Spanish sounds. But that was cheating, somebody shouted, and everyone laughed.

In school, meanwhile, like my brother and sisters, I was required to attend a daily tutoring session. I needed a full year of this special work. I also needed my teachers to keep my attention from straying in class by calling out, *"Rich-heard!"*—their English voices slowly loosening the ties to my other name, with its three notes, *Ri-car-do.* Most of all, I needed to hear my mother and father speak to me in a moment of seriousness in "broken"—suddenly heartbreaking—English. This scene was inevitable. One Saturday morning I entered the kitchen where my parents were talking, but I did not realize that they were talking in Spanish until, the moment they saw me, their voices changed and they began speaking English. The gringo sounds they uttered startled me. Pushed me away. In that moment of trivial misunderstanding and profound insight, I felt my throat twisted by unsounded grief. I simply turned and left the room. But I had no place to escape to where I could grieve in Spanish. My brother and sisters were speaking English in another part of the house.

Again and again in the days following, as I grew increasingly angry, I was obliged to hear my mother and father encouraging me: "Speak to us *en inglés."* Only then did I determine to learn classroom English. Thus, sometime afterward it happened: one day in school, I raised my hand to volunteer an answer to a question. I spoke out in a loud voice and I did not think it remarkable when the entire class understood. That day I moved very far from being the disadvantaged child I had been only days earlier. Taken hold at last was the belief, the calming assurance, that I *belonged* in public.

Shortly after, I stopped hearing the high, troubling sounds of *los gringos*. A more and more confident speaker of English, I didn't listen to how strangers sounded when they talked to me. With so many English-speaking people around me, I no longer heard American accents. Conversations quickened. Listening to persons whose voices sounded eccentrically pitched, I might note their sounds for a few seconds, but then I'd concentrate on what they were saying. Now when I heard someone's tone of voice—angry or questioning or sarcastic or happy or sad—I didn't distinguish it from the words it expressed. Sound and word were thus tightly wedded. At the end of the day I was often bemused, and always relieved, to realize how "soundless," though crowded with words, my day in public had been. An eight-year-old boy, I finally came to accept what had been technically true since my birth: I was an American citizen.

But diminished by then was the special feeling of closeness at home. Gone was the desperate, urgent, intense feeling of being at home among those with whom I felt intimate. Our family remained a loving family, but one greatly changed. We were no longer so close, no longer bound tightly together by the knowledge of our separateness from *los gringos*. Neither my older brother nor my sisters rushed home after school any more. Nor did I. When I arrived home, often there would be neighborhood kids in the house. Or the house would be empty of sounds.

Following the dramatic Americanization of their children, even my parents grew more publicly confident—especially my mother. First she learned the names of all the people on the block. Then she decided we needed to have a telephone in our house. My father, for his part, continued to use the word gringo, but it was no longer charged with bitterness or distrust. Stripped of any emotional content, the word simply became a name for those Americans not of Hispanic descent. Hearing him, sometimes, I wasn't sure if he was pronouncing the Spanish word *gringo*, or saying gringo in English.

There was a new silence at home. As we children learned more and more English, we shared fewer and fewer words with our parents. Sentences needed to be spoken slowly when one of us addressed our mother or father. Often the parent wouldn't understand. The child would need to repeat himself. Still the parent misunderstood. The young voice, frustrated, would end up saying, "Never mind"—the subject was closed. Dinners would be noisy with the clinking of knives and forks against dishes. My mother would smile softly between her remarks; my father, at the other end of the table, would chew and chew his food while he stared over the heads of his children.

My mother! My father! After English became my primary language, I no longer knew what words to use in addressing my parents. The old Spanish words (those tender accents of sound) I had earlier used—*mamá* and *papá*—I couldn't use any more. They would have been all-too-painful reminders of how much had changed in my life. On the other hand, the words I heard neighborhood kids call their parents seemed equally unsatisfactory. "Mother" and "father," "ma, " "papa," "pa," "dad," "pop" (how I hated the all-American sound of that last word)—all these I felt were unsuitable terms of address for *my* parents. As a result, I never used them at home. Whenever I'd speak to my parents, I would try to get their attention by looking at them. In public conversations, I'd refer to them as my "parents" or my "mother" and "father."

My mother and father, for their part, responded differently, as their children spoke to them less. My mother grew restless, seemed troubled and anxious at the scarceness of words exchanged in the house. She would question me about my day when I came home from school. She smiled at my small talk. She pried at the edges of my sentences to get me to say something more. ("What . . . ?") She'd join conversations she overheard, but her intrusions often stopped her children's talking. By contrast, my father seemed to grow reconciled to the new quiet. Though his English somewhat improved, he tended more and more to retire into silence. At dinner he spoke very little. One night his children and even his wife helplessly giggled at his garbled English pronunciation of the Catholic "Grace Before Meals." Thereafter he made his wife recite the prayer at the start of each meal, even on formal occasions when there were guests in the house.

Hers became the public voice of the family. On official business it was she, not my father, who would usually talk to strangers on the phone or in stores. We children grew so accustomed to his silence that years later we would routinely refer to his "shyness." (My mother often tried to explain: both of his parents died when he was eight. He was raised by an uncle who treated him as little more than a menial servant. He was never encouraged to speak. He grew up alone—a man of few words.) But I realized my father was not shy whenever I'd watch him speaking Spanish with relatives. Using Spanish, he was quickly effusive. Especially when talking with other men, his voice would spark, flicker, flare alive with varied sounds. In Spanish he expressed ideas and feelings he rarely revealed when speaking English. With firm Spanish sounds he conveyed a confidence and authority that English would never allow him.

The silence at home, however, was not simply the result of fewer words passing between parents and children. More profound for me was the silence created by my inattention to sounds. At about the time I no longer bothered to listen with care to the sounds of English in public, I grew careless about listening to the sounds made by the family when they spoke. Most of the time I would hear someone speaking at home and didn't distinguish his sounds from the words people uttered in public. I didn't even pay much attention to my parents' accented and ungrammatical speech—at least not at home. Only when I was with them in public would I become alert to their accents. But even then their sounds caused me less and less concern. For I was growing increasingly confident of my own public identity.

I would have been happier about my public success had I not recalled, sometimes, what it had been like earlier, when my family conveyed its intimacy through a set of conveniently private sounds. Sometimes in public, hearing a stranger, I'd hark back to my lost past. A Mexican farm worker approached me one day downtown. He wanted directions to some place. *"Hijito, . . ."* he said. And his voice stirred old longings. Another time I was standing beside my mother in the visiting room of a Carmelite convent, before the dense screen which rendered the nuns shadowy figures. I heard several of them speaking Spanish in their busy, singsong, overlapping voices, assuring my mother that, yes, yes, we were remembered, all our family was remembered, in their prayers. Those voices echoed faraway family sounds. Another day a dark-faced old woman touched my shoulder lightly to steady herself as she boarded a bus. She murmured something to me I couldn't quite comprehend. Her Spanish voice came near, like the face of a never-before-seen relative in the instant before I was kissed. That voice, like so many of the Spanish voices I'd heard in public, recalled the golden age of my childhood.

Bilingual educators say today that children lose a degree of "individuality" by becoming assimilated into public society. (Bilingual schooling is a program popularized in the seventies, that decade when middle-class "ethnics" began to resist the process of assimilation—the "American melting pot.") But the bilingualists oversimplify when they scorn the value and necessity of assimilation. They do not seem to realize that a person is individualized in two ways. So they do not realize that, while one suffers a diminished sense of *private* individuality by being assimilated into public society, such assimilation makes possible the achievement of *public* individuality.

Simplistically again, the bilingualists insist that a student should be reminded of his difference from others in mass society, of his "heritage." But they equate mere separateness with individuality. The fact is that only in private—with intimates—is separateness from the crowd a prerequisite for individuality; an intimate "tells" me that I am unique, unlike all others, apart from the crowd. In public, by contrast, full individuality is achieved, paradoxically, by those who are able to consider themselves members of the crowd. Thus it happened for me. Only when I was able to think of myself as an American, no longer an alien in gringo society, could I seek the rights and opportunities necessary for full public individuality. The social and political advantages I enjoy as a man began on the day I came to believe that my name was indeed *Rich-heard Road-ree-guess*. It is true that my public society today is often impersonal; in fact, my public society is usually mass society. But despite the anonymity of the crowd, and despite the fact that the individuality I achieve in public is often tenuous—because it depends on my being one in a crowd—I celebrate the day I acquired my new name. Those middle-class ethnics who scorn assimilation seem to me filled with decadent self-pity, obsessed by the burden of public life. Dangerously, they romanticize public separateness and trivialize the dilemma of those who are truly socially disadvantaged.

If I rehearse here the changes in my private life after my Americanization, it is finally to emphasize a public gain. The loss implies the gain. The house I returned to each afternoon was quiet. Intimate sounds no longer greeted me at the door. Inside there were other noises. The telephone rang. Neighborhood kids ran past the door of the bedroom where I was reading my schoolbooks—covered with brown shopping-bag paper. Once I learned the public language, it would never again be easy for me to hear intimate family voices. More and more of my day was spent hearing words, not sounds. But that may only be a way of saying that on the day I raised my hand in class and spoke loudly to an entire roomful of faces, my childhood started to end.

I grew up the victim of disconcerting confusion. As I became fluent in English, I could no longer speak Spanish with confidence. I continued to understand spoken Spanish, and in high school I learned how to read and write Spanish. But for many years I could not pronounce it. A powerful guilt blocked my spoken words; an essential glue was missing whenever I would try to connect words to form sentences. I would be unable to break a barrier of sound, to speak freely. I would speak, or try to speak, Spanish, and I would manage to utter halting, hiccuping sounds which betrayed my unease. (Even today I speak Spanish very slowly, at best.)

When relatives and Spanish-speaking friends of my parents came to the house, my brother and sisters would usually manage to say a few words before being excused. I never managed so gracefully. Each time I'd hear myself addressed in Spanish, I couldn't respond with any success. I'd know the words I wanted to say, but I couldn't say them. I would try to speak, but everything I said seemed to me horribly anglicized. My mouth wouldn't form the sounds right. My jaw would tremble. After a phrase or two, I'd stutter, cough up a warm, silvery sound, and stop.

My listeners were surprised to hear me. They'd lower their heads to grasp better what I was trying to say. They would repeat their questions in gentle, affectionate voices. But then I would answer in English. No, no, they would say, we want you to speak to us in Spanish ("*en español*"). But I couldn't do it. Then they would call me *Pocho*. Sometimes playfully, teasing, using the tender diminutive—*mi pochito*. Sometimes not so playfully but mockingly, *pocho*. (A Spanish dictionary defines that word as an adjective meaning "colorless" or "bland." But I heard it as a noun, naming the Mexican-American who in becoming an American, forgets his native society.) "*¡Pocho!*" my mother's best friend muttered, shaking her head. And my mother laughed, somewhere behind me. She said that her children didn't want to practice "our Spanish" after they started going to school. My mother's smiling voice made me suspect that the lady who faced me was not really angry at me. But searching her face, I couldn't find the hint of a smile.

Embarrassed, my parents would often need to explain their children's inability to speak fluent Spanish during those years. My mother encountered the wrath of her brother, her only brother, when he came up from Mexico one summer with his family and saw his nieces and nephews for the very first time. After listening to me, he looked away and said what a disgrace it was that my siblings and I couldn't speak Spanish, "*su propria idioma.*" He made that remark to my mother, but I noticed that he stared at my father.

One other visitor from those years I clearly remember: a long-time friend of my father from San Francisco who came to stay with us for several days in late August. He took great interest in me after he realized that I couldn't answer his questions in Spanish. He would grab me, as I started to leave the kitchen. He would ask me something. Usually he wouldn't bother to wait for my mumbled response. Knowingly, he'd murmur, "*¿Ay pocho, pocho, donde vas?*" And he would press his thumbs into the upper part of my arms, making me squirm with pain. Dumbly I'd stand there, waiting for his wife to notice us and call him off with a benign smile. I'd giggle, hoping to deflate the tension between us, pretending that I hadn't seen the glittering scorn in his glance.

I recount such incidents only because they suggest the fierce power that Spanish had over many people I met at home, how strongly Spanish was associated with closeness. Most of those people who called me a *pocho* could have spoken English to me, but many wouldn't. They seemed to think that Spanish was the only language we could use among ourselves, that Spanish alone permitted our association. (Such persons are always vulnerable to the ghetto merchant and the politician who have learned the value of speaking their clients' "family language" so as to gain immediate trust.) For my part, I felt that by learning English I had somehow committed a sin of betrayal. But betrayal against whom? Not exactly against the visitors to the house. Rather, I felt I had betrayed my immediate family. I knew that my parents had encouraged me to learn English. I knew that I had turned to English with angry reluctance. But once I spoke English with ease, I came to feel guilty. I sensed that I had broken the spell of intimacy which had once held the family so close together. It was this original sin against my family that I recalled whenever anyone addressed me in Spanish and I responded, confounded.

Yet even during those years of guilt, I was coming to grasp certain consoling truths about language and intimacy—truths that I learned gradually. Once, I remember playing with a friend in the backyard when my grandmother appeared at the window. Her face was stern with suspicion when she saw the boy (the *gringo* boy) I was with. She called out to me in Spanish, sounding the whistle of her ancient breath. My companion looked up and watched her intently as she lowered the window and moved (still visible) behind the light curtain, watching us both. He wanted to know what she had said. I started to tell him, to translate her Spanish words into English. The problem was, however, that though I knew how to translate exactly what she told me, I realized that any translation would distort the deepest meaning of her message: it had been directed only to me. This message of intimacy could never be translated because it did not lie in the actual words she had used but passed through them. So any translation would have seemed wrong; the words would have been stripped of an essential meaning. Finally I decided not to tell my friend anything—just that I didn't hear all she had said.

This insight was unfolded in time. As I made more and more friends outside my house, I began to recognize intimate messages spoken in English in a close friend's confidential tone or secretive whisper. Even more remarkable were those instances when, apparently for no special reason, I'd become conscious of the fact that my companion was speaking *only to me*. I'd marvel then, just hearing his voice. It was a stunning event to be able to break through the barrier of public silence, to be able to hear the voice of the other, to realize that it was directed just to me. After such moments of intimacy outside the house, I began to trust what I heard intimately conveyed through my family's English. Voices at home at last punctured sad confusion. I'd hear myself addressed as an intimate—in English. Such moments were never as raucous with sound as in past times, when we had used our "private" Spanish. (Our English-sounding house was never to be as noisy as our Spanish-sounding house had been.) Intimate moments were usually moments of soft sound. My mother would be ironing in the dining room while I did my homework nearby. She would look over at me, smile, and her voice sounded to tell me that I was her son, *Richard*.

Intimacy thus continued at home; intimacy was not stilled by English. Though there were fewer occasions for it—a change in my life that I would never forget—there were also times when I sensed the deep truth about language and intimacy: *Intimacy is not created by a particular language; it is created by intimates.* Thus the great change in my life was not linguistic but social. If, after becoming a successful student, I no longer heard intimate voices as often as I had earlier, it was not because I spoke English instead of Spanish. It was because I spoke public language for most of my day. I moved easily at last, a citizen in a crowded city of words.

As a man I spend most of my day in public, in a world largely devoid of speech sounds. So I am quickly attracted by the glamorous quality of certain alien voices. I still am gripped with excitement when someone passes me on the street, speaking in Spanish. I have not moved beyond the range of the nostalgic pull of those sounds. And there is something very compelling about the sounds of lower-class blacks. Of all the accented versions of English that I hear in public, I hear theirs most intently. The Japanese tourist stops me downtown to ask me a question and I inch my way past his accent to concentrate on what he is saying. The eastern European immigrant in the neighborhood delicatessen speaks to me and again, I do not pay much attention to his sounds, nor to the Texas accent of one of my neighbors or the Chicago accent of the woman who lives in the apartment below me. But when the ghetto black teenagers get on the city bus, I hear them. Their sounds in my society are the sounds of the outsider. Their voices annoy me for being so loud—so self-sufficient and unconcerned by my presence, but for the same reason they are glamorous: a romantic gesture against public acceptance. And as I listen to their shouted laughter, I realize my own quietness. I feel envious of them—envious of their brazen intimacy.

I warn myself away from such envy, however. Overhearing those teenagers, I think of the black political activists who lately have argued in favor of using black English in the public schools—an argument that varies only slightly from that of foreign-language bilingualists. I have heard "radical" linguists make the point that black English is a complex and intricate version of English. And I do not doubt it. But neither do I think that black English should be a language of public instruction. What makes it inappropriate in classrooms is not something in the language itself but, rather, what lower-class speakers make of it. Just as Spanish would have been a dangerous language for me to have used at the start of my education, so black English would be a dangerous language to use in the schooling of teenagers for whom it reinforces feelings of public separateness.

This seems to me an obvious point to make, and yet it must be said. In recent years there have been many attempts to make the language of the alien a public language. "Bilingual education, two ways to understand . . ." television and radio commercials glibly announce. Proponents of bilingual education are careful to say that above all they want every student to acquire a good education. Their argument goes something like this: Children permitted to use their family language will not be so alienated and will be better able to match the progress of English-speaking students in the crucial first months of schooling. Increasingly confident of their ability, such children will be more inclined to apply themselves to their studies in the future. But then the bilingualists also claim another very different goal. They say that children who use their family language in school will retain a sense of their ethnic heritage and their family ties. Thus the supporters of bilingual education want it both ways. They propose bilingual schooling as a way of helping students acquire the classroom skills crucial for public success. But they likewise insist that bilingual instruction will give students a sense of their identity apart from the English-speaking public.

Behind this scheme gleams a bright promise for the alien child: one can become a public person while still remaining a private person. Who would not want to believe such an appealing idea? Who can be surprised that the scheme has the support of so many middle-class ethnic Americans? If the barrio or ghetto child can retain his separateness even while being publicly educated, then it is almost possible to believe that no private cost need be paid for public success. This is the consolation offered by any of the number of current bilingual programs. Consider, for example, the bilingual voter's ballot. In some American cities one can cast a ballot printed in several languages. Such a document implies that it is possible for one to exercise that most public of rights—the right to vote—while still keeping oneself apart, unassimilated in public life.

It is not enough to say that such schemes are foolish and certainly doomed. Middle-class supporters of public bilingualism toy with the confusion of those Americans who cannot speak standard English as well as they do. Moreover, bilingual enthusiasts sin against intimacy. A Hispanic-American tells me, "I will never give up my family language," and he clutches a group of words as though they were the source of his family ties. He credits to language what he should credit to family members. This is a convenient mistake, for as long as he holds on to certain familiar words, he can ignore how much else has actually changed in his life.

It has happened before. In earlier decades, persons ambitious for social mobility, and newly successful, similarly seized upon certain "family words."

Workingmen attempting to gain political power, for example, took to calling one another "brother." The word as they used it, however, could never resemble the word (the sound) "brother" exchanged by two people in intimate greeting. The context of its public delivery made it at best a metaphor; with repetition it was only a vague echo of the intimate sound. Context forced the change. Context could not be overruled. Context will always protect the realm of the intimate from public misuse. Today middle-class white Americans continue to prove the importance of context as they try to ignore it. They seize upon idioms of the black ghetto, but their attempt to appropriate such expressions invariably changes the meaning. As it becomes a public expression, the ghetto idiom loses its sound, its message of public separateness and strident intimacy. With public repetition it becomes a series of words, increasingly lifeless.

The mystery of intimate utterance remains. The communication of intimacy passes through the word and enlivens its sound, but it cannot be held by the word. It cannot be retained or ever quoted because it is too fluid. It depends not on words but on persons.

My grandmother! She stood among my other relations mocking me when I no longer spoke Spanish. *Pocho,* she said. But then it made no difference. She'd laugh, and our relationship continued because language was never its source. She was a woman in her eighties during the first decade of my life—a mysterious woman to me, my only living grandparent, a woman of Mexico in a long black dress that reached down to her shoes. She was the one relative of mine who spoke no word of English. She had no interest in gringo society and remained completely aloof from the public. She was protected by her daughters, protected even by me when we went to Safeway together and I needed to act as her translator. An eccentric woman. Hard. Soft.

When my family visited my aunt's house in San Francisco, my grandmother would search for me among my many cousins. When she found me, she'd chase them away. Pinching her granddaughters, she would warn them away from me. Then she'd take me to her room, where she had prepared for my coming. There would be a chair next to the bed, a dusty jellied candy nearby, and a copy of *Life en Español* for me to examine. "There," she'd say. And I'd sit content, a boy of eight. *Pocho,* her favorite. I'd sift through the pictures of earthquake-destroyed Latin-American cities and blonde-wigged Mexican movie stars. And all the while I'd listen to the sound of my grandmother's voice. She'd pace around the room, telling me stories of her life. Her past. They were stories so familiar that I couldn't remember when I'd heard them for the first time. I'd look up sometimes to listen. Other times she'd look over at me, but she never expected a response. Sometimes I'd smile or nod. (I understood exactly what she was saying.) But it never seemed to matter to her one way or the other. It was enough that I was there. The words she spoke were almost irrelevant to that fact. We were content. And the great mystery remained: intimate utterance.

I learn nothing about language and intimacy listening to those social activists who propose using one's family language in public life. I learn much more simply by listening to songs on a radio, or hearing a great voice at the opera, or overhearing the woman downstairs at an open window singing to herself. Singers celebrate the human voice. Their lyrics are words, but, animated by voice, those words are subsumed into sounds. (This suggests a central truth about language: all words are capable of becoming sounds as we fill them with the "music" of our life.) With excitement I hear the words yielding their enormous power to sound, even though their meaning is never totally obliterated. In most songs, the drama or tension results from the way that the singer moves between words (sense) and notes (song). At one moment the song simply "says" something; at another moment the voice stretches out the words and moves to the realm of pure sound. Most songs are about love: lost love, celebrations of love, pleas. By simply being occasions when sounds soar through words, however, songs put me in mind of the most intimate moments of life.

Finally, among all types of music, I find songs created by lyric poets most compelling. On no other public occasion is sound so important for me. Written poems on a page seem at first glance a mere collection of words. And yet, without musical accompaniment, the poet leads me to hear the sounds of the words that I read. As song, a poem moves between the levels of sound and sense, never limited to one realm or the other. As a public artifact, the poem can never offer truly intimate sound, but it helps me to recall the intimate times of my life. As I read in my room, I grow deeply conscious of being alone, sounding my voice in search of another. The poem serves, then, as a memory device; it forces remembrance. And it refreshes; it reminds me of the possibility of escaping public words, the possibility that awaits me in intimate meetings.

The child reminds the adult: to seek intimate sounds is to seek the company of intimates. I do not expect to hear those sounds in public. I would dishonor those I have loved, and those I love now, to claim anything else. I would dishonor our intimacy by holding on to a particular language and calling it my family language. Intimacy cannot be trapped within words; it passes through words. It passes. Intimates leave the room. Doors close. Faces move away from the window. Time passes, and voices recede into the dark. Death finally quiets the voice. There is no way to deny it, no way to stand in the crowd claiming to utter one's family language.

The last time I saw my grandmother I was nine years old. I can tell you some of the things she said to me as I stood by her bed, but I cannot quote the message of intimacy she conveyed with her voice. She laughed, holding my hand. Her voice illumined disjointed memories as it passed them again. She remembered her husband—his green eyes, his magic name of Narcissio, his early death. She remembered the farm in Mexico, the eucalyptus trees nearby (their scent, she remembered, like incense). She remembered the family cow, the bell around its neck heard miles away. A dog. She remembered working as a seamstress, how she'd leave her daughters and son for long hours to go into Guadalajara to work. And how my mother would come running toward her in the sun—in her bright yellow dress—on her return. "MMMMAAAA-MMMMÁÁÁÁ," the old lady mimicked her daughter (my mother) to her daughter's son. She laughed. There was the snap of a cough. An aunt came into the room and told me it was time I should leave. "You can see her tomorrow," she promised. So I kissed my grandmother's cracked face. And the last thing I saw was her thin, oddly youthful thigh, as my aunt rearranged the sheet on the bed.

At the funeral parlor a few days after, I remember kneeling with my relatives during the rosary. Among their voices I traced, then lost, the sounds of individual aunts in the surge of the common prayer. And I heard at that moment what since I have heard very often—the sound the women in my family make when they are praying in sadness. When I went up to look at my grandmother, I saw her through the haze of a veil draped over the open lid of the casket. Her face looked calm—but distant and unyielding to love. It was not the face I remembered seeing most often. It was the face she made in public when the clerk at Safeway asked her some question and I would need to respond. It was her public face that the mortician had designed with his dubious art.

QUESTIONS FOR REACTION AND DISCUSSION

1. Why does Rodriguez feel that it is not possible for a child to use "his family's language in school"? What is the distinction he makes between the "public uses of schooling" and the "nature of intimate life"?
2. What does English sound like to Rodriguez? How does his own language sound in comparison?
3. What are some of Rodriguez's objections to bilingual education?
4. What does Rodriguez mean when he suggests that bilingual educators oversimplify "when they scorn the value and necessity of assimilation."
5. Rodriguez suggests that the great truth about language and intimacy is that "Intimacy is not created by a particular language; it is created by intimates." How does he learn that truth in his own life?
6. How does Rodriguez equate the issue of teaching or using black English in the schools with foreign-language bilingual education?

QUESTIONS FOR WRITING

1. Interview a classmate or friend who is bilingual. Formulate questions designed to elicit information on the following topics: language spoken at home, early educational experiences, formal instruction in English, and attitudes toward bilingual education. How would this person respond to Rodriguez's experiences? Write an essay in which you describe the responses your subject gave you and speculate on the

implications of this single case study in light of Rodriguez's position in *Hunger of Memory*.

2. After Rodriguez published his essay, his mother wrote him a letter, asking him not to write about what she considered to be their private family life. Throughout this essay, Rodriguez discusses the nature of "private" and "public" life, especially in terms of language. He says "Intimacy is not created by a particular language; it is created by intimates." Write an essay in which you defend or reject that statement, commenting on your own notions of what constitutes private and public life and language.

QUESTIONS FOR FURTHER EXPLORATION

1. Rodriguez, among the first to speak out against bilingual education, touches on a controversial question in public education: Should children be taught in their native language first? Access the Web site of the National Association for Bilingual Education <http://www.nabe.org> and examine their resources and articles about the controversy that has developed among educators. Follow links to other sites, including the National Clearinghouse for Bilingual Education <http://www.ncbe.gwu.edu> and look at the resources in their online library. Write a report for your classmates in which you outline and explain the major issues and questions that bilingual education raises.

2. Since the publication of *Hunger of Memory*, Rodriguez has continued to write about cultural identity. Access his collection of recent, brief essays for the Online NewsHour <http://www.pbs.org/newshour/essays/richard_rodriguez.html> and read several current essays. What issues is he most concerned with today? How are these essays related to the questions he raises in *Hunger of Memory*?

3. Locate a copy of Rodriguez's second book, *Days of Obligation*. Read some of the essays, especially the last chapter, "Nothing Lasts a Hundred Years," and write an essay in which you compare and contrast his view of his father in *Hunger of Memory* with his second book.

4. In this essay, Rodriguez makes a strong case against bilingual education—mostly on the theoretical grounds that assimilation is both valuable and necessary in American society for a successful life as a public individual. Recently, some educators have begun to question the value of bilingual education for practical reasons, pointing, for example, to high drop-out rates and low graduation rates for Hispanic teenagers in the schools. Research the practical problems in bilingual education and prepare a report for your class. You might begin by accessing an article by Rosalie Pedalino Porter, "The Case against Bilingual Education," available online at <http://www.theatlantic.com/issues/98may/biling.htm>.

8

SAVED

Malcolm X (1925–65) was born Malcolm Little in Omaha, Nebraska. The son of Earl Little, an itinerant Baptist minister and supporter of the "back-to-Africa" movement of Marcus Garvey, Malcolm X was placed in a foster home after his father's death and later lived in Boston and in Harlem. With limited economic and social resources, he turned to drug-dealing and robbery, becoming known as "Detroit Red." He was arrested in 1945 for armed robbery and served seven years in prison. In prison, he began to read and became committed to the Black Muslim movement, founded by Elijah Muhammad. When he was released from prison in 1952, he moved to Detroit and changed his name to Malcolm X. He broke with the Black Muslims in 1963 and traveled extensively in the Middle East and Africa. He eventually returned to the United States where he worked to establish the Organization of Afro-American Unity. He was assassinated on February 21, 1965; three Black Muslims were later convicted of his murder. Credited with prompting the black power movement of the 1960s, Malcolm X was a powerful speaker and spirited defender of black nationalism. Later in 1959, Alex Haley, the author of Roots, *became acquainted with Malcolm X after he proposed an article on Black Muslims for* Reader's Digest. *He interviewed Malcolm X for this article, gained his confidence, and then interviewed him for* Playboy Magazine. *The interview was so successful that Haley's agent encouraged him to work with Malcolm X on a book about his life. Malcolm X agreed that Haley could write his life story, and there began a two-year collaboration in which Haley interviewed Malcolm X, and the result was* The Autobiography of Malcolm X. *According to the contract between Haley and Malcolm X, everything in the book had to be what Malcolm X said and nothing could be left out that Malcolm X wanted said. The section of the* Autobiography *printed here is Chapter 11, "Saved," in which Malcolm X explains how his reading and writing in prison changed his life.*

QUESTIONS FOR READING

1. What do you know about the Muslim religion and Black Muslims in America? As you read, make a list of any terms that are unfamiliar to you.
2. Who was Malcolm X and what do you know about him?

MALCOLM X

SAVED

The Autobiography of Malcolm X *(New York: Random House, 1964)*

I did write to Elijah Muhammad. He lived in Chicago at that time, at 6116 South Michigan Avenue. At least twenty-five times I must have written that first one-page letter to him, over and over. I was trying to make it both legible and understandable. I practically couldn't read my handwriting myself; it shames even to remember it. My spelling and my grammar were as bad, if not worse. Anyway, as well as I could express it, I said I had been told about him by my brothers and sisters, and I apologized for my poor letter.

Mr. Muhammad sent me a typed reply. It had an all but electrical effect upon me to see the signature of the "Messenger of Allah." After he welcomed me into the "true knowledge," he gave me something to think about. The black prisoner, he said, symbolized white society's crime of keeping black men oppressed and deprived and ignorant, and unable to get decent jobs, turning them into criminals.

He told me to have courage. He even enclosed some money for me, a five-dollar bill. Mr. Muhammad sends money all over the country to prison inmates who write to him, probably to this day.

Regularly my family wrote to me, "Turn to Allah . . . pray to the East."

The hardest test I ever faced in my life was praying. You understand. My comprehending, my believing the teachings of Mr. Muhammad had only required my mind's saying to me, "That's right!" or "I never thought of that."

But bending my knees to pray—that *act*—well, that took me a week.

You know what my life had been. Picking a lock to rob someone's house was the only way my knees had ever been bent before.

I had to force myself to bend my knees. And waves of shame and embarrassment would force me back up.

For evil to bend its knees, admitting its guilt, to implore the forgiveness of God, is the hardest thing in the world. It's easy for me to see and to say that now. But then, when I was the personification of evil, I was going through it. Again, again, I would force myself back down into the praying-to-Allah posture. When finally I was able to make myself stay down—I didn't know what to say to Allah.

For the next years, I was the nearest thing to a hermit in the Norfolk Prison Colony. I never have been more busy in my life. I still marvel at how swiftly my previous life's thinking pattern slid away from me, like snow off a roof. It is as though someone else I knew of had lived by hustling and crime. I would be startled to catch myself thinking in a remote way of my earlier self as another person.

The things I felt, I was pitifully unable to express in the one-page letter that went every day to Mr. Elijah Muhammad. And I wrote at least one more daily letter, replying to one of my brothers and sisters. Every letter I received from them added something to my knowledge of the teaching of Mr. Muhammad. I would sit for long periods and study his photographs.

I've never been one for inaction. Everything I've ever felt strongly about, I've done something about. I guess that's why, unable to do anything else, I soon began writing to people I had known in the hustling world, such as Sammy the Pimp, John Hughes, the gambling house owner, the thief Jumpsteady, and several dope peddlers. I wrote them all about Allah and Islam and Mr. Elijah Muhammad. I had no idea where most of them lived. I addressed their letters in care of the Harlem or Roxbury bars and clubs where I'd known them.

I never got a single reply. The average hustler and criminal was too uneducated to write a letter. I have known many slick, sharp-looking hustlers, who would have you think they had an interest in Wall Street; privately, they would get someone else to read a letter if they received one. Besides, neither would I have replied to anyone writing me something as wild as "the white man is the devil."

What certainly went on the Harlem and Roxbury wires was that Detroit Red was going crazy in stir, or else he was trying some hype to shake up the warden's office.

During the years that I stayed in the Norfolk Prison Colony, never did any official directly say anything to me about those letters, although, of course, they all passed through the prison censorship. I'm sure, however, they monitored what I wrote to add to the files which every state and federal prison keeps on the conversion of Negro inmates by the teachings of Mr. Elijah Muhammad.

But at that time, I felt that the real reason was that the white man knew that he was the devil.

Later on, I even wrote to the Mayor of Boston, to the Governor of Massachusetts, and to Harry S. Truman. They never answered; they probably never even saw my letters. I handscratched to them how the white man's society was responsible for the black man's condition in this wilderness of North America.

It was because of my letters that I happened to stumble upon starting to acquire some kind of a homemade education.

I became increasingly frustrated at not being able to express what I wanted to convey in letters that I wrote, especially those to Mr. Elijah Muhammad. In the street, I had been the most articulate hustler out there—I had commanded attention when I said something. But now, trying to write simple English, I not only wasn't articulate, I wasn't even functional. How would I sound writing in slang, the way I would *say* it, something such as, "Look, daddy, let me pull your coat about a cat, Elijah Muhammad—"

Many who today hear me somewhere in person, or on television, or those who read something I've said, will think I went to school far beyond the eighth grade. This impression is due entirely to my prison studies.

It had really begun back in the Charlestown Prison, when Bimbi first made me feel envy of his stock of knowledge. Bimbi had always taken charge of any conversation he was in, and I had tried to emulate him. But every book I picked up had few sentences which didn't contain anywhere from one to nearly all of the words that might as well have been in Chinese. When I just skipped those words, of course, I really ended up with little idea of what the book said. So I had come to the Norfolk Prison Colony still going through only book-reading motions. Pretty soon, I would have quit even these motions, unless I had received the motivation that I did.

I saw that the best thing I could do was get hold of a dictionary—to study, to learn some words. I was lucky enough to reason also that I should try to improve my penmanship. It was sad. I couldn't even write in a straight line. It was both ideas together that moved me to request a dictionary along with some tablets and pencils from the Norfolk Prison Colony school.

I spent two days just riffling uncertainly through the dictionary's pages. I'd never realized so many words existed! I didn't know *which* words I needed to learn. Finally, just to start some kind of action, I began copying.

In my slow, painstaking, ragged handwriting, I copied into my tablet everything printed on that first page, down to the punctuation marks.

I believe it took me a day. Then, aloud, I read back, to myself, everything I'd written on the tablet. Over and over, aloud, to myself, I read my own handwriting.

I woke up the next morning, thinking about those words—immensely proud to realize that not only had I written so much at one time, but I'd written words that I never knew were in the world. Moreover, with a little effort, I also could remember what many of these words meant. I reviewed the words whose meanings I didn't remember. Funny thing, from the dictionary first page right now, that "aardvark" springs to my mind. The dictionary had a picture of it, a long-tailed, long-eared, burrowing African mammal, which lives off termites caught by sticking out its tongue as an anteater does for ants.

I was so fascinated that I went on—I copied the dictionary's next page. And the same experience came when I studied that. With every succeeding page, I also learned of people and places and events from history. Actually the dictionary is like a miniature encyclopedia. Finally the dictionary's A section had filled a whole tablet—and I went on into the B's. That was the way I started copying what eventually became the entire dictionary. It went a lot faster after so much practice helped me to pick up handwriting speed. Between what I wrote in my tablet, and writing letters, during the rest of my time in prison I would guess I wrote a million words.

I suppose it was inevitable that as my word-base broadened, I could for the first time pick up a book and read and now begin to understand what the book was saying. Anyone who has read a great deal can imagine the new world that opened. Let me tell you something: from then until I left that prison, in every free moment I had, if I was not reading in the library, I was reading on my bunk. You couldn't have gotten me out of books with a wedge. Between Mr. Muhammad's teachings, my correspondence, my visitors—usually Ella and Reginald—and my reading of books, months passed without my even thinking about being imprisoned. In fact, up to then, I never had been so truly free in my life.

The Norfolk Prison Colony's library was in the school building. A variety of classes was taught there by instructors who came from such places as Harvard and Boston universities. The weekly debates between inmate teams were also held in the school building. You would be astonished to know how worked up convict debaters and audiences would get over subjects like "Should Babies Be Fed Milk?"

Available on the prison library's shelves were books on just about every general subject. Much of the big private collection that Parkhurst had willed to the prison was still in crates and boxes in the back of the library—thousands of old books. Some of them looked ancient: covers faded, old-time parchment-looking binding. Parkhurst, I've mentioned, seemed to have been principally interested in history and religion. He had the money and the special interest to have a lot of books that you wouldn't have in general circulation. Any college library would have been lucky to get that collection.

As you can imagine, especially in a prison where there was heavy emphasis on rehabilitation, an inmate was smiled upon if he demonstrated an unusually intense interest in books. There was a sizable number of well-read inmates, especially the popular debaters. Some were said by many to be practically walking encyclopedias. They were almost celebrities. No university would ask any student to devour literature as I did when this new world opened to me, of being able to read and *understand*.

I read more in my room than in the library itself. An inmate who was known to read a lot could check out more than the permitted maximum number of books. I preferred reading in the total isolation of my own room.

When I had progressed to really serious reading, every night at about ten p.m. I would be outraged with the "lights out." It always seemed to catch me right in the middle of something engrossing.

Fortunately, right outside my door was a corridor light that cast a glow into my room. The glow was enough to read by, once my eyes adjusted to it. So when "lights out" came, I would sit on the floor where I could continue reading in that glow.

At one-hour intervals the night guards paced past every room. Each time I heard the approaching footsteps, I jumped into bed and feigned sleep. And as soon as the guard passed, I got back out of bed onto the floor area of that light-glow, where I would read for another fifty-eight minutes—until the guard approached again. That went on until three or four every morning. Three or four hours of sleep a night was enough for me. Often in the years in the streets I had slept less than that.

The teachings of Mr. Muhammad stressed how history had been "whitened"—when white men had written history books, the black man simply had been left out. Mr. Muhammad couldn't have said anything that would have struck me much harder. I had never forgotten how when my class, me and all of those whites, had studied seventh-grade United States history back in Mason, the history of the Negro had been covered in one paragraph, and the teacher had gotten a big laugh with his joke, "Negroes' feet are so big that when they walk, they leave a hole in the ground."

This is one reason why Mr. Muhammad's teachings spread so swiftly all over the United States, among *all* Negroes, whether or not they became followers of Mr. Muhammad. The teachings ring true—to every Negro. You can hardly show me a black adult in America—or a white one, for that matter—who knows from the history books anything like the truth about the black man's role. In my own case, once I heard of the "glorious history of the black man," I took special pains to hunt in the library for books that would inform me on details about black history.

I can remember accurately the very first set of books that really impressed me. I have since bought that set of books and have it at home for my children to read as they grow up. It's called *Wonders of the World*. It's full of pictures of archeological finds, statues that depict, usually, non-European people.

I found books like Will Durant's *Story of Civilization*. I read H. G. Wells' *Outline of History*. *Souls of Black Folk* by W. E. B. Du Bois gave me a glimpse into the black people's history before they came to this country. Carter G. Woodson's *Negro History* opened my eyes about black empires before the black slave was brought to the United States, and the early Negro struggles for freedom.

J. A. Rogers' three volumes of *Sex and Race* told about race-mixing before Christ's time; about Aesop being a black man who told fables; about Egypt's Pharaohs; about the great Coptic Christian Empires; about Ethiopia, the earth's oldest continuous black civilization, as China is the oldest continuous civilization.

Mr. Muhammad's teaching about how the white man had been created led me to *Findings in Genetics* by Gregor Mendel. (The dictionary's G section was where I had learned what "genetics" meant.) I really studied this book by the Austrian monk. Reading it over and over, especially certain sections, helped me to understand that if you started with a black man, a white man could be produced; but starting with a white man, you never could produce a black man—because the white chromosome is recessive. And since no one disputes that there was but one Original Man, the conclusion is clear.

During the last year or so, in the *New York Times*, Arnold Toynbee used the word "bleached" in describing the white man. (His words were: "White (i.e. bleached) human beings of North European origin. . . .") Toynbee also referred to the European geographic area as only a peninsula of Asia. He said there is no such thing as Europe. And if you look at the globe, you will see for yourself that America is only an extension of Asia. (But at the same time Toynbee is among those who have helped to bleach history. He has written that Africa was the only continent that produced no history. He won't write that again. Every day now, the truth is coming to light.)

I never will forget how shocked I was when I began reading about slavery's total horror. It made such an impact upon me that it later became one of my favorite subjects when I became a minister of Mr. Muhammad's. The world's most monstrous crime, the sin and the blood on the white man's hands, are almost impossible to believe. Books like the one by Frederick Olmstead opened my eyes to the horrors suffered when the slave was landed in the United States. The European woman, Fannie Kimball, who had married a Southern white slaveowner, described how human beings were degraded. Of course I read *Uncle Tom's Cabin*. In fact, I believe that's the only novel I had ever read since I started serious reading.

Parkhurst's collection also contained some bound pamphlets of the Abolitionist Anti-Slavery Society of New England. I read descriptions of atrocities, saw those illustrations of black slave women tied up and flogged with whips; of black mothers watching their babies being dragged off, never to be seen by their mothers again; of dogs after slaves, and of the fugitive slave catchers, evil white men with whips and clubs and chains and guns. I read about the slave preacher Nat Turner, who put the fear of God into the white slavemaster. Nat Turner wasn't going around preaching pie-in-the-sky and "non-violent" freedom for the black man. There in Virginia one night in 1831, Nat and seven other slaves started out at his master's home and through the night they went from one plantation "big house" to the next, killing, until by the next morning 57 white people were dead and Nat had about 70 slaves following him. White people, terrified for their lives, fled from their homes, locked themselves up in public buildings, hid in the woods, and some even left the state. A small army of soldiers took two months to catch, and hang Nat Turner. Somewhere I have read where Nat Turner's example is said to have inspired John Brown to invade Virginia and attack Harper's Ferry nearly thirty years later, with thirteen white men and five Negroes.

I read Herodotus, "the father of History," or, rather, I read about him. And I read the histories of various nations, which opened my eyes gradually, then wider and wider, to how the whole world's white men had indeed acted like devils, pillaging and raping and bleeding and draining the whole world's non-white people. I remember, for instance, books such as Will Durant's story of Oriental civilization, and Mahatma Gandhi's accounts of the struggle to drive the British out of India.

Book after book showed me how the white man had brought upon the whole world's black, brown, red, and yellow peoples every variety of the sufferings of exploitation. I saw how "since the sixteenth century, the so-called

"Christian trader" white man began to ply the seas in his lust for Asian and African empires, and plunder, and power. I read, I saw, how the white man never has gone among the non-white peoples bearing the Cross in the true manner and spirit of Christ's teachings—meek, humble, and Christ-like.

I perceived, as I read, how the collective white man had been actually nothing but a piratical opportunist who used Faustian machinations to make his own Christianity his initial wedge in criminal conquests. First, always "re-ligiously," he branded "heathen" and "pagan" labels upon ancient non-white cultures and civilizations. The stage thus set, he then turned upon his non-white victims his weapons of war.

I read how, entering India—half a *billion* deeply religious brown people—the British white man, by 1759, through promises, trickery and manipulations, controlled much of India through Great Britain's East India Company. The parasitical British administration kept tentacling out to half of the sub-continent. In 1857, some of the desperate people of India finally mutinied—and, excepting the African slave trade, nowhere has history recorded any more unnecessary bestial and ruthless human carnage than the British suppression of the non-white Indian people.

Over 115 million African blacks—close to the 1930's population of the United States—were murdered or enslaved during the slave trade. And I read how when the slave market was glutted, the cannibalistic white powers of Europe next carved up, as their colonies, the richest areas of the black continent. And Europe's chancelleries for the next century played a chess game of naked exploitation and power from Cape Horn to Cairo.

Ten guards and the warden couldn't have torn me out of those books. Not even Elijah Muhammad could have been more eloquent than those books were in providing indisputable proof that the collective white man had acted like a devil in virtually every contact he had with the world's collective non-white man. I listen today to the radio, and watch television, and read the headlines about the collective white man's fear and tension concerning China. When the white man professes ignorance about why the Chinese hate him so, my mind can't help flashing back to what I read, there in prison, about how the blood forebears of this same white man raped China at a time when China was trust-ing and helpless. Those original white "Christian traders" sent into China mil-lions of pounds of opium. By 1839, so many of the Chinese were addicts that China's desperate government destroyed twenty thousand chests of opium. The first Opium War was promptly declared by the white man. Imagine! Declaring *war* upon someone who objects to being narcotized! The Chinese were severely beaten, with Chinese-invented gunpowder.

The Treaty of Nanking made China pay the British white man for the de-stroyed opium; forced open China's major ports to British trade; forced China to abandon Hong Kong; fixed China's import tariffs so low that cheap British articles soon flooded in, maiming China's industrial development.

After a second Opium War, the Tientsin Treaties legalized the ravaging opium trade, legalized a British-French-American control of China's customs. China tried delaying that Treaty's ratification; Peking was looted and burned.

"Kill the foreign white devils!" was the 1901 Chinese war cry in the Boxer Rebellion. Losing again, this time the Chinese were driven from Peking's choicest areas. The vicious, arrogant white man put up the famous signs, "Chinese and dogs not allowed."

Red China after World War II closed its doors to the Western white world. Massive Chinese agricultural, scientific, and industrial efforts are described in a book that *Life* magazine recently published. Some observers inside Red China have reported that the world never has known such a hate-white campaign as is now going on in this non-white country where, present birthrates continuing, in fifty more years Chinese will be half the earth's population. And it seems that some Chinese chickens will soon come home to roost, with China's recent successful nuclear tests.

Let us face reality. We can see in the United Nations a new world order being shaped, along color lines—an alliance among the non-white nations. America's U.N. Ambassador Adlai Stevenson complained not long ago that in the United Nations "a skin game" was being played. He was right. He was facing reality. A "skin game" *is* being played. But Ambassador Stevenson sounded like Jesse James accusing the marshal of carrying a gun. Because who in the world's history ever has played a worse "skin game" than the white man?

————

Mr. Muhammad, to whom I was writing daily, had no idea of what a new world had opened up to me through my efforts to document his teachings in books.

When I discovered philosophy, I tried to touch all the landmarks of philosophical development. Gradually, I read most of the old philosophers, Occidental and Oriental. The Oriental philosophers were the ones I came to prefer; finally, my impression was that most Occidental philosophy had largely been borrowed from the Oriental thinkers. Socrates, for instance, traveled in Egypt. Some sources even say that Socrates was initiated into some of the Egyptian mysteries. Obviously Socrates got some of his wisdom among the East's wise men.

I have often reflected upon the new vistas that reading opened to me. I knew right there in prison that reading had changed forever the course of my life. As I see it today, the ability to read awoke inside me some long dormant craving to be mentally alive. I certainly wasn't seeking any degree, the way a college confers a status symbol upon its students. My homemade education gave me, with every additional book that I read, a little bit more sensitivity to the deafness, dumbness, and blindness that was afflicting the black race in America. Not long ago, an English writer telephoned me from London, asking questions. One was, "What's your alma mater?" I told him, "Books." You will never catch me with a free fifteen minutes in which I'm not studying something I feel might be able to help the black man.

Yesterday I spoke in London, and both ways on the plane across the Atlantic I was studying a document about how the United Nations proposes to insure the human rights of the oppressed minorities of the world. The American black man is the world's most shameful case of minority oppression. What makes the black man think of himself as only an internal United States issue is just a catch-phrase, two words, "civil rights." How is the black man going to get "civil rights" before first he wins his *human* rights? If the American black man will start thinking about his *human* rights, and then start thinking of himself as part of one of the world's great peoples, he will see he has a case for the United Nations.

I can't think of a better case! Four hundred years of black blood and sweat invested here in America, and the white man still has the black man begging for what every immigrant fresh off the ship can take for granted the minute he walks down the gangplank.

But I'm digressing. I told the Englishman that my alma mater was books, a good library. Every time I catch a plane, I have with me a book that I want to read—and that's a lot of books these days. If I weren't out here every day battling the white man, I could spend the rest of my life reading, just satisfying my curiosity—because you can hardly mention anything I'm not curious about. I don't think anybody ever got more out of going to prison than I did. In fact, prison enabled me to study far more intensively than I would have if my life had gone differently and I had attended some college. I imagine that one of the biggest troubles with colleges is there are too many distractions, too much panty-raiding, fraternities, and boola-boola and all of that. Where else but in a prison could I have attacked my ignorance by being able to study intensely sometimes as much as fifteen hours a day?

Schopenhauer, Kant, Nietzsche, naturally, I read all of those. I don't respect them; I am just trying to remember some of those whose theories I soaked up in those years. These three, it's said, laid the groundwork on which the Facist and Nazi philosophy was built. I don't respect them because it seems to me that most of their time was spent arguing about things that are not really important. They remind me of so many of the Negro "intellectuals," so-called, with whom I have come in contact—they are always arguing about something useless.

Spinoza impressed me for a while when I found out that he was black. A black Spanish Jew. The Jews excommunicated him because he advocated a pantheistic doctrine, something like the "allness of God," or "God in everything." The Jews read their burial services for Spinoza, meaning that he was dead as far as they were concerned; his family was run out of Spain, they ended up in Holland, I think.

I'll tell you something. The whole stream of Western philosophy has now wound up in a cul-de-sac. The white man has perpetrated upon himself, as well as upon the black man, so gigantic a fraud that he has put himself into a crack. He did it through his elaborate, neurotic necessity to hide the black man's true role in history.

And today the white man is faced head on with what is happening on the Black Continent, Africa. Look at the artifacts being discovered there, that are proving over and over again, how the black man had great, fine, sensitive civilizations before the white man was out of the caves. Below the Sahara, in the places where most of America's Negroes' foreparents were kidnapped, there is being unearthed some of the finest craftsmanship, sculpture and other objects, that has ever been seen by modern man. Some of these things now are on view in such places as New York City's Museum of Modern Art. Gold work of such fine tolerance and workmanship that it has no rival. Ancient objects produced by black hands . . . refined by those black hands with results that no human hand today can equal.

History has been so "whitened" by the white man that even the black professors have known little more than the most ignorant black man about the talents and rich civilizations and cultures of the black man of millenniums ago. I have lectured in Negro colleges and some of these brainwashed black Ph.D.'s, with their suspenders dragging the ground with degrees, have run to the white man's newspapers calling me a "black fanatic." Why, a lot of them are fifty years behind the times. If I were president of one of these black colleges, I'd hock the campus if I had to, to send a bunch of black students off digging in Africa for more, more, and more proof of the black race's historical greatness. The white man now is in Africa digging and searching. An African elephant can't stumble without falling on some white man with a shovel. Practically every week, we read about some great new find from Africa's lost civilizations. All that's new is white science's attitude. The ancient civilizations of the black man have been buried on the Black Continent all the time.

Here is an example: a British anthropologist named Dr. Louis S. B. Leakey is displaying some fossil bones—a foot, part of a hand, some jaws, and skull fragments. On the basis of these, Dr. Leakey has said it's time to rewrite completely the history of man's origin.

This species of man lived 1,818,036 years before Christ. And these bones were found in Tanganyika. In the Black Continent.

It's a crime, the lie that has been told to generations of black men and white men both. Little innocent black children, born of parents who believed that their race had no history. Little black children seeing, before they could talk, that their parents considered themselves inferior. Innocent black children growing up, living out their lives, dying of old age—and all of their lives ashamed of being black. But the truth is pouring out of the bag now.

Two other areas of experience which have been extremely formative in my life since prison were first opened to me in the Norfolk Prison Colony. For one thing, I had my first experiences in opening the eyes of my brainwashed black brethren to some truths about the black race. And, the other: when I had read enough to know something, I began to enter the Prison Colony's weekly debating program—my baptism into public speaking.

I have to admit a sad, shameful fact. I had so loved being around the white man that in prison I really disliked how Negro convicts stuck together so much. But when Mr. Muhammad's teachings reversed my attitude toward my black brothers, in my guild and shame I began to catch every chance I could to recruit for Mr. Muhammad.

You have to be careful, very careful, introducing the truth to the black man who has never previously heard the truth about himself, his own kind, and the white man. My brother Reginald had told me that all Muslims experienced this in their recruiting for Mr. Muhammad. The black brother is so brainwashed that he may even be repelled when he first hears the truth. Reginald advised that the truth had to be dropped only a little bit at a time. And you had to wait a while to let it sink in before advancing the next step.

I began first telling my black brother inmates about the glorious history of the black man—things they never had dreamed. I told them the horrible slavery-trade truths that they never knew. I would watch their faces when I told them about that, because the white man had completely erased the slaves' past, a Negro in America can never know his true family name, or even what tribe he was descended from: the Mandingos, the Wolof, the Serer, the Fula, the Fanti, the Ashanti, or others. I told them that some slaves brought from Africa spoke Arabic, and were Islamic in their religion. A lot of these black convicts still wouldn't believe it unless they could see that a white man had said it. So, often, I would read to these brothers selected passages from white men's books. I'd explain to them that the real truth was known to some white men, the scholars; but there had been a conspiracy down through the generations to keep the truth from black men.

I would keep close watch on how each one reacted. I always had to be careful. I never knew when some brainwashed black imp, some dyed-in-the wool Uncle Tom, would nod at me and then go running to tell the white man. When one was ripe—and I could tell—then away from the rest, I'd drop it on him, what Mr. Muhammad taught: "The white man is the devil."

That would shock many of them—until they started thinking about it.

This is probably as big a single worry as the American prison system has today—the way the Muslim teachings, circulated among all Negroes in the country, are converting new Muslims among black men in prison, and black men are in prison in far greater numbers than their proportion in the population.

The reason is that among all Negroes the black convict is the most perfectly preconditioned to hear the words, "the white man is the devil."

You tell that to any Negro. Except for those relatively few "integration"-mad so-called "intellectuals," and those black men who are otherwise fat, happy, and deaf, dumb, and blinded, with their crumbs from the white man's rich table, you have struck a nerve center in the American black man. He may take a day to react, a month, a year; he may never respond, openly; but of one thing you can be sure—when he thinks about his own life, he is going to see where, to him, personally, the white man sure has acted like a devil.

And, as I say, above all Negroes, the black prisoner. Here is a black man caged behind bars, probably for years, put there by the white man. Usually the convict comes from among those bottom-of-the-pile Negroes, the Negroes who through their entire lives have been kicked about, treated like children—Negroes who never have met one white man who didn't either take something from them or do something to them.

You let this caged-up black man start thinking, the same way I did when I first heard Elijah Muhammad's teachings: let him start thinking how, with better breaks when he was young and ambitious he might have been a lawyer, a doctor, a scientist, anything. You let this caged-up black man start realizing, as I did, how from the first landing of the first slave ship, the millions of black men in America have been like sheep in a den of wolves. That's why black prisoners become Muslims so fast when Elijah Muhammad's teachings filter into their cages by way of other Muslim convicts. "The white man is the devil" is a perfect echo of that black convict's lifelong experience.

I've told how debating was a weekly event there at the Norfolk Prison Colony. My reading had my mind like steam under pressure. Some way, I had to start telling the white man about himself to his face. I decided I could do this by putting my name down to debate.

Standing up and speaking before an audience was a thing that throughout my previous life never would have crossed my mind. Out there in the streets, hustling, pushing dope, and robbing, I could have had the dreams from a pound of hashish and I'd never have dreamed anything so wild as that one day I would speak in coliseums and arenas, at the greatest American universities, and on radio and television programs, not to mention speaking all over Egypt and Africa and in England.

But I will tell you that, right there, in the prison, debating, speaking to a crowd, was as exhilarating to me as the discovery of knowledge through reading had been. Standing up there, the faces looking up at me, the things in my head coming out of my mouth, while my brain searched for the next best thing to follow what I was saying, and if I could sway them to my side by handling it right, then I had won the debate—once my feet got wet, I was gone on debating. Whichever side of the selected subject was assigned to me, I'd track down and study everything I could find on it. I'd put myself in my opponent's place and decide how I'd try to win if I had the other side; and then I'd figure a way to knock down those points. And if there was any way in the world, I'd work into my speech the devilishness of the white man.

"Compulsory Military Training—Or None?" That's one good chance I got unexpectedly, I remember. My opponent flailed the air about the Ethiopians throwing rocks and spears at Italian airplanes, "proving" that compulsory military training was needed. I said the Ethiopians' black flesh had been spattered against trees by bombs the Pope in Rome had blessed, and the Ethiopians would have thrown even their bare bodies at the airplanes because they had seen that they were fighting the devil incarnate.

They yelled "foul," that I'd made the subject a race issue. I said it wasn't race, it was a historical fact, that they ought to go and read Pierre van Paassen's *Days of Our Years,* and something not surprising to me, that book, right after the debate, disappeared from the prison library. It was right there in prison that I made up my mind to devote the rest of my life to telling the white man about himself—or die. In a debate about whether or not Homer had ever existed, I threw into those white faces the theory that Homer only symbolized how white Europeans kidnapped black Africans, then blinded them so that they could never get back to their own people. (Homer and Omar and *Moor,* you see, are related terms; it's like saying Peter, Pedro, and *petra,* all three of which mean rock.) These blinded Moors the Europeans taught to sing about the Europeans' glorious accomplishments. I made it clear that was the devilish white man's idea of kicks. Aesop's *Fables*—another case in point. "Aesop" was only the Greek name for an Ethiopian.

Another hot debate I remember I was in had to do with the identity of Shakespeare. No color was involved there; I just got intrigued over the Shakespearean dilemma. The King James translation of the Bible is considered the greatest piece of literature in English. Its language supposedly represents the ultimate in using the King's English. Well, Shakespeare's language and the Bible's language are one and the same. They say that from 1604 to 1611, King James got poets to translate, to write the Bible. Well, if Shakespeare existed, he was then the top poet around. But Shakespeare is nowhere reported connected with the Bible. If he existed, why didn't King James use him? And if he did use him, why is it one of the world's best kept secrets?

I know that many say that Francis Bacon was Shakespeare. If that is true, why would Bacon have kept it secret? Bacon wasn't royalty, when royalty sometimes used the *nom de plume* because it was "improper" for royalty to be artistic or theatrical. What would Bacon have had to lose? Bacon, in fact, would have had everything to gain.

In the prison debates I argued for the theory that King James himself was the real poet who used the *nom de plume* Shakespeare. King James was brilliant. He was the greatest king who ever sat on the British throne. Who else among royalty, in his time, would have had the giant talent to write Shakespeare's works? It was he who poetically "fixed" the Bible—which in itself and its present King James version has enslaved the world.

When my brother Reginald visited, I would talk to him about new evidence I found to document the Muslim teachings. In either volume 43 or 44 of The Harvard Classics, I read Milton's *Paradise Lost.* The devil, kicked out of Paradise, was trying to regain possession. He was using the forces of Europe, personified by the Popes, Charlemagne, Richard the Lionhearted, and other knights. I interpreted this to show that the Europeans were motivated and led by the devil, or the personification of the devil. So Milton and Mr. Elijah Muhammad were actually saying the same thing.

I couldn't believe it when Reginald began to speak ill of Elijah Muhammad. I can't specify the exact things he said. They were more in the nature of implications against Mr. Muhammad—the pitch of Reginald's voice, or the way that Reginald looked, rather than what he said.

It caught me totally unprepared. It threw me into a state of confusion. My blood brother, Reginald, in whom I had so much confidence, for whom I had so much respect, the one who had introduced me to the Nation of Islam. I couldn't believe it! And now Islam meant more to me than anything I ever had known in my life. Islam and Mr. Elijah Muhammad had changed my whole world.

Reginald, I learned, had been suspended from the Nation of Islam by Elijah Muhammad. He had not practiced moral restraint. After he had learned the truth, and had accepted the truth, and the Muslim laws, Reginald was still carrying on improper relations with the then secretary of the New York Temple. Some other Muslim who learned of it had made charges against Reginald to Mr. Muhammad in Chicago, and Mr. Muhammad had suspended Reginald.

When Reginald left, I was in torment. That night, finally, I wrote to Mr. Muhammad, trying to defend my brother, appealing for him. I told him what Reginald was to me, what my brother meant to me.

I put the letter into the box for the prison censor. Then all the rest of that night, I prayed to Allah. I don't think anyone ever prayed more sincerely to Allah. I prayed for some kind of relief from my confusion.

It was the next night, as I lay on my bed, I suddenly, with a start, became aware of a man sitting beside me in my chair. He had on a dark suit, I remember. I could see him as plainly as I see anyone I look at. He wasn't black, and he wasn't white. He was light-brown-skinned, an Asiatic cast of countenance, and he had oily black hair.

I looked right into his face.

I didn't get frightened. I knew I wasn't dreaming. I couldn't move, I didn't speak, and he didn't. I couldn't place him racially—other than that I knew he was a non-European. I had no idea whatsoever who he was. He just sat there. Then, suddenly as he had come, he was gone.

Soon, Mr. Muhammad sent me a reply about Reginald. He wrote, "If you once believed in the truth, and now you are beginning to doubt the truth, you didn't believe the truth in the first place. What could make you doubt the truth other than your own weak self?"

That struck me. Reginald was not leading the disciplined life of a Muslim. And I knew that Elijah Muhammad was right, and my blood brother was wrong. Because right is right, and wrong is wrong. Little did I then realize the day would come when Elijah Muhammad would be accused by his own sons as being guilty of the same acts of immorality that he judged Reginald and so many others for.

But at that time, all of the doubt and confusion in my mind was removed. All of the influence that my brother had wielded over me was broken. From that day on, as far as I am concerned, everything that my brother Reginald has done is wrong.

But Reginald kept visiting me. When he had been a Muslim, he had been immaculate in his attire. But now, he wore things like a T-shirt, shabby-looking trousers, and sneakers. I could see him on the way down. When he spoke, I heard him coldly. But I would listen. He was my blood brother.

Gradually, I saw the chastisement of Allah—what Christians would call "the curse"—come upon Reginald. Elijah Muhammad said that Allah was chastising Reginald—and that anyone who challenged Elijah Muhammad would be chastened by Allah. In Islam we were taught that as long as one didn't know the truth, he lived in darkness. But once the truth was accepted, and recognized, he lived in light, and whoever would then go against it would be punished by Allah.

Mr. Muhammad taught that the five-pointed star stands for justice, and also for the five senses of man. We were taught that Allah executes justice by working upon the five senses of those who rebel against His Messenger, or against His truth. We were taught that this was Allah's way of letting Muslims know His sufficiency to defend His Messenger against any and all opposition, as long as the Messenger himself didn't deviate from the path of truth. We were taught that Allah turned the minds of any defectors into a turmoil. I thought truly that it was Allah doing this to my brother.

One letter, I think from my brother Philbert, told me that Reginald was with them in Detroit. I heard no more about Reginald until one day, weeks later, Ella visited me; she told me that Reginald was at her home in Roxbury, sleeping. Ella said she had heard a knock, she had gone to the door, and there was Reginald, looking terrible. Ella said she had asked, "Where did you come from?" And Reginald had told her he came from Detroit. She said she asked him, "How did you get here?" And he had told her, "I walked."

I believed he *had* walked. I believed in Elijah Muhammad, and he had convinced us that Allah's chastisement upon Reginald's mind had taken away Reginald's ability to gauge distance and time. There is a dimension of time with which we are not familiar here in the West. Elijah Muhammad said that under Allah's chastisement, the five senses of a man can be so deranged by those whose mental powers are greater than his that in five minutes his hair can turn snow white. Or he will walk nine hundred miles as he might walk five blocks.

In prison, since I had become a Muslim, I had grown a beard. When Reginald visited me, he nervously moved about in his chair; he told me that each hair on my beard was a snake. Everywhere, he saw snakes.

He next began to believe that he was the "Messenger of Allah." Reginald went around in the streets of Roxbury, Ella reported to me, telling people that he had some divine power. He graduated from this to saying that he was Allah.

He finally began saying he was *greater* than Allah.

Authorities picked up Reginald, and he was put into an institution. They couldn't find what was wrong. They had no way to understand Allah's chastisement. Reginald was released. Then he was picked up again, and was put into another institution.

Reginald is in an institution now. I know where, but I won't say. I would not want to cause him any more trouble than he has already had.

I believe, today, that it was written, it was meant, for Reginald to be used for one purpose only: as a bait, as a minnow to reach into the ocean of blackness where I was, to save me.

I cannot understand it any other way.

After Elijah Muhammad himself was later accused as a very immoral man, I came to believe that it wasn't a divine chastisement upon Reginald, but the pain he felt when his own family totally rejected him for Elijah Muhammad, and this hurt made Reginald turn insanely upon Elijah Muhammad.

It's impossible to dream, or to see, or to have a vision of someone whom you never have seen before—and to see him exactly as he is. To see someone, and to see him exactly as he looks, is to have a pre-vision.

I would later come to believe that my pre-vision was of Master W. D. Fard, the Messiah, the one whom Elijah Muhammad said had appointed him—Elijah Muhammad—as His Last Messenger to the black people of North America.

My last year in prison was spent back in the Charlestown Prison. Even among the white inmates, the word had filtered around. Some of those brainwashed black convicts talked too much. And I know that the censors had reported on my mail. The Norfolk Prison Colony officials had become upset. They used as a reason for my transfer that I refused to take some kind of shots, an inoculation or something.

The only thing that worried me was that I hadn't much time left before I would be eligible for parole-board consideration. But I reasoned that they might look at my representing and spreading Islam in another way: instead of keeping me in they might want to get me out.

I had come to prison with 20/20 vision. But when I got sent back to Charlestown, I had read so much by the lights-out glow in my room at the Norfolk Prison Colony that I had astigmatism and the first pair of the eyeglasses that I have worn ever since.

I had less maneuverability back in the much stricter Charlestown Prison. But I found that a lot of Negroes attended a Bible class, and I went there.

Conducting the class was a tall, blond, blue-eyed (a perfect "devil") Harvard Seminary student. He lectured, and then he started in a question-and-answer session. I don't know which of us had read the Bible more, he or I, but I had to give him credit; he really was heavy on his religion. I puzzled and puzzled for a way to upset him, and to give those Negroes present something to think and talk about and circulate.

Finally, I put up my hand; he nodded. He had talked about Paul.

I stood up and asked, "What color was Paul?" And I kept talking, with pauses, "He had to be black . . . because he was a Hebrew . . . and the original Hebrews were black . . . weren't they?"

He had started flushing red. You know the way white people do. He said "Yes."

I wasn't through yet. "What color was Jesus . . . he was Hebrew, too . . . wasn't he?"

Both the Negro and the white convicts had sat bolt upright. I don't care how tough the convict, be he brainwashed black Christian, or a "devil" white Christian, neither of them is ready to hear anybody saying Jesus wasn't white. The instructor walked around. He shouldn't have felt bad. In all of the years since, I never have met any intelligent white man who would try to insist that Jesus was white. How could they? He said, "Jesus was brown."

I let him get away with that compromise.

Exactly as I had known it would, almost overnight the Charlestown convicts, black and white, began buzzing with the story. Wherever I went, I could feel the nodding. And anytime I got a chance to exchange words with a black brother in stripes, I'd say, "My man! You ever heard about somebody named Mr. Elijah Muhammad?"

QUESTIONS FOR REACTION AND DISCUSSION

1. Why did Malcolm X write a daily letter to Elijah Muhammad?
2. How does Malcolm X describe conditions in the Norfolk Prison Colony? What books were in the library and what did he read?
3. What is the most important book Malcolm X obtains? Why?
4. Choose a book title or author that Malcolm X mentions and prepare a brief report for your class. Comment on why you think Malcolm X specifically mentioned the title or writer.
5. How does Malcolm X respond to the books he reads about slavery?
6. How is Malcolm X's opinion that the collective white man had acted like a devil through history formed?
7. How does Malcolm X compare his "homemade" education with a college education?
8. What becomes of Malcolm X's brother, Reginald? How does this affect Malcolm X?

QUESTIONS FOR WRITING

1. One of the powerful statements in Malcolm X's *Autobiography* is that even though he was imprisoned, through his reading "I never had been so truly free in my life." Write an essay in which you discuss the liberation that reading provided Malcolm X. Consider the following questions: How did the acquisition of language skills and the ability to read widely change Malcolm X's life? What specifically attracted Malcolm X to the teachings of Elijah Muhammad?
2. Malcolm X regarded books and Elijah Muhammad as his teachers. He used his newfound knowledge and beliefs in prison to speak to fellow prisoners. After his release from prison on parole, he began to lecture and speak widely, first as a follower of Elijah Muhammad and then as the independent organizer of the Organization of Afro-American Unity. In the broadest sense, Malcolm X saw himself as a teacher of black persons. What did Malcolm X believe constituted an effective teacher? How does he contrast his own work with that of the Harvard Seminary student who conducts a Bible class in the Charlestown

Prison? Write an essay in which you define and explain Malcolm X's philosophy of teaching according to his experiences as both a student and a teacher himself.

QUESTIONS FOR FURTHER EXPLORATION

1. Alex Haley recounts the story of how he got to know Malcolm X and how he interviewed his subject in the "Epilogue" to *The Autobiography of Malcolm X*. Locate a copy of the book and read Haley's epilogue. Write an essay in which you explain how Haley interviewed Malcolm X, what techniques he used, how he felt about the experience, and how effective this technique was in "Saved."
2. Investigate African-American History sites on the Web; a good place to begin is with The African-American History Historical Text Archive <http://www.geocities.com:80/Athens/Forum/9061/afro/afro.html> which has many links to a wide variety of sites, including The African-American Mosaic, A Library of Congress Resource Guide for the Study of Black History and Culture <http://lcweb.loc.gov/exhibits/african/intro.htm>. What information is available about Malcolm X, Elijah Muhammad, Black Muslims, the Organization of Afro-American Unity, and Alex Haley? Make a list of Internet resources and share them with your classmates.
3. Malcolm X comments in the early 1960s that "You can hardly show me a black adult in America—or a white one, for that matter—who knows from the history books anything like the truth about the black man's role." The erasure of black history was a constant theme of Malcolm X's speeches. What is the importance of knowing about the full history of a country or region? Is Malcolm X's comment true today? Why or why not? What evidence can you collect to prove your position?
4. View Spike Lee's film, *Malcolm X*. How does the movie portray Malcolm X's achievement of full literacy? How is it different from the presentation that Malcolm X recounts in "Saved"? How is it similar? Which is more effective and why?

9

TRANSFORMATION

Lydia Minatoya (1950–) is currently a Counselor at the Counseling Center of North Seattle Community College in Seattle, Washington. Born to Japanese parents in Albany, New York, Minatoya recounted her experience of coming to terms with her Japanese heritage in her autobiography, Talking to High Monks in the Snow. *Minatoya's father, a research scientist training at the University of Chicago, and her mother, a costume designer living in Los Angeles, met at Heart Mountain, Wyoming, one of the many internment camps for Japanese Americans, who forcibly relocated after the Japanese attack on Pearl Harbor in December 1941. The internment camps, established by President Franklin D. Roosevelt by Executive Order, became the temporary homes of nearly 120,000 Japanese Americans (two thirds of them were American citizens) who were compelled to live in the camps until the order was rescinded in 1944. The camps were located in rural areas throughout the interior West, in Arizona, California, Utah, Idaho, Colorado, and Wyoming; the living conditions were notoriously harsh. Although Minatoya was born a few years after her parents had left the camp, their experiences shaped much of the way in which they raised their children. In addition, Minatoya's account of her early life is shaped by her experience of being Japanese and being therefore different and alien to the mostly white society of Albany, New York. This excerpt, "Transformation," is taken from the early part of her autobiography, which won the prestigious 1991 PEN/Jerard Fund Award.*

QUESTIONS FOR READING

1. What do you know about the history of Japanese immigrants to the United States?
2. What do you know about the internment camps and the enforced "relocation" of Japanese Americans during World War II?

3. What does the term "transformation" mean? How does the title create expectations as you read?

LYDIA MINATOYA

TRANSFORMATION

Talking to High Monks in the Snow *(New York: Harper Collins, 1992)*

Perhaps it begins with my naming. During her pregnancy, my mother was reading Dr. Spock. "Children need to belong," he cautioned. "An unusual name can make them the subject of ridicule." My father frowned when he heard this. He stole a worried glance at my sister. Burdened by her Japanese name, Misa played unsuspectingly on the kitchen floor.

The Japanese know full well the dangers of conspicuousness. "The nail that sticks out gets pounded down," cautions an old maxim. In America, Relocation was all the proof they needed.

And so it was, with great earnestness, my parents searched for a conventional name. They wanted me to have the full true promise of America.

"I will ask my colleague Froilan," said my father. "He is the smartest man I know."

"And he has poetic soul," said my mother, who cared about such things.

In due course, Father consulted Froilan. He gave Froilan his conditions for suitability.

"First, if possible, the full name should be alliterative," said my father. "Like Misa Minatoya." He closed his eyes and sang my sister's name. "Second, if not an alliteration, at least the name should have assonantal rhyme."

"Like Misa Minatoya?" said Froilan with a teasing grin.

"Exactly," my father intoned. He gave an emphatic nod. "Finally, most importantly, the name must be readily recognizable as conventional." He peered at Froilan with hope. "Do you have any suggestions or ideas?"

Froilan, whose own American child was named Ricardito, thought a while.

"We already have selected the name for a boy," offered my Father. "Eugene."

"Eugene?" wondered Froilan. "But it meets none of your conditions!"

"Eugene is a special case," said my father, "after Eugene, Oregon, and Eugene O'Neill. The beauty of the Pacific Northwest, the power of a great writer."

"I see," said Froilan, who did not but who realized that this naming business would be more complex than he had anticipated. "How about Maria?"

"Too common," said my father. "We want a *conventional* name, not a common one."

"Hmmm," said Froilan, wondering what the distinction was. He thought some more and then brightened. "Lydia!" he declared. He rhymed the name with media. "Lydia for *la bonita infanta!*"

And so I received my uncommon conventional name. It really did not provide the camouflage my parents had anticipated. I remained unalterably alien. For Dr. Spock had been addressing *American* families, and in those days, everyone knew all real American families were white.

Call it denial, but many Japanese Americans never quite understood that the promise of America was not truly meant for them. They lived in horse stalls at the Santa Anita racetrack and said the Pledge of Allegiance daily. They rode to Relocation Camps under armed guard, labeled with numbered tags, and sang "The Star Spangled Banner." They lived in deserts or swamps, ludicrously imprisoned—where would they run if they ever escaped—and formed garden clubs, and yearbook staffs, and citizen town meetings. They even elected beauty queens.

My mother practiced her okoto and was featured in a recital. She taught classes in fashion design and her students mounted a show. Into exile she had carried an okoto and a sewing machine. They were her past and her future. She believed in Art and Technology.

My mother's camp was the third most populous city in the entire state of Wyoming. Across the barren lands, behind barbed wire, bloomed these little oases of democracy. The older generation bore the humiliation with pride. "*Kodomo no tame ni,*" they said. For the sake of the children. They thought that if their dignity was great, then their children would be spared. Call it valor. Call it bathos. Perhaps it was closer to slapstick: a sweet and bitter lunacy.

Call it adaptive behavior. Coming from a land swept by savage typhoons, ravaged by earthquakes and volcanoes, the Japanese have evolved a view of the world: a cooperative, stoic, almost magical way of thinking. Get along, work hard, and never quite see the things that can bring you pain. Against the tyranny of nature, of feudal lords, of wartime hysteria, the charm works equally well.

And so my parents gave me an American name and hoped that I could pass. They nourished me with the American dream: Opportunity, Will, Transformation.

When I was four and my sister was eight, Misa regularly used me as a comic foil. She would bring her playmates home from school and query me as I sat amidst the milk bottles on the front steps.

"What do you want to be when you grow up?" she would say. She would nudge her audience into attentiveness.

"A mother kitty cat!" I would enthuse. Our cat had just delivered her first litter of kittens and I was enchanted by the rasping tongue and soft mewings of motherhood.

"And what makes you think you can become a cat?" Misa would prompt, gesturing to her howling friends—wait for this; it gets better yet.

"This is America," I stoutly would declare. "I can grow up to be anything that I want!"

My faith was unshakable. I believed. Opportunity. Will. Transformation.

———————

When we lived in Albany, I always was the teachers' pet. "So tiny, so precious, so prettily dressed!" They thought I was a living doll and this was fine with me.

My father knew that the effusive praise would die. He had been through this with my sister. After five years of being a perfect darling, Misa had reached the age where students were tracked by ability. Then, the anger started. Misa had tested into the advanced track. It was impossible, the community declared. Misa was forbidden entry into advanced classes as long as there were white children being placed below her. In her defense, before an angry rabble, my father made a presentation to the Board of Education.

But I was too young to know of this. I knew only that my teachers praised and petted me. They took me to other classes as an example. "Watch now, as Lydia demonstrates attentive behavior," they would croon as I was led to an empty desk at the head of the class. I had a routine. I would sit carefully, spreading my petticoated skirt neatly beneath me. I would pull my chair close to the desk, crossing my swinging legs at my snowy white anklets. I would fold my hands carefully on the desk before me and stare pensively at the blackboard.

This routine won me few friends. The sixth-grade boys threw rocks at me. They danced around me in a tight circle, pulling at the corners of their eyes. "Ching Chong Chinaman," they chanted. But teachers loved me. When I was in first grade, a third-grade teacher went weeping to the principal. She begged to have me skipped. She was leaving to get married and wanted her turn with the dolly.

———————

When we moved, the greatest shock was the knowledge that I had lost my charm. From the first, my teacher failed to notice me. But to me, it did not matter. I was in love. I watched her moods, her needs, her small vanities. I was determined to ingratiate.

Miss Hempstead was a shimmering vision with a small upturned nose and eyes that were kewpie doll blue. Slender as a sylph, she tripped around the classroom, all saucy in her high-heeled shoes. Whenever I looked at Miss Hempstead, I pitied the Albany teachers whom, formerly, I had adored. Poor old Miss Rosenberg. With a shiver of distaste, I recalled her loose fleshy arms, her mottled hands, the scent of lavender as she crushed me to her heavy breasts.

Miss Hempstead had a pet of her own. Her name was Linda Sherlock. I watched Linda closely and plotted Miss Hempstead's courtship. The key was the piano. Miss Hempstead played the piano. She fancied herself a musical star. She sang songs from Broadway revues and shaped her students' reactions. "Getting to know you," she would sing. We would smile at her in a staged manner and position ourselves obediently at her feet.

Miss Hempstead was famous for her ability to soothe. Each day at rest time, she played the piano and sang soporific songs. Linda Sherlock was the only child who succumbed. Routinely, Linda's head would bend and nod until she crumpled gracefully onto her folded arms. A tousled strand of blond hair would fall across her forehead. Miss Hempstead would end her song, would gently lower the keyboard cover. She would turn toward the restive eyes of the class. "Isn't she sweetness itself!" Miss Hempstead would declare. It made me want to vomit.

I was growing weary. My studiousness, my attentiveness, my fastidious grooming and pert poise: all were failing me. I changed my tactics. I became a problem. Miss Hempstead sent me home with nasty notes in sealed envelopes: Lydia is a slow child, a noisy child; her presence is disruptive. My mother looked at me with surprise, *"Nani desu ka?* Are you having problems with your teacher?" But I was tenacious. I pushed harder and harder, firmly caught in the obsessive need of the scorned.

One day I snapped. As Miss Hempstead began to sing her wretched lullabies, my head dropped to the desk with a powerful CRACK! It lolled there, briefly, then rolled toward the edge with a momentum that sent my entire body catapulting to the floor. Miss Hempstead's spine stretched slightly, like a cat that senses danger. Otherwise, she paid no heed. The linoleum floor was smooth and cool. It emitted a faint pleasant odor: a mixture of chalk dust and wax.

I began to snore heavily. The class sat electrified. There would be no drowsing today. The music went on and on. Finally, one boy could not stand it. "Miss Hempstead," he probed plaintively, "Lydia has fallen asleep on the floor!" Miss Hempstead did not turn. Her playing grew slightly strident but she did not falter.

I lay on the floor through rest time. I lay on the floor through math drill. I lay on the floor while my classmates scraped around me, pushing their sturdy little wooden desks into the configuration for reading circle. It was not until penmanship practice that I finally stretched and stirred. I rose like Sleeping Beauty and slipped back to my seat. I smiled enigmatically. A spell had been broken. I never again had a crush on a teacher.

QUESTIONS FOR REACTION AND DISCUSSION

1. Who is Dr. Spock and how is the question of Lydia's name an important one? How did your parents choose your name? Does it reflect a family or ethnic background? How do you feel about your name?
2. What is an okoto, the musical instrument that Minatoya's mother plays?
3. What does Minatoya's assessment of the American dream "Opportunity, Will, Transformation" mean to you?

4. How and why does Minatoya become a teacher's pet?
5. When her family moves to suburban Albany, Minatoya finds that she is no longer a teacher's favorite. How does she rebel?

QUESTIONS FOR WRITING

1. How is this autobiographical sketch an enactment of the American dream of "Opportunity, Will, Transformation"? Write an essay in which you explore how Minatoya as a Japanese American pursues her American dream.
2. In this selection, as in others, teachers are presented as fundamental to the educational experiences of young students—for better and worse. How does Minatoya respond to teachers in Albany? When her family moves to the suburbs? Taking the experiences that Minatoya describes, as well as your own, write an essay in which you evaluate the positive and negative experiences that teachers provide in elementary education.
3. Have you had an educational experience that you might label, as Minatoya does here, a "Transformation"? Write an essay, entitled "Transformation," in which you narrate your own transformative experience as a child in school.

QUESTIONS FOR FURTHER EXPLORATION

1. Many western states where internment camps were located have established archives and resources of information in libraries about the Japanese Americans who were sent there. Three especially good Web sites are in Arizona <http://www.library.arizona.edu/images/jpamer/wraintro.html>, Washington <http://www.lib.washington.edu/exhibits/harmony/default.htm> and Utah <http://www.lib.utah.edu/spc/phot/9066/9066.htm>. Access one of these sites and learn about the internment camps in that state—use the electronic and the print resources. What was everyday life in the camps like? Who was sent to them? What provisions were made for the education of children? Write a report for your class.
2. Minatoya writes movingly about her experiences of growing up Japanese in the United States of the second half of the twentieth century. Read an earlier autobiography of another Japanese American, such as Monica Sone's *Nisei Daughter* (1953) and compare the educational experiences that Minatoya and Sone had. How were they alike? How were they different? What other narratives of Japanese American experiences can you locate?

10

HERALDRY

George Steiner (1929–) is a fellow of Churchill College, Cambridge University, in England. A distinguished literary and cultural critic, Steiner was born in Paris, France, and lived much of his early life there and in New York City. The son of Austrian Jewish parents, Steiner was raised speaking three languages: German, French, and English. Steiner's father, a brilliant man of many talents and much education, suffered from poor health but was nonetheless a success-ful investment banker. He moved his family to Paris from Vienna in 1924 for a less anti-Semitic environment and for the milder weather. The affluence of the Steiner family permitted European travels and the opportunity for significant educational opportunities. A frequent contributor to the New Yorker *and to the* Times Literary Supple-ment, *Steiner is the author of many books, including* After Babel: Aspects of Language and Translation *(1975),* Language and Silence: Essays on Language, Literature, and the Inhuman *(1982),* No Pas-sion Spent: Essays: 1978–1996 *(1996), and his recently published au-tobiography,* Errata: An Examined Life *(1998). Steiner has also published several works of fiction and is himself the subject of a collection of essays,* Reading George Steiner, *edited by Rohams A. Sharp and Scott A. Nathan, Jr. (1998). The essay reprinted here, "Heraldry," was published in* Granta, *a British journal begun in 1889 as a student magazine at Cambridge University that is now a distinguished literary magazine, known for its promotion of newer writers alongside older ones. "Heraldry" was part of a special issue in 1997 on "Ambition," in which fiction writers such as J. M. Coet-zee, Doris Lessing, Joyce Carol Oates, and others recollect their ambitions to be writers in essays that the editor calls "memoirs." Steiner's work—both fiction and nonfiction—has always been shaped by his experiences as a Jew, and as a scholar and a writer he has always been interested in the interactions between Hebraic and Hellenic culture and the ways in which those interactions have shaped western culture. In this essay, he alludes to his abiding*

concern in the developments that led to the Holocaust and to a
world that still seems complacent about such events.

QUESTIONS FOR READING

1. What is "heraldry"? What is a "coat of arms"? Before you read, make notes about your definitions of these terms.
2. What do you know about the history of Germany and Austria in the 1930s? What do you know about the origins and rise of Nazism? What was the position of Jews in Europe at this time?
3. Steiner refers to many writers, artists, musicians, and thinkers such as Freud, Shakespeare, Mahler, Mozart, Wittgenstein, Voltaire, Kant, and Kierkegaard. Are you familiar with these writers? Make a list of names that are unfamiliar to you and look them up in a biographical dictionary.
4. What is a memoir? How is it different from an autobiography?

GEORGE STEINER

HERALDRY

Granta *58 (1997): 147–57*

Rain, particularly to a child, carries distinct smells and colours. Summer rains in the Tyrol are relentless. They have a morose, flogging insistence and come in deepening shades of dark green. At night, the drumming is one of mice on or just under the roof. Even daylight can be sodden. But it is the smell which, after sixty years, stays with me. Of drenched leather and hung game. Or, at moments, of tubers steaming under drowned mud. A world made boiled cabbage.

That summer was already ominous. A family holiday in the dark yet magical landscape of a country condemned. In those mid-1930s, Jew-hatred and a lust for reunification with Germany hung in the Austrian air. My father, convinced that catastrophe was imminent, the gentile husband of my aunt still blandly optimistic, found conversation awkward. My mother and her fitfully hysterical sister sought to achieve an effect of normality. But the planned pastimes, swimming and boating on the lake, walks in the woods and hills, dissolved in the perpetual downpours. My impatience, my demands for entertainment in a cavernous chalet increasingly chill and, I imagine, mildewed, must have been pestilential. One morning Uncle Rudi drove into Salzburg. He brought back with him a small book in blue waxen covers.

It was a pictorial guide to coats of arms in the princely city and surrounding fiefs. Each blazon as reproduced in colour, together with a brief historical notice as to the castle, family domain, bishopric, or abbey which it identified. The little manual closed with a map marking the relevant sites, including ruins, and with a glossary of heraldic terms.

Even today I can feel the pressure of wonder, the inward shock which this chance "pacifier" triggered. What is difficult to render in adult language is the combination, almost the fusion of delight and menace, of fascination and unease I experienced as I retreated to my room, the drains spitting under the rain-lashed eaves, and sat, hour after entranced hour, turning the pages, committing to memory the florid names of those towers, keeps, and high personages.

Though I could not, obviously, have defined or phrased it in any such way, that armorial primer overwhelmed me with a sense of the numberless specificity, of the minutiae, of the manifold singularity of the substance and forms of the world. Each coat of arms differed from every other. Each had its symbolic organization, motto, history, locale, and date wholly proper, wholly integral to itself. It "heralded" a unique, ultimately intractable fact of being. Within its quarterings, each graphic component, colour, and pattern entailed its own prodigal signification. Heraldry often inserts coats of arms within coats of arms. The suggestive French designation of this device is a *mise en abyme*. My treasures included a magnifying glass. I pored over the details of geometric and "bestiary" shapes, the lozenges, diamonds, diagonal slashes of each emblem, over the helmeted crests and "supporters" crowning, flanking the diverse arms. Over the precise number of tassels which graced a bishop's, an archbishop's, or a cardinal's armorials.

The notion which, in some visceral impact, tided over me and held me mesmerized was this: if there are in this obscure province of one small country (diminished Austria) so many coats of arms, each unique, how many must there be in Europe, across the globe? I do not recall what grasp I had, if any, of large numbers. But I do remember that the word "millions" came to me and left me unnerved. How was any human being to see, to master this plurality? Suddenly it came to me, in some sort of exultant but also appalled revelation, that no inventory, no heraldic encyclopedia, no *summa* of fabled beasts, inscriptions, chivalric hallmarks, however compendious, could ever be complete. The opaque thrill and desolation which came over me in that ill-lit and end-of-summer room on the Wolfgangsee—was it, distantly, sexual?—has, in good part, oriented my life.

I grew possessed by an intuition of the particular, of diversities so numerous that no labour of classification and enumeration could exhaust them. Each leaf differed from any other on each differing tree (I rushed out in the deluge to assure myself of this elementary and miraculous truth). Each blade of grass, each pebble on the lake shore was eternally "just so." No repetition of measurement, however closely calibrated, in whatever controlled vacuum it was carried out, could ever be perfectly the same. It would deviate by some trillionth of an inch, by a nanosecond, by the breadth of a hair—itself a teeming immensity—from any preceding measurement. I sat on my bed striving to hold my breath, knowing that the next breath would signal a new beginning, that the past was already unrecapturable in its differential sequence. Did I guess that there could be no perfect *facsimile* of anything, that the identical work spoken twice, even in lightning-quick reiteration, was not and could not be the same (much later, I was to learn that this unrepeatability had preoccupied both Heraclitus and Kierkegaard).

At that hour, in the days following, the totalities of personal experience, of human contacts, of landscape around me became a mosaic, each fragment at once luminous and resistant in its "quiddity"—the scholastic term for integral presence revived by Gerard Manley Hopkins. There could be, I knew, no finality to the raindrops, to the number and variousness of the stars, to the books to be read, to the languages to be learned. The mosaic of the possible could, at any instant, be splintered and reassembled into new images and motions of meaning. The idiom of heraldry, those "gules" and "bars sinister," even if I could not yet make it out, must, I sensed, be only one among countless systems of discourse specifically tailored to the teeming diversity of human purposes, artefacts, representations, or concealments (I still recall the strange excitement I felt at the thought that a coat of arms could hide as well as reveal).

I set out, as many children do, to compile lists. Of monarchs and mythological heroes, of popes, of castles, of numinous dates, of operas—I had been taken to see *Figaro* at the neighbouring Salzburg Festival. The wearied assurance of my parents that such lists already existed, that they could be looked up in any almanac or work of standard reference—my queries about antipopes and how to include them visibly irritated my somewhat ceremonious and Catholic uncle—brought no solace. The available indices of reality, be they a thousand pages thick, the atlases, the children's encyclopedias, could never be exhaustively comprehensive. This or that item, perhaps the hidden key to the edifice, would be left out. There was simply too much to everything. Existence thronged and hummed with obstinate difference like the midges around the light bulb. "Who can number the clouds in wisdom? Or who can stay the bottles of heaven . . . ?" (How did Job 38: 37, already know about rains in the Salzhammergut?) I may not have cited the verse to myself in that drowned August, though the Old Testament was already a tutelary voice, but I did know of those bottles.

If the revelation of incommensurable "singleness" held me spellbound, it also generated fear. I come back to the *mise en abyme* of one blazon within another, to that "setting in the abyss." Consider a fathomless depth of differentiation, of nonidentity, always incipient with the eventuality of chaos. How could the senses, how could the brain impose order and coherence on the kaleidoscope, on the perpetuum mobile of swarming existence? I harboured vague nightmares at the fact, revealed in the nature column of some newspaper, that a small corner of the Amazon forest was habitat to thirty thousand rigorously distinct species of beetles. Gazing at, recopying with watercolours, the baronial or episcopal or civic arms, pondering the unlimited variations possible on formal and iconic motifs, I felt a peculiar dread. Detail could know no end.

How can a human voice cast a huge sickening shadow? On short waves, the wireless chirped and often dissolved in bursts of static. But Hitler's speeches, when broadcast, punctuated my childhood (whence, so many years later, *The Portage to San Cristobal of A.H.*). My father would be close to the wireless, straining to hear. We were in Paris, where I was born in 1929. One of the doctors assisting at my awkward birth then returned to Louisiana to assassinate Huey Long. History was always in attendance.

My parents had left Vienna in 1924. From meagre circumstances, from a Czech-Austrian milieu still in reach of the ghetto, my father had risen to meteoric eminence. Anti-Semitic Vienna, the cradle of Nazism, was, in certain respects, a liberal meritocracy. He had secured a senior legal position in the Austrian Central Bank, with fiacre (the use of a carriage and horses). A brilliant career lay before the youthful Herr Doktor. With grim clairvoyance, my father perceived the nearing disaster. A systematic, doctrinal Jew-hatred seethed and stank below the glittering liberalities of Viennese culture. The world of Freud, of Mahler, of Wittgenstein was also that of Mayor Lueger, Hitler's exemplar. At their lunatic source, Nazism and the final solution are Austrian rather than German reflexes. Like his friend out of Galicia, one Lewis Namier, my father dreamed of England. For the East- and Central-European Jewish intelligentsia, the career of Disraeli had assumed a mythical, talismanic aura. But he suffered from rheumatic fevers, and medical sagacity of the day held France to be the milder climate. So Paris it was, and a new start under strained circumstances (my mother, Viennese to her fingertips, lamented this seemingly irrational move). And to the end of his days, my father never felt at home among what he judged to be the arrogant chauvinism, the frivolities, the myopia of French politics, finance, and society. He would mutter under his breath and unjustly that all nationals will sell you their mothers, but that the French delivered.

Of fragile physique, my father was compounded of formidable will and intellect. He found a surprisingly large portion of mankind unacceptable. Sloppiness, lies, be they "white," evasions of reality, infuriated him. He lacked the art of forgiveness. His contributions to the skills of international investment banking, to the techniques of corporate finance in the period between the wars are on record. His Zionism had the ardour of one who knew, even at the outset, that he would not emigrate to Palestine. His bookplate shows a barque, a seven-branched candelabrum at its bow, approaching Jerusalem. But the holy city remains on the far horizon. Papa embodied, as did every corner of our Paris home, the tenor, the prodigality and glow of Jewish-European and Central-European emancipation. The horrors which reduced this liberal humaneness and vision to ashes have distorted remembrance. Evocations of the Shoah have, tragically, privileged the remembrance of prior suffering, particularly throughout Eastern Europe. The proud Judaism of my father was, like that of an Einstein or a Freud, one of messianic agnosticism. It breathed rationality, the promise of the Enlightenment and tolerance. It owed as much to Voltaire as it did to Spinoza. High holidays, notably the Day of Atonement, were observed not for prescriptive or theological motives, but as a yearly summons to identity, to a homeland in millennial time.

By virtue of what was to become an unbearable paradox, this Judaism of secular hope looked to German philosophy, literature, scholarship, and music for its talismanic guarantees. German metaphysics and cultural criticism, from Kant to Schopenhauer and Nietzsche, the classics of German-language poetry and drama, the master historians, such as Ranke, Mommsen, Gregorovius, crowded the shelves of my father's library. As did first editions of Heine, in whose mordant wit, in whose torn and ambiguous destiny, in whose unhoused virtuosity in both German and French, my father saw the prophetic mirror of modern European Judaism. Like so many German, Austrian, and Central-European Jews, my father was immersed in Wagner. During his very brief spell under arms in Vienna in 1914, he had ridden a horse named Lohengrin; he had then married a woman called Elsa. It was, however, the whole legacy of German-Austrian music: it was Mozart, Beethoven, Schubert, Hugo Wolfe, Mahler who filled the house. As a very young child, at the edge of bedtime and through a crack in the living-room door, I was sometimes allowed to hear chamber music, a lieder recital, being performed by musicians invited into our home. They were, increasingly, refugees in desolate plight. Yet even in the thickening political twilight, a Schubert song, a Schumann study could light up my father's haunted mien. When concessions had to be made to encroaching reality, my father gave them an ironic touch: recordings of Wagner were now played in French.

Only in the posthumously published letters of Gershom Scholem have I come across the same note of helpless clearsightedness and warning. Over and over, even prior to 1933, my father laboured to warn, to alert, to awaken to refuge not only those whom he and my mother had left behind in Prague or in Vienna, but the French political-military establishment with which his international dealings had brought him into contact. His "pessimism," his "alarmist prognostications" elicited only officious dismissal or hostility. Family and friends refused to move. One could come to reasonable terms with Herr Hitler. The unpleasantness would soon pass. The age of pogroms was over. In diplomatic and ministerial circles, my father was regarded as a tedious Cassandra, prone to well-known traits of Jewish hysteria. Papa lived those rancid 1930s like a man trapped in cobwebs, lashing out and sick at heart. There was also, however, a more private and constant regret.

His own studies in law and economic theory had been of exceptional strength. He had published monographs on the utopian economics of Saint-Simon and on the Austrian banking crises of the later nineteenth century. The absolute need to support various less qualified members of his family, the collapse of the dual monarchy, and the aftermath of world war had thrust him into finance. He respected the importance, the technical ingenuities of his craft, but cultivated scant regard for most of those who practiced it (one of the few contemporaries he acknowledged as preeminent, also in integrity and whom he came, in certain outward gestures and tone, to resemble, was Siegmund Warburg). My father's innermost passions lay elsewhere. His uncertain health had barred him from medical studies. He turned to intellectual history, to the history and philosophic aspects of biology. His learning was extensive and exact.

His appetite for languages remained unquenched to the very end (he was systematically acquiring Russian at the time of his death). Investment banking occupied the main of his outward existence. At the core, it left him almost indifferent. From this tension came his uncompromising resolve that his son should know next to nothing of his father's profession. This partition could reach absurd lengths: "I would rather that you did not know the difference between a bond and a share." I was to be a teacher and a thorough scholar. On this last point, I have failed him.

Why this elevation of the teacher-scholar rather than, say, the artist, the writer, the performer in a sensibility so responsive to music, literature, and the arts? There was scarcely a museum in Paris and, later, in New York, to which he did not take me of a Saturday. It is in this instinctive preference for teaching and learning, for the discovery and transmission of the truth, that my father, in his aching stoicism, was most profoundly Jewish. Like Islam, Judaism is iconoclastic. It fears the image; it distrusts the metaphor. Emancipated Judaism delights in the performing artist, especially the musician. It has produced masters of stage and film. Yet even to this day, when it informs so much of American literature, when it can look to a Kafka, a Proust, a Mandelstam or a Paul Celan, Judaism is not altogether at ease with the poetics of invention (*fabulation*), with the mustard seed of "falsehood" or fiction, with the rivalry to God the creator inherent in the arts. Given the limitless wonders of the created universe, when there is such wealth of actual being to be recorded and grasped by reason, when there is history to be untangled, law to be clarified, science to be furthered, is the devising of fictions, of *mimesis* a truly responsible, a genuinely adult pursuit? Freud, for one, did not think so. Fictions were to be outgrown as man ripened into the "reality principle." Somewhere in my father's restless spirit a comparable doubt may have nagged. Even the most Voltairean, perhaps atheist—I do not know—of Jews knows that the word *rabbi* simply means "teacher."

Only later did I come to realize the investment of hope against hope, of watchful inventiveness, which my father made in educating me. This, during years of private and public torment, when the bitter need to find some future for us as Nazism drew near, left him emotionally and physically worn out. I marvel still at the loving astuteness of his devices. No new book was allowed me till I had written down for his inspection a précis of the one I had just read. If I had not understood this or that passage—my father's choices and suggestions aimed carefully above my head—I was to read it to him out loud. Often the voice clears up a text. If misunderstanding persisted, I was to copy the relevant bit in my own writing. At which move, it would usually surrender its lode.

Though I was hardly aware of the design, my reading was held in balance between French, English, and German. My upbringing was totally trilingual, and the background always polyglot. My radiant mama would habitually begin a sentence in one tongue and end it in another. Once a week a diminutive Scottish lady appeared to read Shakespeare to and with me. I entered that world, I am not certain why, via *Richard II*. Adroitly, the first speech I was made to learn by heart was not that of Gaunt, but Mowbray's farewell, with its mordant music of exile. A refugee scholar coached me in Greek and Latin. He exhaled an odour of reduced soap and sorrow.

QUESTIONS FOR REACTION AND DISCUSSION

1. Where is the opening of this memoir set? What is the present, the "pacifier" that Steiner's Uncle Rudi brings?
2. Locate a pictorial guide to coats of arms and bring it with you to class. Ask your classmates to note the "blazons" and also to discuss the purpose and function of coats of arms.
3. What does Steiner mean by the French phrase *mise en abyme?* Why is this phrase important to him?
4. Why does looking at the coats of arms inspire Steiner to compile lists? What is the purpose of these lists for him?
5. Describe Steiner's parents. What is unusual about his father and his background? What is his particular brand of Zionism?
6. Does Steiner feel that he failed to live up to his father's expectations? Why?
7. How effective is the concluding paragraph of the essay?
8. What is the tone of this essay? How does Steiner re-create the dark tragedy of the Holocaust the Nazi era brought?

QUESTIONS FOR WRITING

1. Robert Winder, the editor for the issue of *Granta* in which "Heraldry" appeared, wrote in the introduction that "George Steiner watches the Tyrolean rain drip over his earliest encounters with the guiding principles of scholarship." How did the gift of the pictorial guide to coats of arms in the Tyrolean region shape Steiner's attitudes toward his career as a teacher and a scholar? Write an essay in which you explain what Steiner learned from reading his book on heraldry and what "guiding principles" of scholarship he learned from this early experience.
2. Imagine that you have been invited by the editor of *Granta* to contribute an essay to a follow-up issue on "Ambition." Think of an experience from your childhood or teenage years—an unusual gift, an encounter with an unusual person, a recognition of a special talent—that has been formative in shaping the education and career goals you are now pursuing. Write an essay in which you describe the experience and speculate on the meaning of this experience for you now.

QUESTIONS FOR FURTHER EXPLORATION

1. Access the *Granta* Web site, <http://granta.nybooks.com/magazine.html> and read about the history of the magazine. What is the function of *Granta* today? Browse through the table of contents of recent issues and read some essays or stories by authors whose names you don't know. Write a report of your experience for your classmates, with your positive or negative recommendation of a visit to this site.

2. Visit the Web site of the United States Holocaust Memorial Museum <http://www.ushmm.org>. What is the purpose of this museum? What is its mission? What programs, exhibits, and services does the museum offer? Write an essay in which you describe your "virtual" visit to the museum and explain the effect it had on your attitudes toward the Holocaust.

3. Read some of Steiner's fiction or other essays in the collections mentioned in the Introduction. In what ways does Steiner's interest in the Jewish experience and intellectual tradition shape his works? Write an essay in which you discuss Steiner's use of his background in a work that you read.

SUGGESTIONS FOR FURTHER READING, THINKING, AND WRITING

1. In an article, "Reading Literacy Narratives," Janet Carey Eldred and Peter Mortensen, define the term "literacy narrative" as an account of a person's "ongoing, social process of language acquisition" (512). In that sense, all of the essays in this section of the text are literacy narratives, but each of these essays narrates a different account of language acquisition. Eldred and Mortensen provide some useful refinements to the notion of a "literacy narrative" in their essay (512–513), and they are reprinted here for your information:

> **Narratives of socialization** are stories that chronicle a character's attempt to enter a new social and discursive arena. Many texts, especially coming-of-age stories that show characters negotiating the world around them, often contain detailed and insightful investigations of how language is acquired and how it creates particular regional and private identities. In these narratives, literacy is a necessary component, although it is not emphasized.
>
> **Literature of the contact zone** is that fiction authored in colonial contexts or out of colonial histories. It studies the particular problems of forcing a sanctioned literacy on colonized subjects and examines, among other things, the role of "autoethnography" in resisting legislated representation.
>
> **Literacy narratives** are those stories, like Bernard Shaw's *Pygmalion,* that foreground issues of language acquisition and literacy. These narratives are structured by learned, internalized "literacy tropes," by "prefigured" ideas and images. Literacy narratives sometimes include explicit images of schooling and teaching; they include texts that both challenge and affirm culturally scripted ideas about literacy.

Choose one of the readings in "Literacy Narratives" and write an essay in which you explain how the essay you have read fits into one of the above categories and provide a larger context for that decision. Begin with a clear definition of the category and some specific examples from your essay about how the category works. How does the category help you understand the essay more clearly?

2. Most Americans believe that broader literacy necessarily leads to economic development, cultural progress, and individual improvement for all. But some

scholars believe that this constitutes a "literacy myth" and that we should care-fully question assumptions made about the connections between the achieve-ment of literacy and social mobility or economic success. What essays in this section participate in the "literacy myth"? Which do not? Write an essay in which you compare and contrast two or more of the literacy narratives in this section and demonstrate how literacy leads or does not lead to success in so-cial, economic, or cultural terms.

3. Many of the narratives in this section demonstrate the primary importance of well-trained teachers in formal education. Write an essay in which you define effective teaching by profiling one of the teachers presented by a writer in this section and providing positive and negative examples from the other se-lections. What conclusions can you draw about how teachers affect students?

4. Some of the writers whose works are represented here stress the particular importance—not of teachers—but of books on their development. Consider, for example, the function of *The Columbian Orator* to Frederick Douglass, the pictorial guide to coats of arms to George Steiner, the German Bible to Old Or-der Amish, and *Heart of Darkness* or *On the Road* to Mike Rose. Write an es-say in which you discuss and evaluate the effect of reading on some of the writers presented here. As you prepare to write this essay, think about what the writer learned from the books, what made them special, and in what way the books made a difference to the writer.

5. Consider how many of the writers here present bleak views of their formal educational experiences. Schools are often presented as cold institutions run by thoughtless and insensitive bureaucrats, whether they are Quaker mission schools designed to acculturate Indian children, a public grammar school in Boston, or a Catholic elementary school in South Los Angeles. Compare and contrast the depiction of schools in some of the readings; consider carefully which readings you wish to write about and why.

6. Prepare a questionnaire for your classmates, designed to elicit information about their own literacy narratives. Consider the following: When did you be-come conscious of a desire to achieve literacy? What were your early experi-ences? What kind of school did you attend? Did you have a significant teacher? Were your parents or other family members involved in your education? What books were important to you? Survey your class and write a report of your findings. What are the common experiences among your classmates? What dif-ferences do you detect?

7. Many autobiographies deal with the author's language acquisition, early schooling, and education, especially when the author has been displaced from his or her native culture into that of another. For example, Basil Johnston, an Ojibway Indian, recounts his experiences at a Canadian school for Indian chil-dren in *Indian School Days;* Jill Ker Conway, who grew up on a sheep farm in Australia and became the first woman president of Smith College, reveals her

gradual understanding of how British culture permeated her Australian education in *The Road from Coorain;* Monica Sone narrates her experiences in living in a Japanese internment camp in *Nisei Daughter;* Anna Howard Shaw, an immigrant from Scotland, tells of her experiences in American schools at the turn of the nineteenth into the twentieth century in *The Story of a Pioneer.* Investigate one of these books or another that catches your attention, read it, and write an essay about how the author interprets his or her experience of cultural conflict.

8. In *Hunger of Memory,* Richard Rodriguez suggests that education is a process that remakes a person's life. Explore that assertion in some of the readings in this section and consider whether you agree or disagree with Rodriguez that education must necessarily distance a person from his or her home culture. Write an essay in which you argue your position on this issue.

9. What is the value of reading literacy narratives? What are the lessons that we learn about ourselves, our cultures, our schools, and our teachers? Write an essay in which you evaluate your experience of reading the selections in this section and make a recommendation about the importance of including texts like these in an undergraduate college course.

10. Write your own literacy narrative in which you explore your own process of language acquisition, your relationship with the culture of the school you attended, your experience with books, your interactions with teachers and fellow students, and/or any special circumstances that were a part of your experience.

II

The Purpose of a College Education

INTRODUCTION

Despite the escalating costs, Americans generally regard obtaining a college education as an important goal. The number and sheer variety of institutional kinds—liberal arts colleges, research universities, community colleges, comprehensive state colleges, institutes of technology—all point to a strong desire on the part of Americans to go to college. Whether to a campus in a rural New England setting, to a collection of tall buildings in the middle of a gritty city, or to a campus center located in a business district, Americans are attracted to institutions of higher education and often make great sacrifices in money, energy, and time to achieve the goal of a college degree. But while there is a general consensus about the importance of a college education, what one should know or be or do at the completion of that education is very much open to discussion—among students and parents, and among college administrators and faculty members.

Some of the questions that the writers explore in this section are:

- What are the historical purposes of a college education?
- What are the multiple purposes of a contemporary college education?
- What is a liberal arts education?
- What perceptions and expectations do parents and students have about what a college education means?
- Is there a definable body of knowledge or set of skills that college students should master?
- What is the tension between a liberal arts education and a professional education?
- What is the best training for a student who must deal with the contemporary realities of frequent job and career changes?
- How does contemporary consumer culture influence students and their relationship to a college or university?
- How does a college or university decide on its own mission and curriculum?
- In what ways are students called on to "invent the university" for themselves?

The writers in this section each approach the answers to these and other related questions in a variety of ways and through different genres: investigative reports, surveys, and essays. A historical perspective on the question of what is the purpose of a college education is provided, at least in part, by the extracts from the report of the Committee of the Corporation and Academical Faculty at Yale College in 1828. The works of two college presidents are represented in this section. Richard Hersh, president of Hobart and William Smith Colleges, analyzes the results of a survey on student and parent perspectives on liberal arts education; while George R. Houston, president of Mount St. Mary's College, discusses the relationship between the liberal arts and the professional arts within a college curriculum. A variety of other writers investigate what students should learn in college: Wayne Booth, Mark Edmundson, Martha Nussbaum, and Lisa Schmeiser each offer a different perspective on the knowledge and skills that students need in a contemporary world. Denise Magner reports on a controversial effort to reform the curriculum of one college and demonstrates how complicated such discussions can be for students and faculty members alike. As you read the essays in this section, consider your own purposes for college education and why you chose the institution you did.

I

REPORTS ON THE COURSE OF YALE COLLEGE

Yale University is the third-oldest institution of higher education in the United States, founded in 1701 for men. (Women were not admitted to colleges and universities in this country until Oberlin College was founded in 1833 as the first coeducational college; black men and women were admitted there in 1835). Although Yale was originally known as the Collegiate School, it was renamed "Yale University" in 1716 when Elihu Yale, an English philanthropist who spent part of his childhood in New Haven, Connecticut, gave gifts of books and money to the school. Today "Yale College" refers to the undergraduate school of the university; the college and ten graduate schools in such fields as law, architecture, art, medicine, and music comprise Yale University. In 1828, however, Yale was strictly an undergraduate college. The original mission of Yale College according to its original charter called for the school to train young men "for Publick employment, both in Church and Civil State." In 1828, the Committee of the Corporation and Academical Faculty was formed to study the curriculum and the mission of the College, under the leadership of Jeremiah Day, who was then president of Yale. At the time, the College was under some pressure by students and alumni to change the curriculum from its emphasis on the required study of Latin and Greek—the classical culture of the Old World—to include new information and contemporary fields of study. Such tensions within a college curriculum still exist today, and conversations about the purpose of a college education take place throughout every academic year at virtually every college and university in the United States. The "Mission Statements" that colleges and universities write are the public explanations of the purpose of the educational program available at a particular institution. These mission statements are drafted by faculty members and administrators and are often the result of committee reports such as this early one at Yale. Excerpts from this report make up the text of this reading.

QUESTIONS FOR READING

1. What do you know about the history of colleges and universities in the United States?
2. What do you think are the two or three most important purposes of a college education?

COMMITTEE OF THE CORPORATION
AND THE ACADEMICAL FACULTY

REPORTS ON THE COURSE OF INSTRUCTION IN YALE COLLEGE

(New Haven: Hezekiah Howe, 1828)

At a Meeting of the President and Fellows of Yale College,
Sept. 11th, 1827, the following resolution was passed:

That His Excellency Governor Tomlinson, Rev. President Day, Rev. Dr. Chapin, Hon. Noyes Darling, and Rev. Abel McEwen be a committee to inquire into the expediency of so altering the regular course of instruction in this college as to leave out of said course the study of the *dead languages,* substituting other studies therefore; and either requiring a competent knowledge of said languages as a condition of admittance into the college or providing instruction in the same for such as shall choose to study them after admittance, that the said committee be requested to report at the next annual meeting of this corporation.

This committee, at their first meeting in April, 1828, after taking into consideration the case referred to them, requested the faculty of the college to express their views on the subject of the resolution.

The expediency of retaining the ancient languages as an essential part of our course of instruction is so obviously connected with the object and plan of education in the college that justice could not be done to the particular subject of inquiry in the resolution without a brief statement of the nature and arrangement of the various branches of the whole system. The report of the faculty was accordingly made out in *two parts*: one containing a summary view of the plan of education in the college; the other, an inquiry into the expediency of insisting on the study of the ancient languages.

While this article is reprinted here from its original 1828 text, the punctuation has been updated to reflect modern usage.

This report was read to the committee at their meeting in August. The committee reported their views to the corporation at their session in September, who voted to accept the report and ordered it to be printed, together with the papers read before the committee, or such parts of them as the prudential committee and the faculty should judge it expedient to publish.

PART I

Containing a summary view of the plan of education in the college.

The committee of the corporation, to whom was referred the motion, to inquire into the expediency of dispensing with the study of the ancient languages, as a part of the regular course of instruction in this college, having requested the views of the faculty on the subject, we would respectfully submit the following considerations.

We are decidedly of the opinion that our present plan of education admits of improvement. We are aware that the system is imperfect: and we cherish the hope that some of its defects may ere long be remedied. We believe that changes may, from time to time, be made with advantage, to meet the varying demands of the community, to accommodate the course of instruction to the rapid advance of the country, in population, refinement, and opulence. We have no doubt that important improvements may be suggested, by attentive observation of the literary institutions in Europe and by the earnest spirit of inquiry, which is now so prevalent, on the subject of education.

The guardians of the college appear to have ever acted upon the principle that it ought not to be stationary, but continually advancing. Some alteration has accordingly been proposed almost every year from its first establishment. It is with no small surprise, therefore, we occasionally hear the suggestion that our system is unalterable; that colleges were originally planned in the days of monkish ignorance; and that, "by being immovably moored to the same station, they serve only to measure the rapid current of improvement which is passing by them."

How opposite to all this is the real state of facts, in this and the other seminaries in the United States. Nothing is more common than to hear those who revisit the college, after a few years absence express their surprise at the changes which have been made since they were graduated. Not only the course of studies and the modes of instruction have been greatly varied; but whole sciences have, for the first time, been introduced: chemistry, mineralogy, geology, political economy, and so on. By raising the qualifications for admission, the standard of attainment has been elevated. Alterations so extensive and frequent satisfactorily prove that if those who are intrusted with the superintendence of the institution still firmly adhere to some of its original features, it is from a higher principle than a blind opposition to salutary reform. Improvements, we trust, will continue to be made as rapidly as they can be without hazarding the loss of what has been already attained.

But perhaps the time has come when we ought to pause and inquire whether it will be sufficient to make *gradual* changes, as heretofore and whether the whole system is not rather to be broken up and a better one substituted in its stead. From different quarters, we have heard the suggestion that our colleges must be *new-modeled*; that they are not adapted to the spirit and wants of the age; that they will soon be deserted, unless they are better accommodated to the business character of the nation. As this point may have an important bearing upon the question immediately before the committee, we would ask their indulgence while we attempt to explain, at some length, the nature and object of the present plan of education at the college.

We shall in vain attempt to decide on the expediency of retaining or altering our present course of instruction, unless we have a distinct apprehension of the *object* of a collegiate education. A plan of study may be well adapted to a particular purpose, though it may be very unsuitable for a different one. Universities, colleges, academical, and professional seminaries ought not to be all constituted upon the same model, but should be so varied as to attain the ends which they have severally in view.

What then is the appropriate object of a college? It is not necessary here to determine what it is which, in every case, entitles an institution to the *name* of a college. But if we have not greatly misapprehended the design of the patrons and guardians of this college, its object is to lay the foundation of a superior education: and this is to be done, at a period of life when a substitute must be provided for *parental superintendence*. The ground work of a thorough education must be broad and deep and solid. For a partial or superficial education, the support may be of looser materials and more hastily laid.

The two great points to be gained in intellectual culture are the *discipline* and the *furniture* of the mind, expanding its powers and storing it with knowledge. The former of these is, perhaps, the more important of the two. A commanding object, therefore, in a collegiate course should be to call into daily and vigorous exercise the faculties of the study. Those branches of study should be prescribed and those modes of instruction adopted which are best calculated to teach the art of fixing the attention, directing the train of thought, analyzing a subject proposed for investigation; following, with accurate discrimination, the course of argument; balancing nicely the evidence presented to the judgment; awakening, elevating, and controlling the imagination; arranging, with skill, the treasures which memory gathers; rousing and guiding the powers of genius. All this is not to be effected by a light and hasty course of study, by reading a few books, hearing a few lectures, and spending some months at a literary institution. The habits of thinking are to be formed by long continued and close application. The mines of science must be penetrated far below the surface before they will disclose their treasures. If a dexterous performance of the manual operations in many of the mechanical arts requires an apprentice-ship with diligent attention for years; much more does the training of the pow-ers of the mind demand vigorous and steady and systematic effort.

In laying the foundation of a thorough education, it is necessary that *all* the important mental faculties be brought into exercise. It is not sufficient that one or two be cultivated, while others are neglected. A costly edifice ought not to be left to rest upon a single pillar. When certain mental endowments receive a much higher culture than others, there is a distortion in the intellectual char-acter. The mind never attains its full perfection, unless its various powers are so trained as to give them the fair proportions which nature designed. If the stu-dent exercises his reasoning powers only, he will be deficient in imagination and taste in fervid and impressive eloquence. If he confines his attention to demonstrative evidence, he will be unfitted to decide correctly in cases of prob-ability. If he relies principally on his memory, his powers of invention will be impaired by disuse. In the course of instruction in this college, it has been an object to maintain such a proportion between the different branches of litera-ture and science as to form in a student a proper *balance* of character. From the pure mathematics, he learns the art of demonstrative reasoning. In attending to the physical sciences, he becomes familiar with facts, with the process of in-duction, and the varieties of probable evidence. In ancient literature, he finds some of the most finished models of taste. By English reading, he learns the powers of the language in which he is to speak and write. By logic and mental philosophy, he is taught the art of thinking; by rhetoric and oratory, the art of speaking. By frequent exercise on written composition, he acquires copiousness and accuracy of expression. By extemporaneous discussion, he becomes prompt and fluent and animated. It is a point of high importance that eloquence and solid learning should go together, that he who has accumulated the richest treasures of thought should possess the highest powers of ora-tory. To what purpose has a man become deeply learned if he has no faculty of communicating his knowledge? And of what use is a display of rhetorical elegance from one who knows little or nothing which is worth commun-icating? *Est enim scientia comprehendenda rerum plurimarum, sine qua verborum volubilitas inanis atque irridenda est. Cic.* Our course, therefore, aims at a union of science with literature, of solid attainment with skill in the art of persuasion.

No one feature in a system of intellectual education is of greater moment that such an arrangement of duties and motives as will most effectually throw the student upon the *resources of his own mind.* Without this, the whole ap-paratus of libraries and instruments and specimens and lectures and teachers will be insufficient to secure distinguished excellence. The scholar must form himself by his own exertions. The advantages furnished by a residence at a col-lege can do little more than stimulate and aid his personal efforts. The *inven-tive* powers are especially to be called into vigorous exercise. However abundant may be the acquisitions of the student, if he has no talent at forming new combinations of thought, he will be dull and inefficient. The sublimest efforts of genius consist in the creations of the imagination, the discoveries of the intellect, the conquests by which the dominions of science are extended. But the culture of the inventive faculties is not the *only* object of a liberal education. The most gifted understanding cannot greatly enlarge the amount of science to which the wisdom of ages has contributed. If it were possible for a youth to have his faculties in the highest state of cultivation, without any of the knowledge which is derived from others, he would be but poorly fitted for the business of life. To the discipline of the mind, therefore, is to be added instruction. The analytic method must be combined with the synthetic. Analysis is most efficacious in directing the powers of invention, but is far too slow in its progress to teach, within a moderate space of time, the circle of the sciences.

In our arrangements for the communication of knowledge, as well as in intellectual discipline, such branches are to be taught as will produce a proper symmetry and balance of character. We doubt whether the powers of the mind can be developed, in their fairest proportions, by studying languages alone or mathematics alone or natural or political science alone. As the bodily frame is brought to its highest perfection, not by one simple and uniform motion, but by a variety of exercises, so the mental faculties are expanded and invigorated and adapted to each other by familiarity with different departments of science.

A most important feature in the colleges of this country is that the students are generally of an age which requires that a substitute be provided for *parental superintendence*. When removed from under the roof of their parents, and exposed to the untried scenes of temptation, it is necessary that some faithful and affectionate guardian take them by the hand and guide their steps. This consideration determines the *kind* of government which ought to be maintained in our colleges. As it is a substitute for the regulations of a family, it should approach as near to the character of parental control as the circumstances of the case will admit. It should be founded on mutual affection and confidence. It should aim to effect its purpose, principally by kind and persuasive influence, not wholly or chiefly by restraint and terror. Still, punishment may sometimes be necessary. There may be perverse members of a college as well as of a family. There may be those whom nothing but the arm of law can reach.

The parental character of college government requires that the students should be so collected together as to constitute one family, that the intercourse between them and their instructers may be frequent and familiar. This renders it necessary that suitable *buildings* be provided for the residence of the students— we speak now of colleges in the country, the members of which are mostly gathered from a distance. In a large city, where the students reside with their parents, public rooms only are needed. This may be the case also in professional institutions in which the students are more advanced in age and, therefore, do not require a minute superintendence on the part of their instructers.

The collegiate course of study, of which we have now given a summary view, we hope may be carefully distinguished from several *other* objects and plans with which it has been too often confounded. It is far from embracing *everything* which the student will ever have occasion to learn. The object is not to *finish* his education but to lay the foundation and to advance as far in rearing the superstructure as the short period of his residence here will admit. If he acquires here a thorough knowledge of the principles of science, he may then, in a great measure, educate himself. He has, at least, been taught *how* to learn. With the aid of books and means of observation, he may be constantly advancing in knowledge. Wherever he goes, into whatever company he falls, he has those general views on every topic of interest, which will enable him to understand, to digest, and to form a correct opinion on the statements and discussions which he hears. There are many things important to be known which are not taught in colleges because they may be learned anywhere. The knowledge, though indispensable, comes to us as freely in the way of our business as our necessary supplies of light, and air, and water.

The course of instruction which is given to the undergraduates in the college is not designed to include *professional* studies. Our object is not to teach that which is peculiar to any one of the professions but to lay the foundation which is common to them all. There are separate schools for medicine, law, and theology connected with the college, as well as in various parts of the country, which are open for the reception of all who are prepared to enter upon the appropriate studies of their several professions. With these, the academical course is not intended to interfere.

But, why, it may be asked, should a student waste his time upon studies which have no immediate connection with his future profession? Will chemistry enable him to plead at the bar, or conic sections qualify him for preaching, or astronomy aid him in the practice of physic? Why should not his attention be confined to the subject which is to occupy the labors of his life? In answer to this, it may be observed that there is no science which does not contribute its aid to professional skill. "Everything throws light upon everything." The great object of a collegiate education, preparatory to the study of a profession, is to give that expansion and balance of the mental powers, those liberal and comprehensive views, and those fine proportions of character which are not to be found in him whose ideas are always confined to one particular channel. When a man has entered upon the practice of his profession, the energies of his mind must be given, principally, to its appropriate duties. But if his thoughts never range on other subjects, if he never looks abroad on the ample domains of literature and science, there will be a narrowness in his habits of thinking, a peculiarity of character which will be sure to mark him as a man of limited views and attainments. Should he be distinguished in his profession, his ignorance on other subjects and the defects of his education will be the more exposed to public observation. On the other hand, he who is not only eminent in professional life but has also a mind richly stored with general knowledge has an elevation and dignity of character which gives him a commanding influence in society and a widely extended sphere of usefulness. His situation enables him to diffuse the light of science among all classes of the community. Is a man to have no other object than to obtain a *living* by professional pursuits? Has he not duties to perform to his family, to his fellow citizens, to his country, duties which require various and extensive intellectual furniture?

Professional studies are designedly excluded from the course of instruction at college to leave room for those literary and scientific acquisitions which, if not commenced there, will, in most cases, never be made. They will not grow up spontaneously amid the bustle of business. We are not here speaking of those giant minds which, by their native energy, break through the obstructions of a defective education and cut their own path to distinction. These are honorable exceptions to the general law, not examples for common imitation. Franklins and Marshalls are not found in sufficient numbers to fill a college. And even Franklin would not have been what he was if there had been no colleges in the country. When an elevated standard of education is maintained by the higher literary institutions, men of superior powers, who have not had access to these, are stimulated to aim at a similar elevation by their own efforts and by aid of the light which is thus shining around them.

As our course of instruction is not intended to complete an education in theological, medical, or legal science, neither does it include all the minute details of *mercantile, mechanical,* or *agricultural* concerns. These can never be effectually learned except in the very circumstances in which they are to be practiced. The young merchant must be trained in the counting room; the mechanic, in the workshop; the farmer, in the field. But we have, on our premises, no experimental farm or retail shop, no cotton or iron manufactory, no hatter's or silver-smith's or coach-maker's establishment. For that purpose, then, it will be asked, are young men who are destined to these occupations, ever sent to a college? They should not be sent, as we think, with an expectation of *finishing* their education at the college, but with a view of laying a thorough foundation in the principles of science, preparatory to the study of the practical arts. As everything cannot be learned in four years, either theory or practice must be, in a measure at least, postponed to a future opportunity. But if the scientific theory of the arts is *ever* to be acquired, it is unquestionably first in order of time. The cornerstone must be laid before the superstructure is erected. If suitable arrangements were made, the details of mercantile, mechanical, and agricultural education might be taught at the college to *resident graduates.* Practical skill would then be grounded upon scientific information.

The question may be asked, What is a young man fitted for when he takes his degree? Does he come forth from the college qualified for business? We answer, no—if he stops here. His education is begun, but not completed. Is the college to be reproached for not accomplishing that which it has never undertaken to perform? Do we complain of the mason who has laid the foundation of a house that he has done nothing to purpose, that he has not finished the building, that the product of his labor is not habitable, and that, therefore, there is nothing practical in what he has done? Do we say of the planter who has raised a crop of cotton that he has done nothing practical because he has not given to his product the form of wearing apparel?

In education, as well as in morals, we often hear the suggestion that principles are of no consequence provided the practice is right. Why waste on theories the time which is wanted for acquiring practical arts? We are aware that some operations may be performed by those who have little or no knowledge of the principles on which they depend. The mariner may set his sails to the wind without understanding the laws of the decomposition of forces; the carpenter may square his framework without a knowledge of Euclid's Elements; the dyer may set his colors without being indoctrinated in the principles of chemistry. But the labors of such a one are confined to the narrow path marked out to him by others. He needs the constant superintendence of men of more enlarged and scientific information. If he ventures beyond his prescribed rule, he works at random, with no established principles to guide him. By long continued practice, he may have attained a good degree of manual dexterity. But the arranging of plans of business, the new combinations of mechanical processes, the discoveries and improvements in the arts, must generally come from minds more highly and systematically cultivated. There is a fertility in scientific principles of which the mere artist has no apprehension. A single general law may include a thousand or ten thousand particular cases, each one of which is as difficult to be learned or remembered as the law which explains them all. Men of mere practical detail are wanted, in considerable numbers, to fill the subordinate places in mechanical establishments; but the higher stations require enlightened and comprehensive views.

We are far from believing that theory *alone,* should be taught in college. It cannot be effectually taught, except in connection with practical illustrations. These are necessary in exciting an interest in theoretical instructions and especially important in showing the application of principles. It is our aim, therefore, while engaged in scientific investigations, to blend with them, as far as possible, practical illustrations and experiments. Of what use are all the sublime discoveries which have immortalized the names of Newton, Archimedes, and others if the principles which they have unfolded are never to be taught to those who can reduce them to practice? Why do we bestow such exalted encomiums on inventive genius if the results of original investigations are to be confined to a few scientific men and not diffused among those who are engaged in the active duties of life? To bring down the principles of science to their practical application by the laboring classes is the office of men of superior education. It is the separation of theory and practice which has brought reproach upon both. Their union alone can elevate them to their true dignity and value. The man of science is often disposed to assume an air of superiority when he looks upon the narrow and partial views of the mere artisan. The latter in return laughs at the practical blunders of the former. The defects in the education of both classes would be remedied by giving them a knowledge of scientific principles preparatory to practice.

We are aware that a thorough education is not within the reach of all. Many, for want of time and pecuniary resources, must be content with a partial course. A defective education is better than none. If a youth can afford to devote only two or three years to a scientific and professional education, it will be proper for him to make a selection of a few of the most important branches and give his attention exclusively to these. But this is an imperfection, arising from the necessity of the case. A partial course of study must inevitably give a partial education.

This, we are well convinced, is far preferable to a *superficial* education. Of all the plans of instruction which have been offered to the public, that is the most preposterous which proposes to teach almost everything in a short time. In this way, nothing is effectually taught. The pupil is hurried over the surface so rapidly that scarce a trace of his steps remains when he has finished his course. What he has learned, or thinks he has learned, is just sufficient to inflate his vanity, to expose him to public observation, and to draw on him the ridicule of men of sound judgment and science. A partial education is often expedient; a superficial one, never. Whatever a young man undertakes to learn, however little it may be, he ought to learn it so effectually that it may be of some practical use to him. If there is any way in which everything worth knowing may be taught in four years, we are free to acknowledge that we are not in possession of the secret.

But why, it is asked, should *all* the students in a college be required to tread in the *same steps?* Why should not each one be allowed to select those branches of study which are most to his taste, which are best adapted to his peculiar talents, and which are most nearly connected with his intended profession? To this we answer that our prescribed course contains those subjects only which ought to be understood, as we think, by everyone who aims at a thorough education. They are not the peculiarities of any profession or art. These are to be learned in the professional and practical schools. But the principles of science are the common foundation of all high intellectual attainments. As in our primary schools, reading, writing, and arithmetic are taught to all, however different their prospects, so in a college, all should be instructed in those branches of knowledge of which no one destined to the higher walks of life ought to be ignorant. What subject which is now studied here could be set aside without evidently marring the system. Not to speak particularly in this place of the ancient languages: who that aims at a well-proportioned and superior education will remain ignorant of the elements of the various branches of the mathematics or of history and antiquities or of rhetoric and oratory or natural philosophy or astronomy or chemistry or mineralogy or geology or political economy or mental and moral philosophy?

It is sometimes thought that a student ought not to be urged to the study of that for which he has *no taste or capacity.* But how is he to know whether he has a taste or capacity for a science before he has even entered upon its elementary truths? If he is really destitute of talent sufficient for these common departments of education, he is destined for some narrow sphere of action. But we are well persuaded that our students are not so deficient in intellectual powers as they sometimes profess to be though they are easily made to believe that they have no capacity for the study of that which they are told is almost wholly useless.

When a class have become familiar with the common elements of the several sciences, then is the proper time for them to *divide off* to their favorite studies. They can then make their choice from actual trial. This is now done here, to some extent, in our junior year. The division might be commenced at an earlier period and extended farther, provided the qualifications for admission into the college were brought to a higher standard.

If the view which we have thus far taken of the subject is correct, it will be seen that the object of the system of instruction at this college is not to give a *partial* education, consisting of a few branches only; nor, on the other hand, to give a *superficial* education, containing a smattering of almost everything; nor to *finish* the details of either a professional or practical education; but to *commence a thorough* course and to carry it as far as the time of residence here will allow. It is intended to occupy, to the best advantage, the four years immediately preceding the study of a profession, or of the operations which are peculiar to the higher mercantile, manufacturing, or agricultural establishments.

As the instruction is only preparatory to a profession, the plan upon which it is conducted is not copied from professional schools. There are important differences, arising from the different character of the two courses and the different age at which the student enters upon them. In the professional institution, it is proper that *subjects* should be studied rather than *textbooks*. At this period, the student is engaged, not in learning the mere elements of the various sciences, but in becoming thoroughly acquainted with one great department of knowledge, to the study of which several years are to be devoted. He ought to be allowed time to settle his own opinion on every important point by the slow process of comparing and balancing the various and conflicting opinions of others. A much greater proportion of *lectures* is admissible in this stage of education. The deep interest excited by a long continued pursuit in the same field of inquiry supersedes the necessity of the minute responsibility which is required in elementary studies. The age of the student and the prospect of soon entering on professional practice will commonly be sufficient to secure his assiduous application without the coercive influence of laws and penalties.

Although the restraints in a college are greater than in professional institutions, yet they are less than in common academies. In the latter, the student prosecutes his studies in the presence of his instructer. At the early age of ten or twelve, he needs more frequent assistance and encouragement, in the way of colloquial intercourse than the members of a college, who, though they are young, are not children.

QUESTIONS FOR REACTION AND DISCUSSION

1. What do the committee members regard as the central purpose of education undertaken at Yale College?
2. What does the report mean by suggesting that a college must provide a substitute for "parental superintendence"? Do you think this is a part of a college's mission today? Why or why not?

3. What do the committee members mean by saying that "the *discipline* and the *furniture* of the mind" are the components of intellectual culture?
4. What observations can you make about academic life at Yale College in 1828 for a student? For a faculty member? Using the extracts from the committee report as a departure point, discuss with your classmates what you can glean about the details of the curriculum and course of study.

QUESTIONS FOR WRITING

1. Locate the "Mission Statement" of your own college or university. Begin by consulting the official catalogue of your school. Often these statements are available on the central Web site of your school; an easy tool to find the site of any college is CollegeView <http://www.collegeview.com>, which is actually designed to help prospective students find out information about schools to which they might apply. Read your school's mission statement and, in your own words, write a summary of what the purposes of a college education are according to the statement. In an essay, compare and contrast your college's statement of purpose with what the committee of Yale College determined in 1828. How are the statements alike? How are they different?
2. A central tension within every college and university curriculum is between "liberal education" and "professional training." As the committee members at Yale College explained, they did not see the purpose of college to provide professional studies for students. Rather, their purpose was to educate students broadly in general knowledge, that is, to lay the foundation for future self-study or for professional study. They say, "The object of the undergraduate course is not to finish a preparation for business, but to impart that various and general knowledge which will improve, and elevate, and adorn any occupation." What evidence do you see of this tension within the statements of purpose and general curriculum of your own college? What is your position on this division between liberal and professional education? Determine your position and that of several other students in your class. Write a short defense of your position and organize a panel of papers for your class in which several different opinions are presented.
3. Ask a mix of professors, fellow students, and parents or older relatives about their opinion of the purpose of an undergraduate education. Record their responses and think about the similarities and differences. Does gender or age make a difference in the response you received? Level of education? Write a report for your class of your experiences in asking this question and offer an analysis of the responses you received.

QUESTIONS FOR FURTHER EXPLORATION

1. Investigate the mission statements of several colleges or universities that are similar to the one you are attending. Use your college library to locate college catalogues or, on the Internet, use CollegeView <http://www.collegeview.com> to locate college and university Web sites or <http://www.mit.edu:8001/people/cdemello/univ.html>. Follow the directions to locate the specific site and search for information about the mission statement. How are the mission statements alike? How are they different? Write a report of your research for your class.

2. Research the history of your own college and university. Why was your institution founded and by whom? What was the original purpose? Who were the original students and faculty members? How has the institution changed over time? How different is the institution today from the time when it was founded? Write an essay in which you narrate the important events in the life of your college.

2

INTENTIONS AND PERCEPTIONS: A NATIONAL SURVEY OF PUBLIC ATTITUDES TOWARD LIBERAL ARTS EDUCATION

Richard Hersh is President of Hobart and William Smith Colleges, two four-year liberal arts colleges in central New York that share a central campus. Called "coordinate colleges," Hobart College (for men) and William Smith College (for women) share the same curriculum and faculty, but maintain individual emphases in programming, activities, and athletics. Like most liberal arts colleges, Hobart and William Smith are small, residential, and highly selective in admissions requirements; and because they are private institutions, they must generally charge higher tuition and fees than state schools. Hersh, president of the colleges since 1991, is the author of a number of influential essays on higher education in both academic journals and popular magazines such as Newsweek. *The article printed here is from* Change: The Magazine of Higher Learning, *which is under the editorial leadership of the American Association for Higher Education, an organization of over 9,000 college and university faculty members and administrators. In this article, Hersh reports on his recent survey of attitudes toward liberal arts education, which shows that students and their parents are often uncertain about the value of a liberal arts education and believe a college education should be designed to prepare students for prosperous careers. At the same time, Hersh's survey reveals that business executives and managers overwhelmingly agree that students who have been educated in the liberal arts have better cognitive, presentational, and social skills; candidates who have been broadly and imaginatively educated are greatly preferred. As a result of this gap in expectations, colleges and universities face the difficult challenge of educating students about the importance of the liberal arts for their development as people and as employees.*

QUESTIONS FOR READING

1. What are the liberal arts? What is a liberal arts education? How important is it to you? Why?
2. How would you characterize the college or university you are attending? A community college? A liberal arts college? A liberal arts college within a university? On what basis did you choose the school you are attending?

RICHARD H. HERSH

INTENTIONS AND PERCEPTIONS: A NATIONAL SURVEY OF PUBLIC ATTITUDES TOWARD LIBERAL ARTS EDUCATION

Change *(March/April 1997, pp. 16–22)*

A hundred years ago, liberal arts colleges represented the leading edge of educational quality: 70 percent of college students attended such colleges. That figure is now below 5 percent. As we enter the 21st century, the perceived value of a liberal arts education is seriously questioned by prospective college students and their parents, most of whom view higher education almost exclusively as preparation for jobs.

Indeed, in a review of more than 30 public opinion surveys in the May 12, 1993, *Chronicle of Higher Education,* researchers James Harvey and John Immerwahr found a consistent public belief that higher education was a necessity for employment. Moreover, liberal arts education was generally seen as irrelevant to this purpose, as exemplified by one focus group respondent who said, "If I'm going to be an accountant, what do I care what someone did back in ancient Egypt?"

Contrary to this public view is the one promulgated by liberal arts college presidents and deans at a July 1994 roundtable discussion sponsored by the Pew Charitable Trusts. Convened in acknowledgment of the threat to the survival of liberal arts colleges, the participants concluded—not surprisingly—that the liberal arts college continues to be the gold standard for undergraduate education, one that differentiates it significantly from undergraduate education in large universities. The group affirmed in its written summary that

> It is the liberal arts college—residential, devoted to instruction in a broad curriculum of the arts and sciences, designed as a place of growth and experimentation for the young—that remains the mind's shorthand for an undergraduate education at its best.

ROOT CAUSES OF DISAFFECTION

College presidents, myself included, can easily convince ourselves of our institution's appeal and relevance, but increasing public concern about our cost and value requires that we test those assumptions. To find out more about the root causes of the growing disaffection with liberal arts colleges, I enlisted the support of the AT&T Foundation in commissioning a nationwide survey of constituents—or, in our case, "key liberal arts stakeholders." After all, if prospective students and their parents, for example, no longer desire what my college offers, I'm well advised to know why.

Daniel Yankelovich, chairman of the renowned polling firm DYG Inc., administered both the pilot study focus groups and survey instrument construction and the comprehensive national survey. Our idea was to provide baseline data for a long-term project by first investigating attitudes toward liberal arts colleges themselves as well as liberal arts programs offered within two other types of institutions—universities and specialty schools.

To do so, we needed to ask the following questions: How important is it to go to college? What are the goals of a college education? How familiar are stakeholders with liberal arts education and liberal arts colleges? What are the unique characteristics of liberal arts colleges? How do stakeholders perceive the comparative effectiveness of universities, specialty schools, and liberal arts colleges?

To understand our audience better, we grouped our stakeholders into the following five respondent groups: (1) college-bound juniors and seniors at public and private high schools; (2) parents of college-bound juniors and seniors; (3) CEOs and human resource managers; (4) high school and college faculty and administrators; and (5) recent university and liberal arts college graduates. The variations among the groups' responses reveal much about the disconnect between college intentions and public perceptions.

Below, I highlight twelve of the many findings from this survey. They reveal a continuum of perceptions across groups and a surprising conclusion about the "practicality" of a liberal arts education.

FINDING I

Few people still believe in the importance of learning for learning's sake. The priority on career education becomes clear when respondents are given the opportunity to rate the following four categories according to their levels of importance: "career skills," "personal values," "life skills," and "learning for learning's sake."

Personal values are viewed by the majority of the audiences to be moderately important. Overall, learning for learning's sake is viewed by two-fifths of respondents as least important. (See Table 1.)

TABLE 1 Overall Importance of Various Aspects of Higher Education

	PARENTS %	HIGH SCHOOL STUDENTS %	BUSINESS EXECUTIVES %	FACULTY/ ADMINISTRATORS %	RECENT GRADUATES %
Career Skills					
Most important	42	35	31	20	32
Moderately important	48	58	61	59	53
Least important	10	7	8	21	15
Personal Values					
Most important	15	7	10	10	8
Moderately important	52	61	63	66	63
Least important	33	32	27	24	29
Life Skills					
Most important	9	9	5	9	13
Moderately important	48	59	51	56	51
Least important	43	32	44	25	36
Learning for Learning's Sake					
Most important	6	6	6	18	10
Moderately important	48	59	51	56	51
Least important	46	35	43	26	39

FINDING 2

Parents and high school students have little or no idea what a liberal arts education is. Only twenty-seven percent of parents, and even fewer high school students (fourteen percent), indicate that they are very familiar with a liberal arts education. On the other hand, a majority of faculty and administrators (seventy percent) and business executives (fifty-four percent) indicate that they are very familiar with a liberal arts education. Liberal arts college graduates were, not surprisingly, the most familiar (eighty-six percent), whereas their university and specialty school peers had substantially lower familiarity (thirty-two percent). (See Table 2.)

When asked to volunteer what a liberal arts education means to them, the respondents most often cited "providing a broad introduction to a wide variety of academic disciplines/well-rounded education." But forty-four percent of high school students, along with nineteen percent of parents, were unable to give any answer at all. Only a small number indicated that a liberal arts education "teaches students how to think on their own." (See Table 3.)

TABLE 2   Familiarity with the Liberal Arts Education

	PARENTS %	HIGH SCHOOL STUDENTS %	BUSINESS EXECUTIVES %	FACULTY/ ADMINI- STRATORS %	UNIVERSITY AND SPECIALTY SCHOOL GRADS %	SMALL LIBERAL ARTS COLLEGE GRADS %
Very familiar	27	14	54	70	32	86
Somewhat familiar	46	42	40	27	45	14
Not familiar	27	44	6	3	23	0

FINDING 3

Other than faculty members and liberal arts college graduates, few groups have positive feelings toward liberal arts education. When asked to respond either "very positive," "neutral," or "very negative" to the question, "What is your overall impression of a liberal arts education today?" only a majority of faculty and administrators (fifty-nine percent) and recent liberal arts college graduates (eighty-four percent) indicated a positive overall view of the liberal arts. Approximately one-third of parents and a quarter of high school students and university graduates view the liberal arts positively. Business executives are split between very positive and neutral. (See Table 4.)

FINDING 4

Most people believe you can get a liberal arts education anywhere—it's not unique. To find out how respondents viewed liberal arts education compared to other types of higher education, we asked them to rate which of the twenty-six goals of higher education listed in Table 5 were best provided by either a liberal arts education or by any other higher education curriculum. (High school students were not asked to respond to this question.) Overall, stake-holders believe that the large majority of the goals of higher education can be achieved in any curriculum, especially writing and oral skills, professional school preparation, exposure to the business world, critical thinking, problem-solving, computer literacy, strong work habits, and time management. The only goals of higher education seen as being uniquely provided by liberal education are "developing an appreciation for culture," and "developing basic skills in the sciences, arts, humanities, and social sciences"—goals generally rated as less important by most stakeholders in this survey.

FINDING 5

On a number of measures, business executives have greater faith in the effectiveness of a liberal arts education than do parents. We asked parents and

TABLE 3 Meaning of "Liberal Arts Education" (Volunteered)

	PARENTS %	HIGH SCHOOL STUDENTS %	BUSINESS EXECUTIVES %	FACULTY/ ADMINI- STRATORS %	UNIVERSITY AND SPECIALTY SCHOOL GRADS %	LIBERAL ARTS COLLEGE GRADS %
Broad intro- duction to a wide variety of academic disciplines/well- rounded education	64	23	89	81	58	86
Exposure to different people/ cultures	11	15	9	11	17	10
Exposure to arts/literature/ culture	8	20	51	10	12	11
Helps in choice of a major	7	7	9	12	7	14
Education in general areas of life	7	5	13	13	5	13
Ability to think on one's own	2	3	11	7	6	12
Problem-solving/ critical	1	1	4	9	1	7
Don't know/ no answer	19	44	0	1	10	0

TABLE 4 Overall Impression of a Liberal Arts Education

	PARENTS %	HIGH SCHOOL STUDENTS %	BUSINESS EXECUTIVES %	FACULTY/ ADMINI- STRATORS %	UNIVERSITY AND SPECIALTY SCHOOL GRADS %	LIBERAL ARTS COLLEGE GRADS %
Very positive	34	25	49	59	26	84
Neutral	48	54	46	36	60	15
Very negative	11	14	3	3	11	1

business executives to rate the effectiveness of liberal arts colleges, universities, and specialty schools against each of the twenty-six goals of higher education listed in Table 5. Both groups feel that liberal arts colleges perform better than universities and specialty schools in the following goals:

TABLE 5   Specific Goals of Higher Education

Developing critical thinking skills	Learning foreign language skills
Developing writing, problem-solving, and oral skills	Developing self-discipline
Developing problem-solving skills	Developing one's own ideas
Developing strong work habits	Exposure to diverse ideas
Computer literacy	Learning time management
Adapting to new careers	Experiencing different cultures
Exposure to the business world	Developing a global perspective
Professional school preparation	Making lifelong connections
Teaching technical skills	Teaching business-related skills
Learning for learning's sake	Developing respect for others
Developing basic skills in the sciences, arts, etc.	Developing tolerance for others
	Developing loyalty and integrity
Developing an appreciation for culture	Developing citizenship

- ◆ Developing basic skills in the sciences, arts, etc.
- ◆ Developing respect for others
- ◆ Developing an appreciation for culture
- ◆ Developing loyalty and integrity
- ◆ Learning for learning's sake
- ◆ Developing citizenship
- ◆ Learning foreign language skills
- ◆ Developing tolerance for others

However, parents believe universities perform better on the following goals, while business executives favor liberal arts colleges:

- ◆ Making lifelong connections
- ◆ Developing self-discipline
- ◆ Exposure to diverse ideas
- ◆ Developing a global perspective
- ◆ Learning to live on one's own

With regard to all the other goals, no single type of school dominated the performance ratings.

FINDING 6

Students and parents overwhelmingly believe the reason to go to college is to prepare for a prosperous career—but fewer than forty percent of business executives agree. The large majority of high school students (eighty-five percent) and parents (seventy-five percent) indicate that college is important because it "prepares students to get a better job and/or increases their earning potential."

Table 6 Why It's Important for a Student to Go to College (Volunteered)

	Parents %	High School Students %	Business Executives %	Faculty/ Admini- strators %	University and Specialty School Grads %	Liberal Arts College Grads %
Qualify for better jobs/help increase earning potential/prepare for career	75	85	37	60	59	38
Better lifestyle/ succeed in life	19	29	10	14	13	7
To get an education	17	36	9	6	6	18
Prepare for future	13	10	26	19	8	16
Helps to mature/ become a better person	5	5	16	11	5	13

Faculty and administrators and university graduates also offer "preparing for a career" as the reason to go to college a majority of the time (sixty percent). But only thirty-seven percent of business executives and thirty-eight percent of recent liberal arts college graduates agree. (See Table 6.)

Finding 7

When pushed, most people agree that problem-solving, critical thinking, and writing and oral skills—abilities traditionally imparted by a liberal arts education—are, in fact, career skills and are the most important goals of higher education. Using the twenty-six goals of higher education in Table 5, respondents were asked to rate each on a scale of 1 ("not at all important") to 10 ("very important").

Given the earlier high priority accorded to "career skills," it is interesting to note the common agreement across all stakeholders on the list of most highly rated (eighty percent or better) goals: problem-solving, critical thinking, and writing and oral skills, along with strong work habits, self-discipline, and a respect for others. Liberal arts educators have traditionally embraced these goals as central to a liberal education. The large majority of parents and business executives also view such goals as "exposure to the business world" (seventy-four percent) and "teaching business-related skills" (sixty-eight percent) as very important, whereas faculty and administrators are more likely than others to view "developing basic skills in the sciences, arts, etc." (seventy-three percent), and "developing an appreciation for culture" (seventy percent) as very important.

FINDING 8

Liberal arts colleges should teach skills for the workplace. "More internships," "more emphasis on oral and written communication skills," "greater emphasis on strong work habits," "better development of independent and critical thinking skills," and "offering seminars on how the business world operates" top the list of improvements parents and business executives rate most highly. To a lesser, but nonetheless strong, degree, the other stakeholders agree. "Encouraging tolerance of racial, ethnic, and lifestyle differences," "raising awareness of the need for public service," and "giving more attention to the development of character" are also rated highly by most stakeholders. (See Table 7.)

FINDING 9

No college or university is performing well, say parents and business executives, but small liberal arts colleges excel in certain areas: culture/arts appreciation and foreign language teaching. Parents and business executives generally feel no type of institution is doing as well as it should in fulfilling the goals of higher education. The main exception to this general rating of underperformance across institutions is small liberal arts colleges, which are seen as doing very well in "developing an appreciation for the arts and culture" and "learning foreign language skills." Additionally, business executives feel that small liberal arts colleges do very well on "developing one's own ideals," "exposure to diverse ideas," "making lifelong connections," and "experiencing different cultures." Universities and specialty schools are seen as doing relatively well on "teaching technical skills," "professional school preparation," and "teaching business-related skills."

FINDING 10

More than one-third of parents consider liberal arts education a luxury beyond their reach. Higher education overall is viewed as too expensive by six in ten parents and half of all high school students (fifty-two percent). Moreover, another nineteen percent of parents and twenty-four percent of high school students, along with more than thirty percent in each of the other stakeholder groups, believe the issue of "too expensive" is true only at liberal arts colleges. Additionally, four in ten parents feel that "an education is not a good value for

TABLE 7 **Suggested Improvements to Liberal Arts Curriculum**

	PARENTS %	HIGH SCHOOL STUDENTS %	BUSINESS EXECUTIVES %	FACULTY/ ADMINI- STRATORS %	RECENT GRAD- UATES %
Offer more internships and work-study programs	80	72	87	67	74
More emphasis on oral and written communication skills	79	56	92	85	73
Greater emphasis on self-discipline, time management, and strong work habits	74	71	84	59	63
Better development of independent and critical thinking skills	74	66	84	81	75
Offer more seminars and courses on how the business world operates	72	55	79	46	48
Encourage tolerance of racial, ethnic, and lifestyle differences	71	76	74	72	70
Raise student awareness of the need for public service	70	68	67	69	52
Greater emphasis on cooperative work habits and team problem-solving skills	68	58	82	62	60
More training for specific careers	66	69	68	35	46
More attention to developing character issues	66	75	70	60	55
Higher grading and graduation requirements	46	46	67	48	43
Develop proficiency in a foreign language and encourage study abroad	38	42	45	47	47

the money," with twenty-one percent saying that is true solely at small liberal arts schools. A third of parents agree that "a liberal arts education is a luxury most people cannot afford."

FINDING 11

Belief in the importance of a college education is significantly lower among college and high school faculty and administrators than in society at large. Approximately nine in ten parents (eighty-seven percent), high school students (ninety-two percent), and recent college graduates (eighty-five percent) say that it is very important that a student continue his/her education after high school. Most business executives (seventy-nine percent) agree. But only sixty-two percent of college and high school faculty and administrators share this belief, often declaring in focus groups that "many students are neither socially nor academically prepared for college work."

FINDING 12

Most people believe students at all types of institutions party too much. Liberal arts colleges are criticized along with other institutions for too much partying. A majority of parents (sixty-two percent), high school students (sixty-one percent), business executives (fifty-seven percent), and faculty and administrators (fifty-six percent) agreed that there is an "overindulgence in partying and having a good time" in all three types of institutions. Seventy percent of recent college students agree.

ANALYSIS: SOLVING THE "PRACTICALITY GAP"

The "market" for higher education is growing and will continue to grow for some time to come. Higher education, college and beyond, is seen as the way, indeed, the only way up—the key to financial security and sustained success. New social attitudes about economic uncertainty, the realities of job markets, and demographic imperatives will keep higher education a hot market.

Within that boom market, however, small liberal arts colleges face significant challenges. The findings of this survey suggest that the liberal arts are neither understood well nor held in high esteem by a critical segment of society. Parents and college-bound high school students have very little familiarity with the meaning or purpose of liberal education. An overwhelming majority of parents (seventy-five percent) and college-bound students (eighty-five percent) believe that the ultimate goal of college is to get a practical education and secure a first job.

Choosing an appropriate college or university is a serious and pragmatic decision for families. Financial considerations, preconceptions about colleges and universities, and their perceptions of what employers want often point families in the direction of sure-ticket schools that bestow prestige and, by implication, sure employment. One parent stated plainly, "We live in an environment that can destroy you if you are not practical." The smart choice, they say, is a professional program tailored to specific jobs in business, computer technology, engineering, law, or medicine.

But only about thirty-seven percent of business leaders agree with this belief. CEOs say they value the *long-term* outcomes of a college education—those that prepare one not only for a first job, but for a long and variable career. Employers (represented in our study by CEOs and human resource managers) presumably are every bit as "practical" as parents. But to them, practicality means the ability of higher education to produce people of strong character with generalized intellectual and social skills and a capacity for lifelong learning.

CEOs and human resource managers in our study told us they are looking for three clusters of skills: cognitive, presentational, and social.

Cognitive skills include problem-solving, critical thinking, and "learning to learn." Special emphasis is given to moving up new learning curves rapidly in response to new challenges. This, employers say, requires the ability to see things in a new light and make sense of ideas in old and new contexts, the kind of intellectual agility and enthusiasm they perceive to be found in the traditional notion of a "liberal arts education."

Presentational skills include the ability to write and speak clearly, persuasively, and coherently about oneself, ideas, and data. The ability to communicate—to make sense of and present clearly what appears to others as information chaos across many disciplines—is crucial, say business leaders, if one is to advance in a career.

Social skills include the ability to work cooperatively with others in a variety of settings. Intercultural understanding, the ability to work with people regardless of race, gender, age, and so on, is also crucial. International experience and foreign language facility are considered very desirable.

These are the "well-rounded" *and* "practical" skills business executives want, and they perceive a liberal arts education potentially to be excellent "practical" preparation. Parents, however, reject what they perceive to be "charming" Ivory-Tower liberal arts colleges (and their counterparts within large universities) that profess to turn out "well-rounded" graduates. Hence, an apparent "practicality gap" and a major challenge to liberal education everywhere.

Significantly, the following current developments in the workplace and social trends discerned from a decade of survey research (DYG SCAN, a trend identification program, has tracked since 1986 emerging public and opinion leader attitudes on many values and issues directly relevant to the question of the status of the liberal arts) favor the employers' notion of what makes for a "practical" college education.

A more sober economic outlook. After three decades of a strong "psychology of affluence"—the assumption that America's wealth is unlimited and that economic opportunity is assured—the American public since the mid-1980s has moved steadily toward a psychology of economic limits. Tracking data since 1986 show a precipitous rise in pessimism about our economic future. Central to the new sober outlook is the belief that "it's really rough out there," that

- opportunity is in question,
- well-paying jobs are in short supply, and
- young people will not be able to live or do as well as their parents.

Nowhere is this mentality more evident than among upscale, better-educated managers and professionals and among young adults and teens who see their future as a struggle for economic survival. Down-sizing, right-sizing, and reengineering have put the fear of unemployment—for oneself *and* one's children—in the hearts of the middle and upper classes.

A more practical, non-ideological approach to financial decisions and life choices for ourselves and our children.   Pragmatism and rationality have gained a firm grip on America's psyche. Driven by the new, more sober economic thinking, Americans are applying cost-benefit analysis to all decisions and focusing on the bottom line, examining all expenditures in terms of "What do I get?" and "What's the payoff?" People are doing their homework—seeking information to help them make smart, practical choices. The emphasis is on pursuing what "works," not necessarily what's right or good. The attitude prevails that nothing is more vital than work; launching our children into well-paying jobs is viewed as a necessity.

The nature of the future workplace.   Business is growing more international, more competitive, and more susceptible to technology-driven change. In such a climate, rigid specialists limited to one specific skill are quickly left behind. Graduates must be capable of independent thought, creativity, risk-taking, perseverance, and entrepreneurship, as well as be open to new ideas and willing to express an unpopular point of view. They must be comfortable with different cultures and possess foreign language aptitude.

A preoccupation with value.   Not only are parents and students focused on employment as a goal—part of a response to the last decade's obsession with getting tangible value for every nickel spent—but employers, too, are preoccupied with value. They see college education as a necessary and valuable long-term investment that enhances one's creativity, communication skills, values, and ethics—all attributes for a lifetime.

The pursuit of quality-of-life goals.   Simultaneously, Americans are running away from material expressions of success toward a definition that emphasizes achievement of a better quality of life—less stress; better health; a safe, clean living environment; and the appreciation of art and culture. The notion of a "well-rounded" person may be making a comeback. Interestingly, this is an outcome most parents and employers in our survey identified as a *unique purpose of a liberal arts education.*

Movement away from a focus on self.   The sharp focus on self that has fed hedonism, moral relativity, and overpersonalization is beginning to blur.

Concern for community, more attention to spiritual life, a greater focus on concepts of right and wrong, a search for meaning in life, and a hunger for idealism are all on the rise. These are all identified by parents, students, and employers as *outcomes most associated with the liberal arts.*

CHANGES NEEDED

These trends affirm the importance of the cognitive, presentational, and social skills perceived by business executives to be most important. The unique nature, purpose, and character of liberal arts education, however, are not well defined for most stakeholders in our survey. The survey also substantiates what others have found—a great deal more dissatisfaction with higher education in general than those of us in the profession would like to admit.

Amid the confusion and dissatisfaction, however, there is a potential convergence of views among key stakeholders. All agree on the importance of higher education for the future and on the main goals of a college education. But when thinking of higher education, Americans seem to be operating in a narrow framework of "vocation" versus "learning for learning's sake," an understandable but false dichotomy. The goals traditionally espoused by small liberal arts colleges are seen positively but are not seen as unique to them. Moreover, the chance to learn about business, thought to be necessary by parents and CEOs for tomorrow's world, is perceived to be absent in liberal arts colleges.

To help remedy this situation, changes need to take place in both communications and in the "product." Small liberal arts colleges need to communicate better to their key audiences what the "liberal arts" they offer mean in today's and tomorrow's world and provide evidence that they do offer important skills for the world of work. They need to demonstrate that small liberal arts colleges are "places of value" where intellectual prowess, articulate communication, passion for ideas, engagement with others, the creation of meaning, security in the face of cultural, class, and social differences, and joy in new challenges are learned best with caring and dedicated teachers.

Liberal arts colleges have begun to make these changes. Many place increasing emphasis on business internships, international education, higher writing and speaking standards, and computer literacy—emphases that are no longer seen as mere accessories to a liberal education but as an integral part of an education for the future. Colleges understand as well that it is not business alone that drives the need for change; graduate schools, nonprofit agencies, and state and federal governments are all searching for people who are passionate of spirit, independent yet team players, less preoccupied with their own self-expressiveness, and more capable of coping with a complex world.

The important goals of higher education are shared by stakeholders in our survey. Where and how best to attain such goals is still unsettled in public opinion. Value is often seen to reside in the large, professionally oriented university. How best might liberal arts colleges respond? Eva Brann, dean of St. John's College in Annapolis, suggests in the Fall 1995 *Liberal Education* that

> good education requires devoted, personal teaching, fine subject matter, and supportive communities of learning. This teachers' wisdom is what small independent liberal arts colleges live by, and it is confirmed in the lives of our alumni.

It is now the task of the liberal arts college to demonstrate for stakeholders the assertions of its leaders.

QUESTIONS FOR REACTION AND DISCUSSION

1. Why did Hersh initially undertake this survey? What can you learn about the AT&T Foundation? Why would they wish to underwrite such a survey?
2. Describe and explain the nature of the survey that Hersh undertook. How was the survey structured? What were the central questions? What does he mean by "key liberal arts stakeholders"?
3. Examine Tables 1 and 2 with your classmates. What information can you learn from looking just at the tables?
4. As the president of a small liberal arts college, Hersh is deeply concerned with the results of a survey that suggests the enduring value of a liberal arts education. How does he explain and describe his own position?
5. What are the reactions of your classmates to the findings of this survey? How do your own responses match those of your peers?

QUESTIONS FOR WRITING

1. One of Hersh's key findings is that parents and high school students have little idea of what a liberal arts education is. Why do you think that is true? What did you know about a liberal arts education when you were a high school student thinking about pursuing a college degree? What do you think high school students should know about a liberal arts education *before* they begin to choose a college? Write an essay directed to high school students in which you offer some advice on what to know about a liberal arts education as you choose a college.
2. Examine the "Specific Goals of a Higher Education" listed in Table 5. Discuss these goals with the members of your class or with a small group within your class. Rate each goal as the survey respondents did, using a scale of 1 (not at all important) to a 10 (very important).

What do your classmates view as the most important goals? The least important goals? Have these goals changed since you and your class-mates began to attend college? Write an essay in which you discuss the responses of you and your classmates to the goals and explain the rationale for why some goals are more important than others to you and your group.

3. One of the surprising findings of this survey is what Hersh calls a "practicality" gap between the outcome of a college education that parents and students want—getting a practical education and a job—and the position of business leaders—they want to hire people of "strong character with generalized intellectual and social skills and a capacity for lifelong learning." Look closely at Table 6 and notice the difference in responses. How do you account for the different responses among business executives, parents, and high school stu-dents? Write an essay in which you describe the gap the survey out-lines and persuade a high school student to reconsider his or her position.

4. Hersh explains that business leaders responding to the survey noted three "clusters" of skills that they look for in potential employees. How is your own educational environment contributing to the devel-opment of those skills? What courses or experiences can you under-take at your college or university to ensure that you can graduate with these skills? Write an essay in which you describe how you intend to pursue these clusters of skills.

QUESTIONS FOR FURTHER EXPLORATION

1. Hersh's survey is discussed in the context of the experience of several recent liberal arts graduates in an article, "Life's Ups and Downs" by Dana Cooke in the *Pulteney Street Survey,* the magazine of Hobart and William Smith Colleges. Access this article, <http://www.hws.edu/ NEW/pss/careers.html>, and read about the career experiences of the former students Cooke interviews. Interview older friends and rela-tives who are college graduates and ask them about their career paths. Ask how they got the job they now hold and if they trained for such a position in college. Did a liberal arts education help them or hinder them? Write an article along the lines of "Life's Ups and Downs" in which you provide your own examples from the people you interviewed.

2. As the president of a small liberal arts college, Hersh is particularly concerned with ensuring that parents and potential students under-stand the value of a liberal arts education. One problem that Hersh sees is that liberal arts colleges and perhaps other kinds of institutions as well do not do a sufficiently good job of communicating the

importance of the liberal arts. Check the Web sites or college catalogues of several institutions in your area or in your home state and evaluate how well these institutions communicate the *value* of the education they provide. Use your college library to locate college catalogues or on the Internet, use CollegeView <http://www.collegeview.com> to locate college and university Web sites or <http://www.mit.edu:8001/people/cdemello/univ.html>. How hard is it to find this information? Is such information even available? What does the design of the Web site for the college or university communicate? What are the similarities and differences among schools? How do you think schools might do a more effective job of articulating the value of their programs? Write a report for your classmates on your findings.

3. *Change,* the magazine where this article appeared, is sponsored by the American Association for Higher Education. Visit their Web site <http://www.aahe.org> and prepare a report for your class about the mission, membership, and activities of this organization.

3

Is There Any Knowledge That Men and Women Must Have?

Wayne Booth, an emeritus Professor of English at the University of Chicago, is the author of over a dozen books about literary criticism, literary research, teaching language and literature, and most recently, a book on his lifelong enjoyment of playing the cello and the joys of amateur pursuits, For the Love of It: Amateuring and Its Rivals *(1999). This essay, and the one immediately following, were originally prepared as speeches and both were revised as essays to appear in Booth's books on teaching. The first, "Is There Any Knowledge That a Man Must Have?" is from a collection of essays,* The Knowledge Most Worth Having *(1967), and the second, "Is There Any Knowledge That a Woman Must Have?" was then published as an essay in his collection,* The Vocation of a Teacher *(1988). Booth updated his first essay as a result of complaints that he received, mostly from women. Although, as he has said, he wrote his original essay without thinking to exclude women, his language is clearly masculine in orientation. In commenting on his original essay and in the revisions he made to it for the second version, he said, "Once I reread the essay carefully, however, I discovered, with some shock, that the women had been right to complain. Though I had been thinking of both men and women as I wrote, I had simply failed to consider how my language would strike female readers, consciously or unconsciously, or how it might encourage males to see themselves as the real center of all thought about education. My excuse now is only that I wrote before the feminist critique of language had gotten well underway, and that I was an author who badly needed that critique." In both essays, Booth outlines what* knowledge *he thinks men and women need to possess beyond the basic information needed for functioning in the world.*

QUESTIONS FOR READING

1. These essays were originally delivered as speeches, and the second was
   specifically written for undergraduates. How does a speech differ from
   a written essay? What signals or markers are there in this essay that
   let you know it was originally a speech? Does it make the text harder
   or easier to read and understand? How do you think the audiences
   responded?
2. What does it mean to avoid gender-specific language? How does the
   use of male nouns and pronouns in the first essay affect you as you
   read? How do Booth's explanations for his revision of the essay affect
   you as a reader?
3. Do you think that there is a body of knowledge that is necessary to be
   "fully human" as Booth suggests in these essays? Why or why not?

WAYNE C. BOOTH

IS THERE ANY KNOWLEDGE THAT
A MAN *MUST* HAVE?

The Knowledge Most Worth Having (Chicago: University of Chicago Press, 1967)

Everyone lives on the assumption that a great deal of knowledge is not worth
bothering about; though we all know that what looks trivial in one man's
hands may turn out to be earth-shaking in another's, we simply cannot know
very much, compared with what might be known, and we must therefore
choose. What is shocking is not the act of choice which we all commit openly
but the claim that some choices are wrong. Especially shocking is the claim implied by my title: There is some knowledge that a man *must* have.

There clearly is no such thing, if by knowledge we mean mere acquain-
tance with this or that thing, fact, concept, literary work, or scientific law.
When C. P. Snow and F. R. Leavis exchanged blows on whether knowledge of
Shakespeare is more important than knowledge of the second law of thermodynamics, they were both, it seemed to me, much too ready to assume as indispensable what a great many wise and good men have quite obviously got
along without. And it is not only nonprofessionals who can survive in happy
ignorance of this or that bit of lore. I suspect that many successful scientists (in
biology, say) have lost whatever hold they might once have had on the second
law; I know that a great many literary scholars survive and even flourish without knowing certain "indispensable" classics. We all get along without vast

loads of learning that other men take as necessary marks of an educated man. If we once begin to "reason the need" we will find, like Lear, that "our basest beggars/Are in the poorest thing superfluous." Indeed, we can survive, in a manner of speaking, even in the modern world, with little more than the bare literacy necessary to tell the "off" buttons from the "on."

Herbert Spencer would remind us at this point that we are interpreting need as if it were entirely a question of private survival. Though he talks about what a man must know to stay alive, he is more interested, in his defense of science, in what a *society* must know to survive: "Is there any knowledge that *man* must have?"—not a man; but *man*. This question is put to us much more acutely in our time than it was in Spencer's, and it is by no means as easy to argue now as it was then that the knowledge needed for man's survival is scientific knowledge. The threats of atomic annihilation, of engulfing population growth, of depleted air, water, and food must obviously be met, if man is to survive, and in meeting them man will, it is true, need more and more scientific knowledge; but it is not at all clear that more and more scientific knowledge will by itself suffice. Even so, a modern Herbert Spencer might well argue that a conference like this one, with its emphasis on the individual and his cognitive needs, is simply repeating the mistakes of the classical tradition. The knowledge most worth having would be, from his point of view, that of how to pull mankind through the next century or so without absolute self-destruction. The precise proportions of different kinds of knowledge—physical, biological, political, ethical, psychological, historical, or whatever—would be different from those prescribed in Spencer's essay, but the nature of the search would be precisely the same.

We can admit the relevance of this emphasis on social utility and at the same time argue that our business here is with other matters entirely. If the only knowledge a man *must* have is how to cross the street without getting knocked down—or, in other words, how to navigate the centuries without blowing himself up—then we may as well close the conference and go home. We may as well also roll up the college and mail it to a research institute because almost any place that is not cluttered up with notions of liberal education will be able to discover and transmit practical bits of survival-lore better than we can. Our problem of survival is a rather different one, thrust at us as soon as we change our title slightly once again to "Is there any knowledge (other than the knowledge for survival) that a man must have?" That slight shift opens a new perspective on the problem because the question of what it is to be a man, of what it is to be fully human, is the question at the heart of liberal education.

To be human, to be human, to be fully human. What does it mean? What is required? Immediately, we start feeling nervous again. Is the speaker suggesting that some of us are not fully human *yet?* Here come those hierarchies again. Surely in our pluralistic society we can admit an unlimited number of legitimate ways to be a man, without prescribing some outmoded aristocratic code!

Who—or what—is the creature we would educate? Our answer will determine our answers to educational questions, and it is therefore, I think, worth far more vigorous effort than it usually receives. I find it convenient, and only slightly unfair, to classify the educational talk I encounter these days under four notions of man, three of them metaphorical, only one literal. Though nobody's position, I suppose, fits my types neatly, some educators talk as if they were programming machines, some talk as if they were conditioning rats, some talk as if they were training ants to take a position in the anthill, and some—precious few—talk as if they thought of themselves as men dealing with men.

One traditional division of the human soul, you will remember, was into three parts: the vegetable, the animal, and the rational. Nobody, so far as I know, has devised an educational program treating students as vegetables, though one runs into the analogy used negatively in academic sermons from time to time. Similarly, no one ever really says that men are ants, though there is a marvelous passage in Kwame Nkrumah's autobiography in which he meditates longingly on the order and pure functionality of an anthill. Educators do talk of men as machines or as animals, but of course they always point out that men are much more complicated than any other known animals or machines. My point here is not so much to attack any one of these metaphors—dangerous as I think they are—but to describe briefly what answers to our question each of them might suggest.

Ever since Descartes, La Mettrie, and others explicitly called a man a machine, the metaphor has been a dominant one in educational thinking. Some have thought of man as a very complex machine, needing very elaborate programming; others have thought of him as a very simple machine, requiring little more than a systematic pattern of stimuli to produce foretellable responses. I heard a psychologist recently repeat the old behaviorist claim (first made by John B. Watson, I believe) that if you would give him complete control over any normal child's life from birth, he could turn that child into a great musician or a great mathematician or a great poet—you name it and he could produce it. On being pressed, the professor admitted that this claim was only "in theory," because we don't yet have the necessary knowledge. When I pushed further by asking why he was so confident in advance of experimental proof, it became clear that his faith in the fundamental metaphor of man as a programmable machine was unshakable.

When the notion of man as machine was first advanced, the machine was a very simple collection of pulleys and billiard balls and levers. Such original simplicities have been badly battered by our growing awareness both of how complex real machines can be and of how much more complex man is than any known machine. Modern notions of stimulus-response patterns are immeasurably more complicated than anything Descartes imagined, because we are now aware of the fantastic variety of stimuli that the man-machine is subject to and of the even more fantastic complexity of the responding circuits.

But whether the machine is simple or complex, the educational task for those who think of man under this metaphor is to program the mechanism so that it will produce the results that we have foreordained. We do not simply fill the little pitchers, like Mr. Gradgrind in Dickens' *Hard Times*; we are much too sophisticated to want only undigested "pour-back," as he might have called his product. But we still program the information channels so that the proper if-loops and do-loops will be followed and the right feedback produced. The "programming" can be done by human teachers, of course, and not only by machines; but it is not surprising that those whose thinking is dominated by this metaphor tend to discover that machines are better teachers than men. The more ambitious programmers do not hesitate to claim that they can teach both thought and creativity in this way. But I have yet to see a program that can deal effectively with any subject that cannot be reduced to simple yes and no answers, that is, to answers that are known in advance by the programmer and can thus be fixed for all time.

We can assume that subtler machines will be invented that can engage in simulated dialogue with the pupil, and perhaps even recognize when a particularly bright pupil has discovered something new that refutes the program. But even the subtlest teaching machine imaginable will still be subject, one must assume, to a final limitation: it can teach only what a machine can "learn." For those who believe that man is literally nothing but a very complicated machine, this is not in fact a limitation; machines will ultimately be able to duplicate all mental processes, thus "learning" everything learnable, and they will be able in consequence to teach everything.

I doubt this claim for many reasons, and I am glad to find the testimony of Norbert Wiener, the first and best known cyberneticist, to the effect that there will always remain a radical gap between computers and the human mind. But "ultimately" is a long way off, and I am not so much concerned with whether ultimately man's mind will closely resemble some ultimately inventable machine as I am with the effects, here and now, of thinking about men under the analogy with machines of today. Let me simply close this section with an illustration of how the mechanistic model can permeate our thought in destructive ways. Ask yourselves what picture of creature-to-be-educated emerges from this professor of teacher education:

> To implement the TEAM Project new curriculum proposal . . . our first concerns are with instructional systems, materials to feed the system, and personnel to operate the system. We have defined an instructional system as the optimal bleeding of the demands of content, communication, and learning. While numerous models have been developed, our simplified model of an instructional system would look like Figure 2. . . . We look at the process of communication—communicating content to produce learning—as something involving the senses: . . . [aural, oral, tactile, visual]. And I think in teacher education we had better think of the communications aspect of the instructional system as a package that includes the teacher, textbook, new media, classroom, and environment. To integrate these elements to more effectively transmit content into permanent learning, new and better instructional materials are needed and a new focus on the teacher of teachers is required. The teacher of teachers must: (1) examine critically the content of traditional

courses in relation to desired behavioral outcomes; (2) become more sophisticated in the techniques of communicating course content; and (3) learn to work in concert with media specialists to develop the materials and procedures requisite to the efficient instructional system. And if the media specialist were to be charged with the efficient operation of the system, his upgrading would demand a broad-based "media generalist" orientation.

I submit that the author of this passage was thinking of human beings as stimulus-response systems on the simplest possible model, and that he was thinking of the purpose of education as the transfer of information from one machine to another. Though he would certainly deny it if we asked him, he has come to think about the human mind so habitually in the mechanistic mode that he doesn't even know he's doing it.[1]

But it is time to move from the machine metaphor to animal metaphors. They are closely related, of course, because everybody who believes that man is a machine also believes that animals are machines, only simpler ones. But many people who would resist the word "ma-chine" do tend to analogize man to one or another characteristic of animals. Since man is obviously an animal in one sense, he can be studied as an animal, and he can be taught as an animal is taught. Most of the fundamental research in learning theory underlying the use of teaching machines has been done, in fact, on animals like rats and pigeons. You can teach pigeons to play Ping-Pong rather quickly by rewarding every gesture they make that moves them toward success in the game and refusing to reward those gestures that you want to efface. Though everybody admits that human beings are more complicated than rats and pigeons, just as everyone admits that human beings are more complicated than computers, the basic picture of the animal as a collection of drives or instincts, "conditioned" to learn according to rewards or punishments, has underlain much modern educational theory.

The notion of the human being as a collection of drives different from animal drives only in being more complex carries with it implications for education planners. If you and I are motivated only by sex or hunger or more complex drives like desire for power or for ego-satisfaction, then of course all education depends on the provision of satisfactions along our route to knowledge. If our teachers can just program carrots along the path at the proper distance, we donkey-headed students will plod along the path from carrot to carrot and end up as educated men.

I cannot take time here to deal with this view adequately, but it seems to me that it is highly questionable even about animals themselves. What kind of thing, really, is a rat or a monkey? The question of whether animals have souls has been debated actively for at least nine centuries; now psychologists find themselves dealing with the same question under another guise: What *are* these little creatures that we kill so blithely for the sake of knowledge? What *are* these strangely resistant little bundles of energy that will prefer—as experiments with rats have shown—a complicated interesting maze without food to a dull one *with* food?

There are, in fact, many experiments by now showing that at the very least we must postulate, for animals, a strong independent drive for mastery of the environment or satisfaction of curiosity about it. All the more advanced animals will learn to push levers that produce interesting results—clicks or bells or flashing lights or sliding panels—when no other reward is offered. It seems clear that even to be a fulfilled animal, as it were, something more than "animal satisfaction" is needed!

I am reminded here of the experiments on mother-love in monkeys reported by Harry F. Harlow in the *Scientific American* some years ago. Harlow called his article "Love in Infant Monkeys," and the subtitle of this article read, "Affection in infants was long thought to be generated by the satisfactions of feeding. Studies of young rhesus monkeys now indicate that love derives mainly from close bodily contact." The experiment consisted of giving infant monkeys a choice between a plain wire figure that offered the infant milk and a terry-cloth covered figure without milk. There was a pathetic picture of an infant clinging to the terry-cloth figure, and a caption that read "The infants spent most of their time clinging to the soft cloth 'mother' even when nursing bottles were attached to the wire mother." The article concluded— rather prematurely, I thought—that "contact comfort" had been shown to be a "prime requisite in the formation of an infant's love for its mother," that the act of nursing had been shown to be unimportant if not totally irrelevant in forming such love (though it was evident to any reader, even at the time, that no genuine "*act* of nursing" had figured in the experiment at all), and that "our investigations have established a secure experimental approach to this realm of dramatic and subtle emotional relationships." The only real problem, Harlow said, was the availability of enough infant monkeys for experiment.

Now I would not want to underrate the importance of Harlow's demonstration to the scientific community that monkeys do not live by bread alone. But I think that most scientists and humanists reading the article would have been struck by two things. The first is the automatic assumption that the way to study a subject like love is to break it down into its component parts; nobody looking at that little monkey clinging to the terry-cloth could possibly have said, "This is love," unless he had been blinded by a hidden conviction that love in animals is—must be— a mere cumulative result of a collection of drive satisfactions. This assumption is given quite plainly in Harlow's concluding sentence: "Finally with such techniques established, there appears to be no reason why we cannot at some future time investigate the fundamental neurophysiological and biochemical variables underlying affection and love." For Harlow monkeys (and people) seem to be mere collections of neurophysiological and biochemical variables, and love will be best explained when we can explain the genesis of each of its parts. The second striking point is that for Harlow animals do not matter, except as they are useful for experiment. If he had felt that they mattered, he might have noticed the look on his infant's face—a look that predicted for me, and for other readers of the *Scientific American* I've talked with, that these monkeys were doomed.

And indeed they were. A year or so later another article appeared, reporting Harlow's astonished discovery that all of the little monkeys on which he had earlier experimented had turned out to be incurably psychotic. Not a single monkey could mate, not a single monkey could play, not a single monkey could in fact become anything more than the twisted half-creatures that Harlow's deprivations had made of them. Harlow's new discovery was that monkeys needed close association with their peers during infancy and that such association was even more important to their development than genuine mothering. There was no sign that Harlow had learned any fundamental lessons from his earlier gross mistakes; he had landed nicely on his feet, still convinced that the way to study love is to break it down into its component parts and that the way to study animals is to maim them or reduce them to something less than themselves. As Robert White says, summarizing his reasons for rejecting similar methods in studying human infancy, it is too often assumed that the scientific way is to analyze behavior until one can find a small enough unit to allow for detailed research, but in the process "very vital common properties" are lost from view.

I cite Harlow's two reports not, of course, to attack animal experimentation—though I must confess that I am horrified by much that goes on in its name—nor to claim that animals are more like human beings than they are. Rather, I want simply to suggest that the danger of thinking of men as animals is heightened if the animals we think of are reduced to machines on a simple model.

The effects of reducing education to conditioning can be seen throughout America today. Usually they appear in subtle forms disguised with the language of personalism; you will look a long time before you find anyone (except a very few Skinnerians) saying that he thinks of education as exactly like conditioning pigeons. But there are plenty of honest, blunt folk around to let the cat out of the bag—like the author of an article this year in *College Composition and Communications*: "The Use of a Multiple Response Device in the Teaching of Remedial English." The author claimed to have evidence that if you give each student four buttons to be pushed on multiple-choice questions, with all the buttons wired into a lighted grid at the front of the room, the resulting "instantaneous feedback"—every child learning immediately whether he agrees with the rest of the class—speeds up the learning of grammatical rules considerably over the usual workbook procedures. I daresay it does—but meanwhile what has happened to education? Or take the author of an article on "Procedures and Techniques of Teaching," who wrote as follows: "If we expect students to learn skills, they have to practice, but practice doesn't make perfect. Practice works if the learner *learns the results* of his practice, i.e., if he receives feedback. Feedback is most effective when it is contiguous to the response being learned. One of the chief advantages of teaching machines is that the learner finds out quickly whether his response is right or wrong . . . [Pressey] has published the results of an extensive program of research with tests that students score for themselves by punching alternatives until they hit the correct one . . . [Thus] teaching machines or workbooks have many theoretical advantages over lecturing or other conventional methods of instruction." But according to what theory, one must ask, do systematic feedback mechanisms, perfected to whatever degree, have "theoretical advantages" over human contact? Whatever else can be said for such a theory, it will be based on the simplest of comparisons with animal learning. Unfortunately, the author goes on, experimental evidence is on the whole rather discouraging: "Experiments at the Systems Development Corporation . . . suggest that teaching incorporating . . . human characteristics is more effective than the typical fixed-sequence machines. (In this experiment instead of using teaching machines to simulate human teachers, the experimenters used humans to simulate teaching machines.)"

So far I have dealt with analogies for man that apply only to individuals. My third analogy turns to the picture of men in groups, and it is given to me partly by discussions of education, like those of Admiral Rickover, that see it simply as filling society's needs. I know of only one prominent educator who has publicly praised the anthill as a model for the kind of society a university should serve—a society of specialists each trained to do his part. But the notion pervades many of the defenses of the emerging multiversities.

If knowledge is needed to enable men to function as units in society, and if the health of society is taken as the purpose of their existence, then there is nothing wrong in training the ants to fill their niches; it would be wrong not to. "Education is our first line of defense—make it strong," so reads the title of the first chapter of Admiral Rickover's book, *Education and Freedom* (New York: Dutton, 1959). "We must upgrade our schools" in order to "guarantee the future prosperity and freedom of the Republic." You can tell whether the ant-analogy is dominating a man's thinking by a simple test of how he orders his ends and means. In Admiral Rickover's statement, the schools must be upgraded in order to guarantee future prosperity; that is, we improve education for the sake of some presumed social good.

I seldom find anyone putting it the other way round: we must guarantee prosperity so that we can improve the schools, and the reason we want to improve the schools is that we want to insure the development of certain kinds of persons, both as teachers and as students. You cannot even say what I just said so long as you are really thinking of ants and anthills. Ants are not ends in themselves, ultimately more valuable than the hills they live in (I *think* they are not; maybe to themselves, or in the eyes of God, even ants are ultimate, self-justifying ends). At least from our point of view, ants are expendable, or to put it another way, their society is more beautiful, more interesting, more admirable than they are. And I would want to argue that too many people think of human beings in the same way when they think of educating them. The Communists make this quite explicit: the ends of Communist society justify whatever distortion or destruction of individual purposes is necessary to achieve them; men are educated for the state, not for their own well-being. They are basically political animals, not in the Aristotelian sense that they require society if they are to achieve their full natures and thus their own special, human kind of happiness, but in the sense that they exist, like ants, for the sake of the body politic.

If the social order is the final justification of what we do in education, then a certain attitude toward teaching and research will result: all of us little workmen, down inside the anthill, will go on happily contributing our tiny bit to the total scheme without worrying much about larger questions of the why and wherefore. I know a graduate student who says that she sometimes sees her graduate professors as an army of tiny industrious miners at the bottom of a vast mine, chipping away at the edges and shipping their bits of knowledge up to the surface, blindly hoping that someone up there will know what to do with it all. An order is received for such-and-such new organic compounds; society needs them. Another order is received for an atomic bomb; it is needed, and it is therefore produced. Often no orders come down, but the chipping goes on anyway, and the shipments are made, because everyone knows that the health of the mine depends on a certain tonnage of specialized knowledge each working day.

We have learned lately that "they" are going to establish a great new atom-smasher, perhaps near Chicago. The atom-smasher will employ two thousand scientists and technicians. I look out at you here, knowing that some of you are physics majors, and I wonder whether any of you will ultimately be employed in that new installation, and if you are, whether it will be an ant or as a human being. Which it will be must depend not on your ultimate employers but on yourself and on what happens to your education between now and then: if you have been given nothing but training to be that ultimate unit in that ultimate system, only a miracle can save you from formic dissolution of your human lineaments.

But it is long past time for me to turn from these negative, truncated portraits of what man really is not and attempt to say what he is. And here we encounter a difficulty that I find very curious. You will note that each of these metaphors has reduced man to something less than man, or at least to a partial aspect of man. It is easy to say that man is not a machine, though he is in some limited respects organized like a machine and even to some degree "programmable." It is also easy to say that man is not simply a complicated rat or monkey, though he is in some ways like rats and monkeys. Nor is man an ant, though he lives and must function in a complicated social milieu. All these metaphors break down not because they are flatly false but because they *are* metaphors, and any metaphorical definition is inevitably misleading. The ones I have been dealing with are especially misleading because in every case they have reduced something more complex to something much less complex. But even if we were to analogize man to something more complex, say, the universe, we would be dissatisfied. What we want is some notion of what man really *is,* so that we will know what or whom we are trying to educate.

And here it is that we discover something very important about man, something that even the least religious person must find himself mystified by:

man is the one "thing" we know that is completely resistant to our efforts at metaphor or analogy or image-making. What seems to be the most important literal characteristic of man is his resistance to definitions in terms of anything else. If you call me a machine, even a very complicated machine, I know that you deny what I care most about, my selfhood, my sense of being a person, my consciousness, my conviction of freedom and dignity, my awareness of love, my laughter. Machines have none of these things, and even if we were generous to their prospects, and imagined machines immeasurably superior to the most complicated ones now in existence, we would still feel an infinite gap between them and what we know to be a basic truth about ourselves: machines are expendable, ultimately expendable, and men are mysteriously ends in themselves.

I hear people deny this, but when they do they always argue for their position by claiming marvelous feats of super-machine calculation that machines can now do or will someday be able to do. But that is not the point; of course machines can outcalculate us. The question to ask is entirely a different one: Will they ever outlove us, outlive us, outvalue us? Do we build machines because machines are good things in themselves? Do we nurture them for their own good, as we nurture our children? An obvious way to test our sense of worth in men and machines is to ask ourselves whether we would ever campaign to liberate the poor downtrodden machines who have been enslaved. Shall we form a National Association for the Advancement of Machinery? Will anyone ever feel a smidgeon of moral indignation because this or that piece of machinery is not given equal rights before the law? Or put it another way: Does anyone value Gemini more than the twins? There may be men now alive who would rather "destruct," as we say, the pilot than the experimental rocket, but most of us still believe that the human being in the space ship is more important than the space ship.

When college students protest the so-called depersonalization of education, what they mean, finally, is not simply that they want to meet their professors socially or that they want small classes or that they do not want to be dealt with by IBM machines. All these things are but symptoms of a deeper sense of a violation of their literal reality as persons, ends in themselves rather than mere expendable things. Similarly, the current deep-spirited revolt against racial and economic injustice seems to me best explained as a sudden assertion that people, of whatever color or class, are not reducible to social conveniences. When you organize your labor force or your educational system as if men were mere social conveniences, "human resources," as we say, contributors to the gross national product, you violate something that we all know, in a form of knowledge much deeper than our knowledge of the times tables or the second law of thermodynamics: those field hands, those children crowded into the deadening classroom, those men laboring without dignity in the city anthills are *men*, creatures whose worth is mysteriously more than any description of it we might make in justifying what we do to them.

Ants, rats, and machines can all learn a great deal. Taken together they "know" a very great part of what our schools and colleges are now designed to teach. But is there any kind of knowledge that a creature must have to qualify as a man? Is there any part of the educational task that is demanded of us by virtue of our claim to educate this curious entity, this *person* that cannot be reduced to mechanism or animality alone?

You will not be surprised, by now, to have me sound, in my answer, terribly traditional, not to say square: the education that a *man* must have is what has traditionally been called liberal education. The knowledge it yields is the knowledge or capacity or power of how to act free as a man. That's why we call liberal education liberal: it is intended to liberate from whatever it is that makes animals act like animals and machines act like machines.

I'll return in a moment to what it means to act freely as a man. But we are already in a position to say something about what knowledge a man must have—he must first of all be able to learn for himself. If he cannot learn for himself, he is enslaved by his teachers' ideas, or by the ideas of his more persuasive contemporaries, or by machines programmed by other men. He may have what we call a good formal education, yet still be totally bound by whatever opinions happen to have come his way in attractive garb. One wonders how many of our graduates have learned how to take hold of a subject and "work it up," so that they can make themselves experts on what other men have concluded. In some ways this is not a very demanding goal, and it is certainly not very exciting. It says nothing about the popular concept creativity, or about imagination or originality. All it says is that anyone who knows how to learn for himself is less like animals and machines than anyone who does not know how to learn for himself.

We see already that a college is not being merely capricious or arbitrary when it insists that some kinds of learning are more important than some others. The world is overflowing with interesting subjects and valuable skills, but surely any college worth the name will put first things first: it will try to insure, as one inescapable goal, that every graduate can dig out from the printed page what he needs to know. And it will not let the desire to tamp in additional tidbits of knowledge, however delicious, interfere with training minds for whom a formal teacher is no longer required.

To put our first goal in this way raises some real problems that we cannot solve. Obviously, no college can produce self-learners in very many subjects. Are we not lucky if a graduate can learn for himself even in one field, now that knowledge in all areas has advanced as far as it has? Surely we cannot expect our graduates to reach a stage of independence in mathematics and physics, in political science and psychology, in philosophy and English, *and* in all the other nice subjects that one would like to master.

Rather than answer this objection right away, let me make things even more difficult by saying that it is not enough to learn how to learn. The man who cannot *think* for himself, going beyond what other men have learned or thought, is still enslaved to other men's ideas. Obviously the goal of learning to think is even more difficult than the goal of learning to learn. But difficult as it is we must add it to our list. It is simply not enough to be able to get up a subject on one's own, like a good encyclopedia employee, even though any college would take pride if all its graduates could do so. To be fully human means in part to think one's own thoughts, to reach a point at which, whether one's ideas are different from or similar to other men's, they are truly one's own.

The art of asking oneself critical questions that lead either to new answers or to genuine revitalizing of old answers, the art of making thought live anew in each new generation, may not be entirely amenable to instruction. But it is a necessary art nonetheless, for any man who wants to be free. It is an art that all philosophers have tried to pursue, and many of them have given direct guidance in how to pursue it. Needless to say, it is an art the pursuit of which is never fully completed. No one thinks for himself very much of the time or in very many subjects. Yet the habitual effort to ask the right critical questions and to apply rigorous tests to our hunches is a clearer mark than any other of an educated man.

But again we stumble upon the question, "Learn to think about *what?*" The modern world presents us with innumerable subjects to think about. Does it matter whether anyone achieves this rare and difficult point in more than one subject? And if not, won't the best education simply be the one that brings a man into mastery of a narrow specialty as soon as possible so that he can learn to think for himself as soon as possible? Even at best most of us are enslaved to opinions provided for us by experts in *most* fields. So far, it might be argued, I still have not shown that there is any kind of knowledge that a man must have, only that there are certain skills that he must be able to exercise in at least one field.

To provide a proper grounding for my answer to that objection would require far more time than I have left, and I'm not at all sure that I could do so even with all the time in the world. The question of whether it is possible to maintain a human stance toward any more than a tiny fraction of modern knowledge is not clearly answerable at this stage in our history. It will be answered, if at all, only when men have learned how to store and retrieve all "machinable" knowledge, freeing themselves for distinctively human tasks. But in the meantime, I find myself unable to surrender, as it were, three distinct kinds of knowledge that seem to me indispensable to being human.

To be a man, a man must first know something about his own nature and his place in Nature, with a capital N—something about the truth of things, as men used to say in the old-fashioned days before the word "truth" was banned from academia. Machines are not curious, so far as I can judge: animals are, but presumably they never go, in their philosophies, even at the furthest, beyond a kind of solipsistic existentialism. But in science, in philosophy (ancient and modern), in theology in psychology and anthropology, and in literature (of some kinds), we are presented with accounts of our universe and of our place in it that as men we can respond to in only one manly way: by thinking about them, by speculating and testing our speculations.

We know before we start that our thought is doomed to incompleteness and error and downright chanciness. Even the most rigorously scientific view will be changed, we know, within a decade, or perhaps even by tomorrow. But to refuse the effort to understand is to resign from the human race; the unexamined life can no doubt be worth living in other respects—after all, it is no mean thing to be a vegetable, an oak tree, an elephant, or a lion. But a man, a man will want to see, in this speculative domain, beyond his next dinner.

By putting it in this way, I think we can avoid the claim that to be a man I must have studied any one field—philosophy, science, theology. But to be a man, I *must speculate,* and I must learn how to test my speculations so that they are not simply capricious, unchecked by other men's speculations. A college education, surely, should throw every student into a regular torrent of speculation, and it should school him to recognize the different standards of validation proper to different kinds of claims to truth. You cannot distinguish a man who in this respect is educated from other men by whether or not he believes in God, or in UFOs. But you can tell an educated man by the way he takes hold of the question of whether God exists, or whether UFOs are from Mars. Do you know your own reasons for your beliefs, or do you absorb your beliefs from whatever happens to be in your environment, like plankton taking in nourishment?

Second, the man who has not learned how to make the great human achievements in the arts his own, who does not know what it means to *earn* a great novel or symphony or painting for himself, is enslaved either to caprice or to other men's testimony or to a life of ugliness. You will notice that as I turn thus to "beauty"—another old-fashioned term—I do not say that a man must know how to prove what is beautiful or how to discourse on aesthetics. Such speculative activities are pleasant and worthwhile in themselves, but they belong in my first domain. Here we are asking that a man be educated to the experience of beauty; speculation about it can then follow. My point is simply that a man is less than a man if he cannot respond to the art made by his fellow man.

Again I have tried to put the standard in a way that allows for the impossibility of any one man's achieving independent responses in very many arts. Some would argue that education should insure some minimal human competence in all of the arts, or at least in music, painting, and literature. I suppose I would be satisfied if all of our graduates had been "hooked" by at least one art, hooked so deeply that they could never get free. As in the domain of speculation, we could say that the more types of distinctively human activity a man can master, the better, but we are today talking about floors, not ceilings, and I shall simply rest content with saying that to be a man, a man must know artistic beauty, in some form, and know it in the way that beauty can be known. (The distinction between natural and man-made beauty might give me trouble if you pushed me on it here, but let me just say, dogmatically, that I would not be satisfied simply to know natural beauty—women and sunsets, say—as a substitute for art.)

Finally, the man who has not learned anything about how to understand his own intentions and to make them effective in the world, who has not, through experience and books, learned something about what is possible and what impossible, what desirable and what undesirable, will be enslaved by the political and social intentions of other men, benign or malign. The domain of practical wisdom is at least as complex and troublesome as the other two, and at the same time it is even more self-evidently indispensable. How should a man live? How should a society be run? What direction should a university take in 1966? For that matter what should be the proportion, in a good university, of inquiry into truth, beauty, and "goodness"? What kind of knowledge of self or of society is pertinent to living the life proper to a man? In short, the very question of this conference falls within his final domain: What knowledge, if any, is most worthy of pursuit? You cannot distinguish the men from the boys according to any one set of conclusions, but you can recognize a man, in this domain, simply by discovering whether he can think for himself about practical questions, with some degree of freedom from blind psychological or political or economic compulsions. Ernest Hemingway tells somewhere of a man who had "moved one dollar's width to the [political] right for every dollar that he'd ever earned." Perhaps no man ever achieves the opposite extreme, complete freedom in his choices from irrelevant compulsions. But all of us who believe in education believe that it is possible for any man, through study and conscientious thought, to school his choices—that is, to free them through coming to understand the forces working on them.

Even from this brief discussion of the three domains, I think we are put in a position to see how it can be said that there is some knowledge that a man must have. The line I have been pursuing will not lead to a list of great books, or even to a list of indispensable departments in a university. Nor will it lead, in any clear-cut fashion, to a pattern of requirements in each of the divisions. Truth, beauty, and goodness (or "right choice") are relevant to study in every division within the university; the humanities, for example, have no corner on beauty or imagination or art, and the sciences have no corner on speculative truth. What is more, a man can be ignorant even of Shakespeare, Aristotle, Beethoven, and Einstein, and be a man for a' that—*if* he has learned how to think his own thoughts, experience beauty for himself, and choose his own actions.

It is not the business of a college to determine or limit what a man will know; if it tries to, he will properly resent its impositions, perhaps immediately, perhaps ten years later when the imposed information is outmoded. But I think that it *is* the business of a college to help teach a man how to use his mind for himself, in at least the three directions I have suggested . . . To think for oneself is, as we all know, hard enough. To design a program and assemble faculty to assist rather than hinder students in their efforts to think for themselves is even harder. But in an age that is oppressed by huge accumulations of unassimilated knowledge, the task of discovering what it means to educate a man is perhaps more important than ever before.

WAYNE C. BOOTH

IS THERE ANY KNOWLEDGE THAT
A WOMAN MUST HAVE?

The Vocation of a Teacher (Chicago: University of Chicago Press, 1988)

About thirteen years ago, our College ran a Liberal Arts Conference, so-called. Incredible as it may seem to you, the College Council voted to suspend classes for two or three days, to allow for about a dozen big public lectures and scores of panels and discussion groups packed into a very tight schedule, centering on the topic "The Knowledge Most Worth Having." We were initially warned—those of us who thought the conference a good idea—that U. of C. undergraduates could not be tempted to attend so many weird and dubiously profitable events, and as the conference approached we found ourselves almost in panic, as delegations of concerned students arrived to warn that vast hordes of students were not even aware of the conference yet, let alone planning to attend. Several of us then went from dormitory to dormitory talking it up, gadflying about the questions the conference would deal with. We plastered the campus with enough advertising to carry the Chrysler Corporation through a bad year.

This is not the place to describe all that happened. But I must confess that the happiest moment I can remember as dean of the College was when I arrived at Breasted Hall to give the opening statement and introduce the first major speaker, fearing that "nobody would come," and found so many people that we had to walk over to Mandel and filled it! The whole College, it seemed, had gathered to listen and think about what we're thinking about here today—the goals of liberal education.

As some of you know, I later revised and expanded my brief statement that opened the conference to make the opening essay in a little book that came out of the conference. I called the essay, "Is There any Knowledge that a Man *Must* Have?" The piece ended up in the *Norton Anthology of Expository Prose*, and I began to get letters about it. At first the letters were friendly, but as the sixties turned into the seventies, there was a flood of letters (well, there *were* three) from women who were angered or shocked by what they took to be the male chauvinism not only in the title but in my use of "man" for humankind, and not only in the title but throughout the essay. I answered those letters as well as I could, on the assumption that obviously I was not guilty as charged. But I didn't get around to rereading the essay until last week, when I sat down to prepare this talk.

What I found rather shocked *me*. The essay *is* male-chauvinist, at least to some degree. It is not only male-centered in the sense that the author is clearly a male seeing the world through masculine eyes. It is chauvinist also in the sense of failing to think about how its language would strike *female* readers, consciously or unconsciously. I ask you to remember, as a kind of self-defense, that it was written before the feminist critique of language and literature had got well under way. It was written by a man who had all his life attended and taught at co-educational schools. He thought of himself as considerably more enlightened on the subject of women than most men. He had contracted formally, when he married at the age of twenty-five, to be responsible for 50 percent of the housework and child-rearing—and that was in 1946, mind you! What's more, he believed, or said he believed, in equal careers for women and men. Needless to say, however, he had not lived up to the contract: the fifty percent had shrunk, as the children came along and his professional commitments came to seem more and more important to him, to forty, then thirty, then perhaps twenty, with only brief bursts of one-hundred percent at times of illness, pregnancy, or uncharacteristic self-reproach. And of course the "equal careers" had quickly been thrown off balance, leaving Phyllis's "half" to wait, as we put it, until the children were in school.

Well, that flaming liberal, that youngish dean, talking about liberal education for all people, not only let himself ring a chime of scores of "man"s and "men"s where words like "people" or "students" or "human beings" would have done as well, he let himself write a passage like this:

> The distinction between natural and man-made beauty might give me trouble if you pushed me on it here, but let me just say, dogmatically, that I would not be satisfied simply to know natural beauty—women and sunsets, say—as a substitute for art.

Now of course I did not mean even to hint at the notion that women, unlike men, are merely natural objects designed to serve as ornaments for a man's world. I can remember defending myself to one protesting woman by saying that my point was about people, and that it could just as well have been made about women admiring male beauty. But does the point really go as well the other way round?

Let's try it: "A woman should not be satisfied simply to know natural beauty—men and sunsets, say—as a substitute for art." It seems obvious that no woman would ever have thought of putting it that way, unless she were trying to make a dishonest buck writing for *Playgirl* or trying to make an ironic point about men. Yet that way seemed to me an acceptable way to write and talk.

Most of that essay, I'm glad to say, translates fairly easily when we switch sexes. In fact, I thought for a wild moment last week that I would try the experiment of simply delivering the same talk, with proper changes of nouns and pronouns, cleaned up like this:

> Second, the woman who has not learned how to make the great human achievements in the arts her own, who does not know what it means to earn a great novel or symphony or painting for herself, is enslaved either to caprice or to other women's testimony or to a life of ugliness. You will notice that as I turn thus to "beauty"—another old-fashioned term—I do not say that a woman must know how to prove what is beautiful. . . . Here we are asking that a woman be educated to the experience of beauty: speculation about it can then follow. My point is simply that a woman is less than a woman if she cannot respond to the art made by her fellow women.

Something's wrong, there. "By her fellows"? Not too good. "By other women?" That loses the force of community sought in that word "fellow."

Thus I discovered that I could not make an effective verbal translation. But even if I had been able to, the essay would still trouble me. I simply cannot stretch it, try as I will, to cover the ideas that occur when we ask the simple question that obviously never occurred to me at the time: "Is There Any Knowledge That a *Woman* Must Have?" Or, to read it with the intonation that the original title was supposed to have, "Is There Any Knowledge That a Woman *Must* Have?" If there is, we may decide that men will want it, too.

I'm going to dwell on that question for a while today, but I should hasten to make clear, first, that I am not taking a stand on the much-debated question of whether women are essentially different from men. My hunch is that, except for the anatomical consequences of the ancient dictum "Know Thyself," there is no essential difference in what men and women must know to be liberally educated—that is, there would be no essential difference if men and women found themselves in essentially similar circumstances in the world. But we all know that men and women do not find themselves in essentially similar circumstances. In our society, every woman's circumstances—her "surrounding positions," to translate that tired old word—are largely constructed by men, men who, even after some decades of consciousness-raising, have seldom even tried to imagine what treating women as equals might entail. We might, of course, try to imagine a utopian world in which those circumstances no longer existed, a world like Plato's imaginary one, in which men and women were treated exactly alike from birth and therefore experienced no different educational needs. But we do not live in that world, and our thinking about liberal education, an education that would in fact liberate, ought to have some connection with the world we all live in—from birth, through graduation, to death.

Women in our society need, then, to learn something that men don't need in quite the same way: how to cope with men, men who think of women largely in reductive metaphors labeled "woman" or "chick" or "broad" or "better half." One way of coping is, of course, to take on protective camouflage, to learn to think and act like a male. Some of you may be fearing that I shall now try to tell women what they need, instead of sitting back as I should and letting women tell *me* what they want. Well, like every other male academic, I do have some ideas about what women need, and I shall no doubt offer some of them before I'm through. But I hope that I'm a bit more sensitive to the ravages of egoism than I once was, and I'm more interested today in what a male can teach himself about liberal education, using the simple device of asking a simple question: What were you led to overlook because you failed to think about the special needs and problems of women in a male-dominated world?

So I'm going to dwell on the shortcomings of that original essay for a while, salvaging briefly what seems to me still valid in it, from the perspective of one whose eyes are slowly opening. Then I'll go on to add a bit about what it conspicuously ignores. We shall find, I'm sorry to say, that what it ignores runs far deeper than the simple failure to sprinkle in a few "she"s or "her"s.

II

My speculation about education, like almost everybody else's, began with a critique of other people's wrong ideas. The first two-thirds of the essay dismissed a passel of wrong-headed notions, starting with the widespread claim that we can't really *think* together about why some kinds of knowledge or pursuit of knowledge are superior to other kinds. With a passing shot at the conception of knowledge as mere information, I then gave a perfunctory refutation of the chief rival to my enterprise—the view that education should be controlled by social utility. In what seems to me now a misleading dichotomy between social utility and personal fulfillment, I took pot shots at a couple of easy targets, in order to leave the field clear for the question that really interested me then, and that still interests me now: "To be human, to be human, to be fully human. What does it mean? What is required? . . . Who—or what—is the creature we would educate?"

After six pages, I come at last to a section that I can still read without embarrassment. It classifies educational theories under four notions of human nature, three of them metaphorical, only one of them literal. Human beings, I argue, are not likely to be educated well if educators think of their charges as merely complicated machines, or rats, or ants. People are really people. I would now put my rejection of the three destructive metaphors differently, because I have discovered since then just how difficult it is to criticize a metaphorical view cogently enough to make those who hold it sit up and take notice. It seems obvious to me now that the few pages I devote to each metaphor work better as rhetoric addressed to the preconverted than as rhetoric addressed to those who *think with* one or the other of the three metaphors. But it still seems to me true that genuine education, whether for men or women, is threatened by those who think of themselves as programming complex machines, by those who think of themselves as conditioning complicated animals, and by those who think of themselves as training units for an ant-like social utility.

So it is mainly the last third of the essay that leaves me squirming, the constructive third, the third that offers the knowledge that every . . . woman must have. What it offers to you women is the overwhelmingly original doctrine that to achieve your full status as human beings, you oughta just take good courses that teach you first how to think about what is true, second how to respond to what is beautiful, and third how to choose what is good.

Now obviously I'm not going to quarrel with such bromides today: they say nothing downright false. When I think, for example, of the education I would have wanted for my two daughters, I do not find myself having to discard anything that I said about what every man, meaning every man and woman, should have. I would still want to stress as strongly as I ever did the need for steady and sustained attention to the three domains I described: the speculative, the aesthetic, and the practical; or if you prefer, the domains of science and philosophy, of art, and of politics and ethics. I would feel about my daughters, as strongly as about my son, that they would be maimed in life—not just life in our time but life in any time of human history—if their natural curiosity about the truth of things were allowed to wither, or if they had no regular loving experience of the beautiful—that is, of those things in the world that are lovable for their own sake, without utilitarian qualification (and I would hope, incidentally, that they would not confine their appreciation to natural beauty—"men, say, or sunsets"). And I would hope to see them steadily growing in what Aristotle calls "practical wisdom"—able to make their way through the moral tangles of modern life with some sense of the difficulties, the excitement, and the sense of well-being ("happiness," "eudaimonia") to be derived from carving out a character for oneself, a character that can in turn to some degree master the choices life presents rather than being mastered by them.

But you see how general such talk is, and it was not much more precise in the developed speech. Instead of trying to cover the whole range once more, for the rest of my time today I'd like to concentrate on those matters that the young half-chauvinist either left undeveloped or didn't even mention. And instead of trying to think about the education every woman needs, in every age or clime, let's try to think about the education every woman needs in the 1980s.

To do that would seem to require us to describe what the world is like in 1980. If we are to educate ourselves to live in the eighties, we ought to know what the eighties are. But nobody knows for sure how to describe a given period, present or past, let alone what the future will bring. Every seemingly literal description I might offer you would be at best a part of the whole, and thus not really a literal picture at all but a reduction: a selection of parts that I would ask you to accept as the whole. In short, even the most literal picture would be metaphorical, in the sense of the word that includes that good old term *metonymy*: the part standing for the whole. And, thus, in choosing how to describe our times, we are already engaged in the task of criticizing metaphors, selecting those that somehow do least violation to the actual richness of our lives.

Some people, searching for an accurate picture of the condition of women in our time, might attempt a hard social survey on income or expenditure, or purchasing power, or expressed goals. We might ask NORC [National Opinion Research Center] to do a poll, a vast questionnaire duplicating the coverage of the census. My sampling technique is slightly less scientific in appearance, though perhaps no less reliable in the long run.

I just happen to have with me this afternoon a beautifully edited little treatise on the nature and condition of women in our time. This glossy 250-page vade mecum to the good life, the good life for both women *and* men, was purchased by more than five million people last month, including me. Like Aristotle, the editors knew that all men, all *men,* I say, desire happiness, and all men pursue the good. So what they offer us, us *men,* is an unremitting picture of what the goods are in life that will produce happiness.

Look at the cover with me for a moment. This treatise on the good life is called *Penthouse: The International Magazine for Men.* Five million of us men bought copies of it last month, no doubt because many of us half believed that happiness could be found if we just had a "penthouse." A penthouse—that is, by implication, a place with unlimited and totally irresponsible sex can be had three times nightly, and twice as often on Sundays—a penthouse, we infer from this cover, is a place where it is okay to bind, and strip, and presumably whip certain anonymous females, whose eyes are mercifully shaded from us. Along with the photo of the writhing lady that we see here on the cover, we are offered an article entitled "Women Who Flirt with Pain"—that is, obviously, women who like to have us international-minded men, us cosmopolites, inflict pain on them.

Women who flirt with pain! Wow! We American males buy that, in more ways than one. We buy this version of happiness in a penthouse, at three dollars a throw, and we turn eagerly to the section on the pain women flirt with. Saving for later the "Free 31-inch by 21-inch Pet Poster Inside," saving the article on teenage sexuality, saving the "Forum" of fantasies fulfilled, we hurry to the series of paintings by Pater Sato, with the heading "Sato-Masochism: A Japanese master illustrator [Sato] . . . evokes the electricity of desire in women flirting with pain." Each painting shows ecstatic women either suffering or inflicting that marvelous electric shock they are supposed to enjoy whenever pain comes their way. And the paintings are accompanied with selections of poetry, so-called, all by males, of course, poetry that reads like this:

> Hurt me with kisses, kill me with desire
> Consume me and destroy me with the fire
> of blasting passion

That's Aleister Crowley. Or—
> My passion excites the tormentor.

That's Baudelaire. Or—

> I have placed you
> In the hollow of my hand
> Little toy-woman,
> And I gaze at you disdainfully.

That's by somebody named Joseph King. Or—

> No stirrup, no saddle.
> Just a touch of my boot, and you're off.

That's from a poem called "To my mouse twin" by Tristan Corbière.

The best metaphor for happiness, then, is a toy-woman who wants you to hurt her. Right? With a sense that my education in women is moving along nicely, I turn next to a sequence of photos of a lovely, gamboling, naked young woman called Tamara. Here the quotations claim to be from Tamara herself, though they were very likely written by flunkies in *Penthouse's* editorial offices. "I like to take unsuspecting men by storm—like a friendly cyclone!" Tamara says, as she runs through the jungle in what the caption calls "savage splendor." Tamara is described, as some of you will, I'm sure, remember, as "The Pet of the Month"—to be replaced, in her mindlessness, by another pet of next month and another of the month after that. I can't bring myself to read aloud—not from prudery but from sheer impatience—many of the inane words that *Penthouse* puts into her mouth, a mouth that, so far as one can tell, is always breathlessly open. But I give you two of *Penthouse's* visions of bliss, free for nothing: "Becoming a *Penthouse* Pet, claims our jubilant jungle lady, is 'a marvelous high—it appeals to my natural cockiness!'" Get it? She admits that her power over men has always been considerable. "'They tend to fall harder than I do,' she says. 'Even if a man stalks me [note that metaphor!] and claims me [*claims* me!] for the night . . . there's no guarantee I'll be there when he wakes the next morning. I'm very young and very restless, and I'm not ready to settle for one kind of man or one kind of life.'" And Tamara goes on—that is, they go on for her: "'I think I radiate a certain kind of animal appeal that makes a lot of dialogue unnecessary . . . I would love to see myself on the giant screen. It would be similar . . . to appearing here in *Penthouse*—knowing that thousands and thousands of otherwise indifferent men would be sharing one common passion: Me!'" And she concludes: "'I hate to say it, but when it comes to getting my attention, nice guys finish last!'"

Well, like, man! I turn fifty-nine this week, and I confess that all my life that's exactly the kind of woman I've been looking for, a *real* woman who is *all* woman. None of this nonsense about having to *talk* with her, none of this nonsense about having to be *nice*. The un-nicer I get, the more she'll like it. The less chatter I get from her empty (and for the most part almost invisible) face, the better. Sheer mindless passion is what I have always longed for and somehow have never been able to find. Where do they *find* these wonderful creatures who will guarantee that when I wake next morning they won't be around to interfere with my life? Clearly there are thousands and thousands of these creatures *somewhere,* eager to be screwed without being nailed. They are so eager, indeed, and loving, that they somehow are forced, *Penthouse* implies, to spend their whole time masturbating. Here they are, page after page, so desperate for a one-night stand that they have either to masturbate, or, for want of a male, to make love with other women.

I spare you most of the details of a long photo sequence called "The Art of Loving," featuring two women flopping about in wet paint and ending up in position sixty-nine, but I must share one bit of immortally poetic prose: "Breasts and buttocks splashed with rainbows of color [rainbows of what? color? Know any other rainbows?], voluptuous loins warmly massaged with sensuous brushstrokes. . . . 'You're a work of art,' breathed the sorceress to her swooning apprentice. 'Please excuse my free-form lust!'"

So now we men know what happiness is. Or at least we know something about it. It is inflicting pain and degradation on mindless and faceless animals who *want* nothing but pain and degradation. In a penthouse, don't forget. And—to make a long summary of the rest of the magazine short—wearing denim. "For the man who doesn't try too hard. He doesn't have to. Things come easy for the man who wears denim." Or perhaps he is sprayed by Chaz, "the fragrance that's almost as interesting as the men who wear it," or English Leather, because "all men wear English Leather . . . or they wear nothing at all"; drinking Ballantine's, "the oldest and most expensive scotch in the world"; smoking Winston cigarettes, for men "whose taste has grown up," or Camels, which offer satisfaction, since "some men taste it all"; listening to Panasonic stereo, which offers "for your eyes: sleek, sophisticated lines, a contemporary look, and a dazzling display of fluorescent meters and light emitting diodes," and for your ears, an "incredibly smooth, clean power"; all the while driving a new rotary-engine RX-7 Mazda, the "seductive sedan."

Well, that's perhaps more than enough time spent on that kind of thing. My point is not to tell you women how to read *Penthouse*; most of you know how to reject such trash by virtue of being who you are. The point is that you are surrounded by men who read *Penthouse* and its kind, men like me whose fantasies about the ideal life are fed by such tripe. Five million copies in one month!—for only one of the scores of magazines selling the metaphor of happiness-as-the-quick-lay, the instantly gratified desire, the totally irresponsible pursuit of you and your sisters as machines of gratification, candy machines that ideally should cost nothing and that at most should cost somewhere between the world's most expensive scotch and the world's best stereo. Go inquire, I dare you, at your university bookstore as to how many copies of *Penthouse* they sold last month, as compared with copies of any novel you love that shows women as human beings. The best novel I have read this month is *Plains Song: for Female Voices,* by Wright Morris. It is a loving hymn to three lonely women who suffer much from their uncomprehending menfolk. If Wright Morris is lucky, he may be read by ten thousand readers, a majority of them women—even though critics have called *Plains Song* "the perfect novel," and good old Dick Cavett has interviewed Morris about it on TV.

You are surrounded, I am saying, by men whose education about who you are is partly conducted by the sort of thing I have read to you. What kind of education might help you cope with that?

I'm afraid I don't find much in my earlier essay to help you. It describes what you need in a general way, when it says that all of us need to learn how to read critically, how to distinguish between the beautiful and the ugly, and how to make practical choices in the world. Sure. But *what* choices—and how do you learn how to make them, except by making all the bad ones and then suffering the consequences, perhaps fatal?

My essay gave scant help in how to choose models for one's self, in how to protect one's *self* from seductive models or metaphors that are offered by those who pretend to be friends but who are really exploiters; and it did not even mention how to combat the basic threats to the self that come from a given social or political order. Aristotle once said that you can't become a fully good man (read "woman") in a corrupt state. But Wayne Booth did not even mention the possibility of a corrupt society that might threaten anyone's effort to achieve freedom in each of his three lovely domains.

In short, I ignored the arts of self-defense, what today we shall think of as the womanly arts of self-defense. Self-defense can be a misleading concept, if we think of it as simply preserving selves that are already complete and whole. But if we think of the metaphor as suggesting our need both to build a self and to protect it from all of the social acids that might dissolve it, we may get somewhere.

I am suggesting that I did not think in these terms then because I was in fact thinking more about males than about females. And I suspect that it is thinking about women's special needs now that leads me into this talk of defensive stances. One need not read very far in feminist literature to see that as soon as women start thinking about themselves in our society, they start thinking defensively, and then quite naturally they start thinking of aggressive strategies that might fight off the forces that too often destroy them. I won't debate today the question of whether women are in fact more vulnerable to self-annihilation than men. A good case could be made, on another occasion, for the claim that more women achieve full selfhood in our society, or achieve it earlier in their lives, than men. In fact, if I am right, it is the special failure of men to grow up that constitutes the main threat to women. But for now we are thinking of women, and doing so leads us to think of their special vulnerability to exploitation and loss of selfhood, and we are looking for ways to help diminish that vulnerability.

I have in mind four neglected liberal arts that every woman must, in our society, master if she is not to end up less than herself. They are, of course, arts that every man ought to master too—now that we've thought about them they become just as important for men as for women. Please relax: they are not the quadrivium, though they will be practiced best by those who master those traditional arts too.

The first one has long since occurred to many feminists here. But on the whole it has been practiced very badly. It is the art of strategy, the art of planning a political or military campaign in such a way as to win. In preparing a talk recently for the PERL program [Politics, Economics, Rhetoric, and Law], I noticed a peculiar omission in the disciplines that PERL covers. The PERL program claims, as you may know, to educate people liberally while preparing them for practical affairs in government or business. When we devised that program, we tried to think of the arts or disciplines that are indispensable to the practical man or woman who intends to engage in what are sometimes called "public affairs." We thought of law, obviously indispensable. We thought of political science and of economics, almost as obvious. We thought of ethics and history and sociology and anthropology—and ruled them all out, sometimes for good reasons, sometimes just because we couldn't get anybody who teaches these subjects to take an interest in our program. We even thought of rhetoric, sometimes considered as merely the art of winning with words, but considered by us to be the whole art of thinking and communicating with various human languages. What we did not think of was one that was automatically included in many ancient programs designed to train citizens: strategy—how to outsmart your opponent and ensure victory. So far as I know, it never even occurred to any of us, though we can be sure that in some law courses and in some political science courses it has been taught under other names. I suppose if we *had* thought of it we would have rejected it, on the grounds that strategy connotes military strategy, and we would have shrunk from having PERL identified with the Vietnam War, or indeed with any war. So far as I know, there has never been a required course in strategy in this or any other nonmilitary college in this century, and the result has been, I suspect, that whenever American citizens spot an enemy, foreign or domestic, they tend to conduct their strategy very badly. Believing, as I long believed, that the very notion of trying to outsmart somebody was wicked, we find ourselves, when the occasion to fight occurs, falling back on a very simple repertory of devices, which depends on whatever is fashionable. If sit-ins are in, we sit in. If strikes have been tried with some success, we strike again. If hiring an advertising firm to change our image is what people are doing, we compete for the advertising firm that charges most. But what we don't do is study strategy.

This is not the time to relate all of the ineffective strategies that have been used by feminists in their efforts to combat male chauvinism. Nor can I claim to know many better strategies that might have had more chances of success. But it takes no very subtle analysis to see that American women have on the whole not fought the feminist wars very successfully. If ERA is not passed, we shall all of course blame the arch-conservatives for the defeat. But if ever a constitutional amendment had everything going for it—except the strategic ignorance of us defenders—ERA is it. We defenders of ERA had no know-how at all about how to win a political battle. How could we have obtained that know-how? Not in most college courses. The very thought of introducing such a course would have led to branding the proposer as illiberal or commercial or anti-intellectual. Learn how to think about how to win in a good cause? Terrible. Corrupt. Let's read more D. H. Lawrence or Ionesco or Stevens instead.

Just think of the energy that we academics have expended trying to get our professional organizations to boycott the cities that are in states that have not ratified ERA. Boycotting Chicago to punish Illinois is, after all, a piece of strategy, a piece of strategy that has been employed by a fair number of organizations, including some I belong to. So far as I can tell, the chief effect has been to make enemies for ERA. Boycotting, useful in some contexts when other methods of persuasion have failed, was unthinkingly and self-righteously adopted as appropriate to a situation in which the problem was to win the votes of legislators. To win votes in regions where your policies are opposed, you do not set out to punish people in other regions where your policies are approved, thus confirming the worst prejudices that your enemies already hold. To win votes you attempt to win votes. Mike Royko has playfully suggested that we feminists should learn to win votes in the Illinois legislature with bribery. That would be immoral, but it would at least have some chance of success. But the boycott of Chicago to punish Springfield is both immoral and almost certainly ineffective. It is just plain bad strategy.

I do not know what an effective strategy for ERA might have been (I'm afraid that the past tense looks more and more appropriate). But I do know that lots of people know a lot about such matters, and that it is a curious gap in our general education that we do not require of everyone some experience with current strategies for political victory. Courses dealing with strategy would seem to be required both for self-defense—how can you fight 'em if you don't recognize what they're doing to you—and for offensives, when we see a good cause that deserves our support.

You may want to point out that we do have, in America, plenty of courses in strategy: courses offered by advertising departments and business schools. That's true: professionals do spend time and money training, or claiming to train, in the arts of producing the *Penthouse* magazine kind of advertising copy, and its hundreds of equivalents, some of them even having nothing to do with sex. But where are the courses designed to train us in the art of combatting the image-makers who make their livings by degrading us?

(Incidentally, if you want an account of what we're up against, I suggest you take a look at the TV criticism written by Michael J. Arlen. His little book called *Thirty Seconds* describes the enormous care and skill going into a single commercial spot; it is especially revealing about the way the advertisers study how you and I tick, in order to hit us where we live. Or you might look at his recent piece in *The New Yorker,* where *Thirty Seconds* originally appeared, this one on how television sells political candidates. Interviewing, a "television media consultant," David Sawyer, he reports on the strategies that apparently work on those of us who do not have counter-strategies for self-defense.)

I have time only to touch on the second art, which is not quite so badly neglected as strategy. I mean the art of persuasion (I won't call it rhetoric), conceived of as an arm of strategy. To learn how to speak and write in such a way as to increase the chances of winning is by no means the whole end of education in speaking and writing. But it is no mean art, and in a world in which too many people see themselves as winning by deception or by preventing thought in language, the art of using thought in language to persuade people to a cause is a relatively noble one. I've talked about it so much around here on various occasions, however, that I can perhaps take it for granted for today and hurry on.

The trouble with both of the first two arts, important as they can be, is that they presuppose practitioners who already have the right view of the world and of themselves, and who thus can wholeheartedly plunge into the effort to sway the world to their correct views. But some of you are old enough to have discovered that the cause you fight to support one year may actually turn out to work against your own true interests, and that the self you fling into combat today may look pretty puny and misguided tomorrow. The third and fourth neglected arts, then, are arts of criticism: first, the criticism of metaphors for human life and metaphors for the self; and second, the criticism of situations or circumstances.

The first of these twin arts, criticism of metaphor, I've been engaged in most of the time today. When I made fun of *Penthouse's* metaphors for happiness, what I was trying to do was to stimulate you to think about what a woman really is or *is like*. It is clear that *Penthouse* magazine has decided that all people, not just women, are reducible to one of two metaphors. Everyone I meet can be considered as *either* a useful tool, an exploitable means to some end I care about, a kind of tool box; *or* as a candy machine, a source of pleasure that will be mine when I insert something into a convenient slot. The only limits to exploitation of people as tools or as candy machines are the limits of the given market; other markets exploit the hard-core audience, and others still, the hard-core with open violence.

We all reject, or I hope we do, the notion that other people are merely our tools or candy machines, but what, then, are they, really? They are, we say, people, persons, selves. What it means to develop a self—what used to be called a soul—is never easy to say. The history of thought is full, in fact, of efforts to find the right metaphor, or analogy, for what a soul is. We used to be told that men are made in the image of God, meaning that the closest analogy to the mystery of selfhood is the mystery of universehood. The soul, like God, is too complex to be compared with anything else that is. For Plato, the soul is more like a commonwealth than like a god: a healthy soul is like a well-ordered state, in which each of many complex parts does its proper job, in harmony with the other parts, all under the direction of the part that *should* be in charge; a corrupt soul is one in which insurrection has occurred, this or that inferior part taking charge. Aristotle's picture is in some ways the same, though it could be argued that his good man's soul, identical with the happy man's soul, is far less turbulent than Plato's, far less subject to insurrection, far less like an angry and threatened slave master beating down the revolutionary forces of anger and desire. In Aristotle, the goal of life seems to be quite clearly cultivation of a self whose deepest desires and appetites are for kinds of activity that by definition preserve the soul's integrity and defend it from its enemies.

Though Aristotle's notion may come closer than the others to being literal and distinctive to human nature, it is still essentially metaphorical, since it inevitably reduces the soul to a finite and literal range of parts and habits, something that each of us struggling to find a self knows that a self is not. What is more, it comes uncomfortably close to the metaphor of a programmed machine, as we can see in various corrupt Aristotelianisms that have been offered throughout history.

In my original conception of this talk, I had planned to offer at this point a section on some of the metaphors for the self that feminists have themselves employed. For completeness, the talk should take on some of these serious efforts to construct an image that might rival in its richness and power the traditional views I have mentioned. But time's a-wasting, and I must just ask you to take my word for it that there is almost as much need for critical acumen in appraising metaphors offered by would-be feminists as in reading *Penthouse*. Perhaps the need is greater because I suspect that for most women (unlike most men) the crippling metaphors offered in a work like Erica Jong's *Fear of Flying* (say) will be more seductive than anything offered in the popular media. Women can simply dismiss the hacks of *Penthouse*, except insofar as males are seduced by them. But the serious contenders for a feminist vision require a criticism as subtle as we can manage: Just what *is* a model for a life worth having?

My point is that there is an immense gap in almost all programs in liberal education: the study of how to appraise metaphors. You will look a long time in any catalogue before you find a course titled "Criticism of Metaphor 101," or another, "Metaphorical Defenses Against Reductive Metaphor 299, for fourth-year students only." Yet every day selves are being destroyed before our eyes for lack of effective defenses against plausible metaphors.

I must hurry on to a fourth art, one that can be developed above and beyond the art of winning though strategy or rhetoric and the art of criticizing metaphors. The trouble with both strategy and the rhetoric designed to win is that, though both are necessary in our world, their use depends on our accepting a basic and uncriticized metaphor for our circumstances: the metaphor of warfare. And they assume that we know who we are and what we want. Who we are can be stated easily: we are the decent folks who want what's good and right. What we want is victory over those fools and knaves who are essentially beneath consideration: people we can deal with only by fighting them.

But we don't have to be sentimentalists to recognize that when we treat each other as unreconstructible enemies, we usually make disastrous mistakes. I think that Mayor Byrne, for example, has let herself fall into frozen postures of opposition that may very well destroy her and bring our houses down with her. Watching her, I have no doubt that she is sincere, courageous, convinced of her own rectitude, and frightened because she is surrounded by enemies who can understand nothing but power. She *is* surrounded by enemies, of course, more of them every day. And she seems to have no suspicion that there might be a kind of strategy, a kind of rhetoric, a kind of metaphorical criticism, a transforming art of thinking that would refuse to accept her *circumstances,* her surrounding positions, as fixed, and then would seek imaginatively for metaphors other than the stand-off, the battle-line, the righteous last-ditch defense of truth and justice against the selfish monsters who have no public interest.

Just how she might do that I cannot pretend to know; my education in the higher strategies and the higher rhetoric of diplomacy was faulty. But the sad truth is that the first woman mayor of Chicago, probably the first woman leader of a city of this size in the history of the world, seems so badly educated in the arts we are talking about that she is "blowing" one of the biggest opportunities anyone ever had to show what she can do. And I don't have to tell you that she is surrounded—again those *circum-stances*—by hundreds of thousands of men who are secretly pleased to watch her painting herself into corners: "Just what we would expect, from a *woman.*" From a *woman.* Woman as metaphor, again, the proper metaphor for political ineptitude and shrill intransigence. One hardly knows what to be angrier about: the men who think this way, Mayor Byrne for falling into these traps, or a culture that educates us all to be as ignorant as she is about how to remake our selves and our circumstances by exercising habits of freedom.

I have suggested four arts that every woman must master, if she is to achieve any kind of genuine liberation in a world that from her birth seems determined to bind her to its enslaving metaphors. Two of them are arts of winning, given the selves and circumstances we find ourselves in. The other two are arts of reconstitution, the reconstitution of selves by a vigorous criticism of metaphors for the self, and the art of reconstituting circumstances, by a vigorous criticism of metaphors for situations. These arts are not dispensable frills on education. We cannot afford to leave them, as we now do, to the accidents of teacher preferences and the vagaries of the registration schedule. They are matters of life and death, sometimes quite literally, as when a Janis Joplin is killed by a society willing to use her and use her and use her, until what self she has is used up into nothingness. They are more often matters of life and death metaphorically: the life and death of our selves, our souls, depends on our mastery of these arts.

You may have noticed that though I began by talking of education as simply a kind of glorified self-defense, the distinction between what is defensive and what is constructive has somehow disappeared. Whenever I work to *defend* myself I am simultaneously *constructing* myself, building habits of self, habits of courage, skills of thought, powers of action. I thus want to conclude, as perhaps I should have begun, with some hints about what seem to me the ultimate rewards of thinking about education in these ways.

The woman who successfully resists the reductive metaphors I have described, and thus builds a self for herself, discovers somewhere along the line a marvelous and perhaps unexpected reward: friendship has become possible. Instead of conceiving of happiness as we are told Tamara conceives it—a solitary gambol through the jungle, with pauses only to masturbate and to drift "restlessly" (her word) from one-night stand to one-night stand—this self will conceive of happiness as the knowing of other selves and dwelling with them.

Some people, some selves, manage in a miraculous way to get beyond warfare and manipulation and achieve a mutual relation of loving respect, a relation in which each party works as hard to develop a self for the other as for her self. In such relations it is not just that number one wishes for the welfare of number two because number two is necessary for number one's happiness—a very refined tool box but a tool box still. No, here number one simply loses track of which is number one and which is number two. Both become number one for both. In the words of E. E. Cummings' poem:

> now i love you and you love me . . .
> there's somebody calling who's we . . .
> we're anything brighter than even the sun
> (we're everything greater
> than books
> might mean)
> we're everyanything more than believe
> (with a spin
> leap
> alive we're alive)
> we're wonderful one times one

Now you'll look a long way in current literature about education before you'll find someone saying that the knowledge most worth having is the knowledge of how to become a self capable of true friendship, of how to multiply one by one to get one. The goal is certainly implicit in much that your best teachers try to teach you, but it is also repudiated in many of the good things we try to do together in the academy. In most graduate study it is either repudiated directly, as in the economic theories that reduce friendship and love to their cash value, or it is simply ignored. Perhaps more surprising, even in our so-called liberal education, even in our required courses, too often the subject matter, aims, and methods seem almost deliberately chosen to reduce education to an exclusive training of what is called the "mind," rather than education of what I am calling a "self."

I cite only one example. For decades here at Chicago, Aristotle's *Ethics* has been taught in many required courses. It has often been taught well, and it has no doubt had fine ethical effect in leading students to recognize that if happiness is one's goal in life, one had better stop *pursuing* it, as if it were something that could be advertised in *Penthouse* or *The New Yorker*, and learn instead to develop a self, a character, capable of happiness. But so far as I know, no one in all those decades of required reading has until this year ever led first-year students to read the two books in the *Ethics* on friendship and the final book on pleasure and happiness, the books, note well, that provide the metaphoric culmination of the work and thus reward us for our journey through the whole treatise. Students have thus been left to discover on their own that for Aristotle the reward for studying ethics is a self capable of living in friendship.

But it is not my point to indict but to incite. I should like to incite you all, male and female, to turn your lives towards the active reshaping of yourselves and your circumstances. You are not helpless clay in the hands of Hugh Hefner and Bob Guccione and all they stand for. And you can begin to fight back by turning each course you take, each book and magazine you read, into an active critique of the basic metaphors for human life on which it depends. Further, you can seek out those courses that will help you develop the rhetorical and strategic skills for combatting—both within yourselves and in your circumstances—those who, for good motives or bad, are busily reducing your metaphoric world to tool boxes, candy machines, and sophisticated biofeedback mechanisms.

It should be obvious, here at the end, that this knowledge that every woman must have is a knowledge every man must have, too. But there is one kind of knowledge that every man should have that is not available to women: namely, how to listen to those who have been the chief victims of our vast hordes of hirelings, our hack metaphorists. The chances are very high that each of you men, sitting here, has been seriously maimed already by your culture. The chances are high that you have, even during this lecture, thought occasionally of the woman sitting next to you as a toolbox, or as a candy machine, rather than as a potential friend who might teach you something about how to become a self.

How do I know? Because it takes one to know one. Let's step over into the corner here, and I'll tell you a wonderful joke about this beautiful chick who comes into this bar, and she walks up to this cool stud, and she says . . .

Will you let me finish that story without criticism? If you do, you're no friend of mine.

NOTES

1. I am not of course suggesting that any us of teaching machines implies a mechanistic reduction of persons to machines; programmers rightly point out that machines can free teachers from the mechanical and save time for the personal.

QUESTIONS FOR REACTION AND DISCUSSION

1. Why is the question of what it is to be "fully human" at the heart of liberal education? How does describing what "fully human" means help us determine the nature of a liberal education? Is this an effective opening for the first essay? Why or why not?

2. Booth said that after he reread this essay, he realized that the criticisms about sexist use of language were correct and that he needed the feminist critique of language that he received. Do you agree? Does this essay sound dated or inappropriate to you? Why or why not? Booth uses his experiences in rereading this essay to introduce his second essay. How effective are his examples? How important is avoiding gender-specific language for a writer or a speaker? Why?

3. Booth uses a series of analogies to define "man" so that he can discuss what educational strategies work best: as a machine, as an animal, and as a member of a group. How effectively does Booth use these metaphors in this essay? What are the implications of each? How does he point out the limitations of each? Are these effectively described and used in the essay? Why or why not?

4. Booth believes that a liberal education is crucial because it yields the knowledge of "how to act free as a 'man.'" The first goal toward gaining this knowledge is avoiding dependence on teachers and learning by one's self. Do you agree or disagree? Why or why not?

5. One goal of Booth's liberal education is the ability to speculate. What does he mean by this term? What are examples you can think of from your own educational experience?

6. In his second essay, Booth uses more examples from his personal life (he mentions his wife and three children), and he uses *Penthouse: The International Magazine for Men* ironically as an extended example of a contemporary statement on the nature and condition of women. In the first essay he used virtually no personal examples and nothing as provocative as *Penthouse*. Are these effectively used here? What does this suggest about the tone of this essay?

QUESTIONS FOR WRITING

1. Booth revised this essay after he listened to criticisms of his use of gender-specific language. But his second essay is considerably more than just a revision of his first, and he demonstrates clearly that a few nouns and pronouns cannot simply be substituted in order to effect the changes he wished to make. Analyze the difference between the two essays. What are the similarities and differences in language, tone, and substance? Which essay is more effective? Write an essay in which you compare and contrast the two essays.

2. Write an essay in which you write your own response to the following alteration to the question Booth set for himself: Is there any knowledge that men and women must have at the beginning of the twenty-first century? In this essay, describe your sense of common ground that men and women occupy as well as any differences that you think are important.

3. In writing his second essay, Booth decided that he wished to add a component to the nature of a liberal education, something that women need to learn and not men. He says that women need to know "how to cope with men" and they must "learn to think and act like a male." As for men, Booth suggests that men should ask themselves a simple question: "What were you led to overlook because you failed to think about the special needs and problems of women in a male-dominated world?" Are there further problems and difficulties that he has not foreseen in making these suggestions? Do you agree that women must learn to cope with men and men must learn to take into account the achievements of women? Why or why not? After considering Booth's position carefully, write a response to his essays in the form of a formal letter to him.

4. Booth discusses four "liberal arts" that he considers crucial for women but possibly as important for men: the arts of strategy and persuasion and two arts of the criticism of metaphor, which he calls "the criticism of metaphors for human life and for the self and the criticism of situations and circumstances." How valuable are these additional four liberal arts? For women? For men? How would a college or a university teach them? Using examples from your own experience and education, write an essay in which you defend or reject the addition of these "liberal arts" as a part of the knowledge that men and women must have.

Questions for Further Exploration

1. Examine several current grammar handbooks (readily available in any library in print, packaged with many word processing programs, or online) and read what each says about the use of gender-specific language. What is the usual definition? What are the common suggestions? What are the most useful? Why is it important to avoid gender-specific language? Prepare a report for your class on your findings.

2. Evaluate the official statements that your own college or university has made about what students need to know and what they will learn in the process of their educational experience. Look at the mission statements and descriptions of the general education requirements. Is there any evidence that students—male or female—will learn strategy,

persuasion, and the criticism of metaphors? Check the mission statement or curriculum description of the University of Chicago (where Booth was a member of the English Department). Look at the college catalogue or access the Web site. Report on your findings to your class.

4

ON THE USES OF A LIBERAL EDUCATION: I. AS LITE ENTERTAINMENT FOR BORED COLLEGE STUDENTS

Mark Edmundson is a professor of English at the University of Virginia, where he teaches courses in British literature and literary theory. In addition to his teaching responsibilities at the university, he writes academic books and articles and is a contributing editor for Harper's Magazine, *one of the oldest magazines in America. Founded in 1850 as* Harper's New Monthly Magazine *by book publishers, the magazine printed the works of well-known American writers, such as Mark Twain and Henry James, in the nineteenth century. Today the magazine is known for its award-winning fiction and essays, as well as for features such as* Harper's Index, *a list of unusual statistics that serve as a guide to contemporary American culture. An online version, <http://www.harpers.org>, includes archives and historical information about the magazine.* Harper's *frequently publishes essays about contemporary issues in education, such as this one by Edmundson. In this essay, Edmundson provides an unusual contribution to the debate about the purpose of a liberal arts education. While other writers in this section speak mainly about the ineffectiveness of the college curriculum, Edmundson analyzes the culture of the college campus itself and provides a striking profile of the contemporary college student.*

QUESTIONS FOR READING

1. What does the title, especially the use of the phrase "lite entertainment," suggest to you about the nature of this essay?
2. Are you a "bored" college student? Why or why not?
3. What is the procedure for student evaluation of instruction on your campus? When does it take place? How are the results used? What are student attitudes toward the process?

MARK EDMUNDSON

On the Uses of a Liberal Education: I. As Lite Entertainment for Bored College Students

Harper's Magazine (September 1997, pp. 39–49)

Today is evaluation day in my Freud class, and everything has changed. The class meets twice a week, late in the afternoon, and the clientele, about fifty undergraduates, tends to drag in and slump, looking disconsolate and a little lost, waiting for a jump start. To get the discussion moving, they usually require a joke, an anecdote, an off-the-wall question—When you were a kid, were your Halloween getups ego costumes, id costumes, or superego costumes? That sort of thing. But today, as soon as I flourish the forms, a buzz rises in the room. Today they write their assessments of the course, their assessments of *me,* and they are without a doubt wide-awake. "What is your evaluation of the instructor?" asks question number eight, entreating them to circle a number between five (excellent) and one (poor, poor) Whatever interpretive subtlety they've acquired during the term is now out the window. Edmundson: one to five, stand and shoot.

And they do. As I retreat through the door—I never stay around for this phase of the ritual—I look over my shoulder and see them toiling away like the devil's auditors. They're pitched into high writing gear, even the ones who struggle to squeeze out their journal entries word by word, stoked on a procedure they have by now supremely mastered. They're playing the informed consumer, letting the provider know where he's come through and where he's not quite up to snuff.

But why am I so distressed, bolting like a refugee out of my own classroom, where I usually hold easy sway? Chances are the evaluations will be much like what they've been in the past—they'll be just fine. It's likely that I'll be commended for being "interesting" (and I am commended, many times over), that I'll be cited for my relaxed and tolerant ways (that happens, too), that my sense of humor and capacity to connect the arcana of the subject matter with current culture will come in for some praise (yup). I've been hassled this term, finishing a manuscript, and so haven't given their journals the attention I should have, and for that I'm called—quite civilly, though—to account. Overall, I get off pretty well.

Yet I have to admit that I do not much like the image of myself that emerges from these forms, the image of knowledgeable, humorous detachment and bland tolerance. I do not like the forms themselves, with their number ratings, reminiscent of the sheets circulated after the TV pilot has just been played to its sample audience in Burbank. Most of all I dislike the attitude of calm consumer expertise that pervades the responses. I'm disturbed by the serene belief that my function—and, more important, Freud's, or Shakespeare's, or Blake's—is to divert, entertain, and interest. Observes one respondent, not at all unrepresentative: "Edmundson has done a fantastic job of presenting this difficult, important & controversial material in an enjoyable and approachable way."

Thanks but no thanks. I don't teach to amuse, to divert, or even, for that matter, to be merely interesting. When someone says she "enjoyed" the course—and that word crops up again and again in my evaluations—somewhere at the edge of my immediate complacency I feel encroaching self-dislike. That is not at all what I had in mind. The off-the-wall questions and the sidebar jokes are meant as lead-ins to stronger stuff—in the case of the Freud course, to a complexly tragic view of life. But the affability and the one-liners often seem to be all that land with the students; their journals and evaluations leave me little doubt.

I want some of them to say that they've been changed by the course. I want them to measure themselves against what they've read. It's said that some time ago a Columbia University instructor used to issue a harsh two-part question. One: What book did you most dislike in the course? Two: What intellectual or characterological flaws in you does that dislike point to? The hand that framed that question was surely heavy. But at least it compels one to see intellectual work as a confrontation between two people, student and author, where the stakes matter. Those Columbia students were being asked to relate the quality of an *encounter*, not rate the action as though it had unfolded on the big screen.

Why are my students describing the Oedipus complex and the death drive as being interesting and enjoyable to contemplate? And why am I coming across as an urbane, mildly ironic, endlessly affable guide to this intellectual territory, operating without intensity, generous, funny, and loose?

Because that's what works. On evaluation day, I reap the rewards of my partial compliance with the culture of my students and, too, with the culture of the university as it now operates. It's a culture that's gotten little exploration. Current critics tend to think that liberal arts education is in crisis because universities have been invaded by professors with peculiar ideas: deconstruction, Lacanianism, feminism, queer theory. They believe that genius and tradition are out and that P.C., multiculturalism, and identity politics are in because of an invasion by tribes of tenured radicals, the late millennial equivalents of the Visigoth hordes that cracked Rome's walls.

But mulling over my evaluations and then trying to take a hard, extended look at campus life both here at the University of Virginia and around the country eventually led me to some different conclusions. To me, liberal arts education is as ineffective as it is now not chiefly because there are a lot of strange theories in the air. (Used well, those theories *can* be illuminating.) Rather, it's that university culture, like American culture writ large, is to put it crudely, ever more devoted to consumption and entertainment, to the using and using up of goods and images. For someone growing up in America now, there are few available alternatives to the cool consumer worldview. My students didn't ask for that view, much less create it, but they bring a consumer weltanschauung to school, where it exerts a powerful, and largely unacknowledged, influence. If we want to understand current universities, with their multiple woes, we might try leaving the realms of expert debate and fine ideas and turning to the classrooms and campuses, where a new kind of weather is gathering.

From time to time I bump into a colleague in the corridor and we have what I've come to think of as a Joon Lee fest. Joon Lee is one of the best students I've taught. He's endlessly curious, has read a small library's worth, seen every movie, and knows all about showbiz and entertainment. For a class of mine he wrote an essay using Nietzsche's Apollo and Dionysus to analyze the pop group The Supremes. A trite, cultural-studies bonbon? Not at all. He said striking things about conceptions of race in America and about how they shape our ideas of beauty. When I talk with one of his other teachers, we run on about the general splendors of his work and presence. But what inevitably follows a JL fest is a mournful reprise about the divide that separates him and a few other remarkable students from their contemporaries. It's not that some aren't nearly as bright—in terms of intellectual ability, my students are all that I could ask for. Instead, it's that Joon Lee has decided to follow his interests and let them make him into a singular and rather eccentric man; in his charming way, he doesn't mind being at odds with most anyone.

It's his capacity for enthusiasm that sets Joon apart from what I've come to think of as the reigning generational style. Whether the students are sorority/fraternity types, grunge aficionados, piercer/tattooers, black or white, rich or middle class (alas, I teach almost no students from truly poor backgrounds), they are nearly across the board, very, very self-contained. On good days they display a light, appealing glow; on bad days, shuffling disgruntlement. But there's little fire, little passion to be found.

This point came home to me a few weeks ago when I was wandering across the university grounds. There, beneath a classically cast portico, were two students, male and female, having a rip-roaring argument. They were incensed, bellowing at each other, headstrong, confident, and wild. It struck me how rarely I see this kind of full-out feeling in students anymore. Strong emotional display is forbidden. When conflicts arise, it's generally understood that one of the parties will say something sarcastically propitiating ("whatever" often does it) and slouch away.

How did my students reach this peculiar state in which all passion seems to be spent? I think that many of them have imbibed their sense of self from consumer culture in general and from the tube in particular. They're the progeny of 100 cable channels and omnipresent Blockbuster outlets. TV, Marshall McLuhan famously said, is a cool medium. Those who play best on it are low-key and nonassertive; they blend in. Enthusiasm, à la Joon Lee, quickly looks absurd. The form of character that's most appealing on TV is calmly self-interested though never greedy, attuned to the conventions, and ironic. Judicious timing is preferred to sudden self-assertion. The TV medium is inhospitable to inspiration, improvisation, failures, slipups. All must run perfectly.

Naturally, a cool youth culture is a marketing bonanza for producers of the right products, who do all they can to enlarge that culture and keep it grinding. The Internet, TV, and magazines now teem with what I call persona ads, ads for Nikes and Reeboks and Jeeps and Blazers that don't so much endorse the capacities of the product per se as show you what sort of person you will be once you've acquired it. The Jeep ad that features hip, outdoorsy kids whipping a Frisbee from mountaintop to mountaintop isn't so much about what Jeeps can do as it is about the kind of people who own them. Buy a Jeep and be one of them. The ad is of little consequence in itself, but expand its message exponentially and you have the central thrust of current consumer culture—buy in order to be.

Most of my students seem desperate to blend in, to look right, not to make a spectacle of themselves. (Do I have to tell you that those two students having the argument under the portico turned out to be acting in a role-playing game?) The specter of the uncool creates a subtle tyranny. It's apparently an easy standard to subscribe to, this Letterman-like, Tarantino-like cool, but once committed to it, you discover that matters are rather different. You're inhibited, except on ordained occasions, from showing emotion, stifled from trying to achieve anything original. You're made to feel that even the slightest departure from the reigning code will get you genially ostracized. This is a culture tensely committed to a laid-back norm.

Am I coming off like something of a crank here? Maybe. Oscar Wilde, who is almost never wrong, suggested that it is perilous to promiscuously contradict people who are much younger than yourself. Point taken. But one of the lessons that consumer hype tries to insinuate is that we must never rebel against the new, never even question it. If it's new—a new need, a new product, a new show, a new style, a new generation—it must be good. So maybe, even at the risk of winning the withered, brown laurels of crankdom, it pays to resist newness-worship and cast a colder eye.

Praise for my students? I have some of that too. What my students are, at their best, is decent. They are potent believers in equality. They help out at the soup kitchen and volunteer to tutor poor kids to get a stripe on their resumés, sure. But they also want other people to have a fair shot. And in their commitment to fairness they are discerning; there you see them at their intellectual best. If I were on trial and innocent, I'd want them on the jury.

What they will not generally do, though, is indict the current system. They won't talk about how the exigencies of capitalism lead to a reserve army of the unemployed and nearly inevitable misery. That would be getting too loud, too brash. For the pervading view is the cool consumer perspective, where passion and strong admiration are forbidden. "To stand in awe of nothing, Numicus, is perhaps the one and only thing that can make a man happy and keep him so," says Horace in the *Epistles,* and I fear that his lines ought to hang as a motto over the university in this era of high consumer capitalism.

It's easy to mount one's high horse and blame the students for this state of affairs. But they didn't create the present culture of consumption. (It was largely my own generation, that of the sixties, that let the counterculture search for pleasure devolve into a quest for commodities.) And they weren't the ones responsible, when they were six and seven and eight years old, for unplugging the TV set from time to time or for hauling off and kicking a hole through it. It's my generation of parents who sheltered these students, kept them away from the hard knocks of everyday life, making them cautious and overfragile, who demanded that their teachers, from grade school on, flatter them endlessly so that the kids are shocked if their college profs don't reflexively suck up to them.

Of course, the current generational style isn't simply derived from culture and environment. It's also about dollars. Students worry that taking too many chances with their educations will sabotage their future prospects. They're aware of the fact that a drop that looks more and more like one wall of the Grand Canyon separates the top economic tenth from the rest of the population. There's a sentiment currently abroad that if you step aside for a moment, to write, to travel, to fall too hard in love, you might lose position permanently. We may be on a conveyor belt, but it's worse down there on the filth-strewn floor. So don't sound off, don't blow your chance.

But wait. I teach at the famously conservative University of Virginia. Can I extend my view from Charlottesville to encompass the whole country, a whole generation of college students? I can only say that I hear comparable stories about classroom life from colleagues everywhere in America. When I visit other schools to lecture, I see a similar scene unfolding. There are, of course, terrific students everywhere. And they're all the better for the way they've had to strive against the existing conformity. At some of the small liberal arts colleges, the tradition of strong engagement persists. But overall, the students strike me as being sweet and sad, hovering in a nearly suspended animation.

Too often now the pedagogical challenge is to make a lot from a little. Teaching Wordsworth's "Tintern Abbey," you ask for comments. No one responds. So you call on Stephen. Stephen: "The sound, this poem really flows." You: "Stephen seems interested in the music of the poem. We might extend his comment to ask if the poem's music coheres with its argument. Are they consistent? Or is there an emotional pain submerged here that's contrary to the poem's appealing melody?" All right, it's not usually that bad. But close. One friend describes it as rebound teaching: they proffer a weightless comment, you hit it back for all you're worth, then it comes dribbling out again. Occasionally a professor will try to explain away this intellectual timidity by describing the students as perpetrators of postmodern irony, a highly sophisticated mode. Everything's a slick counterfeit, a simulacrum, so by no means should any phenomenon be taken seriously. But the students don't have the urbane, Oscar

Wilde–type demeanor that should go with this view. Oscar was cheerful, funny, confident, strange. (Wilde, mortally ill, living in a Paris flophouse: "My wallpaper and I are fighting a duel to the death. One or the other of us has to go.") This generation's style is considerate, easy to please, and a touch depressed.

Granted, you might say, the kids come to school immersed in a consumer mentality—they're good Americans, after all—but then the university and the professors do everything in their power to fight that dreary mind-set in the interest of higher ideals, right? So it should be. But let us look at what is actually coming to pass.

Over the past few years, the physical layout of my university has been changing. To put it a little indecorously, the place is looking more and more like a retirement spread for the young. Our funds go to construction, into new dorms, into renovating the student union. We have a new aquatics center and ever-improving gyms, stocked with StairMasters and Nautilus machines. Engraved on the wall in the gleaming aquatics building is a line by our founder, Thomas Jefferson, declaring that everyone ought to get about two hours' exercise a day. Clearly even the author of the Declaration of Independence endorses the turning of his university into a sports-and-fitness emporium.

But such improvements shouldn't be surprising. Universities need to attract the best (that is, the smartest *and* the richest) students in order to survive in an ever more competitive market. Schools want kids whose parents can pay the full freight, not the ones who need scholarships or want to bargain down the tuition costs. If the marketing surveys say that the kids require sports centers, then, trustees willing, they shall have them. In fact, as I began looking around, I came to see that more and more of what's going on in the university is customer driven. The consumer pressures that beset me on evaluation day are only a part of an overall trend.

From the start, the contemporary university's relationship with students has a solicitous, nearly servile tone. As soon as someone enters his junior year in high school, and especially if he's living in a prosperous zip code, the informational material—the advertising—comes flooding in. Pictures, testimonials, videocassettes, and CD ROMs (some bidden, some not) arrive at the door from colleges across the country, all trying to capture the student and his tuition cash. The freshman-to-be sees photos of well-appointed dorm rooms; of elaborate phys-ed facilities; of fine dining rooms; of expertly kept sports fields; of orchestras and drama troupes; of students working alone (no overbearing grown-ups in range), peering with high seriousness into computers and microscopes; or of students arrayed outdoors in attractive conversational garlands.

Occasionally—but only occasionally, for we usually photograph rather badly; in appearance we tend at best to be styleless—there's a professor teaching a class. (The college catalogues I received, by my request only, in the late sixties were austere affairs full of professors' credentials and course descriptions; it was clear on whose terms the enterprise was going to unfold.) A college financial officer recently put matters to me in concise, if slightly melodramatic terms: "Colleges don't have admissions offices anymore; they have marketing departments." Is it surprising that someone who has been approached with photos and tapes, bells and whistles, might come in thinking that the Freud and Shakespeare she had signed up to study were also going to be agreeable treats?

How did we reach this point? In part the answer is a matter of demographics and (surprise) of money. Aided by the G.I. bill, the college-going population in America dramatically increased after the Second World War. Then came the baby boomers, and to accommodate them, schools continued to grow. Universities expand easily enough, but with tenure locking faculty in for lifetime jobs, and with the general reluctance of administrators to eliminate their own slots, it's not easy for a university to contract. So after the baby boomers had passed through—like a fat meal digested by a boa constrictor—the colleges turned to energetic promotional strategies to fill the empty chairs. And suddenly college became a buyer's market. What students and their parents wanted had to be taken more and more into account. That usually meant creating more comfortable, less challenging environments, places where almost no one failed, everything was enjoyable, and everyone was nice.

Just as universities must compete with one another for students, so must the individual departments. At a time of rank economic anxiety, the English and history majors have to contend for students against the more success-insuring branches, such as the sciences and the commerce school. In 1968, more than twenty-one percent of all the bachelor's degrees conferred in America were in the humanities; by 1993, that number had fallen to about thirteen percent. The humanities now must struggle to attract students, many of whose parents devoutly wish they would study something else.

One of the ways we've tried to stay attractive is by loosening up. We grade much more softly than our colleagues in science. In English, we don't give many Ds, or Cs for that matter. (The rigors of Chem 101 create almost as many English majors per year as do the splendors of Shakespeare.) A professor at Stanford recently explained grade inflation in the humanities by observing that the undergraduates were getting smarter every year; the higher grades simply recorded how much better they were than their predecessors. Sure.

Along with softening the grades, many humanities departments have relaxed major requirements. There are some good reasons for introducing more choice into curricula and requiring fewer standard courses. But the move, like many others in the university now, jibes with a tendency to serve—and not challenge—the students. Students can also float in and out of classes during the first two weeks of each term without making any commitment. The common name for this time span—shopping period—speaks volumes about the consumer mentality that's now in play. Usually, too, the kids can drop courses up until the last month with only an innocuous "W" on their transcripts. Does a course look too challenging? No problem. Take it pass-fail. A happy consumer is, by definition, one with multiple options, one who can always have what he wants. And since a course is something the students and their parents have bought and paid for, why can't they do with it pretty much as they please?

A sure result of the university's widening elective leeway is to give students more power over their teachers. Those who don't like you can simply avoid you. If the clientele dislikes you en masse, you can be left without students, period. My first term teaching I walked into my introduction to poetry course and found it inhabited by one student, the gloriously named Bambi Lynn Dean. Bambi and I chatted amicably awhile, but for all that she and the pleasure of her name could offer, I was fast on the way to meltdown. It was all a mistake, luckily, a problem with the scheduling book. Everyone was waiting for me next door. But in a dozen years of teaching I haven't forgotten that feeling of being ignominiously marooned. For it happens to others, and not always because of scheduling glitches. I've seen older colleagues go through hot embarrassment at not having enough students sign up for their courses: they graded too hard, demanded too much, had beliefs too far out of keeping with the existing disposition. It takes only a few such instances to draw other members of the professoriat further into line.

And if what's called tenure reform—which generally just means the abolition of tenure—is broadly enacted, professors will be yet more vulnerable to the whims of their customer-students. Teach what pulls the kids in, or walk. What about entire departments that don't deliver? If the kids say no to Latin and Greek, is it time to dissolve classics? Such questions are being entertained more and more seriously by university administrators.

How does one prosper with the present clientele? Many of the most successful professors now are the ones who have "decentered" their classrooms. There's a new emphasis on group projects and on computer-generated exchanges among the students. What they seem to want most is to talk to one another. A classroom now is frequently an "environment," a place highly conducive to the exchange of existing ideas, the students' ideas. Listening to one another, students sometimes change their opinions. But what they generally can't do is acquire a new vocabulary, a new perspective, that will cast issues in a fresh light.

The Socratic method—the animated, sometimes impolite give-and-take between student and teacher—seems too jagged for current sensibilities. Students frequently come to my office to tell me how intimidated they feel in class; the thought of being embarrassed in front of the group fills them with dread. I remember a student telling me how humiliating it was to be corrected by the teacher, by me. So I asked the logical question: "Should I let a major factual error go by so as to save discomfort?" The student—a good student, smart and earnest— said that was a tough question. He'd need to think about it.

Disturbing? Sure. But I wonder, are we really getting students ready for Socratic exchange with professors when we push them off into vast lecture rooms, two and three hundred to a class, sometimes face them with only grad students until their third year, and signal in our myriad of professorial ways that we often have much better things to do than sit in our offices and talk with them? How bad will the student-faculty ratios have to become, how teeming the lecture courses, before we hear students righteously complaining, as they did thirty years ago, about the impersonality of their schools, about their decline into knowledge factories? "This is a firm," said Mario Savio at Berkeley during the Free Speech protests of the sixties, "and if the Board of Regents are the board of directors, . . . then . . . the faculty are a bunch of employees and we're the raw material. But we're a bunch of raw material that don't mean . . . to be made into any product."

Teachers who really do confront students, who provide significant challenges to what they believe, *can* be very successful, granted. But sometimes such professors generate more than a little trouble for themselves. A controversial teacher can send students hurrying to the deans and the counselors, claiming to have been offended. ("Offensive" is the preferred term of repugnance today, just as "enjoyable" is the summit of praise.) Colleges have brought in hordes of counselors and deans to make sure that everything is smooth, serene, unflustered, that everyone has a good time. To the counselor, to the dean, and to the university legal squad, that which is normal, healthy, and prudent is best.

An air of caution and deference is everywhere. When my students come to talk with me in my office, they often exhibit a Franciscan humility. "Do you have a moment?" "I know you're busy. I won't take up much of your time." Their presences tend to be very light; they almost never change the temperature of the room. The dress is nondescript: clothes are in earth tones; shoes are practical—cross-trainers, hiking boots, work shoes, Dr. Martens, with now and then a stylish pair of raised-sole boots on one of the young women. Many, male and female both, peep from beneath the bills of monogrammed baseball caps. Quite a few wear sports, or even corporate, logos, sometimes on one piece of clothing but occasionally (and disconcertingly) on more. The walk is slow; speech is careful, sweet, a bit weary, and without strong inflection. (After the first lively week of the term, most seem far in debt to sleep.) They are almost unfailingly polite. They don't want to offend me; I could hurt them, savage their grades.

Naturally, there are exceptions, kids I chat animatedly with, who offer a joke, or go on about this or that new CD (almost never a book, no). But most of the traffic is genially sleepwalking. I have to admit that I'm a touch wary, too. I tend to hold back. An unguarded remark, a joke that's taken to be off-colored, or simply an uncomprehended comment can lead to difficulties. I keep it literal. They scare me a little, these kind and melancholy students, who themselves seem rather frightened of their own lives.

Before they arrive, we ply the students with luscious ads, guaranteeing them a cross between summer camp and lotusland. When they get here, flattery and nonstop entertainment are available, if that's what they want. And when they leave? How do we send our students out into the world? More and more, our administrators call the booking agents and line up one or another celebrity to usher graduates into the millenium. This past spring, Kermit the Frog won himself an honorary degree at Southampton College on Long Island; Bruce Willis and Yogi Berra took credentials away at Montclair State; Arnold Schwarzenegger scored at the University of Wisconsin–Superior. At Wellesley, Oprah Winfrey gave the commencement address. (*Wellesley*—one of the most rigorous academic colleges in the nation.) At the University of Vermont, Whoopi Goldberg laid down the word. But why should a worthy administrator contract the likes of Susan Sontag, Christopher Hitchens, or Robert Hughes—someone who might actually say something, something disturbing, something "offensive"—when he can get what the parents and kids apparently want and what the newspapers will softly commend—more lite entertainment, more TV?

Is it a surprise, then, that this generation of students—steeped in consumer culture before going off to school, treated as potent customers by the university well before their date of arrival, then pandered to from day one until the morning of the final kiss-off from Kermit or one of his kin— are inclined to see the books they read as a string of entertainments to be placidly enjoyed or languidly cast down? Given the way universities are now administered (which is more and more to say, given the way that they are currently marketed), is it a shock that the kids don't come to school hot to learn, unable to bear their own ignorance? For some measure of self-dislike, or self-discontent—which is much different than simple depression—seems to me to be a prerequisite for getting an education that matters. My students, alas, usually lack the confidence to acknowledge what would be their most precious asset for learning: their ignorance.

Not long ago, I asked my Freud class a question that, however hoary, never fails to solicit intriguing responses: Who are your heroes? Whom do you admire? After one remarkable answer, featuring T.S. Eliot as hero, a series of generic replies rolled in, one gray wave after the next: my father, my best friend, a doctor who lives in our town, my high school history teacher. Virtually all the heroes were people my students had known personally, people who had done something local, specific, and practical, and had done it for them. They were good people, unselfish people, these heroes, but most of all they were people who had delivered the goods.

My students' answers didn't exhibit any philosophical resistance to the idea of greatness. It's not that they had been primed by their professors with complex arguments to combat genius. For the truth is that these students don't need debunking theories. Long before college, skepticism became their habitual mode. They are the progeny of Bart Simpson and David Letterman, and the hyper-cool ethos of the box. It's inane to say that theorizing professors have created them, as many conservative critics like to do. Rather, they have substantially created a university environment in which facile skepticism can thrive without being substantially contested.

Skeptical approaches have *potential* value. If you have no all-encompassing religious faith, no faith in historical destiny, the future of the West, or anything comparably grand, you need to acquire your vision of the world somewhere. If it's from literature, then the various visions literature offers have to be inquired into skeptically. Surely it matters that women are denigrated in Milton and in Pope, that some novelistic voices assume an overbearing godlike authority, that the poor are, in this or that writer, inevitably cast as clowns. You can't buy all of literature wholesale if it's going to help draw your patterns of belief.

But demystifying theories are now overused, applied mechanically. It's all logocentrism, patriarchy, ideology. And in this the student environment—laid-back, skeptical, knowing—is, I believe, central. Full-out debunking is what plays with this clientele. Some have been doing it nearly as long as, if more crudely than, their deconstructionist teachers. In the context of the contemporary university, and cool consumer culture, a useful intellectual skepticism has become exaggerated into a fundamentalist caricature of itself. The teachers have buckled to their students' views.

At its best, multiculturalism can be attractive as well-deployed theory. What could be more valuable than encountering the best work of far-flung cultures and becoming a citizen of the world? But in the current consumer environment, where flattery plays so well, the urge to encounter the other can devolve into the urge to find others who embody and celebrate the right ethnic origins. So we put aside the African novelist Chinua Achebe's abrasive, troubling *Things Fall Apart* and gravitate toward hymns on Africa, cradle of all civilizations.

What about the phenomenon called political correctness? Raising the standard of civility and tolerance in the university has been—who can deny it?—a very good thing. Yet this admirable impulse has expanded to the point where one is enjoined to speak well—and only well—of women, blacks, gays, the disabled, in fact of virtually everyone. And we can owe this expansion in many ways to the student culture. Students now do not wish to be criticized, not in any form. (The culture of consumption never criticizes them, at least not *overtly*.) In the current university, the movement for urbane tolerance has devolved into an imperative against critical reaction, turning much of the intellectual life into a dreary Sargasso Sea. At a certain point, professors stopped being usefully sensitive and became more like careful retailers who have it as a cardinal point of doctrine never to piss the customers off.

To some professors, the solution lies in the movement called cultural studies. What students need, they believe, is to form a critical perspective on pop culture. It's a fine idea, no doubt. Students should be able to run a critical commentary against the stream of consumer stimulations in which they're immersed. But cultural-studies programs rarely work, because no matter what you propose by way of analysis, things tend to bolt downhill toward an uncritical discussion of students' tastes, into what they like and don't like. If you want to do a Frankfurt School–style analysis of *Braveheart*, you can be pretty sure that by mid-class Adorno and Horkheimer will be consigned to the junk heap of history and you'll be collectively weighing the charms of Mel Gibson. One sometimes wonders if cultural studies hasn't prospered because, under the guise of serious intellectual analysis, it gives the customers what they most want—easy pleasure, more TV. Cultural studies becomes nothing better than what its detractors claim it is—Madonna studies—when students kick loose from the critical perspective and groove to the product, and that, in my experience teaching film and pop culture, happens plenty.

On the issue of genius, as on multiculturalism and political correctness, we professors of the humanities have, I think, also failed to press back against our students' consumer tastes. Here we tend to nurse a pair of—to put it charitably—disparate views. In one mode, we're inclined to a programmatic debunking criticism. We call the concept of genius into question. But in our professional lives per se, we aren't usually disposed against the idea of distinguished achievement. We argue animatedly about the caliber of potential colleagues. We support a star system, in which some professors are far better paid, teach less, and under better conditions than the rest. In our own profession, we are creating a system that is the mirror image of the one we're dismantling in the curriculum. Ask a professor what she thinks of the work of Stephen Greenblatt, a leading critic of Shakespeare, and you'll hear it for an hour. Ask her what her views are on Shakespeare's genius and she's likely to begin questioning the term along with the whole "discourse of evaluation." This dual sensibility may be intellectually incoherent. But in its awareness of what plays with students, it's conducive to good classroom evaluations and, in its awareness of where and how the professional bread is buttered, to self-advancement as well.

My overall point is this: It's not that a left-wing professorial coup has taken over the university. It's that at American universities, left liberal politics have collided with the ethos of consumerism. The consumer ethos is winning.

Then how do those who at least occasionally promote genius and high literary ideals look to current students? How do we appear, those of us who take teaching to be something of a performance art and who imagine that if you give yourself over completely to your subject you'll be rewarded with insight beyond what you individually command?

I'm reminded of an old piece of newsreel footage I saw once. The speaker (perhaps it was Lenin, maybe Trotsky) was haranguing a large crowd. He was expostulating, arm waving, carrying on. Whether it was flawed technology or the man himself, I'm not sure, but the orator looked like an intricate mechanical device that had sprung into fast-forward. To my students, who mistrust enthusiasm in every form, that's me when I start riffing about Freud or Blake. But more and more, as my evaluations showed, I've been replacing enthusiasm and intellectual animation with stand-up routines, keeping it all at arm's length, praising under the cover of irony.

It's too bad that the idea of genius has been denigrated so far, because it actually offers a live alternative to the demoralizing culture of hip in which most of my students are mired. By embracing the works and lives of extraordinary people, you can adapt new ideals to revise those that came courtesy of your parents, your neighborhood, your clan—or the tube. The aim of a good liberal arts education was once, to adapt an observation by the scholar Walter

Jackson Bate, to see that "we need not be the passive victims of what we deterministically call 'circumstances' (social, cultural, or reductively psycho-logical-personal), but that by linking ourselves through what Keats calls an 'immortal free-masonry' with the great we can become freer—freer to be our-selves, to be what we most want and value."

But genius isn't just a personal standard; genius can also have political ef-fect. To me, one of the best things about democratic thinking is the conviction that genius can spring up anywhere. Walt Whitman is born into the working class and thirty-six years later we have a poetic image of America that gives a passionate dimension to the legalistic brilliance of the Constitution. A democ-racy needs to constantly develop, and to do so it requires the most powerful vi-sionary minds to interpret the present and to propose possible shapes for the future. By continuing to notice and praise genius, we create a culture in which the kind of poetic gamble that Whitman made—a gamble in which failure would have entailed rank humiliation, depression, maybe suicide—still takes place. By rebelling against established ways of seeing and saying things, genius helps us to apprehend how malleable the present is and how promising and fraught with danger is the future. If we teachers do not endorse genius and self-overcoming, can we be surprised when our students find their ideal images in TV's latest persona ads?

A world uninterested in genius is a despondent place, whose sad denizens drift from coffee bar to Prozac dispensary, unfired by ideals, by the glowing image of the self that one might become. As Northrop Frye says in a beautiful and now dramatically unfashionable sentence, "The artist who uses the same energy and genius that Homer and Isaiah had will find that he not only lives in the same palace of art as Homer and Isaiah, but lives in it at the same time." We ought not to deny the existence of such a place sim-ply because we, or those we care for, find the demands it makes intimidat-ing, the rent too high.

What happens if we keep trudging along this bleak course? What happens if our most intelligent students never learn to strive to overcome what they are? What if genius, and the imitation of genius, become silly, outmoded ideas? What you're likely to get are more and more one-dimensional men and women. These will be people who live for easy pleasures, for comfort and pros-perity, who think of money first, then second, and third, who hug the status quo; people who believe in God as a sort of insurance policy (cover your bets); people who are never surprised. They will be people so pleased with themselves (when they're not in despair at the general pointlessness of their lives) that they cannot imagine humanity could do better. They'll think it their highest duty to clone themselves as frequently as possible. They'll claim to be happy, and they'll live a long time.

It is probably time now to offer a spate of inspiring solutions. Here ought to come a list of reforms, with due notations about a core curriculum and var-ious requirements. What the traditionalists who offer such solutions miss is that no matter what our current students are given to read, many of them will simply translate it into melodrama, with flat characters and predictable morals. (The unabated capitalist culture that conservative critics so often endorse has put students in a position to do little else.) One can't simply wave a curricular wand and reverse acculturation.

Perhaps it would be a good idea to try firing the counselors and sending half the deans back into their classrooms, dismantling the football team and making the stadium into a playground for local kids, emptying the fraternities, and boarding up the student-activities office. Such measures would convey the message that American colleges are not northern outposts of Club Med. A willingness on the part of the faculty to defy student conviction and affront them occasionally—to be usefully offensive—also might not be a bad thing. We professors talk a lot about subversion, which generally means subverting the views of people who never hear us talk or read our work. But to subvert the views of our students, our customers, that would be something else again.

Ultimately, though, it is up to individuals—and individual students in particular—to make their own way against the current sludgy tide. There's still the library, still the museum, there's still the occasional teacher who lives to find things greater than herself to admire. There are still fellow students who have not been cowed. Universities are inefficient, cluttered, archaic places, with many unguarded corners where one can open a book or gaze out onto the larger world and construe it freely. Those who do as much, trusting themselves against the weight of current opinion, will have contributed something to bringing this sad dispensation to an end. As for myself, I'm canning my low-key one-liners; when the kids' TV-based tastes come to the fore, I'll aim and shoot. And when it's time to praise genius, I'll try to do it in the right style, full-out, with faith that finer artistic spirits (maybe not Homer and Isaiah quite, but close, close), still alive somewhere in the ether, will help me out when my invention flags, the students doze, or the dean mutters into the phone. I'm getting back to a more exuberant style; I'll be expostulating and arm waving straight into the millennium, yes I will.

QUESTIONS FOR REACTION AND DISCUSSION

1. In the opening of this essay, Edmundson discusses his reactions to student evaluations at his institution. How would you characterize his response? What is your response to evaluating instructors? What do you think this process tells administrators, faculty members, and students about the quality of instruction on a campus?

2. Edmundson feels that passion and enthusiasm are conspicuously absent from the "cool youth culture" he observes on his campus. Does his description of his campus fit yours? Why or why not?

3. What does Edmundson mean by a "cool consumer perspective" that most students share? Do you agree with his analysis of how the media has enforced such a perspective? Why or why not?

4. What positive attributes in his students does Edmundson stress?

5. Edmundson suggests that the physical layouts of many campuses are changing, including his own; he says humorously that the campus "is looking more and more like a retirement spread for the young." Is this true of your campus? What is the purpose of these recreational facilities? How important do you think these facilities are in attracting students? Are they important to you?

QUESTIONS FOR WRITING

1. One of Edmundson's key concerns about contemporary college campus culture is that students have become consumers in a marketplace. This metaphor has a variety of implications for Edmundson, mostly negative. How do you see yourself in such a view of college culture? Are you a consumer who, if offended, will "shop" elsewhere? Are you a student who wants to be confronted and criticized? Is there some other more effective description that fits you? Write an essay in which you agree or disagree with Edmundson's position and provide examples and details from your own educational experience.

2. Assume that you are a student in a class who is asked to describe your hero, or the person you most admire. Who is that person? Why? What do our choices of heroes suggest about ourselves? How would Edmundson respond to the choice you made? Write an essay in which you describe your hero and then evaluate your choice.

3. Edmundson suggests at the end of his essay that liberal arts education today is ineffective because colleges and universities are fighting a losing battle against the forces of a consumer culture that promotes passivity, contentment with the status quo, comfort, and prosperity. Do you agree or disagree with Edmundson's analysis of contemporary culture? Do you agree with his characterization of the majority of today's college students? Write a position paper in which you defend or reject Edmundson's thesis.

4. With one or two other students, survey the physical layout of your campus and interview students about their daily activities. Construct some questions that you can ask of students: How much time do they spend at various campus facilities? What groups do they belong to? Why did they come to college? Who are their heroes? What are their favorite classes and why? How do they feel when they are corrected in a classroom? What are the characteristics of professors they admire the most? In discussion with your small group, prepare a report on the culture of your campus.

QUESTIONS FOR FURTHER EXPLORATION

1. Edmundson says that the promotional materials that colleges and universities send to prospective students suggest "the contemporary university's relationship with students has a solicitous, nearly servile tone." Locate such materials from the admissions office of your own campus and investigate the college Web site section for prospective students. Bring the materials with you to class and ask your classmates to evaluate what the materials suggest about the attitude toward students that is presented by the university's materials. Write a report of your classmates' responses for them.

2. One of Edmundson's particular criticisms of the consumer culture he depicts is television. Specifically he points to the importance of appealing characters on programs that blend in, are attuned to the "conventions," and that convey a laid-back persona. Choose one or two current or recent popular television programs and watch a few episodes. Do you see what Edmundson sees? Why or why not? In an essay, explain why you chose the programs you did, describe what you have seen, and write an analysis of the programs.

5

THE OLD EDUCATION AND THE THINK-ACADEMY

Martha C. Nussbaum is a professor of philosophy and law at the University of Chicago, where she teaches courses in philosophy and classical literature. Her book, Cultivating Humanity, *is based on her travels to several colleges and universities to study how institutions are coping with contemporary demands on the curriculum and with efforts to reform higher education generally. Drawing on her extensive knowledge of classical literature, Nussbaum takes her title from a phrase from Seneca, a Stoic philosopher who believed that the true philosopher's greatest role is as a teacher of humanity. As such, his works encourage individuals to avoid the material excess of the world and cultivate the virtue within. Nussbaum's subtitle is from* The Clouds *by Aristophanes, the greatest comic dramatist of ancient times. In* The Clouds *(BC 423), Aristophanes reveals his conservative impulses. Socrates, the educational innovator, is presented as an evil influence on society and savagely criticized for his rhetorical powers. Although Nussbaum alludes to ancient philosophy and literature, her critique of higher education is strikingly contemporary. Throughout her book, she emphasizes the importance for students and faculty members to develop global perspectives in a multicultural world. In this essay, taken from the introduction to her book, Nussbaum's position is that a liberal arts education is defined by what a citizen of the world today "should be and know."*

QUESTIONS FOR READING

1. What does the title suggest to you about this essay?
2. The title is actually an allusion to Aristophane's comedy, *The Clouds.* What do you know about this play? Where would you look to find information about Greek drama?
3. What do you know about a Socratic argument or the Socratic method?

4. What does it mean to be a professor of philosophy and law? What information do you know about your professors and their backgrounds? How can you find out more about them?

MARTHA C. NUSSBAUM

THE OLD EDUCATION AND
THE THINK-ACADEMY

*Cultivating Humanity: A Classical Defense of Reform in Liberal Education
(Cambridge: Harvard University Press, 1997)*

In Aristophanes's great comedy *The Clouds*, a young man, eager for the new learning, goes to a "Think-Academy" run by that strange, notorious figure, Socrates. A debate is staged for him, contrasting the merits of traditional education with those of the new discipline of Socratic argument. The spokesman for the Old Education is a tough old soldier. He favors a highly disciplined patriotic regimen, with lots of memorization and not much room for questioning. He loves to recall a time that may never have existed—a time when young people obeyed their parents and wanted nothing more than to die for their country, a time when teachers would teach that grand old song "Athena, glorious sacker of cities"—not the strange new songs of the present day. Study with me, he booms, and you will look like a real man—broad chest, small tongue, firm buttocks, small genitals (a plus in those days, symbolic of manly self-control).

His opponent is an arguer, a seductive man of words—Socrates seen through the distorting lens of Aristophanic conservatism. He promises the youth that he will learn to think critically about the social origins of apparently timeless moral norms, the distinction between convention and nature. He will learn to construct arguments on his own, heedless of authority. He won't do much marching. Study with me, he concludes, and you will look like a philosopher: you will have a big tongue, a sunken, narrow chest, soft buttocks, and big genitals (a minus in those days, symbolic of lack of self-restraint). Socrates's self-advertisement, of course, is being slyly scripted by the conservative opposition. The message? The New Education will subvert manly self-control, turn young people into sex-obsessed rebels, and destroy the city. The son soon goes home and produces a relativist argument that he should beat his father. The same angry father then takes a torch and burns down the Think-Academy. (It is not made clear whether the son is still inside.) Twenty-five years later, Socrates, on trial for corrupting the young, cited Aristophanes' play as a major source of prejudice against him.

In contemporary America as in ancient Athens, liberal education is changing. New topics have entered the liberal arts curricula of colleges and universities: the history and culture on non-Western peoples and of ethnic and racial minorities within the United States, the experiences and achievements of women, the history and concerns of lesbians and gay men. These changes have frequently been presented in popular journalism as highly threatening, both to traditional standards of academic excellence and to traditional norms of citizenship. Readers are given the picture of a monolithic, highly politicized elite who are attempting to enforce a "politically correct" view of human life, subverting traditional values and teaching students, in effect, to argue in favor of father-beating. Socratic questioning is still on trial. Our debates over the curriculum reveal the same nostalgia for a more obedient, more regimented time, the same suspiciousness of new and independent thinking, that finds expression in Aristophanes' brilliant portrait.

This picture of today's campuses bears little resemblance to the daily reality of higher education in America, as faculty and students grapple with issues of human diversity. Sensationalistic descriptions of horrors may sometimes be more fun to read than nuanced accounts of responsible decision making, but the latter are badly needed, since they represent the far more common reality. In order to evaluate the changes that are taking place in colleges and universities, we have to look more closely to see exactly what is changing, and why. What are faculty and students really doing, and how do newly fashionable issues about human diversity affect what they do? What sort of citizens are our colleges trying to produce, and how well are they succeeding in that task? To answer these questions, we need to look not only at one or two well-known institutions but at a wide range, representative of the variety that currently exists in American higher education: institutions public and private, religious and secular, large and small, rural and urban, four-year and university.

When we look in this way, we do see problems; and we do see tendencies that ought to be criticized. But on the whole, higher education in America is in a healthy state. Never before have there been so many talented and committed young faculty so broadly dispersed in institutions of so many different kinds, thinking about difficult issues connecting education with citizenship. The shortage of jobs in the humanities and social sciences has led to hardships; many have left the professions they love. But those who have stayed are intensely dedicated; furthermore, the ablest teachers and scholars are now no longer concentrated in a few elite schools. They are all over the country, reflecting about the mission of higher education, trying out strategies to enliven the thinking of the students who come their way. The real story of higher education in America is the story of the daily struggles of these men and women to reason well about urgent questions and to engage the hearts and minds of their students in that search.

At St. Lawrence University, a small liberal arts college in upstate New York, near the Canadian border, the snow is already two feet deep by early January. Cars make almost no sound rolling slowly over the packed white surface. But the campus is well plowed, even at Christmas. In a brightly lit seminar room young faculty, gathering despite the vacation, talk with excitement about their month-long visit to Kenya to study African village life. Having shared the daily lives of ordinary men and women, having joined in local debates about nutrition, polygamy, AIDS, and much else, they are now incorporating the experience into their teaching—in courses in art history, philosophy, religion, women's studies. Planning eagerly for the following summer's trip to India, they are already meeting each week for an evening seminar on Indian culture and history. Group leaders Grant Cornwell from Philosophy and Eve Stoddard from English talk about how they teach students to think critically about cultural relativism, using careful philosophical questioning in the Socratic tradition to criticize the easy but ultimately (they argue) incoherent idea that toleration requires us not to criticize anyone else's way of life. Their students submit closely reasoned papers analyzing arguments for and against outsiders' taking a stand on the practice of female circumcision in Africa.

In Riverside, California, already at 8 a.m. a brown haze blankets the mountains and the orange groves. It is the first day of the summer session at the University of California campus, and the ethnically mixed student body, more than forty percent minority, crowds the campus green. Richard Lowy, a young white instructor in Ethnic Studies, talks rapidly to my research assistant Yasmin Dalisay, herself a daughter of two Filipino doctors who immigrated to Orem, Utah. Lowy speaks in a low, gentle voice, peering through his thick glasses. He describes the difficulty of teaching about immigration, assimilation, and the political struggles of new minorities in a political climate saturated with sensationalism, mistrust, and appeals to irrational emotion. "Certainly there are some people who teach multiculturalism in a provocative way. I choose a more gentle approach. I try to tell everybody I'm not here to degrade you and I'm not here to condemn anybody for what your ancestors, relatives, or anybody did; I just try to explain what's going on, and I hope that the knowledge I present will begin to affect people, whereas the emotionalism of some people is what turns people off. I think that for people to be orienting their humanity only in political terms is too narrow, and I always tell people that you can either package your humanity in your politics or you can package your politics in your humanity, and if you're really a decent human being with the right attitude and the right heart and good faith toward people, it will come out. So I try to put things in that kind of perspective."

In Reno the University of Nevada campus is a small enclave of red brick and manicured lawns in the middle of casino-land. Yasmin talks with Eric Chalmers, a senior health science major from Carson City, who describes himself as having "more bigoted ideas than some people at the university level." Chalmers, who has never heard of the recently introduced "diversity requirement," requiring new freshman to take one course on a non-Western culture or on an ethnic or gender issue within the United States, applauds the trend to internationalizing, wishing he had had the opportunity to study Islam and the Middle East. But he criticized a course on domestic violence taught by a "liberated woman professor" because it seemed to him "too demeaning to men." As the interview is drawing to an end, he laughs, remembering something. "Here's another interesting thing. In English 102 we had to write a letter putting ourselves in the shoes of a gay person, like breaking the news to our parents saying we were gay, and explaining our lifestyle to them. At the time, when I was a freshman, it seemed really off the wall to me, and it was kind of an uncomfortable assignment, but now, looking back on it, it seems as though I can understand why he would do something like that—because you come into contact with people like—you know, different types of people—all the time, and maybe it's an understanding of their belief system." He laughs nervously.

On a dark afternoon in February 1995, I go to my Cambridge, Massachusetts, health club. There is a young man behind the check-in desk whom I haven't seen before—tall, beefy, red cheeked, in his late teens, wearing a red baseball cap and a bright purple sweatshirt with "Washington" in silver letters across the top and a glow-in-the-dark picture of the White House. He tells me his name is Billy. He is reading Plato's *Apology* and *Crito*. So you're reading Plato, I say. "Yeah. You like that stuff?" he asks, and his eyes light up. I tell him I like that stuff a lot, and I ask him about his class. It's at Bentley, a college in nearby Waltham, focused on business education. Who's the instructor? "I don't remember," he says. "She's foreign." The syllabus reads, "Dr. Krishna Mallick." Krishna Mallick, originally from Calcutta, has written some wonderful study questions about Socrates's mission of self-examination, his obedience to the laws of Athens, his willingness to die for the sake of the argument. Soon students will go on to use the techniques they have learned from Plato to stage debates about moral dilemmas of our time. Before I head for the Stairmaster, we talk for a while about why Socrates did not escape from prison when he had the chance, and it's plain that Krishna Mallick has produced real excitement. "You know, I really like this philosophy. Most courses, you have to remember lots of little facts, but in this one they want you to think and ask questions."

At the University of Chicago, a chain-link fence out back of the law school parking lot marks the line between the university campus and the impoverished black community that surrounds it. Black children sometimes climb over the fence or get round it by the driveway, but they are not allowed to stay long. On a May afternoon seventy students, one black, sit in a law school classroom discussing Richard Wright's *Native Son,* a novel set in that very part of Chicago in 1940. They talk about the "line" that Bigger Thomas thought of as the symbol of white hatred and black shame, and they argue intensely over Bigger's state of mind and the degree of his criminal responsibility. Since Justice Clarence Thomas has recently made a statement opposing mitigation in sentencing for blacks who trace their criminal tendencies to their deprived backgrounds, they ask whether Wright's novel supports or subverts Thomas's claims.

Scott Braithwaite, a young gay Mormon, recent graduate of Brigham Young University, gives a Sacrament meeting talk referring to the importance of including discussion of the history and variety of human sexuality in the liberal arts curriculum. This is currently a topic of intense controversy at BYU, and Braithwaite's talk is thick with references both to biblical texts and to Mormon scripture and history. "Ideally, " he concludes, "we should love everyone. Yet it is often difficult to love someone unknown, or different from oneself."

As Richard Lowy justly remarks, it is easier in our culture to purvey an emotion-laden sensationalizing message than to tell, with accurate information and humanity and even humor, stories of people's real diversity and complexity. Individuals can all too easily be forgotten when we engage in political debate. This book will let the voices of these representative yet highly individual teachers and students be heard—in the hope that the reader will decide to "package his politics in his humanity," imagining the concrete situations of the teachers who are making curricular choices and thinking about the issues with flexibility and empathy, rather than making a political prejudgment about the faculty who are actually teaching in our universities.

Today's teachers are shaping future citizens in an age of cultural diversity and increasing internationalization. Our country is inescapably plural. As citizens we are frequently called upon to make decisions that require some understanding of racial and ethnic and religious groups in our nation, and of the situation of its women and its minorities in terms of sexual orientation. As citizens we are also increasingly called upon to understand how issues such as agriculture, human rights, ecology, even business and industry, are generating discussions that bring people together from many nations. This must happen more and more if our economy is to remain vital and effective solutions to pressing human problems are to be found. The new emphasis on "diversity" in college and university curricula is above all a way of grappling with the altered requirements of citizenship, an attempt to produce adults who can function as citizens not just of some local region or group but also, and more importantly, as citizens of a complex interlocking world.

When I arrived at Harvard in 1969, my fellow first-year graduate students and I were taken up to the roof of Widener Library by a well-known professor of classics. He told us how many Episcopal churches could be seen from that vantage point. As a Jew (in fact a convert from Episcopalian Christianity), I knew that my husband and I would have been forbidden to marry in Harvard's Memorial Church, which had just refused to accept a Jewish wedding. As a woman I could not eat in the main dining room of the faculty club, even as a member's guest. Only a few years before, a woman would not have been able to use the undergraduate library. In 1972 I became the first female to hold the Junior Fellowship that relieved certain graduate students from teaching so that they could get on with their research. At that time I received a letter of congratulation from a prestigious classicist saying that it would be difficult to know what to call a female fellow, since "fellowess" was an awkward term. Perhaps the Greek language could solve the problem: since the masculine for "fellow" was *hetairos,* I could be called a *hetaira. Hetaira,* however, as I knew, is the ancient Greek word not for "fellowess" but for "courtesan."

In a setting in which such exclusions and such "jokes" were routine, is it any wonder that the academic study of women's history, of literature written by women, of the sociology and politics of gender—that all these perfectly normal and central topics were unavailable for serious study? They were just as available as was (in most places) the serious academic study of Judaism, of African and of African-American cultures, of many other ethnic minorities, of many non-Western religions and cultures, of the variety and diversity of human sexuality. Exclusions of people and exclusions of their lives from the domain of knowledge went hand in hand. The exclusions seemed natural and apolitical; only the demand for inclusion seemed motivated by a "political agenda." From the rooftop of Widener, there were many people and many lives that my colleague could not see.

We are now trying to build an academy in which women, and members of religious and ethnic minorities, and lesbians and gay people, and people living in non-Western cultures can be seen and also heard, with respect and love, both as knowers and as objects of study, an academy in which to be a "fellowess" need not mean being called "courtesan," an academy in which the world will be seen to have many types of citizens and in which we can all learn to function as citizens of that entire world.

Inevitably there is pain and turmoil in these attempts to bring about change, and not all proposals for change are healthy ones. Some faculty pursue the diversification of the curriculum in a way that ultimately subverts the aims of citizenship, focusing on interest-group identity politics rather than on the need of all citizens for knowledge and understanding. Some, too, have become unjustly skeptical of rational argument, thinking of its abuses as if they were part of the essence of rationality itself. These errors and excesses, however, are neither ubiquitous nor uncontroverted. Instead of a monolithic "politically correct" orthodoxy, what I hear when I visit campuses are the voices of many diverse individual faculty, administrators, and students, confronting curricular issues with, for the most part, resourcefulness, intelligence, and good faith. This means confronting it locally, understanding the nature of one's students and the resources of one's own institution. Any single set of curricular proposals for citizenship indicts itself by its very singleness, since U.S. college students are an extraordinarily heterogeneous group. So the heroes and heroines of my book are the many thousands of instructors who are working with dedication on this task: instructors like Richard Lowy, Eve Stoddard, Grant Cornwell, and Krishna Mallick, each going to work in a concrete context to create a conception of citizenship for the future. They are thinking searchingly, disagreeing fruitfully, and coming up with concrete solutions that should command our respect even where we do not fully agree.

Our campuses are producing citizens, and this means that we must ask what a good citizen of the present day should be and should know. The present-day world is inescapably multicultural and multinational. Many of our most pressing problems require for their intelligent, cooperative solution a dialogue that brings together people from many different national and cultural and religious backgrounds. Even those issues that seem closest to home—issues, for example, about the structure of the family, the regulation of sexuality, the future of children—need to be approached with a broad historical and cross-cultural understanding. A graduate of a U.S. university or college ought to be the sort of citizen who can become an intelligent participant in debates involving these difference, whether professionally or simply as a voter, a juror, a friend.

When we ask about the relationship of a liberal education to citizenship, we are asking a question with a long history in the Western philosophical tradition. We are drawing on Socrates' concept of "the examined life," on Aristotle's notions of reflective citizenship, and above all on Greek and Roman Stoic notions of an education that is "liberal" in that it liberates the mind from the bondage of habit and custom, producing people who can function with sensitivity and alertness as citizens of the whole world. This is what Seneca means by the cultivation of humanity. The idea of the well-educated person as a "citizen of the world" has had a formative influence on Western thought about education: on David Hume and Adam Smith in the Scottish/English tradition, on Immanuel Kant in the continental Enlightenment tradition, on Thomas Paine and other Founding Fathers in the American tradition. Understanding the classical roots of these ideas helps us to recover powerful arguments that have exercised a formative influence on our own democracy.

Our democracy, indeed, has based its institutions of higher learning on these ideals to a degree unparalleled in the world. In most nations students enter a university to pursue a single subject, and that is all they study. The idea of "liberal education"—a higher education that is a cultivation of the whole human being for the functions of citizenship and life generally—has been taken up most fully in the United States. This noble ideal, however, has not yet been fully realized in our colleges and universities. Some, while using the words "liberal education," subordinate the cultivation of the whole person to technical and vocational education. Even where education is ostensibly "liberal," it may not contain all that a citizen really needs to know. We should ask, then, how well our nation is really fulfilling a goal that it has chosen to make its own. What does the "cultivation of humanity" require?

The classical ideal of the "world citizen" can be understood in two ways, and "cultivation of humanity" along with it. The sterner, more exigent version is the ideal of a citizen whose *primary* loyalty is to human beings the world over, and whose national, local, and varied group loyalties are considered distinctly secondary. Its more relaxed version allows a variety of different views about what our priorities should be but says that, however we order our varied loyalties, we should still be sure that we recognize the worth of human life wherever it occurs and see ourselves as bound by common human abilities and problems to people who lie at a great distance from us. These two different versions have existed at least since ancient Rome, when statesman and philosopher Cicero softened the stern demands of Greek Stoicism for a Roman audience. Although I do sympathize with the sterner thesis, it is the more relaxed and inclusive thesis that will concern me here. What, then, does this inclusive conception ask us to learn?

Three capacities, above all, are essential to the cultivation of humanity in today's world. First is the capacity for critical examination of oneself and one's traditions—for living what, following Socrates, we may call "the examined life." This means a life that accepts no belief as authoritative simply because it has been handed down by tradition or become familiar through habit, a life that questions all beliefs and accepts only those that survive reason's demand for consistency and for justification. Training this capacity requires developing the capacity to reason logically, to test what one reads or says for consistency of reasoning, correctness of fact, and accuracy of judgment. Testing of this sort frequently produces challenges to tradition, as Socrates knew well when he defended himself against the charge of "corrupting the young." But he defended his activity on the grounds that democracy needs citizens who can think for themselves rather than simply deferring to authority, who can reason together about their choices rather than just trading claims and counterclaims. Like a gadfly on the back of a noble but sluggish horse, he said, he was waking democracy up so that it could conduct its business in a more reflective and reasonable way. Our democracy, like ancient Athens, is prone to hasty and sloppy reasoning, and to the substitution of invective for real deliberation. We need Socratic teaching to fulfill the promise of democratic citizenship.

Citizens who cultivate their humanity need, further, an ability to see themselves not simply as citizens of some local region or group but also, and above all, as human beings bound to all other human beings by ties of recognition and concern. The world around us is inescapably international. Issues from business to agriculture, from human rights to the relief of famine, call our imaginations to venture beyond narrow group loyalties and to consider the reality of distant lives. We very easily think of ourselves in group terms—as Americans first and foremost, as human beings second—or, even more narrowly, as Italian-Americans, or heterosexuals, or African-Americans first, Americans second, and human beings third if at all. We neglect needs and capacities that link us to fellow citizens who live at a distance or who look different from ourselves. This means that we are unaware of many prospects of communication and fellowship with them, and also of responsibilities we may have to them. We also sometimes err by neglect of differences, assuming that lives in distant places must be like ours and lacking curiosity about what they are really like. Cultivating our humanity in a complex, interlocking world involves understanding the ways in which common needs and aims are differently realized in different circumstances. This requires a great deal of knowledge that American college students rarely got in previous eras, knowledge of non-Western cultures, of minorities within their own, of differences of gender and sexuality.

But citizens cannot think well on the basis of factual knowledge alone. The third ability of the citizen, closely related to the first two, can be called the narrative imagination. This means the ability to think what it might be like to be in the shoes of a person different from oneself, to be an intelligent reader of that person's story, and to understand the emotions and wishes and desires that someone so placed might have. The narrative imagination is not uncritical, for we always bring ourselves and our own judgments to the encounter with another; and when we identify with a character in a novel, or with a distant person whose life story we imagine, we inevitably will not merely identify; we will also judge that story in the light of our own goals and aspirations. But the first step of understanding the world from the point of view of the other is essential to any responsible act of judgment, since we do not know what we are judging until we see the meaning of an action as the person intends it, the meaning of a speech as it expresses something of importance in the context of that person's history and social world. The third ability our students should attain is the ability to decipher such meanings through the use of the imagination.

Intelligent citizenship needs more than these three abilities. Scientific understanding is also of the first importance. My excuse for not dwelling on this aspect of a liberal education is that others are far better placed to describe it than I. The same is true for economics, which I shall approach only in its relationship to philosophy and political theory. I focus on the parts of a liberal education that have by now become associated with "the humanities" and to some extent "the social sciences": above all, then, on philosophy, political science, religious studies, history, anthropology, sociology, literature, art, music, and studies of language and culture. Nor do I describe everything in these areas that a good citizen should know. I focus on areas of current urgency and controversy. (Even within the areas of controversy I am selective, allowing the example of African-American studies to stand for more complex debates about ethnic studies generally. Issues of poverty and social class, which I have treated elsewhere, are treated selectively, within chapters organized along other lines.)

It was through ancient Greek and Roman arguments that I came upon these ideas in my own history. The Greek and Roman versions of these ideas are immensely valuable to us as we pursue these debates today, and I shall focus on that contribution. But ideas of this sort have many sources in many traditions. Closely related notions can be found in India, in Africa, in Latin America, and in China. One of the errors that a diverse education can dispel is the false belief that one's own tradition is the only one that is capable of self-criticism or universal aspiration.

Consider my examples of contemporary liberal education in the light of the three goals of world citizenship. The St. Lawrence program focuses on the second goal, that of producing students who are well informed about the lives of people different from themselves, and who can participate in debates about these lives with interest in the future of humanity. But the program leaders hold that any responsible teaching on the first issues must also be Socratic teaching, training logical abilities to think critically and to construct an argument. This training is built into the program, in the central role it gives to philosophy. Finally, the program's emphasis on travel develops imagination as well as factual knowledge. Living with people in Kenya expands one's ability to see the world from those people's point of view, and to approach new knowledge in a more empathetic spirit.

Richard Lowy's ethnic studies classes face an uphill battle: the tenacious loyalty of students to their group identities. He faces a classroom already politicized by these identities, and he must struggle to create a community of learning and dialogue within that situation. Like the St. Lawrence teachers, he emphasizes the importance of thinking of humanity in broader and more flexible terms than those dictated by ideological focusing on group loyalty; like them, he thinks of his goal as one of world citizenship and understanding. The Socratic logical abilities are less stressed in his approach, largely because of the nature of his discipline and subject matter. But imagination and empathy are clearly in evidence in the way in which he appeals to students to transcend their narrow sympathies.

Billy Tucker's philosophy class, by contrast, focuses on the Socratic ability to question and to justify, using this as the underpinning of a concept of citizenship. Krishna Mallick and Richard Lowy are pursuing related goals, each starting from a different disciplinary perspective: goals of broad understanding and respectful dialogue. But there is no doubt that the philosophical contribution to Tucker's education has been important to him as a citizen; it could not have been replaced by factual knowledge alone. Tucker is acquiring a new mode of approaching political debate, one that focuses on issues rather than on personalities, on reasoned analysis rather than on name-calling or sloganeering. He will need facts in order to make his arguments well, and the course stresses this requirement when it asks debaters to do research on their subjects. But the facts would not have produced a dialogue without the course's strong emphasis on Socratic argumentation, and without Mallick's ability to get students interested in such apparently boring phenomena as detecting fallacies and formalizing arguments.

Eric Chambers's English class focused on the imagination, pursuing the goal of world citizenship through practice in narrative understanding. Chalmers resisted courses presented in what he took to be an ideological or politically partisan manner. But the invitation to present the world from the point of view of a person different from himself did engage him, producing a person who was still capable of critical judgment, but who probably will relate to gay people, as a health care worker, in a more knowledgeable and sympathetic manner.

Scott Braithwaite did not encounter such instruction. Indeed, his training at Brigham Young was constructed in deliberate opposition to all three of my goals. It has more in common with Aristophanes' portrait of the Old Education than with the Socratic approach of the world citizen. Braithwaite was not taught to think critically about his tradition; he was taught to internalize its teachings. In a sense, as a young Mormon in a highly international church, he was taught to interact with others from different parts of the world—but usually in the mode of proselytizing, and never with the thought that learning might move in both directions. Finally, as he reports, his education did not invite his fellow students to imagine or know someone like him, nor did it invite him to know himself. He argues that this failure of knowledge entails a failure in the kind of love his own religion asks all people to have for one another.

Law students at the University of Chicago will soon be influencing life in our country in many ways. A large proportion will soon clerk for judges and write judicial opinions. Others will be involved in public service projects; still others will move directly into work with firms in a variety of capacities. Most will at one or another time deal with the problem of race—as clerks researching cases on affirmative action and minority hiring, as lawyers representing minority clients. Most of these law students, like Wright's character Mary Dalton, have never been into a tenement such as those that still exist several blocks from their classroom. If they are going to become good citizens in their future roles, they need not only logical ability and knowledge, aspects of citizenship already amply stressed in their curriculum. They also need to be able to participate imaginatively in a life such as that of Bigger Thomas, seeing how aspiration and emotion are shaped by their social setting.

In five of six cases, then, nontraditional studies, studies that would not have been in the curriculum twenty-five years ago, are supplying essential ingredients for citizenship. Billy Tucker's class is the closest to one that might have been taught in the last generation, but even that class has a focus on citizenship and on issues of the day that would not have been characteristic of the philosophical academy a while back. The St. Lawrence program involves a radical reform of a curriculum formerly focused on Europe and North America. The emphasis on ethnic studies at Riverside is part of a complex transformation of that curriculum to incorporate a variety of approaches to human diversity. Eric Chalmers encountered an English assignment that would have been unknown in Reno, Nevada, until very recently, part of a diversity movement that still generates intense controversy on campus. Scott Braithwaite laments the absence of such changes in the BYU curriculum. The University of Chicago, like most major U.S. law schools, devotes more attention to issues of race in response to interests of students and faculty. Unlike many such efforts, Chicago's focuses on the humanistic imagination as well as on factual knowledge.

Our campuses educate our citizens. Becoming an educated citizen means learning a lot of facts and mastering techniques of reasoning. But it means something more. It means learning how to be a human being capable of love and imagination. We may continue to produce narrow citizens who have difficulty understanding people different from themselves, whose imaginations rarely venture beyond their local setting. It is all too easy for the moral imagination to become narrow in this way. Think of Charles Dickens's image of bad citizenship in *A Christmas Carol*, in his portrait of the ghost of Jacob Marley, who visits Scrooge to warn him of the dangers of a blunted imagination. Marley's ghost drags through all eternity a chain made of cash boxes, because in life his imagination never ventured outside the walls of his successful business to encounter the lives of the men and women around him, men and women of different social class and background. We produce all too many citizens who are like Marley's ghost, and like Scrooge before he walked out to see what the world around him contained. But we have the opportunity to do better, and now we are beginning to seize that opportunity. That is not "political correctness"; that is the cultivation of humanity.

QUESTIONS FOR REACTION AND DISCUSSION

1. Nussbaum begins this essay by recounting part of the plot of *The Clouds*. What is your understanding of the difference between the "Think-Academy" and the Old Education? How effective is the contrast between Socrates and the old soldier? Is this an effective introduction to this essay? In what ways does Nussbaum return to this account of education in ancient Athens?

2. Nussbaum is considerably more positive and optimistic than other writers about the current state of higher education. In what ways is this tone reflected in her examples? In her commentary on her examples? How does this tone affect you as a reader?

3. Nussbaum blends examples from both her personal and professional experience in her essay. Are these effective? Why or why not?

4. In this essay, Nussbaum narrates accounts of her visits to St. Lawrence University, the University of California at Riverside, the University of Nevada at Reno, and the University of Chicago. What is the most striking example that Nussbaum uses from her travels to different campuses? What makes the example interesting, readable, or relevant? How effective do you think it is for a writer to use a series of examples in this way?

5. What does Nussbaum mean by a "world citizen" and the "cultivation of humanity"? What is the relationship between these terms and her definition of a liberal arts education?

QUESTIONS FOR WRITING

1. An assumption of Nussbaum's argument is that America is an "inescapably plural" society and that the goals of education must take this pluralism into account. In what ways does the curriculum of your college reflect the pluralism of the United States? How are the issues of cultural, racial, and gender diversity dealt with on your campus? Do you feel excluded or included in conversations and activities on your campus? What experiences have you had with these issues and what has been your reaction? In an essay, discuss your experience with the plurality of American society and how your education is helping or hindering your understanding.

2. Eric Chalmers, a student at the University of Nevada, Reno, is Nussbaum's example of a student who has resisted courses that he thought presented material in an "ideological or politically partisan" manner. In addition, faculty members often report that students frequently resist courses in women's history, African-American literature, and non-Western cultures, to name just a few examples. Do you sympathize with Eric's resistance? Why or why not? How can colleges and universities help students and faculty members communicate more effectively about the goals and purposes of courses and experiences aimed to promote diversity? Assume that you are a student representative on a campus committee to investigate resistance to cultural diversity courses and programs on your campus. Write an essay in which you discuss the problem, analyze the significance, and make specific recommendations for your committee to pursue.
3. Nussbaum explains her view of the major goals for a liberally educated world citizen: the ability to critically examine one's self and one's traditions, the ability to perceive the complexity of an interlocking global culture, and the ability to cultivate a narrative imagination. Write an essay in which you defend or reject Nussbaum's goals and offer specific examples from your own experience about how such goals (and those that you might propose as additions) can be accomplished in your undergraduate education.

QUESTIONS FOR FURTHER EXPLORATION

1. On March 5, 1998, Nussbaum participated in an interview about her book, *Cultivating Humanity*, on Jim Lehrer's *The Newshour* for the Public Broadcasting Corporation. Access the transcript on the PBS Web site <http://www.pbs.org/newshour> and read the interview. What did you learn from the interview that you didn't learn from your reading of the chapter of her book? Write a summary of the interview for your class and conclude it with your recommendation of whether others would benefit from reading it.
2. Read Aristophanes's play, *The Clouds*, and write an essay in which you relate the events of the play to the current debate of the nature of a liberal arts education. As you plan your essay, consider how you might use the characters of the play in a similar or different way from Nussbaum.
3. Read Charles Dickens's short novel, *A Christmas Carol*, and write an essay in which you develop Nussbaum's discussion about the image of Jacob Marley as a "bad citizen." Is this an effective example? Can you think of another character from your reading that would be equally or more effective to make Nussbaum's point that our educational institutions should avoid producing narrow citizens who cannot understand the views of others?

6

PROFESSORS AND INFLUENTIAL ALUMNI JOIN FORCES TO PROTECT BROOKLYN COLLEGE'S CORE CURRICULUM

Denise K. Magner is the senior editor of "The Faculty Section" of The Chronicle of Higher Education, *a weekly newspaper published in printed form and on the Internet <http://chronicle.com>. The* Chronicle *covers higher education in the United States and abroad and is read by more than 400,000 college and university administrators and faculty members. Each issue includes news about campuses in the United States and abroad, articles on developments in scholarly research, features on professional issues, articles and reviews on information technology, reports on state and federal government actions that affect higher education, statistical reports on varied topics like student enrollment and tuition figures, lists of new scholarly books, job listings, and a calendar of events. The* Chronicle *is an excellent source of information on all aspects of higher education. The Faculty Section is devoted to professional issues involving professors and graduate students, including teaching, the curriculum, affirmative action, and tenure. In recent years, many colleges and universities have revised their general education or core curriculum requirements. In this article, Magner reports on a recent controversy at Brooklyn College, one of the ten senior colleges within the City University of New York. Established in 1930 through the combination of a men's and women's college, Brooklyn was the first public, coeducational liberal arts college in New York City. With an enrollment of over fifteen thousand students, Brooklyn has been frequently acclaimed for its successful general education program.*

QUESTIONS FOR READING

1. What is your understanding of a "core curriculum" or "general education" requirements at a college or university? Are such requirements in existence on your campus? What are they?
2. How are core curriculum or general education requirements established at a college or university?

DENISE K. MAGNER

PROFESSORS AND INFLUENTIAL ALUMNI JOIN FORCES TO PROTECT BROOKLYN COLLEGE'S CORE CURRICULUM

ADMINISTRATION SCALES BACK A PLAN TO "REORIENT" THE INSTITUTION BY FOCUSING ON FOUR THEMES

The Chronicle of Higher Education (October 17, 1997)

The first official word on "Brooklyn Connections" was that it would transform the undergraduate curriculum at Brooklyn College.

A year later, the only thing that's been transformed is the administration's lofty rhetoric about the plan.

An ambitious effort to "reorient" the curriculum has been scaled back, and Brooklyn's core curriculum—the pride of many professors and alumni—has emerged unscathed. The president now says he always viewed the reform as a "small change" that would lead to only a few new majors and minors. In fact, says the provost, the name "Brooklyn Connections" has outlived its usefulness and may soon be retired.

How a curricular reform aimed at "transformation" turned into small potatoes is not just a matter of semantics. It is part of a continuing national battle among academics over the appropriate balance between a traditional liberal arts education and new interdisciplinary fields of study.

Three factors account for the straitened fortunes of Brooklyn Connections: a persistent circle of faculty critics, the intervention of a national alumni group, and bad publicity in a media-drenched town.

Faculty members on this campus of the City University of New York are fiercely protective of the liberal arts. Since 1981, the college has required all students to take ten "core" courses, on such topics as the classical origins of Western culture, power and politics, music and art, mathematics, and the basic sciences.

The announcement of a plan to reorient the curriculum around four new themes—communications, community studies, environmental studies, and science education—did not sit well with some members of the faculty. They viewed Brooklyn Connections as little more than an administrative marketing scheme, even though some professors were involved all along.

A turning point, most here agree, came in July, with the release of a letter from fifteen Brooklyn alumni, including such prominent academics as Eugene D. Genovese, Gertrude Himmelfarb, and Donald Kagan. It would be a "tragic mistake," they wrote, if money were diverted from the college's nationally acclaimed core curriculum to Brooklyn Connections. The letter, signed by members of the "Committee For the Brooklyn Core," was sent under the address of the National Alumni Forum, a Washington-based group that has won a reputation as a champion of the Western canon in the college curriculum.

"An administration steamroller was pushing the changes through at Brooklyn College," says Jerry L. Martin, president of the forum. "The alumni response took the steam out of the steamroller."

But where Dr. Martin sees a victory for educational standards, some here see a defeat for academic debate. Administrators and professors alike who helped design the plan are troubled by the "misinformation" they say was circulated about it, and by the interference in a campus debate of a national group with its own agenda.

The core curriculum was never in danger, they say. "You need continuity, but you need change too," says Nancy Hager, director of the college's Conservatory of Music and chairwoman of the Faculty Council. "The core itself was an example of radical change. A lot of people thought it was a big mistake, too. Brooklyn Connections was an opportunity to get the faculty thinking about where the college was going and its connection to the outside world."

Christopher M. Kimmich, the provost and the lead administrator behind Brooklyn Connections, characterizes the furor as a skirmish in the culture wars: "This is clearly part of a larger discussion taking place around the higher-education world between people concerned with change and people who find change disturbing."

He is "baffled," he says, at how people came to see Brooklyn Connections as a threat. "I saw it as providing opportunities beyond the core."

If the provost is puzzled, critics say, he need only look at his own memos for an explanation.

Most professors first heard of the plan about a year ago, when they assembled for a September faculty meeting. Dr. Kimmich stood up to describe it and noted that a memorandum on Brooklyn Connections was on its way to faculty mailboxes. The memo, from the provost's office, outlined a curricular effort to help the college become a model urban liberal arts institution of the twenty-first century.

You can't get much more urban than Brooklyn College, which is located in the Flatbush section of town. Most of its roughly fifteen thousand students come from the diverse ethnic mix of the borough.

The memo spoke of a need to engage the college in "issues that animate the vital and complex metropolitan community where our students live and work."

But two other sentences aroused immediate suspicion on a campus that has faced years of cuts in public financing. After listing the four themes, the memo said: "Decisions on resources in the years to come will proceed from these priorities. For example, they will be dispositive in decisions to hire new faculty for the fall of 1997."

Two months later, when the provost announced how twenty faculty slots open for 1997–98 would be distributed among departments, he noted that "most, though not all, of the allocations reflect the priorities set forth in Brooklyn Connections, with emphasis on communications and community studies."

It was impossible to miss the drift, says Margaret L. King, a professor of history. "It's true that faculty create the curriculum, and the provost assigns the faculty lines. But what if the lines are assigned according to radically new concepts that not only had the faculty not approved but had never even been presented with?"

After playing "zero role" in campus politics for years, Dr. King says, she has been unsparing in her criticism of the four themes, calling them a "hodge-podge of goofiness" and arguing that they emphasize only skills and tactics, not bodies of knowledge.

She found an ally in Abigail L. Rosenthal, a professor of philosophy. Rather than prepare students for the outside world, Dr. Rosenthal says, Brooklyn Connections would prepare them for living in Brooklyn.

She had always thought that the college was safe from the trendiness of much of the rest of academe, she says. The college, she says, offers its students—many of them new to the United States—the kind of strong liberal arts education that they could otherwise find only at far more expensive private colleges. "Here you have people who *are* diverse," Dr. Rosenthal says. "You don't have to instill that with community studies."

Departments in need of new professors after years of cutbacks were forced to tailor their personnel requests to one of the four themes, she says. "Faculty were not able to deliberate the fundamental worth of the innovation. They were encountered with a fait accompli and told, 'If you don't recast positions, you will be starved.'"

The two professors took it upon themselves to lead the opposition. Last February they helped engineer a resolution to create a faculty panel to evaluate Brooklyn Connections, since no elected body of professors had yet reviewed it. The resolution failed, but the close vote—119 in favor and 122 against—underscored the divisions over the plan.

The opposition was bolstered in May, when the Faculty Council's Committee on the Core Curriculum voted unanimously that the core should remain an important priority in the distribution of faculty slots. The core could "fall victim to passive euthanasia," the committee said, if faculty members were hired to focus on new priorities that had yet to be approved by the larger campus community.

But the momentum on campus still seemed to be swinging in favor of Brooklyn Connections, say Drs. King and Rosenthal. That's when Dr. Rosenthal contacted the National Alumni Forum. "It seemed like we'd tried every recourse internal to the college, and there was no sign of any change of course," she says. "I thought, They're going to win because we'll be exhausted."

As it turns out, she wasn't the only one to make that telephone call.

"We were contacted by both alums and faculty," says Dr. Martin, head of the national forum. "The alums were trying to figure out what to do. They'd heard bits and pieces and wanted to be better informed." The initial report on Brooklyn Connections, he says, "was so deeply flawed I found it embarrassing to read. It was presented at a level of vacuous slogans. No real case was made for these particular themes."

The forum helped organize the letter signed by the fifteen Brooklyn alumni, among whom were recent graduates as well as well-known scholars who had graduated well before the current core was in place, including Eugene Genovese, of the University Center in Georgia, and Donald Kagan, of Yale University.

Gertrude Himmelfarb, a professor emeritus of history at CUNY and a 1942 graduate, also signed the letter. When she read about Brooklyn Connections, she says, "I was appalled. It struck me as the kind of thing that community colleges and vocational schools do and do very well. It seems to be a shame to convert a very successful liberal arts college into that."

A 1992 graduate, Patrice P. Rankin, also signed the alumni letter after being contacted by the forum. Mr. Rankin, who is pursuing a Ph.D. in classical languages and literature at Yale University, says he was concerned about what he saw as the political slant of the forum. But he believes that alumni should have a say in campus curricular matters, and says the forum was the only group that provided a platform for alumni to express their views.

The alumni letter led to largely unfavorable articles in New York City's newspapers. An August editorial in the *New York Post* was headlined, "Attack on academic standards."

Then Brooklyn College's president, Vernon E. Lattin, stepped into the fray with a statement that critics of Brooklyn Connections saw as a sign of retreat. In a September 3 letter to the college's faculty members, he wrote that he was "alarmed" that a "legitimate curriculum debate has been so misunderstood at such an inopportune time, a time when CUNY is being bombarded by negative publicity." He insisted that Brooklyn Connections would have "no effect" on the "superb" core curriculum. But he also acknowledged that early documents about the project had contributed to the "confusion about the scope of 'Brooklyn Connections.'"

In an interview, he adds: "There were some hyperbolic statements early on."

Still, the plan's supporters insist that they have not backpedaled. "Nothing has changed as far as the faculty continuing to look at the four themes and come up with majors and minors," the president says.

What has changed, the plan's advocates say, is that people are finally beginning to understand that no new offerings will be created without faculty approval. While critics say the concept of Brooklyn Connections was never put to a faculty vote, President Lattin points out that a piece of it was: The faculty approved the creation of a new major in environmental studies, which awaits final approval by the CUNY central administration.

Dr. Kimmich, the provost, says the college hired sixteen new faculty members for this fall, nine of them in departments that teach courses in the core curriculum. Professors always have multiple teaching obligations and would never have been hired to teach solely in Brooklyn Connections, he says.

Descriptions of the four themes as "vocational" education came as a surprise to the provost, who says he views them as "theory based," and have incensed some faculty members, who have pushed for the new programs. For instance, they say, the new major in environmental studies will combine science and public-policy issues; it won't train students as sanitation engineers.

"I'd have had much less trouble with people going outside the faculty walls if their facts were clear," says Timothy Gura, a professor of speech who has taken a lead role in organizing the proposed new major in communications.

"Someone was jumping the gun to short-circuit academic discussion of our mission," says Louise Hainline, dean of graduate studies and research.

These faculty members say the reason Brooklyn Connections was not put to a vote of the faculty was that it was still in the planning stages, and there was nothing concrete to vote on.

They also question the idea that the expenditures of college dollars has to focus, first and foremost, on the core. "The core itself is 30 credits out of 120," says Dr. Hainline. "It's an important part of the curriculum, but not the only part."

At any rate, these supporters say, let the critics of Brooklyn Connections think they've won. Groups of professors are now quietly debating how to design new interdisciplinary majors and minors that in the end, they say, may prove transformative.

The critics, for their part, are not worried. They say the defenders of Brooklyn Connections are trying to rewrite history and are just sore because their pet projects are no longer a sure thing.

"Officials are responsible for the language of documents they've issued," Dr. Rosenthal says. "It's not enough to say—a year later, after alumni pressure and press attention—that they never meant it."

BROOKLYN COLLEGE'S CURRICULUM

Brooklyn College requires all undergraduates to complete ten "core" courses. A new program, "Brooklyn Connections," was announced last fall as an attempt to "reorient" the curriculum around four broad themes. Administrators and professors have been at odds over how those themes will affect the core courses.

THE CORE CURRICULUM

Classical Origins of Western Culture

Introduction to Art and Introduction to Music

People, Power, and Politics

The Shaping of the Modern World

Introduction to Mathematical Reasoning and Computer Programming

Landmarks of Literature

Science in Modern Life I: Chemistry and Physics
Science in Modern Life II: Biology and Geology
Studies in African, Asian, and Latin American Cultures
Knowledge, Existence, and Values

THE THEMES OF "BROOKLYN CONNECTIONS"

Community Studies
Communications
Environmental Studies
Science Education

QUESTIONS FOR REACTION AND DISCUSSION

1. What was "Brooklyn Connections" and how was it to be different from the core curriculum in place at Brooklyn College?
2. Who were the principal supporters of the new curriculum? Why did alumni groups oppose the new curriculum? Why did some members of the faculty oppose it?
3. Why did a core curriculum requirement at one college in New York City receive so much national attention?

QUESTIONS FOR WRITING

1. In the catalogue or on the Web site for your college or university, read the description of the core curriculum or general education requirements. What goals are these requirements intended to accomplish? Are they closer in spirit to the ten-course requirement at Brooklyn or to the four themes that had been proposed? In an essay, describe the core curriculum on your campus and compare it with the ten-course requirement at Brooklyn.
2. Magner suggests that at least part of the tension among the faculty members at Brooklyn were over traditional disciplinary boundaries (such as history, art, and literature) and new "interdisciplinary" fields of study. What is an interdisciplinary field? What are prominent examples on your campus? Investigate interdisciplinary study on your campus and write a report for your classmates of your findings. Interview some students involved in interdisciplinary study and ask them to evaluate their program. Include such information as the number and kinds of programs, examples of courses, mission or purpose state-

ments, sources of information on campus, faculty members, and numbers of students enrolled.

3. Throughout this essay, Magner quotes the opinions of vocal former students about the efforts to change the curriculum at Brooklyn College. At many campuses, students participate in curriculum discussion by serving as representatives on faculty curriculum committees. What system is in place on your campus for expressing your opinion about the curriculum? What is the responsibility of current and former students for the curriculum of the schools they attend? Write a letter to your campus newspaper in which you outline a statement of responsibilities of students for voicing opinions about the curriculum.

QUESTIONS FOR FURTHER EXPLORATION

1. Access the Brooklyn College Web site <http://www.brooklyn.cuny.edu>, and read the mission statement of the college as well as the description of the core curriculum. How well do you think the curriculum suits the mission of the college? Are there any gaps? Is there anything you would add or delete? What is the purpose of a liberal arts education, according to the mission statement? Write an essay in which you evaluate the current curriculum against the goals outlined in the mission statement.

2. A number of other institutions have been deeply involved in curriculum debates during the last decade, such as the State University of New York system, Duke University, Rice University, and Columbia University. Investigate how the curriculum of an institution becomes national news. What are the major issues? What are dividing lines for faculty, administrators, and students? How did the institution resolve the conflict? Write a report of your findings and present it to your classmates.

7

BURY THE LIBERAL VS. PROFESSIONAL ARTS DEBATE

George R. Houston is the President of Mount Saint Mary's College, a Catholic, coeducational, liberal arts college in rural Maryland. Founded in 1808, the college is one of the oldest in the country. Like other church-related schools, the college strives to provide an education within a religious tradition, which in this case is the Roman Catholic Church. This essay first appeared in Education, *an academic journal that publishes essays, reviews, and research reports on innovations in teaching and all levels of education. In this essay, Houston confronts a central issue for colleges and universities: the tension between traditional undergraduate liberal arts programs (such as philosophy, history, and literature) and professional programs (such as business and education). On many campuses, this issue is not a central one. For example, traditional liberal arts colleges often do not offer courses in business, engineering, or education. On the other hand, many large public and private institutions have departments and even undergraduate colleges devoted to professional offerings; in some cases several colleges within a single university will have different sets of curriculum and graduation requirements for undergraduates. Houston provides a historical context for the debate that often divides faculty members and students, suggesting that the divide between the liberal arts and the "professional arts" is a false one and one that we should "bury."*

QUESTIONS FOR READING

1. How are the traditional liberal arts and courses designed for professional training handled on your campus? Is there a division that is institutionalized (through departments, colleges, or schools)?
2. Do you consider yourself a student involved in a liberal arts program, a professional program, or both?

3. Houston suggests in his essay that many students pursuing professional degrees are often made to feel like second-class citizens. Is this true on your campus? Why or why not?

GEORGE R. HOUSTON, JR.

BURY THE LIBERAL VS. PROFESSIONAL ARTS DEBATE

Education 117 (1996)

The purpose of education is to provide a foundation for how to live life. Clearly both liberal arts education and professional education contribute to this goal. The future requires that America's college and university graduates possess the ability to think, reason, and communicate, but it also demands that they have the knowledge and skills needed for employment and career building.

The debate between the relative value of a pure "liberal arts" education and one that combines the liberal arts with professional arts has been fueling academic fires for decades. The debate has no place in the modern academy. Historically some students who pursued the professional arts—business and education on the undergraduate level—were made to feel "second class" citizens of the university. Frequently, students admitted to these programs were accused of entering the university through the "back door." And frequently this was a "self-fulfilling" prophecy. Many of these students were "less credentialed" than their counterparts in the arts and sciences. However, a review of the history of the academy should eliminate this accusation. Some of the oldest universities were founded for professional purposes.

The University of Salerno, one of Europe's oldest, was founded for the study of medicine. A college was founded at Cambridge almost seven hundred years ago to provide "clerks for the King's service." Law, medicine, arts, and theology are the four original higher faculties in a university. Historically, "The universities have trained the intellectual pioneers of our civilization [sic]—the priests, the lawyers, the statesman, the doctors, the men of science, and the men of letters."[1] Then, what is the question of the place of "liberal" versus "professional" arts in the university?

To get a good understanding of the debate, one only has to read two books. One is John Henry Newman's *The Idea of a University* (1852) and the other is Alfred North Whitehead's *The Aims of Education and Other Essays*

(1929). These two authors go to the heart of the debate. For Alfred North Whitehead, the essence of a liberal education was:

> . . . an education for thought and for aesthetic appreciation. It proceeds by imparting a knowledge of the masterpieces of thought, of imaginative literature, and of art. The action which it contemplates is command. It is an aristocratic education implying leisure. This Platonic ideal has rendered imperishable services to European civilization [sic]. It has encouraged art, it has fostered that spirit of disinterested curiosity which is the origin of science, it has maintained the dignity of mind in the face of material force, a dignity which claims freedom of thought . . . For centuries, from Pope Nicholas V to the school of the Jesuits, and from the Jesuits to the modern . . . schools, this educational ideal has had the strenuous support of the clergy.
>
> For certain people it is a very good education. It suits their type of mind and the circumstances amid which their life is passed. But more has been claimed for it than this. All education has been judged adequate or defective according to its approximation to this type.[2]

Whitehead saw the value of other types of education. It is no wonder that Harvard chose him to be the inaugural speaker at the founding of its famous Business School.

For Newman (1852), education was for education's sake. He believed: "This process of training, by which the intellect, instead of being formed or sacrificed to some particular or accidental purpose, some specific trade or profession, or study of science, is disciplined for its sake, for the perception of its own proper object, and for its own highest culture, is called Liberal Education . . ."[3] The essence of a good liberal education for Newman was "the cultivation of the 'understanding,'" a "talent for speculation and original inquiry," and "the habit of pushing things up to their first principles."[4]

This, I would posit, is the origin of the issue. For the disciples of John Henry Newman, a pure liberal arts education is the only type of education. To enter into this debate, we must first ask: "What is the purpose of education?"

There is only one subject matter for education and that is how to live. To learn how to live, education must be useful. "Education is the acquisition of the art of the utilization [sic] of knowledge."[5] Neither John Henry Newman nor Alfred North Whitehead could have predicted the "knowledge explosion" that has taken place since their lifetimes. Something like eighty percent of written documents have been produced in the last half century. Thus, Newman was confined to less than twenty percent of the journals and books available to us today, let alone the information through information networks. Newman wrote for an English audience in an English world in an English century.

It must also be kept in mind that Newman's "liberal arts" education that studied the classics was the norm throughout the world of education in his time. A knowledge of Greek and Latin was required because those were the languages used by scholars. That is gone for ever. When classics were the normal road to advancement, classics were popular. But classics were not studied for "education's sake."

Both Alfred North Whitehead and John Henry Newman concur on the role of a "liberal education." Few today would question its value. The best preparation for any profession or vocation is a sound grounding in liberal education. A program where students learn to communicate and develop intellectual and interpersonal skills. A program where students are exposed to three general areas of knowledge:

- Understanding of historical events and of different cultures.
- Interaction with diverse groups on various intellectual levels.
- Appreciation of global economic, political and social forces present in the world today.

Today's educational experience should draw from both Newman and Whitehead. The purpose of education, identified by Newman, is the formation of a philosophical habit rooted in freedom, equitableness, calmness, moderation, and wisdom. It is exercises of mind, reason, reflection. These are good and every student should be exposed to a curriculum that develops these "goods." Whitehead's belief that education should produce people who possess both culture and expert knowledge of some particular field should also be accommodated. Both men linked culture and education. General culture of mind is the best aid to professional and scientific study. There does not have to be any distinction between the professional and liberal arts in acquiring this "general culture of mind."

The antithesis between a technical and a liberal education is fallacious. There can be no adequate technical education which is not liberal, and no liberal education which is not technical; that is, no education which does not impart both technique and intellectual vision. In simpler language, education should turn out the pupil with something he knows well and something he can do well. This intimate union of practice and theory aids both. The intellect does not work best in a vacuum. The stimulation of creative impulse requires, especially in the case of a child, the quick transition to practice. Geometry and mechanics, followed by a workshop practice, gain that reality without which mathematics is verbiage.[6]

In the fields of accounting, education, medicine and law, the combining of a "practicum" and "theory" has long been the practice. Those who have chosen the vocation of "teaching" at the primary and secondary levels have a period of "practice teaching" as part of their curriculum. As an aside, many a university professor would have benefited from some practice teaching before being thrown into the undergraduate classroom. Accountants have long required "experience" before one is fully admitted to the profession. Many law schools offer "clinics" where their students get "hands on" experience while assisting those in need of legal services. Moot Courts are just another example of offering "experience" in the legal curriculum. Even in the formation of priests, "field work" is a component of the educational process.

How courses are taught, whether they be the "classics" or "professional arts," is the determinant as to whether an education is liberal or not. Frequently it has been argued that the memorization of lines of poetry improves the memory. Then that same argument would hold true for the memorization of mathematical equations or marketing definitions in a business curriculum. Accounting can be taught where the student is encouraged to memorize a series of transactions and then regurgitate them during examinations. That is not a liberal education. On the other hand, accounting principles can be taught and the student then must analyze a business transaction, breaking it into its components, applying the correct principle, to obtain the correct answer. That is a liberal learning experience.

At Mount Saint Mary's College in Emmitsburg, Maryland, a Junior Honors Seminar on "The Many Faces of Leadership: An Interdisciplinary View" is offered. The seminar's purpose is:

> . . . to create an interdisciplinary synthesis of the phenomenon of leadership based on multiple modes of inquiry and knowledge bases housed in different disciplines. It is hoped that out of this seminar students will acquire an appreciation of an interdisciplinary framework that can be used to guide their critical thinking and inform their practice of leadership in a number of diverse contexts. The goal of the seminar is to help students better formulate their own model of leadership by providing them with a variety of useful lenses through which to view and reflect on their own philosophy and practice of leadership.

During the course of the year, leadership is discussed from a number of views. Ethics is discussed by a professor from the Philosophy Department; Religion by a professor from Theology. Non-Western culture and gender differences are also introduced by appropriate professors. Fact and fiction and persuasive languages are discussed by professors from English and from Rhetoric and Writing Departments. The seminar is offered by the Chair of the Business, Accounting, and Economics Department. Hence, it would be labeled one of the "professional arts" in many a college. At that same academy, if the identical seminar was offered by the Philosophy Department, it would be a "liberal arts" course. So what? What difference does the label make? It is the course content and the learning that make the difference in determining whether a course contributes to a "liberal education."

When you have learned to think and reason, to compare, to discriminate, to analyze, if you have refined your taste, formed your judgments, and sharpened your mental vision, you have acquired an "education" and are prepared to take up any calling. This is the purpose of education. How you acquire some of the characteristics is immaterial. For example, whether you learn to "think and reason" by studying Aristotelian logic or by "flow-charting" an accounting process, or "writing a computer program" is unimportant. What is important is that the student learns to think and reason. This point of view forces the academy to place learning above teaching. This will bring on cardiac arrest in many. But this shift is taking place, and those of us who are going not only to survive, but also to thrive are going to have to change also.

For all the differences between Newman and Whitehead and perhaps Newman's inability to foresee the accessibility of various types of university education in the twentieth century, his aim of a university is quite desired today:

> But a University training is the great ordinary means to a great but ordinary end; it aims at raising the intellectual tone of society, at cultivating the public mind, at purifying the national taste, at supplying true principles to popular enthusiasm and fixed aims to popular aspiration, at giving enlargement and sobriety to the ideas of the age, at facilitating the exercise of political power, and refining the intercourse of private life. It is the education which gives a man a clear conscious view of his own opinions and judgments, a truth in developing them, an eloquence in expressing them, and a force in urging them. It teaches him to see things as they are, to go right to the point, to disentangle a skein of thought, to detect what is sophistical, and to discard what is irrelevant. It prepares him to fill and post with credit, and to master any subject with facility. It shows him how to accommodate himself to others, how to throw himself into their state of mind, how to bring before them his own, how to influence them, how to come to an understanding with them, how to be with them. He is at home in any society; he has common ground with every class; he knows when to speak and when to be silent; he is able to converse; he is able to listen; he can ask a question pertinently, and gain a lesson seasonably, when he has nothing to impart himself; he is ever ready, yet never in the way; he is a pleasant companion, and a comrade you can depend upon; he knows when to be serious and when to trifle, and he has a sure tact which enables him to trifle with gracefulness and to be serious with effect. He has the repose of a mind which lives in itself, while it lives in the world, and which has resources for its happiness at home when it cannot go abroad. He has a gift which serves him in public, and supports him in retirement, without which good fortune is but vulgar, and with which failure and disappointment have a charm. The art which tends to make a man all of this is in the object which it pursues as useful as the art of wealth or the art of health, though it is less susceptible of method, and less tangible, less certain, less complete in its result.[7]

If the graduates of all of our academies possessed the above characteristics, regardless of whether they pursued professional or liberal arts, they would have received a life long education. And in a well-designed program, of either stripe, it can be accomplished.

Today, the higher education "industry" is in a mature market. This means that consumers focus more on cost than quality. They are used to living on tight budgets that have acquired a "markdown" mentality. They have already forced the medical and legal professions to cut or at least contain their costs. And we are beginning to see this same impact on higher education. And that impact is being felt in the once sacred faculty preserve of curriculum development.

Curriculum reviews now are ongoing, not periodic, in the best of our academic houses, and they are being dictated by the mission of the academy and not faculty interest. For those who will survive, that mission will include not only an "education for life" but an education that provides the skills, wisdom, and knowledge to get employed. There is nothing wrong with providing an education that enables one to be hired. To work is not a sin. Clearly the academy does not want to train for a very narrow "first task." That could defeat the development of an "imaginative learning" process. It would not provide the necessary tools for advancement both in employment and life skills. Combining the liberal and professional arts in a liberal education is the current challenge.

Today, we do not educate for a leisure society. Work is good. To prepare the next generation to take its place in the work force, in the professions, in our communities, and in the Republic is also good. Let's bury the liberal versus professional arts debate and get on with providing an education—a learning experience—that meets the challenges and needs of the next generation for the Third Millennium.

NOTES

1. A. N. Whitehead, *The Aims of Education and Other Essays* (New York: The Free Press, 1929) 95.
2. Whitehead 46.
3. J. H. Newman, as cited in C. B. Schmersahl and M. Sollenberger, *Choices* (Acton, MA: Copely Publishing Group).
4. Newman 183.
5. Whitehead 48.
6. Ibid.
7. Newman 193–194.

QUESTIONS FOR REACTION AND DISCUSSION

1. How effective is Houston's example of the University of Salerno at the beginning of his essay? Houston suggests that the description of this old university answers—at least partly—the question he raises about the origins of the division between the liberal arts and the professional. Do you agree or disagree?
2. Houston draws heavily on John Henry Newman and Alfred North Whitehead throughout this essay. How effective is his use of these sources? How are the quotations from each introduced and integrated into Houston's own argument?
3. In your own words, what is the thesis of Houston's essay? What are his major sources of support for his thesis?
4. How would you characterize the tone of this essay? Does the tone strengthen or weaken the argument of the essay?

QUESTIONS FOR WRITING

1. Houston says, "There is only one subject matter for education and that is how to live. To learn how to live, education must be useful."

Do you agree or disagree? How would other writers in this section respond to this statement? Write an essay in which you compare and contrast the views of Houston with those of Nussbaum, Booth, or Edmundson.

2. Houston describes a junior seminar in the Mount Saint Mary's curriculum, "The Many Faces of Leadership: An Interdisciplinary View." Reread Houston's account of the success of this course. How important is teaching in Houston's assessment of the success of this course? How does this course attempt to bridge the divide between the liberal arts and the professional? How effective do you think such a course would be? Is there a similar course offered on your campus? Write an essay in which you evaluate how a course at your institution or at Mount Saint Mary's can successfully blend the purposes of the liberal arts with professional training.

3. Consider the curriculum for your major or, if you are undecided, consider the curriculum for the major that is now closest to your interest. What constitutes the liberal arts part of it? The professional part? Is there an institutional effort to blend the two through courses, programs, and departments? Write an essay in which you describe and analyze the curriculum in terms of Houston's position that combining the liberal and professional arts curriculum is the best education for the next century.

QUESTIONS FOR FURTHER EXPLORATION

1. Read the full text of John Henry Newman's *The Idea of a University,* which was originally a set of lectures delivered in Dublin in 1852. What was the particular historical context for Newman's lectures? What special kind of university did he envision? How relevant are his arguments for contemporary universities? Assume that you have been asked by the editor of this text to include a selection from Newman's works that you think would be appropriate for this section of this textbook. Choose the selection, write a headnote for it that justifies its inclusion, and design a set of reading and discussion questions for students.

2. Read Alfred North Whitehead's *The Aims of Education and Other Essays.* Write a short introduction to this text, describing Whitehead's life and career, and include an explanation of why a contemporary audience of college faculty members and students should read and know his book.

3. Access the Mount Saint Mary's College Web Site <www.msmary.edu> and read the mission statement, purpose, and description of the curriculum. What evidence do you see that this college has closed the gap between the liberal arts and professional education? Write a report for class.

8

Do Geeks Need to Go to College?

Lisa Schmeiser is the author or coauthor of three books on Web site design and maintenance. As a freelance writer, Schmeiser also contributes to online magazines; this article appears in the award-winning Salon Magazine *<http://www.salon.com>. Founded in 1995 by David Talbot, former Arts and Features Editor of the* San Francisco Examiner, Salon *is an Internet magazine that publishes original book and media reviews, articles on the arts, interviews, technology, news commentary, travel essays, and a "Table Talk Forum," an online chat group on some one thousand five hundred topics with over ninety thousand registrants. Contributing writers for the magazine include such well-known writers as Garrison Keillor (who writes a funny advice column), David Horowitz, Camille Paglia, and Christopher Hitchens. According to the editor's statistics, more than 9.5 million page views of the magazine had occurred by July 1998 (a "page view" is the way in which Web site managers determine how frequently their sites are accessed). This article appeared in the "Technology" section of the magazine and takes up the topic of the appropriate kind of education for a person who seeks a career in computer technology.*

Questions for Reading

1. What does the title suggest to you about the thesis of this essay?
2. This article has never been published in print form until its appearance in this text; it is a publication of an online magazine. What effect does reading the printed version have on you as a reader?

LISA SCHMEISER

DO GEEKS NEED TO GO TO COLLEGE?

Salon Magazine (April 12, 1999)
<http://www.salonmagazine.com/tech/feature/1999/04/12/college/index.html>

When Brad Scott of *Clear Ink* has to devise the information architecture for a new Web site, he just asks himself where the site's bathrooms will be.

Scott, a one-time interior design major turned information architect, is speaking only metaphorically, of course. But he says learning about "critical adjacencies of space"—such as putting restrooms near conference rooms so that meeting attendees can quickly duck in and out—carries over to Web design, where the "critical adjacencies" are of information.

Scott's migration from architecture into the technology industry isn't atypical: Talk to a group of tech workers, and you may find that the majority of them drifted into the industry from a completely different discipline.

The Web industry is creating jobs at a clip, and many of those jobs are going to college graduates without academic computing experience—and people who skipped college altogether. No one has taken a formal count of these two groups, but they haven't gone unnoticed. And their success raises the question of whether a computer science education, or even any higher education, is a prerequisite to competing in the high-tech job market.

The relevance of higher education to high-tech jobs is under scrutiny, thanks to the rising number of success stories featuring someone who majored in a right-brained specialty, bypassed college or dropped out—the most famous example being Harvard dropout Bill Gates. In December, *Forbes* asked if investing in a college education was a smart way to spend time investing in a career. Among the numbers the article cited: Close to fifteen percent of the Forbes 400 either dropped out of college or avoided it altogether, and those executives boast an average net worth of $4.8 billion. A few weeks later, *U.S. News and World Report* ran a related article: More boys are opting out of college to pursue jobs in a booming economy.

There is ample incentive to trade higher education for high-salaried, high-tech jobs. *Forbes* noted that a college degree costing $120,000 might actually be worth more as a mutual fund with a five percent interest rate; if a teenager's parents sink the $30,000 they would have spent on the first year's tuition into a mutual fund for their child, he'll have $500,000 by the time he turns fifty. Many college graduates, especially those who spend their early postgraduate years paying off student loans, will never see that much in the bank. The article also contends that colleges are unable to keep up with the proliferation of programming languages and technologies driving today's job market, and thus do not outfit their students with the necessary job skills. Is it any wonder would-be tech tyros rethink college?

The übergeek news portal *Slashdot* posted a link to the *Forbes* article and found itself hosting a three hundred-plus-message argument on the merits of education in relation to high-tech jobs. The respondents were evenly split: Some younger programmers argued that their practical experience and high salaries offset the disadvantages of lacking a degree, while others argued that a formal education leads to a higher caliber of technical work later in life.

But does that formal education even have to be in engineering, or will any old degree do? Scott is joined by Web producer Satya Kuner and Jason Monberg, the CTO of Sparks, in believing that their nontechnical degrees have enhanced their work in the tech industry.

Kuner contends that her background as a dance major improved her job performance when she was charged with doing technical support for Unix, C, and Perl programming. As part of her job, she had to walk users through solutions to thorny code errors, then log the events in a database for other workers. She credits the improvements she made to the company's database to the communication skills she learned in college, saying, "Lots of geeks I know can't provide clear instructions because they can't fathom that someone couldn't know something."

Humanities-based skills can also improve the traditional code-writing process. According to Kuner, artists bring a novel perspective to code composition, allowing them to extend the uses to which a programming language is put. Monberg, who holds a degree in sociology, has noticed that coding and engineering groups that include people trained outside the discipline are more open to innovation. "It opens the door to a more engaging cross-pollinating environment," he says. "Individual contributors are not completely locked into thinking only about their specific task."

Nor are individuals locked into one set of job skills: Scott, Kuner, and Monberg all acquired specific technical skills on a compressed schedule in response to job demands, and they believe that their college education helped flatten the learning curve—even if the connections between Unix and dancing, interior design or sociology aren't readily apparent.

College provided a mental model for learning subsequent skills, which complements the one constant in high tech: the need to keep learning. Any high-tech worker, regardless of academic background, must stay abreast of new skills to keep up in the field.

Perhaps, as those *Slashdot* posters argued, the learning can take place on site at a sixty thousand dollar programming job. But judging by the posts complaining, "if only Bill Gates took an OS class," there are also unarguable merits to a technical university education for engineers. Monberg himself admits that there are times when a computer science education would have come in handy: "When you get down to it, earning a CS degree provides one with some very basic practical experience."

At the heart of the higher-education debate lies the question: Do high-tech workers miss out on some crucial educational event if they skip college? There's no denying that high tech offers something few other disciplines do—

the ability to enter and move up in an industry based on applicable skills and experience, instead of requiring a degree to even enter the arena. But having a degree doesn't prevent high-tech workers from picking up experience elsewhere. The learning skills one uses to pick up programming languages and systems operations are highly individual and can be acquired from disciplines as diverse as music or biology. They can also be picked up through a combination of time spent on a computer and a curiosity to learn more: Kuner, Monberg, and Scott all honed their technical chops through self-teaching.

What can't be picked up through hard programming experience is the discipline-specific experience that any college graduate possesses. To a biology major like me, object-oriented programming didn't make much sense when it was explained in terms of classes and constructors. But when I could map the general ideas to familiar ground—the immune system's different types of cells and the chemical signals they send to each other are similar to classes of code objects and the embedded functional signals they each have—I picked up the programming concept and expanded on it in ways my computer-engineering coworkers hadn't pondered yet.

As more graduates combine their intellectual experience with practical technical skills, observers may recast the higher-education question. Instead of wondering whether college is relevant, we may ask what kind of degrees will allow high-tech workers and companies to stay fresh and keep innovating.

QUESTIONS FOR REACTION AND DISCUSSION

1. Were you surprised about the number of people mentioned in this article who work in the computer industry with nontechnical backgrounds? Why or why not?
2. What is the argument for *not* going to college if you wish to pursue a high-tech job? Is it persuasive? Why or why not?
3. What arguments do several of the people mentioned in this article offer for going to college and pursuing a nontechnical major?

QUESTIONS FOR WRITING

1. In this article, Schmeiser interviews several people with high-tech jobs and nontechnical education. Make a list of the skills and abilities that these people have in common. Write an essay in which you describe the kind of education that a person needs in order to develop these skills and abilities.
2. Although this essay is not explicitly concerned with explaining the goals and purposes of a liberal arts education, Schmeiser's argument is that people who have one may be better prepared than others with no

education or a highly technical one. Do you agree or disagree? On what basis? Interview some of your classmates or friends who intend to pursue high-tech careers. What courses and/or majors do they intend to pursue? Why? Write an essay in which you challenge or support Schmeiser's argument, providing examples and details from your own experiences and your reading.

QUESTIONS FOR FURTHER EXPLORATION

1. In an interview with Amazon.com (http://www.amazon.com), Schmeiser was asked when and how she began writing. Her response was "I don't have a good 'why'—writing is an involuntary brain stem function for me. I've been writing since I was old enough to form letters; when we cleaned out my grandfather's things after his death, I discovered a stash of stories I wrote him through elementary school. However, I didn't start writing publication-ready stuff until college. I still don't consider myself a 'writer'—I guess I'm waiting for some sort of divine sign like a burning bestseller or something." Access the interview by searching for her recent book *The Complete Website Kit* and read her additional comments. Do you consider Schmeiser's essay well written? Why or why not? What is effective about the essay and what is not? Do you feel with Schmeiser that writing is "an involuntary brain stem function"? Write an essay in which you evaluate Schmeiser's writing style in this essay.

2. Research the opinions of others who have written about the appropriate background for a career in computer technology. Use *The Reader's Guide to Periodical Literature* to locate articles and information; you might begin by reading the articles in *Forbes* and *U.S. News and World Report* mentioned in this article. What are the major issues? Do many experts agree with Schmeiser about the importance of a broad, liberal arts background? Write a report of your findings and present them to your class.

Suggestions for Further Reading, Thinking, and Writing

1. Several of the writers whose works are represented in this section take different positions on the purposes of a liberal education: especially Wayne Booth, Mark Edmundson, George Houston, and Martha Nussbaum. Write an essay in which you compare and contrast the views of several writers about the purpose of a liberal education, being careful to provide a clear explanation for the differing views of each writer.

2. In *What's College For: The Struggle to Define American Higher Education*, Zachary Karabell observes:

> At the close of the twentieth century, possessing a diploma is not necessarily enough to guarantee one either a good job or even any job. As business is now organized, most jobs are not lifelong, and career changes occur frequently. And here, it is skills rather than credentials, even the skill to be able to learn what needs to be learned to shift careers midway through life, that seem more influential in determining who best weathers career crises (viii).

Several writers in this section touch on the contemporary reality that most jobs are not lifelong. What are the implications for you as a student and potential job-seeker? Drawing on your readings from this section as well as your own views, write an essay in which you describe the difference between "skills" and "credentials."

3. Many of the writers in this section speak about college faculty members and administrators and the roles they play in developing missions statements that outline the purposes and goals of a liberal education. Few discuss the role of students. Should students be involved in constructing the goals for their own educations? To what extent? Write an essay in which you discuss the absence of student perspective in one or more of the essays you have read and propose a role for students.

4. Several of the writers presented in this section teach at colleges and universities that are among the oldest in the country. Investigate the early history of

higher education in the United States. What was the purpose? Who was educated? What were the costs? What did the curriculum look like? Write a report of your findings for your classmates.

5. Research the history of your own college or university. Where and why was it founded? By whom? For what purpose? Who was the first president? How was the institution governed? Who served on the faculty? Assume that you are on a committee to revamp the campus Web site. Write an account of the history of your school that would be suitable for mounting on the site.

6. Investigate the requirements of the core curriculum of your college or university. In a letter to a potential student, explain the history and purpose of the requirements and describe the courses or experiences that students undertake.

7. Construct a questionnaire in which you ask a dozen classmates and friends their purposes in going to college. Ask them why they chose the college they did, what major they plan, what career expectations they have in mind, and other questions of your own devising. Using your survey, create tables that illustrate the responses you receive and write a narrative about your results. What conclusions can you draw from this limited survey?

8. Assume that Mark Edmundson and Martha Nussbaum have been invited to your campus to talk about their contrasting views on the nature of a liberal education. You have been assigned the task of interviewing them for the campus newspaper. Write a series of questions and, using the articles in this section as your source of information, prepare written responses to the questions in the way that you think Edmundson and Nussbaum would answer them.

9. Take Wayne Booth's general question, "Is there any knowledge that a man or woman must have?" and write an essay in which you compare and contrast the responses that several of the writers (especially Houston, Nussbaum, and Edmundson) in this section would make to this question.

10. This chapter of the text, "The Purpose of a College Education," is designed to invite you to read and think about a variety of issues related to how colleges and universities determine the goals of the education they provide. What have you learned from your reading, thinking, and writing about the purpose of a college education? What are the major issues for college students? What do you need to know more about? Send an e-mail message to your classmates, inviting them to participate in an electronic discussion with you about the issues most crucial to them. Summarize the results and post them to your class.

III

LITERACIES FOR
A DIVERSE WORLD

INTRODUCTION

In *Talking Back*, bell hooks, a professor at City College in New York and the author of several books on her experiences as a black academic, observes that "The most powerful resource any of us can have as we study and teach in university settings is full understanding and appreciation of the richness, beauty, and primacy of our familial and community backgrounds. . . . Education as the practice of freedom [is] not a force which fragments or separates, but one that brings us closer, expanding our definitions of home and community." How our educations separate us and/or bring us closer together is the central topic of this section, which is a collection of readings that explore the differing notions of what constitutes the various literacies that are necessary for a full understanding of American culture. Cultural diversity has emerged as a major topic of concern on campuses across the country since the late 1980s and has, in most cases, affected almost every part of the college curriculum. Initially, the question, especially as raised by E. D. Hirsch in his best-selling *Cultural Literacy*, was whether there should be a relationship between the cultural pluralism of our society and the college curriculum. As he outlines in the section of *Cultural Literacy* reprinted here, his answer was largely negative. But since the publication of *Cultural Literacy* and in the aftermath of spirited response to the book both in the academic and in the larger world, much has changed. What some writers in this section call a quiet revolution has occurred on college campuses. The question today is not whether there should be a relationship between a culturally diverse society and the college curriculum, but what form the relationship should take. Writers in this section take up the following questions:

- What is "cultural literacy," as it was first defined by E. D. Hirsch? Why did this become such a controversial issue for the American public and for higher education?

- Is it possible to define a core of knowledge that all students must have?

- What was the nature of the response to Hirsch and what are the issues in the debate over "multicultural literacy"?

- What is the relationship between general education and cultural diversity?

- How do teaching methods reflect philosophies of education?

- What is "civil literacy" and how is it related to the purposes of a college education?

- How does religious diversity constitute a part of cultural diversity?

- How do campuses handle the issues of religious diversity among students?

- What is "cultural pluralism" and how is it related to "multi-culturalism"?

- How and why does authority become an issue in a culturally diverse classroom?

- How have programs such as Native American Studies helped colleges and universities provide culturally diverse experiences for students? What have been the problems and conflicts?

- How can campuses deal more effectively with the diversity of students that exists now and in the future?

- How can the tensions between freedom of speech and campus codes of conduct be resolved?

The writers in this section explore the answers to these and related questions in a variety of ways. We begin with Hirsch, because his provocative book might well be said to have opened the debate. Like Hirsch, almost all of the writers in this section are professors; they come from a variety of racial and ethnic heritages and teach in a variety of institutional contexts, public and private, large and small. Many of them, such as Hirsch, Barber, Shapiro, and Gates, have extended themselves beyond an academic audience to write about the complex issues of cultural diversity for popular magazines and newspapers. Paulo Friere was among the most influential educators of his time, both in the United States and Latin America. Kidwell outlines the special problems for Native Americans within the complex cultural diversity of the United States, while Garcia discusses frankly her experiences of teaching courses that integrate writers of many backgrounds to mostly white students. Several of the professors have written and edited textbooks for higher education; some, like Hirsch, Purves, Moffett, and Cortés, have also written texts for primary and secondary school programs as well. Although Simonson and Walker, the two writers in this section who are not professors, are professionals in commercial publishing, the texts they have edited are primarily designed for use by students in both schools and colleges. All of the readings in this section ask you to consider what educational experience is appropriate for the education of the future citizens of an increasingly complex society.

I

LITERACY AND CULTURAL LITERACY
WHAT LITERATE AMERICANS KNOW:
A PRELIMINARY LIST

E. D. Hirsch is a professor of English at the University of Virginia and currently the president of a nonprofit educational foundation, The Core Knowledge Foundation. The author of books on literary criticism and British poetry, he became famous almost overnight when his best-selling book, Cultural Literacy, *was published in 1988. This book, along with Allen Bloom's* The Closing of the American Mind, *launched the beginning of an ongoing and often fierce debate about how schools and colleges train students to be fully literate in today's society. The phrase "cultural literacy" means, in Hirsch's formulation, "to possess the basic information needed to thrive in the modern world." What constitutes that basic information is the subject of Hirsch's book; in an appendix to the original book, Hirsch lists a large number of terms, which he believes are departure points for the shared body of information that literate Americans need to have in common in order to communicate with one another. This view of literacy—that it is primarily information—is at odds with other definitions that literacy is a set of skills. Hirsch believes that an emphasis on skills in our schools has eliminated what he calls "core knowledge" from the curriculum. In his book, he outlines his rationale for adopting a curriculum that includes elements of knowledge (his list of names, dates, events, and terms). Indeed, Hirsch has since published a series of books for the elementary and secondary schools,* What Your Kindergartner–Sixth Grader Needs to Know, The Dictionary of Cultural Literacy, *and most recently,* The Schools We Need and Why We Don't Have Them, *all of which work out the details of such a curriculum. This reading is taken from the first chapter of his book; the terms at the end of the reading are taken from his article, "What Literate Americans Know: A Preliminary List."*

QUESTIONS FOR READING

1. What prior knowledge do you have about the term "cultural literacy"? What does it mean to you?

2. Are you aware of the debates of cultural and/or multicultural literacy? What is your understanding of these terms?

E. D. HIRSCH

LITERACY AND CULTURAL LITERACY

Cultural Literacy (New York: Vintage, 1988)

THE DECLINE OF LITERATE KNOWLEDGE

This book explains why we need to make some very specific educational changes in order to achieve a higher level of national literacy. It does not anatomize the literacy crisis or devote many pages to Scholastic Aptitude Test scores. It does not document at length what has already been established, that Americans do not read as well as they should. It takes no position about methods of initial reading instruction beyond insisting that content must receive as much emphasis as "skill." It does not discuss teacher training or educational funding or school governance. In fact, one of its major purposes is to break away entirely from what Jeanne S. Chall has called "the great debate" about methods of reading instruction. It focuses on what I conceive to be the great hidden problem in American education, and I hope that it reveals this problem so compellingly that anyone who is concerned about American education will be persuaded by the book's argument and act upon it.

The standard of literacy required by modern society has been rising throughout the developed world, but American literacy rates have not risen to meet this standard. What seemed an acceptable level in the 1950s is no longer acceptable in the late 1980s, when only highly literate societies can prosper economically. Much of Japan's industrial efficiency has been credited to its almost universally high level of literacy. But in the United States, only two thirds of our citizens are literate, and even among those the average level is too low and should be raised. The remaining third of our citizens need to be brought as close to true literacy as possible. Ultimately our aim should be to attain universal literacy at a very high level, to achieve not only greater economic prosperity but also greater social justice and more effective democracy. We Americans have long accepted literacy as a paramount aim of schooling, but only recently have some of us who have done research in the field begun to realize that literacy is far more than a skill and that it requires large amounts of specific information. That new insight is central to this book.

Professor Chall is one of several reading specialists who have observed that "world knowledge" is essential to the development of reading and writing skills.[1] What she calls world knowledge I call cultural literacy, namely, the network of information that all competent readers possess. It is the background information, stored in their minds, that enables them to take up a newspaper and read it with an adequate level of comprehension, getting the point, grasping the implications, relating what they read to the unstated context which alone gives meaning to what they read. In describing the contents of this neglected domain of background information, I try to direct attention to a new opening that can help our schools make the significant improvement in education that has so far eluded us. The achievement of high universal literacy is the key to all other fundamental improvements in American education.

Why is literacy so important in the modern world? Some of the reasons, like the need to fill out forms or get a good job, are so obvious that they needn't be discussed. But the chief reason is broader. The complex undertakings of modern life depend on the cooperation of many people with different specialties in different places. Where communications fail, so do the undertakings. (That is the moral of the story of the Tower of Babel.) The function of national literacy is to foster effective nationwide communications. Our chief instrument of communication over time and space is the standard national language, which is sustained by national literacy. Mature literacy alone enables the tower to be built, the business to be well managed, and the airplane to fly without crashing. All nationwide communications, whether by telephone, radio, TV, or writing are fundamentally dependent upon literacy, for the essence of literacy is not simply reading and writing but also the effective use of the standard literate language. In Spain and most of Latin America the literate language is standard written Spanish. In Japan it is standard written Japanese. In our country it is standard written English.

Linguists have used the term "standard written English" to describe both our written and spoken language, because they want to remind us that standard spoken English is based upon forms that have been fixed in dictionaries and grammars and are adhered to in books, magazines, and newspapers. Although standard written English has no intrinsic superiority to other languages and dialects, its stable written forms have now standardized the oral forms of the language spoken by educated Americans.[2] The chief function of literacy is to make us masters of this standard instrument of knowledge and communication, thereby enabling us to give and receive complex information orally and in writing over time and space. Advancing technology, with its constant need for fast and complex communications, has made literacy ever more essential to commerce and domestic life. The literate language is more, not less, central in our society now than it was in the early days before television and the silicon chip.

The recently rediscovered insight that literacy is more than a skill is based upon knowledge that all of us unconsciously have about language. We know instinctively that to understand what somebody is saying, we must understand more than the surface meanings of words; we have to understand the context as well. The need for background information applies all the more to reading and writing. To grasp the words on a page we have to know a lot of information that isn't set down on the page.

Consider the implications of the following experiment described in an article in *Scientific American*.[3] A researcher goes to Harvard Square in Cambridge, Massachusetts, with a tape recorder hidden in his coat pocket. Putting a copy of the *Boston Globe* under his arm, he pretends to be a native. He says to passers-by, "How do you get to Central Square?" The passers-by, thinking they are addressing a fellow Bostonian, don't even break their stride when they give their replies, which consist of a few words like "First stop on the subway."

The next day the researcher goes to the same spot, but this time he presents himself as a tourist, obviously unfamiliar with the city. "I'm from out of town," he says. "Can you tell me how to get to Central Square?" This time the tapes show that people's answers are much longer and more rudimentary. A typical one goes, "Yes, well, you go down on the subway. You can see the entrance over there, and when you get downstairs you buy a token, put it in the slot, and you go over to the side that says Quincy. You take the train headed for Quincy, but you get off very soon, just the first stop is Central Square, and be sure you get off there. You'll know it because there's a big sign on the wall. It says Central Square." And so on.

Passers-by were intuitively aware that communication between strangers requires an estimate of how much relevant information can be taken for granted in the other person. If they can take a lot for granted, their communications can be short and efficient, subtle and complex. But if strangers share very little knowledge, their communications must be long and relatively rudimentary.

In order to put in perspective the importance of background knowledge in language, I want to connect the lack of it with our recent lack of success in teaching mature literacy to all students. The most broadly based evidence about our teaching of literacy comes from the National Assessment of Educational Progress (NAEP). This nationwide measurement, mandated by Congress, shows that between 1970 and 1980 seventeen-year-olds declined in their ability to understand written materials, and the decline was especially striking in the top group, those able to read at an "advanced" level.[4] Although these scores have now begun to rise, they remain alarmingly low. Still more precise quantitative data have come from the scores of the verbal Scholastic Aptitude Test (SAT). According to John B. Carroll, a distinguished psychometrician, the verbal SAT is essentially a test of "advanced vocabulary knowledge," which makes it a fairly sensitive instrument for measuring levels of literacy.[5] It is well known that verbal SAT scores have declined dramatically in the past fifteen years, and though recent reports have shown them rising again, it is from a very low base. Moreover, performance on the verbal SAT has been slipping steadily *at the top*. Ever fewer numbers of our best and brightest students are making high scores on the test.

Before the College Board disclosed the full statistics in 1984, antialarmists could argue that the fall in average verbal scores could be explained by the rise in the number of disadvantaged students taking the SATs. That argument can no longer be made. It's now clear that not only our disadvantaged but also our best educated and most talented young people are showing diminished verbal skills. To be precise, out of a constant pool of about a million test takers each year, fifty-six percent more students scored above six hundred in 1972 than did so in 1984. More startling yet, the percentage drop was even greater for those scoring above 650—seventy-three percent.[6]

In the mid-1980s American business leaders have become alarmed by the lack of communication skills in the young people they employ. Recently, top executives of some large U.S. companies, including CBS and Exxon, met to discuss the fact that their younger middle-level executives could no longer communicate their ideas effectively in speech or writing. This group of companies has made a grant to the American Academy of Arts and Sciences to analyze the causes of this growing problem. They want to know why, despite breathtaking advances in the technology of communication, the effectiveness of business communication has been slipping, to the detriment of our competitiveness in the world. The figures from NAEP surveys and the scores on the verbal SAT are solid evidence that literacy has been declining in this country just when our need for effective literacy has been sharply rising.

I now want to juxtapose some evidence for another kind of educational decline, one that is related to the drop in literacy. During the period 1970–1985, the amount of shared knowledge that we have been able to take for granted in communicating with our fellow citizens has also been declining. More and more of our young people don't know things we used to assume they knew.

A side effect of the diminution in shared information has been a noticeable increase in the number of articles in such publications as *Newsweek* and the *Wall Street Journal* about the surprising ignorance of the young. My son John, who recently taught Latin in high school and eighth grade, often told me of experiences which indicate that these articles are not exaggerated. In one of his classes he mentioned to his students that Latin, the language they were studying, is a dead language that is no longer spoken. After his pupils had struggled for several weeks with Latin grammar and vocabulary, this news was hard for some of them to accept. One girl raised her hand to challenge my son's claim. "What do they speak in Latin America?" she demanded.

At least she had heard of Latin America. Another day my son asked his Latin class if they knew the name of an epic poem by Homer. One pupil shot up his hand and eagerly said, "The Alamo!" Was it just a slip for *The Iliad?* No, he didn't know what the Alamo was, either. To judge from other stories about information gaps in the young, many American schoolchildren are less well informed than this pupil. The following, by Benjamin J. Stein, is an excerpt from one of the most evocative recent accounts of youthful ignorance.

> I spend a lot of time with teenagers. Besides employing three of them part-time, I frequently conduct focus groups at Los Angeles area high schools to learn about teenagers' attitudes towards movies or television shows or nuclear arms or politicians. . . .

I have not yet found one single student in Los Angeles, in either college or high school, who could tell me the years when World War II was fought. Nor have I found one who could tell me the years when World War I was fought. Nor have I found one who knew when the American Civil War was fought. . . .

A few have known how many U.S. senators California has, but none has known how many Nevada or Oregon has. ("Really? Even though they're so small?"). . . . Only two could tell me where Chicago is, even in the vaguest terms. (My particular favorite geography lesson was the junior at the University of California at Los Angeles who thought that Toronto must be in Italy. My second-favorite geography lesson is the junior at USC, a prelaw student, who thought that Washington, D.C. was in Washington State.). . .

Only two could even approximately identify Thomas Jefferson. Only one could place the date of the Declaration of Independence. None could name even one of the first ten amendments to the Constitution or connect them with the Bill of Rights. . . .

On and on it went. On and on it goes. I have mixed up episodes of ignorance of facts with ignorance of concepts because it seems to me that there is a connection. . . . The kids I saw (and there may be lots of others who are different) are not mentally prepared to continue the society because they basically do not understand the society well enough to value it.[7]

My son assures me that his pupils are not ignorant. They know a great deal. Like every other human group they share a tremendous amount of knowledge among themselves, much of it learned in school. The trouble is that, from the standpoint of their literacy and their ability to communicate with others in our culture, what they know is ephemeral and narrowly confined to their own generation. Many young people strikingly lack the information that writers of American books and newspapers have traditionally taken for granted among their readers from all generations. For reasons explained in this book, our children's lack of intergenerational information is a serious problem for the nation. The decline of literacy and the decline of shared knowledge are closely related, interdependent facts.

The evidence for the decline of shared knowledge is not just anecdotal. In 1978 NAEP issued a report which analyzed a large quantity of data showing that our children's knowledge of American civics had dropped significantly between 1969 and 1976.[8] The performance of thirteen-year-olds had dropped an alarming eleven percentage points. That the drop has continued since 1976 was confirmed by preliminary results from a NAEP study conducted in late 1985. It was undertaken both because of concern about declining knowledge and because of the growing evidence of a causal connection between the drop in shared information and in literacy. The Foundations of Literacy project is measuring some of the specific information about history and literature that American seventeen-year-olds possess.

Although the full report will not be published until 1987, the preliminary field tests are disturbing.[9] If these samplings hold up, and there is no reason to think they will not, then the results we will be reading in 1987 will show that two thirds of our seventeen-year-olds do not know that the Civil War occurred between 1850 and 1900. Three quarters do not know what *reconstruction* means. Half do not know the meaning of *Brown decision* and cannot identify either Stalin or Churchill. Three quarters are unfamiliar with the names of standard American and British authors. Moreover, our seventeen-year-olds have little sense of geography or the relative chronology of major events. Reports of youthful ignorance can no longer be considered merely impressionistic.[10]

My encounter in the seventies with this widening knowledge gap first caused me to recognize the connection between specific background knowledge and mature literacy. The research I was doing on the reading and writing abilities of college students made me realize two things.[11] First, we cannot assume that young people today know things that were known in the past by almost every literate person in the culture. For instance, in one experiment conducted in Richmond, Virginia, our seventeen- and eighteen-year-old subjects did not know who Grant and Lee were. Second, our results caused me to realize that we cannot treat reading and writing as empty skills, independent of specific knowledge. The reading skill of a person may vary greatly from task to task. The level of literacy exhibited in each task depends on the relevant background information that the person possesses.

The lack of wide-ranging background information among young men and women now in their twenties and thirties is an important cause of the illiteracy that large corporations are finding in their middle-level executives. In former days, when business people wrote and spoke to one another, they could be confident that they and their colleagues had studied many similar things in school. They could talk to one another with an efficiency similar to that of native Bostonians who speak to each other in the streets of Cambridge. But today's high school graduates do not reliably share much common information, even when they graduate from the same school. If young people meet as strangers, their communications resemble the uncertain, rudimentary explanations recorded in the second part of the Cambridge experiment.

My father used to write business letters that alluded to Shakespeare. These allusions were effective for conveying complex messages to his associates, because, in his day, business people could make such allusions with every expectation of being understood. For instance, in my father's commodity business, the timing of sales and purchases was all-important, and he would sometimes write or say to his colleagues, "There is a tide," without further elaboration. Those four words carried not only a lot of complex information, but also the persuasive force of a proverb. In addition to the basic practical meaning, "Act now!" what came across was a lot of implicit reasons why immediate action was important.

For some of my younger readers who may not recognize the allusion, the passage from *Julius Caesar* is:

There is a tide in the affairs of men
Which taken at the flood leads on to fortune;
Omitted, all the voyage of their life

Is bound in shallows and in miseries.
On such a full sea are we now afloat,
And we must take the current when it serves,
Or lose our ventures.

To say "There is a tide" is better than saying "Buy (or sell) now and you'll cover expenses for the whole year, but if you fail to act right away, you may regret it the rest of your life." That would be twenty-seven words instead of four, and while the bare message of the longer statement would be conveyed, the persuasive force wouldn't. Think of the demands of such a business communication. To persuade somebody that your recommendation is wise and well-founded, you have to give lots of reasons and cite known examples and authorities. My father accomplished that and more in four words, which made quoting Shakespeare as effective as any efficiency consultant could wish. The moral of this tale is not that reading Shakespeare will help one rise in the business world. My point is a broader one. The fact that middle-level executives no longer share literate background knowledge is a chief cause of their inability to communicate effectively.

THE NATURE AND USE OF CULTURAL LITERACY

The documented decline in shared knowledge carries implications that go far beyond the shortcomings of executives and extend to larger questions of educational policy and social justice in our country. Mina Shaughnessy was a great English teacher who devoted her professional life to helping disadvantaged students become literate. At the 1980 conference dedicated to her memory, one of the speakers who followed me to the podium was the Harvard historian and sociologist Orlando Patterson. To my delight he departed from his prepared talk to mention mine. He seconded my argument that shared information is a necessary background to true literacy. Then he extended and deepened the ideas I had presented. Here is what Professor Patterson said, as recorded in the *Proceedings* of the conference.

> Industrialized civilization [imposes] a growing cultural and structural complexity which requires persons to have a broad grasp of what Professor Hirsch has called cultural literacy: a deep understanding of mainstream culture, which no longer has much to do with white Anglo-Saxon Protestants, but with the imperatives of industrial civilization. It is the need for cultural literacy, a profound conception of the whole civilization, which is often neglected in talk about literacy.

Patterson continued by drawing a connection between background information and the ability to hold positions of responsibility and power. He was particularly concerned with the importance for blacks and other minorities of possessing this information, which is essential for improving their social and economic status.

> The people who run society at the macro-level must be literate in this culture. For this reason, it is dangerous to overemphasize the problems of basic literacy or the relevancy of literacy to specific tasks, and more constructive to emphasize that blacks will be condemned in perpetuity to oversimplified, low-level tasks and will never gain their rightful place in controlling the levers of power unless they also acquire literacy in this wider cultural sense.

Although Patterson focused his remarks on the importance of cultural literacy for minorities, his observations hold for every culturally illiterate person in our nation. Indeed, as he observed, cultural literacy is not the property of any group or class.

> To assume that this wider culture is static is an error; in fact it is not. It's not a WASP culture; it doesn't belong to any group. It is essentially and constantly changing, and it is open. What is needed is recognition that the accurate metaphor or model for this wider literacy is not domination, but dialectic; each group participates and contributes, transforms and is transformed, as much as any other group. . . . The English language no longer belongs to any single group or nation. The same goes for any other area of the wider culture.[12]

As Professor Patterson suggested, being taught to decode elementary reading materials and specific, job-related texts cannot constitute true literacy. Such basic training does not make a person literate with respect to newspapers or other writings addressed to a general public. Moreover, a directly practical drawback of such narrow training is that it does not prepare anyone for technological change. Narrow vocational training in one state of a technology will not enable a person to read manuals that explain new developments in the same technology. In modern life we need general knowledge that enables us to deal with new ideas, events, and challenges. In today's world, general cultural literacy is more useful than what Professor Patterson terms "literacy to a specific task," because general literate information is the basis for many changing tasks.

Cultural literacy is even more important in the social sphere. The aim of universal literacy has never been a socially neutral mission in our country. Our traditional social goals were unforgettably renewed for us by Martin Luther King, Jr., in his "I Have a Dream" speech. King envisioned a country where the children of former slaves sit down at the table of equality with the children of former slave owners, where men and women deal with each other as equals and judge each other on their characters and achievements rather than their origins. Like Thomas Jefferson, he had a dream of a society founded not on race or class but on personal merit.

In the present day, that dream depends on mature literacy. No modern society can hope to become a just society without a high level of universal literacy. Putting aside for the moment the practical arguments about the economic uses of literacy, we can contemplate the even more basic principle that underlies our national system of education in the first place—that people in a democracy can be entrusted to decide all important matters for themselves because they can deliberate and communicate with one another. Universal literacy is inseparable from democracy and is the canvas for Martin Luther King's picture as well as for Thomas Jefferson's.

Both of these leaders understood that just having the right to vote is meaningless if a citizen is disenfranchised by illiteracy or semiliteracy. Illiterate and semiliterate Americans are condemned not only to poverty, but also to the powerlessness of incomprehension. Knowing that they do not understand the issues, and feeling prey to manipulative oversimplifications, they do not trust the system of which they are supposed to be the masters. They do not feel themselves to be active participants in our republic, and they often do not turn out to vote. The civic importance of cultural literacy lies in the fact that true enfranchisement depends upon knowledge, knowledge upon literacy, and literacy upon cultural literacy.

To be truly literate, citizens must be able to grasp the meaning of any piece of writing addressed to the general reader. All citizens should be able, for instance, to read newspapers of substance, about which Jefferson made the following famous remark:

> Were it left to me to decide whether we should have a government without newspapers, or newspapers without a government, I should not hesitate a moment to prefer the latter. But I should mean that every man should receive those papers and be capable of reading them.[13]

Jefferson's last comment is often omitted when the passage is quoted, but it's the crucial one.

Books and newspapers assume a "common reader," that is, a person who knows the things known by other literate persons in the culture. Obviously, such assumptions are never identical from writer to writer, but they show a remarkable consistency. Those who write for a mass public are always making judgments about what their readers can be assumed to know, and the judgments are closely similar. Any reader who doesn't possess the knowledge assumed in a piece he or she reads will in fact be illiterate with respect to that particular piece of writing.

Here, for instance, is a rather typical excerpt from the *Washington Post* of December 29, 1983.

> A federal appeals panel today upheld an order barring foreclosure on a Missouri farm, saying that U.S. Agriculture Secretary John R. Block has reneged on his responsibilities to some debt ridden farmers. The appeals panel directed the USDA to create a system of processing loan deferments and of publicizing them as it said Congress had intended. The panel said that it is the responsibility of the agriculture secretary to carry out this intent "not as a private banker, but as a public broker."

Imagine that item being read by people who are well trained in phonics, word recognition, and other decoding skills but are culturally illiterate. They might know words like *foreclosure,* but they would not understand what the piece means. Who gave the order that the federal panel upheld? What is a federal appeals panel? Where is Missouri, and what about Missouri is relevant to the issue? Why are many farmers debt ridden? What is the USDA? What is a public broker? Even if culturally illiterate readers bothered to look up individual words, they would have little idea of the reality being referred to. The explicit words are just surface pointers to textual meaning in reading and writing. The comprehending reader must bring to the text appropriate background information that includes knowledge not only about the topic but also the shared attitudes and conventions that color a piece of writing.

Our children can learn this information only by being taught it. Shared literate information is deliberately sustained by national systems of education in many countries because they recognize the importance of giving their children a common basis for communication. Some decades ago a charming book called 1066 *and All That* appeared in Britain.[14] It dealt with facts of British history that all educated Britons had been taught as children but remembered only dimly as adults. The book caricatured those recollections, purposely getting the "facts" just wrong enough to make them ridiculous on their face. Readers instantly recognized that the book was mistaken in its theory about what Ethelred-the-Unready was unready for, but, on the other hand, they couldn't say precisely what he *was* unready for. The book was hilarious to literate Britons as a satire of their own vague and confused memories. But even if their schoolchild knowledge had become vague with the passage of time, it was still functional, because the information essential to literacy is rarely detailed or precise.

This haziness is a key characteristic of literacy and cultural literacy. To understand the *Washington Post* extract literate readers have to know only vaguely, in the backs of their minds, that the American legal system permits a court decision to be reversed by a higher court. They would need to know only that a judge is empowered to tell the executive branch what it can or cannot do to farmers and other citizens. (The secretary of agriculture was barred from foreclosing a Missouri farm.) Readers would need to know only vaguely what and where Missouri is, and how the department and the secretary of agriculture fit into the scheme of things. None of this knowledge would have to be precise. Readers wouldn't have to know whether an appeals panel is the final judicial level before the U.S. Supreme Court. Any practiced writer who feels it is important for a reader to know such details always provides them.

Much in verbal communication is necessarily vague, whether we are conversing or reading. What counts is our ability to grasp the general shape of what we are reading and to tie it to what we already know. If we need details, we rely on the writer or speaker to develop them. Or if we intend to ponder matters in detail for ourselves, we do so later, at our leisure. For instance, it is probably true that many people do not know what a beanball is in baseball. So in an article on the subject the author conveniently sets forth as much as the culturally literate reader must know.

Described variously as the knockdown pitch, the beanball, the duster and the purpose pitch—the Pentagon would call it the peacekeeper—this delightful stratagem has graced the scene for most of the 109 years the major leagues have existed. It starts fights. It creates lingering grudges. It sends people to the hospital. . . . "You put my guy in the dirt, I put your guy in the dirt."[15]

To understand this text, we don't have to know much about the particular topic in advance, but we do require quite a lot of vague knowledge about baseball to give us a sense of the whole meaning, whether our knowledge happens to be vague or precise.

The superficiality of the knowledge we need for reading and writing may be unwelcome news to those who deplore superficial learning and praise critical thinking over mere information. But one of the sharpest critical thinkers of our day, Dr. Hilary Putnam, a Harvard philosopher, has provided us with a profound insight into the importance of vague knowledge in verbal communication.[16]

Suppose you are like me and cannot tell an elm from a beech tree. . . . [I can nonetheless use the word "elm" because] *there is a division of linguistic labor.* . . . It is not at all necessary or efficient that everyone who wears a gold ring (or a gold cufflink, etc.) be able to tell with any reliability whether or not something is really gold. . . . Everyone to whom the word "gold" is important for any reason has to *acquire* the word "gold"; but he does not have to acquire the *method of recognizing* if something is or is not gold.

Putnam does acknowledge a limit on the degrees of ignorance and vagueness that are acceptable in discourse. "Significant communication," he observes, "requires that people know something of what they are talking about." Nonetheless, what is required for communication is often so vague and superficial that we can properly understand and use the word *elm* without being able to distinguish an elm tree from a beech tree. What we need to know in order to use and understand a word is an initial stereotype that has a few vague traits.

Speakers are *required* to know something about (stereotypic) tigers in order to count as having acquired the word "tiger"; something about elm trees (or anyway about the stereotype thereof) to count as having acquired the word "elm," etc. . . . The nature of the required minimum level of competence depends heavily upon both the culture and the topic, however. In our culture speakers are not . . . required to know the fine details (such as leaf shape) of what an elm tree looks like. English speakers are *required by their linguistic community* to be able to tell tigers from leopards; they are not required to be able to tell beech trees from elm trees.

When Putnam says that Americans can be depended on to distinguish tigers and leopards but not elms and beeches, he assumes that his readers will agree with him because they are culturally literate. He takes for granted that one literate person knows approximately the same things as another and is aware of the probable limits of the other person's knowledge. That second level of awareness—knowing what others probably know—is crucial for effective communication. In order to speak effectively to people we must have a reliable sense of what they do and do not know. For instance, if Putnam is right in his example, we should not have to tell a stranger that a leopard has spots or a tiger stripes, but we would have to explain that an elm has rough bark and a beech smooth bark if we wanted that particular piece of information conveyed. To know what educated people know about tigers but don't know about elm trees is the sort of cultural knowledge, limited in extent but possessed by all literate people, that must be brought into the open and taught to our children.

Besides being limited in extent, cultural literacy has another trait that is important for educational policy—its national character. It's true that literate English is an international language, but only so long as the topics it deals with are international. The background knowledge of people from other English-speaking nations is often inadequate for complex and subtle communications within our nation. The knowledge required for national literacy differs from country to country, even when their national language is the same. It is no doubt true that one layer of cultural literacy is the same for all English-speaking nations. Australians, South Africans, Britons, and Americans share a lot of knowledge by virtue of their common language. But much of the knowledge required for literacy in, say, Australia is specific to that country, just as much of ours is specific to the United States.

For instance, a literate Australian can typically understand American newspaper articles on international events or the weather but not one on a federal appeals panel. The same holds true for Americans who read Australian newspapers. Many of us have heard "Waltzing Matilda," a song known to every Australian, but few Americans understand or need to understand what the words mean.

Once a jolly swagman camped by a billy-bong,
Under the shade of a kulibar tree,
And he sang as he sat and waited for his billy-boil,
"You'll come a-waltzing, Matilda, with me."

Waltzing Matilda doesn't mean dancing with a girl; it means walking with a kind of knapsack. A *swagman* is a hobo, a *billy-bong* is a brook or pond, a *kulibar* is a eucalyptus, and *billy-boil* is coffee.

The national character of the knowledge needed in reading and writing was strikingly revealed in an experiment conducted by Richard C. Anderson and others at the Center for the Study of Reading at the University of Illinois. They assembled two paired groups of readers, all highly similar in sexual balance, educational backgrounds, age, and social class.[17] The only difference between the groups was that one was in India; the other, in the United States. Both were given the same two letters to read. The texts were similar in overall length, word-frequency distribution, sentence length and complexity, and number of explicit propositions. Both letters were on the same topic, a wedding, but one described an Indian wedding; the other, an American wedding. The reading performances of the two groups—their speed and accuracy of comprehension—split along national lines. The Indians performed well in reading about the Indian wedding but poorly in reading about the American one, and the Americans did the opposite. This experiment not only reconfirmed the dependence of reading skill on cultural literacy; it also demonstrated its national character.

Although nationalism may be regrettable in some of its worldwide political effects, a mastery of national culture is essential to mastery of the standard language in every modern nation. This point is important for educational policy, because educators often stress the virtues of multicultural education. Such study is indeed valuable in itself; it inculcates tolerance and provides a perspective on our own traditions and values. But however laudable it is, it should not be the primary focus of national education. It should not be allowed to supplant or interfere with our schools' responsibility to ensure our children's mastery of American literate culture. The acculturative responsibility of the schools is primary and fundamental. To teach the ways of one's own community has always been and still remains the essence of the education of our children, who enter neither a narrow tribal culture nor a transcendent world culture but a national literate culture. For profound historical reasons, this is the way of the modern world.[18] It will not change soon, and it will certainly not be changed by educational policy alone.

THE DECLINE OF TEACHING CULTURAL LITERACY

Why have our schools failed to fulfill their fundamental acculturative responsibility? In view of the immense importance of cultural literacy for speaking, listening, reading, and writing, why has the need for a definite, shared body of information been so rarely mentioned in discussions of education? In the educational writings of the past decade, I find almost nothing on this topic, which is not arcane. People who are introduced to the subject quickly understand why oral or written communication requires a lot of shared background knowledge. It's not the difficulty or novelty of the idea that has caused it to receive so little attention.

Let me hazard a guess about one reason for our neglect of the subject. We have ignored cultural literacy in thinking about education—certainly I as a researcher also ignored it until recently—precisely because it was something we have been able to take for granted. We ignore the air we breathe until it is thin or foul. Cultural literacy is the oxygen of social intercourse. Only when we run into cultural illiteracy are we shocked into recognizing the importance of the information that we had unconsciously assumed.

To be sure, a minimal level of information is possessed by any normal person who lives in the United States and speaks elementary English. Almost everybody knows what is meant by *dollar* and that cars must travel on the right-hand side of the road. But this elementary level of information is not sufficient for a modern democracy. It isn't sufficient to read newspapers (a sin against Jeffersonian democracy), and it isn't sufficient to achieve economic fairness and high productivity. Cultural literacy lies *above* the everyday levels of knowledge that everyone possesses and *below* the expert level known only to specialists. It is that middle ground of cultural knowledge possessed by the "common reader." It includes information that we have traditionally expected our children to receive in school, but which they no longer do.

During recent decades Americans have hesitated to make a decision about the specific knowledge that children need to learn in school. Our elementary schools are not only dominated by the content-neutral ideas of Rousseau and Dewey; they are also governed by approximately sixteen thousand independent school districts. We have viewed this dispersion of educational authority as an insurmountable obstacle to altering the fragmentation of the school curriculum even when we have questioned that fragmentation. We have permitted school policies that have shrunk the body of information that Americans share, and these policies have caused our national literacy to decline.

At the same time we have searched with some eagerness for causes such as television that lie outside the schools. But we should direct our attention undeviatingly toward what the schools teach rather than toward family structure, social class, or TV programming. No doubt, reforms outside the schools are important, but they are harder to accomplish. Moreover, we have accumulated a great deal of evidence that faulty policy in the schools is the chief cause of deficient literacy. Researchers who have studied the factors influencing educational outcomes have found that the school curriculum is the most important controllable influence on what our children know and don't know about our literate culture.[19]

It will not do to blame television for the state of our literacy. Television watching does reduce reading and often encroaches on homework. Much of it is admittedly the intellectual equivalent of junk food. But in some respects, such as its use of standard written English, television watching is acculturative.[20] Moreover, as Herbert Walberg points out, the schools themselves must be held partly responsible for excessive television watching, because they have not firmly insisted that students complete significant amounts of homework, an obvious way to increase time spent on reading and writing.[21] Nor should our schools be excused by an appeal to the effects of the decline of the family or the vicious circle of poverty, important as these factors are. Schools have, or should have, children for six or seven hours a day, five days a week, nine months a year, for thirteen years or more. To assert that they are powerless to make a significant impact on what their students learn would be to make a claim about American education that few parents, teachers, or students would find it easy to accept.

Just how fragmented the American public school curriculum has become is described in *The Shopping Mall High School*, a report on five years of firsthand study inside public and private secondary schools. The authors report that our high schools offer courses of so many kinds that "the word 'curriculum' does not do justice to this astonishing variety." The offerings include not only academic courses of great diversity, but also courses in sports and hobbies and a "services curriculum" addressing emotional or social problems. All these courses are deemed "educationally valid" and carry course credit. Moreover, among academic offerings are numerous versions of each subject, corresponding to different levels of student interest and ability. Needless to say, the material covered in these "content area" courses is highly varied.[22]

Cafeteria-style education, combined with the unwillingness of our schools to place demands on students, has resulted in a steady diminishment of commonly shared information between generations and between young people themselves. Those who graduate from the same school have often studied different subjects, and those who graduate from different schools have often studied different material even when their courses have carried the same titles. The inevitable consequence of the shopping mall high school is a lack of shared knowledge across and within schools. It would be hard to invent a more effective recipe for cultural fragmentation.

The formalistic educational theory behind the shopping mall school (the theory that any suitable content will inculcate reading, writing, and thinking skills) has had certain political advantages for school administrators. It has allowed them to stay scrupulously neutral with regard to content.[23] Educational formalism enables them to regard the indiscriminate variety of school offerings as a positive virtue, on the grounds that such variety can accommodate the different interests and abilities of different students. Educational formalism has also conveniently allowed school administrators to meet objections to the traditional literate materials that used to be taught in the schools. Objectors have said that traditional materials are class-bound, white, Anglo-Saxon, and Protestant, not to mention racist, sexist, and excessively Western. Our schools have tried to offer enough diversity to meet these objections from liberals and enough Shakespeare to satisfy conservatives. Caught between ideological parties, the schools have been attracted irresistibly to a quantitative and formal approach to curriculum making rather than one based on sound judgments about what should be taught.

Some have objected that teaching the traditional literate culture means teaching conservative material. Orlando Patterson answered that objection when he pointed out that mainstream culture is not the province of any single social group and is constantly changing by assimilating new elements and expelling old ones.[24] Although mainstream culture is tied to the written word and may therefore seem more formal and elitist than other elements of culture, that is an illusion. Literate culture is the most democratic culture in our land: it excludes nobody; it cuts across generations and social groups and classes; it is not usually one's first culture, but it should be everyone's second, existing as it does beyond the narrow spheres of family, neighborhood, and region.

As the universal second culture, literate culture has become the common currency for social and economic exchange in our democracy, and the only available ticket to full citizenship. Getting one's membership card is not tied to class or race. Membership is automatic if one learns the background information and the linguistic conventions that are needed to read, write, and speak effectively. Although everyone is literate in some local, regional, or ethnic culture, the connection between mainstream culture and the national written language justifies calling mainstream culture *the* basic culture of the nation.

The claim that universal cultural literacy would have the effect of preserving the political and social status quo is paradoxical because in fact the traditional forms of literate culture are precisely the most effective instruments for political and social change. All political discourse at the national level must use the stable forms of the national language and its associated culture. Take the example of *The Black Panther,* a radical and revolutionary newspaper if ever this country had one. Yet the *Panther* was highly conservative in its language and cultural assumptions, as it had to be in order to communicate effectively. What could be more radical in sentiment but more conservative in language and assumed knowledge than the following passages from that paper?

> The present period reveals the criminal growth of bourgeois democracy since the betrayal of those who died that this nation might live "free and indivisible." It exposes through the trial of the Chicago Seven, and its law and order edicts, its desperate turn toward the establishment of a police state. (January 17, 1970)

> In this land of "milk and honey," the "almighty dollar" rules supreme and is being upheld by the faithful troops who move without question in the name of "law and order." Only in this garden of hypocrisy and inequality can a murderer not be considered a murderer—only here can innocent people be charged with a crime and be taken to court with the confessed criminal testifying against them. Incredible? (March 28, 1970)

> In the United States, the world's most technologically advanced country, one million youths from twelve to seventeen years of age are illiterate—unable to read as well as the average fourth grader, says a new government report. Why so much illiteracy in a land of so much knowledge? The answer is because there is racism. Blacks and other Nonwhites receive the worst education. (May 18, 1974)

The last item of the Black Panther Party platform, issued March 29, 1972, begins

> 10. WE WANT LAND, BREAD, HOUSING, EDUCATION, CLOTHING, JUSTICE, PEACE AND PEOPLE'S CONTROL OF MODERN TECHNOLOGY.
> When in the course of human events it becomes necessary for one people to dissolve the political bands which have connected them with another, and to assume among the powers of the earth the separate and equal station to which the laws of nature and nature's God entitle them, a decent respect to the opinions of mankind requires that they should declare the causes which impel them to the separation.

And so on for the first five hundred of Jefferson's words without the least hint, or need of one, that this is a verbatim repetition of an earlier revolutionary declaration. The writers for *The Black Panther* had clearly received a rigorous traditional education in American history, in the Declaration of Independence, the Pledge of Allegiance to the Flag, the Gettysburg Address, and the Bible, to mention only some of the direct quotations and allusions in these passages. They also received rigorous traditional instruction in reading, writing, and spelling. I have not found a single misspelled word in the many pages of radical sentiment I have examined in that newspaper. Radicalism in politics, but conservatism in literate knowledge and spelling: to be a conservative in the *means* of communication is the road to effectiveness in modern life, in whatever direction one wishes to be effective.

To withhold traditional culture from the school curriculum, and therefore from students, in the name of progressive ideas is in fact an unprogressive action that helps preserve the political and economic status quo. Middle-class children acquire mainstream literate culture by daily encounters with other literate persons. But less privileged children are denied consistent interchanges with literate persons and fail to receive this information in school. The most straightforward antidote to their deprivation is to make the essential information more readily available inside the schools.

Providing our children with traditional information by no means indoctrinates them in a conservative point of view. Conservatives who wish to preserve traditional values will find that these are not necessarily inculcated by a traditional education, which can in fact be subversive of the status quo. As a child of eleven, I turned against the conservative views of my family and the Southern community in which I grew up, precisely because I had been given a traditional education and was therefore literate enough to read Gunnar Myrdal's *An American Dilemma*, an epoch-making book in my life.

Although teaching children national mainstream culture doesn't mean forcing them to accept its values uncritically, it does enable them to understand those values in order to predict the typical attitudes of other Americans. The writers for *The Black Panther* clearly understood this when they quoted the Declaration of Independence. George Washington, for instance, is a name in our received culture that we associate with the truthfulness of the hero of the story of the cherry tree. Americans should be taught that value association, whether or not they believe the story. Far from accepting the cherry-tree tale or its implications, Oscar Wilde in "The Decay of Lying" used it ironically, in a way that is probably funnier to Americans than to the British audience he was addressing.

> [Truth telling is] vulgarizing mankind. The crude commercialism of America, its materializing spirit, its indifference to the poetical side of things, and its lack of imagination and of high unattainable ideals, are entirely due to that country having adopted for its national hero a man who, according to his own confession, was incapable of telling a lie, and it is not too much to say that the story of George Washington and the cherry tree has done more harm, and in a shorter space of time, than any other moral tale in the whole of literature. . . . And the amusing part of the whole thing is that the story of the cherry tree is an absolute myth.[25]

For us no less than for Wilde, the values affirmed in traditional literate culture can serve a whole spectrum of value attitudes. Unquestionably, decisions about techniques of conveying traditions to our children are among the most sensitive and important decisions of a pluralistic nation. But the complex problem of how to teach values in American schools mustn't distract attention from our fundamental duty to teach shared content.

The failure of our schools to create a literate society is sometimes excused on the grounds that the schools have been asked to do too much. They are asked, for example, to pay due regard to the demands of both local and national acculturation. They are asked to teach not only American history but also state and city history, driving, cardiopulmonary resuscitation, consumerism, carpentry, cooking, and other special subjects. They are given the task of teaching information that is sometimes too rudimentary and sometimes too specialized. If the schools did not undertake this instruction, much of the information so provided would no doubt go unlearned. In some of our national moods we would like the schools to teach everything, but they cannot. There is a pressing need for clarity about our educational priorities.

As an example of the priorities we need to set, consider the teaching of local history in the Commonwealth of Virginia. Suppose Virginians had to choose between learning about its native son Jeb Stuart and Abraham Lincoln. The example is arbitrary, but since choices have to be made in education, we might consider the two names emblematic of the kind of priority decision that has to be made. Educational policy always involves choices between degrees of worthiness.

The concept of cultural literacy helps us to make such decisions because it places a higher value on national than on local information. We want to make our children competent to communicate with Americans throughout the land. Therefore, if Virginians did have to decide between Stuart and Lincoln, they ought to favor the man from Illinois over the one from Virginia. All literate Americans know traditional information about Abraham Lincoln but relatively few know about Jeb Stuart. To become literate it's therefore more important to know about Lincoln than about Stuart. The priority has nothing to do with inherent merit, only with the accidents of culture. Stuart certainly had more merit than Benedict Arnold did, but Arnold also should be given educational priority over Stuart. Why? Because Benedict Arnold is as much a part of our national language as is, say, Judas.

To describe Benedict Arnold and Abraham Lincoln as belonging to the national language discloses another way of conceiving cultural literacy—as a vocabulary that we are able to use throughout the land because we share associations with others in our society. A universally shared national vocabulary is analogous to a universal currency like the dollar. Of course the vocabulary consists of more than just words. *Benedict Arnold* is part of our national cultural literacy; *eggs Benedict* isn't.

THE CRITICAL IMPORTANCE
OF EARLY SCHOOLING

Once we become aware of the inherent connection between literacy and cultural literacy, we have a duty to those who lack cultural literacy to determine and disclose its contents. To someone who is unaware of the things a literate person is expected to know, a writer's assumption that readers possess cultural literacy could appear to be a conspiracy of the literate against the illiterate, for the purpose of keeping them out of the club. But there is no conspiracy. Writers *must* make assumptions about the body of information their readers know. Unfortunately for the disadvantaged, no one ever spells out what that information is. But, as the Appendix illustrates, the total quantity of commonly shared information that the schools need to impart is less daunting than one might think, for the crucial background knowledge possessed by literate people is, as I have pointed out, telegraphic, vague, and limited in extent.

Preschool is not too early for starting earnest instruction in literate national culture. Fifth grade is almost too late. Tenth grade usually *is* too late. Anyone who is skeptical of this assertion should take a look at a heterogeneous class of fifth-graders engaged in summarizing a piece they have read. There are predictable differences between the summaries given by children with culturally adequate backgrounds and those given by children without. Although disadvantaged children often show an acceptable ability to decode and pronounce individual words, they are frequently unable to gain an integrated sense of a piece as a whole. They miss central implications and associations because they don't possess the background knowledge necessary to put the text in context. Hearing they hear not, and seeing they do not understand.[26]

Yet if you observe a kindergarten or first-grade class in which pupils have the same diversity of family background, you will *not* find a similar spread in the reading performances of pupils from different social classes. Disadvantaged first-graders do as well as middle-class ones in sounding out letters and simple words.[27] What happens between first grade and fifth grade to change the equality of performance? The impression that something significant has occurred or has failed to occur in these early grades is confirmed by international comparisons of reading attainment at early ages in different countries. Before grade three, when reading skills are more mechanical than interpretive, the United States stands in the top group of countries. Later, when reading requires an understanding of more complex content, our comparative ranking drops.[28] Although our schools do comparatively well in teaching elementary decoding skills, they do less well than schools of some other countries in teaching the background knowledge that pupils must possess to succeed at mature reading tasks.

The importance of this evidence for improving our national literacy can scarcely be overemphasized. If in the early grades our children were taught texts with cultural content rather than "developmental" texts that develop abstract skills, much of the specific knowledge deficit of disadvantaged children could be overcome. For it is clear that one critical difference in the reading performances of disadvantaged fifth-graders as compared with advantaged pupils is the difference in their cultural knowledge. Background knowledge does not take care of itself. Reading and writing are cumulative skills; the more we read the more necessary knowledge we gain for further reading.

Around grade four, those who lack the initial knowledge required for significant reading begin to be left behind permanently. Having all too slowly built up their cultural knowledge, they find reading and learning increasingly toilsome, unproductive, and humiliating. It follows that teaching cultural information in the early grades would do more than just improve the reading performance of all our children. By removing one of the causes of failure, it would especially enhance the motivation, self-esteem, and performance of disadvantaged children.

Really effective reforms in the teaching of cultural literacy must therefore begin with the earliest grades. Every improvement made in teaching very young children literate background information will have a multiplier effect on later learning, not just by virtue of the information they will gain but also by virtue of the greater motivation for reading and learning they will feel when they actually understand what they have read.

Young children enjoy absorbing formulaic knowledge. Even if they did not, our society would still find it essential to teach them all sorts of traditions and facts. Critical thinking and basic skills, two areas of current focus in education, do not enable children to create out of their own imaginations the essential names and concepts that have arisen by historical accident. The Rio Grande, the Mason-Dixon line, "The Night Before Christmas," and *Star Wars* are not products of basic skills or critical thought. Many items of literate culture are arbitrary, but that does not make them dispensable. Facts are essential components of the basic skills that a child entering a culture must have.

I'm not suggesting that we teach our children exactly what our grandparents learned. We should teach children current mainstream culture. It's obvious that the content of cultural literacy changes over the years. Today the term "Brown decision" belongs to cultural literacy, but in 1945 there hadn't been any Brown decision. The name Harold Ickes was current in 1945 but no longer is. Such mutability is the fate of most names and events of recent history. Other changes come through the contributions of various subnational cultures. Ethnic words (like *pizza*) and art forms (like *jazz*) are constantly entering and departing from mainstream culture. Other subnational cultures, including those of science and technology, also cause changes in the mainstream culture. DNA and quarks, now part of cultural literacy, were unknown in 1945. In short, terms that literate people know in the 1980s are different from those they knew in 1945, and forty years hence the literate culture will again be different.

The flux in mainstream culture is obvious to all. But stability, not change, is the chief characteristic of cultural literacy. Although historical and technical terms may follow the ebb and flow of events, the more stable elements of our national vocabulary, like George Washington, the tooth fairy, the Gettysburg Address, Hamlet, and the Declaration of Independence, have persisted for a long time. These stable elements of the national vocabulary are at the core of cultural literacy, and for that reason are the most important contents of schooling. Although the terms that ebb and flow are tremendously important at a given time, they belong, from an educational standpoint, at the periphery of literate culture. The persistent, stable elements belong at the educational core.

Let me give some concrete examples of the kinds of core information I mean. American readers are assumed to have a general knowledge of the following people (I give just the beginning of a list): John Adams, Susan B. Anthony, Benedict Arnold, Daniel Boone, John Brown, Aaron Burr, John C. Calhoun, Henry Clay, James Fenimore Cooper, Lord Cornwallis, Davy Crockett, Emily Dickinson, Stephen A. Douglas, Frederick Douglass, Jonathan Edwards, Ralph Waldo Emerson, Benjamin Franklin, Robert Fulton, Ulysses S. Grant, Alexander Hamilton, and Nathaniel Hawthorne. Most of us know rather little about these people, but that little is of crucial importance, because it enables writers and speakers to assume a starting point from which they can treat in detail what they wish to focus on.

Here is another alphabetical list that no course in critical thinking skills, however masterful, could ever generate: Antarctic Ocean, Arctic Ocean, Atlantic Ocean, Baltic Sea, Black Sea, Caribbean Sea, Gulf of Mexico, North Sea, Pacific Ocean, Red Sea. It has a companion list: Alps, Appalachians, Himalayas, Matterhorn, Mount Everest, Mount Vesuvius, Rocky Mountains. Because literate people mention such names in passing, usually without explanation, children should acquire them as part of their intellectual equipment.

Children also need to understand elements of our literary and mythic heritage that are often alluded to without explanation, for example, Adam and Eve, Cain and Abel, Noah and the Flood, David and Goliath, the Twenty-third Psalm, Humpty Dumpty, Jack Sprat, Jack and Jill, Little Jack Horner, Cinderella, Jack and the Beanstalk, Mary had a little lamb, Peter Pan, and Pinocchio. Also Achilles, Adonis, Aeneas, Agamemnon, Antigone, and Apollo, as well as Robin Hood, Paul Bunyan, Satan, Sleeping Beauty, Sodom and Gomorrah, the Ten Commandments, and Tweedledum and Tweedledee.

Our current distaste for memorization is more pious than realistic. At an early age when their memories are most retentive, children have an almost instinctive urge to learn specific tribal traditions. At that age they seem to be fascinated by catalogues of information and are eager to master the materials that authenticate their membership in adult society. Observe for example how they memorize the rather complex materials of football, baseball, and basketball, even without benefit of formal avenues by which that information is inculcated.

The weight of human tradition across many cultures supports the view that basic acculturation should largely be completed by age thirteen. At that age Catholics are confirmed, Jews bar or bat mitzvahed, and tribal boys and girls undergo the rites of passage into the tribe. According to the anthropological record, all cultures whose educational methods have been reported in the *Human Relations Area Files* (a standard source for anthropological data) have used early memorization to carry on their traditions.[29]

In Korea, "numerous books must be memorized, including the five *Kyung,* and the four *Su.*" In Tibet, "from eight to ten years of age, the boy spends most of his time reading aloud and memorizing the scriptures." In Chile, the Araucanian Indians use the memorization of songs as an educational technique to teach "the subtleties of the native tongue, and an insight into the customs and traditions of their tribe." In southern Africa, the children of Kung bushmen listen for hours to discussions of which they understand very little until they "know the history of every object, every exchange between their families, before they are ten or twelve years old." In Indonesia, "memorization is the method commonly used." In Thailand, children "repeat their lessons until they know them by heart." In Arizona, the Papago Indians take children through the lengthy rituals "as many times as needed for the learner to say it all through, which may take a year."[30]

The new kind of teaching espoused by Rousseau and Dewey, which avoids rote learning and encourages the natural development of the child on analogy with the development of an acorn into an oak, has one virtue certainly: it encourages independence of mind. But the theory also has its drawbacks, one of which is that a child is not in fact like an acorn. Left to itself, a child will not grow into a thriving creature; Tarzan is pure fantasy. To thrive, a child needs to learn the traditions of the particular human society and culture it is born into.[31] Like children everywhere, American children need traditional information at a very early age.

A great deal is at stake in understanding and acting on this essential perception as soon as possible. The opportunity of acquiring cultural literacy, once lost in the early grades, is usually lost for good. That is most likely to be true for children of parents who were not themselves taught the literate national culture.

In the technological age, Washington and the cherry tree, Scrooge and Christmas, the fights historical, the oceans geographical, the "beings animalculus," and all the other shared materials of literate culture have become more, not less, important. The more computers we have, the more we need shared fairy tales, Greek myths, historical images, and so on. That is not really the paradox it seems to be. The more specialized and technical our civilization becomes, the harder it is for nonspecialists to participate in the decisions that deeply affect their lives. If we do not achieve a literate society, the technicians, with their arcane specialties, will not be able to communicate with us nor we with them. That would contradict the basic principles of democracy and must not be allowed to happen.

The antidote to growing specialization is to reinvigorate the unspecialized domain of literate discourse, where all can meet on common ground. That this ideal *can* be achieved is proved by such admirable writers as Theodore H. White, John Kenneth Galbraith, Lewis Thomas, Peter Medawar, and Richard Feynman, who are able to communicate their complex expertise to a wide audience of educated people. We will be able to achieve a just and prosperous society only when our schools ensure that everyone commands enough shared background knowledge to be able to communicate effectively with everyone else.

NOTES

1. For rising standards of literacy, see R. L. Thorndike, *Reading Comprehension Education in Fifteen Countries: An Empirical Study* (New York: Wiley, 1973). On the connection between high literacy and Japan's economic performance, see Thomas R. Rohlen, "Japanese Education: If They Can Do It, Should We?" *American Scholar* 55, I (Winter 1985–86): 29–44. For American literacy rates see Jeanne Chall, "Afterward," in R. C. Anderson et. al., *Becoming a Nation of Readers: The Report of the Commission on Reading* (Washington, D. C.: National Institute of Education, 1985), 123–24. On "world knowledge" in literacy, see Jeanne C. Chall, *Stages of Reading Development* (New York: McGraw-Hill, 1983), 8.

2. The two classical discussions of the stabilizing effects of mass literacy on oral speech are Henry Bradley, *The Making of English,* revised edition by Simeon Potter (London: Macmillan, 1968), and Otto Jespersen, *Mankind, Nation, and Individual from a Linguistic Point of View,* Midland edition (Bloomington: Indiana University Press, 1964). Wider bibliographical references to this subject may be found in the first two chapters of my *Philosophy of Composition* (Chicago: University of Chicago Press, 1977).

3. The experiment is described in R. M. Krauss and S. Glucksberg, "Social and Nonsocial Speech," *Scientific American* 236 (February 1977): 100–105.

4. National Assessment of Educational Progress, *Three National Assessments of Reading: Changes in Performance, 1970–1980* (Report 11-R-01) (Denver: Education Commission of the States, 1981). The percentage of students scoring at the "advanced" level (4.9 percent) has climbed back to the very low levels of 1970. See *The Reading Report Card: Progress Toward Excellence in Our Schools, Trends in Reading over Four National Assessments, 1971–1984* (Princeton, N.J.: Educational Testing Service No. 15-R-01, 1986).

5. John B. Carroll, "Psychometric Approaches to the Study of Language Abilities," in C. J. Fillmore, D. Kempler, and S.-Y. Wang, eds., *Individual Differences in Language Abilities and Language Behavior* (New York: Academic Press, 1979), 29.

6. The College Board, *College-Bound Seniors: Eleven Years of National Data from the College Board's Admission Testing Program, 1973-83* (New York, 1984). The College Board has sent me further details from an unpublished report that shows the breakdown of scores over 600 between 1972 and 1984. The percentage of students who scored over 600 was 7.3 percent in 1984 and 11.4 percent in 1972. The percentage scoring over 650 was 3.0 percent in 1984 and 5.29 percent in 1972.

7. Benjamin J. Stein, "The Cheerful Ignorance of the Young in L.A.," *Washington Post,* October 3, 1983. Reprinted with the kind permission of the author.

8. *Changes in Political Knowledge and Attitudes, 1969-76: Selected Results from the Second National Assessments of Citizenship and Social Studies* (Denver: National Assessment of Educational Progress, 1978).

9. The Foundations of Literacy Project under a grant from the National Endowment for the Humanities, has commissioned NAEP, now conducted by the Educational

Testing Service of Princeton, to probe the literacy and historical knowledge of American seventeen-year-olds.

10. I am breaking no confidences as a member of the NAEP panel in revealing these pretest figures. They were made public on October 8, 1985, in a press release by NEH Chairman John Agresto, which stated in part: "Preliminary findings indicate that two-thirds of the seventeen-year-old students tested could not place the Civil War in the correct half century; a third did not know that the Declaration of Independence was signed between 1750 and 1800; half could not locate the half century in which the First World War occurred; a third did not know that Columbus sailed for the New World 'before 1750'; three fourths could not identify Walt Whitman or Thoreau or E. E. Cummings or Carl Sandburg. And one-half of our high school seniors did not recognize the names of Winston Churchill or Joseph Stalin."

11. See Chapter 2, pages 42-47.

12. Orlando Patterson, "Language, Ethnicity, and Change," in S. G. D'Eloia, ed., *Toward a Literate Democracy: Proceedings of the First Shaughnessy Memorial Conference, April 3, 1980,* special number of *The Journal of Basic Writing* III (1980): 72–73.

13. Letter to Colonel Edward Carrington, January 16, 1787, taken from *The Life and Selected Writings of Thomas Jefferson,* ed. A. Koch and W. Peden (New York: Random House, 1944), 411–12.

14. W. C. Sellar and R. J. Yeatman, *1066 and All That: A Memorable History of England, Comprising All the Parts You Can Remember, Including 103 Good Things, 5 Bad Kings, and 2 Genuine Dates* (London: Methuen, 1947).

15. Melvin Durslag, "To Ban the Beanball," *TV Guide,* June 8–14, 1985, 9.

16. H. Putnam, "The Meaning of Meaning," in *Philosophical Papers, Volume 2: Mind, Language and Reality* (Cambridge: Cambridge University Press, 1975), 227–48.

17. See M. S. Steffenson, C. Joag-Des, and R. C. Anderson, "A Cross-Cultural Perspective on Reading Comprehension," *Reading Research Quarterly* 15, 1 (1979): 10–29.

18. This is fully discussed in Chapter 3.

19. See H. J. Walberg and T. Shanahan, "High School Effects on Individual Students," *Educational Researcher* 12 (August–September 1983): 4–9.

20. "Up to about ten hours a week, there is actually a slight positive relationship between the amount of time children spend watching TV and their school achievement, including reading achievement. Beyond this point, the relationship turns negative and, as the number of hours per week climbs, achievement declines sharply." R. C. Anderson et al., *Becoming a Nation of Readers,* 27.

21. Walberg and Shanahan, "High School Effects on Individual Students," 4–9.

22. Arthur G. Powell, Eleanor Farrar, and David K. Cohen, *The Shopping Mall High School: Winners and Losers in the Educational Marketplace* (Boston: Houghton Mifflin, 1985), 1–8.

23. The neutrality and avoidance of the schools are described in detail in *The Shopping Mall High School.*

24. Patterson, "Language, Ethnicity, and Change," 72–73.

25. Oscar Wilde, "The Decay of Lying" (1889).

26. Jeanne S. Chall, "Afterword," in R. C. Anderson et al., *Becoming a Nation of Readers,* 123–25.

27. J. S. Chall, C. Snow, et al., *Families and Literacy,* Final Report to the National Institute of Education, 1982.

28. R. L. Thorndike, *Reading Comprehension Education in Fifteen Countries: An Empirical Study* (New York: Wiley, 1973). There is also recent evidence that advanced reading skills have declined in the United States while elementary skills have risen. See J. S. Chall, "Literacy: Trends and Explanations," *Educational Researcher* 12 (1983): 3–8, and R. C. Anderson et al., *Becoming a Nation of Readers*, 2.
29. *Human Relations Area Files,* microfiches (New Haven: Human Relations Area Files, 1899–1956).
30. Ibid. My examples are from more than two hundred entries, stretching from 1899 to 1949, under the topics "Educational Theories and Methods" and "Transmission of Beliefs."
31. L. A. Cremin, *The Transformation of the American School: Progressivism in American Education, 1876–1957* (New York: Knopf, 1964).

E. D. HIRSCH, JR., JOSEPH KETT,
AND JAMES TREFIL

FROM WHAT LITERATE AMERICANS KNOW: A PRELIMINARY LIST

Cultural Literacy *(New York: Vintage, 1988)*

1066	absolute monarchy
1492	absolute zero
1776	abstract art
1861–1865	abstract expressionism
1914–1918	academic freedom
1939–1945	a capella
1984 (title)	accelerator, particle
Aaron, Hank	accounting
Abandon hope, all ye who enter here.	acculturation
abbreviation	AC/DC
Aberdeen	Achilles
abolitionism	Achilles' heel
abominable snowman	acid
abortion	acid rain
Absence makes the heart grow fonder.	acquittal
absenteeism	acronym

acrophobia

Acropolis

Actions speak louder than words.

act of God

actuary

acupuncture

A.D.

ad absurdum

adagio

Adam and Eve

Adams, John

Adams, John Quincy

adaptation

Addams, Jane

Addis Ababa

Adeste Fideles (song)

ad hoc

ad hominem

adieu

ad infinitum

adiós

Adirondack Mountains

adjective

Adonis

adrenal gland

adrenaline (fight or flight)

adultery

adverb

AEC (Atomic Energy Commission)

Aegean, the

Aeneas

Aeneid, The (title)

aerobic

Aeschylus

Aesop's fables

aesthetics

affirmative action

affluent society

Afghanistan

aficionado

AFL-CIO

Africa

Agamemnon

Age cannot wither her, nor custom stale/Her infinite variety.

aggression

agnosticism

agreement

agribusiness

Ahab, Captain

AIDS

air pollution

Air Quality Index

Akron, OH

Alabama

á la carte

Aladdin's lamp

Alamo

Alaska

Alaskan pipeline

Alas, poor Yorick . . .

Albania

Albany, NY

albatross around one's neck

Albuquerque, NM

alchemy

Alcott, Louisa May

Aleutian Islands

Alexander the Great

Alexandria, Egypt

al fresco

algae

Alger, Horatio

Algeria

Algiers

alias

Alice in Wonderland (title)

Alien and Sedition Acts

alienation

Ali Muhammad

alkaline

Allah

All animals are equal, but some animals are more equal than others.

Allegheny Mountains

allegory

allegro

Allen, Woody

allergy

Alliance for Progress

alliteration

alloy

All roads lead to Rome.

All's fair in love and war.

All's well that ends well.

All that glitters is not gold.

All the news that's fit to print

All the world's a stage.

all things to all men

allusion

All work and no play makes Jack a dull boy.

alma matter

alpha and omega

alpha radiation

Alps, the

alter ego

QUESTIONS FOR REACTION AND DISCUSSION

1. What does Hirsch say is the purpose of his book? Why has he written it?
2. What does Hirsch mean by "cultural literacy"? Why is it necessary? How does one obtain it? What does it mean to say that cultural literacy is more than a skill?
3. What is a literacy rate? How are such rates determined?

4. How does Hirsch use standardized test scores in his argument that students are slipping in their mastery of communication skills? Is this effective? Why or why not?
5. What are the principal examples Hirsch gives as evidence for a lack of shared cultural knowledge? How effective are these? Why or why not?
6. Hirsch quotes from a variety of experts in this chapter from his book. How well does he identify them? How useful do you find the quotations he uses? Can you understand them all? If not, which ones cause problems for you as a reader? Why?
7. To what does Hirsch attribute to the decline of teaching? Why?
8. Any list is exclusionary by its very nature. Of what value is a list of terms for students? Can any list open or close our minds? Why or why not?

QUESTIONS FOR WRITING

1. Hirsch suggests that secondary schools in the United States offer a "cafeteria-style education." What does he mean by this term? In an essay, describe your secondary education and explain whether it fits this category.
2. In this essay, Hirsch states, "The concept of cultural literacy . . . places a higher value on national than on local information. We want to make our children competent to communicate with Americans throughout the land. Therefore, if Virginians did have to decide between [Jeb] Stuart and [Abraham] Lincoln, they ought to favor the man from Illinois over the one from Virginia." In an essay, defend or reject this position, citing details and examples from your own schooling and life experiences.
3. With some members of your class, examine the extract from the "Preliminary List" of terms that Hirsch and his colleagues have assembled. What are your reactions to the construction of such a list? What are the advantages of constructing what Hirsch calls a "provisional" list of terms from "mainstream" culture, as Hirsch defines it? The disadvantages? Test your classmates on their understanding of the terms given here. How much information do you have on these terms? Write an essay in which you report on the responses of your classmates to the concept of a list and their ability to explain or define the terms. What conclusions can you draw?

QUESTIONS FOR FURTHER EXPLORATION

1. Visit the Core Knowledge Foundation Web site <http://www.core-knowledge.org> and examine the mission statement, programs, and

Core Knowledge Sequence for the schools. What are your impressions? What do you think of the model curriculum guidelines? How do such guidelines compare with what you recall of the curriculum of your elementary school experience? Investigate (through some library and/or Internet research) the experiences of some of the schools using the core knowledge program and write a report for your classmates.

2. When *Cultural Literacy* was published in 1988, it was widely and thoroughly reviewed by major magazines, newspapers, and journals. By using *The Book Review Digest* or *The Reader's Guide to Periodical Literature*, locate several reviews of the book, read them carefully, and write an assessment of how Hirsch's book was received when it was first published.

3. In *The Opening of the American Mind: Canons, Culture, and History,* Lawrence W. Levine observes, "The historical pattern of American higher education . . . has been toward increasing openness, greater inclusiveness, expanded choice, the study of the modern as well as the ancient, a concentration on American, African, and Asian as well as European culture. These have not been inventions of our own time; they have not resulted from the plots of New Left Activists, the chauvinism of Afrocentrists, the philistinism of unsophisticated, gullible students, or the Machiavellianism of crafty faculty. This pattern has been the result of fundamental changes in the nature and composition of our society and has emanated from continuous encounters with those who have held a more fixed, Eurocentric, past-oriented, hierarchical conception of education." Write an essay in which you discuss how Hirsch would respond to this statement.

2

INTRODUCTION AND OPENING
THE AMERICAN MIND:
A PRELIMINARY LIST

*In an almost immediate response to E. D. Hirsch, Rick Simonson
and Scott Walker edited and published* Multi-cultural Literacy, *an
anthology of readings written by writers of a variety of racial and
ethnic backgrounds, such as James Baldwin, Paula Gunn Allen, Carlos Fuentes, David Mura, Gloria Anzaldúa, and Ishmael Reed. Simonson is a bookseller and Scott Walker is the editor of the
Graywolf Press, a small publishing company which is well known for
its series in contemporary literature, the Graywolf Annual. This collection was intended for use in college and university courses and as
a counter to* Cultural Literacy. *In preparing this anthology, Simonson
and Walker wished to demonstrate the narrowness of Hirsch's conception of "mainstream" literacy and proposed to broaden and update the list of what literate people need to know. In addition, they
wished to provide an additional list of terms, in part to point out
what they saw as the deficiencies in Hirsch's list.*

QUESTIONS FOR READING

1. What is your understanding of "multicultural literacy"? Is this term in
   opposition to "cultural literacy"? Why or why not?
2. What do you think the primary criticism that Simonson and Walker
   have for Hirsch will be?

RICK SIMONSON AND
SCOTT WALKER

INTRODUCTION

Multi-cultural Literacy *(St. Paul: Graywolf Press, 1988)*

In 1987, two serious books about American education became surprise best-sellers and the focal points of a renewed national debate about values and education. To date, the two books have sold nearly two million copies. The books are, simultaneously, impassioned pleas for making education a higher priority and blueprints for the revival of a conservative system of education utterly out of date with contemporary cultural and political realities.

Allan Bloom's *The Closing of the American Mind* is a "lack of" book, a book that complains of contemporary America's lack of values, our educational system's lack of purpose, and the average American's lack of vision, lack of understanding, and lack of knowledge. Bloom seems to long for a Reaganesque return to simpler times, when men were men, when we all—meaning white folk more than colored, meaning more men than women—learned the 3-Rs by way of the certain classic texts, in our little schoolhouses on the prairies.

E. D. Hirsch, Jr.'s *Cultural Literacy* gives alarming examples of high school and college graduates' ignorance of what Hirsch perceives to be the "basic" terms, facts, and concepts of our culture. He argues for a "return" to a system of education that teaches all citizens an established vocabulary of culture, so that we can talk together using the same system of cultural referents.

Hirsch's examples—the high school boy who, when asked to name an epic poem by Homer, answered, "The Alamo!"; the college junior who thought Toronto was a city in Italy; the alarming decline in college entrance examination scores—provided thundering first paragraphs to editorial writers across the U.S. Hirsch, Joseph Kett, and James Trefil compiled a list of five thousand things, names, proverbs, quotes, and concepts that "literate Americans know."

The renewed national debate about education and values has become something of a fad, which started in 1986 on publication of Jonathan Kozol's *Illiterate America*, a book that delivered the disturbing news that one in six of us can't read the Surgeon General's warnings or know what we're going to eat for dinner before opening the can. The books by Hirsch and Bloom settled onto bestseller lists in hardcover and paperback. William Bennett, President Reagan's former Secretary of Education, has for years stumped cross-country advocating "back-to-basics" education. Duke University's and Stanford University's amendments to their core reading lists became a national controversy. Stanford's previous "Western Culture Program," with its Eurocentric, exclusively male list of authors, will in the future give way to a "Cultures, Values, and Ideas Program" which broadens in gender and national origin the list of great books read as part of a student's fundamental education.

The editors of this *Graywolf Annual* agree with Hirsch, Bloom, and the editorial writers of America that education should be among the highest of national priorities, and that our current educational system is desperately wanting of both vision and financing. The need for change is urgent.

We do take issue with Hirsch's and Bloom's definitions of what (or whose) culture should be taught. We are alarmed by the number of people who are so enthusiastically in agreement with the Hirsch/Bloom argument for educational reform that they fail to discern its overridingly static, and so shallow, definition of culture. Both writers seem to think that most of what constitutes contemporary American and world culture was immaculately conceived by a few men in Greece, around 900 BC, came to its full expression in Europe a few centuries later, and began to decline around the middle of the nineteenth century.

Much of the Hirsch/Bloom world view is outdated. Most Americans are now aware of the contributions of repressed cultures, more alert to how history has been rewritten and molded to the vision of the majority population, and accustomed to the notion that culture, like language, changes, and that we ought to be sensitive to those changes. Though Hirsch is right, as far as he goes, in his list of five thousand things that savvy folk ought to know, he doesn't go far or deep enough. We need to know much more.

America's historians have enjoyed thinking of the country as a melting pot into which all ethnic populations thoroughly mixed. This may have been a faulty notion in the first place, and it is certainly no longer true. Here, as everywhere in the world, ethnic, minority populations (usually defined as "people of color"; and in many places actually the majority population) find ways to succeed within the mainstream culture while at the same time proudly preserving their own languages and cultures. Exemplifying this trend are the growing Latino populations in the United States, particularly in New York and the Southwest; the more recently arrived Southeast Asian population; the identity-seeking revival of Germanic and Nordic traditions among people long since considered fully "melted" Americans; and the admirable reculturing of the American Indians. At a time when one in four Americans is a person of color, none of us can afford to remain ignorant of the heritage and culture of any part of our population. Watching Jesse Jackson's political campaigns, as the Rainbow Coalition's broad appeal finds common ground, we have witnessed the development of a new definition of what comprises "mainstream" culture.

The twentieth century revolution in communications, the rise and pervasiveness of mass media, and dramatic changes in the world economy have led to a softening of political and cultural boundaries. As the world is "made smaller" and cultures become more uniform (imperialism taking on cultural as well as political forms), we are simultaneously brought closer together and suffer the destruction of individual languages, imagination, and cultural meaning. As we learn more about ecology and of ways to preserve nature, we should also learn the great value of diversity and seek to preserve a diverse cultural heritage. Economic development has historically led the way to cultural expansion. As the world becomes more of a single economic entity, there is a corresponding need for all citizens to have not only a fundamental understanding of their own culture (in part to conserve it), but also a knowledge of the cultures of the rest of the world. However, the citizens of the United States are profoundly ignorant of world literatures, histories, mythologies, and politics. For the United States to continue to have cultural and economic relevance, this inadequacy must be addressed.

2

Hirsch, Kett, and Trefil admit to knowing they were asking for trouble by compiling their list, "What Literate Americans Know." The list (which in its revised paperback edition is still called "preliminary") is peculiarly and appropriately wide-ranging. It includes *the Beatles, weather map, realpolitik, A rolling stone gathers no moss, Verdi, Bronze Age, tectonic plates,* and *Ty Cobb.* But Hirsch is disturbingly ignorant of some very common aspects of culture.

Women, for example. Though Hirsch's list does include *penis envy, macho,* and *vasectomy,* he fails to find significant *mastectomy, gynecology,* or *Georgia O'Keeffe.* Nor does he deem it important for culturally literate Americans to know about *alcoholism, internment camps, Bhagavad Gita, Pelé, rhythm and blues, computer crash, El Salvador,* or *One Hundred Years of Solitude.* Hirsch doesn't seem to consider it of value for Americans to know about food and agriculture, the environment, world geography, non-European history, or the plants and animals with whom we share the planet. Some of these omissions are the result of oversight. Many result from a particular white, male, academic, eastern U.S., Eurocentric bias that severely limits Hirsch's and Bloom's and Reagan's and Bennett's concept of American culture.

Despite our own best judgment, the editors of this anthology have compiled the beginnings of a list of words, concepts, names, and titles that were omitted by Hirsch and Co. Our list, presented as an appendix to this volume, is offered simply to show some aspects of our culture that are not deemed significant by our more conservative educators and policy makers. These educators and politicians form U.S. educational policy and therefore our future, and they too often ignore the part that women and/or people of color play in making this culture and country what it is.

3

In researching material for this anthology, the editors spoke to many people who for years have thought and written about issues of multiculturalism, the history of civilizations, feminist literature and culture, ethnicity, and the literature and histories of many non-White and non-European cultures. It was surprising to find how few of these people knew about either the Bloom or the Hirsch books. When informed of the books, most dismissed them as hapless throwbacks to a more conservative time. The issues of the contributions to our culture made by women and people of color, and of the importance of developing a worldwide view of culture, had, to these people, been settled years ago.

Clearly, though, the issues of what our culture is and how it can be taught have not been settled. They have not been settled in the academic world nor in the everyday world in which we all live and work. Americans need to have a better grasp of the European heritage and a clearer understanding of American history and culture to know its depths and soul. Americans need to broaden their awareness and understanding of the cultures of the rest of the world. Other histories and cultures reveal ancestry and knowledge that has bearing on who we are and where we are going. By understanding more about our immediate locale, the native soil we stand on and the other living things that share our world, we expand our imaginations and expand our culture. The language of the academic world, of government, of business, of mass media so easily becomes abstract, distancing, manipulative. Such language cannot, with its nervous speed, its strip-mined, appropriating qualities, touch the deep, turned-over ground of our culture. Such language can, and often does, seek to bury it.

RICK SIMONSON AND
SCOTT WALKER

OPENING THE AMERICAN MIND: A PRELIMINARY LIST

E. D. Hirsch, Jr., Joseph Kett, and James Trefil, all of whom are professors at the University of Virginia, Charlottesville, compiled, for inclusion in Hirsch's book, *Cultural Literacy,* a list they called "What Literate Americans Know." They admitted that the list was preliminary and provisional, and added a few things to the list for the paperback printing of the book. Their list includes approximately five thousand names, dates, places, phrases, terms, and concepts that they believe knowledgeable citizens should know.

Rick Simonson and Scott Walker, editors of *The Graywolf Annual 5: Multi-Cultural Literacy,* think the list compiled by Hirsch and his colleagues is fine as far as it goes, but that their list is alarmingly deficient in its male and European bias.

The brief list printed below is intended only to suggest the sorts of things not included in the Hirsch book, the sorts of things too commonly excluded from U.S. educational texts, political thinking, or social planning. The list could be considerably lengthened, and we prefer to think of this list as simply the start of a discussion among friends who hope to improve the educational system of this country, and to make its citizens more aware of the important roles played in our lives by a great many cultures.

THE LIST

100,000 Songs of Milarepa
AA (Alcoholics Anonymous)
AAA (American Automobile
    Association)
Abdul-Jabbar, Kareem
aborigine
abstract expressionism
Absurd, Theater of the
Achebe, Chinua
ACOA (Adult Children of
    Alcoholics)
action painting
Ade, King Sunny
Adler, Alfred
adobe
advertising
African diaspora
Afro-American
Agent Orange
Akhmatave, Anna
Al-Anon
alcoholism
Allende, Salvador
alphabet
altar
Amado, Jorge
amen
Anasazi (tribe)
ancestor worship
anima/animus
anthology
antiwar movement
apse
aquaculture
Aquarius

Arabic
Arafat, Yasir
Aries
Art Deco
Ashé
ashram
Asian Exclusion Act
attention span
Baal
Baha'i
Baja California
Baldwin, James
Bannister, Roger
barrio
Bartók, Béla
Bashō
Batman
Bay of Bengal
Beamon, Bob
beat, the
beatnick
Beckett, Samuel
Belize
Bell's Theorem
Benedict, Ruth
Bergman, Ingmar
Bhagavad Gita
Biko, Steve
bilingual
biodegradable
biological clock
biopsy
bioregional
birds and the bees, the
Black and Tans

Black Elk
Bloody Sunday
bluegrass (music)
Bly, Robert
Bogotá
Bolívar, Simón
Bonhoeffer, Dietrich
boom box
boot up
Borges, Jorge Luis
braille
Brecht, Bertolt
Breton, André
Bringing in the Sheaves (song)
Brodsky, Joseph
Brooks, Gwendolyn
Buchenwald
Buñuel, Luis
Cage, John
Cajun
Campbell, Joseph
Camus, Albert
Capone, Al
Capricorn
Cardenal, Ernesto
Carver, George Washington
Castaneda, Carlos
Castro Street
cathouse
cause and effect
Cavafy, Constantine
Cavell, Edith
celibacy
Celtic
Chandler, Raymond
chaos (science term)
charge
Charlotte's Web (title)
chautauqua
Chernobyl
chess
Cheyenne (tribe)
child abuse
Chinese New Year

chiropractic
cholera
Chopin, Kate
Christian radicalism
church
Cinco de Mayo
Cinderella
cinéma verité
clan
co-parenting
Cochise
codependency
Cole, Nat King
Colette
community
condom
cool (personality attribute)
corporate/party line
corruption
Cosby, Bill
covert operation
Coyote
crash (computer)
cultural materialism
cybernetics
dadaism
Damballah
Dar-es-Salaam
Davis, Miles
de Beauvoir, Simone
Decline and Fall of the Roman
    Empire, The (title)
deep ecology
defoliation
Dhammapada
Diamond Sutra
diaspora
Díaz del Castillo, Bernal
Díaz, Porfirio
Diddley, Bo
Dinesen, Isak
Disappeared, The
disinformation
divorce

Dixieland jazz
Djakarta
domestic violence
dope
downtime
down under
Dr. J
Dresden
Druids
drum
dub poetry
Earhart, Amelia
Easter Island
Easter, 1916
economic violence
El Salvador
Elegba
Elytis, Odysseus
endangered species
environment impact statement
environmental movement
Evers, Medgar
extinction
facts of life
fallout
Farsi
fax
fertility
film noir
Fonda, Jane
football
FORTRAN
Franklin, Aretha
Freud, Anna
Freidan, Betty
Fromm, Erich
fructose
Fuentes, Carlos
funk
Gaia hypotheses
García Lorca, Federico
Garcìa Márquez, Gabriel
Gaye, Marvin
Gemini

genitals
get down
Gesundheit
ghost dance
Gide, André
gift
Gilgamesh
Ginsberg, Allen
Golden Bough, The (title)
Gorbachev, Mikhail
gospel (music)
Grass, Günter
Great Mother
Green party movement
Greenpeace
griot
Guadalajara
Guarani (tribe)
Guatemala
Guevara, Che
gulag
gynecology
Haida (tribe)
Hall, Radclyffe
Halloween
Hamburger Hill
Hamilton, Edith
Hansberry, Lorraine (Raisin in
  the Sun)
Happy Birthday (song)
Harlem Renaissance
Hasidic
Health Maintenance Organization
Heaney, Seamus
Heaven
Hebrew
Hell
Hidalgo, Miguel
History is bunk
Holiday, Billie
homeopathy
homophobia
Hopi
hostile takeover

Hughes, Langston
Hurston, Zora Neale
Hydra
hyperspace
hysterectomy
I Ching
I heard it through the grape vine
I will fight no more forever
Ibn al-'Arabī
"If you want to see a mask dancing,
you cannot stand in one place."—Ibo
proverb
Inanna
indigenous
Indonesia
infertility
infiltration
instant replay
internment camps
Inuit (tribe)
Isis
issei
It ain't me, babe
Ivory Coast
Iztapalapa
jam session
jazz-rock fusion (music)
Jeffers, Robinson
jit (music)
jive
Johnson, Robert
joint custody
Jones, Mother
Jones, Quincy
juju music
Kaballah
Kahlo, Frida
Kalahari Desert
Kali
karma
Kawabata, Yasunari
Kenya
Kerouac, Jack
Khmer Rouge

Killing Fields
Kiowa (tribe)
kiva
Krishna
kundalini yoga
Kundera, Milan
Kung (tribe)
Kurosawa, Akira
Kyoto
Lagos
land ethic
land stewardship
Lao Tzu
Laveau, Marie
Lawrence, Jacob
learning disability
Lem, Stanislaw
Leo
Lessing, Doris
Li Po
liberation theology
Libra
Little Red Book, The
Lone Ranger
loom (weaver's)
Los Alamos, New Mexico
Love Canal
Mabinogion, The
macrobiotic
magical realism
Magritte, René
Maharishi Mahesh Yogi
makossa (music)
Mandela, Nelson
Marley, Bob
mastectomy
mbaqanga (music)
McCarthy, Joseph
McCoy, Elijah
McCullers, Carson
Mead, Margaret
Means, Russell
Mekong Delta
mercenary soldier

prayer
premenstrual syndrome
prime time
prison
prophylactic
prostitution
protein debt
provincial
psyche
public relations
pueblo
Puget Sound
Puig, Manuel
put to bed (finish)
Quetzalcoatl
quilt
racial slur
Rainbow Coalition
randomness (science term)
rap (music)
rape
Rasta
Ray, Man
recycling
Reed, Ishmael
reforestation
refusenik
reggae
REM (rapid eye movement)
reservation (Indian)
retrograde
revolution
Rexroth, Kenneth
rhythm and blues (music)
Rich, Adrienne
riff
right brain/left brain
Rilke, Rainer Maria
rock 'n' roll
Rome
Rumi
safe sex
Sagittarius
samba

Sand Creek
Sandinismo
Sands, Bobby
Sanger, Margaret
sansei
scat
Seattle, Chief
selective perception
semiotics
sexism
shadow (psychological term)
shaman
shaman(ism)
shango
Shinto
Shiva
ska (music)
Smith, Bessie
Smokey the Bear
Snyder, Gary
soca music
soccer
socialized medicine
socially responsible investing
solar energy
Solidarity movement
Somoza
Sonoran Desert
soukous (music)
soul
soul food
soul music
Souls of Black Folk, The (title)
Soweto, South Africa
Soyinka, Wole
spirituals (music)
Springsteen, Bruce
St. Patrick's Day
strange particles
Stuart Little (title)
subatomic particles
substance abuse
sucrose
Sufi

QUESTIONS FOR REACTION AND DISCUSSION

1. Is the portrayal of Hirsch fair in this essay? Why or why not?
2. What do you learn implicitly about the background of Simonson and Walker through reading this "Introduction"?
3. What is the central contribution of this anthology? Why?
4. What is the rationale for a "multicultural" literacy?
5. Examine the list of terms that Simonson and Walker attach as their Appendix. How many do you know? Discuss the list with your classmates.

QUESTIONS FOR WRITING

1. How do you think E. D. Hirsch responded to the publication of *Multi-cultural Literacy*? Write an essay in which you speculate on how he would answer the criticisms that Simonson and Walker raise about his idea of the importance of mainstream culture.
2. Many colleges and universities have responded to the need for students to understand diverse cultures by imposing gender and cultural diversity requirements. Others have worked to infuse multiculturalism into many aspects of the curriculum through existing courses. What is the case at your own institution? Investigate how multiculturalism is taught on your campus and write a description of the requirements, programs, or courses. How effective do you think the requirements are? Why or why not?
3. Although Simonson and Walker criticize Hirsch's list as inevitably prescriptive and narrow, they offer their own supplementary list. How effective do you think lists are generally as a way of suggesting information that students should know? What are the limitations of such lists? Write an essay in which you evaluate the use of lists of terms that Americans should know.

QUESTIONS FOR FURTHER EXPLORATION

1. How much evidence is there that multiculturalism has become a part of the curriculum of American colleges and universities? Choose four or five different schools in your part of the country and investigate their Web sites and catalogues. Do these schools have mission statements that incorporate multiculturalism? Are there course or program requirements? Write a report of your findings.

2. How is the debate over multiculturalism reported in the popular press? Using the *Reader's Guide to Periodical Literature* (either in print or online), investigate multiculturalism as a topic in magazines such as *Time, Newsweek,* and other magazines designed for the general American public. What about general magazines designed for specialized audiences such as women and minorities? Write a report in which you summarize and analyze your findings.

3

GENERAL EDUCATION AND THE SEARCH FOR A COMMON CULTURE

Alan C. Purves (1931–1996) was Director of the Center for Writing and Literacy and a professor in the English Department at the State University of New York at Albany. Internationally known as a consultant on college curricula, literature instruction, and assessment of students' works, Purves wrote nearly two dozen books on a wide range of topics in higher education—from the assessment of writing instruction to literary criticism. His last book, published posthumously, is The Web of Text and the Web of God: An Essay on the Third Information Transformation *(1998), an analysis of ways in which electronic technology has affected cultural, intellectual, and religious beliefs. The essay below was published in a collection by the National Society for the Study of Education, which sponsors an annual academic conference and publishes a yearly series on issues in contemporary education. In this essay, Purves introduces a group of essays that were written in response to the general topic of cultural literacy and the idea of general education. But more than merely an introduction to a book, Purves discusses his own view of the main issues involved in the relationship between the demands of cultural literacy and the traditional requirements of general education for contemporary college students.*

QUESTIONS FOR READING

1. What does the term "general education" suggest to you? Are you currently taking courses in a general education program or division? What are the courses intended to do?
2. This essay begins with a quotation, the first three lines of a poem by W. B. Yeats. What do the lines suggest about the nature of the essay to follow?

ALAN C. PURVES

GENERAL EDUCATION AND THE
SEARCH FOR A COMMON CULTURE

*Cultural Literacy and the Idea of General Education, ed. Ian Westbury and Alan C. Purves
(Chicago: NSSE, 1988)*

*Turning and turning in a widening gyre,
The falcon cannot hear the falconer;
Things fall apart, the center cannot hold.*
W. B. YEATS
"THE SECOND COMING"

General education might best be defined as the purposeful attempt to provide
a particular group of students with a common core of knowledge, skills, and
values. The term "general" refers not to the people who will undergo that education, but to the substance that is imparted. Paradoxically, general education, in many cases, is "caviar to the general," and is not to be equated with
common schooling or basic education. At times it has been equated with "liberal education," that which traditionally includes training in the modes of
thought of the humanities, including foreign languages, the natural and physical sciences, and the social sciences. At times it has been seen as encompassing
a broader set of studies. General education, as applied to colleges and universities, appears to be a peculiarly American conception. It is often viewed as also
the province of secondary schools, particularly by those who recall the fact
that many universities ran their own preparatory schools to provide students
with sufficient "general education" to be ready to begin specialized university
training. Such schools no longer exist, but the very idea of university entrance
or high school graduation requirements may be seen as vestiges of this earlier
state of affairs.

GENERAL EDUCATION AND
CULTURAL LITERACY

The idea of general education is related to the idea of culture, which is something to which people are affiliated as opposed to their natural filiation. General education has come into the news during the 1980s, thanks to an article by
E. D. Hirsch, Jr.[1] and the addition of a measure of cultural knowledge in the
National Assessment of Educational Progress. The idea of culture goes back at
least as far as the eighteenth century and was spurred in the nineteenth century
by the nationalist impetus. Culture may best be defined as Edward Said has

defined it: "[C]ulture is used to designate not merely something to which one belongs but something that one possesses, and along with that proprietary process, culture also designates a boundary by which the concepts of what is extrinsic or intrinsic to the culture comes into forceful play."[2] Anthropologists tend to see culture somewhat differently from literary people, but this root definition of possession and being possessed seems to apply both to those societies that operate through what might be called natural filiation (a system of intergenerational and familial relationships), and those that operate through affiliation to some arbitrarily instituted set of relationships. Current "American" culture is a culture of affiliation, whether it be the culture of Hawthorne and Harriet Beecher Stowe, the culture of Black Studies, the culture of feminism, or the culture of "hard science." Some have argued that the idea of general education came to America in its attempt to define itself as America and to define American culture. Others have seen general education as an attempt by American educational institutions to ensure that the European heritage remained part of the American culture.

Any culture serves to isolate its members from other cultures and any culture is elitist in some senses. As Said points out, "What is more important in culture is that it is a system of values saturating downward almost everything within its purview, yet paradoxically culture dominates from above without at the same time being available to everything and everyone that it dominates."[3] Cultures are exclusionary by definition; people who have a culture see others as outside or beneath them, and certainly very few people transcend cultures or are full members of more than one culture, although they may be members of several subcultures, such as that of mycologists, joggers, or film aficionados as well as of the broader culture of "generally educated" Americans.

To be a member of a culture, one must possess a fair amount of knowledge, some of it tacit, concerning the culture: its rules, its rituals, its mores, its heroes, gods, and demigods. This knowledge lies at the heart of cultural literacy, and such knowledge is brought into play when people read and respond to a text that comes from the same culture. It is such knowledge that, in fact, enables them to read that text and is brought into play when we read and write as social beings within a particular community. The lack of such knowledge keeps us outside, as witness the problems of visitors to a national or disciplinary culture who often suffer trifling embarrassments or serious misunderstandings.

Cultural literacy may be thought of as language learning, for the study of any discipline or field of knowledge involves the learning of a language which represents a mode of thought culturally appropriate to the discipline. Judit Kádár-Fülöp[4] has written that there are three major functions of the language curriculum in school (and by extension the curriculum in any discipline) that accord with the definitions of language functions proposed by Uriel Weinreich.[5] The first of these functions is the promotion of cultural communication so as to enable the individual to communicate with other members of the culture or discipline. Such a function clearly calls for the individual to learn the cultural norms of semantics, morphology, syntax, text structure, and pragmatics and some common procedural routines so as to operate within those norms and be understood. The second function is the promotion of cultural loyalty or the acceptance and valuing of those norms and routines and the inculcation of a desire to have them remain. A culturally loyal literate in physics, for example, would have certain expectations about how texts are to be written or to be read as well as what they should look like, and would expect others in the culture to follow those same norms. The third - function of language education may be the development of individuality. Once one has learned to communicate within the culture and developed a loyalty to it, then one is able to become independent of it. Before then, independence of those norms and values is seen as naive, illiterate, or childish. As Lev Vygotsky wrote (1956): "In reality a child's thought progresses from the social to the individual not from the individual to the socialized."[6]

When writers such as Hirsch speak of cultural literacy, they are clearly advocating the first two goals set forth by Kádár-Fülop and restrict the sense of the term to literacy in a particular culture, as did William Bennett in his report, *To Reclaim a Legacy,*[7] or that segment of general education which is defined as "the humanities" or "American classics." Hirsch and other advocates of cultural literacy refer to a definite body of knowledge (although Hirsch might not include specific titles, the National Assessment suggested that specific titles are necessary) that enables readers to read certain kinds of texts—notably texts that are shared by a group that one might define as "highly literate Americans." These would be people, for example, who can read the *New York Times* with understanding and can also read books and such journals as the *Atlantic Monthly.*[8]

The argument for this sort of cultural literacy is the argument that supported the Chicago Great Books Program, Harvard's General Education proposal, and Columbia's Humanities and Contemporary Civilization program in the early part of this century: such literacy brings together a disparate immigrant population and helps the melting pot do its job.[9] Such proposals bore with them the arguments of Matthew Arnold that a common culture based on the western heritage forged society into unity through affiliation and prevented anarchy and mobocracy. It does so not without cost. Again to cite the comments of Edward Said: "When our students are taught such things as 'the humanities' they are almost always taught that these classic texts embody, express, represent what is best in our, that is, the only, tradition. Moreover, they are taught that such fields as the humanities and such subfields as 'literature' exist in a relatively neutral political element, that they are to be appreciated and venerated, that they define the limits of what is acceptable, appropriate, and legitimate as far as culture is concerned."[10]

THE LIMITATIONS OF THE EQUATION OF GENERAL EDUCATION AND CULTURAL LITERACY

But it is at this point that the similarity between the concern for general education and the current definitions of cultural literacy begin to break down, for those who advocate cultural literacy appear to think of the culture primarily in belle-lettristic terms. Such a conception seems hardly appropriate in an age of American culture in which science and technology play so large a part. One must consider the nature of American culture in broader terms. In part it is those terms which this volume sets out to consider and debate. Some of the points raised in the debate include the following:

1. Given a comprehensive secondary and initial tertiary educational system, more diverse groups with their distinctive cultural heritages are now passing through the system and we must attend to the needs and values of those groups. The current conception does not adequately address these minority groups.

2. Education should meet the functional needs of the students and the workplace; there is little room in life for the sort of culture that is implied by any of the definitions of general education.

3. Any concept of general education must recognize the technological and scientific nature of our society. The emphasis on the humanities must be lessened; otherwise American society will lose out to the technologically more sophisticated nations.

4. In current academic practice, general education exists in the curriculum of both higher and secondary educational institutions. It is often defined in terms that resemble a menu in a mediocre Chinese restaurant; a person has attained a general education if the requisite number of hours have been spent in certain portions of the course catalog, instead of particular kinds of knowledge, skill, or attitude. It is also generally defined in terms of a limited number of academic fields (literature and history, with the social, natural, and physical sciences playing a secondary role). Yet one could easily make the argument that the fine arts, physical education, and the practical and technical arts should be included in general education. These areas, too, are constituents of our culture.

5. At the same time the very notion of the culture that a general education was to support has come to be challenged on a number of fronts: the culture appears too "Western" and too masculine and in defining itself has excluded much of the world in which Americans play an important but perhaps small part; the culture appears to have excluded the tremendous flow of information and the social and intellectual changes brought about by the new technologies; the culture has neglected the fact that people in various occupations have had to become so specialized in order to keep up with the occupation that they have "no time" to be cultured, and in many cases it has tended to see people in those occupations as without culture.

These are but some of the challenges to those planning general education for the students of the next century. To meet these challenges, educational planners and policy makers must face issues that are intellectual, political (both nationally and within the various educational institutions), and practical. This volume explores the challenges and the issues arising from them.

The volume, then, explores the possible collapse of general education and of the broad cultural literacy that Hirsch proposes for our schools. This volume is in one sense a somber one. The high hopes for general education and the bringing together of a diverse people into a broad educated culture appears to be diminishing as the century wanes. It may be that we are in a *fin de siècle* mood, a point in our history where we find the lines of Yeats which began this introduction to be even more apposite than they were when written over sixty years ago. Yeats raised the question of a second coming and wondered "what rough beast [was] slouching towards Bethlehem to be born." In our world of schools and colleges, the shape of the rough beast is yet indistinct and may remain so for years to come.

NOTES

1. E. D. Hirsch, Jr., "Cultural Literacy," *American Scholar* 52 (Spring 1983): 159–69.
2. Edward Said, *The World, the Text, and the Critic* (Cambridge, MA: Harvard University Press, 1983).
3. Said, 9.
4. Judit Kádár-Fülop, "Culture, Writing, and the Curriculum," in *Writing across Languages and Cultures: Theory and Method in Contrastive Rhetoric,* ed. Alan C. Purves (Beverly Hills, CA: Sage Publications, in press).
5. Uriel Weinreich, *Languages in Contact: Findings and Problems* (The Hague: Mouton, 1963).
6. Lev Vygotsky, *Izbrannye psikhologicheskie isseldovaniia* (Moscow: RSFR Academy of Pedagogical Science, 1956), quoted in A. K. Markova, *The Teaching and Mastery of Language* (London: Croom Helm, 1979).
7. William J. Bennett, *To Reclaim a Legacy: A Report on the Humanities in Higher Education* (Washington, DC: National Endowment for the Humanities, 1984).
8. It is important to note that in his reworking of that article into a book, *Cultural Literacy: What Every American Needs to Know* (Boston: Houghton Mifflin, 1987), Hirsch has extended his view of cultural literacy to include much in science and the practical arts as well as current events and popular culture. It would seem that he is no longer in the same camp as Bennett.
9. Daniel Bell, *The Reforming of General Education* (New York and London: Columbia University Press, 1966).
10. Said, *The World, the Text, and the Critic,* 21.

QUESTIONS FOR REACTION AND DISCUSSION

1. How is general education a particularly American conception? What do you know about the structure of higher education in other countries?
2. What does Purves mean when he says that current American culture is a culture of "affiliation"? What are the implications for general education?
3. How might cultural literacy be construed as language learning? How useful is it to define cultural literacy in this way?
4. How does Purves situate E. D. Hirsch's definition of cultural literacy within the structure of definitions he provides? Is this fair or appropriate, based on your reading of Hirsch?
5. What does Purves mean when he says that some current definitions of cultural literacy are "belle-lettristic"?

QUESTIONS FOR WRITING

1. Purves suggests that as social beings within a particular community we possess a fair amount of knowledge that is specific to that community. Outsiders to a community are immediately identified by their lack of knowledge about community culture and can sometimes, as Purves suggests, suffer "trifling embarrassments or serious misunderstandings." A campus is a particular community with its own culture and special knowledge, and new students often feel like outsiders as they learn the campus culture. Consider your own experience in learning about your campus. What information did you need to know that was campus-specific? What did you find hardest to learn? Were there expressions and phrases that were new to you? Do you still feel like an outsider? Why? Write an essay in the form of a letter to a friend or a parent, in which you describe your acquisition of campus cultural literacy. Use specific details and examples, such as any embarrassments or misunderstandings you experienced in the process.
2. Purves suggests that the general education program at many campuses resembles a menu in a mediocre Chinese restaurant. Other writers about higher education have referred to general education as a cafeteria approach to learning where students pick and choose from a conventional menu of choices; others have compared the student's experience of these programs to that of a shopper at a mall, going aimlessly from one store to the next. What do these comparisons have in common? Do these comparisons provide any commentary on the general education program on your campus? Why or why not? Write an essay in which you defend or reject the way in which the general education program is defined on your campus.

3. One of the points that is raised in the debate about a definition of cultural literacy as a specific body of knowledge (such as the program that Hirsch advocates) is that technology and science are deemphasized in favor of the humanities. How crucial do you think general education in science and technology is? Write an essay in which you describe what you regard as basic knowledge in these areas, why it is important, and how it might be best learned by students.

QUESTIONS FOR FURTHER EXPLORATION

1. Locate a copy of W. B. Yeats's "The Second Coming," which was published in 1920. Write an essay in which you explore the imagery of the destruction of the familiar world in the poem and relate it to Purves's notion of the possibilities for a common culture and a general education.
2. Locate a copy of the provocative report published in 1984 by the National Endowment for the Humanities: William J. Bennett, *To Reclaim a Legacy: A Report on the Humanities in Higher Education.* What general assumptions about cultural literacy and American education have guided the author of this report? In what way is Purves commenting on Bennett? Write a report for your classmates.
3. Many of the writers in this section, including Purves, allude to the numbers of minority students who are currently enrolled in a college or university. Where would you look to find current figures on the numbers of people enrolled in colleges and universities this year, along with information on gender, race, ethnicity, and age? Use your library and the Internet to locate this information and prepare a report for your classmates on the current statistics.

4

THE BANKING CONCEPT OF EDUCATION

Paulo Freire (1927–1997) was a teacher and author whose books on education and teaching methods have made a significant impact on American educators. In Recife, Brazil, Freire was born to a lower middle-class family living in one of poorest and most underdeveloped parts of the Third World. The economic crisis in the United States in 1929 affected Brazil as well, and Freire's family experienced great hardship. These experiences shaped Freire's lifelong concern with people who were oppressed by poverty, ignorance, and repressive governments. Working as a teacher of the illiterate peasants of his country, Freire became interested in developing a pedagogical practice based on his philosophy that education should be liberating. In 1959, he earned a Ph.D. and became a professor at the University of Recife. In 1963, he was appointed director of the Brazilian National Literary Program. Following a military coup in Brazil the next year, he was jailed for what were considered his subversive educational activities. He spent the next fifteen years in exile, living and writing in Chile, Nicaragua, Switzerland, and the United States, where he served as a consultant to the Harvard University School of Education. He returned permanently to Brazil in 1980 under a political amnesty agreement. In 1989, he was named education secretary of Sao Paulo and also returned to university teaching at the Catholic University of Sao Paulo.

Freire published over twenty books during his lifetime, but none has been more influential than Pedagogy of the Oppressed, *published in 1970. Here Freire maintains that traditional teaching subscribes to the "banking concept of education," in which the student is conceived of as a piggy bank into which a teacher deposits knowledge. Taking the view that such an approach is oppressive because it negates inquiry and places all the authority in the teacher, Freire advocated a "pedagogy of liberation," in which teacher and student relinquish the traditional roles and engage in an active dialogue, using the everyday words and experiences of the student as a departure point. The essay printed here is from the second chapter of* Pedagogy of the Oppressed *and outlines the implications of the "banking concept of education."*

Questions for Reading

1. What does the word "pedagogy" mean?
2. What is your initial reaction to the phrase, "pedagogy of the oppressed"?
3. How do you view the roles of teacher and student? What responsibilities does each have?

PAULO FREIRE

Chapter 2

Pedagogy of the Oppressed *(Translated by Myra Bergman Ramos)*

A careful analysis of the teacher-student relationship at any level, inside or outside the school, reveals its fundamentally *narrative* character. This relationship involves a narrating Subject (the teacher) and patient, listening objects (the students). The contents, whether values or empirical dimensions of reality, tend in the process of being narrated to become lifeless and petrified. Education is suffering from narration sickness.

The teacher talks about reality as if it were motionless, static, compartmentalized, and predictable. Or else he expounds on a topic completely alien to the existential experience of the students. His task is to "fill" the students with the contents of his narration—contents which are detached from reality, disconnected from the totality that engendered them and could give them significance. Words are emptied of their concreteness and become a hollow, alienated, and alienating verbosity.

The outstanding characteristic of this narrative education, then, is the sonority of words, not their transforming power. "Four times four is sixteen; the capital of Pará is Belém." The student records, memorizes, and repeats these phrases without perceiving what four times four really means, or realizing the true significance of "capital" in the affirmation "the capital of Pará is Belém," that is, what Belém means for Pará and what Pará means for Brazil.

Narration (with the teacher as narrator) leads the students to memorize mechanically the narrated content. Worse yet, it turns them into "containers," into "receptacles" to be "filled" by the teacher. The more completely she fills the receptacles, the better a teacher she is. The more meekly the receptacles permit themselves to be filled, the better students they are.

Education thus becomes an act of depositing, in which the students are the depositories and the teacher is the depositor. Instead of communicating, the teacher issues communiqués and makes deposits which the students patiently receive, memorize, and repeat. This is the "banking" concept of education, in which the scope of action allowed to the students extends only as far as receiving, filing, and storing the deposits. They do, it is true, have the opportunity to become collectors or cataloguers of the things they store. But in the last analysis, it is the people themselves who are filed away through the lack of creativity, transformation, and knowledge in this (at best) misguided system. For apart from inquiry, apart from the praxis, individuals cannot be truly human. Knowledge emerges only through invention and reinvention, through the restless, impatient, continuing, hopeful inquiry human beings pursue in the world, with the world, and with each other.

In the banking concept of education, knowledge is a gift bestowed by those who consider themselves knowledgeable upon those whom they consider to know nothing. Projecting an absolute ignorance onto others, a characteristic of the ideology of oppression, negates education and knowledge as processes of inquiry. The teacher presents himself to his students as their necessary opposite; by considering their ignorance absolute, he justifies his own existence. The students, alienated like the slave in the Hegelian dialectic, accept their ignorance as justifying the teacher's existence—but, unlike the slave, they never discover that they educate the teacher.

The *raison d'être* of libertarian education, on the other hand, lies in its drive towards reconciliation. Education must begin with the solution of the teacher-student contradiction, by reconciling the poles of the contradiction so that both are simultaneously teachers *and* students.

This solution is not (nor can it be) found in the banking concept. On the contrary, banking education maintains and even stimulates the contradiction through the following attitudes and practices, which mirror oppressive society as a whole:

(a) The teacher teaches and the students are taught.

(b) The teacher knows everything and the students know nothing.

(c) The teacher thinks and the students are thought about.

(d) The teacher talks and the students listen—meekly.

(e) The teacher disciplines and the students are disciplined.

(f) The teacher chooses and enforces his choice, and the students comply.

(g) The teacher acts and the students have the illusion of acting through the action of the teacher.

(h) The teacher chooses the program content, and the students (who were not consulted) adapt to it.

(i) The teacher confuses the authority of knowledge with his or her own professional authority, which she and he sets in opposition to the freedom of the students.

(j) The teacher is the Subject of the learning process, while the pupils are mere objects.

It is not surprising that the banking concept of education regards men as adaptable, manageable beings. The more students work at storing the deposits entrusted to them, the less they develop the critical consciousness which would result from their intervention in the world as transformers of that world. The more completely they accept the passive role imposed on them, the more they tend simply to adapt to the world as it is and to the fragmented view of reality deposited in them.

The capability of banking education to minimize or annul the students' creative power and to stimulate their credulity serves the interests of the oppressors, who care neither to have the world revealed nor to see it transformed. The oppressors use their "humanitarianism" to preserve a profitable situation. Thus they react almost instinctively against any experiment in education which stimulates the critical faculties and is not content with a partial view of reality but always seeks out the ties which link one point to another and one problem to another.

Indeed, the interests of the oppressors lie in "changing the consciousness of the oppressed, not the situation which oppresses them";[1] for the more the oppressed can be led to adapt to that situation, the more easily they can be dominated. To achieve this end, the oppressors use the banking concept of education in conjunction with a paternalistic social action apparatus, within which the oppressed receive the euphemistic title of "welfare recipients." They are treated as individual cases, as marginal persons who deviate from the general configuration of a "good, organized, and just" society. The oppressed are regarded as the pathology of the healthy society, which must therefore adjust these "incompetent and lazy" folk to its own patterns by changing their mentality. These marginals need to be "integrated," "incorporated" into the healthy society that they have "forsaken."

The truth is, however, that the oppressed are not "marginals," are not people living "outside" society. They have always been "inside"—inside the structure which made them "beings for others." The solution is not to "integrate" them into the structure of oppression, but to transform that structure so that they can become "beings for themselves." Such transformation, of course, would undermine the oppressors' purposes; hence their utilization of the banking concept of education to avoid the threat of student *conscientização*.

The banking approach to adult education, for example, will never propose to students that they critically consider reality. It will deal instead with such vital questions as whether Roger gave green grass to the goat, and insist upon the importance of learning that, on the contrary, Roger gave green grass to the *rabbit*. The "humanism" of the banking approach masks the effort to turn women and men into automatons—the very negation of their ontological vocation to be more fully human.

Those who use the banking approach, knowingly or unknowingly (for there are innumerable well-intentioned bank-clerk teachers who do not realize that they are serving only to dehumanize), fail to perceive that the deposits themselves contain contradictions about reality. But, sooner or later, these contradictions may lead formerly passive students to turn against their domestication and the attempt to domesticate reality. They may discover through existential experience that their present way of life is irreconcilable with their vocation to become fully human. They may perceive through their relations with reality that reality is really a *process*, undergoing constant transformation. If men and women are searchers and their ontological vocation is humanization, sooner or later they may perceive the contradiction in which banking education seeks to maintain them, and then engage themselves in the struggle for their liberation.

But the humanist, revolutionary educator cannot wait for this possibility to materialize. From the outset, her efforts must coincide with those of the students to engage in critical thinking and the quest for mutual humanization. His efforts must be imbued with a profound trust in people and their creative power. To achieve this, they must be partners of the students in their relations with them.

The banking concept does not admit to such partnership—and necessarily so. To resolve the teacher-student contradiction, to exchange the role of depositor, prescriber, domesticator, for the role of student among students would be to undermine the power of oppression and serve the cause of liberation.

Implicit in the banking concept is the assumption of a dichotomy between human beings and the world: a person is merely *in* the world, not *with* the world or with others; the individual is spectator, not re-creator. In this view, the person is not a conscious being (*corpo consciente*); he or she is rather the possessor of *a* consciousness: an empty "mind" passively open to the reception of deposits of reality from the world outside. For example, my desk, my books, my coffee cup, all the objects before me—as bits of the world which surround me—would be "inside" me, exactly as I am inside my study right now. This view makes no distinction between being accessible to consciousness and entering consciousness. The distinction, however, is essential: the objects which surround me are simply accessible to my consciousness, not located within it. I am aware of them, but they are not inside me.

It follows logically from the banking notion of consciousness that the educator's role is to regulate the way the world "enters into" the students. The teacher's task is to organize a process which already occurs spontaneously, to "fill" the students by making deposits of information which he or she considers to constitute true knowledge.[2] And since people "receive" the world as passive entities, education should make them more passive still, and adapt them to the world. The educated individual is the adapted person, because she or he is better "fit" for the world. Translated into practice, this concept is well suited to the purposes of the oppressors, whose tranquility rests on how well people fit the world the oppressors have created, and how little they question it.

The more completely the majority adapt to the purposes which the dominant minority prescribe for them (thereby depriving them of the right to their own purposes), the more easily the minority can continue to prescribe. The theory and practice of banking education serve this end quite efficiently. Verbalistic lessons, reading requirements,[3] the methods for evaluating "knowledge," the distance between the teacher and the taught, the criteria for promotion: everything in this ready-to-wear approach serves to obviate thinking.

The bank-clerk educator does not realize that there is no true security in his hypertrophied role, that one must seek to live *with* others in solidarity. One cannot impose oneself, nor even merely co-exist with one's students. Solidarity requires true communication, and the concept by which such an educator is guided fears and proscribes communication.

Yet only through communication can human life hold meaning. The teacher's thinking is authenticated only by the authenticity of the students' thinking. The teacher cannot think for her students, nor can she impose her thought on them. Authentic thinking, thinking that is concerned about *reality,* does not take place in ivory tower isolation, but only in communication. If it is true that thought has meaning only when generated by action upon the world, the subordination of students to teachers becomes impossible.

Because banking education begins with a false understanding of men and women as objects, it cannot promote the development of what Fromm calls "biophily," but instead produces its opposite: "necrophily."

> While life is characterized by growth in a structured, functional manner, the necrophilous person loves all that does not grow, all that is mechanical. The necrophilous person is driven by the desire to transform the organic into the inorganic, to approach life mechanically, as if all living persons were things. . . . Memory, rather than experience; having, rather than being, is what counts. The necrophilous person can relate to an object—a flower or a person—only if he possesses it; hence a threat to his possession is a threat to himself; if he loses possession he loses contact with the world. . . . He loves control, and in the act of controlling he kills life.[4]

Oppression—overwhelming control—is necrophilic; it is nourished by love of death, not life. The banking concept of education, which serves the interests of oppression, is also necrophilic. Based on a mechanistic, static, naturalistic, spatialized view of consciousness, it transforms students into receiving objects. It attempts to control thinking and action, leads women and men to adjust to the world, and inhibits their creative power.

When their efforts to act responsibly are frustrated, when they find themselves unable to use their faculties, people suffer. "This suffering due to impotence is rooted in the very fact that the human equilibrium has been disturbed."[5] But the inability to act which causes people's anguish also causes them to reject their impotence, by attempting

> . . . to restore [their] capacity to act. But can [they], and how? One way is to submit to and identify with a person or group having power. By this symbolic participation in another person's life, [men have] the illusion of acting, when in reality [they] only submit to and become a part of those who act.[6]

Populist manifestations perhaps best exemplify this type of behavior by the oppressed, who, by identifying with charismatic leaders, come to feel that they themselves are active and effective. The rebellion they express as they emerge in the historical process is motivated by that desire to act effectively. The dominant elites consider the remedy to be more domination and repression, carried out in the name of freedom, order, and social peace (that is, the peace of the elites). Thus they can condemn—logically, from their point of view—"the violence of a strike by workers and [can] call upon the state in the same breath to use violence in putting down the strike."[7]

Education as the exercise of domination stimulates the credulity of students, with the ideological intent (often not perceived by educators) of indoctrinating them to adapt to the world of oppression. This accusation is not made in the naïve hope that the dominant elites will thereby simply abandon the practice. Its objective is to call the attention of true humanists to the fact that they cannot use banking educational methods in the pursuit of liberation, for they would only negate that very pursuit. Nor may a revolutionary society inherit these methods from an oppressor society. The revolutionary society which practices banking education is either misguided or mistrusting of people. In either event, it is threatened by the specter of reaction.

Unfortunately, those who espouse the cause of liberation are themselves surrounded and influenced by the climate which generates the banking concept, and often do not perceive its true significance or its dehumanizing power. Paradoxically, then, they utilize this same instrument of alienation in what they consider an effort to liberate. Indeed, some "revolutionaries" brand as "innocents," "dreamers," or even "reactionaries" those who would challenge this educational practice. But one does not liberate people by alienating them. Authentic liberation—the process of humanization—is not another deposit to be made in men. Liberation is a praxis: the action and reflection of men and women upon their world in order to transform it. Those truly committed to the cause of liberation can accept neither the mechanistic concept of consciousness as an empty vessel to be filled, nor the use of banking methods of domination (propaganda, slogans—deposits) in the name of liberation.

Those truly committed to liberation must reject the banking concept in its entirety, adopting instead a concept of women and men as conscious beings, and consciousness as consciousness intent upon the world. They must abandon the educational goal of deposit-making and replace it with the posing of the problems of human beings in their relations with the world. "Problem-posing" education, responding to the essence of consciousness—*intentionally*—rejects communiqués and embodies communication. It epitomizes the special characteristic of consciousness: being *conscious of*, not only as intent on objects but as turned in upon itself in a Jasperian "split"—consciousness as consciousness *of* consciousness.

Liberating education consists in acts of cognition, not transferrals of information. It is a learning situation in which the cognizable object (far from being the end of the cognitive act) intermediates the cognitive actors—teacher on the one hand and students on the other. Accordingly, the practice of problem-posing education entails at the outset that the teacher-student contradiction be resolved. Dialogical relations—indispensable to the capacity of cognitive actors to cooperate in perceiving the same cognizable object—are otherwise impossible.

Indeed, problem-posing education, which breaks with the vertical patterns characteristic of banking education, can fulfill its function as the practice of freedom only if it can overcome the above contradiction. Through dialogue, the teacher-of-the-students and the students-of-the-teacher cease to exist and a new term emerges: teacher-student with students-teachers. The teacher is no longer merely the-one-who-teaches, but one who is himself taught in dialogue with the students, who in turn while being taught also teach. They become jointly responsible for a process in which all grow. In this process, arguments based on "authority" are no longer valid; in order to function, authority must be *on the side of* freedom, not *against* it. Here, no one teaches another, nor is anyone self-taught. People teach each other, mediated by the world, the cognizable objects which in banking education are "owned" by the teacher.

The banking concept (with its tendency to dichotomize everything) distinguishes two stages in the action of the educator. During the first, he cognizes a cognizable object while he prepares his lessons in his study or his laboratory; during the second, he expounds to his students about that object. The students are not called upon to know, but to memorize the contents narrated by the teacher. Nor do the students practice any act of cognition, since the object towards which that act should be directed is the property of the teacher rather than a medium evoking the critical reflection of both teacher and students. Hence in the name of the "preservation of culture and knowledge" we have a system which achieves neither true knowledge nor true culture.

The problem-posing method does not dichotomize the activity of the teacher-student: she is not "cognitive" at one point and "narrative" at another. She is always "cognitive," whether preparing a project or engaging in dialogue with the students. He does not regard cognizable objects as his private property, but as the object of reflection by himself and the students. In this way, the problem-posing educator constantly re-forms his reflections in the reflection of the students. The students—no longer docile listeners—are now critical coinvestigators in dialogue with the teacher. The teacher presents the material to the students for their consideration, and reconsiders her earlier considerations as the students express their own. The role of the problem-posing educator is to create, together with the students, the conditions under which knowledge at the level of the *doxa* is superseded by true knowledge, at the level of the *logos*.

Whereas banking education anesthetizes and inhibits creative power, problem-posing education involves a constant unveiling of reality. The former attempts to maintain the *submersion* of consciousness; the latter strives for the *emergence* of consciousness and *critical intervention* in reality.

Students, as they are increasingly posed with problems relating to themselves in the world and with the world, will feel increasingly challenged and obliged to respond to that challenge. Because they apprehend the challenge as interrelated to other problems within a total context, not as a theoretical question, the resulting comprehension tends to be increasingly critical and thus constantly less alienated. Their response to the challenge evokes new challenges, followed by new understandings; and gradually the students come to regard themselves as committed.

Education as the practice of freedom—as opposed to education as the practice of domination—denies that man is abstract, isolated, independent, and unattached to the world; it also denies that the world exists as a reality apart from people. Authentic reflection considers neither abstract man nor the world without people, but people in their relations with the world. In these relations consciousness and world are simultaneous: consciousness neither precedes the world nor follows it.

> La conscience et le monde sont dormés d'un même coup: extérieur par essence à la conscience, le monde est, par essence relatif à elle.[8]

In one of our culture circles in Chile, the group was discussing (based on a codification[9]) the anthropological concept of culture. In the midst of the discussion, a peasant who by banking standards was completely ignorant said: "Now I see that without man there is no world." When the educator responded: "Let's say, for the sake of argument, that all the men on earth were to die, but that the earth itself remained, together with trees, birds, animals, rivers, seas, the stars . . . wouldn't all this be a world?" "Oh no," the peasant replied emphatically. "There would be no one to say: 'This is a world.'"

The peasant wished to express the idea that there would be lacking the consciousness of the world which necessarily implies the world of consciousness. *I* cannot exist without a *non-I*. In turn, the *not-I* depends on that existence. The world which brings consciousness into existence becomes the world *of* that consciousness. Hence, the previously cited affirmation of Sartre: "*La conscience et le monde sont dormés d'un même coup.*"

As women and men, simultaneously reflecting on themselves and on the world, increase the scope of their perception, they begin to direct their observations towards previously inconspicuous phenomena:

> In perception properly so-called, as an explicit awareness [*Gewahren*], I am turned towards the object, to the paper, for instance. I apprehend it as being this here and now. The apprehension is a singling out, every object having a background in experience. Around and about the paper lie books, pencils, inkwell, and so forth, and these in a certain sense are also "perceived," perceptually there, in the "field of intuition"; but whilst I was turned towards the paper there was no turning in their direction, nor any apprehending of them, not even in a secondary sense. They appeared and yet were not singled out, were not posited on their own account. Every perception of a thing has such a zone of background intuitions or background awareness, if "intuiting" already includes the state of being turned towards, and this also is a "conscious experience," or more briefly a "consciousness of" all indeed that in point of fact lies in the co-perceived objective background.[10]

That which had existed objectively but had not been perceived in its deeper implications (if indeed it was perceived at all) begins to "stand out," assuming the character of a problem and therefore of challenge. Thus, men and women begin to single out elements from their "background awareness" and to reflect upon them. These elements are now objects of their consideration, and, as such, objects of their action and cognition.

In problem-posing education, people develop their power to perceive critically *the way they exist* in the world *with which* and *in which* they find themselves; they come to see the world not as a static reality, but as a reality in process, in transformation. Although the dialectical relations of women and men with the world exist independently of how these relations are perceived (or whether or not they are perceived at all), it is also true that the form of action they adopt is to a large extent a function of how they perceive themselves in the world. Hence, the teacher-student and the students-teachers reflect simultaneously on themselves and the world without dichotomizing this reflection from action, and thus establish an authentic form of thought and action.

Once again, the two educational concepts and practices under analysis come into conflict. Banking education (for obvious reasons) attempts, by mythicizing reality, to conceal certain facts which explain the way human beings exist in the world; problem-posing education sets itself the task of demythologizing. Banking education resists dialogue; problem-posing education regards dialogue as indispensable to the act of cognition which unveils reality. Banking education treats students as objects of assistance; problem-posing education makes them critical thinkers. Banking education inhibits creativity and domesticates (although it cannot completely destroy) the *intentionality* of consciousness by isolating consciousness from the world, thereby denying people their ontological and historical vocation of becoming more fully human. Problem-posing education bases itself on creativity and stimulates true reflection and action upon reality, thereby responding to the vocation of persons as beings who are authentic only when engaged in inquiry and creative transformation. In sum: banking theory and practice, as immobilizing and fixating forces, fail to acknowledge men and women as historical beings; problem-posing theory and practice take the people's historicity as their starting point.

Problem-posing education affirms men and women as beings in the process of *becoming*—as unfinished, uncompleted beings in and with a likewise unfinished reality. Indeed, in contrast to other animals who are unfinished, but not historical, people know themselves to be unfinished; they are aware of their incompletion. In this incompletion and this awareness lie the very roots of education as an exclusively human manifestation. The unfinished character of human beings and the transformational character of reality necessitate that education be an ongoing activity.

Education is thus constantly remade in the praxis. In order to *be*, it must *become*. Its "duration" (in the Bergsonian meaning of the word) is found in the interplay of the opposites *permanence* and *change*. The banking method emphasizes permanence and becomes reactionary; problem-posing education— which accepts neither a "well-behaved" present nor a predetermined future—roots itself in the dynamic present and becomes revolutionary.

Problem-posing education is revolutionary futurity. Hence, it is prophetic (and, as such, hopeful). Hence it corresponds to the historical nature of humankind. Hence, it affirms women and men as beings who transcend themselves, who move forward and look ahead, for whom immobility represents a fatal threat, for whom looking at the past must only be a means of understanding more clearly what and who they are so that they can more wisely build the future. Hence, it identifies with the movement which engages people as beings aware of their incompletion—a historical movement which has its point of departure, its Subjects and its objective.

The point of departure of the movement lies in the people themselves. But since people do not exist apart from the world, apart from reality, the movement must begin with the human-world relationship. Accordingly, the point of departure must always be with men and women in the "here and now," which constitutes the situation within which they are submerged, from which they emerge, and in which they intervene. Only by starting from this situation—which determines their perception of it—can they begin to move. To do this authentically they must perceive their state not as fated and unalterable, but merely as limiting—and therefore challenging.

Whereas the banking method directly or indirectly reinforces men's fatalistic perception of their situation, the problem-posing method presents this very situation to them as a problem. As the situation becomes the object of their cognition, the naïve or magical perception which produced their fatalism gives way to perception which is able to perceive itself even as it perceives reality, and can thus be critically objective about that reality.

A deepened consciousness of their situation leads people to apprehend that situation as an historical reality susceptible of transformation. Resignation gives way to the drive for transformation and inquiry, over which men feel themselves to be in control. If people, as historical beings necessarily engaged with other people in a movement of inquiry, did not control that movement, it would be (and is) a violation of their humanity. Any situation in which some individuals prevent others from engaging in the process of inquiry is one of violence. The means used are not important; to alienate human beings from their own decision-making is to change them into objects.

This movement of inquiry must be directed toward humanization—the people's historical vocation. The pursuit of full humanity, however, cannot be carried out in isolation or individualism, but only in fellowship and solidarity; therefore it cannot unfold in the antagonistic relations between oppressors and oppressed. No one can be authentically human while he prevents others from being so. Attempting *to be more* human, individualistically, leads to *having more*, egotistically, a form of dehumanization. Not that it is not fundamental *to have* in order *to be* human. Precisely because it *is* necessary, some men's *having* must not be allowed to constitute an obstacle to others' *having*, must not consolidate the power of the former to crush the latter.

Problem-posing education, as a humanist and liberating praxis, posits as fundamental that the people subjected to domination must fight for their emancipation. To that end, it enables teachers and students to become Subjects of the educational process by overcoming authoritarianism and an alienating intellectualism; it also enables people to overcome their false perception of reality. The world—no longer something to be described with deceptive words—becomes the object of that transforming action by men and women which results in their humanization.

Problem-posing education does not and cannot serve the interests of the oppressor. No oppressive order could permit the oppressed to begin to question: Why? While only a revolutionary society can carry out this education in systematic terms, the revolutionary leaders need not take full power before they can employ the method. In the revolutionary process, the leaders cannot utilize the banking method as an interim measure, justified on grounds of expediency, with the intention of *later* behaving in a genuinely revolutionary fashion. They must be revolutionary—that is to say, dialogical—from the outset.

NOTES

1. Simone de Beauvoir, *La Pensée de Droite, Aujord'hui* (Paris); ST, *El Pensamiento político de la Derecha* (Buenos Aires, 1963), 34.
2. This concept corresponds to what Sartre calls the "digestive" or "nutritive" concept of education, in which knowledge is "fed" by the teacher to the students to "fill them out." See Jean-Paul Sartre, "Une idée fundamentale de la phénomeno-logic de Husserl: L'intentionalité, *Situations I* (Paris, 1947).
3. For example, some professors specify in their reading lists that a book should be read from pages 10 to 15—and do this to "help" their students!
4. Fromm, 41.
5. Fromm, 31.
6. Fromm.
7. Reinhold Niebuhr, *Moral Man and Immoral Society* (New York, 1960), 130.
8. Sartre, 32.
9. See chapter 3.—Translator's note.
10. Edmund Husserl, *Ideas—General Introduction to Pure Phenomenology* (London, 1969), 105–106.

QUESTIONS FOR REACTION AND DISCUSSION

1. Freire describes the teacher-student relationship as having a "narrative" character. What is your understanding of the meaning of this idea? What are the implications?
2. What, in your own words, is the banking concept of education? Why does Freire find this "oppressive"?
3. In what situations have you experienced the banking concept of education?

4. What is the concept of education that Freire would substitute? Why would this be a view that an authoritarian government would find objectionable?
5. What does Freire mean by the term "humanist"? Do you consider yourself a humanist? Why or why not?

QUESTIONS FOR WRITING

1. Other writers in this section have presented their views of what constitutes a cultural and/or multicultural literacy. Does the "banking concept of education" serve cultural literacy as a primary pedagogical strategy? Why or why not? In what ways does Freire's pedagogy of liberation negate the goals of cultural literacy? In an essay, discuss the conflicts between the banking concept of education and the problem-posing education that Freire advocates.
2. In the "banking concept of education," Freire conceives of the relationship between student and teacher as oppositional. Do you think this is always true? Are there situations in which the banking concept of education might be useful or necessary? Write an essay in which you describe your reaction to the banking concept of education and explain specific situations that you think complicate Freire's notion of the oppositional relationship between teacher and learner.
3. Freire was exiled from Brazil after a military coup because the new government considered his educational practice subversive. In any reading of Freire's views on education, we find that authority and power are very much at issue. What is subversive about the pedagogy of liberation? Where are authority and power situated in the banking concept of education? Where are authority and power situated in the pedagogy of liberation? Write an essay in which you describe the subversive aspects of the pedagogy of liberation.
4. How would you describe the major teaching strategies of your secondary education? Were you exposed to the banking concept of education, problem-posing education, or some other method that you can describe? Write an essay in which you describe your educational experience and explain the primary pedagogical strategies that were used. Give specific examples and details from your experience.

QUESTIONS FOR FURTHER EXPLORATION

1. Locate and read Freire's autobiography, which he wrote in the unusual form of a series of letters to his niece: *Letters to Cristina: Reflections on My Life and Work* (London: Routledge 1996). How does he explain his educational theory and philosophy? In what ways did his

childhood experience in Brazil influence his life as a teacher? Write a review of this book and post it to the review section of an online bookstore such as <http://www.amazon.com>.

2. The Paulo Freire Institute Web site <http://paulofreire.org> is largely written in Portuguese. Even if you do not speak this language, visit the Web site and search for other sites that provide information about Freire's life and work. Create an annotated list of Web sites and e-mail it to your classmates.

3. The School Partnership Program at New York University is a collaborative venture between several inner-city high schools in New York City and the university. Part of the program is devoted to training teachers to use the methods of Paulo Freire. Research this program by checking the Web site <http://www.nyu.edu/education/metrocenter/spp/spp.html> and by searching the site for their activities and program. Write a report about the ways in which Freire's methods are discussed in the description of the program and how they are used in the schools.

5

AMERICA SKIPS SCHOOL: WHY WE TALK SO MUCH ABOUT EDUCATION AND DO SO LITTLE

Benjamin R. Barber is a professor in the political science department at Rutgers University and the director of the Whitman Center for the Culture and Politics of Democracy. Barber has written several books on education and politics; and, with Patrick Watson, he wrote the ten-part PBS/CBS television series, The Struggle for Democracy. *Barber writes frequently on educational issues for* The Atlantic Monthly, The New York Times, *and* Harper's Magazine, *one of the oldest magazines in America. Founded in 1850 as* Harper's New Monthly Magazine *by book publishers, the magazine printed the works of well-known American writers, such as Mark Twain and Henry James in the nineteenth century. Today the magazine is known for its award-winning fiction and essays, as well as for features such as* Harper's Index, *a list of unusual statistics that serve as a guide to contemporary American culture. An online version, <http://www.harpers.org>, includes archives and historical information about the magazine.* Harper's Magazine *frequently publishes essays about contemporary issues in education, such as this one by Barber. In this essay, Barber suggests that despite the hundreds of reports, books, and essays about what students need to know, in reality, education is not finally truly important to Americans. He makes the provocative assertion that as a society, we have grown comfortable with the game of "let's pretend we care."*

QUESTIONS FOR READING

1. The title of this essay is deliberately provocative. What message does Barber send with such a title? How is the title an invitation to read further?
2. How does the fact that this essay was published in a magazine like *Harper's* influence your reading? Why?

BENJAMIN R. BARBER

AMERICA SKIPS SCHOOL: WHY WE TALK SO MUCH ABOUT EDUCATION AND DO SO LITTLE

Harper's Magazine *(November 1993, pp. 40–48)*

On September 8, the day most of the nation's children were scheduled to return to school, the Department of Education Statistics issued a report, commissioned by Congress, on adult literacy and numeracy in the United States. The results? More than ninety million adult Americans lacked simple literacy. Fewer than twenty percent of those surveyed could compare two metaphors in a poem; not four percent could calculate the cost of carpeting at a given price for a room of a given size, using a calculator. As the DOE report was being issued, as if to echo its findings, two of the nation's largest school systems had delayed their openings: in New York, to remove asbestos from aging buildings; in Chicago, because of a battle over the budget.

Inspired by the report and the delays, pundits once again began chanting the familiar litany of the education crisis. We've heard it all many times before: 130,000 children bring guns along with their pencils and books to school each morning; juvenile arrests for murder increased by eighty-five percent from 1987 to 1991; more than three thousand youngsters will drop out today and every day for the rest of the school year, until about 600,000 are lost by June— in many urban schools, perhaps half the enrollment. A lot of the dropouts will end up in prison, which is a surer bet for young black males than college: one in four will pass through the correctional system, and at least two out of three of those will be dropouts.

In quiet counterpoint to those staggering facts is another set of statistics: teachers make less than accountants, architects, doctors, lawyers, engineers, judges, health professionals, auditors, and surveyors. They can earn higher salaries teaching in Berlin, Tokyo, Ottawa, or Amsterdam than in New York or Chicago. American children are in school only about 180 days a year, as against 240 days or more for children in Europe or Japan. The richest school districts (school financing is local, not federal) spend twice as much per student as poorer ones do. The poorer ones seem almost beyond help: children with venereal disease or AIDS (2.5 million adolescents annually contract a sexually transmitted disease), gangs in the schoolyard, drugs in the classroom, children doing babies instead of homework, playground firefights featuring Uzis and Glocks.

Clearly, the social contract that obliges adults to pay taxes so that children can be educated is in imminent danger of collapse. Yet for all the astonishing statistics, more astonishing still is that no one seems to be listening. The education crisis is kind of like violence on television: the worse it gets the more inert we become, and the more of it we require to rekindle our attention. We've had a "crisis" every dozen years or so at least since the launch of *Sputnik,* in 1957, when American schools were accused of falling behind the world standard in science education. Just ten years ago, the National Commission on Excellence in Education warned that America's pedagogical inattention was putting America "at risk." What the commission called "a rising tide of mediocrity" was imperiling "our very future as a Nation and a people." What was happening to education was an "act of war."

Since then, countless reports have been issued decrying the condition of our educational system, the DOE report being only the most recent. They have come from every side, Republican as well as Democrat, from the private sector as well as the public. Yet for all the talk, little happens. At times, the schools look more like they are being dismantled than rebuilt. How can this be? If Americans over a broad political spectrum regard education as vital, why has nothing been done?

I have spent thirty years as a scholar examining the nature of democracy, and even more as a citizen optimistically celebrating its possibilities, but today I am increasingly persuaded that the reason for the country's inaction is that Americans do not really care about education—the country has grown comfortable with the game of "let's pretend we care."

As America's educational system crumbles, the pundits, instead of looking for solutions, search busily for scapegoats. Some assail the teachers—those "Profscam" pedagogues trained in the licentious sixties who, as aging hippies, are supposedly still subverting the schools—for producing a dire illiteracy. Others turn on the kids themselves, so that at the same moment as we are transferring our responsibilities to the shoulders of the next generation, we are blaming them for our own generation's most conspicuous failures. Allan Bloom was typical of the many recent critics who have condemned the young as vapid, lazy, selfish, complacent, self-seeking, materialistic, small-minded, apathetic, greedy, and, of course, illiterate. E. D. Hirsch in his *Cultural Literacy* and Diane Ravitch and Chester E. Finn, Jr., in their *What Do Our Seventeen-Year-Olds Know?* have lambasted the schools, the teachers, and the children for betraying the adult generation from which they were to inherit, the critics seemed confident, a precious cultural legacy.

How this captious literature reeks of hypocrisy! How sanctimonious all the hand-wringing over still another "education crisis" seems. Are we ourselves really so literate? Are our kids stupid or smart for ignoring what we preach and copying what we practice? The young, with their keen noses for hypocrisy, are in fact adept readers—but not of books. They are society-smart rather than school-smart, and what they read so acutely are the social signals emanating from the world in which they will have to make a living. Their teachers in that world, the nation's true pedagogues, are television, advertising, movies, politics, and the celebrity domains they define. We prattle about deficient schools and the gullible youngsters they turn out, so vulnerable to the siren song of drugs, but think nothing of letting the advertisers into the classroom to fashion what an *Advertising Age* essay calls "brand and product loyalties through classroom-centered, peer-powered lifestyle patterning."

Our kids spend nine hundred hours a year in school (the ones who go to school) and from twelve hundred to eighteen hundred hours a year in front of the television set. From which are they likely to learn more? Critics such as Hirsch and Ravitch want to find out what our seventeen-year-olds know, but it's really pretty simple: they know exactly what our forty-seven-year-olds know and teach them by example—on television, in the boardroom, around Washington, on Madison Avenue, in Hollywood. The very first lesson smart kids learn is that it is much more important to heed what society teaches implicitly by its deeds and reward structures than what school teaches explicitly in its lesson plans and civic sermons. Here is a test for adults that may help reveal what the kids see when they look at our world.

REAL-WORLD CULTURAL LITERACY

1. According to television, having fun in America means

   a. going blond
   b. drinking Pepsi
   c. playing Nintendo
   d. wearing Air Jordans
   e. reading Mark Twain

2. A good way to prepare for a high-income career and to acquire status in our society is to

   a. win a slam-dunk contest
   b. take over a company and sell off its assets
   c. start a successful rock band
   d. earn a professional degree
   e. become a kindergarten teacher

3. Book publishers are financially rewarded today for publishing

   a. mega-cookbooks
   b. mega-cat books
   c. megabooks by Michael Crichton
   d. megabooks by John Grisham
   e. mini-books by Voltaire

4. A major California bank that advertised "no previous credit history required" in inviting Berkeley students to apply for Visa cards nonetheless turned down one group of applicants because

a. their parents had poor credit histories
b. they had never held jobs
c. they had outstanding student loans
d. they were "humanities majors"

5. Colleges and universities are financially rewarded today for

a. supporting bowl-quality football teams
b. forging research relationships with large corporations
c. sustaining professional programs in law and business
d. stroking wealthy alumni
e. fostering outstanding philosophy departments

6. Familiarity with *Henry IV, Part II* is likely to be of vital importance in

a. planning a corporate takeover
b. evaluating budget cuts in the Department of Education
c. initiating a medical-malpractice lawsuit
d. writing an impressive job résumé
e. taking a test on what our seventeen-year-olds know

7. To help the young learn that "history is a living thing," Scholastic, Inc., a publisher of school magazines and paperbacks, recently distributed to forty thousand junior and senior high-school classrooms

a. a complimentary video of the award-winning series *The Civil War*
b. free copies of Plato's *Dialogues*
c. an abridgment of Alexis de Tocqueville's *Democracy in America*
d. a wall-size Periodic Table of the Elements
e. gratis copies of Billy Joel's hit single "We Didn't Start the Fire" (which recounts history via a vaguely chronological list of warbled celebrity names)

My sample of forty-seven-year-olds scored very well on the test. Not surprisingly, so did their seventeen-year-old children. (For each question, either the last entry is correct or all responses are correct *except* the last one.) The results of the test reveal again the deep hypocrisy that runs through our lamentations about education. The illiteracy of the young turns out to be our own reflected back to us with embarrassing force. We honor ambition, we reward greed, we celebrate materialism, we worship acquisitiveness, we cherish success, and we commercialize the classroom—and then we bark at the young about the gentle arts of the spirit. We recommend history to the kids but rarely consult it ourselves. We make a fuss about ethics but are satisfied to see it taught as an "add-on," as in "ethics in medicine" or "ethics in business"— as if Sunday morning in church could compensate for uninterrupted sinning from Monday to Saturday.

The children are onto this game. They know that if we really valued schooling, we'd pay teachers what we pay stockbrokers; if we valued books, we'd spend a little something on the libraries so that adults could read, too; if we valued citizenship, we'd give national service and civic education more than pilot status; if we valued children, we wouldn't let them be abused, manipulated, impoverished, and killed in their beds by gang-war cross fire and stray bullets. Schools can and should lead, but when they confront a society that in every instance tells a story exactly opposite to the one they are supposed to be teaching, their job becomes impossible. When the society undoes each workday what the school tries to do each school day, schooling can't make much of a difference.

Inner-city children are not the only ones who are learning the wrong lessons. TV sends the same messages to everyone, and the success of Donald Trump, Pete Rose, Henry Kravis, or George Steinbrenner makes them potent role models, whatever their values. Teen dropouts are not blind; teen drug sellers are not deaf; teen college students who avoid the humanities in favor of prebusiness or prelaw are not stupid. Being apt pupils of reality, they learn their lessons well. If they see a man with a rubber arm and an empty head who can throw a ball at ninety-five miles per hour pulling down millions of dollars a year while a dedicated primary-school teacher is getting crumbs, they will avoid careers in teaching even if they can't make the major leagues. If they observe their government spending up to $35,000 a year to keep a young black behind bars but a fraction of that to keep him in school, they will write off school (and probably write off blacks as well).

Our children's illiteracy is merely our own, which they assume with commendable prowess. They know what we have taught them all too well: there is nothing in Homer or Virginia Woolf, in Shakespeare or Toni Morrison, that will advantage them in climbing to the top of the American heap. Academic credentials may still count, but schooling in and of itself is for losers. Bookworms. Nerds. Inner-city rappers and fraternity-house wise guys are in full agreement about that. The point is to start pulling down the big bucks. Some kids just go into business earlier than others. Dropping out is the national pastime, if by dropping out we mean giving up the precious things of the mind and the spirit in which America shows so little interest and for which it offers so little payback. While the professors argue about whether to teach the ancient history of a putatively white Athens or the ancient history of a putatively black Egypt, the kids are watching televised political campaigns driven by mindless image-mongering and inflammatory polemics that ignore history altogether. Why, then, are we so surprised when our students dismiss the debate over the origins of civilization, whether Eurocentric or Afrocentric, and concentrate on cash-and-carry careers? Isn't the choice a tribute not to their ignorance but to their adaptive intelligence? Although we can hardly be proud of ourselves for what we are teaching them, we should at least be proud of them for how well they've learned our lessons.

Not all Americans have stopped caring about the schools, however. In the final irony of the educational endgame, cynical entrepreneurs like Chris Whittle are insinuating television into the classroom itself, bribing impoverished

Bill for the More General Diffusion of Knowledge in Virginia as a center-
e of his career (although it failed passage as legislation—times were per-
not so different). John Adams, too, boasted regularly about
sachusetts's high literacy rates and publicly funded education.

Jefferson and Adams both understood that the Bill of Rights offered little
ection in a nation without informed citizens. Once educated, however, a
le was safe from even the subtlest tyrannies. Jefferson's democratic pro-
ies rested on his conviction that education could turn a people into a safe
e—indeed "the only safe depository" for the ultimate powers of society.
rish therefore the spirit of our people," he wrote to Edward Carrington in
, "and keep alive their attention. Do not be severe upon their errors, but
m them by enlightening them. If once they become inattentive to public
s, you and I and Congress and Assemblies, judges and governors, shall all
ne wolves."

he logic of democracy begins with public education, proceeds to in-
d citizenship, and comes to fruition in the securing of rights and liberties.
ve been nominally democratic for so long that we presume it is our nat-
ondition rather than the product of persistent effort and tenacious re-
bility. We have decoupled rights from civic responsibilities and severed
ship from education on the false assumption that citizens just happen.
ve forgotten that the "public" in public schools means not just paid for
public but procreative of the very idea of a public. Public schools are
public—a citizenry—is forged and how young, selfish individuals turn
nscientious, community-minded citizens.

nong the several literacies that have attracted the anxious attention of
ntators, civic literacy has been the least visible. Yet this is the funda-
literacy by which we live in a civil society. It encompasses the compe-
o participate in democratic communities, the ability to think critically
t with deliberation in a pluralistic world, and the empathy to identify
ntly with others to live with them despite conflicts of interest and dif-
s in character. At the most elementary level, what our children suffer
ost, whether they're hurling racial epithets from fraternity porches or
g one another down in schoolyards, is the absence of civility. Security
and metal detectors are poor surrogates for civility, and they make our
look increasingly like prisons (though they may be less safe than pris-
fferson thought schools would produce free men: we prove him right by
dropouts in jail.

lity is a work of the imagination, for it is through the imagination that
er others sufficiently like ourselves for them to become subjects of tol-
nd respect, if not always affection. Democracy is anything but a "nat-
rm of association. It is an extraordinary and rare contrivance of
d imagination. Give the uneducated the right to participate in making
e decisions, and what results is not democracy but, at best, mob rule:
rnment of private prejudice once known as the tyranny of opinion. For
, the difference between the democratic temperance he admired in

school boards by offering free TV sets on which they ca
children—sold to sponsors at premium rates. Whittle,
sitions mogul of education, is trying to get rich off
schools and the fears of parents. Can he really believe a
enhances education? Or is he helping to corrupt publ
will make parents even more anxious to use vouchei
which might one day be run by Whittle's latest entr
Edison Project.

According to Lifetime Learning Systems, an edi
pany, "kids spend forty percent of each day . . . whe
can't reach them." Not to worry, says Lifetime Learni
promo: "Now, you can enter the classroom through c
terials created with your specific marketing objectiv
with young spenders directly and, through them, the
well." If we redefine young learners as "young spenc
to be blamed for acting like mindless consumers?
spenders and still become young critical thinkers, le
If we are willing to give TV cartoons the governmei
tional television" (as we did a few years ago, until t
can we blame kids for educating themselves on tele

Everyone can agree that we should educate our chi
than young spenders molded by "lifestyle patterr
goals of the classroom be? In recent years it has be
educational crisis in terms of global competition a
if schools were no more than vocational instituti
sensibly about education, the Clinton Administra
approach, under the tutelage of Secretary of Labo

The classroom, however, should not be mere
mental task of education in a democracy is wha
apprenticeship of liberty: learning to be free. I wo
believe liberty has to be learned and that its skill
they been deluded by two centuries of rhetoric
"natural" and can be taken for granted?

The claim that all men are born free, upon v
at best a promising fiction. In real life, as eve
born fragile, born needy, born ignorant, born ur
ish, born dependent—born in chains. We acqui
all. Embedded in families, clans, communities,
be free. We may be natural consumers and borr
be made. Liberal arts education actually means
the "servile arts" were the trades learned by
the vocational education of their day. Perhar
preferred to memorialize his founding of th
tombstone rather than his two terms as presid

agrarian America and the rule of the rabble he condemned when viewing the social unrest of Europe's teeming cities was quite simply education. Madison had hoped to "filter" out popular passion through the device of representation. Jefferson saw in education a filter that could be installed within each individual, giving to each the capacity to rule prudently. Education creates a ruling aristocracy constrained by temperance and wisdom; when that education is public and universal, it is an aristocracy to which all can belong. At its best, the American dream of a free and equal society governed by judicious citizens has been this dream of an aristocracy of everyone.

To dream this dream of freedom is easy, but to secure it is difficult as well as expensive. Notwithstanding their lamentations, Americans do not appear ready to pay the price. There is no magic bullet for education. But I no longer can accept that the problem lies in the lack of consensus about remedies—in a dearth of solutions. There is no shortage of debate over how to repair our educational infrastructure. National standards or more local control? Vouchers or better public schools? More parental involvement or more teacher autonomy? A greater federal presence (only five or six percent of the nation's education budget is federally funded) or fairer local school taxes? More multicultural diversity or more emphasis on what Americans share in common? These are honest disputes. But I am convinced that the problem is simpler and more fundamental. Twenty years ago, writer and activist Frances Moore Lappé captured the essence of the world food crisis when she argued that starvation was caused not by a scarcity of food but by a global scarcity in democracy. The education crisis has the same genealogy. It stems from a dearth of democracy: an absence of democratic will and a consequent refusal to take our children, our schools, and our future seriously.

Most educators, even while they quarrel among themselves, will agree that a genuine commitment to any one of a number of different solutions could help enormously. Most agree that although money can't by itself solve problems, without money few problems can be solved. Money also can't win wars or put men in space, but it is the crucial facilitator. It is also how America has traditionally announced, We are serious about this!

If we were serious, we would raise teachers' salaries to levels that would attract the best young professionals in our society: starting lawyers get from $70,000 to $80,000—why don't starting kindergarten teachers get the same? Is their role in vouchsafing our future less significant? And although there is evidence suggesting that an increase in general educational expenditures doesn't translate automatically into better schools, there is also evidence that an increase aimed specifically at instructional services does. Can we really take in earnest the chattering devotion to excellence of a country so wedded in practice to mediocrity, a nation so ready to relegate teachers—conservators of our common future—to the professional backwaters?

If we were serious, we would upgrade physical facilities so that every school met the minimum standards of our better suburban institutions. Good buildings do not equal good education, but can any education at all take place in leaky, broken-down habitats of the kind described by Jonathan Kozol in his *Savage Inequalities?* If money is not a critical factor, why are our most successful suburban school districts funded at nearly twice the level of our inner-city schools? Being even at the starting line cannot guarantee that the runners will win or even finish the race, but not being even pretty much assures failure. We would rectify the balance not by penalizing wealthier communities but by bringing poorer communities up to standard, perhaps by finding other sources of funding for our schools besides property taxes.

If we were serious, we'd extend the school year by a month or two so that learning could take place throughout the year. We'd reduce class size (which means more teachers) and nurture more cooperative learning so that kids could become actively responsible for their own education and that of their classmates. Perhaps most important, we'd raise standards and make teachers and students responsible for them. There are two ways to breed success: to lower standards so that everybody "passes" in a way that loses all meaning in the real world; and to raise standards and then meet them, so that school success translates into success beyond the classroom. From Confucian China to Imperial England, great nations have built their success in the world upon an education of excellence. The challenge in a democracy is to find a way to maintain excellence while extending educational opportunity to everyone.

Finally, if we were serious, parents, teachers, and students would be the real players while administrators, politicians, and experts would be secondary, at best advisers whose chief skill ought to be knowing when and how to facilitate the work of teachers and then get out of the way. If the Democrats can clean up federal government bureaucracy (the Gore plan), perhaps we can do the same for educational bureaucracy. In New York up to half of the city's teachers occupy jobs outside the classroom. No other enterprise is run that way: Half the soldiers at company headquarters? Half the cops at stationhouse desks? Half the working force in the assistant manager's office? Once the teachers are back in the classroom, they will need to be given more autonomy, more professional responsibility for the success or failure of their students. And parents will have to be drawn in not just because they have rights or because they are politically potent but because they have responsibilities and their children are unlikely to learn without parental engagement. How to define the parental role in the classroom would become serious business for educators.

Some Americans will say this is unrealistic. Times are tough, money's short, and the public is fed up with almost all of its public institutions: the schools are just one more frustrating disappointment. With all the goodwill in the world, it is still hard to know how schools can cure the ills that stem from the failure of so many other institutions. Saying we want education to come first won't put it first.

America, however, has historically been able to accomplish what it sets its mind to. When we wish it and will it, what we wish and will has happened. Our successes are willed; our failures seem to happen when will is absent. There are, of course, those who benefit from the bankruptcy of public education and the failure of democracy. But their blame is no greater than our own; in a world where doing nothing has such dire consequences, complacency has become a greater sin than malevolence.

In wartime, whenever we have known why we were fighting and believed in the cause, we have prevailed. Because we believe in profits, we are consummate salespersons and efficacious entrepreneurs. Because we love sports, ours are the dream teams. Why can't a Chicago junior high school be as good as the Chicago Bulls? Because we cherish individuality and mobility, we have created a magnificent (if costly) car culture and the world's largest automotive consumer market. Even as our lower schools are among the worst in the Western world, our graduate institutions are among the very best—because professional training in medicine, law, and technology is vital to our ambitions and because corporate America backs up state and federal priorities in this crucial domain. Look at the things we do well and observe how very well we do them: those are the things that as a nation we have willed.

Then observe what we do badly and ask yourself, Is it because the challenge is too great? Or is it because, finally, we aren't really serious? Would we will an end to the carnage and do whatever it took—more cops, state militias, federal marshals, the Marines?—if the dying children were white and middle class? Or is it a disdain for the young—white, brown, and black—that inures us to the pain? Why are we so sensitive to the retirees whose future (however foreshortened) we are quick to guarantee—don't worry, no reduced cost-of-living allowances, no taxes on social security except for the well-off—and so callous to the young? Have you noticed how health care is on every politician's agenda and education on no one's?

To me, the conclusion is inescapable: we are not serious. We have given up on the public schools because we have given up on the kids; and we have given up on the kids because we have given up on the future—perhaps because it looks too multicolored or too dim or too hard. "Liberty," said Jean-Jacques Rousseau, "is a food easy to eat but hard to digest." America is suffering from a bad case of indigestion. Finally, in giving up on the future, we have given up on democracy. Certainly there will be no liberty, no equality, no social justice without democracy, and there will be no democracy without citizens and the schools that forge civic identity and democratic responsibility. If I am wrong (I'd like to be), my error will be easy to discern, for before the year is out we will put education first on the nation's agenda. We will put it ahead of the deficit, for if the future is finished before it starts, the deficit doesn't matter. Ahead of defense, for without democracy, what liberties will be left to defend? Ahead of all the other public issues and public goods, for without public education there can be no public and hence no truly public issues or public goods to advance. When the polemics are spent and we are through hyperventilating about the crisis in education, there is only one question worth asking: are we serious? If we are, we can begin by honoring that old folk homily and put our money where for much too long our common American mouth has been. Our kids, for once, might even be grateful.

QUESTIONS FOR REACTION AND DISCUSSION

1. What does Barber mean by the "familiar litany of the education crisis"? What has happened to add to this list since the 1993 publication date of this essay?
2. Why does Barber see the great number of reports and articles about the education crisis as hypocritical and sanctimonious?
3. Discuss the cultural literacy test that Barber constructs with your classmates. What was Barber's purpose in including it? How effective is this test within the context of his essay?
4. How effectively does Barber use statistical and factual information in this article? What examples surprised you? Why?
5. How does Barber use the definition of "public" in the term "public school"? In Barber's view, what are the responsibilities of a public school?
6. What is Barber's suggestion for education reform?

QUESTIONS FOR WRITING

1. Barber suggests several "goals of the classroom" beyond the "lifestyle patterning" that he thinks is currently taking place. The goals he proposes begin with his position that a liberal arts education is actually "education in the arts of liberty." In an essay, describe Barber's definition of the purposes of an education and defend or reject his position.
2. A central concern of Barber's is civil literacy, which he says is fundamental to a democratic society. As he suggests, "Security guards and metal detectors are poor surrogates for civility, and they make our schools look increasingly like prisons." Since the publication of Barber's essay, general violence in the schools has actually decreased. At the same time, a few extraordinarily violent and tragic episodes occurred at schools in the late 1990s, including the mass killings in Littleton, Colorado. In what ways do these episodes point to the failure of our schools and societies to teach civil literacy? Did the secondary school you attended promote civil literacy? How? Is civil literacy a part of your undergraduate education? How? Write an essay in which you define civil literacy and suggest some ways in which the schools with which you are familiar did or did not teach civil literacy.
3. At the end of his essay, Barber makes several recommendations for improving America's schools, such as raising teacher salaries; upgrading physical facilities; extending the school year; and broadening the role of parents, teachers, and students within the school structure. How would you go about collecting information about

these recommendations and how they might be enacted? Would one of these recommendations make a difference in the school you attended? Why or why not? Choose one of these recommendations and investigate what it would take to accomplish it generally. What would be the potential cost of the recommendation you choose? Write an essay in the form of a response to Barber in which you support or reject one of his recommendations.

QUESTIONS FOR FURTHER EXPLORATION

1. Barber suggests that children spent nine hundred hours a year in school and from twelve hundred to eighteen hundred hours a year in front of television. In the years since Barber wrote this essay, computers have become a standard purchase for homes as well as schools and businesses. What are the current statistics for the number of hours that children spend in school, watching television, and using a computer for recreation? Are there variations in these numbers according to age, geographic location, ethnicity, race, or gender? Research these questions and write a report for your classmates.
2. Barber refers to the launch of Sputnik in 1957 when American schools were thought to be falling behind international standards in science education. Investigate the Sputnik episode in history and its effects on educational theory and practice. What was Sputnik? Why was it such a visible event? What actions were taken by American politicians and educators? Write an essay in which you describe the launch of Sputnik as the first crisis in postwar American education.

6

CENSORSHIP AND SPIRITUAL EDUCATION

James Moffett has taught at a number of different kinds of schools and colleges, including Phillips Exeter Academy; Harvard University; the University of California, Berkeley; San Diego State University; and Middlebury College. A well-known educator and consultant to schools and colleges, Moffett is the author of nearly twenty books about reform in higher education, language education, writing-across-the-curriculum, and the teaching of writing. His latest book, The Universal Schoolhouse: Spiritual Awakening through Education, *is a proposal for a radical change in the way Americans think about public primary and secondary education that calls for the end of the traditional school and school district with national standards and a national curriculum and a move to a system of what he calls "decentralized community-learning networks." Moffett challenges individuals to pursue a spiritual education, by which he means a sense of oneness with all others, and to act appropriately. In this essay, he draws on his investigation into the violent 1974 textbook controversy in Kanawha County, West Virginia, which resulted in the firebombing of a school, the result of a clash between those favoring textbooks supporting a multicultural curriculum and fundamentalists opposed to the teaching of multiple viewpoints and ideas. Moffett analyzes the fundamentalist opposition carefully, deeply aware of the concern of many of the adults in the community that their children would grow up with ideas in conflict with family and religious values. The Kanawha County case is important because it demonstrates clearly the dilemma of what Moffett terms "a single curriculum for a pluralistic populace."*

QUESTIONS FOR READING

1. What does censorship mean to you? Is it an important issue in your life or that of your family and friends? Why or why not?

2. What is spiritual education? What expectations do you have for an essay that purports to be about spiritual education?

JAMES MOFFETT

CENSORSHIP AND SPIRITUAL EDUCATION

The Right to Literacy, *ed. Andrea A. Lunsford, Helene Maglen, and James Slevin*
(New York: MLA, 1990)

In addressing this subject, I wish to distinguish spirituality from morality and religion. Morality concerns good and bad behavior. As the root meanings of both *morals* and *ethics* indicate, these words derive from the customs of some group, an ethos, and too often tend to apply only to members of that group. As its root meaning suggests, religion aims to tie individuals back to some less apparent reality from which they have been diverted by, presumably, people and other attractive hazards in the environment. However divinely inspired, any religion partakes of a certain civilization, functions through human institutions, and is, therefore, culturally biased. Precisely because of this partiality and even partisanship, our devoutly Christian Founding Fathers refrained from making theirs the state religion and rightly forbade any theocracy.

Spirituality, by contrast, is the perception of oneness behind the plurality of things, peoples, and other forms; spiritual behavior is the acting on this perception. Thus, morality follows from spirituality, because the more that people identify with others, the better they act toward them. The supreme identification, of oneself with the One, brings about that reunion toward which religions work at the same time that it makes morality apply beyond the in-group to the world at large. So a spiritual education can accomplish moral and religious education but without moralizing or indoctrinating.

American schools have had to face directly the dilemma of *e pluribus unum*—a single curriculum for a pluralistic populace. In 1974 the most tumultuous and significant textbook controversy that North America has ever known broke out in Kanawha County, West Virginia. The textbooks teachers choose from today are limited by what happened there then. Ignoring the fundamentalist Appalachian part of its constituency, the district selected $450,000 worth of reading and language arts textbooks that fulfilled a state mandate for multicultural materials. Among these was a K–12 program that I had directed called Interaction.

By the time school started on 3 September, book protesters, stirred into action by a new school board member, had organized themselves for tough activist tactics borrowed from the labor movement. Led by fundamentalist ministers from the hills and hollows of the upper valley, they kept their children home from school and threatened other parents who did not, picketed mines until the miners struck, barricaded some trucking companies, demonstrated outside the board building in defiance of court injunctions, and on 10 September got city bus drivers to suspend service in sympathy.

The next day, the school board announced that it was withdrawing the books until a citizens review committee could report on them. But disruption escalated. At each of two picket points a man was wounded by gunfire. Cars were smashed, and a CBS television crew was roughed up. Extremist protesters fired on school buses returning from their rounds and even firebombed two elementary schools at night. Leaders of both sides were threatened and guarded. On 13 September, the safety of both children and adults seemed so much at risk that the superintendent shut down all public schools for a four-day weekend, during which he and the school board slipped out of town. The whole county bordered on anarchy.

After delaying its climactic meeting for a week following a dynamite blast in its building, the school board voted 8 November on the recommendations of its citizens review committee. The majority of the committee members asked for the return of virtually all the books to the classrooms, and the minority rejected virtually all the books. The board decided to return all but the most controversial series and the senior high portion of Interaction, which were consigned to libraries. Protest activities abated when Governor Arch Moore finally allowed state troopers to reinforce county sheriffs, and they ended in the spring, after one of the ministers leading the revolt was sentenced to three years in prison for his part in firebombing a school.

The creek preachers have done me a great favor. They have made me think about the many ways we all suppress knowledge outside and repress it inside and about why we do so. Let me mention what these fundamentalists objected to in our books. In 1982 I interviewed three of the protest leaders in Kanawha County. I have studied carefully the criticisms that dissenting members of the citizens review committee wrote about particular selections in the disputed books. I have written an account and interpretation of the Kanawha County controversy as a book, *Storm in the Mountains: A Case Study of Censorship, Conflict, and Consciousness.* In trying to see more deeply by the light of this incendiary episode, I have honored most what meant most to the objectors, their religious beliefs and values.

In plain human terms the protesters feared losing their children. Books (like television) bypass the oral culture—hearth and ethos—and thus may weaken local authority and control. Perhaps all parents fear having their children mentally kidnapped by voices from other milieus and ideologies. The rich range of ideas and viewpoints, the multicultural smorgasbord, of the books adopted in Kanawha County were exactly what fundamentalists don't want. They believe that most of the topics English teachers think make good discussion are about matters they consider already settled. The invitation to reopen such subjects through pluralistic readings, role-playing, values clarification, personal writing, and open-ended discussion can only be taken as an effort to indoctrinate their children in the atheistic freethinking of the Eastern-seaboard liberal establishment that scoffs at them and runs the country according to a religion of secular humanism.

In fending off other ethnicity, the book protesters objected again and again to selections by blacks and Chicanos, of whom there are few in West Virginia. However disguised as complaints about bad grammar and foul language, this objection has to be recognized as racism. But the real enemy is the outsider, the Other. Exclusion practically defines ethnocentricity, which is a failure to identify outside a certain reference group. Hence, bigotry and intolerance. About this censors may be extreme, but they are not unique. They are insisting, in fact, on a principle that public schools seem founded on—the transmission of culture. They are saying: "Those books are not passing on *our* heritage and values. They are indoctrinating our children with someone *else's* way of life." And, indeed, the educational goal of transmitting the culture always begs the question, "*Whose* culture?" America is and always has been a pluralistic nation.

The book protesters charged that our books attacked family, church, and state—authority in general. As the most exclusive social unit, the family is the heart of hearts of the culture. Hearth and ethos. Blood and soil. And so the profamily movement serves as the nucleus for the New Right and its anti-Communist jihad.

Examples of works attacking the family were Gina Berriault's short story "The Stone Boy" and an excerpt from Oscar Lewis' anthropological study *The Children of Sanchez,* both of which the censors claimed presented parents as failures. This accusation has to be understood as part of an ongoing fight with schools about whether the family or the classroom should bear the blame for children who turn out badly and for society's ills in general.

All the programs denounced in Kanawha County contained modern poems that try to make Christ real to today's secular readers. One of the poems was T. S. Eliot's "Journey of the Magi." The reviewers there consistently branded these selections as mocking and blasphemous, though none of them were. As for attacks on the state, a couple of books in my own program contained interviews and trial transcripts that allowed students to hear what a number of participants in the Vietnam war had to say, including some involved in the civilian massacre of My Lai. The objection to these selections was that they were "not necessary for education" and seemed to be included only to make students "feel guilt and shame."

The issue of this Vietnam material was self-examination, which the censors chronically resisted. In fact, one of the set terms used throughout the censorship network in reviewing books is "invasion of privacy," a liberal-sounding objection that is invoked whenever, for example, students are invited to relate literature to their own experiences or to talk or write about their thoughts and feelings. One of the set terms used in the literature of psychological research on authoritarian or dogmatic personality is "anti-intraception"—fear of inwardness—something, incidentally, that women frequently attribute to men. Indeed, we shouldn't lay just at the door of conservative censors this preference for projecting onto others, instead of looking within, for self-exoneration over self-examination. As John Barth quipped in his novel *Giles Goat Boy*, "Self-knowledge is bad news."

"Know thyself" is the supreme tenet of spiritual education, already well attested before. Oedipus discovered that he was the culprit he sought. But this principle was never meant to carry a guilt trip. That is the negative view, based on a low self-concept—the master trait, by the way, that researchers find in the authoritarian or dogmatic personality. "Know thyself" pertains not simply to our personal makeup but to our transpersonal nature. It asks, "Who am I?" to whatever depth and height we can bear the answer. It is a cosmic voyage that should be the first-goal statement in every school district's curriculum guide, before that stuff about being good citizens and productive workers. Those results will follow as fallout from self-development.

It is not difficult to connect invasion of privacy with another of the most common objections in the censorship network—morbidity and negativity, which, if denied in oneself, become targets in books. Here are examples listed by one Kanawha County reviewer:

"The Highwayman," Alfred Noyes—Girl shoots herself through the breast.

"Lord Randall," traditional ballad—The main character is poisoned.

"Danny Deaver," Rudyard Kipling—Poem concerning a military hanging.

"The Tell-Tale Heart," E. A. Poe—A man cunningly contrives to kill an old man whom he loves, carries this out, and dismembers the body.

"To Build a Fire," Jack London—A man freezes to death.

On this basis, we could dismiss John Keats's "Ode to a Nightingale" as suicidal and Matthew Arnold's "Dover Beach" as nihilistic and proceed to eliminate not only tragedy but virtually all literature. Why avoid negativity within only to meet it in books?

And yet, the case that the censors make differs not a great deal from Plato's reason for banishing the poets. Dwelling on Barth's "bad news" just keeps you down. Why not keep fixed on the good news, gospel, the word of God? Indeed, another ancient spiritual dictum is "You become what you think." If you focus on the negative, you will become or remain negative. If you meditate on the divine, you will bring out your divinity.

Literary artists themselves, I wager, see their work as gospel, as good news, even though it may be wrought from the bad news of self-examination and other worldly realities, because they feel the transformative effect of the imagination. In its secular way literature tries to act as gospel. But if read shallowly, both holy writ and literature can be dangerous, because their rhetorical power and spellbinding stories can attach readers even more to surface forms than they already are.

As religious education was phased out of public schools in the last century, English education was phased in. Literature took over from scripture, literary criticism from biblical exegesis, textual performance from liturgical service. The syllabus is now the canon; the literature professor, the hierophant. Has English teaching extended religious teaching in a secular way? If so, is that right? If not, should it? I think fundamentalists are right to hold out for spiritual education, but that cannot come about by controlling reading matter or by teaching morality and religion as such. The fundamentalists are right, too, that our secular society tends to censor out spirituality in its distrust of religion.

But education can be spiritual without manipulating minds, without teaching Spirituality 101, replete with textbooks, lectures, and mid-terms (open to qualified juniors and seniors only). In fact, I think schools will become spiritual to the extent that they reduce manipulation. Some of it—the overcontrolling of texts to read and subjects to write on and of the situations in which reading and writing occur—is designed to direct thought where adults think it should go. Some of the manipulation—the obsessive testing and the military-industrial managerial systems—is just bureaucratic self-accommodation. One way or another, in the name of "structure," youngsters are infantalized. The first step toward spiritual education is to put them in a stance of responsible decision making and in an unplanned interaction with other people and the environment. As part of this change, I would drop textbooks in favor of trade books, a syllabus in favor of a classroom library, and go strongly for individual and small-group reading. Any specific presenting and sequencing of texts, whether done in the editorial offices of amoral corporations or within the somewhat more sanctified walls of the faculty conference room, short-circuits the learning process and undermines the will of the student.

The solution to censorship may also be the way to a spiritual education. A single course of reading for a pluralistic populace doesn't make sense unless we really do want a cookie-cutter curriculum. If students are routinely reading individually and in small groups, negotiating different reading programs with the teacher, parents, and classmates, no family can object that their child is being either subjected to or barred from certain books or ideas. Teachers and librarians can point out thin or skewed reading fare in conferring with students and parents and can keep students and books constantly circulating.

Pluralism is central to this process because spirituality depends on widening the identity. Every social system is a knowledge system and has limitations that must be overcome. Learning to think and rejoining the All both require expanding the frequency spectrum to which we can attune. Great books, yes, but youngsters need to experience *all* kinds of discourse and all kinds of voices and viewpoints and styles—hear out the world. Our heritage, yes, but we need to encompass *all* heritages, cross cultures, raise consciousness enough to peer over the social perimeters that act as parameters of knowledge. The Kanawha County imbroglio taught me that the same attachments to blood and soil, hearth and ethos, that Christ vividly enjoined us not to put before him work

against intellectual understanding as well as spiritual development. As we identify, so we know. As we know, so we identify.

But our self and very life depend, we feel, on identifications with family,
neighborhood, ethnic group, church, nation, and language. We have an investment in not knowing anything that will disturb such identifications. So we tend
to limit what we are willing to know to what is known and accepted in our reference group. In my book *Storm in the Mountains* I call this not-wanting-to-
know agnosis, partly to contrast it with *gnosis,* the esoteric term for direct
and total revelation, but partly also to create an analogy with clinical states
like anesthesia, amnesia, and aphasia. Just as our inner system may block
sensory perception, memories, or abstraction, our acculturation may block
any knowledge from within or without that threatens our identities. Agnosis is
self-censorship.

Creek preachers aren't the only ones afraid of reading and writing. We all
are, and that is the real reason that reading and writing have proved inordi-
nately difficult to teach. Literacy is dangerous and has always been so regarded. It naturally breaks down barriers of time, space, and culture. It
threatens one's original identity by broadening it through vicarious experiencing and the incorporation of somebody else's hearth and ethos. So we feel profoundly ambiguous about literacy. Looking on it as a means of transmitting
our culture to our children, we give it priority in education, but, recognizing
the threat of its backfiring, we make it so tiresome and personally unreward-
ing that youngsters won't want to do it on their own, which is when it becomes
dangerous. This is an absurd state of affairs, but it is a societal problem going
beyond schools alone to the universal fear of literacy—a fear based on ethnocentricity—and to the educational goal of transmitting the culture.

At bottom, this goal embodies a needless worry. By definition, culture is
self-transmitting—caught, not taught. It is transmitted through every detail of
our daily lives and our environment. It does not depend on books, but great
books are great because they have passed into and shaped the culture even for
those who never heard of them. This does not argue for neglecting great books,
but if we pulled out all the stops on literacy, quit fearing it, and gave it to
youngsters wholeheartedly for personal inquiry, we would produce a nation of
real readers who would be far more familiar with great books than they are today. Over-controlling the content of reading, writing, and discussing has the
same effect as censorship. Let's not castigate those bigots over there if we're doing our own version of the same thing.

One generation of teachers has somehow got to bring through one generation of students who will have thoughts we have not had before. It is clear
that the nation's and the planet's problems cannot be solved by just thinking
along the lines we do now, according to our heritage. These truly new ways of
thinking will come from the same expanded consciousness that I have called
spiritual. Practically, we must decondition ourselves, jump cultures, slip outside
the cage of mere genetic and environmental inheritance. Transmit the culture,
yes, but subordinate that to transcending the culture, which after all isn't doing

very well right now, like the others. The world is warring right and left because the various cultures strive so intently to perpetuate themselves that they end by imposing themselves on each other. These lethal efforts to make others like oneself burlesque the expanded identity that would make possible real global unity. The secret of war is that nations need enemies to maintain definition, because differences define.

The exclusivity of cultures is so dangerous that each must build into itself the means of transcending itself. Actually, I think the deepest spiritual teachings in all cultures have tried to achieve this goal but, in doing so, seem subversive, which is why they had to go underground, where historians rarely find them. If schools took on the transcending of cultural conditioning, it would hardly mean more than fulfilling the already professed goal of teaching the young to think for themselves. But truly free inquiry has conflicted so much with the old goal of cultural transmission and identity maintenance that we have sabotaged our own noble aim. If we educate youngsters to transcend their heritage, they will be able to transform it and lead other cultures to do the same. The American way is to pioneer. If we don't transform our culture, we won't have a culture to transmit. So the practical way is, after all, the spiritual way.[1]

NOTE

1. Parts of this article appeared in "Censorship and Spiritual Education," *English Education* 21 (1989): 70–87.

QUESTIONS FOR REACTION AND DISCUSSION

1. What does Moffett mean by spiritual education? Do you accept or reject his definition? Why or why not?
2. In your own words, explain your understanding of the Kanawha County textbook protest. Do you think Moffett explains the positions on both sides fairly? Why or why not?

QUESTIONS FOR WRITING

1. Moffett says that "'Know thyself' . . . is a cosmic voyage that should be the first-goal statement in every school district's curriculum guide, before that stuff about being good citizens and productive workers. Those results will follow as fallout from self-development." What does Moffett mean by self-knowledge as the central tenet of spiritual education? How would the textbook protesters view Moffett's definitions of the most important goal? What would a curriculum look like that supported Moffett's goal? Were you spiritually educated, in Moffett's sense of the term? Write an essay in which you discuss specifically how your secondary education did or did not help

you know yourself and explain what you think the effects have been on your educational experience.

2. One of Moffett's more provocative suggestions is that students are "infantalized" by an overly bureaucratic system of control and manipulation. He says, "The first step toward spiritual education is to put them in a stance of responsible decision making and in unplanned interaction with other people and the environment." In other words, Moffett suggests putting the student at the center of the learning process. How does Moffett think such a system might work? How would such a system overturn the objections of fundamentalists? Write an essay in which you describe an educational institution based on Moffett's ideas in this essay.

3. Another writer in this section, E. D. Hirsch, thinks that conversancy in the products of mainstream culture is crucial to communication for all Americans. What would Moffett's positions be on Hirsch's "cultural literacy"? Write a set of questions for the two writers, and devise answers to them, according to your reading of these essays. Some possible questions are: What is the goal of education? What is the role of books in education? Where is the student situated within the educational system?

QUESTIONS FOR FURTHER EXPLORATION

1. Kanawha County, West Virginia, is not the only place in the United States where there have been heated book and curriculum protests. Investigate protests in other parts of the country. You might begin your research by accessing Lexis-Nexis Academic Universe, which provides access to news and reference resources <http://web.lexis-nexis.com/universe>. What are the issues? What are the backgrounds of the protesters? How do school districts handle the adoption of textbooks? Choose a controversy and write a case study of it, including information about the nature of the protest and the final outcome.

2. One of the issues Moffett touches on throughout this essay is the separation of church and state, which is a fundamental aspect of the Constitution of the United States. Investigate the historical bases on which this separation was created. In what ways are textbook controversies related to this separation? Write a report for your classmates in which you summarize the origins of the separation of church and state.

3. Locate a copy of Gina Berriault's short story, "The Stone Boy," and read it carefully. Moffett explains that many of the book protesters were specifically opposed to the inclusion of this story because they felt it attacked the family. Do you agree or disagree with this assessment of the story? Is it appropriate or inappropriate in a secondary school curriculum? Why or why not? Write an essay in which you support or reject the inclusion of this story within a curriculum, carefully explaining the reasons for your opinion.

7

A PARENT'S DILEMMA: PUBLIC VS. JEWISH EDUCATION

Svi Shapiro is a professor of education and chair of the Department of Educational Leadership and Cultural Foundations at the University of North Carolina, Greensboro. Primarily for the professional training of central school administrators (such as principals and superintendents), the department also offers interdisciplinary graduate courses and programs in the social, cultural, and philosophical foundations of education. Shapiro teaches courses in political change and educational policy as well as methods of research and teaching. He is also the author or editor of several books on educational policy and reform, including Between Capitalism and Democracy *(1990), in which he presents his thesis that educational policy is the result of contradictory and unresolved political and ideological viewpoints in our society. His latest book,* Strangers in a Strange Land: Modernity, Pedagogy, and Jewish Identity *(1999), is a collection of accounts from Jewish scholars about their experiences in the academic world, reflecting Shapiro's concern with Jews as an oppressed and marginalized group within the United States. The essay reprinted here originally appeared in* Tikkun, *a bimonthly magazine of politics, culture, and society from a Jewish perspective. In "A Parent's Dilemma," Shapiro writes about how and why he decided to send his daughter to a Jewish school, despite his long-time, personal and professional support of public education.*

QUESTIONS FOR READING

1. The title of the magazine, *Tikkun,* is taken from the Hebrew word "tikkun," "to mend, repair, and transform the world." How does the nature of the magazine in which this essay first appeared shape your reading?
2. What is the nature of the "dilemma" that you think Shapiro intends to discuss? What issues do you think he will raise? Why?

SVI SHAPIRO

A PARENT'S DILEMMA:
PUBLIC VS. JEWISH EDUCATION

Tikkun *(November/December 1996, pp. 59–64)*

The time for decision always seemed to be far off. It would be six years from the beginning of kindergarten before my daughter would complete her elementary schooling—a seemingly endless period of time during which I would surely find the clarity of thinking to decide on the future course of her education. Yet fifth grade at B'nai Shalom Day School had arrived far more rapidly than I wanted. I would now have to seriously confront my own commitments to public education, and to Jewish education—to say nothing of my ambivalence about private schooling and the privileges of class, the rootlessness of a postmodern America, and the comforts of parochial communities.

For leftist academics, there is always the danger of allowing the particularities of one person's life to become lost in the much grander narratives of moral, ideological, and political considerations. This is, after all, a decision about where my eleven-year-old daughter Sarah is to spend her sixth grade. Nor, as I have reminded myself many times, can I hold her needs hostage to my own heavily worked concerns about the course of social justice and identity in this country.

We live in Greensboro, North Carolina. This is not New York or Philadelphia. The Jewish community (well established and comfortable as it is) exists as a very small island in an overwhelmingly dominant Christian milieu. This is what is sometimes referred to as the New South—middle class, moderately conservative. Greensboro is a city of several colleges and universities; we recycle garbage; our mayor is a woman and an environmentalist. Despite a notorious 1979 shoot-out involving the Ku Klux Klan, this is not Klan country.

To grow up Jewish here is certainly a minority experience. But it is far from the culturally marginalizing and politely silent experience I had growing up Jewish in England in the 1950s. Here, Jewish holidays are visibly and positively commented on in the local media, the television stations wish their viewers a happy Chanukah, and the downtown Christmas decorations are referred to as the "Festival of Lights." Even our supermarkets consult with our Conservative rabbi on Jewish dietary laws and culinary tastes.

The Jewish day school my daughter attends is a quite beautiful institution. Its enrollment is about 190 students—fairly remarkable in a city of about 1,200 Jewish families. Recently celebrating its twenty-fifth anniversary, the school provides a warm, very *haimish* Jewish environment, where holidays and Shabbat are richly celebrated, and the Hebrew language ubiquitous. Its religiosity is traditional though nondogmatic, and it affirms the notions of *tikkun olam*. While I find the pedagogy too conventional, my daughter has found the place to be nurturant and loving. She has, for the most part, found delight in being there—a place where schooling has sustained her, not opposed her life.

What was at stake in my choice of Sarah's schooling was no abstract pedagogic exercise. I want my daughter's heart and soul to be shaped and nurtured by a *Yiddishkeyt* that would ensure her allegiance to a Jewish identity. As spiritually or historically compelling as this might be, I make no claim that this is not, at root, a selfish act. Such an education would ensure my continuing ability to recognize my own self in my daughter's being—the natural, if not entirely laudable, desire of most parents. Until now, my decision has been richly repaid; she had indeed absorbed not only some of the knowledge and culture of Jewish life, but more significantly its texture and feel. She senses its importance and its uniqueness. The joys and significance of this belong not only to the private sphere of family life, but also for her to the sphere of communal participation. Jewish life exists not merely in home or synagogue, but richly and vibrantly in the everyday, Monday-through-Friday world from which, for most of us, it is abstracted.

The mobilization of support for a politics that eviscerates public institutions is bound up with the widely felt hostility in modern societies toward the state, with all of its impersonality, inefficiency, and waste. It is precisely this perception that has fueled the relentless drive of the Right to gut almost everything that has the word "public" in it.

At the heart of this assault is an ideology that lionizes the marketplace and scorns society's attempts to ameliorate social injustice. In this view, the marketplace and market forces are regarded as the only legitimate means to allocate resources and to assign economic or cultural values. The resultant push for smaller government and a balanced budget has the effect of drastically reducing the scope and scale of the social safety net. It means ever more drastic cutbacks in society's supports to the elderly, children, the unemployed, the poor, and the sick.

So our culture continues to foster self-interest and a lack of concern for the common good. Where the marketplace alone is to be arbiter of economic investment and social values, attempts are made to eliminate or reduce publicly financed education and culture. Prisons become one of the few areas of public investment. And where public policy collides with the imperatives of the market, as in environmental and consumer regulation, then the latter need be scaled back if not eradicated.

The political discourse that has sought to achieve these ends is not without its own conflicts and contradictions. It is clear, for example, that many people subscribe to the notion of smaller, less wasteful government, but also support a state that lessens the hazards and dangers of the free market. In this sense the state is, paradoxically, both the focus of much popular anger and repository of much of our needs and aspirations as a community. It irks us with its demands and intrusiveness, but it also instantiates our collective responsibilities and obligations. For all of its flaws, the state embodies some notion of a shared purpose; its ultimate client purports to be the public good, not simply the desirous ego.

The irony is that those conservatives who have often been the loudest in their condemnation of the decline of community and an ethic of responsibility have pursued a politics that has sought to allow the standards and ethics of the market to exert ever more freedom and dominance in our social, economic, and cultural lives. In working to ensure a world in which private interests and profits are less and less hindered by broad public responsibilities, and where the public arena is endlessly demeaned and savagely attacked, these free-marketeers have helped create a society that more and more resembles a predatory jungle. The violence of the Oklahoma bombing and the shut-down of the federal government, with its callous layoffs of workers and undelivered unemployment checks, are the most recent visible evidence of a discourse which has effectively trashed the public domain.

Sadly, it is often only when cuts in services and benefits are directly felt that individuals become more critical of what is happening on a broader level. Until then, the politics of racism and division succeed in legitimating the Right's social policies. A bunker mentality spreads, which calls for a social ethic of each for him or herself; individualism, separateness, and isolation frame our disposition toward the rest of the world. All of this has been given added impetus by corporate behavior in the 1980s and '90s, replete with layoffs, downsizing, closings, and relocations. It is a world that mocks any notions of obligation or commitment to workers, consumers, or community. Nothing really counts except the hunt for immediate profitability. Public accountability is a barrier to be subverted by whatever means necessary.

Yet in spite of all of this, there is still a deep hunger for communal life and the public good in America. Despite the shift to the Right, large majorities continue to affirm the importance of protecting our environment, maintaining investments in public libraries and cultural resources, and ensuring the availability of health care. Sometimes it becomes crystallized in ways that seem narrow or even repressive (protecting "our" flag). Yet behind these can be heard a cry for a society in which our collective concerns, not just our private interests, are honored, and where there is a strong sense of the public good instantiated in our civic world and in our social institutions.

Perhaps nowhere has this struggle been more focused than around the institutions of public education. Indeed, all of our societal schizophrenia around questions of public and private, marketplace and equity, democracy and capitalism, are in evidence there. In its most ideal rendering, public schooling represents a space where all of our children may be educated, a place where the rights of citizenship take precedence over the privileges or disadvantages of social and economic life. Understood in this way, public education becomes a crucial element in the making of a democratic civil society. It is an indispensable site for the nurturing of a new generation in those attitudes and values that ensure the possibility of meaningful democratic life.

Public school brings together in one setting children who, regardless of their class, race, gender or ethnicity, may acquire the capacity for critical intelligence, the sense of community, and the cultural literacy that are requisites for democracy. As many political commentators have pointed out, the current crisis of democracy in the United States is closely related to the decline of meaningful public spaces where citizens can engage in a thoughtful and critical consideration of our society's pressing issues and concerns. In a world where commercial malls and presidential debates simulate real public interaction and involvement, there is a growing urgency to preserve those places where notions of equity, community, citizenship, and the public good still have validity.

Sadly, the reality of public schools has always been a long way from its democratic promise. The fundamental ideal of a place where the offspring of all citizens might meet and come together as a community has always been upset by the harsh realities of privilege, inequity, and racism. The historic struggles to eradicate the effects of a racially segregated system of public education are well known. Less obvious have been the continuing pernicious effects of class and race in maintaining schools vastly different in their resources, funding, expectations of students, and educational climate. Jonathan Kozol, among others, vividly documented the horrendous conditions that beset schools in poor and underfunded districts, producing debilitating and demoralizing third-world environments for kids in many of this nation's cities.

This public sphere mirrors the increasing polarization of wealth and opportunity found in the wider society. Urban schools with their violence, high drop-out rates, low achievement, and poor morale exist as altogether different institutions from those in suburban areas that function as conduits to good colleges and economic well-being.

Far from equalizing opportunities for diverse groups of students, education typically reinforces the already existing advantages and disadvantages found in the larger culture. The bitter irony of the process is that it occurs under the apparently well-meaning rhetoric of educational theories that promise to teach to the intellectual and emotional differences among students. Yet, in practice, the effect is usually to rationalize racism and classism. The ubiquitous grouping and tracking of students become little more than a way of affirming the "cultural capital" of some individuals and invalidating that of others. It takes only a cursory look at many schools to see how education dignifies the knowledge and experiences of some young people and silences and marginalizes that of others.

Typically, schooling represents a process of mindless absorption of knowledge separated from any notion of existential or social meaning. Successful learning comes to be seen as a regurgitation of bits and pieces of knowledge abstracted from a context that might provide them with relevance to the lives, hopes, interests, and dreams of kids' lives. And the "hidden curriculum" of schooling is such that the emphasis on achievement, individual success, and competition undermines efforts to build communities of respect and care. Indeed, where the latter are taken seriously, they must confront the contradictions not only of school culture but that of the large social milieu. The daily grind of public school life with its boredom, alienation, and bureaucratic regimentation are the resonant features of contemporary, adolescent popular culture.

In my struggle to decide the fate of my fifth-grade daughter, I am mindful of the desperate need to sustain the promise of public life in this country. The withdrawal of the middle class from public institutions is the certain vehicle for their demoralization and decline. Not only in this country but in other places such as the United Kingdom, the turn toward more individualistic lifestyles and privatized institutions, promoted by conservative governments, has turned the public space into one of neglect and decay. Whether in health care, housing, or in education, the story is one of double standards—where publicly provided institutions or systems are synonymous with the poor, and where standards are increasingly inferior as compared to those found in the private domain.

In wrestling with whether to send my daughter to a public school, I feel compelled to weigh my own moral responsibility as to whether I am to be part of the flight from our public world into the safety and privileges of a private institution. A commitment to progressive politics would seem to demand commitment to those public institutions where we may share, to some degree, our lives with those who inhabit economic, cultural or racial worlds quite different from our own.

Among all these concerns, one is of particular significance to me. How do we reconcile a commitment to public education with the need to recognize and affirm cultural, religious, or other differences? For many on the Left, this validation of difference has been central to the contemporary struggle to deepen the meaning of democratic life. It has been seen as a critical feature of democracy in a "postmodern" world. The struggle to recognize the multiplicity of voices and the diversity of histories and experiences of those who inhabit our nation and world has been a key focus of progressive educators.

And there has been increasing recognition of the ways that education has for so long denied the contributions and presence of many kinds of people. Whether because of class or race or ethnicity or gender or religion or nationality, it has become clear just how much we have ignored or invalidated the knowledge and traditions of others—those who fall outside the constructed norms of the culture. As educators, we have come to see how this process demeans and silences our students as the classroom becomes a place that is quite foreign to their homes, neighborhood, or communities.

In this regard, the emergence of a "multicultural" awareness in our schools is an important and liberating phenomenon. It is certainly a mark of progress that children are being taught to question the notion that "Columbus discovered America" with all its ethnocentric and racist assumptions about civilization; or that history, social studies, and English are beginning to be taught in more expansive and inclusive ways. Even where there are good-faith efforts, multiculturalism too often becomes trivialized—a matter of food, fiestas, and dressing up. It offers a very superficial appreciation indeed of what difference has meant to communities often denigrated or despised by those in the mainstream of society. Whatever its limitations, these efforts represent real cracks in the wall of cultural assumptions that have confronted generations of young people, shutting out or silencing those whose language, history, beliefs, and culture have been made to seem peripheral to the society.

Yet even where difference is valued and the plural nature of cultures in America is celebrated, the texture of the particular cultures recognized by our public schools is likely to be "thin." For my daughter, no multicultural environment can offer the judaically rich, evocative, and full experience that would be available to her in a Jewish day school. Only in that environment does Jewishness become a form of life that colors moral expression, joyful celebration, the moments of soulful reflection and sadness, and the days and seasons of the calendar. Jewishness becomes more than an abstract focus of intellectual discussion: the living vehicle through which my daughter can construct her identity and articulate her ethical and spiritual commitments.

Such a voice is a matter of both the heart and the mind, and only a pedagogic environment that is flooded with the resonance of Jewish memory and experience can nurture it. Nor is a deep sense of value about Jewish life easily available outside of a context which integrates it into a community's daily practice—one that draws in some way from the moral and spiritual meanings of our people's historical wisdom. The "thick" texture of Jewish life—the pervasive sounds of Hebrew, the smell of challah, the *niggunim* and Israeli songs, the benching after meals—are the resources upon which are built an identity that contains an enduring commitment to Jewish life and continuity.

The intensity of this experience, however, holds the potential danger of nurturing parochial or arrogant attitudes. Such schooling may produce a *shtetl* consciousness that shuns or disparages anything foreign—one that later fuels the intolerance of "*goyim*-bashing," or the self-righteousness that underlays so much of the American-Jewish support for chauvinistic, right-wing Israeli politics.

While at B'nai Shalom, much hard work goes toward developing a sense of social responsibility and celebrating the values of human community and global connectedness, the school my daughter attends is nevertheless a sheltered, limited community that is separated from much that other children must confront and deal with in their lives. Certainly its ambiance is too competitive, oriented to the goals of individual success and achievements. Its selectivity as a Jewish and predominantly middle- and upper-middle-class institution ensures that it is the kind of secure and cohesive community so appealing to parents. Yet in this sense it also provides a powerful, if disturbing, answer to some of the dilemmas of a postmodern world.

In their observations of postmodern society, there is a surprising convergence among both left- and right-wing critics. At the center is the belief that the world we have entered is one in which barriers—spatial, moral, political, intellectual, and aesthetic—have collapsed. Even the boundaries of gender appear permeable in an age in which sexual borders are easily crossed and labile. Our age is one of unfixity, uncertainty, and flux.

There is much to celebrate in all of this. The unfixing of boundaries, verities, and distinctions has given us the promise of a world that is more fluid, open, and free. Yet there is a price to pay—one, I believe, that has traumatic consequences for the young. And in this the conservative critique finds a powerful resonance in the anguish of many parents, by no means all of whom can be dismissed as simply and predictably right wing.

It is quite clear that the desire for discipline and structure in the raising of the young now hits a powerful chord across a wide range of parents. This desire emanates from the increasing recognition of a world in which a moral and spiritual homelessness is the prevailing sensibility. More and more there is the sense of being uprooted from the stabilities of place, family, and normative communities. The postmodern world is one in which individuals increasingly feel as if they are in exile—existentially and morally adrift in a world that constantly disrupts and dissolves any sense of situatedness in an enduring web of meaning and community. Indeed, far from acknowledging the pain of so much alienation, we are urged by Madison Avenue as well as the hipper cultural critics to enjoy the tumultuous ride.

In ways that distort the broad concern for the disintegration of ethical life and the erosion of the sense of social responsibility, talk of tradition, values, and discipline is mistakenly understood as only a discourse of the Right. Yet a world in which all that is solid melts—moral commitment, identity, community, social connection—is a matter that confronts all of us. And nowhere is this more painfully so than in regard to the upbringing of our own children. Daily, all of us, especially parents, are forced to confront the fallout from the postmodern condition—the self-destructiveness of adolescent suicide, drugs, alcoholism and compulsive dieting, widespread depression and generalized rage, and a cynical detachment from social institutions. However manipulative or distorting, conservative discourse succeeds because it speaks to the widespread anguish of an older generation.

In this context of disintegration, rootlessness, and the culture of images, Jewish schooling offers a sense of possibility not easily found elsewhere. Here there is the hope of nurturing an identity grounded in the Jewish people's long history—a history rich with the struggles for a world of justice and freedom. Here, too, is the real possibility of transmitting what it means to be a "stranger in the land"—developing personalities, empathic to the pain of exclusion and human indignity.

Jewish "memory" roots us in a temporal community of unbelievable human tragedies, celebrations, suffering, courage, and the will for physical and spiritual survival. And such history makes powerful claims on the living—an insistence on the vision of *tikkun olam;* to act as if we ourselves had experienced the bondage of Egypt. Far from the Disney World theme park of historical images, Jewish pedagogy can offer a deep sense of historic and communal identification. Such identification is one of connectedness to an enduring moral and spiritual vision.

The religious sensibility forged in this history is one that continually demands that we create and recognize boundaries—distinctions within our world between ways of living that express the sacred and those that are profane. Judaism is a religion of everyday life that constantly seeks to make sacred the so-called ordinary, taken-for-granted acts of daily existence. Those of us who grew up in Orthodox homes know the rigidity and frequently stultifying nature of halakhic Judaism. Yet, at the same time, one can find here a powerful rejoinder to the dehumanization and degradation of our common world—one that insists that we seek to make holy human life and behavior, as well as the whole environment that makes life possible.

Certainly Judaism, like all religions, can become dogmatic and reified; a series of mindless rituals and practices. Yet I have reason to believe that B'nai Shalom offers my daughter the beginning of a deeper set of meanings that points to the limits and boundaries that structure our relationship to the world as one of respect, consciousness of the needs of others, and responsibility toward them. In this school's Judaism there is, too, a sense of celebration and festivity—one that seeks to teach the young something about experiencing lives of joy, wonder and appreciation. It is, I believe, in this synthesis of social responsibility and joyful mindfulness that we can find the beginnings of a meaningful response to the rampant cynicism and nihilism of our culture.

It is true that the school offers an environment that is only very cautiously questioning or critical of the injustices of our world. And I am concerned lest it limit the importance of developing the critical mind and spirit—the lifeblood of a democratic culture. But beyond the need for our young to be educated to enable them to challenge their world, there is a need for the sense of hope and possibility that the world can be changed and transformed. And this, I believe, happens best in an environment where we feel a deeply shared, and inspiring, sense of connected fate. For Jews, there is our long history of struggle in a harsh world of brutality and oppression, and the will to maintain our hope for a better world.

Without this communal rootedness and affirmation of a way of life there is, I think, little emotional capacity to act in the world—at least not where acting means trying to transform the moral character of our lives and the political shape of our society. There is only disconnected apathy and cynicism—the world of the young so well reflected in the recent popular movies, *Slacker* and *Clueless*.

The Right is correct to argue that without an internalized discipline the self becomes passive, unable to act in the world. Yet the discipline that empowers is not that of the obedient drone but the structure that comes from participation and responsibility in the life of a meaningful and enduring community.

These are not easy times. Such communities are not easy to find. All of us must somehow find the capacity for commitment in a world where all beliefs seem uncertain, visions uncertain, and social relations fragile or broken. Yet the need to find a place in which our commitments are shared and our identities confirmed is the necessary ground of our being as moral agents in the world.

Let me be clear that my real interest is not in what is referred to today as "Jewish continuity." The continuation of a set of practices and rituals is of no particular significance to me. The ultimate value of Jewish education is not found in my daughter's capacity to read or speak Hebrew, or her knowledge of Judaica, but in whether she will become a human being deeply concerned for the worth and dignity of all the lives that share our world. My hope is that her Jewish education will be a powerful vehicle for developing such a way of being. The particular here, I hope, will provide a gateway to the universal.

Yet I worry that my desire for this education will also boost the arguments of those who favor "school choice." These are often no more than thinly veiled attempts to promote educational policies that are elitist, racially separatist, or religiously fundamentalist, and have little to do with creating a more compassionate or respectful civic culture. As I wrestle with my daughter's future, I feel the strong and inescapable claims of the particular in a world that more and more demands a recognition of our universal connectedness and responsibilities.

QUESTIONS FOR REACTION AND DISCUSSION

1. How would you describe the organization of this essay? How effectively does Shapiro use narration, description, and classification in his essay?
2. What do you know about private schools with a religious affiliation? Did you attend one or know someone well who did? Was attending such a school a mostly positive or mostly negative experience? Why?
3. What does Shapiro say when he comments that "our culture continues to foster self-interest and a lack of concern for the common good"? How does he support this contention?
4. How does Shapiro rate the effects of multiculturalism in the public school curriculum?
5. What is Shapiro's assessment of the kind of education his daughter will receive in a Jewish school?

QUESTIONS FOR WRITING

1. Shapiro makes an eloquent case for his decision to send his daughter to a Jewish school. Is it convincing? Why or why not? Do you agree with his position? Write an essay in the form of a letter to the editor of *Tikkun* in which you defend or reject his position with examples and details from your reading and your own educational experience.

2. Would you consider sending a child of your own to a private, religious-affiliated school? Why or why not? Write an essay in which you describe and defend your decision. To support and justify your opinion, use details and examples from your own cultural, educational, and religious background as appropriate.

3. While Shapiro acknowledges that the emergence of multiculturalism within a school curriculum is "an important and liberating phenomenon," he raises his concerns about superficial appreciation of other cultures and suggests that the celebration of other cultures often becomes trivialized. Consider the positions of other writers in this section on the value of multiculturalism, especially Simonson and Walker and Gates. How would they respond to his concern? How would you? Write an essay in which you describe and analyze the ways in which multiculturalism may be trivialized and give examples from your own experiences.

QUESTIONS FOR FURTHER EXPLORATION

1. Shapiro mentions two popular movies of the 1990s, *Clueless* and *Slacker,* as examples of the "disconnected apathy and cynicism" of the "world of the young." Locate a videotape of one of these movies and watch it with a group of your classmates. Afterwards, discuss the movie in the context of Shapiro's point about the rootlessness and lack of structure in the contemporary world. Consider some of the following questions as a departure point for your discussion: What depictions of educational institutions are there in the movies? Who or what is responsible for the exiled status of the young people depicted?

2. "School choice" and the movement for vouchers for private schools are increasingly becoming topics on the political agenda. Research the status of the movement to allow tax monies to help finance a student at a private school. What are the various positions in the debate? What is happening in the state where you live or attend college? Is this movement important to you? Why or why not?

3. Access the Web site for *Tikkun* <http://www.tikkun.org> and read Shapiro's 1998 essay, "Public School Reform: The Mismeasure of Education," and the accompanying response by Bruce S. Cooper <http://www.tikkun.org/9801/9801shapiro.html>. What is the nature of the debate between the two writers? What ideas of Shapiro do you recognize from his earlier essay, "A Parent's Dilemma"? Write a response to both Shapiro and Cooper, in the style that is used in *Tikkun.*

8

THE DEBATE HAS BEEN MISCAST
FROM THE START

Henry Louis Gates, Jr. is a professor of the humanities at Harvard University, where he also chairs the Afro-American Studies Department and directs the W. E. B. Du Bois Institute for Afro-American Research. Gates is the author of several works of literary criticism about African-Americans; he has also written on multiculturalism and higher education and on his experiences as a black man in the academic world. Gates is regarded by many as a "public intellectual," a professor with an audience and influence far beyond the academic world of colleges and universities. In 1997, Time *listed him as among the "Twenty-five Most Influential Americans." One of his recent books is* Colored People: A Memoir *(1994), an account of his childhood in a small West Virginia town in the 1950s and 1960s. Gates also writes frequently for magazines and newspapers, including* Time, *the* New Yorker, *and* The Boston Globe, *where the article reprinted here was first published in the Sunday magazine. The* Boston Globe *was established in 1872 to serve Boston and the surrounding communities. During its long history, the* Globe *has emerged as one of the top-rated newspapers in the United States and has been awarded several Pulitzer Prizes in investigative reporting, editorial cartoons, local reporting, commentary, and criticism. In this essay, Gates describes his position on the central issues in the debate over multiculturalism in the curriculum of American higher education.*

QUESTIONS FOR READING

1. What is your understanding of the sides or points of view that people have taken on the multicultural debate? How would you describe the current state of the debate? Why?
2. What does the title suggest about the content of this article?

HENRY LOUIS GATES, JR.

THE DEBATE HAS BEEN MISCAST FROM THE START

The Boston Globe *(October 13, 1991)*

What is multiculturalism and why are they saying such terrible things about it?

We've been told that it threatens to fragment American culture into a warren of ethnic enclaves, each separate and inviolate. We've been told that it menaces the Western tradition of literature and the arts. We've been told that it aims to politicize the school curriculum, replacing honest historical scholarship with a "feel-good" syllabus designed solely to bolster the self-esteem of minorities. The alarm has been sounded, and many scholars and educators—liberals as well as conservatives—have responded to it. After all, if multiculturalism is just a pretty name for ethnic chauvinism, who needs it?

But I don't think that's what multiculturalism is—at least, I don't think that's what it ought to be. And because the debate has been miscast from the beginning, it may be worth setting the main issues straight.

To both proponents and antagonists, multiculturalism represents—either refreshingly or frighteningly—a radical departure. Like most claims for cultural novelty, this one is more than a little exaggerated. For the challenges of cultural pluralism—and the varied forms of official resistance to it—go back to the very founding of our republic.

In the university today, it must be admitted, the challenge has taken on a peculiar inflection. But the underlying questions are time tested. What does it mean to be an American? Must academic inquiry be subordinated to the requirements of national identity? Should scholarship and education reflect our actual diversity, or should they, rather, forge a communal identity that may not yet have been achieved?

For answers, you can, of course, turn to the latest jeremiad on the subject from, say, George Will, Dinesh D'Souza, or Roger Kimball. But in fact these questions have always occasioned lively disagreement among American educators. In 1917, William Henry Hulme decried "the insidious introduction into our scholarly relations of the political propaganda of a wholly narrow, selfish, and vicious nationalism and false patriotism." His opponents were equally emphatic in their beliefs. "More and more clearly," Fred Lewis Pattee ventured in 1919, "is it seen now that the American soul, the American conception of democracy, Americanism, should be made prominent in our school curriculums, as a guard against the rising spirit of experimental lawlessness." Sound familiar?

Given the political nature of the debate over education and the national interest, the conservative penchant for charging the multiculturalists with "politics" is a little perplexing. For conservative critics, to their credit, have never hesitated to provide a political defense of what they consider to be the "traditional" curriculum: The future of the republic, they argue, depends on the inculcation of proper civic virtues. What these virtues are is a matter of vehement dispute. But to imagine a curriculum untouched by political concerns is to imagine—as no one does—that education can take place in a vacuum.

So where's the beef? Granted, multiculturalism is no panacea for our social ills. We're worried when Johnny can't read. We're worried when Johnny can't add. But shouldn't we be worried, too, when Johnny tramples gravestones in a Jewish cemetery or scrawls racial epithets on a dormitory wall? And it's because we've entrusted our schools with the fashioning of a democratic polity that education has never been exempt from the kind of debate that marks every other aspect of American political life.

Perhaps this isn't altogether a bad thing. As the political theorist Amy Gutmann has argued: "In a democracy, political disagreement is not something that we should generally seek to avoid. Political controversies over our educational problems are a particularly important source of social progress because they have the potential for educating so many citizens."

And while I'm sympathetic to what Robert Nisbet once dubbed the "academic dogma"—the ideal of knowledge for its own sake—I also believe that truly humane learning, unblinkered by the constraints of narrow ethnocentrism, can't help but expand the limits of human understanding and social tolerance. Those who fear that "Balkanization" and social fragmentation lie this way have got it exactly backward. Ours is a world that already is fissured by nationality, ethnicity, race, and gender. And the only way to transcend those divisions—to forge, for once, a civic culture that respects both differences and commonalities—is through education that seeks to comprehend the diversity of human culture. Beyond the hype and the high-flown rhetoric is a pretty homely truth: There is no tolerance without respect—and no respect without knowledge.

The historical architects of the university always understood this. As Cardinal Newman wrote more than a century ago, the university should promote, "the power of viewing many things at once, as one whole, of referring them severally to their true place in the universal system, of understanding their respective values, and determining their mutual dependence." In just this vein, the critic Edward Said has recently suggested that "our model for academic freedom should therefore be the migrant or traveler: for if, in the real world outside the academy, we must needs be ourselves and only ourselves, inside the academy we should be able to discover and travel among other selves, other identities, other varieties of the human adventure. But, most essentially, in this joint discovery of self and other, it is the role of the academy to transform what might be conflict, or context, or assertion into reconciliation, mutuality, recognition, creative interaction."

But if multiculturalism represents the culmination of an age-old ideal—the dream known in the seventeenth century as *mathesis universalis*—why has it been the target of such ferocious attacks? On this point, I'm often reminded of a wonderfully wicked piece of nineteenth-century student doggerel about

Benjamin Jowett, the great Victorian classicist and master of Balliol College, Oxford:

Here stand I, my name is Jowett,
If there's knowledge, then I know it;
I am the master of this college,
What I know not, is not knowledge.

Of course, the question of how we determine what is worth knowing is now being raised with uncomfortable persistence. So that in the most spirited attacks on multiculturalism in the academy today, there's a nostalgic whiff of the old sentiment: We are the masters of this college; what we know not is not knowledge.

I think this explains the conservative desire to cast the debate in terms of the West vs. the Rest. And yet that's the very opposition that the pluralist wants to challenge. Pluralism sees cultures as porous, dynamic, and interactive, rather than the fixed property of particular ethnic groups. Thus the idea of a monolithic, homogenous "West" itself comes into question (nothing new here: Literary historians have pointed out that the very concept of "Western culture" may date back only to the eighteenth century). But rather than mourning the loss of some putative ancestral purity, we can recognize what's valuable, resilient, even cohesive, in the hybrid and variegated nature of our modernity.

Genuine multiculturalism is not, of course, everyone's cup of tea. Vulgar cultural nationalists—like Allan Bloom or Leonard Jeffries—correctly identify it as the enemy. These polemicists thrive on absolute partitions: between "civilization" and "barbarism," between "black" and "white," between a thousand versions of Us and Them. But they are whistling in the wind.

For whatever the outcome of the culture wars in the academy, the world we live in is multicultural already. Mixing and hybridity is the rule, not the exception. As a student of African-American culture, of course, I've come to take this kind of cultural palimpsest for granted. Duke Ellington, Miles Davis, John Coltrane have influenced popular musicians the world over. Wynton Marsalis is as comfortable with Mozart as he is with jazz; Anthony Davis writes operas in a musical idiom that combines Bartok with the blues.

In dance, Judith Jamison, Alvin Ailey, Katherine Dunham all excelled at "Western" cultural art forms, melding these with African-American styles to produce performances that were neither, and both. In painting, Romare Bearden and Jacob Lawrence, Martin Puryear and Augusta Savage learned to paint and sculpt by studying Western masters, yet each has pioneered the construction of a distinctly African-American visual art.

And in literature, of course, the most formally complex and compelling black writers—such as Jean Toomer, Sterling Brown, Langston Hughes, Zora Hurston, Richard Wright, Ralph Ellison, James Baldwin, and Gwendolyn Brooks—have always blended forms of Western literature with African-American vernacular and written traditions. Then, again, even a vernacular form such as the spiritual took for its texts the King James version of the Old and New Testaments. Toni Morrison's master's thesis was on Virginia Woolf and Faulkner; Rita Dove is as comfortable with German literature as she is with the blues.

Indeed, the greatest African-American art can be thought of as an exploration of that hyphenated space between the African and the American. As James Baldwin once reflected during his long European sojourn, "I would have to appropriate these white centuries; I would have to make them mine. I would have to accept my special attitude, my special place in this scheme; otherwise I would have no place in this scheme."

"Pluralism," the American philosopher John Dewey insisted early in this century, "is the greatest philosophical idea of our times." But he recognized that it was also the greatest problem of our times: "How are we going to make the most of the new values we set on variety, difference, and individuality—how are we going to realize their possibilities in every field, and at the same time not sacrifice that plurality to the cooperation we need so much?" It has the feel of a scholastic conundrum: How can we negotiate between the one and the many?

Today, the mindless celebration of difference has proven as untenable as that bygone model of monochrome homogeneity. If there is an equilibrium to be struck, there's no guarantee we will ever arrive at it. The worst mistake we can make, however, is not to try.

Questions for Reaction and Discussion

1. Describe your understanding of the debate over multiculturalism. How is Gates's analysis different from your own? Has your understanding changed as a result of reading this article? Why or why not?

2. What does Gates mean by his questions: "Must academic inquiry be subordinated to the requirements of national identity"? How might Hirsch or Freire respond to this question?

3. How do you interpret Gates's observation that conservatives cast the debate in terms of "the West vs. the Rest"? Is this fair? Why or why not?

4. As a student of African-American culture, Gates explains that he brings a particular perspective to the debate on multiculturalism because of the hybrid nature of his own background. What is that perspective and how does he explain it? How many of the examples he mentions are familiar to you?

5. What does Gates mean by "multiculturalism"? What does he mean by "cultural pluralism"?

Questions for Writing

1. Gates explains that a time-tested question in universities is "What does it mean to be an American?" Based on your own experience, what is your definition of an American? Write an essay in which you

define Americanism and give specific examples from your own educational and cultural background as well as your reading of Gates and other writers.

2. In paragraph ten, Gates says: "Ours is a world that already is fissured by nationality, ethnicity, race, and gender. And the only way to transcend those divisions—to forge, for once, a civic culture that respects both difference and commonalities—is through education that seeks to comprehend the diversity of human culture." What does such an education look like in curricular terms? How would such an educational program be accomplished? Assume that you are a representative on a student committee to revise the general curriculum on your campus. What recommendation would you make to ensure that your curriculum would "comprehend the diversity of human culture"? Write a recommendation with a rationale for its acceptance for presentation to your committee.

3. At the end of his essay, Gates cautions that the "mindless celebration of difference" is as problematic as the "bygone model of monochrome homogeneity." What experiences have you had in your education that would suggest the truth of this statement? Write an essay in which you contrast these two curricular models and give examples from your own experience and reading.

QUESTIONS FOR FURTHER EXPLORATION

1. Gates mentions the names of several writers, George Will, Dinesh D'Souza, Allan Bloom, Leonard Jeffries, and Roger Kimball, all of whom have written books and articles about their concerns about a multicultural curriculum for students. Investigate and read some of the works of one of these writers and write a brief summary of the viewpoint you find. How does this viewpoint compare with that of Gates or another writer in this section of your text? Report your findings to your class.

2. Investigate the W. E. B. Du Bois Institute for Afro-American Research at Harvard University <http://web-dubois.fas.harvard.edu>. What is the purpose and mission of the Institute? What programs and projects does it sponsor? What role does the Institute play in the Harvard curriculum? What other sites of interest are linked to the Institute? Write a report of your investigation of the Web site and present it to your class.

3. Gates suggests that his African-American heritage has taught him that we already live in a multicultural world. He gives examples from African-American music, dance, art, and literature. Choose the area with which you are least familiar and investigate one of the artists or writers Gates mentions. Write a brief report for your class in which you introduce the artist or writer you've chosen and discuss the "mixing and hybridity" that you find in his or her work.

9

EMOTIONAL BAGGAGE IN A COURSE ON BLACK WRITERS

Claire Oberon Garcia teaches a variety of courses in American literature in the English Department at Colorado College, a private, liberal arts and sciences college in Colorado Springs, Colorado. The article reprinted here was first published in the Chronicle of Higher Education, *a weekly newspaper published in printed form and on the Internet <http://chronicle.com>. The* Chronicle *covers higher education in the United States and abroad and is read by more than 400,000 college and university administrators and faculty members. Each issue includes news about campuses in the United States and abroad, articles on developments in scholarly research, features on professional issues, articles and reviews on information technology, reports on state and federal government actions that affect higher education, statistical reports on varied topics like student enrollment and tuition figures, lists of new scholarly books, job listings, and a calendar of events. The* Chronicle *is an excellent source of information on all aspects of higher education. "Emotional Baggage in a Course on Black Writers" appeared in the "Opinion" section, which includes essays on a range of topics, generally written by professors. In this essay, Garcia recounts her experiences in teaching black writers in courses to mostly white students.*

QUESTIONS FOR READING

1. What is "emotional baggage"? What kinds of emotional baggage might students of any race or background bring to a course on black writers?
2. Have you taken a course on black writers? Do you plan to do so? Why or why not?

CLAIRE OBERON GARCIA

EMOTIONAL BAGGAGE IN A COURSE
ON BLACK WRITERS

The Chronicle of Higher Education *(July 27, 1994, B1)*

During a class I was teaching a few years ago on novels written by black women, we discussed *The Street,* Ann Petry's study of a black single mother's doomed struggle to achieve the American dream in the inner city. In a conversation after class with some of my students—most of whom were white—I happened to mention that I had gone to school in Switzerland. One young woman expressed astonishment: "I pictured you working your way through high school and college, in somewhere like Chicago, struggling through with all your children, and then finally getting this job at our college."

Laughing, I explained to her that, although I am black, I had had a rather middle-class life. I had attended private schools, married a lawyer, had children. I wondered how many other students—not knowing anything about my personal life—had seen me as a local version of struggling and heroic black womanhood as exemplified by Ms. Petry's Lutie Johnson, Gloria Naylor's *The Women of Brewster Place,* or the up-close-and-personal interviewees on network news stories about successful workfare programs.

I do not think my experience is unique. In discussions with other faculty members from minority groups, I hear similar tales of students who assume that their professors personally represent the experiences of the fictional minority characters they are studying. The new emphasis on multiculturalism in education has exposed more white undergraduates to the creative and scholarly work of members of minority groups. And, thanks to increased recruitment efforts, more faculty members from racial- and ethnic-minority backgrounds are teaching in predominantly white institutions. These changes suggest questions about how students deal with multicultural material, what they expect from minority-group faculty members, and how such faculty members should address their expectations.

I teach several courses on African-American and American literature at my small, predominantly white liberal arts college. I have never had more than two black students in a single class; at most, I have had four students of color in one class. Although I teach the work of writers from racial-minority groups in all of my courses, I have found that some unique dynamics develop in my African-American literature classes.

As in all English classes, the question of which readings are superior to others raises the issues of authority and values. Who determines what is "good literature" and why? Is Zora Neale Hurston as "good" a writer as D. H. Lawrence? Can you understand Frances E. W. Harper's stylistic decision in

Iola Leroy without knowing something about turn-of-the-century feminism, the conventions of the domestic novel, and the backlash against Reconstruction? Do we need historical background to understand Mark Twain's works? Questions such as these help students think about reading and evaluating literature, but the racial dimension adds an extra twist or two to already complex problems.

Many white students express the fear that they won't understand texts by minority-group writers because they and the authors come from very different worlds. Several times, especially in my classes on fiction written by black women, I've had students preface remarks with statements such as, "As a white, middle-class male, I can't really speak to" a particular aspect of a story. Sometimes the qualifier is merely an excuse for not fully engaging in the discussion. But more often it reveals the speaker's anxiety that he isn't "getting" something that is apparent to readers who have either race or gender in common with the author of the book.

Although some of the texts that I use in my African-American literature classes are also taught in American literature classes (Toni Morrison's *Beloved*, for example), students seem to be more confused by these texts when they read them in African-American literature courses. Perhaps this is because they come into those classes expecting to learn not only about the development of the African-American novel or African-American theater or poetry, but also about "blackness." They expect an answer to the "unasked question" with which W. E. B. DuBois commenced the classic *The Souls of Black Folk*: "How does it feel to be the problem?" And many students expect an answer not only from the texts they are reading, but from personal testimonials of their black professors.

When I taught "Black Literature in America" last year, at least half of the twenty-five students in the class came to me individually to express consternation that there weren't any minority-group students in the class. I decided that we needed to talk about those feelings together. I asked: "What is it that you expect any minority student, as a minority, to contribute to the class?" We had been reading texts ranging from narratives written by slaves to sketches of black bourgeois angst. The ideological attitudes of the writers spanned a spectrum from the uncompromising anger of Richard Wright to the genteel humanism of Charles Johnson. Yet the consensus was that any black student, no matter what his or her background, would be able to "help the white students understand the books better," because the black student would have "actually lived" the emotions—if not the exact situations—depicted in the various texts. The texts would resonate with black students, and white students could learn from the vibrations.

This conversation led to the discussion of two issues: my authority, as the only black person in the room, as an interpreter of texts, and whether or not students would take the class if it were taught by a white person. The vast majority of the class said that they wouldn't, even though most teachers on our English faculty include texts by writers of color in their courses. I then asked the students if they felt that I shouldn't teach Henry James (on whom I had done my dissertation) and other white writers. Perhaps out of politeness, they agreed that this was all right, as black Americans "have always had to learn the ways of the dominant culture." And anyway, some said, I had a Ph.D. from a "white" university. I ended the discussion by encouraging my students to think about the study of black literature as an area of scholarship and research just like any other in the discipline of literary studies. After all, I pointed out, we don't demand that only British scholars interpret Thomas Hardy or only women interpret Jane Austen.

But I concluded privately that the issue of authority is a double-edged sword. I know that I will always be expected to have extra insight into black texts—especially texts by black women. A working-class Jewish woman from Brooklyn could become an expert on Shakespeare or Baudelaire, my students seemed to believe, if she mastered the language, the texts, and the critical literature. But they would not grant that a middle-class white man could ever be a trusted authority on Toni Morrison.

The other side of this seeming consensus is that many of my students come to the first class assuming that much black literature is not "literary" in the ways that they learned to define literature in high school: It does not have universal appeal (because it is too immersed in the problems of a particular people) and it is not "beautiful" (because it is too concerned with cruelty and injustice). Although fewer students come to my classes with these preconceptions now than at the beginning of my teaching career in the 1980s (the influence, I suppose, of multiculturalism in the high-school curriculum), a significant number still hold assumptions about the inferiority of black literature.

Because we live in such a racially polarized society, students bring a lot of emotional baggage with them to a black-literature class. Their experiences with black boyfriends or black maids, their perceptions of cliquish black students in their high schools, their impressions of black life gleaned from television sitcoms and MTV or from driving by an infamous Chicago housing project all influence their perception of what African-American literature is about.

My challenge as a teacher is to discern which of the experiences, assumptions, questions, and interpretations that make up the baggage my students bring with them are worth unpacking and analyzing for the educational benefit of the whole class, and which the individual students must deal with in other areas of their lives. At the beginning of my teaching career, I thought that I could begin to change the attitudes bred in American hearts and minds over four hundred years of racial conflict during the course of a dozen conversations about books. I used to set aside a session early in my black-literature classes that I called, to myself, "a rap session." I encouraged the students "to let it all hang out" in a freewheeling conversation in which they could confront and share their own doubts, prejudices, fears, questions, and notions about race. I thought that these rap sessions would allow us to clear the air and then get down to the business of reading texts.

However, I found that emotions came up that I was unprepared to handle: A biracial student exploded in anger over high-school slights that still smarted.

A white student expressed wonder at how much he didn't know about the life of a black maid who had served his family for more than twenty years. The descendant of Virginia slave owners wept guiltily. I often found that I had opened a Pandora's box of emotion, which I would then clumsily try to relate to whatever text had been assigned for the day. But I simply didn't have the wisdom, experience, or professional training to handle the emotions and conflicts over race that students brought to my classroom.

My pedagogical goals are now much more modest: I want the literature to be meaningful to my students. Early in the course we still discuss basic questions such as: "What is race?" "What is art?" "What is culture?" I still encourage my students to become self-aware readers: to examine their emotions, their assumptions, and the way they ask questions. But we never stray far from the texts and the issues raised by the texts themselves. For example, I'll use a student's comments about his relationship with his family's black maid to focus and enrich our discussions of Lutie Johnson's perceptions of her white employers.

I also try to establish a classroom climate in which students can actively question their own biases as well as those of the author and literary critics and other students in the class. I encourage students to feel that they can speak freely without being self-conscious about their lack of knowledge, experience, or political savvy. Merely telling them they are free in this way is not enough, of course. I give them the freedom in various ways. For example, I assign a lot of work to be done in small groups, knowing that students can sometimes be more adventurous in them. Or I might take lines of interpretation that students would not expect from a minority faculty member. For example, I question Ann Petry's relentlessly deterministic depiction of Lutie's life. The author attempts to show that her character's struggle to achieve the American dream is doomed from the start because she is black, female, a mother, and poor. I argue that the problem is not that Lutie does not have choices, but that she makes the wrong choices.

I also share my own ignorance and the evolution of my understanding of the texts we read. When teaching Ralph Ellison's *Invisible Man,* I compare my initial rather confused readings of the book with later readings, when I was more familiar with Ellison's allusions. I didn't grasp the bitter irony in the protagonist's graduation speech to his town's white elite, for instance, until I learned that it was a direct quotation of Booker T. Washington's speech advocating that black Americans abandon the struggle for political enfranchisement.

In addition, I try to convey to students that there are no privileged readings in my class—only readings that are more, or less, interesting than others. And, of course, the texts themselves challenge any preconceptions the students may have about a monolithic black experience in the United States. Readings as varied as James Weldon Johnson's *Autobiography of an Ex-Coloured Man,* Zora Neale Hurston's *Their Eyes Were Watching God,* Charles Johnson's *Middle Passage,* and Jamaica Kincaid's *Lucy* undermine any notion of black consensus and convey to students the rich variety of black literature, aesthetics, and ideologies.

I am always impressed by how brave most of the students who take my classes are. They are eager and willing to have their own world views challenged, changed, and enriched. Many of them have read works by black authors before they take my class—either in other classes or, more often, on their own. They are excited by African-American literature and open to new perspectives on history, social structures, relationships, and their own privileges.

Teaching in a predominantly white college where there is only one other African-American woman on the faculty can be bewildering and lonely: I never feel as conscious of my race as I do when I stand before a class of twenty-five young men and women eager to learn about what it is to be black in America. But my students' enthusiasm and patience sustain me. I always try to meet them wherever they are intellectually, and to guide them to places that they might not have imagined.

I certainly haven't discovered all of the most effective strategies for dealing with the racial dynamics of black-literature classes in predominantly white institutions. But as more and more faculty members of color join the teaching ranks at predominantly white colleges and universities—and as scholars turn more attention to literature by writers from minority groups—we're going to need much more frank discussion about the resulting intellectual and social dynamics than we encounter in our classrooms.

QUESTIONS FOR REACTION AND DISCUSSION

1. What is your response to Garcia's opening anecdote? What expectations do you have about professors based on their race, ethnicity, or gender?
2. What is your experience in taking courses specifically on black writers? Where and when have you taken such courses? If you have not taken one, do you plan to? Why or why not?
3. Garcia suggests that many white students express anxieties about their abilities to understand texts written by minority writers. Do you fear an inability to understand texts written by persons with a different racial or ethnic background than your own? Why or why not?
4. What does Garcia mean by saying that "the issue of authority is a double-edged sword" when it comes to teaching the works of minorities?
5. According to Garcia, what kinds of emotional baggage do students— white, black, or other minorities—bring to classes on African-American literature? What lessons about handling emotional responses in class has Garcia learned through her teaching experience?

QUESTIONS FOR WRITING

1. In paragraph eleven, Garcia suggests that the effects of multiculturalism in the high-school curriculum have resulted in students having fewer negative assumptions about black literature. What assumptions or pre-conceptions do you carry about black literature? Are they positive or negative? How have you formed these assumptions? Write an essay in which you describe your experiences in reading and studying black literature and explain your current sense of black literature as "literary."

2. Garcia explains that in an effort to establish a climate for active discussion in the classroom, she encourages students to speak freely and to work in small groups where students can be more "adventurous." Are these techniques appealing to you? Do you speak up in class discussions? Under what circumstances? Do you find group work an effective way to learn? What experiences have you had in your educational background that have helped you question your own biases? Write an essay in which you describe a class (in any subject) in which you were able to question your own ideas and those of others freely and without self-consciousness. Evaluate what you learned from this class.

3. A central issue that any professor must face is authority. Garcia explains that her students often feel that she has special authority as a black woman to teach black literature. The majority of one of her classes said they would not take a course in black literature taught by a white person. What is your opinion about what establishes a professor's authority? Would you take a course in black literature taught by a white person or a person of another minority background? Why or why not? Write an essay in which you explore your definition of authority for the teacher in the classroom. Give specific details and examples from your own educational experience and reading.

4. In another section, Garcia discusses a student's authority in the classroom. She explains that in a class on "Black Literature in America," students were concerned that there were no minority students to "help the white students understand the books better" because black students would know more about the emotions and experiences of the characters. What is your response to that contention by white students? What does the authority of a student mean to you? Write an essay in which you explore your definition of authority for the student in the classroom.

QUESTIONS FOR FURTHER EXPLORATION

1. Garcia mentions the names of a variety of African-American authors, including Gloria Naylor, Zora Neale Hurston, Frances E. W. Harper, Toni Morrison, W. E. B. DuBois, and Charles Johnson. Have you read

the works of any of these writers? Under what circumstances? Are these writers taught in courses on your campus? Investigate the sources of information available on your campus for courses (catalogues, the Web site, and/or class schedules) and write a brief e-mail message to your classmates in which you explain what courses they might take in order to read and study African-American writers.

2. One of the novels that Garcia routinely teaches is Toni Morrison's *Beloved*. Morrison, who also teaches creative writing at Princeton University, is among America's most distinguished writers of essays. She was the first black woman writer to be awarded the Nobel Prize, which she won in 1993. What do you know about the Nobel Prize in Literature? How many black American writers have won the award? Investigate the Nobel Prize Web site <http://nobelprizes.com> and learn what you can about the Prize—its history, purpose, and why Morrison was awarded the prize. What was the response to Morrison as the winner? Investigate the articles and stories that were written about Morrison at the time by using print indices or Lexis-Nexis Academic Universe <http://web.lexis-nexis.com/universe>. Write a brief report about the Nobel Prize and the reaction of the popular press to Morrison as an award winner.

10

THE VANISHING NATIVE REAPPEARS
IN THE COLLEGE CURRICULUM

*The first Native American to graduate from college in the United
States was Caleb Cheeshateaumuck, an Algonquin Indian, who graduated in 1865 from Harvard College, whose charter provided for the
education of English and Indian youth. As a student at Harvard at that
time, Cheeshateaumuck followed the standard curriculum prescribed
for all students and learned to read and write in Latin and Greek, but
he lived in the Indian College. Higher education for Native Americans
was often a matter of establishing Indian colleges, primarily designed
to Christianize and civilize the Indians in European ways. The history
of American Indians and their experience in higher education is a
troubled one; today less than forty percent of Indians who finish secondary school choose to go to college, and that number represents less
than two percent of the total college population. The presence and absence of American Indians in higher education has become an increasing topic of interest, as has the study of Native American history and
culture. Clara Sue Kidwell is the director of the Native American Studies Program at the University of Oklahoma. Kidwell, a member of the
Choctaw/Chippewa tribes, has taught at several colleges and universities and has also served as associate director of the National Museum
of the American Indian, Smithsonian Institution. Kidwell teaches
courses on the history of Native Americans and on Indian philosophy
and medicine. The article printed here is from* Change: The Magazine
of Higher Learning, *which is under the editorial leadership of the
American Association for Higher Education, an organization of over
nine thousand college and university faculty members and administrators. Kidwell's essay discusses the history of Native American studies
programs and the current conflicts and problems.*

QUESTIONS FOR READING

1. What do you know about programs in Native American Studies?
2. What knowledge do you have of American Indians in higher education?
3. Why do you think Kidwell calls the native "vanishing" in her title?

CLARA SUE KIDWELL

THE VANISHING NATIVE REAPPEARS IN THE COLLEGE CURRICULUM

Change *(March/April 1991, pp. 19–23)*

In the early 1970s, Native American or American Indian studies programs first appeared at numerous colleges and universities throughout the country. Some programs, such as the one at the University of Minnesota, were established through negotiation between student groups and university administrators. Minnesota, which started a full-fledged American Indian Studies Department in 1970 with strong administrative support, offered a bachelor's degree by 1974. Its curriculum, which included courses in two Indian languages, was highly regarded by leaders of the Minnesota Chippewa tribe.

Other programs evolved out of active student protest and confrontation. The University of California at Berkeley was the scene of a student strike inspired in part by the abrupt cancellation of a class that was to have been offered by African-American activist Stokely Carmichael. In response to the strike and student demands for academic programs, the faculty senate passed a resolution calling for the creation of an Ethnic Studies department, which included a Native American studies program. By 1974, Berkeley's program also offered a bachelor's degree and had a complement of eight faculty members.

A 1978 survey of Indian studies programs conducted for the Western Interstate Commission for Higher Education garnered one hundred responses out of a mailing to one hundred seventy institutions. The programs surveyed ranged in scope from one or two courses taught in history, anthropology, or education departments, and perhaps a counselor with some special responsibility for Indian student concerns, to full-fledged departments with their own faculty and degree programs such as the American Indian Studies Department at Minnesota.

THE POLITICS

Ethnic studies curricula were very much a product of the rapid growth of colleges and universities fueled by federal funding for higher education throughout the early 1960s. The choice of Native American Studies as a program name often reflected a political statement as people sought to disassociate themselves from the idea that they had been discovered by Columbus and named Indians by accident. Both terms, Native American and American Indian, of course subsume a wide diversity of different tribal names by which people identify themselves. For purposes of this article, the terms are used interchangeably.

The civil rights movement of the mid- and late-1960s raised issues of equal access and affirmative action in higher education. The political activism spawned by U.S. involvement in the Vietnam War increased sensitivity to racism. The massacre of Vietnam villagers at My Lai was compared, not without reason, with the massacre of Cheyenne families at Sand Creek in 1861, or of Big Foot's band of Sioux at Wounded Knee in 1890.

CHANGING FORTUNES

Any academic program that springs from an ostensibly political agenda is bound to be suspect in the supposedly objective and dispassionate halls of academe. That suspicion, combined with the lack of academic sophistication of many faculty members who were hastily recruited from the ranks of activists to teach, undermined the stability of many programs. By the early 1980s, many of the programs that had begun with such optimism and potential promise ten years earlier had shrunk considerably or disappeared entirely. At Minnesota, the American Indian Studies Department was dismantled after a period of internal turmoil, and its faculty members were distributed throughout other departments. At the University of California at Davis, the Native American Studies degree program was suspended for a time when faculty retirements seemed to threaten the department's stability.

Given the highly variable definitions of what constitutes a Native American or American Indian studies program, it is difficult to say how many have actually existed over time. One measure of their shifting fortunes, however, is found in two studies—one the survey of 100 programs in 1976–77, and the other a survey of 107 institutions conducted in 1980–81 by the American Indian Culture and Research Center at UCLA. The overlap between the two surveys was only fifty-seven institutions, from which we can infer that although new programs had emerged, many programs that existed in 1976–77 had changed or disappeared by 1981.

INCREASING POPULATION

As the historical vagaries of federal policy have affected the health, well-being, and political status of Indian tribes, so the vagaries of academic politics have affected Indian studies programs. When they began, they were generally suspected of being simply political advocacy organizations for Indian causes. By the early 1980s, however, the civil rights movement had given rise to affirmative action programs, and colleges began to be concerned about their recruitment policies. In 1982, Alexander Astin et al. published an influential study, *Minorities in Higher Education* (San Francisco: Jossey-Bass, 1982), and college administrators, confronted with appalling statistics on minority attrition rates, saw Indian studies programs as mechanisms to recruit and retain American Indian students.

The driving political force in the late 1980s became demography and American competitiveness in a global economy. Another influential report, *One Third of a Nation,* appeared in 1988. It projected that, by the year 2000, a third of the U.S. population will be composed of members of minority groups—Asian, African-American, Hispanic, and American Indian. The report brought home to politicians the fact that, unless the U.S. population's growing diversity is matched by those groups' participation in higher education, America's competitiveness in the world economy will suffer.

Although institutions of higher education are often notoriously slow to respond to social change, they have become acutely aware of the impact of demography in the age distribution of the American population, as well as its complexion. The traditional college-age cohort (eighteen to twenty-four) is shrinking progressively, and because of differences in birth rates, more of it is made up of members of ethnic minorities, who have traditionally attended college at lower rates than their white counterparts.

DIVERSIFYING THE CURRICULUM

The politics of demography have brought ethnic studies programs, including Native American studies, back into the academic spotlight. Although critics such as Alan Bloom, in *The Closing of the American Mind,* have castigated the politicization of knowledge by minority groups, college and universities throughout the country have joined the movement to diversify their curricula to match the growing diversity of their student bodies. The loose cannon of curriculum reform is rattling through many college classrooms.

One approach to diversity has been to require an ethnic studies or non-European culture class for graduation. Variants of this approach have been implemented at the University of Minnesota, the University of Wisconsin, Penn State University, and the University of California at Santa Cruz and Santa Barbara, to name only a few institutions. At San Francisco State University, selected courses from the Ethnic Studies Department, including some from American Indian studies, can fulfill the ethnic studies graduation requirement.

At UCLA, the effort is a voluntary one, as faculty are being encouraged to integrate ethnic and women's studies scholarship into their existing courses. At Stanford University, in a move perceived by some as an outright attack on the canon, the faculty senate voted to broaden the existing Western culture humanities requirement into a "Cultures, Ideas, and Values" requirement. The change gives individual instructors much greater latitude in selecting readings that deal with class, ethnicity, and gender. It may now be possible for N. Scott Momaday's *House Made of Dawn* to take its place beside Nathaniel Hawthorne's *House of the Seven Gables* in discussions of American literature.

The University of California at Berkeley, considered itself—as always—a leader in educational innovation, has taken yet another approach to the issue of curriculum diversity. In a long process marked by sometimes heated debate, the faculty senate approved establishing a new graduation requirement in American cultures. Courses that satisfy this requirement must be "integrative and comparative and address theoretical and analytical issues relevant to understanding race, culture, and ethnicity in American history and society." They must also deal with at least three of five major ethnic groups—African-Americans, American Indians, Asian-Americans, Chicano/Latinos, and European Americans.

Rather than simply using existing courses, or grafting new material onto them, the American Cultures requirement challenges faculty members to develop entirely new courses. Since few have any real expertise in scholarship on American Indians, the Native American Studies program—its library and its faculty—constitutes an important resource for the campus. As requirements are implemented at colleges and universities throughout the country, enrollments in courses dealing with American Indian history and culture will increase, and, at least in theory, the resources of programs offering those courses should also increase.

TOO POPULAR?

Although it may be true that Native American or American Indian studies programs will benefit from implementing new requirements, there is a hidden hazard. Courses that fulfill graduation requirements often become service courses for large groups of students who have little or no intrinsic interest in the subject matter. They consume the time and energy of faculty to the disadvantage of program development, and unless the institution commits additional money for them, they shift programmatic resources and emphasis away from the core curriculum. Native American studies programs may benefit from increased enrollments, and since numbers usually drive budgets, they may gain additional resources. However, they face the danger of being relegated to the status of service units at a time when some are finally beginning to achieve a measure of academic respectability.

COMPETING DEMANDS AND BURNOUT

The identity crisis of Native American studies has been an ongoing one. Outsiders' perceptions of the program and their usefulness have changed over time as social and political change has impinged on colleges and universities. Insiders' perceptions, those of American Indian faculty and students, have also changed.

Initially, Indian students demanded "relevance" of education to their real-life situations. Students expected faculty members to be role models, community activists, personal counselors, sources of student loans, skillful teachers, and critics of existing academic disciplines such as history and anthropology. Some wanted knowledge that would prepare them for professional careers in

Indian communities so they could provide needed services, while others wanted instruction in traditional practices and values in order to affirm their own identities. Few had college-educated parents or relatives who could give them any idea of what college education was like. Today, Indian students are more likely to know someone who has been to college and are likely to see college as a steppingstone to a graduate degree and a professional career. Their expectations seem to be more realistic.

Another constituency, non-Indian students, flocked to classes in the early 1970s, many of them seeking truth and beauty through the Indian way of life and expecting easy enlightenment instead of intellectual rigor. Although their numbers justified the existence of the programs in the beginning, many dropped away when courses proved to be demanding in terms of reading and writing assignments. There has, however, been a relatively consistent core of genuine intellectual interest in American Indian topics among non-Indian students. Although enrollments might have declined somewhat, student interest seems much more serious.

Yet another audience, faculty members in other departments, expected Indian faculty members, and sometimes students, to serve on committees, give guest lectures on Indian topics in other classes, conduct research, and publish path-breaking studies from new perspectives (without, however, getting too far from the bounds of traditional scholarship). Administrators wanted Indian studies programs as some tangible demonstration of their institution's sensitivity to large societal concerns.

Indian community leaders wanted Indian faculty members to give expert advice, free consultation, and articulate Indian causes to non-Indians. Many, however, were highly suspicious of any hint of intellectual elitism in Indian college students or faculty, and Indian students who did return to their home reservations or Indian communities were often told that the knowledge they had gained at college was not practical or applicable to community needs. Today, a generation of Indian college graduates has begun to change the perceptions of tribal leaders about the value of a college education.

Should Indian studies programs be concerned with professional skills or cultural values? Should they teach Indian students how to be Indian, or should they sensitize non-Indian students to Indian concerns? Should faculty man the barricades or blockade themselves in the libraries and do research? Should programs offer courses that challenge stereotypes and criticize past scholarship and thus risk rapid demise, or should they adapt as quickly as possible to the models of existing academic disciplines in order to survive? Or can they do all these things at once?

It is clear that American Indian programs with any academic component were, in the early 1970s and are still to a remarkable degree today, faced with a number of competing and sometimes contradictory demands. The rate of faculty burnout has been high and program stability often uncertain, and, despite the existence of these programs, the numbers of American Indian college students have not increased dramatically over the past decade. In fact, in absolute numbers, the college enrollment of Indians peaked at about 87,700 in 1982 and declined to about 83,000 in 1984. Although the percentage of Indians completing four years or more of college doubled from 1970 to 1980 (from twenty-two percent to fifty-five percent), the gap in the rate between Indians and whites actually increased.

As sociologist and demographer C. Matthew Snipp notes in his recent book, *American Indians: The First of This Land* (Russell Sage Foundation, 1989), "the percentage of the American Indian population with advanced education grew during the 1970s, but it expanded less than the percentage of the white population pursuing college educations." Nevertheless, if one cannot point to Indian studies programs as successfully raising Indian participation in college education to the same level as that of whites, one can point to the significant increase in the number of students completing degrees and wonder whether it would have been that great if such programs did not exist.

THE FUTURE

As each new political issue has arisen—civil rights and equal access in the 1960s, social protest and student antiwar activism in the 1970s, affirmative action programs in the 1980s, economic competitiveness and the education of the workforce in the 1990s—Indian studies programs have had to respond. Faculties have had to juggle competing demands while struggling to achieve the intellectual respectability necessary to survive in the academic establishment. Remarkably, many Indian faculty members have published and not perished; they have received tenure. Their numbers are still very small, however.

According to statistics compiled by the National Research Council, the number of doctoral degrees awarded to American Indians reached a high of 116 in 1987, but declined to 99 in 1988. A directory compiled by the Indian studies program at the University of Wisconsin at Milwaukee in 1985 listed only 134 people with academic or professional doctorates (including Juris Doctore degrees). The list is admittedly incomplete since it depended upon self-identification or nomination. Because of that fact, however, the individuals on it actively identified themselves as Indians and took initiative to be included, rather than simply checking a box on a census form.

The small number of American Indians with the credentials to teach in academic institutions does not bode well for the future expansion of Indian studies programs. Even if the demand for courses increases as more institutions establish so-called "cultural diversity requirements" for graduation, it will be very difficult to find qualified American Indian faculty to staff their programs. Institutions must find ways of encouraging Indian students to pursue graduate degrees and college teaching careers, such as giving Indian faculty members special support in their efforts to recruit students and serve as role models for them. Some release time from teaching, or special assistance to meet the demands of research, or substitution of service to an Indian community for service to the university would be important.

Despite political vagaries and academic politics, American Indian and Native American studies programs are here to stay, partly because they have helped to bring Indians out of the anthropology and history texts and into the classrooms as students and faculty members, and also because they have been among the forces that have inspired or compelled institutions to change.

As interviews with Native American students attest, the existence of programs or departments has been crucial to their success. Students need to feel they can be part of the institution and that it is in some way responsive to their interests. At Berkeley, for instance, students have gotten financial support from the administration to hold colloquia on issues of American Indian religious freedom. Some have served on campus committees to consider whether Indian remains and funerary objects in the anthropology museum should be returned to Indian communities. This kind of student activism serves to raise important ethical and cultural issues that probably would not appear otherwise—issues that are pertinent to the larger concerns of academic freedom and ethics in research. Faculty and administrators may try to dismiss Indian remains as a political issue, but they must face the fact that these issues are very much a part of the intellectual life of the institution. They are, indeed, part of what intellectual diversity is all about.

As American Indians still exist in society as identifiable cultural groups despite change and adaptation, so Indian studies programs will continue to survive through adaptation to the changing political environment of higher education. Institutions where they exist will benefit from the rich cultural heritages and unique perspectives that Indian students and faculty represent.

QUESTIONS FOR REACTION AND DISCUSSION

1. What is the difference between the terms "Native American" and "American Indian"? What is the effect of Kidwell's usage in this article?
2. What prompted the origins of Native American Studies programs? Why did they shrink in the 1980s? What has prompted the revival of interest?
3. Why and how has the movement toward multiculturalism influenced the development of new Native American Studies programs?
4. What does Kidwell mean when she suggests that Native American Studies has had an ongoing identity crisis?

QUESTIONS FOR WRITING

1. Unlike other minority studies programs, those in Native American have often carried the expectation of providing professional training for careers in Indian communities. Kidwell asks, "Should Indian Studies programs be concerned with professional skills or cultural values?" What is your view on this topic? Is there a special case to be made for

Native American Studies that one would not make for another ethnic studies program? Why or why not? Write an essay in which you explain what you think should be the purpose of a Native American Studies program.

2. To what degree are you familiar with Native American history and culture? If you were a student member on a committee to design an introductory course for your campus, what would you include? With a small group of other students, discuss what you would want to learn. Write a formal proposal for such a course, including the purpose, goals, topics for study, and a reading list.

3. A question that Kidwell asks is whether Indian Studies programs should "sensitize non-Indian students to Indian concerns." Recognizing that there may be several purposes to accomplish for Native American Studies programs, write an essay in which you support or reject the idea that a central purpose should be to teach non-Indians about Native American history and culture. Use examples from your own educational experience and your reading.

QUESTIONS FOR FURTHER EXPLORATION

1. Does your campus have a Native American Studies program? If so, investigate the purpose of the program, course offerings, and the numbers of faculty members and students involved. You can access the Native American Studies program at the University of Oklahoma <http://www.ou.edu/cas/nas> to learn about the program Kidwell directs. Research the number and diversity of Native American Studies programs in the United States and Canada by accessing a guide to the programs on a Web site maintained by the Association for the Study of American Literatures <http://www.richmond.edu/faculty/ASAIL/guide/guide.html>. Investigate some of the programs you find listed there and compare them with the program on your campus (if you have one) or with one another. What commonalities are there? What differences? Write a brief summary of your findings and present them to your classmates.

2. Investigate the history of Native Americans in higher education. What were the first Indian colleges like? What colleges and universities established mission statements that included Indians? You might, for example, investigate Dartmouth College and the University of Tulsa, both established first as Indian schools. What is the situation for Indians today in higher education? How do some tribes view higher education? How many Indians attend college and what is the relationship between that number and the total college-age Indian population? Create an annotated list of resources and write a brief report of your findings for your classmates.

II

PLURIBUS & UNUM:
THE QUEST FOR COMMUNITY
AMID DIVERSITY

Carlos E. Cortés is a professor of history at the University of California, Riverside, where he teaches courses in Latin American and Chicano history, as well as in the history of the mass media. Deeply interested in multicultural education, Cortés has published several books on education reform, including Understanding You and Them. *He has served as a consultant for many government agencies, school districts, and universities, and was the central presenter in a widely used education training video, "Diversity in the Classroom." The article printed here was first published in* Change: The Magazine of Higher Learning, *which is under the editorial leadership of the American Association for Higher Education, an organization of over nine thousand college and university faculty members and administrators. As an editor of three book series on Hispanic American culture and literature, Cortés is keenly interested in the Hispanic presence in American culture. But as he explains in this essay, he is an "E Pluribus Unum Multiculturalist."*

QUESTIONS FOR READING

1. The Latin phrase "E Pluribus Unum" ("from many, one") appears on the Great Seal of the United States. What do you infer from the rewording of this phrase in the title of this essay?
2. Is it possible to have "community amid diversity"? Under what circumstances?

CARLOS E. CORTÉS

PLURIBUS & UNUM: THE QUEST FOR COMMUNITY AMID DIVERSITY

Change *(September/October 1991, pp. 9–13)*

"Life is like a game of cards. The hand that is dealt you is determinism; the way you play it is free will." So said India's Nehru. Ethnic diversity comprises a critical aspect of America's future, including the future of our nation's colleges and universities. According to a 1989 Census Bureau projection, during the next four decades (1900–2030), the white population of the United States will grow by about 25 percent. During that same 40-year period, the African-American population will increase by 68 percent, the Asian-American, Pacific Island-American, and American Indian populations will grow by 79 percent, and the Latino or Hispanic population of the United States will leap by 187 percent. That's determinism!

The Population Reference Bureau has projected that, by the year 2080, the United States of America may well be twenty-four percent Latino, fifteen percent African-American, and twelve percent Asian-American—more than half of the nation's population. Even recognizing that intermarriage complicates most racial and ethnic statistics and that all projections are merely informed guesswork, the United States has obviously reached merely the diversity take-off stage. What we now call "ethnic diversity" may well be viewed as relative homogeneity from a twenty-first century perspective.

Which brings me to the second part of Nehru's wise adage. While this Diversity Revolution provides a major element of our nation's future determinism, the way that we play it involves a great degree of free will.

Colleges and universities face two main questions in addressing the Diversity Revolution. First, how can they help American society make the best of these inevitable demographic changes? Second, how can they deal more effectively with campus diversity in the quest for better institutional climate and community?

I would like to suggest one constructive response to both questions—Multiculturalism, the omnipresent, often-celebrated, often-excoriated "M" word. Barbara Tuchman once wrote: "Bias is only misleading when it is concealed." So let me unconceal my bias. I am a Multiculturalist. However, since so many scholars and pundits have been defining, redefining, and distorting this concept, and since not all Multiculturalists think alike, I need to further situate myself in the Multiculturalist cosmos.

I am an E Pluribus Unum (EPU) Multiculturalist. That is, I see the Diversity Revolution's opportunities and challenges in terms of the historical American Pluribus-Unum balancing act described incisively by R. Freeman Butts in *The Revival of Civic Learning.* Such Pluribus values as freedom, individualism, and diversity live in constant and inevitable tension with such Unum values as authority, conformity, and commonality. Constructive EPU Multiculturalism involves responding thoughtfully to both powerful Pluribus and necessary Unum imperatives, as well as carefully setting limits to Pluribus and to Unum when they become poisonous to climate and destructive to community.

The United States has been involved in this Pluribus-Unum balancing act since its inception. That's what federalism and the separation of powers are all about. That's what much of the Constitution, myriad laws, and many Supreme Court decisions have addressed. But the Diversity Revolution has added a major new dimension to the Pluribus-Unum relationship.

For colleges and universities, the Diversity Revolution has had Pluribus-Unum demographic and psychological ramifications for campus climate. Demographically, it has expanded the presence of women and persons of nonwhite backgrounds. Psychologically, it has led to a "revolution of rising expectations" that colleges and universities should not only welcome diversity, but also become more responsive to increasingly voiced ethnic and women's perspectives and concerns.

At one time happy just to be admitted to the higher education party, minorities and women now rightfully want a larger role in its planning and implementation. The result has been inevitable disagreements and ultimately a basic rethinking of the role and operation of higher education. While this diversity-impelled reconsideration of the college as an educational community has affected many areas of campus life, I will focus on the implications of four critical Pluribus-Unum areas for college climate:

1. Multicultural curricular reform,
2. Ethnic isolation and multicultural integration,
3. Language and accent diversity, and
4. Free speech and campus codes of conduct.

MULTICULTURAL CURRICULAR REFORM

The process of multicultural curricular reform provides the cornerstone for EPU campus climate. Beginning in the 1960s, spurred by the civil rights movement and the growing minority presence on college campuses, the push came for more curricular Pluribus—the establishment of minority content courses and ethnic studies programs, a call paralleled in the area of women's studies. Supporters of these Pluribus efforts saw such courses and programs as the most viable avenues for providing alternative scholarly interpretations and pedagogical perspectives seldom found in the traditional college curriculum. Although success has varied—some ethnic and women's studies programs have flourished, while others have collapsed—the new knowledge, insights, critical questions, and interpretative challenges generated by these scholarly and pedagogical movements have fueled the current second wave of multicultural reform.

While generally still supporting separate ethnic and women's studies programs as important loci of teaching and research about gender and ethnicity, EPU Multiculturalists no longer accept the sufficiency of Pluribus isolationist specialization. Rather, they have drawn upon new multicultural knowledge and insights to rethink the very bases of mainstream scholarship and to work toward a more capacious, future-oriented Unum curricular climate.

This curricular transformation has taken many forms: the establishment of required world civilization courses (incorporating, not defrocking, Western civilization); the institution of diversity-oriented course graduation requirements; and the greater integration of multicultural perspectives into mainstream courses in such areas as American history, literature, and society. In short, EPU Multiculturalists have championed the transformation of the Unum college curriculum to expose all students to national and world Pluribus in order to help better prepare them for the guaranteed future of ethnic diversity and global interdependence. For the Macbeths of traditionalist curricular Unum, Birnam wood, safely marginalized in the 1960s and 70s, has come to high Dunsinane hill.

This multicultural transformation of curricular Unum is no clash between liberal, illiberal, and non-illiberal educators, no joust between accused closers and self-anointed openers of the American mind—as satisfyingly simplistic and journalistically marketable as these polarizing dichotomies may be. Highly publicized curricular debates and student demonstrations at a few major universities have dominated media attention. Yet, on most campuses such curricular changes have occurred not because of student protest or the imposition of supposed "political correctness" on spineless colleagues by campus radicals.

Curricular change has generally come through the serious, contemplative implementation of a new multicultural educational vision based on the desire to help students more effectively engage the future, in particular, the opportunities and challenges of the Diversity Revolution as well as growing global interdependence. Even American business in-service education has gone multicultural—witness the rapid rise of company-instituted diversity training—while some of K-12 education has progressed multiculturally far beyond colleges and universities. In carrying out such reforms, multicultural reformers have followed Charles Kettering's injunction: "My interest is in the future because I am going to spend the rest of my life there."

Overwhelmingly, this curricular reform has involved no rejection of American Unum, no repudiation of Western civilization, no adoption of valueless, nonjudgmental relativism. Rather, it has involved a serious recasting of the meaning of American Unum as a more Pluribus concept that recognizes the importance and value of engaging and considering previously marginalized voices and perspectives. In the words of Arnita Jones, executive secretary of the Organization of American Historians, Multiculturalism is "not a problem. It's a wonderful opportunity to bring some excellent new scholarship to all levels of education." Multicultural reform-oriented college campuses have merely been heeding the advice of that old radical, Queen Victoria, when she admonished her followers: "Change must be accepted . . . when it can no longer be resisted."

ETHNIC ISOLATION AND MULTICULTURAL INTEGRATION

While the process of multicultural curricular reform has been one major influence on campus climate, it has been accomplished by other Pluribus-Unum issues, including ethnic isolation and multicultural integration. Colleges and universities have historically supported the right of *temporary* Pluribus group isolationism, emerging from the desire of people to spend time with others of shared concerns and interests.

Such isolationism has taken many forms. It encompasses students who feel like being around those of the same gender in sororities and fraternities. It involves persons who want to worship a deity together, usually within an isolationist religious setting, or to socialize with persons who share the same religious beliefs, like a Hillel or a Newman Club. It includes students who gather around common interests like a school newspaper, common pursuits like a football team, common pleasures like a chess club, or common social goals like working in a K-12 outreach tutorial program. And, or course, those groupings may be based on race, ethnicity, and culture, like African-American, Latino, American Indian, Asian-American, Italian-American, Arab-American, or Polish-American student associations, in which people gather periodically in ethnic comfort zones of shared experiences, identities, and concerns.

Yet some campus denizens and off-campus critics, who accept, support, or even participate in other types of Pluribus isolationism without labeling them as "Balkanization" or "tribalism," become apoplectic about isolationism, no matter how transitory, involving race or ethnicity. When students, staff, or faculty of visibly similar ethnic appearance eat together in school cafeterias, sit together in classrooms, or, most terrifyingly, form organizations, such alarmist critics proclaim this as indisputable evidence of a collapsing Unum, even a disintegrating society.

But since all of us, at various times and places, function as Pluribus isolationists—even professors gather in their own disciplinary isolationism in department meetings or scholarly conventions—then there is nothing *intrinsically* wrong with temporary isolationism, even when based on race and ethnicity. The Unum problem for campus climate and, likewise, for society, occurs when racial, ethnic, cultural, religious, gender, political, disciplinary, or any other type of isolationism—what The Carnegie Foundation for the Advancement of Teaching report, *Campus Life: In Search of Community,* has called, "little loyalties"—becomes an overly encompassing element of one's life. Isolationism becomes injurious to a sense of campus community when people decide that only their groups matter, when they lose (or fail to develop) concern and consideration for other individuals, other groups, the campus at large, and society as a whole.

The danger of Pluribus isolationism, then, lies not in its unavoidable existence, but in its avoidable extremism. The challenge for college campuses is to create a climate in which temporary Pluribus isolationism and continuous Unum integration operate in a mutually constructive fashion.

LANGUAGE AND ACCENT DIVERSITY

Related to the isolation-integration issue is the growing controversy over foreign languages and accents. Bilingual students, staff, and faculty, many of whom speak English as a second language, are increasing on college campuses. While necessarily using English throughout most of their campus life, many bilingual speakers enjoy moments of non-English conversational respite from the demanding labor of listening to and speaking English. During these intervals they can relax by speaking their strongest language, a relief from the stresses and strains of operating continuously in a sometimes wearying "foreign-language" English environment.

Such actions are as natural and American as apple pie. When Americans run into each other in a foreign country, even if they speak that nation's language, they normally switch to English. Why? Because it is easier and more comfortable as well as emotionally relaxing and cognitively rejuvenating after hours of speaking and hearing the foreign language. Why shouldn't the same occur for English-as-a-second-language speakers on college campuses? Yet participants in such Pluribus speech behavior, particularly college employees, have become targets of extremist Unum criticism.

Now the U. S. Supreme Court has pushed the language issue one step further into the area of accents. In 1990, the Court let stand a Ninth Circuit Court of Appeals ruling in the case of *Fragante v. the Honolulu Department of Motor Vehicles.* A Filipino immigrant, Manuel Fragante had been denied a position with the Department not because of his command of English, which he had already demonstrated on the written examination, but on the grounds that his accent would restrict his ability to deal with the public. The Supreme Court upheld the Department, ruling that such discrimination is acceptable if an accent "interferes materially" with the ability to perform a job. (In the meantime, Fragante was hired by the state of Hawaii for a position in which he conducted telephone surveys—in English.)

Of course, the Court did not establish guidelines for determining when an accent "interferes materially" with job performance or what accents are acceptable or unacceptable for a particular endeavor. Did Henry Kissinger's thick accent "interfere materially" with his ability to teach history or serve as Secretary of State? *Everybody* speaks with an accent—just listen to a conversation between an American, a Jamaican, and a Kenyan, or throw in a couple of people from England or India. They all speak English, but each will notice the others' accents.

However, I don't want to trivialize the accent issue. I have had students—mainly immigrant and refugee students—whose accents severely impeded their ability to communicate orally and probably rendered them less able to perform certain jobs where oral communication was important. Moreover, American universities are currently experiencing a sharp rise in student dissatisfaction with some foreign-born professors and teaching assistants—particularly in such areas as mathematics and the sciences—because of their accents and limited ability in oral English.

Such complaints raise perplexing Pluribus-Unum issues. Students have an Unum right to take courses from professors whose English they can understand, but professors also have a Pluribus right not to be victimized by students who simply don't like their accents. The *Fragante* case has added a new legal twist to this Pluribus-Unum issue, with serious implications for multicultural campus climate. In what respects do professorial accents actually "interfere materially" with student opportunities to learn? Or in what respects do some student complaints simply reflect "accentism," plain old Unum anti-accent nativist bigotry (maybe we should call it "AC"—accent correctness)?

FREE SPEECH AND CAMPUS CODES OF CONDUCT

This brings us inevitably to the most controversial current Pluribus-Unum issue spawned by the Diversity Revolution—the balancing of the Pluribus value of free speech and the Unum value of creating a campus climate of civility, in which people of diverse backgrounds can flourish. Racist, sexist, anti-religious, and homophobic incidents have hypertrophied in recent years—not only on college campuses, but also in society at large. How should colleges respond to these reprehensible acts, which poison campus climate and threaten campus community?

Some responses have increased polarization. On the one hand has come rising petulance by some students and faculty, who appear to be engaged in a never-ending search for statements and acts that they somehow can construe as racist, sexist, or other kinds of "ist." Moreover, some campuses have instituted ill-conceived speech codes that have reached ludicrous extremes of attempting to micro-manage the "unacceptable." Such actions have had the unfortunate side effect of trivializing the critical issue of continuing campus and societal bigotry, while at the same time casting a pall on the entire higher educational struggle against prejudice and for multicultural understanding: witness the growing charges of supposed "political correctness" reigns of terror.

At the other extreme stand the anti-PC demonologists, who have etched minicareers of modern academic witch-hunting, even branding the scarlet PC on moderate multiculturalist scholarly or curricular initiatives and reforms.

Despite their self-righteous claims to being champions of societal Unum through unfettered Pluribus speech (provided, of course, that it is in English), they further polarize campus climate by disregarding variations in ethnic, gender, or multicultural perspectives.

As the *Los Angeles Times* pointed out in a May 13, 1991, editorial on PC, "the label is often misused, for example, as the new acceptable way to denigrate laudable and necessary attempts to make the college curriculum inclusive of the history and achievements of women and minorities." Even the 1991 *Random House Webster's College Dictionary* has been accused of being PC because it has taken such steps as indicating that certain derogatory terms may be offensive. In truth, professional anti-PCers have personified H. L. Mencken's warning that "criticism is prejudice made plausible."

Caught in the middle, college administrators try to contend with the extremes of insult-hunters and anti-multiculturalism demagogues, as well as with the wearying expressions of individual hypersensitivity and the appalling expressions of continuing racism, sexism, and homophobia. But the issues are not simple.

Should campus free speech reign supreme as a Pluribus absolute? (Remember, the First Amendment has long been limited by libel, slander, and defamation laws.) Or should colleges take careful, limited, selective actions to restrict certain kinds of Pluribus expression that erode the Unum civility of campus climate by making some institutions unwelcome for certain groups of students? These EPU administrative dilemmas defy the types of facile answers currently colliding in the rhetorical arena.

Aesop once warned: "Beware lest you lose the substance by grasping at the shadow." The sound and fury over such overblown, media-hyped topics as political correctness have obscured the larger, deeper, more significant diversity-related issues facing higher education: the creation of a better E Pluribus Unum campus climate and the role that colleges and universities can play in contributing to our students' and our nation's successful response to the Diversity Revolution.

The challenge of building campus community is a multicultural society involves balancing Pluribus and Unum imperatives, avoiding Pluribus and Unum extremism, and rejecting the prophets of polarization. For the complex dilemmas raised by the Diversity Revolution, there are no simple solutions. However, as Einstein pointed out, "the formulation of a problem is often more essential than its solution."

By providing a framework for weighing and responding to both Pluribus and Unum as basic, sometimes conflicting values of our society, EPU Multiculturalism can help colleges and universities reformulate, clarify, and thereby more effectively address these perplexing issues. Moreover, it also provides an educational vision for better preparing college students to participate more constructively in what will inevitably be a multicultural future.

QUESTIONS FOR REACTION AND DISCUSSION

1. What is the effect of the statistical information Cortés offers in the introduction to his essay? Were you surprised by the projections? Why or why not?
2. What, in your own words, does Cortés mean when he describes himself as an "E Pluribus Unum (EPU) Multiculturalist"?
3. What does he mean by the Diversity Revolution? What have been the implications for college campuses?
4. What is the "second wave of multicultural reform"? What evidence is there of such a second wave on your campus?
5. What is the tension between ethnic isolation and the overall campus climate?
6. What are the conflicts that arise because of language and accent diversity among students and professors?
7. Why are free speech and campus codes of conduct the most controversial issue in the Diversity Revolution?

QUESTIONS FOR WRITING

1. Cortés suggests that most campuses have already experienced a curricular transformation along the lines of what he refers to as "EPU Multiculturalism." In paragraph eleven, he suggests some of the ways this transformation has been accomplished. What is the situation on your campus? Do any of these transformations describe what you observe when you study your curriculum? Write an essay in which you defend or reject the statement that your college curriculum has been influenced by EPU Multiculturalism.
2. As anyone visiting a college campus knows, students congregate according to common interests and pursuits. Cortés suggests that these are temporary groupings, that the isolationism is not harmful unless it becomes ingrained into campus life. What is the climate like on your campus? Do you think that the groups that have formed are isolationist and extreme? Why or why not? Write an essay in which you describe the climate on your campus and suggest ways in which "Pluribus isolationism and continuous Unum integration" might be achieved.
3. Among the most difficult issues for colleges and universities to handle today is what Cortés refers to as free speech and campus codes of conduct. Does your campus have a code of conduct? Investigate current policies on your campus. Have there been incidents of problems with the code on your campus? Why or why not? Write an essay in which you summarize the code of conduct for your campus and discuss the implications for students and faculty members.

4. What is your understanding of the often-used phrase "politically correct"? Cortés suggests that many commentators have used this phrase to trivialize efforts by colleges and universities to overcome prejudice and strengthen multicultural understanding. Investigate some recent examples of free speech conflicts on college campuses and write an essay in the form of an editorial for your campus newspaper in which you explain your position on how the term "political correctness" has affected free speech on campuses.

QUESTIONS FOR FURTHER EXPLORATION

1. The phrase "E Pluribus Unum," which is taken from the poem "Moretum" attributed to the ancient Latin poet Vergil, was not the first choice for the motto for the Seal of the United States. Benjamin Franklin, a member of the committee formed to prepare a seal on July 4, 1776, favored "Rebellion to Tyrants Is Obedience to God." Investigate the circumstances for the choice of this motto. What is the symbolic power that it has carried for the debate over multiculturalism in the last decade? Write an essay in which you comment on the history of the motto and its relevance for education today.

2. Does your campus have a Latino or Hispanic Studies program? If so, investigate the purpose of the program, course offerings, and the numbers of faculty members and students involved. Research the number of Hispanic Studies programs in the United States and Canada by accessing the César E. Chávez Instructional Center in Interdisciplinary Chicana and Chicano Studies at the University of California, Los Angeles <http://www.sscnet.ucla.edu/chavez>. Investigate this Web site and follow links to other programs, such as CLNet <http://latino.sscnet.ucla.edu>. Investigate some of the programs you find listed there and compare them with the program on your campus (if you have one) or with one another. What commonalities are there? What differences? Write a brief summary of your findings and present them to your classmates.

3. Closely connected with efforts to make the college curriculum more representative of the range of cultural backgrounds of students and faculty are concerns about language and accent diversity, and while Cortés raises this issue, he does not offer specific solutions for how campuses can deal with the sometimes daunting language gaps that exist between professors and students. How many languages are spoken on your campus? How does your campus deal with students for whom English is not a first language? What services, classes, or programs does your campus offer to nonnative speakers of English? Is your campus working to close what Cortés calls the isolation-integration problem for language? Investigate the ways in which your campus handles students who need assistance with learning the English language and write a report for your class.

SUGGESTIONS FOR FURTHER READING, THINKING, AND WRITING

1. E. D. Hirsch's thesis that there is a core of knowledge that all Americans should know was a major factor in launching a national debate on what constitutes an appropriate curriculum. As many writers in this section have demonstrated, that thesis provoked an immediate challenge by educators who regarded themselves as multiculturalists. Compare and contrast the different definitions of what constitutes literacy within a diverse society among the writers in this section.

2. In *Culture of Intolerance: Chauvinism, Class, and Racism in the United States*, Mark Nathan Cohen suggests that "The media bombard people with messages about being number one, as if nothing else mattered. The popular media—movies, television, advertising, music, magazines—teach us that violence is the path to glamour and success. They teach that money, profit, and material goods are all that matter: basketball shoes, not the ideas in people's heads, the cultural or natural beauty around them, not even the other people in their lives." Do you agree or disagree? How do the popular media support or undermine the agenda of multicultural education? Write an essay in which you investigate the tensions between the mass media's emphasis on the individual and the goals of multicultural education.

3. Two of the writers in this section, Moffett and Shapiro, raise the question of how religious diversity is handled in our educational institutions. But this topic has largely been unaddressed in the years of debate over how to construct a curriculum for an increasingly diverse country. What are the pressures in both public and private colleges and universities to assimilate to a predominately Christian view of the world? What can a campus do to promote toleration for other religious beliefs? Investigate how your own campus handles the question of religious diversity and write an essay in the form of a letter to the editor of the student newspaper suggesting some additional ways in which your campus might increase tolerance for religious viewpoints, especially the non-Christian.

4. A number of writers in this section comment on the ways in which colleges and universities have worked to diversify their curriculum. A common method has been to add specialized courses in the curriculum, such as in African-American writers or in women's literature. Many commentators on higher education have raised concerns that the addition of such courses will not by themselves assist in making the curriculum diverse because not all students will take these courses. Based on your reading and your own educational experience, how do you think ensuring exposure to cultural diversity is best treated in a college curriculum? Study the curriculum of your own campus and write your own opinion about how much or how little most students learn about gender and cultural diversity in their educational experiences.

5. In order to promote an understanding of diverse cultures, many campuses have developed centers—among them, Women's Studies, African-American, Native American, and Hispanic-American. What are the advantages and disadvantages of the presence of these centers on campuses? What are their primary functions and goals? Write an essay in which you comment on the presence of a center or centers and discuss how the center contributes both to the individual lives of students and to the collective life of the campus.

6. In response to a question from an interviewer about the importance of free speech on campus, the President of Dartmouth College commented that "My sense is that the campus should be free from behavior that is harassing. But that the remedy for speech that is harassing has to be more speech and the self-discipline of civility." (*Change,* September/October 1991, 29). Several of the writers in this section touch on the conflicts that often occur on a campus when sensitive issues of race, gender, and ethnic background are raised. What is your position on how a campus should define and handle codes of behavior and the enforcement of the First Amendment? What can a campus do to promote what Benjamin Barber in this section has called "civil literacy."

7. To Hirsch, cultural literacy means possessing core knowledge. To Friere, any educational system that is teacher centered adheres to what he called the "banking" concept of education. Consider the assumptions about teaching that underlie two or three of the writers' positions in this section, and write an essay in which you compare and contrast the various concepts of education. Which position is closest to your own? Why?

8. Interview a dozen of your classmates about their experiences in learning about cultures different from their own. Some questions to ask are: What is your perception of the value of an educational experience that is multicultural? What are your attitudes in learning about people of different backgrounds and experiences? How important do you regard learning about differences? Have you experienced classrooms in which students voice resistance to some subject

matters? How have professors handled such resistance? Write a report of the responses and share them with your classmates.

9. One of the topics that few commentators on multicultural education address is the economic imperatives that drive colleges and universities. Many large state university systems have experienced dramatic funding cuts in recent years, including New York, Connecticut, California, Illinois, and Oregon. What do you know about the way in which both public and private colleges and universities are funded? What is the impact on curricular programs of all kinds when funding is reduced? By using Lexis-Nexis Academic Universe <http://web.lexis-nexis.com/universe>, investigate recent articles about funding for higher education. Choose a college or university system that has suffered recent cutbacks and share your feelings about how those cutbacks have altered curricular programs with your classmates.

10. The purpose of this chapter of the text, "Literacies for a Diverse World," is to invite you to read and think about the variety of ways in which we define cultural and multicultural literacy and how these definitions impact your own education. What have you learned from your reading, thinking, and writing? What are the major issues for college students? What do you need to know more about? Send an e-mail message to your classmates, inviting them to participate in an electronic discussion with you about the issues most crucial to them. Summarize the results and post them to your class.

IV

CYBERLITERACY

INTRODUCTION

No one in contemporary American society would disagree with the statement that the Internet and the World Wide Web have dramatically changed how we communicate, the way we find and locate information of all kinds, how we manage businesses, the way we educate ourselves and others, and the way we speak and write. We "access" a "site" where our "hit" may be recorded, we refer to ourselves as @ an address, and even the most technologically challenged person possesses more common knowledge about URLs and the availability of ISDN lines in a particular geographic area than he or she probably realizes. News programs and even entertainment shows have begun to take on the look of a sophisticated Web site with scrolling images, running titles, split screens, and multiple presentations of the same information. Elementary school children sit down in front of computer screens with easy familiarity and have Internet assignments from the early grades. Although few would deny that computers have changed our lives, there is considerable disagreement about whether those changes have been uniformly positive. The writers whose works are represented in this section explore many of the following questions:

- How are new technologies changing our educational lives by changing college and university structures?
- What difference does the Internet make to college students and to the ways in which students read, conduct research, and write essays and term papers?
- How does computer technology alter our notions of what constitutes a book or a text?
- How is hypertext altering linear narrative as a means of telling a story, providing information, or writing a report?
- How are colleges and universities coping with the costs of wiring, purchasing equipment, supporting computer use, and developing technology policies for students and faculty?
- How significant for students is the issue of access to sophisticated technology?
- What are the limitations of computers and the Internet? Has there been an unthinking acceptance of computer technology in our society?

- Is using computer technology a different experience for male and female students?
- What legal and ethical issues are involved in using new technologies?

The complex questions raised here do not have easy answers. But they constitute a framework of inquiry for investigating *cyberliteracy*—an understanding and consciousness of the ways in which electronic culture is changing our practices of reading, writing, and knowing.

The authors of the readings in this section explore the ways in which the new electronic technology at once contributes to and shapes our negotiation of the academic world. They use a variety of approaches and styles to construct their arguments and support their opinions. Many are professors whose field of study is electronic culture and new forms of narrative, and in the cases of Janet Murray, they encourage us to investigate the Web site versions of the books excerpted here. Others are journalists like Todd Oppenheimer, Kelly McCollum, Barbara Kantrowitz, Kevin Hunt, and Laura Miller, who write professionally for newspapers and magazines for both popular and specialized audiences. Some have written for periodicals that exist exclusively on the Internet and are not available in printed form. Some, like Sven Birkerts, are award-winning authors of best-selling books; others, like John Hickman, are recent college graduates with considerable expertise in using the new technology. Many of the writers are deeply optimistic about technology and the possibilities for teaching and learning, while other writers, like Gertrude Himmelfarb, are clearly skeptical about the promises of new technology and raise serious concerns about what might be lost when we are all online. But a common thread in all the articles is a passionate interest in print and electronic culture as well as a joyful interest in writing well. As you read, note the background of the writer and the intended audience for the essay and consider carefully how the writer develops his or her perspective.

I

LORD BURLEIGH'S KISS

Janet H. Murray is Director of the Laboratory for Advanced Computing Initiatives at the Georgia Institute of Technology. Although she has worked as a computer programmer and was trained as a traditional literary scholar, her recent work has been in developing applications for the use of computers in the humanities. She also teaches courses in interactive narrative at Georgia Tech. Her book Hamlet on the Holodeck *is an exploration of the future of narrative, an increasingly important topic in literary study today. Murray is especially interested in analyzing the implications of what happens when print culture gives way to an electronic culture, where virtual reality is an actuality and not simply a feature of science fiction like the holodeck, the vacation retreat for characters of the television series* Star Trek: The Next Generation. *In this reading, taken from the beginning of the book, Murray takes up the serious questions that confront us as we consider how the new medium of communication might alter narrative, story, and the development of characters into a new form that she calls "cyberliterature."*

QUESTIONS FOR READING

1. Murray draws heavily on examples from the television program *Star Trek: The Next Generation* and introduces an array of terms: photon weapons, tricorders, the transporter room, replicators, and, of course, the holodeck. Have these terms and others from science fiction become a part of general cultural literacy? What examples from your own life can you think of?

2. Murray also mentions a number of literary works in this text and assumes some degree of familiarity with them. What do you know about *Beowulf, Jane Eyre, Brave New World,* and *Fahrenheit 451*? What do the terms "utopian literature" and "dystopian literature"

mean? How does background information about literature help you understand this reading?

JANET H. MURRAY

LORD BURLEIGH'S KISS

Hamlet on the Holodeck: The Future of Narrative in Cyberspace
(New York: The Free Press, 1997)

In a far distant corner of the galaxy sometime in the twenty-fourth century, the brisk and competent Kathryn Janeway, captain of the starship *Voyager,* is taking a break from her duties with her favorite "holonovel." Exchanging her spandex-sleek Starfleet uniform for a hugely crinolined Victorian dress, Janeway enters one of the ship's "holosuites," which is running a three-dimensional simulation of a richly furnished English drawing room, complete with cozy armchairs and a roaring fire. Brooding by the fire is the handsome romantic hero, who greets her as she enters as his governess, Lucy Davenport. He gives her a meaningful look, and she returns it earnestly.

"Lord Burleigh, is something wrong?"

"Yes, terribly wrong."

He suddenly steps toward her, takes her in his arms, and kisses her passionately. "I have fallen in love with you, Lucy." They stare deeply into one another's eyes.

But it is teatime, and they are interrupted by the arrival of the sinister housekeeper and Lord Burleigh's two anxious and secretive young children. His little daughter, Beatrice, drops her teacup with alarm when questioned about the mysterious piano music that Lucy has been hearing.

Beatrice's precocious brother, Henry, is quick to silence her.

As soon as they are again alone, Lucy confronts Lord Burleigh: "What's happening in this house? How can you not know that Beatrice plays the piano? Why shouldn't I go to the fourth floor? What's up there?"

"Those are questions you must not ask," he declares imperiously.

"But I am asking them," comes her fervent reply. "I'm worried about the children. Beatrice fantasizes that her mother is still alive."

"Don't pursue this, I beg you," he says, looking deep into her eyes.

The confrontation is escalating dramatically and Lucy is breathless with excitement when suddenly another voice is heard:

"Bridge to Captain."

"Freeze program," says Lucy/Janeway, reluctantly backing away from the now frozen image of Lord Burleigh. "Janeway here."

"We've been hailed by a representative of the Bothan government. They'd like to talk to you."

"I'll be right there."

As she turns to leave, Janeway pauses before the stilled hologram of her would-be lover. "Sorry, my lord. Duty calls," she says, grinning, before striding back to resume command of the ship.[1]

Captain Janeway's Victorian excursion takes place on *Star Trek: Voyager,* the latest of four *Star Trek* television series in which gloriously equipped starships and space stations serve the ideals of the peace-seeking interplanetary United Federation of Planets.[2] There are many technical wonders in the *Star Trek* vision of the future, including lightspeed travel; photon weapons; medical "tricorders," which diagnose and heal with the wave of a wand; the well-known "transporter" room, in which technicians "beam" the crew up and down from dangerous planets by decomposing and reassembling their molecular patterns; and the conveniently wall-mounted "replicators," which can materialize hot and cold snacks on demand. The holodeck is an appropriate entertainment medium for the fortunate citizens of such a world: a utopian technology applied to the age-old art of storytelling.[3]

First introduced on *Star Trek: The Next Generation* in 1987, the holodeck consists of an empty black cube covered in white gridlines upon which a computer can project elaborate simulations by combining holography with magnetic "force fields" and energy-to-matter conversions. The result is an illusory world that can be stopped, started, or turned off at will but that looks and behaves like the actual world and includes parlor fires, drinkable tea, and characters, like Lord Burleigh and his household, who can be touched, conversed with, and even kissed. The *Star Trek* holodeck is a universal fantasy machine, open to individual programming: a vision of the computer as a kind of storytelling genie in the lamp. In the three series in which the holodeck has been featured, crew members have entered richly detailed worlds, including the tribal manor house of the Old English *Beowulf* saga, a gaslit London street, and a San Francisco speakeasy, in order to participate in stories that change around them in response to their actions.[4]

Lucy Davenport (as we can call Janeway's unnamed adventure) is in many ways typical of the holonovel form. It is a period piece and a work of genre fiction in which the elaborate set design and recognizable story conventions (an arrival in the rain, ghostly noises at the window, a forbidden attic) are playfully savored, as if put there by a very thorough and well-read programmer. Holonovels provide customized entertainment for a variety of tastes. They reveal unexpected sides of familiar characters. Just as Jean-Luc Picard, the highly cultured captain of *Star Trek: The Next Generation,* enjoys film noir, his android crewman, Commander Data, identifies with Sherlock Holmes, and the sensitive Dr. Julian Bashir of *Star Trek: Deep Space Nine* prefers James Bond spy adventures, so the conscientious Captain Janeway turns to gothic fiction in her well-earned leisure hours.

But Janeway's holonovel marks a milestone in this virtual literature of the twenty-fourth century as the first holodeck story to look more like a nineteenth-century novel than an arcade shoot-'em up. Unlike virtually all the holodeck stories run by male crew members, *Lucy Davenport* is not focused on a violent central conflict that is resolved within a single *Star Trek* episode. Instead, Janeway is involved in a more leisurely and open-ended exploration of the Burleigh household, a continuing avocation that she takes up regularly on her days off and that is presented over several episodes.[5] From Janeway's references to events that are not dramatized, it seems that she is spending long periods of time in the household, participating in a daily routine, giving lessons to the children, having tea at regular hours, and getting to know each individual character. Like *Jane Eyre*, Charlotte Brontë's 1847 novel, which established the governess gothic genre, *Lucy Davenport* takes place in a mysteriously haunted household and emphasizes the perils of the governess's intense social relationships rather than the physical terrors of the situation. When Janeway is shown relishing a verbal contest with the sinister housekeeper, promising the reluctant Henry that she will be a challenging math teacher, or trying to assuage the grief of the clearly anguished young Beatrice, we can understand what engages the resourceful starship captain in this particular virtual world. As her name implies, Janeway has much in common with her fictional predecessor Jane Eyre, including a strong resistance to being bullied, a willingness to stand on principle, and the courage to face fear and isolation head-on. The Lucy Davenport story therefore suits her well, making the holodeck form itself seem worthy of adult attention.

Janeway's attraction to the illusory Lord Burleigh is taken seriously as an exercise posing psychological and moral questions for her. After she is surprised by his teatime embrace, Janeway is tormented by visions of the holonovel characters walking around the ship. She thinks she is hallucinating until it is discovered that a telepathic enemy alien is fabricating these visions as a way of incapacitating the crew members and taking over the starship. At the dramatic climax of the episode, almost all of *Voyager's* crew are lost in hallucinatory trances, transfixed by apparitions of distant spouses welcoming them home or disapproving parents sapping their confidence.

Janeway responds to the crisis much like a Victorian gothic heroine: she holds firmly to reason and duty, though all around her are going mad. But then the alien appears to her in the shape of her lover, Mark, whom she may never see again since her ship is stranded at the farthest corner of the known galaxy. The apparition tries to embrace her, but she pushes him away:

MARK: What's the matter? You used to love it when I kissed you there.
JANEWAY: I don't know who you are, what you are. But I won't let you touch me.
MARK: What about the man on the holodeck? You didn't seem to mind him touching you, did you? In fact, I think you liked it. Now I ask you, Kath, is that fair to me? I stayed faithful to you. I vowed to wait for you no matter how long it takes. Shouldn't you do the same?
JANEWAY: *(stung, and turning to him)* I haven't been unfaithful.
MARK: Oh, Kath . . .

She kisses him and enters a catatonic trance.

The story of the rational and courageous Captain Janeway seduced and undone by a simulated kiss reflects a common anxiety about the new technologies of simulation. Do we believe that kissing a hologram (or engaging in cybersex) is an act of infidelity to a flesh-and-blood partner? If we could someday make holographic adventures as compelling as *Lucy Davenport,* would the power of such a vividly realized fantasy world destroy our grip on the actual world? Will the increasingly alluring narratives spun out for us by the new digital technologies be as benign and responsible as a nineteenth-century novel or as dangerous and debilitating as a hallucinogenic drug?

ALIEN KISSES

The paralyzing alien kiss is the latest embodiment of the fear with which we have greeted every powerful new representational technology—from the bardic lyre, to the printing press, to the secular theater, to the movie camera, to the television screen. We hear versions of the same terror in the biblical injunction against worshiping graven images; in the Homeric depiction of the alluring Sirens' songs, drawing sailors to their death; and in Plato's banishing of the poet from his republic because "he stimulates and strengthens an element which threatens to undermine the reason" with his fraudulent "phantasms."[6] All the representational arts can be considered dangerously delusional, and the more entrancing they are, the more disturbing. The powerful new storytelling technologies of the twentieth century have brought on an intensification of these fears. While the *Star Trek* writers imagine holodeck versions of *Beowulf* and *Jane Eyre,* a widely read and influential dystopian tradition has depicted such futuristic entertainment forms as intrinsically degrading.

Aldous Huxley's *Brave New World* (1932), set six hundred years from now, describes a society that science has dehumanized by eliminating love, parenthood, and the family in favor of genetic engineering, test-tube delivery, and state indoctrination. Books are banned, and science has come up with a substitute form of storytelling to delight the masses. In one of the novel's most memorable scenes the unspoiled hero, called the Savage (since he grew up with a biological mother in a far-off American Indian village), goes on a date to the "feelies" with Lenina, a satisfied child of the state. They are seated in the popular Alhambra theater, which is a kind of high-tech version of the plush movie palaces of the 1930s:

> Sunk in their pneumatic stalls, Lenina and the Savage sniffed and listened . . .
>
> The house lights went down; fiery letters stood out solid and as though self-supported in the darkness. THREE WEEKS IN A HELICOPTER. AN ALL-SUPER-SINGING, SYNTHETIC-TALKING, COLOURED, STEREO-SCOPIC FEELY, WITH SYNCHRONIZED SCENT-ORGAN ACCOMPANIMENT.
>
> "Take hold of those metal knobs on the arms of your chair," whispered Lenina. "Otherwise you won't get any of the feely effects." (134)

The attraction of the feely is an extension of the attraction of the movie and the talkie. The exuberant musicals of the early sound era are parodied by Huxley's description of the feely's foolish plot, which relies on arresting helicopter views, lots of sex, and characters who are constantly bursting into song. Writing in the age of the Hollywood star, Huxley describes the feely actors as simultaneously larger than life and less than human: a "gigantic Negro" and "a golden-haired young brachycephalic Beta-Plus female" who look "dazzling and incomparably more solid-looking than they would have seemed in actual flesh and blood, far more real than reality" (134). When these too-real characters kiss, the Savage experiences for the first time the wonders of erotic engineering:

> The Savage started. That sensation on his lips! He lifted a hand to his mouth; the titillation ceased; let his hand fall back on the metal knob; it began again. . . . "Ooh-ah! Ooh-ah!" the stereoscopic lips came together again, and once more the facial erogenous zones of the six thousand spectators in the Alhambra tingled with almost intolerable galvanic pleasure. "Ooh . . . " (134–35)

After the movie, the Savage feels debased by his own arousal. He rejects the eager Lenina and goes home instead to read *Othello*.

The horror of the feely theater lies in knowing that your intense responses have been calculated and engineered, in knowing that a technician has set the male voice at "less than thirty-two vibrations per second" to achieve an automatic erotic effect and has reduced the lips of all the individual audience members to just so many "facial erogenous zones" to be stimulated by galvanic means, like so many light bulbs to be flipped on.

Ray Bradbury offered a remake of the same media nightmare at the beginning of the television era. In *Fahrenheit 451* (1953), a future dictatorship keeps the populace amused and docile with raucous "televisors," sound and image systems embedded in living room walls at great expense and dedicated to incoherent but arresting entertainment. Televisor parlors are primitive holodecks in which housewife viewers converse with on-screen characters by reading from scripts in answer to their cues. Bradbury's hero, Montag (named after a paper company), is a "fireman" whose job is burning books. The novel charts his awakening from destroyer to preserver of book culture. Montag's wife, who has forgotten all the actual events of her life, has pressured him into buying three televisor walls and is pleading for the fourth so that she can be with her "parlor families" all day. In one key scene, Montag observes his wife and her friends sitting in rapt enjoyment of the disturbingly nonlinear televisor presentations:

> On one wall a woman smiled and drank orange juice simultaneously. How does she do both at once? thought Montag, insanely. In the other walls an x-ray of the same woman revealed the contracting journey of the refreshing beverage on its way to her delighted stomach! Abruptly the room took on a rocket flight into the clouds, it plunged into the lime-green sea where blue fish ate red and yellow fish. A minute later, Three White Cartoon Clowns chopped off each other's limbs to the accompaniment of immense incoming tides of laughter. Two minutes more and the room whipped out of town to the jet cars

wildly circling an arena, bashing and backing up and bashing each other again. Montag saw a number of bodies fly in the air. (93–94)

As the housewives exclaim with delight at the entertainment, Montag pulls the switch, causing the images to drain away "as if the water had been let from a gigantic crystal bowl of hysterical fish." But the damage remains, for when Montag tries to engage them in conversation about the coming war, the women cannot take in the reality of the situation. "It's always someone else's husband dies," they agree, fidgeting anxiously before the now empty walls (94). Like Janeway and her crew in the grip of the alien hallucination, the televisor viewers are mesmerized by an illusion so intense that it blocks out imminent danger.

The housewives' psychological and moral paralysis is a direct consequence of the virtues of the technology, namely, its power to appeal to the senses of vision and hearing with stunning immediacy. In the words of Montag's mentor, Faber (named for the pencil), the televisors are evil because they create "an environment as real as the world." Books are praised as a better representational technology by virtue of their limitations; their meager sensory input makes their illusions easier to resist. "You can shut them and say, 'Hold on a moment'" (84). But with the new multisensory media, the populace is overpowered.

For Huxley and Bradbury, the more persuasive the medium, the more dangerous it is. As soon as we open ourselves to these illusory environments that are "as real as the world" or even "more real than reality," we surrender our reason and join with the undifferentiated masses, slavishly wiring ourselves into the stimulation machine at the cost of our very humanity. In this dystopian view, the new entertainment technologies are a means of stripping away the language and culture that give life meaning and of reducing us to a state of abject bestiality. When the Savage complains that he prefers the works of Shakespeare because the feelies "don't mean anything," the spokesman for the technostate assures him that "they mean a lot of agreeable sensations for the audience" (391). Why would the docile populace want a narrative art form that helps them to better understand themselves when they can enjoy a love scene on a sensuous bearskin rug whose "every hair . . . [can] be separately and distinctly felt"?

Starting in the 1970s and 1980s, the same fears provoked by the advent of film and television began to be expressed against videogames, which added interactivity to the sensory allures of sight, sound, and motion. Critics have condemned the too-easy stimulation of electronic games as a threat to the more reflective delights of print culture. A prominent film critic, for instance, recently lamented the fact that his sons have deserted Dickens for shoot-'em-up computer games, which "offer a kind of narrative, but one that yields without resistance to the child's desire for instant gratification."[7] In recent dystopian literature, the computer screen or virtual reality helmet is as addictive and delusional as the feely or televisor. The nightmare vision of a future totalitarian state has been replaced by the equally frightening picture of a violently fragmented world organized around cyberspace, where ruthless international corporations, secret agencies, and criminal conspiracies struggle for control.

These accounts of a digital dystopia both eroticize and demonize the computer. Cyberpunk surfers are like cowboys on a new frontier or motorcycle hoodlums with a joystick in their hand instead of a motorcycle between their legs. They are outlaw pirates on an endless voyage of exploration throughout the virtual world, raiding and plundering among the invisible data hoards of the world and menaced by the stronger pirate barons who reach in and reprogram their minds. In this world, first popularized in William Gibson's *Neuromancer* (1983), the addictive delusional experience is vividly imagined as "jacking in," that is, wiring your neurons directly into the immaterial world of "cyberspace," a word coined by the novelist to describe the virtual terrain of databanks along a surfable Internet. The popular entertainment form in Gibson's gritty world is the "simstim," a way of riding in someone else's consciousness and thus experiencing the world through that person's sensorium by seeing, hearing, and feeling whatever he or she does. Case, the hero of *Neuromancer,* is addicted to the thrill of jacking in to the cyberspace databanks but is bored by the simstim as a mere "meat toy," for meat is what the body becomes when the mind finds its narcissistic love object within the machine. Yet it is hard to know which of these virtual experiences—jacking in to cyberspace or hitching a ride in a simstim—is more disturbing. In *Neuromancer* the human condition is to be faced with such choices and to flip back and forth between them with a kind of ultimate feely knob. The illusory world has become so powerfully enticing that it has subsumed physical reality itself.

But it is not just the essayists and novelists who have expressed their terrors of the emerging virtual landscape. Television shows and films have also targeted the computer as a dehumanizing representational technology. The television series *Tek War* (produced in the early 1990s by William Shatner, the actor who played the optimistic and heroic Captain Kirk on the original *Star Trek* series) is set in a future America destroyed by the illegal traffic in Tek, a hallucinogenic technology resembling a virtual reality headset. In the first episode of the series, for instance, the hero is paralyzed by powerful Tek programs, bought on the black market, that simulate his ex-wife returning to love him. When his partner arrives to tear off the helmet and bring him back to chasing bad guys, it is a scene very like the classic Western cliché of the sheriff sobering up the drunken deputy but with darker urban overtones suggesting a heroin or cocaine habit. Throughout the *Tek War* series, virtual reality technologies are explicitly equated with lethal drugs as the source of addiction, destitution, bad trips, overdose deaths, and gangster violence.

Movies have been even more lurid in their depiction of computer-based entertainment. Perhaps the most explicit filmic statement of the dangers of cyberspace is *Lawnmower Man* (1992), in which a virtual reality researcher turns a simpleminded gardener into a digital monster. In this retelling of the Frankenstein story, Dr. Larry Angelo experiments with Jobe Smith with the intention of expanding his mental abilities. Larry's first step in sending Jobe down the road to psychosis is to invite him in to play virtual reality videogames that speed up his mind, awakening neurons the rest of us leave dormant. Soon Jobe rejects books as too slow a means of learning and listens to music by jumping from one short excerpt to another. Once he has left the world of linear media behind, he quickly turns to horror-movie-style slaughter, accomplished by the sheer power of his unnaturally augmented brain. The movie climaxes with Jobe leaving his body and entering the machine, where he appears as a kind of videogame character. The virtual Jobe easily outfights the virtual image of his creator and eventually escapes into the Internet. At the very end of the movie, we hear the sound of all the telephones in the world ringing simultaneously, signaling that this superior being is on the verge of taking over the planet. In effect, the videogame will play us from now on. *Lawnmower Man* is the most extreme version of the dystopian vision: the representational technology as both diversion and dictator all in one.

THE THINKING WOMAN'S FEELY

Which vision of digital storytelling are we to believe? Will the literature of cyberspace be continuous with the literary traditions of the *Beowulf* poet, Shakespeare, and Charlotte Brontë as the *Star Trek* producers portray it, or will it be the dehumanizing and addictive sensation machine predicted by the dystopians? Is the optimistic *Star Trek* view too pat and sentimental to be credible at all in the light of Huxleyan criticism?

We can certainly see Captain Janeway's experience as dystopian. The holodeck is in many ways exactly the sort of entertainment machine Huxley dreaded: a masterpiece of engineering aimed at inducing delusional physical sensations. No doubt the appropriate moisture and temperature of Lord Burleigh's kiss have been as carefully calculated as the sensations produced by the feely knob. But unlike the helpless fantasy addicts of the dystopian stories, Janeway is the master of the apparatus that is creating the illusion. This is made clear when 'she returns to the holodeck after her initial hallucinations to check it for a malfunction and is eagerly greeted by her virtual lover:

BURLEIGH: Lucy, thank God you've come back. (*Notices her uniform*) But why are you dressed so strangely?
JANEWAY: It's a costume.
BURLEIGH: You'd look lovely in anything. (*Takes her hand*) I've thought of you constantly, remembered your touch, your perfume, your lips.
JANEWAY: (*Eyes closed, as if surrendering to his magnetism*) Computer, delete character!

Even as she swoons in an embrace, Janeway is in control of the mirage. In Bradbury's terms, she can shut the book. Lord Burleigh is deliciously enticing but unenslaving, just as movie and television heart throbs from Clark Gable's Rhett Butler to George Clooney's Dr. Doug Ross have proved to be, despite dystopian fears.

The *Star Trek* story can be seen as a fable differentiating humane and meaningful digital storytelling from the dehumanizing illusions that the dystopians warn about. Janeway is paralyzed by her hallucination of her lover, Mark, because it is too literal a transcription of her fantasies. The alien treats human consciousness like a stimulus–response machine. The holonovel, on the other hand, is aimed not at Janeway's neurons but at her imagination. Although it offers the pleasures of an art form "more real than reality," it is clearly make-believe. At the end of the episode, Janeway is skipping her regular visit to the holodeck to think about the issues the enemy hallucinations have raised. Now that the alien is defeated by the superior telepathic powers of another female crew member, Janeway thinks, "In a way, maybe he did us all a favor. Maybe it's better to look those feelings in the eye than to keep them locked up inside." The holodeck, like any literary experience, is potentially valuable in exactly this way. It provides a safe space in which to confront disturbing feelings we would otherwise suppress; it allows us to recognize our most threatening fantasies without becoming paralyzed by them. Like a magical starship designed for safely exploring the distant quadrants of the galaxy, the holodeck is an optimistic technology for exploring inner life. For Captain Janeway, a person of Victorian integrity, such an exploration brings the benefit of self-knowledge. It is not paralyzing. It sends her back to the real world all the stronger.

The holonovel offers a model of an art form that is based on the most powerful technology of sensory illusion imaginable but is nevertheless continuous with the larger human tradition of storytelling, stretching from the heroic bards through the nineteenth-century novelists. The feely (and its successors) offers an opposing image of a sensation-based storytelling medium that is intrinsically degrading, fragmenting, and destructive of meaning, a medium whose success implies the death of the great traditions of humanism, or even a fundamental shift in human nature itself. Neither vision of the future refutes the other. Together they sum up the hopes and fears aroused by the increasingly visceral representational technologies of the twentieth century. As these utopian and dystopian fictions remind us, we rely on works of fiction, in any medium, to help us understand the world and what it means to be human. Eventually all successful storytelling technologies become "transparent": we lose consciousness of the medium and see neither print nor film but only the power of the story itself. If digital art reaches the same level of expressiveness as these older media, we will no longer concern ourselves with how we are receiving the information. We will only think about what truth it has told us about our lives.

NOTES

1. From the episode "Persistence of Vision" in the series *Star Trek: Voyager.* (See bibliography for production credits.)

2. *Star Trek* was created by Gene Roddenberry. The original series went on the air in 1966 and lasted for three seasons and seventy-nine episodes. As of 1997, the franchise includes seven movies and three additional television series—*Star Trek: The Next Generation* (debut, 1988), *Star Trek: Deep Space 9* (debut, 1993), and *Star Trek: Voyager* (debut, 1995). Although *The Next Generation* went off the air after seven seasons, it continues to be seen in reruns, as does the original or "classic" series. (See bibliography for production credits.)

3. Lawrence Krauss, in *The Physics of Star Trek* (99–108), has analyzed the series' combination of plausible and wildly fanciful inventions. He considers the three-dimensional images of the holodeck possible although its use of "matter replicators," which make things out of thin air, is unrealistic. We could therefore imagine a future holodeck theater in which images would surround us but would be incapable of being touched. Janeway would not be able to drink holodeck tea or sit on a holodeck parlor chair, let along receive a holodeck embrace from Lord Burleigh.

4. Although *Star Trek* holodeck adventures were originally referred to as holodeck programs, the producers have come to distinguish between programs, which simulate a place and its inhabitants, and "holonovels," which offer complex narratives. Crew members might run a holodeck program of sailing on Lake Como or of a nineteenth-century French billiard parlor, complete with flirtatious men and easy women, to enjoy as a recreation environment, but they run a holonovel to participate in a story as *Beowulf* or as a Victorian governess.

5. The Lucy Davenport story appeared in three episodes of *Star Trek: Voyager*: "Cathexis," "Learning Curve," and "Persistence of Vision." (See bibliography for production credits.)

6. *The Republic of Plato*, chapter XXXVI.

7. Denby, "Buried Alive: Our Children and the Avalanche of Crud" 48–58.

REFERENCES

"Cathexis." Episode 12 of *Star Trek: Voyager*, (Season 1, initial broadcast on May 1, 1995). Written by Brannon Braga, directed by Kim Friedman. Television Program.

Denby, David. "Buried Alive: Our Children and the Avalanche of Crud." *The New Yorker* (July 15, 1996): 48–58.

Krauss, Lawrence. *The Physics of Star Trek.* New York: Harper Perennial, 1996.

"Learning Curve." Episode 15 of *Star Trek: Voyager* (Season 1, initial broadcast on May 22, 1995). Written by Ronald Wilderson and Jean Louise Matthias; directed by David Livingston. Television Program.

"Persistence of Vision." Episode 23 of *Star Trek: Voyager* (Season 1, initial broadcast on October 30, 1995). Written by Jeri Taylor, directed and produced by James L. Conway. Television Program.

Plato. *The Republic of Plato*. Translated by Francis MacDonald Cornford. Oxford: Oxford University Press, 1970.

QUESTIONS FOR REACTION AND DISCUSSION

1. Murray begins this reading with a "story," a summary of part of an actual *Star Trek* episode, and then a discussion. How effective is this beginning? What is the purpose of this story and how does it demonstrate or explain Murray's concept of the "holonovel"?

2. Murray contrasts holonovels with other futuristic entertainment forms she refers to as dystopian. *Brave New World* is one example and she mentions others. What are the characteristics of this dystopian tradition? What is degrading and horrifying about this vision?

3. Many people have expressed concern about the interactivity of videogames as additional enhancements to the sensory experiences of sight, sound, and motion. How does Murray analyze these computer-based entertainments? What value does she see in them?

4. Murray suggests in this reading and in her book as a whole that story-telling is a necessary part of human life and that we rely on it "to help us understand the world and what it means to be human." To what extent does her discussion overlook the negative aspects of a person's ability to enter a narrative and alter the ending?

5. At the end of this reading, Murray offers us two views of the future of digital storytelling. Describe them and explain their relationship. Consider the title of this reading, "Lord Burleigh's Kiss." Why is this an effective title? How does it prepare you for the reading that follows?

QUESTIONS FOR WRITING

1. Consider objections that you have read or heard about the negative effects of narrative-based videogames on children and teenagers. Does Murray's analysis of the tensions in digital storytelling provide any useful insights? Think about her statement, "The feely (and its successors) offers an opposing image of a sensation-based storytelling medium that is intrinsically degrading, fragmenting, and destructive of meaning, a medium whose success implies the death of the great traditions of humanism, or even a fundamental shift in human nature itself." Write a position paper in which you defend or reject that statement.

2. With a group of your classmates, view the movie of Ray Bradbury's *Fahrenheit 451*. Discuss the negative view of technology that is presented here. Write an essay for your classmates in which you discuss how Bradbury demonstrates the dangers of technology. Consider these questions as you draft your essay: Is this movie relevant today? Do you recommend it? What does Bradbury suggest about the future of narrative?

3. Murray suggests elsewhere in her book *Hamlet on the Holodeck* that it is important to remember that narrative traditions do not arise out of the blue. She reminds her readers that the first published books were taken from written manuscripts, which were in turn taken from centuries of oral storytelling. Remnants of these traditions remain in published books. During the last part of the twentieth century, we have also seen films, television programs, and plays strain the

boundaries of linear storytelling; as just one example, a characteristic of a television series in the 1980s, *Moonlighting,* was that the characters would suddenly move from the set onto the parking lot of the studio lot and consequently move out of the "story" they were making. Murray refers to these as "harbingers of the holodeck." Think of examples from your experience as a media watcher and write an essay in which you describe how contemporary media have altered the ways you respond to novels.

QUESTIONS FOR FURTHER EXPLORATION

1. On the <http://www.amazon.com> Web site, Janet H. Murray, janet.murray@lcc.gatech.edu, <http://www.lcc.gatech.edu/~murray/>, July 1, 1997, made the following comments in an electronic interview:

   > I really welcome reader comments on the book. I wrote this book in order to celebrate and inspire creative storytelling in the new digital medium. I sympathize with many of the fears computers inspire, but I am mostly exhilarated by the possibilities they offer for human expression. I would be happy to hear from people who agree, disagree, or who have suggestions on how I can offer support over the Web for those who want more information. Most of all, I hope people write to tell me about their most compelling narrative experiences with hypertexts, MUDS, games, or virtual reality environments.

   Take Professor Murray up on her offer and write her an e-mail message about your "most compelling narrative experiences." Apart from merely summarizing your experience, however, comment on how this experience differs from reading a narrative in print. Finally, offer some of your own conclusions about the difference between narrative creativity in print and in the electronic medium.

2. Find Janet H. Murray's Home Page on the Internet <http://www.lcc.gatech.edu/~murray/> and follow the links to her Resource Page for *Hamlet on the Holodeck.* Investigate a link in her expanded Table of Contents that interests you—her debate with Sven Birkerts, her account of MUDs, or one of her new projects. What is your assessment of this expanded version of her book? How is following the links different from the experience of reading "Lord Burleigh's Kiss" in this text? Write an essay in which you discuss the differences between your experience in using Murray's Internet version of her book and your experience in reading a chapter from a printed text.

2

WWW.CLAPTRAP.COM

Laura Miller is a senior editor, covering books and cultural events in New York City, for Salon Magazine *<http://www.salonmagazine. com>. Founded in 1995 by David Talbot, former Arts and Features Editor of the* San Francisco Examiner, Salon *is an Internet magazine that publishes original book and media reviews, articles on the arts, interviews, news commentary, travel essays and a "Table Talk Forum," an online chat group on some fifteen hundred topics with over ninety thousand registrants. Contributing writers for the magazine include such well-known writers as Garrison Keillor (who writes a funny advice column), David Horowitz, Camille Paglia, and Christopher Hitchens. According to the editor's statistics, more than 9.5 million page views of the magazine had occurred by July 1998 (a "page view" is the way in which Web site managers determine how frequently their sites are accessed). This article, "www.claptrap. com," was not published in* Salon, *however, but in the prestigious* New York Times Book Review, *a supplement to the Sunday edition of the* New York Times, *which includes reviews of current books and occasional essays like this one on the final "Bookend" page. In this article, Miller offers her own position on the future of fiction in print and on the Internet.*

QUESTIONS FOR READING

1. What does the title of this article suggest about Miller's thesis?
2. Miller mentions one writer whose works are included in this reader— Janet H. Murray. Why does she mention Murray as an example? Are you familiar with the other writers she mentions?
3. How does the fact that this essay was published in print and in the *New York Times Book Review* shape your reading?

L A U R A   M I L L E R

WWW.CLAPTRAP.COM

The New York Times Book Review *(March 15, 1998, p. 43)*

Shortly after personal computers and word processing programs became commonplace tools for writers, a brave new future for fiction was trumpeted. In 1992, Robert Coover informed the readers of the Book Review that the novel, "as we know it, has come to its end." Hypertext, "writing done in the nonlinear or nonsequential space made possible by the computer," would at last enable the reader to amble through a network of linked text blocks, or "lexias." Instead of following a linear story dictated by the author, the reader could now navigate at will through an "endless expansion" of words.

Proclamations about the death of the novel (or, as Coover's essay was titled, "The End of Books") can still get a rise out of a surprising number of people, even though, so far, they've all proved to be little more than empty, apocalyptic showboating. Six years after Coover's essay was published, and five years after a second article by him, this one recommending several "hyperfictions" for the curious reader, the market for hardcover books may be flat, but over a million people have nevertheless bought Charles Frazier's literary novel *Cold Mountain,* and I've yet to encounter anyone who reads hypertext fiction. No one, that is, who isn't also a hypertext author or a journalist reporting on the trend.

Surely those readers, however few, must exist, but what's most remarkable about hyperfiction is that no one really *wants* to read it, not even out of idle curiosity. The most adventurous souls I know, people amenable to sampling cryptic performance art and even those most rare and exotic of creatures, readers of poetry who aren't poets themselves—all shudder at the thought, for it's the very concept of hypertext fiction that strikes readers as dreary and pointless. Yet Coover's announcement wasn't the last of its kind; recently Janet H. Murray examined the future of reader-controlled narratives at length in her book, "Hamlet on the Holodeck: The Future of Narrative in Cyberspace," and Mark Amerika started "Grammatron" (www.grammatron.com), a "novel-length hypertext work" on the World Wide Web. The promise that the fiction of the future will have no story, or a story of the reader's own devising, recalls a Lily Tomlin joke about the afterlife: it turns out that there is sex in heaven; you just can't feel it.

That Coover and hypertext authors and theorists like Michael Joyce, George P. Landow, Stuart Moulthrop, and Mark Amerika apparently still believe in the eventual triumph of hyperfiction over the novel becomes less baffling when you understand that hypertext is a form of writing perfectly suited to contemporary literary theory. In his aptly titled book/Web site, "Hypertext: The Convergence of Contemporary Critical Theory and Technology"

<www.stg.brown.edu/projects/hypertext/landow/ht/contents2.html>, Landow observes that "using hypertext, critical theorists will have, or now already have, a laboratory with which to test their ideas." In fact, he says, hypertext is "an almost embarrassingly literal embodiment" of key poststructuralist notions. What the laboratory of hyperfiction demonstrates, though, is how alienated academic literary criticism is from actual readers and their desires.

The theory of hyperfiction insists that readers ought to be, and long to be, liberated from two mainstays of the traditional novel: linear narrative and the author. The reader, cruelly forced to read one word after another to reach the end of a sentence, one paragraph after another to reach the end of a scene, will rejoice to learn that, according to Coover, "true freedom from the tyranny of the line is perceived as only really possible now at last with the advent of hypertext." In reality, the common reader most likely will be surprised to be told that structured storytelling—from the most basic beginning-middle-end scheme of fairy tales to more elaborately constructed, nonchronological literary narratives and frolics like murder mysteries—is actually a form of oppression, rather than the source of delight it has always seemed in the past.

In Jostein Gaarder's novel "Sophie's World" (proof that a story can transform a seemingly uncommercial primer on philosophy into a popular book), a character describes a cat and a little girl in a room. If a ball rolls across the floor, the cat will chase it, but the little girl will look to see where the ball came from. Story—the idea that events happen in a specific, casual order—is both the way we see the world and what interests us most about it, and story is fiction's trump card. People who read for nothing else will read for plot, yet hyperfiction's advocates maintain that we find it "confining" and chafe against its "limitations."

A primary source for the peculiar notion that linear narratives "tyrannize" their readers and need to be broken is the French critic Roland Barthes, who in "S/Z," his book-length dissection of a Balzac story, champions an ideal that he calls "the writerly text": "It has no beginning; it is reversible; we gain access to it by several entrances, none of which can be authoritatively declared to be the main one." Barthes complains of "the pitiless divorce which the literary institution maintains between the producer of the text and its user, between its owner and its consumer, between its author and its reader," which prevents the reader from "gaining access to . . . the pleasure of writing."

That last point is true enough: reading doesn't offer the pleasure of writing. But it does offer the pleasure of *reading*, a practice much undervalued by literary critics and hyperfiction advocates. Meandering through the lexias of hypertext works like Michael Joyce's "Afternoon, A Story," Stuart Moulthrop's "Victory Garden" (both published on floppy disks by Eastgate Systems; www.eastgate.com) and even the floridly naughty "Grammatron" is a listless task, a matter of incessantly having to choose among alternatives, each of which, I'm assured, is no more important than any other. This process, according to Landow, makes me "a truly active reader," but the experience feels profoundly meaningless and dull. If any decision is as good as any other, why bother? Hypertext is sometimes said to mimic real life, with its myriad opportunities and surprising outcomes, but I already have a life, thank you very much, and it is hard enough putting that in order without the chore of organizing someone else's novel. Hyperfiction, Coover promises, will make me a "cowriter" by enabling me to rearrange its text blocks however I choose. Of course, I could just write my own book if writing is what I really want to do.

Readers like me stubbornly resist hyperfiction's efforts to free them from what Coover calls "domination by the author." Instead, I persist, like Lynne Sharon Schwartz, the author of "Ruined by Reading: A Life in Books," in perceiving my readerly enslavement as "a delectable exercise for the mind." Since Schwartz's anecdotal memoir could hardly be called plot-driven, why do I find following its aimless course so pleasant? The answer lies in the author herself, whom I experience as confiding, amusing, and enlightening, not domineering. Like her, I consider a book to be "a solitary voice whispering in your ear," providing the possibility of an encounter with the author, whose theoretical "death" I neither long for nor believe in, however ingeniously Barthes and others may argue for it. Schwartz gracefully assumes the "authority" implicit in the profession of author. She knows what she thinks and she selects what she wishes to say, and in what order. She doesn't needlessly defer to me the option of rearranging her book. Yet at no point did I feel her boot on my throat.

I am not, however, an academic. The downtrodden reader depicted in hypertext manifestoes and poststructuralist literary theory is the creature of a world where books are assigned, not chosen. To the academic, a book is often a stony monument from which the relatively insignificant scholar must wring some drop of fresh commentary. As a result, the rhetoric of hyperfiction can be warlike, full of attacks launched against texts that can offer no "defense," prove "vulnerable" and ultimately "yield." Coover sees "readers who fall asleep on four or five books a year" and "surrender to novels as a way of going on holiday from themselves" as weaklings insufficiently girded for the glorious battle ahead.

That surrender, though, and the intimacy to be had in allowing a beloved author's voice into the sanctums of our minds, are what the common reader craves. We want to experience how someone as acerbic as Jane Austen, as morally passionate as Dostoyevsky, as psychologically astute as Henry James makes sense of the chaos of this world, and our passage through it, because making sense of it is humanity's great collective project. Is it merely a holiday or is it an expansion of ourselves when we issue this invitation to guests whose appeal lies precisely in their distinctive, unequivocal, undeniably authoritative voices? Hyperfiction's champions aren't the first self-styled revolutionaries threatening to liberate other people from their pleasures, but they make one of the weakest cases. The end of books will come only when readers abandon novels for the deconstructed stories of hypertext and that exodus is strictly a fiction.

QUESTIONS FOR REACTION AND DISCUSSION

1. What is Miller's central thesis and what are her principal supporting ideas and examples?

2. Compare and contrast Miller's views on the hypertext fiction with those of Janet H. Murray.

3. A point that Miller makes in this essay is that no one wants to read hypertext fiction. How does she know that? What is her evidence for this statement?

4. Miller explains the "theory of hypertext fiction" by suggesting such a theory depends on the notion that readers ought to be liberated from two restrictions: the confines of a linear narrative and the control of an author. Describe these restrictions. Based on what you know about hypertext fiction, is this definition fair?

QUESTIONS FOR WRITING

1. Miller refutes the claims of hypertext fiction by providing a spirited defense of the linear narrative and the presence of an author—the two hallmarks of the traditional print novel. Write an essay in which you agree or disagree with her assessment of the importance of these aspects of the novel, using examples from your own reading (in print or electronic forms).

2. Using the positions of other writers in this section (Janet Murray or Sven Birkerts), compose a list of questions in which you ask these writers about their responses to Miller's essay. Imagine that you have been asked to publish a written "interview" for a magazine. Prepare your account by writing your questions followed by the "answers" you compose for each writer and identify each respondent with their names. As the interviewer, prepare a final summation of the experience as a concluding paragraph.

QUESTIONS FOR FURTHER EXPLORATION

1. Access *Salon Magazine* <http://www.salonmagazine.com> and read a variety of articles of interest to you from the various sections in the current issue. Participate in one of the Table Talk Forum sessions. Write an essay in which you describe the process of reading an Internet magazine and evaluate your experience. Think carefully about the experience of reading a print magazine and an online magazine. What are the major differences? Similarities?

2. Miller suggests that she knows no one who has actually read a hypertext fiction. Locate such a fiction. Miller suggests two—Michael Joyce's "Afternoon, a Story" or Stuart Moulthrop's "Victory Garden"—both available on diskettes from Eastgate Systems <http://www.eastgate.com>; alternatively, there are many Web sites of hypertext fiction on the Internet (Miller mentions Mark Amerika's "Grammatron," <http://www.grammatron.com>. Read a short work and write an essay in which you agree or disagree with Miller's position that reading a hypertext fiction is "meaningless and dull."

3

THE CULTURAL CURRENCY OF THE BOOK

Kevin Hunt is a freelance writer who, as a graduate student at Rens-sailer Polytechnic Institute, reviewed books for CMC Magazine, *one of the first Internet magazines (the CMC stands for Computer Mediated Communication). Begun in May 1994, CMC Magazine was published as a commercial venture of December Communications, Inc., with the ambitious purpose of providing news and reports about human communication and interaction in online environments. Sponsored exclusively by advertising (the way most online magazines are supported), CMC existed only on the Internet. A user could access and print articles, but paper copies of the magazine were not available. Like many print periodicals that suffer short publication spans, CMC ceased online publication in January 1999. The site, however, is still available, and users can access the complete archive for the publication through the home page <http://www.de-cember.com/cmc/mag>. Although this article is at least in part a book review of* Rewired: A Brief (and Opinionated) Net History *by David Hudson (New York: Macmillan, 1997), Hunt provides an interesting perspective on the difference between reading books and visiting a Web site.*

QUESTIONS FOR READING

1. What does the phrase "cultural currency" mean to you?
2. What is the purpose of a book review and how does it affect the way you approach reading this work?
3. Have you read articles on the Internet in the past? Have you read books on the Internet? How is that experience of reading a text on a computer screen different from reading an article or book in print? Make a list of the differences and similarities.

KEVIN HUNT

THE CULTURAL CURRENCY
OF THE BOOK

CMC Magazine *(August 1998<http://www.december.com/cmc/mag/1998/aug/hunt.html>)*

In *Being Digital,* first published in 1995, Nicholas Negroponte described how "bits" are beginning to replace atoms as the basic commodity of human interaction. In other words, the words we write and speak increasingly take the form of bits and are transmitted to others over various electronic networks. The results of this digitization, as Negroponte details at length in the book, promise to be revolutionary, changing how we work, play, and live.

In the three years since Negroponte wrote *Being Digital,* the Web has indeed begun to transform the way some of us work, play, and live (though perhaps not in the ways that Negroponte imagined). Yet despite the advantages and revolutionary effects of the Web as a digital medium, the primary means of communicating grand ideas, opinions, or experiences continues to be via the atoms that make up a book. Whenever anyone wants to showcase the fruits of their mental labors, or make a detailed, extensive argument, or present their side of a story, they turn to book publishers. And when anyone wants to read about the details of someone else's ideas or stories, they go to their favorite bookstore.

The question is, why? Given the Web's potential as a medium for communicating and expressing ideas and experiences in ways that blow away the limitations of print, why aren't we bypassing Border's or Amazon.com, and instead going directly to URLs for books online, to "book webs," if you will? Think of the possibilities. Imagine going to a book web detailing the experiences Jon Krakauer described in *Into Thin Air,* the bestseller about the deadly climbing debacle on Mount Everest in 1996. Why aren't we clamoring to visit an *Into Thin Air* book web, complete with a VRML climb up Everest, 3-D models of the lethal Everest weather patterns, color photos and film clips of the 1996 expeditions, and, of course, the searchable text of his book (and perhaps even his complete, unedited travel diaries, as well). And why aren't publishers beginning to develop sites such as this?

I first thought about this question when I read David Hudson's *Rewired: A Brief (and Opinionated) Net History* (reviewed in the December 1997 issue of *CMC Magazine*). As the title suggests, Hudson presents his own ideas on how the Internet has been developed, and the direction it's heading in, and in the process takes issue with some of the ideas others have presented about the Net. What I found interesting about Hudson's book, aside from many of the excellent points he makes about the past and future of the Net, is the fact that he chose to convey these points in a *book*. In presenting his case, Hudson primarily builds upon, reformulates, and supports his arguments based on discussions and ideas that were originally presented in digital form—in e-mail and news-group communiques and in articles published in e-zines and at other Web sites. And all these digital sources are cited at the end of each section within the book.

Given that Hudson's book is about the effects of digital communication, and given that it draws upon primarily digital sources, why didn't the book take the form of a Web site, especially since most readers of the book are very Web-literate and are familiar with many of the electronic discussions that Hudson cites in his book? After all, it would have made the citation process, via hyper-links, easier and more immediate, allowing readers to go to various online sources to get the full details of the various viewpoints Hudson presents or critiques.

The basic answer is, of course, one of economics. Nobody—neither au-thors nor publishers—would make any money by publishing their works on-line. If we've learned anything from the economics of the Web so far, it's that, except in a few cases, few people will pay to visit Web sites. And, of course, with the exception of books such as Hudson's, still fewer of the potential read-ership of an author's work even have Web access at this point. The bottom line is that the big numbers, both in terms of sales and in terms of the market for readers, still favor books.

Another answer is that the technology has not evolved to the point where reading online makes for an optimal experience. Reading text on a screen still strains the eyes. And computers are not yet as portable as books are. As the oft-repeated line goes: you can't curl up in bed with your computer just yet.

But even if publishing book webs were profitable, and even if the technol-ogy were developed to the point where reading from your computer in bed is comfortable, would you favor bits over atoms as the information commodity of choice? My feeling is that for people raised in a print culture, books still carry a certain amount of cultural capital that digital technology will not erase anytime soon. Books still carry an authority and sense of permanence that Web sites do not. Would Gerry Spence's book, O. J.: The Last Word—on the O. J. Simpson case—convey the same sense of finality if it were a Web site? Given that effective Web sites are interactive and dynamic, requiring fresh content if they are to remain relevant and well visited, my sense is that it wouldn't.

In addition to the permanence and authority that books convey to those of us brought up in a print culture, books tend to have a standard structure that we expect, a structure that is conducive to developing a detailed, linear argu-ment or for building and sustaining a coherent narrative. The hypertextual na-ture of the Web tends to break free of this structure, as chunks of information can be linked together for quick access from a variety of entry points (though if you've followed this essay this far, you know this isn't always the case). The result is that the experience of going to a Web site is far different from reading a book. A visit to a Web site has the potential to be unique for each reader, no two paths through the content the same. And this is one of the reasons that books will remain relevant for a while. Part of the allure of books is the role they play in our culture as social currency: we like to talk about books. In

Interface Culture, author Steven Johnson reasons that this is the reason interactive fiction has not become popular. Each reader emerges with a different reading experience, rendering discussions of interactive books impossible.

In the end, the experience of reading books and using the Web are profoundly different, and so the revolutionary effects of digital media will not come about merely by translating the atoms of books into bits for online consumption. Although something like the book webs I imagine will evolve at some point—perhaps initially as a way of marketing printed books, as is already happening now—books will remain for quite some time because they're artifacts that embody the way those of us brought up in a print culture work, play, and live.

QUESTIONS FOR REACTION AND DISCUSSION

1. How would you characterize Hunt's attitude toward technology? Positive? Negative? Somewhere in the middle? Explain your response.
2. Hunt uses the colorful example of Jon Krakauer's *Into Thin Air* as an example of a book that could easily be expanded into a "book web." What books have you read that might work equally well? How and why?

QUESTIONS FOR WRITING

1. Hunt's position is that one major reason that neither authors nor publishers are eager to publish works online is economics. As he says, except in a few cases, few people pay to visit Web sites. How are most Web sites supported? Is the fact that *CMC Magazine* folded evidence of the economic complexities posed by virtual publishing? Investigate freely accessible Web sites that publish literature (such as a magazine like *Atlantic Unbound* or *Salon Magazine*) as well as subscription Web sites (like *The Chronicle of Higher Education* or *The New York Times*) and find out what you can about what money is being made and by whom. Write a report for your classmates in which you explain the economic advantages and/or disadvantages for online publication.
2. Hunt comments that "My feeling is that for people raised in a print culture, books still carry a certain amount of cultural capital that digital technology will not erase anytime soon. Books still carry an authority and sense of permanence that Web sites do not." Do you agree or disagree? Write an opinion paper in which you defend or reject Hunt's position. Be sure to include examples from books you have read and Web sites you have visited.

3. Hunt raises questions that other writers, such as Murray and Miller in this chapter, suggest about the linearity of print texts and the nonlinear quality of hypertexts. Hunt suggests that we continue to cling to texts because they carry "social currency." What does he mean by this phrase? Do you think this is true? Do visits to Web sites ever carry "social currency"? Do books really share the standard structure that Hunt suggests? How would Hunt account for differing interpretations of books? Write an essay in which you agree or disagree with Hunt's position that books carry social currency that Web sites do not.

QUESTIONS FOR FURTHER EXPLORATION

1. Hunt implies that book webs are already in place—as a way of marketing printed books. Visit online bookstores such as <www.amazon.com> or <www. Borders.com>. How do these sites promote the social currency of printed books? What special features do they use to attract readers and shoppers? Select some of the titles that Hunt mentions or choose your own, and read reviews and author interviews on the site. What services do these sites offer? Do the sites promote the notion of a community of readers? How and why? Write a report for your class in which you evaluate online bookstores as "book webs."

2. Read David Hudson's *Rewired*. Write a review of it and post it to the review section of the page devoted to *Rewired* on <www.amazon.com>. How does your review compare to the comments of others? Do you think the book would have been more compelling or interesting if it had been published as a "book web"? Why or why not?

4

PERSEUS UNBOUND

Sven Birkerts teaches literature at Mt. Holyoke College and is a dis-
tinguished reviewer and author of books of literary criticism and the
editor of several collections of fiction and poetry. His most recent
books are collections of essays; in Tolstoy's Dictaphone: Technology
and the Muse *(1996), Birkerts collected a variety of essays from au-*
thors writing in response to The Gutenberg Elegies. *His latest book is*
a collection of his own essays, Readings *(1999), in which he develops*
the theme of how electronic technology is altering reading and the
nature of books. Birkerts has won a number of awards, including the
National Book Critics Circle Citation for Excellence in Reviewing, as
well as fellowships from the Lila Wallace-Reader's Digest Foundation
and the Guggenheim Foundation. He writes frequently for The New
York Times Book Review, The Atlantic Monthly, Harper's Magazine,
and The New Republic. *At last report, Birkerts neither owned nor*
used a computer, and his position on the new technology can be char-
acterized as skeptical and negative. In his best-selling The Gutenberg
Elegies, *Birkerts outlines his views about the implications for the shift*
from print to screen and writes movingly about his love of printed
books and reading. Birkerts explains his view of the gains of elec-
tronic postmodernity for individuals, which he suggests are an in-
creased awareness of the big picture or a global perspective,
expanded neural capacity, a relativistic comprehension of situations
that promotes the erosion of old biases, and a matter-of-fact and un-
encumbered readiness to try new situations and arrangements. On
the other hand, Birkerts sees the losses as a fragmented sense of time,
reduction in attention span, shattered faith in institutions and in ex-
planatory narratives, an unhealthy divorce from the past, estrange-
ment from geographic place and community, and the absence of any
strong vision of a personal or collective future. These are serious is-
sues. Whether you are equally comfortable in front of a screen or a
book, Birkerts offers important points about how electronic tech-
nology is changing our ways of living—not just reading.

QUESTIONS FOR READING

1. How does the title of Birkerts's book shape your expectations about this selection? Who was Gutenberg? What is an elegy? And why does he mention Perseus in this selection?
2. What is your own position on reading and technology? Has technology changed the ways people read printed text? How does your position shape your response to this selection?

SVEN BIRKERTS

PERSEUS UNBOUND

The Gutenberg Elegies: The Fate of Reading in an Electronic Age
(New York: Fawcett Columbine, 1994)

Like it or not, interactive video technologies have muscled their way into the formerly textbound precincts of education. The videodisc has mated with the microcomputer to produce a juggernaut: a flexible and encompassing teaching tool that threatens to overwhelm the linearity of print with an array of option-rich multimedia packages. And although we are only in the early stages of implementation—institutions are by nature conservative—an educational revolution seems inevitable.

Several years ago in *Harvard Magazine,* writer Craig Lambert sampled some of the innovative ways in which these technologies have already been applied at Harvard. Interactive video programs at the Law School allow students to view simulated police busts or actual courtroom procedures. With a tap of a digit they can freeze images, call up case citations, and quickly zero-in on the relevant fine points of precedent. Medical simulations, offering the immediacy of video images and instant access to the mountains of data necessary for diagnostic assessment, can have the student all but performing surgery. And language classes now allow the learner to make an end run around tedious drill repetitions and engage in protoconversations with video partners.

The hot news in the classics world, meanwhile, is Perseus 1.0, an interactive database developed and edited by Harvard associate professor Gregory Crane. Published on CD-ROM and videodisc, the program holds, according to its publicists, "the equivalent of twenty-five volumes of ancient Greek literature by ten authors (one million Greek words), roughly four thousand glosses in the online classical encyclopedia, and a thirty-five thousand-word online Greek lexicon." Also included are an enormous photographic database (six thousand images), a short video with narration, and "hundreds of descriptions and drawings of art and archeological objects." The package is affordable, too: Perseus software can be purchased for about $350. Plugged in, the student can call up a text, read it side-by-side with its translation, and analyze any word using the Liddell-Scott lexicon; he can read a thumbnail sketch on any mythic figure cited in the text, or call up images from an atlas, or zoom in on color Landsat photos; he can even study a particular vase through innumerable angles of vantage. The dusty library stacks have never looked dustier.

Although skepticism abounds, most of it is institutional, bound up with established procedures and the proprietorship of scholarly bailiwicks. But there are grounds for other, more philosophic sorts of debate, and we can expect to see flare-ups of controversy for some time to come. For more than any other development in recent memory, these interactive technologies throw into relief the fundamental questions about knowledge and learning. Not only what are its ends, but what are its means? And how might the means be changing the ends?

From the threshold, I think, we need to distinguish between kinds of knowledge and kinds of study. Pertinent here is German philosopher Wilhelm Dilthey's distinction between the natural sciences *(Naturwissenschaften),* which seek to explain physical events by subsuming them under causal laws, and the so-called sciences of culture *(Geisteswissenschaften),* which can only understand events in terms of the intentions and meanings that individuals attach to them.

To the former, it would seem, belong the areas of study more hospitable to the new video and computer procedures. Expanded databases and interactive programs can be viewed as tools, pure and simple. They give access to more information, foster cross-referentiality, and, by reducing time and labor, allow for greater focus on the essentials of a problem. Indeed, any discipline where knowledge is sought for its application rather than for itself could only profit from the implementation of these technologies. To the natural sciences one might add the fields of language study and law.

But there is a danger with these sexy new options—and the rapture with which believers speak warrants the adjective—that we will simply assume that their uses and potentials extend across the educational spectrum into realms where different kinds of knowledge, and hence learning, are at issue. The realms, that is, of *Geisteswissenschaften,* which have at their center the humanities.

In the humanities, knowledge is a means, yes, but it is a means less to instrumental application than to something more nebulous: understanding. We study history or literature or classics in order to compose and refine a narrative, or a set of narratives about what the human world used to be like, about how the world came to be as it is, and about what we have been—and are— like as psychological or spiritual creatures. The data—the facts, connections, the texts themselves—matter insofar as they help us to deepen and extend that narrative. In these disciplines the *process* of study may be as vital to the understanding as are the materials studied.

Given the great excitement generated by Perseus, it is easy to imagine that in the near future a whole range of innovative electronic-based learning packages will be available and, in many places, in use. These will surely include the manifold variations on the electronic book. Special new software texts are already being developed to bring us into the world of, say, Shakespeare, not only glossing the literature, but bathing the user in multimedia supplements. The would-be historian will step into an environment rich in choices, be they visual detailing, explanatory graphs, or suggested connections and sideroads. And so on. Moreover, once the price is right, who will be the curmudgeons who would deny their students access to the state-of-the-art?

Being a curmudgeon is a dirty job, but somebody has to do it. Someone has to hoist the warning flags and raise some issues that the fast-track proselytizers might overlook. Here are a few reservations worth pondering.

1. Knowledge, certainly in the humanities, is not a straightforward matter of access, of conquest via the ingestion of data. Part of any essential understanding of the world is that it is opaque, obdurate. To me, Wittgenstein's famous axiom, "The world is everything that is the case," translates into a recognition of otherness. The past is as much about the disappearance of things through time as it is about the recovery of traces and the reconstruction of vistas. Say what you will about books, they not only mark the backward trail, but they also encode this sense of obstacle, of otherness. The look of the printed page changes as we regress in time; under the orthographic changes are the changes in the language itself. Old-style textual research may feel like an unnecessarily slow burrowing, but it is itself an instruction: It confirms that time is a force as implacable as gravity.

Yet the multimedia packages would master this gravity. For opacity they substitute transparency, promoting the illusion of access. All that has been said, known, and done will yield to the dance of the fingertips on the terminal keys. Space becomes hyperspace, and time, hypertime ("hyper–" being the fashionable new prefix that invokes the nonlinear and nonsequential "space" made possible by computer technologies). One gathers the data of otherness, but through a medium which seems to level the feel—the truth—of that otherness. The field of knowledge is rendered as a lateral and synchronic enterprise susceptible to collage, not as a depth phenomenon. And if our media restructure our perceptions, as McLuhan and others have argued, then we may start producing generations who know a great deal of "information" about the past but who have no purchase on pastness itself.

Described in this way, the effects of interactive programs on users sound a good deal like the symptoms of postmodernism. And indeed, this recent cultural aesthetic, distinguished by its flat, bright, and often affectless assemblages of materials may be a consequence of a larger transformation of sensibility by information-processing technologies. After all, our arts do tend to mirror who we are and anticipate what we might be becoming. Changes of this magnitude are of course systemic, and their direction is not easily dictated. Whether the postmodern "vision" can be endorsed as a pedagogic platform, however, is another question.

2. Humanistic knowledge, as I suggested earlier, differs from the more instrumental kinds of knowledge in that it ultimately seeks to fashion a

comprehensible narrative. It is, in other words, about the creation and expansion of meaningful contexts. Interactive media technologies are, at least in one sense, anticontextual. They open the field to new widths, constantly expanding relevance and reference, and they equip their user with a powerful grazing tool. One moves at great rates across subject terrains, crossing borders that were once closely guarded. The multimedia approach tends ineluctably to multidisciplinarianism. The positive effect, of course, is the creation of new levels of connection and integration; more and more variables are brought into the equation.

But the danger should be obvious: The horizon, the limit that gave definition to the parts of the narrative, will disappear. The equation itself will become nonsensical through the accumulation of variables. The context will widen until it becomes, in effect, everything. On the model of Chaos science, wherein the butterfly flapping its wings in China is seen to affect the weather system over Oklahoma, all data will impinge upon all other data. The technology may be able to handle it, but will the user? Will our narratives—historical, literary, classical—be able to withstand the data explosion? If they cannot, then what will be the new face of understanding? Or will the knowledge of the world become, perforce, a map as large and intricate as the world itself?

3. We might question, too, whether there is not in learning as in physical science a principle of energy conservation. Does a gain in one area depend upon a loss in another? My guess would be that every lateral attainment is purchased with a sacrifice of depth. The student may, through a program on Shakespeare, learn an immense amount about Elizabethan politics, the construction of the Globe theater, the origins of certain plays in the writings of Plutarch, the etymology of key terms, and so on, but will this dazzled student find the concentration, the will, to live with the often burred and prickly language of the plays themselves? The play's the thing—but will it be? Wouldn't the sustained exposure to a souped-up cognitive collage not begin to affect the attention span, the ability if not willingness to sit with one text for extended periods, butting up against its cruxes, trying to excavate meaning from the original rhythms and syntax? The gurus of interaction love to say that the student learns best by doing, but let's not forget that *reading* a work is also a kind of doing.

4. As a final reservation, what about the long-term cognitive effects of these new processes of data absorption? Isn't it possible that more may be less, and that the neural networks have one speed for taking in—a speed that can be increased—and quite another rate for retention? Again, it may be that our technologies will exceed us. They will make it not only possible but irresistible to consume data at what must strike people of the book as very high rates. But what then? What will happen as our neural systems, evolved through millennia to certain capacities, modify themselves to hold ever-expanding loads? Will we simply become smarter, able to hold and process more? Or do we have to reckon with some other gain/loss formula? One possible cognitive response, call it the "S.A.T. cram-course model"—might be an expansion of the short-term memory banks and a correlative atrophying of long-term memory.

But here our technology may well assume a new role. Once it dawns on us, as it must, that our software will hold all the information we need at ready access, we may very well let it. That is, we may choose to become the technicians of our auxiliary brains, mastering not the information but the retrieval and referencing functions. At a certain point, then, we could become the evolutionary opposites of our forebears, who, lacking external technology, committed everything to memory. If this were to happen, what would be the status of knowing, of being educated? The leader of the electronic tribe would not be the person who knew most, but the one who could execute the broadest range of technical functions. What, I hesitate to ask, would become of the already antiquated notion of wisdom?

I recently watched a public television special on the history of the computer. One of the many experts and enthusiasts interviewed took up the knowledge question. He explained how the formerly two-dimensional process of book-based learning is rapidly becoming three-dimensional. The day will come, he opined, when interactive and virtual technologies will allow us to more or less dispense with our reliance on the sequence-based print paradigm. Whatever the object of our study, our equipment will be able to get us there directly: inside the volcano or the violin-maker's studio, right up on the stage. I was enthralled, but I shuddered, too, for it struck me that when our technologies are all in place—when all databases have been refined and integrated—that will be the day when we stop living in the old hard world and take up residence in some bright new hyperworld, a kind of Disneyland of information. I have to wonder if this is what Perseus and its kindred programs might not be edging us toward. That program got its name, we learn from the brochure, from the Greek mythological hero Perseus, who was the explorer of the limits of the known world. I confess that I can't think of Perseus without also thinking of Icarus, heedless son of Daedalus, who allowed his wings to carry him over the invisible line that was inscribed across the skyway.

QUESTIONS FOR REACTION AND DISCUSSION

1. Birkerts alludes to philosophers and other writers and uses German words. Some partial meanings can be gleaned from the context. Construct a vocabulary list along with identifications and definitions for any names or terms that are unfamiliar to you.
2. Summarize the reservations Birkerts offers about multimedia packages like Perseus. Why does he label these the response of a "curmudgeon"? Does that make you more or less sympathetic with his position? Why?
3. Birkerts uses Perseus as the figure who explores the unknown, then makes a negative connection. What positive "explorers" of the unknown could Birkerts have used instead of Daedalus?

QUESTIONS FOR WRITING

1. An important distinction that Birkerts makes is one between kinds of knowledge and kinds of study. He suggests that there are certain areas that are more hospitable to electronic technologies than others. Based on your own knowledge of the curriculum you are undertaking as a college student, is this true? Write a position paper, outlining your sense of what fields of knowledge and fields of study are more generally aided by technology.

2. Birkerts says elsewhere in *The Gutenberg Elegies* that "Wisdom has nothing to do with the gathering or organizing of facts—this is basic. Wisdom is a seeing through facts, a penetration to the underlying laws and patterns." In "Perseus Unbound," Birkerts suggests that some students might think that access to the texts and apparatus offered by a program like Perseus was the same thing as acquiring knowledge or even wisdom. What is the distinction between access and wisdom? What is Birkerts's concern about the easy accessibility that computer technology fosters? Write a position paper on your view of the distinction between access and wisdom. What examples from your own educational experience can you draw on to use in support of your view?

3. Are you as convinced about the negative effects of the new technology as Birkerts? Write a position paper in which you agree or disagree with his reservations.

QUESTIONS FOR FURTHER EXPLORATION

1. On May 30, 1995, Sven Birkerts participated in an online conference for the *Atlantic Monthly Online* on the America Online network. Access the site for this conference at <http://www.theatlantic.com/unbound/aandc/trnscrpt/birkerts.htm> and read the discussion between the host, Scott Stossel, and Birkerts. Analyze Birkerts's remarks and write an informal essay in which you agree or disagree with his position.

2. Imagine a debate between Janet Murray and Sven Birkerts. Write a "transcript" of a conversation between them in response to questions that you, as an interviewer, ask. Think carefully about points on which they might agree, as well as the points on which they would surely disagree.

3. Use *Book Review Digest* or *The Reader's Guide to Periodical Literature* to find reviews of Birkerts's book. What is the consensus of the reviewers? Can you draw any conclusions about how this book has been received and who is reading it? Write a review following the format for an online bookstore (like <http://www.amazon.com>) in which you give your "review" of the selection you read.

5

Virtual Grub Street

Paul Roberts is a writer who lives in Seattle. In this essay, he describes his experiences as a multimedia writer engaged in digital publishing. Trained as a journalist, Roberts gives a firsthand account of the way in which text is produced for CD-ROM companies. As the original subtitle of his essay suggests ("Sorrows of a Multimedia Hack"), the essay is an account of one person's deeply felt concerns about the future of writing in the electronic age. This essay appeared in Harper's Magazine, *one of the oldest magazines in America. Founded in 1850 as* Harper's New Monthly Magazine *by book publishers, the magazine printed the works of well-known American writers, such as Mark Twain and Henry James in the nineteenth century. Today the magazine is known for its award-winning fiction and essays, as well as for features such as* Harper's Index, *a list of unusual statistics that serve as a guide to contemporary American culture. An online version, <http://www.harpers.org>, includes archives and historical information about the magazine. "Virtual Grub Street" appeared in the "Criticism," a section of the magazine devoted to commentary on a variety of aspects of American life.*

Questions for Reading

1. The title of this essay refers to Grub Street, once an actual street near the section of London called Moorfields. In the seventeenth and eighteenth century, the street was home to a number of professional writers who produced poems, short essays, and dictionaries. "Grub Street" came to refer to writers, or "hacks," who made a meager living from their work. With this reference in mind, what does the title suggest about the essay?
2. What are some of the points that Roberts makes about the process of writing itself? Make notes about his comments as you read, indicating those that describe your own experiences in writing essays for classes.

PAUL ROBERTS

VIRTUAL GRUB STREET:
SORROWS OF A MULTIMEDIA HACK

Harper's Magazine *(June 1996, pp. 71-77)*

It's Wednesday, late afternoon, and I'm writing about classical composers—Bach, Beethoven, Mozart, and so on, thirty of them—for a multimedia product on European history. It's an odd assignment. I've never written about music or studied the people who make it. My specialty, before I started writing for CD-ROM companies, was environmental journalism, and what I know about classical composers is, basically, *Amadeus*. But ignorance, in the new electronic literature, isn't always an obstacle. The irony of the information revolution is that consumers neither like nor expect long, densely written texts on their computer screens. Long texts addle the eyes; they slow the rapid-fire "interactive" process, steal precious screen space from the animation, video, and multimedia's other, more marketable gewgaws. So we writers needn't be experts so much as filters whose task is to absorb and compress great gobs of information into small, easily digestible, on-screen chunks. Brevity and blandness: these are the elements of the next literary style. Of roughly one thousand "essays" I've "written" for CD-ROM companies here in Seattle over the last year and a half, fewer than forty ran longer than two hundred words—about the length of the paragraph you're reading now—and most were much, much shorter.

I never expected to be working like this. I once earned a respectable living writing long, earnest articles about spotted owls, riparian buffer zones, even, on one occasion, a ten thousand-word treatise on the Douglas fir, hero tree of the Pacific Northwest. Nowadays, whole months go by when I do nothing but crank out info-nuggets on whatever topics the multimedia companies believe will sell: dead composers, large African mammals, sports stars of yore. It is, without question, hack writing, the kind of pap (I used to think) only the feckless and unprincipled had the nerve or need to take. But if the emergence of the so-called new media has clarified anything, it's just how malleable literary standards and professional expectations are, how quickly they can wither or mutate or be ignored altogether in the presence of powerful novelty and cold cash. In early 1994, just before I joined the digital revolution, few of my writer friends had any understanding of what CD-ROM was, much less any desire to write for it. Today, half of the writers I know in this town are either working in electronic publishing or trying to.

> A brilliant performer from a young age, Austria's Wolfgang Amadeus Mozart (1756–1791) was perhaps the most influential composer of the eighteenth century. He wrote more than 130 works, including the operas *Don Giovanni* and *The Marriage of Figaro*, and is noted for his purity of form and melody. Despite such talents, Mozart struggled financially, earning a meager living as a pianist and tutor. He died a pauper at age thirty-five.

An economist might explain the current literary redeployment as a simple shift in supply and demand. Between Christmas 1993 and Christmas 1995, consumer ownership of CD-ROM drives jumped from fewer than nine million to an estimated forty million, with another seventeen million purchases projected by the end of 1996. What was accurately described a few years ago as a garage industry is now very much a mass market, and to keep it that way multimedia companies like Microsoft and Voyager and Broderbund are spending billions of dollars developing thousands of new CD-ROM titles in virtually every category one can imagine: games, naturally, but also encyclopedias, interactive magazines, children's products, how-tos, history, science, wildlife, even pornography. This title wave has generated a massive demand for what multimedia executives glibly call "content," launching the industry on an enormous hiring binge: software engineers and digital artists, of course, but also legions of writers and editors, lured away from newspapers, film companies, magazines, and publishing houses, plucked from the ranks of the un- and underemployed (or "freelance," to use the more generous term) and offered more money a week than many previously had made in a month. For those of us raised to believe that a career in writing meant a life at or near the poverty line, multimedia feels like a gold rush, a wartime buildup, a massive new government program.

But the new media's appeal to writers goes beyond dollars. There's the allure of a sexy new technology, sharpened by a fear of professional obsolescence. The fact is, multimedia can do things the printed page never even dreamed about. It's digital, which means that obscene amounts of data can be encoded and stored on a four-inch, wafer-thin laser disc. It's also *interactive,* which means that all those digitized artifacts—hundreds of photos and graphics, video clips, my own wee texts—can be linked together in a kind of electronic-semantic web. You can access my "essay" on Mozart, for example, from any number of other texts on the disc, simply by finding the word "Mozart" in highlighted, or "hot," text and clicking on it with your mouse. You could be reading something on eighteenth-century music, say, or Viennese opera, and—*click*—up pops my terse little bio. But there's more. Once inside my text, you might click on the words "Don Giovanni," and get yet another text, or perhaps a few seconds of music from the opera, or a video clip from *Amadeus.* And once in "Don Giovanni," you might encounter the word "Italy" and click up a nice little geopolitical summary. And so on. Each multimedia text—and, theoretically, each word in each text—can serve as an electronic portal to an infinite number of other digital locations. With a series of clicks, you can hop from one object of fascination to any number of others, branching this way and that along various semantic trails, creating your very own, custom-built, nonlinear narrative from a vast reservoir of recombinant texts.

> Clear waters and abundant marine life make Mafia, an island off the coast of Tanzania, one of the best diving spots in the world. Tropical temperatures are ideal for many varieties of crustaceans, including lobsters. Divers also encounter huge schools of fantastically colored fish and can swim with sea turtles, octopuses, large but docile whale sharks, and occasionally, the manatee-like dugong.

Nonlinearity might seem like little more than channel surfing, but its proponents—ranging from wealthy software gurus to tenured English professors—champion it as an authentic yet functional postmodern form, a critical break from the age-old, rigidly linear format of the printed page. Nonlinearity, we're told, redistributes narrative power to readers. It undermines the tyranny of the Author. Its branching "intertextuality" is a much closer match to the brain's own networks. Indeed, advocates believe that with nonlinear text, or *hypertext*, literature can at last give full expression to the kinds of unconventional discursive impulses that folks like Joyce and Barthes were forced to convey via the grotesquely obsolete linear format. For that matter, nonlinearity provides a kind of running critique of the linear format, laying open the myth that "stories" can be told only one way, in only one direction, and toward only one conclusion: toward "closure." With nonlinearity, as with thought itself, there is no closure, only additional links. Thus nonlinearity, to its proponents, is the beginning of a new, more honest and complex literature—and, perhaps, the beginning of the end of an old one. "The printed book . . . seems destined to move to the margin of our literature culture," writes Jay David Bolter, a Georgia Tech professor of communications and one of the more articulate exponents of electronic texts. "Print will no longer define the organization and presentation of knowledge, as it has for the past five centuries."

Personally, I've never achieved the degree of literary transcendence that these advocates describe. Down at the level where I operate, the digital "revolution" is actually something of a bust, a high-tech revival of the piecemeal sensibility that animated the pulp magazines and the early broadsheets. But mine, it seems, is a minority view. Even as you read this, editors and publishers the world over are practically wetting themselves in the rush to get their content "on disc" or "online." Meanwhile, my brethren are flocking in ever greater numbers to digital-writing conferences with an enthusiasm more typically encountered at Tony Robbins seminars. Last year, to offer just one example, a Seattle arts organization sponsored a workshop for writers hoping to break into multimedia—nothing special, just a local CD-ROM producer sharing insights and showing demos. It sold out. Tickets, at forty dollars each, were snapped up weeks in advance. The night of the event, organizers ran out of chairs, and folks who hadn't bothered to preregister actually had to wait on standby, like fans at a rock concert, praying for no-shows. What a poignant comment on the digital revolution: an overflow crowd of writers—sensitive, struggling artistic types, by and large—forking over a week's grocery money to hear not some world-famous poet or author but a mid-level exec in an industry whose greatest hit is an interactive game called Myst and whose primary unit of literary meaning is a toneless, unsigned blurb that, for all the cleverness of its high-tech format, could have been written anytime during the previous five hundred years.

Tormons Tablets cure all disorders of the Liver, Stomach, and Bowels, Headache, Dyspepsia, Constipation, Biliousness, Dizziness; Clear the Complexion, Increase the Appetite, Tone the System, and are a sure Remedy for Depression of Spirits, General Debility, Kidney Complaints, Nervousness, Sour Stomach, Disturbed Sleep, etc.

I'm making most of these examples up, by necessity. The multimedia industry is hugely paranoid about leaks and we're all required to sign fiercely worded nondisclosure agreements, or NDAs, before we're even told the topic of our next assignment. Such secrecy usually baffles the newly initiated, particularly after they see what they'll be writing and how unlikely a target of industrial espionage it is. Still, I can't reveal the names of my client companies and bosses, or the CD-ROM titles I've worked on. Technically, I'm not even supposed to disclose the existence of the nondisclosure agreements. It's as if multimedia companies want deniability, as if the transaction between writer and publisher never occurred. In multimedia, as in other instances of corporate creativity, text simply *happens*. It appears on-screen without any evidence of being authored by a single, living individual.

NDAs notwithstanding, it's probably safe to reveal that I am, in fact, a real person, thirty-four, married, with a two-year-old daughter and four-year communications degree. Like many multimedia writers, I got my literary start in newspapers and magazines, settling finally at an alternative newsweekly in Seattle. Also like many multimedia writers, I work mostly at home. My text-production facility is a small second-floor study in my eighty-year-old house, in a wooded, hillside neighborhood seven miles from downtown Seattle. My workspace resembles that of any busy writer: computer, reference books, coffee cups. The giveaway is the floor. It's almost always buried beneath thick strata of mimeographed articles on a range of topics too diverse for a normal journalist: Roman history, Greek philosophy, rain forest ecology, medieval battle tactics, Mayan archaeology, Romantic poets, mountain climbing.

Sadly, multimedia writers are too harried to savor the variety of subject matter. Although a single CD-ROM title might contain several thousand separate text blocks, text budgets are typically small in comparison with budgets for the more time- and memory-consuming video or audio components. Thus, the famously high wages for writers—anywhere from eighteen dollars to thirty dollars an hour—are based on the expectation that we will extrude texts with machine-like efficiency. Producers are always encouraging us, dropping such helpful comments as "These really shouldn't take more than thirty minutes apiece" and "I was getting about three of these done an hour." I've no idea where they get these estimates, but the tactic is effective. Before I developed the rhythms and strategies of the seasoned multimedia writer, I kept a stopwatch by my computer, struggling to crank out each blurb in under fifteen minutes. This follows another irony of the information revolution: the texts of the next century are being manufactured much like the products of the last one—on an hourly basis in a vast, decentralized electronic sweatshop.

For a time I was able to take a romantic pleasure in the frenzied pace of the work. It seemed so classic, so nineteenth century. Dostoevsky and Dickens both poured forth prodigious streams of words every week. George Gissing hammered out the 220,000-word novel *New Grub Street*, the portrait of a hack writer, at the rate of about three thousand, five hundred words a day— half again as much as my best performance. But my fantasies soon buckled under the load. Those walking word machines wound up with true works of art. All I have at the end of the day is screen after screen of blurbs.

> Invented by Christopher Sholes in 1867, the typewriter transformed both the process and content of written communication. Typewritten letters were initially dismissed as cold and impersonal but quickly came to dominate business writing, while the typewriters themselves helped open office work to women. Mechanical typewriters were eventually replaced by electric models, which in turn have been rendered all but obsolete by computer word processors.

Most multimedia writers I know didn't plan their move into electronic publishing. I, for example, was never a computer enthusiast. To the degree that I considered it at all, the entire phenomenon of interactive CD-ROM—which even then was being invented in suburban office parks just a few miles east of my house—seemed like a brush war in another hemisphere: vaguely interesting, mostly irrelevant. But things change. My newspaper's rumor mill warned of impending layoffs, my daughter arrived, and I began to notice that many of my writer-acquaintances were disappearing, one by one, from the freelance ranks. I'd meet them at parties and no sooner had talk turned to jobs than they'd launch into breathless depictions of the *work* they were doing, and the *technology* they were using, and, more to the point, the buckets of money they were earning. No one had ever talked this way about writing. It was like hearing some just-returned settler describing the frontier: wide-open and mine for the taking.

My first multimedia assignment, finagled through a friend of a friend, came in the spring of 1994. A man called me at home and asked whether I knew what CD-ROM was and if I had ever written for digital publications. I mumbled an ambiguous reply and found myself the following afternoon in a small beige office in the suburban megalopolis known hereabouts as the Eastside. The voice on the phone turned out to belong to the project producer, a gaunt fellow in his thirties whom I'll call Bob. Bob shook hands hastily. He wore faded blue jeans and an untucked polo shirt. A year before, he'd been editing a magazine somewhere east of the Rockies. Today, he seemed harassed and tired and in serious need of cigarettes. Bob asked a few perfunctory questions about my writing, interrupting my answers with a staccato "uh-huh, uh-huh," then, apparently satisfied, hauled out a nondisclosure agreement. I signed it. Bob explained that I was now legally barred from telling anyone, including family and friends, anything about the Project. I laughed. Bob looked cross. He related a story of several loose-lipped former employees who had been tracked down and prosecuted. "They're serious about this," said Bob, catching and holding my gaze.

Later, as I learned more about the industry, the NDAs became more understandable. Title budgets can top one million dollars, with no profits expected for three years. The more excited a company is about a project under development, the more paranoid its staff becomes that a single leak might let a rival get to market first with a similar product. I'm still not sure if these fears are valid or simply an extension of the militaristic paranoia and manic team-spiritedness that have long energized the software industry. In any case, secrecy remains a central component of multimedia's corporate character, infusing what is essentially an entertainment business with a gravity both absurd and titillating.

At least, I found it so. Bob, apparently, was well past the philosophizing stage and was also in a hurry. He moved deftly from the NDA to a terse discussion of production schedules, software requirements, and, finally, the Assignment, handing me a list of fifty subjects, somewhat historical in nature, and a thick stack of reference materials. He wanted seventy-five words on each by the start of the following week. Nothing fancy. Simple declarative sentences. High school reading level. Tight. No one had ever talked to me about writing like this before, either. I felt disoriented, like Barton Fink after he receives his first assignment for a "wrestling movie." I scanned Bob's office, looking for clues as to what I'd gotten myself into. On the wall, I spied a chalkboard sketch, a series of small circles, each labeled with an abbreviation ("Intro.," "Vid.," "Aud.") and all interconnected by spokes. A nonlinear conceptual blueprint, Bob explained vaguely, waving at it. For the project. For the first time, he smiled. "But you guys don't need to worry about that."

The truth is that multimedia writers needn't worry about a great many things. We get our assignments, write our texts, and some months later, a shiny disc wrapped in an inordinate amount of packaging hits the shelves at Egghead or Waldenbooks. No one expects us to understand or care what happens to our texts in the interim, because writers are mere cogs in the multimedia machine. We're never asked to generate story ideas and pitch them to editors. We needn't concern ourselves with story structure, or themes, or any of the other, more celebrated elements of traditional writing. All that is handled by the engineers and designers and scriptwriters who lay out the disc's schematic, who decide where and when the digital objects will appear, which object will be linked to which, and why. Questions traditional writers might agonize over for hours or days—lead paragraphs, say, or transitions—have been rendered moot by the peculiarities of the nonlinear narrative.

What remains for CD-ROM writers isn't so much writing as tailoring; tucking specified content into a specified space. Producers send us off with sage, neo-Strunkish advice: avoid complex syntax and vocabulary; suppress "voice" or "attitude"; do not, under any circumstances, exceed the specific word count. It's a strange way to write. Strange, too, to see how easily the brain shifts from the extended symphonic rhythms of a longer article to the staccato jingle of the one-hundred word blurb. Dismaying, actually. Yet the self-disgust pales, at least initially, against the sensation of relief. Conventional, linear writing can be a gruesome task. Beyond the lame pay and the feast-or-famine job cycle, the pounding of disparate facts and feelings into a tightly structured narrative is like digging a ditch across a concrete parking lot. By contrast, squirting out blurbs is a cakewalk, a lower-order process managed, I'm sure, by the same lobe that handles heart rate and knitting. For the first few months, I felt as if I'd entered a writers' fairy land, where one could earn a good living without anxieties or writer's block, without the corrosive oscillations between depression and ecstasy—just a steady putt-putt-putt of words. I'd fire up the computer at 8:00 a.m., shut it down at supper, and by the time I'd raised the fork to my lips, whatever I had been working on six minutes earlier had evaporated from my head.

> The fifty-word caption typically begins with a declarative sentence summarizing the photographed subject. The second sentence puts the first in context with a general topic statement. The third adds interesting, even humorous detail. Beginning multimedia writers are often advised to study magazines famous for their captions, including *National Geographic* and *Life*.

My disillusionment with multimedia grew less out of any principled objection than from a slow accretion of insults and revelations. There was the sheer tedium of blurb writing. There were also the routine demonstrations of text's low rank on the CD-ROM totem pole: whenever software engineers had trouble cramming all the visual components onto a disc, we writers would simply be told to chop our texts in half. As my meager status sunk in, I found it ever harder at parties to wax enthusiastic about my job. My humor darkened. I took to introducing myself as a hack, a blurbmeister, affecting a cynicism that I didn't quite feel but I knew was coming.

From a distance, a multimedia text looks exactly like a paragraph plucked from a standard linear narrative. But closer inspection reveals important differences. In "normal" writing, the writer uses the paragraph as a bridge between specific points. Not so with the multimedia text block. Each blurb must, almost by definition, carry out its minimal literary function in virtual independence from the rest of the story. If I'm writing multimedia Text A, for example, I can assume no specific prior knowledge on the part of the reader, because he or she may be arriving at Text A from any of a number of previous texts. Similarly, I can't use Text A to set up Text B, because the reader may be bouncing to any number of Text Bs. For that matter, I can't even infuse Text A with a meaning or sentiment that is essential to the reader's understanding of, or pleasure in, the larger narrative, because the reader, as narrative boss, may skip Text A entirely. The style of the multimedia text, if you want to call it a style, is one of expendability.

I realize that even in a conventional article, I can't make my "linear" readers read what I write in the order that I write it. Linear readers skim. They jump ahead, looking for interesting parts, then refer back for context—behaving, in some respects, like the multimedia user. But the nonlinear interactive process undeniably accelerates this haphazardness. The nexus of creativity is shifted from the writer to either the producers, who lay out the text links, or the readers, who make use of those links.

To be fair, if a multimedia writer has the technical expertise and the financial resources to control the entire story-line process, some interesting literary and journalistic forms are possible. Allowing readers to choose their own research paths, or, in the case of nonlinear fiction, to choose among multiple outcomes, probably qualifies as a genuine step forward in literary evolution. The reality, however, is that most multimedia writers are not (and, given the complexity and expense of production, aren't likely to be) in control of the entire process or even a large chunk thereof. Multimedia is the epitome of corporate production, of breaking projects into elements and doling them out. As such, the average writer is effectively, if not intentionally, sealed off from the larger narrative, and quickly learns not even to think about how the texts will be used or where the writing is going, because it doesn't matter. One text is pretty much like another, a self-contained literary unit: modular, disposable, accessible from any angle, leading both everywhere and nowhere.

> Larger text blocks, though providing more freedom than captions, often prove harder to write. Readers anticipate more information, so more hard data— distances, ages, sizes, dates, etc.—are critical. Larger texts also require some adherence to standard writing "rules," such as varying sentence length, as well as some degree of structural innovation. Themes raised in an opening sentence, for example, may require mention or resolution in the conclusion. Ultimately, however, larger texts can grant only the temporary illusion of conventional writing, such that writers embark in directions that, while interesting, simply cannot be explored within the allotted space.

Nonlinearity advocates often claim that a conventional writer's frustration with this new form stems from the loss of authorial control. We are angry that readers can pick and choose among our ideas—can mix our texts with information from entirely separate sources. Mostly, though, we are threatened by the new kind of mind that such writing requires. "A philosophy of mind for the coming age of writing," Bolter writes, "will have to recognize the mind as a network . . . spreading out beyond the individual mind to embrace other texts, written in other minds. . . . The most radical solution would dispense altogether with the notion of intentionality: there is no privileged author but simply textual networks that are always open to interpretation. Such a philosophy may be nothing less than the end of the ego, the end of the Cartesian self as the defining quality of humanity."

I admit that the thought of losing narrative control is excruciating. But is my frustration so selfish or authoritarian? We hardly expect musicians or sculptors to allow their work to be pulled apart and reassembled with bits and pieces from other artists. We writers are no less invested in our work and cannot be expected to delight in the prospect of merely contributing to a collective, egoless supertext. Nor are we likely to be persuaded that the journalistic imperative—to educate and inform a readership—can come about via a format that is so antithetical to persuasion or extended analysis.

Ultimately, what depresses me most about multimedia writing is its sheer pleasurelessness. Conventional writing, even at its low-paying, psychotic worst, provides me with an intellectual challenge, and lets me attempt a mastery of language and form. Writing allows me to tell stories. Multimedia writing is not about telling a story. It's about telling fragments of stories, fragments that may or may not add up to anything. It's about preparation and research—everything but the actual narrative release. At the end of the project, you're left saturated and unfulfilled, ready to burst. One Saturday night, at a friend's house for dinner, having spent the previous four weeks writing tidbits for a science title, I found myself rambling almost uncontrollably about the project. For a full forty-five minutes, I flouted the nondisclosure agreement, marshaling facts and figures, prying open one-hundred word capsules and spreading their contents into a tale I'd been unable to tell for nearly a month.

> The universe is believed to be between ten billion and twenty billion years old. Composed mainly of empty space, the universe is dotted with countless stars, galaxies, and planets. Some scientists theorize the universe began as a single, ultradense ball of matter, which exploded. This so-called Big Bang Theory may explain why all known objects, including those in our galaxy, are moving away from one another at high speeds.

We are living, according to some high-tech advocates, in the "late age of print," and I have to say that the business of writing is being transformed with amazing speed. Publishers continue to pour out new discs by the cargo-container load. Conferences go on inviting neo-luminati to discuss the shape and substance of the new New Literature. Phone and cable and computer companies, meanwhile, are developing fantastic new technologies to bring interactive everything to consumers' fingertips. So while the explosive growth of the CD-ROM industry is waning somewhat, the creative slack is being vacuumed up by online services, whose technical criteria place similar requirements on writing and whose managers seem to be hiring writers with almost as much vigor.

Indeed, I can imagine a not-so-distant future when a sizable fraction of professional writers won't ever enter the world of print but will go directly from school to digital publishing. Maybe they'll be constrained at first by the needs of older readers who were raised on print and who have only recently and partially and timidly converted to the nonlinear faith. But in time, this will change, as printing comes to be seen as too expensive and cumbersome, as computers become more powerful and more interlinked, and as they show up in every classroom and office, in every living room and den. My twelve-year old nephew lives in a small, rural eastern Washington town, yet he is as comfortable with on-screen multimedia presentations as with comic books. He represents the mind that writers will write for. Perhaps his generation will perceive language in a different way. Perhaps the understanding and meaning and pleasure they will derive from creating and consuming nonlinear text will be as significant and as beautiful as anything that has come during print's three thousand, five hundred-year reign. Yet I can't help viewing this future with alarm and sadness, not simply because I question the quality of the literature these people will have but because I can already see that I won't be capable of comprehending it. I have participated in, and in some small way precipitated, my own obsolescence. For those raised in the tradition of linear print, this may represent the bleakest irony of the digital revolution—that we so willingly took part in our own extinction.

QUESTIONS FOR REACTION AND DISCUSSION

1. What is multimedia writing? What examples do you know of or have you used?
2. How does Roberts describe the "nonlinearity" of hypertext? Explain his definition in your own words.
3. What is a nondisclosure agreement? Why does Roberts have to sign one in order to work for the companies who employ him?
4. Roberts describes himself as working in a "vast, decentralized electronic sweatshop." What does he mean by using these terms? What is the effect on you as a reader?
5. What depresses Roberts the most about multimedia writing?

QUESTIONS FOR WRITING

1. Summarize the differences Roberts sees between multimedia writing and an essay like "Virtual Grub Street." What are the major differences? What does Roberts see as being lost in multimedia writing? Write an essay, incorporating your summary and commenting on Roberts's negative view of the new writing.
2. Roberts's essay is a personal experience essay that invites readers to share his opinion about the future of writing in an electronic age. Write an essay in which you use your personal experience in the world of electronic writing—whether positive or negative—and present your opinion about the future.
3. Roberts quotes Jay David Bolter, author of *Writing Space: The Computer, Hypertext, and the History of Writing* in this essay when he says that "The Printed book . . . Seems destined to move to the margin of our literate culture." Other writers in this section (Hunt, Birkerts, and Himmelfarb) also comment on the way in which the position of printed texts is changing in our culture. Write an essay in which you

compare and contrast the views of Roberts and another writer on the demise of the printed book.

QUESTIONS FOR FURTHER EXPLORATION

1. Check the reference holdings of your library and access a CD-ROM of the kind that Roberts might have written for—some standard examples are both general and specialized encyclopedias such as the *Encyclopedia Britannica* and the *Catholic Encyclopedia*. Read some random entries and write a brief commentary on their effectiveness.
2. Locate a reference work such as *CD-ROMs in Print* or access an on-line catalogue of CD-ROMs. Select a topic—such as tourism in your state, science for children, or an activity like fishing or cooking. What kinds of CD-ROMs are available? What companies prepare such titles? What can you find out about writers they use? Research one of the companies that produces titles on your topic and prepare a brief report for your class.

6

"RAMPING UP" TO SUPPORT 42,000 STUDENT COMPUTERS ON A SINGLE CAMPUS

Every college and university in the country has to deal with a serious issue in technology: how to provide computer access to students. This article about the efforts of the University of Florida to require all students to have computers describes one of dozens of ways that institutions have worked to insure that students will have access to the tools and information computers provide. Kelly McCollum is a senior reporter on information technology issues for The Chronicle of Higher Education, *a weekly newspaper published in printed form and on the Internet <http://chronicle.com>. The* Chronicle *covers higher education in the United States and abroad and is read by more than 400,000 college and university administrators and faculty members. Each issue includes news about campuses in the United States and abroad, articles on developments in scholarly research, features on professional issues, articles and reviews on information technology, reports on state and federal government actions that affect higher education, statistical reports on varied topics like student enrollment and tuition figures, lists of new scholarly books, job listings, and a calendar of events. The* Chronicle *is an excellent source of information on all aspects of higher education. This article, a feature story in the "Information Technology" section of the* Chronicle, *is a report and commentary on the decision of the University of Florida to dramatically increase computer use on its campus.*

QUESTIONS FOR READING

1. As you read, make notes on how the article is organized. Is it easy to follow? Why or why not? How is unfamiliar information handled? What terms do you need to know in order to understand this article fully?

2. Think about your own access to sophisticated computer technology. Do you own your own machine? How were you trained to use it? Does your college or university make computers available to its students? Do you believe students should be required to use computers?

KELLY McCOLLUM

AT UNIVERSITY OF FLORIDA, "RAMPING UP" TO SUPPORT 42,000 STUDENT COMPUTERS ON A SINGLE CAMPUS

The Chronicle of Higher Education *(March 20, 1998, pp. 427–29)*

Last spring, when they announced that all 42,000 students at the University of Florida would soon be required to own personal computers, administrators were fully aware that neither the faculty, the support-services staff, nor the campus network was ready for such an onslaught. But that was part of their plan.

"The requirement is actually not for the students—it's for the university," says John V. Lombardi, Florida's president, a sometime computer-magazine columnist who is by all accounts the motivating force behind the new requirement. Up to seventy percent of Florida's students already own personal computers, he and others here estimate, but making computers an official requirement will let all students add the cost of the machines into financial-aid calculations. At the same time, it will force the university to bolster its support structure for information technology. The new policy goes into effect this summer and will be phased in through 1999.

The requirement recognizes that students are "all showing up with the things," says the president. "I'm trying to bring some order out of how they show up, and some structure to the support for them showing up."

But preparing for the demands the requirement will create—"ramping up," as technology people like to call it—may seem like anything but an orderly process over the next year and a half. The time frame means the university must simultaneously upgrade its campus network and modem banks, seek vendors to sell machines to students, help faculty members prepare to take advantage of the new technology, and strengthen user-support services to handle what is expected to be a flood of questions and minor crises.

The total cost for the ramping up is, by Mr. Lombardi's estimate, "in the millions," which will come in dribs and drabs from many sources. A big dedicated tuition increase, which is how other universities have paid for such projects, would not have fared well in a state that, as Mr. Lombardi says, "believes in its heart of hearts that higher education should be a free entitlement." Nor are administrators banking on a proposed student-technology fee that the Legislature will soon consider. Some money will come from a portion of a 1997 tuition increase, and a recently proposed increase for 1998–99 includes a portion reserved for technology spending.

Several universities, including Virginia Tech, Georgia Tech, and Sonoma State University, have instituted computer requirements, but none on as large a scale as Florida's. Wake Forest University's plan, perhaps the most widely talked about, phases in a computer requirement over four years and adds three thousand dollars to the annual tuition to provide a new laptop for each of six thousand undergraduates. The University of North Carolina wants all new students to be equipped with laptops beginning in 2000, although the students will have to buy their own computers—possibly at a discount through the university.

Florida's new policy does not provide computers for students. But once computers are a university requirement, students can claim them as a cost of attendance when they're filling out financial-aid forms. Like textbooks and fees, the computer's cost is then factored in when the student's scholarships, grants, or loans are calculated. Students who qualify would be eligible for up to one thousand dollars a year in aid to buy or upgrade their computers, pay for technical support or repairs, and purchase software.

Strictly speaking, Florida's computer requirement does not force students to purchase computers. Nor does it require professors to incorporate computers in their lessons. But students will be expected to have the access and tools that a computer can provide.

Both students and professors, however, compare computers to textbooks—a student might get by without one, but for all practical purposes, it's a required purchase. Some students feel that the requirement is an unfair additional cost, especially when some can barely afford textbooks and fees. But since most students buy computers anyway, the complaints have been muted.

Students are free to choose their own brands, configurations, and operating systems. The new requirement just specifies the capabilities that a student's computer should have: standard word processing and spreadsheet software, a World Wide Web browser, and an e-mail program. The computers must also have modems or network cards that allow them to connect to the campus network and the Internet. The policy recommends that students bring a printer, although the university has some public-use printers, which students can use for a fee.

This fall, the requirement will apply to freshmen and juniors. By the fall of 1999, it will apply to everyone. Computing requirements in individual majors already cover most upperclassmen, administrators note.

The requirement also allows students to choose between desktop and laptop models. Some administrators argued that the university should require laptops, which would give professors the option of using them in classroom lessons. On the other hand, giving students a choice lets them buy the computer most appropriate to their major. Some programs at the university, including those in the business school, specify that students must have laptops, while students in some art-and-design programs benefit from the large-screen displays that desktop computers provide.

Assuring that students can find somewhere to buy computers is another of the issues that administrators have considered. Beyond the campus, Gainesville is a typical small Southern city. An assortment of computer stores serves the technology needs of the university and the city's 85,000 residents, but the local market is not big enough to attract a superstore like CompUSA or Office Depot. To guarantee that students will have access to the hardware, software, and service they will need, administrators are seeking to bring a major vendor to campus.

In January, the university solicited proposals from more than thirty computer manufacturers and sellers for ways to provide students with computers as efficiently as possible. Among the requests is that the companies offer a "Gator-ready" computer—one that comes with university-required software and that is configured to connect easily to the campus network.

Ed Poppell, associate vice-president for administrative affairs, says the university is looking not for the company that can offer students the cheapest computers, but for one that can provide the best computers at a reasonable price. In fact, he says the university changed the proposal it sent out to vendors after students suggested putting less emphasis on price. After all, he says, "the university isn't buying anything; the students are buying."

Once the new computers are unwrapped, students will need a way to hook in to the campus network and the Internet. The university has begun to play the role of Internet service provider by offering fifteen hours per month of free dial-up Internet access with every computer account. Other universities have shied away from offering home Internet service to students because of the costs and headaches involved in keeping hundreds or thousands of modems and telephone lines running.

Mark P. Hale, director of the university's computer-services department, acknowledges that providing Internet access to tens of thousands of potential users is a daunting proposition, but he says it's worthwhile. "We wanted a baseline service that would be no charge to students." The university explored Internet-service agreements with companies including IBM and Sprint but could not reach any agreement that would provide free access for students.

Mr. Hale says the university is making room for more users by expanding the number of modems—currently seven hundred—to which students can connect. But, he says many students come to the campus with Internet accounts of their own and never use the campus connections. The modem pool will also get some relief because an increasing number of students will be using hardwired connections on campus.

The university is in the process of wiring on-campus residences, which house about nine thousand students—who are facing rent increases to pay for the new wires. Mr. Hale says the university plans to have "a port per pillow"—one network connection for each student—by January 1999. The residence halls are mostly older structures, which complicates the task. Wires must be run to buildings and holes cut in walls to accommodate the new connections.

Because students tend to get in the way of network installation, Mr. Hale hopes that much of the work will be done during the summer. At the same time, the university will be installing connections in its classroom buildings—a few rooms per building at first, and then more, as professors work the Internet into their teaching. Mr. Hale says he's also looking into installing both hallway terminals, which would allow students to check e-mail quickly, and "walk-up ports," connections in public areas where students with laptops can plug in to the campus network.

Adding so many ports will place additional demands on the network, which is why officials are also upgrading its backbone to allow for much higher capacity. The costs and benefits of the upgrade are shared by another project—the university's involvement with Internet 2, the proposed high-speed national computer network that would connect member institutions and be used for advanced research and educational applications. A fast local network is a requirement for universities participating in the new Internet, Mr. Lombardi says, "so that the Internet 2 pipe doesn't run into a string and a tin can."

But the hardware issues pale beside the challenge of keeping 42,000 student computers running and up to date. Mr. Poppell, the administrative vice-president, says Florida is emphasizing support and service in choosing a preferred computer vendor, because the university will probably never be capable of maintaining 42,000 computers on its own. He predicts that the local computer-service industry, like the pizza-delivery business in any college town, will blossom.

The university's user-support task may be eased slightly, Mr. Poppell adds, because not all students will necessarily buy computers. "Not every student buys a textbook," he notes, and similarly, students will probably end up sharing their computers and technical know-how. "Just like students do now when they can't figure out a calculus problem, they'll ask their friend down the hall," he says. "It'll be, 'Help me install this software, and I'll buy the pizza tonight.'"

"Those kinds of things will happen informally. Right now we've got to be ready to fill in the blanks that will occur."

One blank is the need for computer training. Students will arrive with varying levels of computer experience. To help everyone attain at least a basic understanding of the technology, the university has arranged for students, professors, and staff members to have access to hundreds of Web-based courses on computer-related topics, along with some courses on CD-ROM.

The courses are provided by the Gartner Group, a company that markets consulting and training services to corporations and has recently begun working with universities as well. Florida's three-year, $600,000 per-year contract with the company offers anyone on campus a range of courses, from a general introduction to computers and the Internet to lessons in programming languages.

Marie Dence, associate director of the Northeast Regional Data Center, an arm of the university that coordinates many of its computing and information-technology activities, sees the online courses supplementing the university's own help-desk services. "We're going to have a lot of people with computers who may not have had them before, and we want to provide some kind of really accessible training," she says. Users can reach the Web courses from campus computer labs, wired classrooms, or from their homes, if they're dialed in to the campus network. Ms. Dence says professors can assign lessons on various topics in the online resources to help prepare students for their courses.

The online courses may relieve some of the tech-support burden, but the university is also taking steps to make sure that "The computer ate my homework" doesn't become too common an excuse.

"Rather than building a new support agency with one hundred fifty new employees and so many millions of dollars, we're coordinating efforts around campus to try to make something happen," says Mr. Hale, who directs the Center for Instructional Research Computing Activities here. "This is an implementation without any real new money in the picture." A proposal to train technology assistants, who would be employed by colleges, would take more pressure off the central help desk, which is operated by the center. The new assistants would be paid by the colleges.

Still, says Mr. Hale, expanding the central help desk is inevitable, and the center has already begun hiring additional student assistants of its own. The university also plans to move the central help desk from its current location—a fifth-floor office to a more user-friendly space on a ground floor.

At the same time, the university is moving to provide more computer support to faculty members. They will have access to the same help services as students, but faculty members are also likely to need help finding teaching resources and incorporating them into the curriculum. The campus office responsible for instructional materials already has begun training professors to create Web pages and use computers in class.

Making sure that professors have computers of their own is still an issue, though. Elizabeth D. Capaldi, Florida's provost, says the university is trying to determine how best to provide money for faculty computers.

Getting professors to use computers in their teaching is another matter, she says. "Even if we bought every faculty member a computer, some would just let them sit there."

Some professors are worried nonetheless that the requirement for computers will put pressure on faculty members to use the machines in their teaching, whether they feel it's warranted or not. Greg Ulmer, an English professor who already uses computers and the Internet in class, offers another textbook analogy: "I'm requiring this beautiful fifty-five dollar book here, and if I don't use it, I'm going to have some ticked-off students."

Mr. Hale and others at the university say wired teaching will follow naturally once most students have their own computers. "Instead of spending two or three years getting faculty ready," he says, "we're bringing the wave over the wall. Here come the students with computers, faculty—let's look at it and face up to it."

Other institutions may not have chosen such a strategy, but administrators here think it's the best choice for a university like Florida. "We're a large public institution, but we're not a well-funded large public institution," Mr. Hale says. "You can't make a big investment in course development for every faculty member, but you need to create the incentive and the environment in which the faculty say, 'I want to keep up, I want to change my courses, and you don't have to give me extra money.'"

"Students will drive the faculty," says Mr. Lombardi, in the same way that students showing up with computers will drive the university's support services. The computing requirement, says the president, guarantees that the university will stay focused on fulfilling students' technological needs. "We were going to be overwhelmed by student demand if we weren't focused. The computer requirement has committed the university to do it right."

QUESTIONS FOR REACTION AND DISCUSSION

1. John V. Lombardi, the President of the University of Florida, is quoted at the beginning of this article as saying that the requirement for students to own their own computers is "actually not for the students— it's for the university." What does he mean by that? In what way do student-owned computers help the university?
2. What specifically is the University of Florida requiring students to do? How are students being helped to pay for computers? What capabilities are the students supposed to have?
3. How is the university coping with the enormous problem of supporting 42,000 students with computers on the campus? What networking solutions are being pursued? How will the university handle computer support?
4. What are the concerns of faculty members for this computer initiative? Are they realistic?

QUESTIONS FOR WRITING

1. In this essay, McCollum quotes the university president, the provost, and directors of several offices on the campus. No student is quoted— the writer merely mentions that "complaints have been muted." Interview the students in your class and ask for their response to the computer initiative at Florida. Write an essay in the form of a letter to the editor of the *Chronicle*, responding to this article either positively or negatively. As you question your classmates and consider your own response, take a clear stand about whether or not you think computer ownership should be a requirement at your institution.
2. McCollum mentions several institutions in this article—Virginia Tech, Georgia Tech, Wake Forest University, and Sonoma State University— that have computer requirements, and there have been more since this article was published. What are the requirements for computer usage at your institution? Is there an expectation that all students have

access to computers? How does your institution provide access? Write an essay in which you evaluate the access to computers on your own campus and conclude with a recommendation for improving or increasing the access.

3. Research the policies and technical goals of your own college or university. You might begin by locating the office of information resources on your campus or even by calling the help desk at the computer center and asking what materials are available. In what ways has your institution planned and implemented policies for students? Are students involved in the process? Why or why not? What changes would you like to see at your own institution? Write an essay in which you summarize the computer policies at your institution and propose some changes or additions.

QUESTIONS FOR FURTHER EXPLORATION

1. By checking the *Chronicle* archive <http://chronicle.com> and the University of Florida Web site <http://www.ufl.edu>, find out what has happened at Florida since the publication of this article. Do all students now registered at the university own computers? What evidence of ongoing technical and financial support can you find? What problems have there been? What can you find out about student attitudes and concerns? Faculty attitudes and concerns? Write a brief report for your class.

2. Check the Web sites for the colleges and universities mentioned in this article. What progress has been made at these schools to achieve the goal of computers for every student? What problems have there been? What kinds of support are available?

3. The administrators interviewed in this article have a generally positive view of technology and evidently see few problems ahead for students once they are "wired." Prepare a survey for students in which you develop questions designed to elicit their responses about how they see their own educations as being reconfigured as a result of the increased use of technology in education. Consider asking such questions as: How does access to so much information affect your work? What new skills in critical thinking do you need to learn? How are you handling e-mail and e-lists as additional places for "classroom" discussion? Invite a dozen students to respond to the survey, compile the results, and write an essay describing what these students had to say about their experiences.

7

THE COMPUTER DELUSION

Todd Oppenheimer is the associate editor of Newsweek Interactive *and writes frequently on technology and education in journals such as the* Columbia Journalism Review *and* Mother Jones. *This essay, which offers a set of challenges to assumptions about the positive effect of computer use in the schools, appeared in the* Atlantic Monthly, *a magazine devoted to essays and articles on politics, culture, and the arts. Founding the magazine in 1857 as an antislavery magazine, the original editors also determined to publish "the efforts of the best writers upon literature and politics, under the light of the highest morals." Originally the magazine published a great deal of original literary works, including stories and poems by some of America's leading writers. Although contemporary literature is still published in the* Atlantic, *today the magazine is designed more for general interest and includes mostly articles and reviews on social and political topics. Oppenheimer's essay is typical of the length and scope of a feature article for the* Atlantic *today. The* Atlantic *also has an Internet version: "Atlantic Unbound"* <http://www.theatlantic.com>. *In this essay, Oppenheimer contends that while there is limited evidence that computer use significantly enhances teaching and learning, schools are eliminating important programs in art and music—lifelong skills—to pay for glamorous tools that will become quickly outdated.*

QUESTIONS FOR READING

1. "Delusion" is a word that typically refers to a serious psychological condition. What does the arresting title of this essay suggest about the author's argument?
2. Oppenheimer uses observations from his own experiences in the classroom as well as expert testimony throughout this essay. What strikes you as particularly effective evidence in support of his thesis?

TODD OPPENHEIMER

THE COMPUTER DELUSION

Atlantic Monthly 280 (July 1997, pp. 45–59)

*There is no good evidence that most uses of computers
significantly improve teaching and learning, yet school
districts are cutting programs—music, art, physical
education—that enrich children's lives to make room
for this dubious nostrum, and the Clinton
Administration has embraced the goal of "computers in
every classroom" with credulous and costly
enthusiasm.*

In 1922 Thomas Edison predicted that "the motion picture is destined to rev-
olutionize our educational system and . . . in a few years it will supplant
largely, if not entirely, the use of textbooks." Twenty-three years later, in 1945,
William Levenson, the director of the Cleveland public schools' radio station,
claimed that "the time may come when a portable radio receiver will be as
common in the classroom as is the blackboard." Forty years after that the
noted psychologist B. F. Skinner, referring to the first days of his "teaching machines," in the late 1950s and early 1960s, wrote "I was soon saying that, with
the help of teaching machines and programmed instruction, students could
learn twice as much in the same time and with the same effort as in a standard
classroom." Ten years after Skinner's recollections were published, President
Bill Clinton campaigned for "a bridge to the twenty-first century . . . where
computers are as much a part of the classroom as blackboards." Clinton was
not alone in his enthusiasm for a program estimated to cost somewhere between forty billion dollars and one hundred billion dollars over the next five
years. Speaker of the House Newt Gingrich, talking about computers to the
Republican National Committee early this year, said, "We could do so much to
make education available twenty-four hours a day, seven days a week, that
people could literally have a whole different attitude toward learning."

If history really is repeating itself, the schools are in serious trouble. In
Teachers and Machines: The Classroom Use of Technology Since 1920 (1986),
Larry Cuban, a professor of education at Stanford University and a former
school superintendent, observed that as successive rounds of new technology
failed their promoters' expectations, a pattern emerged. The cycle began with
big promises backed by the technology developers' research. In the classroom,
however, teachers never really embraced the new tools, and no significant
academic improvement occurred. This provoked consistent responses: the
problem was money, spokespeople argued, or teacher resistance, or the paralyzing school bureaucracy. Meanwhile, few people questioned the technology

advocates' claims. As results continued to lag, the blame was finally laid on the machines. Soon schools were sold on the next generation of technology, and the lucrative cycle started all over again.

Today's technology evangels argue that we've learned our lesson from past mistakes. As in each previous round, they say that when our new hot technology—the computer—is compared with yesterday's, today's is better. "It can do the same things, plus," Richard Riley, the U.S. Secretary of Education, told me this spring.

How much better is it, really?

The promoters of computers in schools again offer prodigious research showing improved academic achievement after using their technology. The research has again come under occasional attack, but this time quite a number of teachers seem to be backing classroom technology. In a poll taken early last year U.S. teachers ranked computer skills and media technology as more "essential" than the study of European history, biology, chemistry, and physics; than dealing with social problems such as drugs and family breakdown; than learning practical job skills; and than reading modern American writers such as Steinbeck and Hemingway or classic ones such as Plato and Shakespeare.

In keeping with these views New Jersey cut state aid to a number of school districts this past year and then spent $10 million on classroom computers. In Union City, California, a single school district is spending $27 million to buy new gear for a mere eleven schools. The Kittridge Street Elementary School, in Los Angeles, killed its music program last year to hire a technology coordinator; in Mansfield, Massachusetts, administrators dropped proposed teaching positions in art, music, and physical education, and then spent $333,000 on computers; in one Virginia school the art room was turned into a computer laboratory. (Ironically, a half dozen preliminary studies recently suggested that music and art classes may build the physical size of a child's brain, and its powers for subjects such as language, math, science, and engineering—in one case far more than computer work did.) Meanwhile, months after a New Technology High School opened in Napa, California, where computers sit on every student's desk and all academic classes use computers, some students were complaining of headaches, sore eyes, and wrist pain.

Throughout the country, as spending on technology increases, school book purchases are stagnant. Shop classes, with their tradition of teaching children building skills with wood and metal, have been almost entirely replaced by new "technology education programs." In San Francisco only one public school still offers a full shop program—the lone vocational high school. "We get kids who don't know the difference between a screwdriver and a ball peen hammer," James Dahlman, the school's vocational-department chair, told me recently. "How are they going to make a career choice? Administrators are stuck in this mindset that all kids will go to a four-year college and become a doctor or a lawyer, and that's not true. I know some who went to college, graduated, and then had to go back to technical school to get a job." Last year the school superintendent in Great Neck, Long Island, proposed replacing elementary school shop classes with computer classes and training the shop teachers as computer coaches. Rather than being greeted with enthusiasm, the proposal provoked a backlash.

Interestingly, shop classes and field trips are two programs that the National Information Infrastructure Advisory Council, the Clinton Administration's technology task force, suggests reducing in order to shift resources into computers. But are these results what technology promoters really intend? "You need to apply common sense," Esther Dyson, the president of EDventure Holdings and one of the task force's leading school advocates, told me recently. "Shop with a good teacher probably is worth more than computers with a lousy teacher. But if it's a poor program, this may provide a good excuse for cutting it. There will be a lot of trials and errors with this. And I don't know how to prevent those errors."

The issue, perhaps, is the magnitude of the errors. Alan Lesgold, a professor of psychology and the associate director of the Learning Research and Development Center at the University of Pittsburgh, calls the computer an "amplifier," because it encourages both enlightened study practices and thoughtless ones. There's a real risk, though, that the thoughtless practices will dominate, slowly dumbing down huge numbers of tomorrow's adults. As Sherry Turkle, a professor of the sociology of science at the Massachusetts Institute of Technology and a longtime observer of children's use of computers, told me, "The possibilities of using this thing poorly so outweigh the chance of using it well, it makes people like us, who are fundamentally optimistic about computers, very reticent."

Perhaps the best way to separate fact from fantasy is to take supporters' claims about computerized learning one by one and compare them with the evidence in the academic literature and in the everyday experiences I have observed or heard about in a variety of classrooms.

Five main arguments underlie the campaign to computerize our nation's schools.

- Computers improve both teaching practices and student achievement.
- Computer literacy should be taught as early as possible; otherwise students will be left behind.
- To make tomorrow's workforce competitive in an increasingly high-tech world, learning computer skills must be a priority.
- Technology programs leverage support from the business community—badly needed today because schools are increasingly starved for funds.
- Work with computers—particularly using the Internet—brings students valuable connections with teachers, other schools and students, and a wide network of professionals around the globe. These connections spice the school day with a sense of real-world relevance, and broaden the educational community.

"THE FILMSTRIPS OF THE 1990S"

Clinton's vision of computerized classrooms arose partly out of the findings of the presidential task force—thirty-six leaders from industry, education, and several interest groups who have guided the Administration's push to get computers into the schools. The report of the task force, "Connecting K–12 Schools to the Information Superhighway" (produced by the consulting firm McKinsey & Co.), begins by citing numerous studies that have apparently proved that computers enhance student achievement significantly. One "meta-analysis" (a study that reviews other studies—in this case 130 of them) reported that computers had improved performance in "a wide range of subjects, including language arts, math, social studies, and science." Another found improved organization and focus in students' writing. A third cited twice the normal gains in math skills. Several schools boasted of greatly improved attendance.

Unfortunately, many of these studies are more anecdotal than conclusive. Some, including a giant, oft-cited meta-analysis of 254 studies, lack the necessary scientific controls to make solid conclusions possible. The circumstances are artificial and not easily repeated, results aren't statistically reliable, or, most frequently, the studies did not control for other influences, such as differences between teaching methods. This last factor is critical because computerized learning inevitably forces teachers to adjust their style—only sometimes for the better. Some studies were industry funded and thus tended to publicize mostly positive findings. "The research is set up in a way to find benefits that aren't really there," Edward Miller, a former editor of the *Harvard Education Letter,* says. "Most knowledgeable people agree that most of the research isn't valid. It's so flawed it shouldn't even be called research. Essentially, it's just worthless." Once the faulty studies are weeded out, Miller says, the ones that remain "are inconclusive"—that is, they show no significant change in either direction. Even Esther Dyson admits the studies are undependable. "I don't think those studies amount to much either way," she says. "In this area there is little proof."

Why are solid conclusions so elusive? Look at Apple Computer's "Classrooms of Tomorrow," perhaps the most widely studied effort to teach using computer technology. In the early 1980s Apple shrewdly realized that donating computers to schools might help not only students but also company sales, as Apple's ubiquity in classrooms turned legions of families into Apple loyalists. Last year, after the *San Jose Mercury News* (published in Apple's Silicon Valley home) ran a series questioning the effectiveness of computers in schools, the paper printed an opinion-page response from Terry Crane, an Apple vice-president. "Instead of isolating students," Crane wrote, "technology actually encouraged them to collaborate more than in traditional classrooms. Students also learned to explore and represent information dynamically and creatively, communicate effectively about complex processes, become independent learners and self-starters and become more socially aware and confident."

Crane didn't mention that after a decade of effort and the donation of equipment worth more than $25 million to thirteen schools, there is scant evidence of greater student achievement. To be fair, educators on both sides of the computer debate acknowledge that today's tests of student achievement are shockingly crude. They're especially weak in measuring intangibles such as enthusiasm and self-motivation, which do seem evident in Apple's classrooms and other computer-rich schools. In any event, what is fun and what is educational may frequently be at odds. "Computers in classrooms are the filmstrips of the 1990s," Clifford Stoll, the author of *Silicon Snake Oil: Second Thoughts on the Information Highway* (1995), told *The New York Times* last year, recalling his own school days in the 1960s. "We loved them because we didn't have to think for an hour, teachers loved them because they didn't have to teach, and parents loved them because it showed their schools were high-tech. But no learning happened."

Stoll somewhat overstates the case—obviously, benefits can come from strengthening a student's motivation. Still, Apple's computers may bear less responsibility for that change than Crane suggests. In the beginning, when Apple did little more than dump computers in classrooms and homes, this produced no real results, according to Jane David, a consultant Apple hired to study its classroom initiative. Apple quickly learned that teachers needed to change their classroom approach to what is commonly called "project-oriented learning." This is an increasingly popular teaching method, in which students learn through doing and teachers act as facilitators or partners rather than as didacts. (Teachers sometimes refer to this approach, which arrived in classrooms before computers did, as being "the guide on the side instead of the sage on the stage.") But what the students learned "had less to do with the computer and more to do with the teaching," David concluded. "If you took the computers out, there would still be good teaching there." This story is heard in school after school, including two impoverished schools—Clear View Elementary School, in southern California, and the Christopher Columbus Middle School, in New Jersey—that the Clinton Administration has loudly celebrated for turning themselves around with computers. At Christopher Columbus, in fact, students' test scores rose before computers arrived, not afterward, because of relatively basic changes: longer class periods, new books, after-school programs, and greater emphasis on student projects and collaboration.

During recent visits to some San Francisco–area schools I could see what it takes for students to use computers properly, and why most don't.

On a bluff south of downtown San Francisco, in the middle of one of the city's lower-income neighborhoods, Claudia Schaffner, a tenth-grader, tapped away at a multimedia machine in a computer lab at Thurgood Marshall Academic High School, one of half a dozen special technology schools in the city. Schaffner was using a physics program to simulate the trajectory of a marble on a small roller coaster. "It helps to visualize it first, like 'A is for Apple' with kindergartners," Schaffner told me, while mousing up and down the virtual roller coaster. "I can see how the numbers go into action." This was lunch hour, and the students' excitement about what they can do in this lab was palpable. Schaffner could barely tear herself away. "I need to go eat some food," she finally said, returning within minutes to eat a rice dish at the keyboard.

Schaffner's teacher is Dennis Frezzo, an electrical-engineering graduate from the University of California at Berkeley. Despite his considerable knowledge of computer programming, Frezzo tries to keep classwork focused on physical projects. For a mere $8,000, for example, several teachers put together a multifaceted robotics lab, consisting of an advanced Lego engineering kit and twenty-four old 386-generation computers. Frezzo's students used these materials to build a tiny electric car, whose motion was to be triggered by a light sensor. When the light sensor didn't work, the students figured out why. "That's a real problem—what you'd encounter in the real world," Frezzo told me. "I prefer they get stuck on small real-world problems instead of big fake problems"—like the simulated natural disasters that fill one popular educational game. "It's sort of the Zen approach to education," Frezzo said. "It's not the big problems. Isaac Newton already solved those. What comes up in life are the little ones."

It's one thing to confront technology's complexity at a high school—especially one that's blessed with four different computer labs and some highly skilled teachers like Frezzo, who know enough, as he put it, "to keep computers in their place." It's quite another to grapple with a high-tech future in the lower grades, especially at everyday schools that lack special funding or technical support. As evidence, when *U.S. News & World Report* published a cover story last fall on schools that make computers work, five of the six were high schools—among them Thurgood Marshall. Although the sixth was an elementary school, the featured program involved children with disabilities—the one group that does show consistent benefits from computerized instruction.

ARTIFICIAL EXPERIENCE

Consider the scene at one elementary school, Sanchez, which sits on the edge of San Francisco's Latino community. For several years Sanchez, like many other schools, has made do with a roomful of basic Apple IIs. Last year, curious about what computers could do for youngsters, a local entrepreneur donated twenty costly Power Macintoshes—three for each of five classrooms, and one for each of the five lucky teachers to take home. The teachers who got the new machines were delighted. "It's the best thing we've ever done," Adela Najarro, a third-grade bilingual teacher, told me. She mentioned one boy, perhaps with a learning disability, who had started to hate school. Once he had a computer to play with, she said, "his whole attitude changed." Najarro is now a true believer, even when it comes to children without disabilities. "Every single child," she said, "will do more work for you and do better work with a computer. Just because it's on a monitor, kids pay more attention. There's this magic to the screen."

Down the hall from Najarro's classroom her colleague Rose Marie Ortiz had a more troubled relationship with computers. On the morning I visited, Ortiz took her bilingual special-education class of second-, third-, and fourth-graders into the lab filled with the old Apple IIs. The students look forward to this weekly expedition so much that Ortiz gets exceptional behavior from them all morning. Out of date though these machines are, they do offer a range of exercises, in subjects such as science, math, reading, social studies, and problem solving. But owing to this group's learning problems and limited English skills, math drills were all that Ortiz could give them. Nonetheless, within minutes the kids were excitedly navigating their way around screens depicting floating airplanes and trucks carrying varying numbers of eggs. As the children struggled, many resorted to counting in whatever way they knew how. Some squinted at the screen, painstakingly moving their fingers from one tiny egg symbol to the next. "*Tres, cuatro, cinco, seis. . . .*" one little girl said loudly, trying to hear herself above her counting neighbors. Another girl kept a piece of paper handy, on which she marked a line for each egg. Several others resorted to the slow but tried and true—their fingers. Some just guessed. Once the children arrived at answers, they frantically typed them onto the screen, hoping it would advance to something fun, the way Nintendos, Game Boys, and video-arcade games do. Sometimes their answers were right, and the screen did advance; sometimes they weren't, but the children were rarely discouraged. As schoolwork goes, this was a blast.

"It's highly motivating for them," Ortiz said as she rushed from machine to machine, attending not to math questions but to computer glitches. Those she couldn't fix she simply abandoned. "I don't know how practical it is. You see," she said, pointing to a girl counting on her fingers, "these kids still need the hands-on"—meaning the opportunity to manipulate physical objects such as beans or colored blocks. The value of hands-on learning, child-development experts believe, is that it deeply imprints knowledge into a young child's brain, by transmitting the lessons of experience through a variety of sensory pathways. "Curiously enough," the educational psychologist Jane Healy wrote in *Endangered Minds: Why Children Don't Think and What We Can Do About It* (1990), "visual stimulation is probably not the main access route to nonverbal reasoning. Body movements, the ability to touch, feel, manipulate, and build sensory awareness of relationships in the physical world, are its main foundations." The problem, Healy wrote, is that "in schools, traditionally, the senses have had little status after kindergarten."

Ortiz believes that the computer-lab time, brief as it is, dilutes her students' attention to language. "These kids are all language-delayed," she said. Though only modest sums had so far been spent at her school, Ortiz and other local teachers felt that the push was on for technology over other scholastic priorities. The year before, Sanchez had let its librarian go, to be replaced by a part-timer.

When Ortiz finally got the students rounded up and out the door, the kids were still worked up. "They're never this wired after reading group," she said, "They're usually just exhausted because I've been reading with them, making them write and talk." Back in homeroom Ortiz showed off the students' monthly handwritten writing samples. "Now, could you do that on the computer?" she asked. "No, because we'd be hung up on finding the keys." So why does Ortiz bother taking her students to the computer lab at all? "I guess I come in here for the computer literacy. If everyone else is getting it, I feel these kids should get it too."

Some computerized elementary school programs have avoided these pitfalls, but the record subject by subject is mixed at best. Take writing, where by all accounts and by my own observations the computer does encourage practice—changes are easier to make on a keyboard than with an eraser, and the lettering looks better. Diligent students use these conveniences to improve their writing, but the less committed frequently get seduced by electronic opportunities to make a school paper look snazzy. (The easy "cut and paste" function in today's word processing programs, for example, is apparently encouraging many students to cobble together research materials without thinking them through.) Reading programs get particularly bad reviews. One small but carefully controlled study went so far as to claim that Reader Rabbit, a reading program now used in more than 100,000 schools, caused students to suffer a fifty percent drop in creativity. (Apparently, after forty-nine students used the program for seven months, they were no longer able to answer open-ended questions and showed a markedly diminished ability to brainstorm with fluency and originality.) What about hard sciences, which seem so well suited to computer study? Logo, the high-profile programming language refined by Seymour Papert and widely used in middle and high schools, fostered huge hopes of expanding children's cognitive skills. As students directed the computer to build things, such as geometric shapes, Papert believed, they would learn "procedural thinking," similar to the way a computer processes information. According to a number of studies, however, Logo has generally failed to deliver on its promises. Judah Schwartz, a professor of education at Harvard and a codirector of the school's Educational Technology Center, told me that a few newer applications, when used properly, can dramatically expand children's math and science thinking by giving them new tools to "make and explore conjectures." Still, Schwartz acknowledges that perhaps "ninety-nine percent" of the educational programs are "terrible, really terrible."

Even in success stories important caveats continually pop up. The best educational software is usually complex—most suited to older students and sophisticated teachers. In other cases the schools have been blessed with abundance— fancy equipment, generous financial support, or extra teachers—that is difficult if not impossible to duplicate in the average school. Even if it could be duplicated, the literature suggests, many teachers would still struggle with technology. Computers suffer frequent breakdowns; when they do work, their seductive images often distract students from the lessons at hand—which many teachers say makes it difficult to build meaningful rapport with their students.

With such a discouraging record of student and teacher performance with computers, why has the Clinton Administration focused so narrowly on the hopeful side of the story? Part of the answer may lie in the makeup of the Administration's technology task force. Judging from accounts of the task force's deliberations, all thirty-six members are unequivocal technology advocates. Two thirds of them work in the high-tech and entertainment industries. The effect of the group's tilt can be seen in its report. Its introduction adopts the authoritative posture of impartial fact-finder, stating that "this report does not attempt to lay out a national blueprint, nor does it recommend specific public policy goals." But it comes pretty close. Each chapter describes various strategies for getting computers into classrooms, and the introduction acknowledges that "this report does not evaluate the relative merits of competing demands on educational funding (e.g., more computers versus smaller class sizes)."

When I spoke with Esther Dyson and other task-force members about what discussion the group had had about the potential downside of computerized education, they said there hadn't been any. And when I asked Linda Roberts, Clinton's lead technology adviser in the Department of Education, whether the task force was influenced by any self-interest, she said no, quite the opposite: the group's charter actually gave its members license to help the technology industry directly, but they concentrated on schools because that's where they saw the greatest need.

That sense of need seems to have been spreading outside Washington. Last summer a California task force urged the state to spend $11 billion on computers in California schools, which have struggled for years under funding cuts that have driven academic achievement down to among the lowest levels in the nation. This task force, composed of forty-six teachers, parents, technology experts, and business executives, concluded, "More than any other single measure, computers and network technologies, properly implemented, offer the greatest potential to right what's wrong with our public schools." Other options mentioned in the group's report—reducing class size, improving teachers' salaries and facilities, expanding hours of instruction—were considered less important than putting kids in front of computers.

"HYPERTEXT MINDS"

Today's parents, knowing firsthand how families were burned by television's false promises, may want some objective advice about the age at which their children should become computer literate. Although there are no real guidelines, computer boosters send continual messages that if children don't begin early, they'll be left behind. Linda Roberts thinks that there's no particular minimum age—and no maximum number of hours that children should spend at a terminal. Are there examples of excess? "I haven't seen it yet," Roberts told me with a laugh. In schools throughout the country administrators and teachers demonstrate the same excitement, boasting about the wondrous things that children of five or six can do on computers: drawing, typing, playing with elementary science simulations and other programs called "educational games."

The schools' enthusiasm for these activities is not universally shared by specialists in childhood development. The doubters' greatest concern is for the very young—preschool through third grade, when a child is most impressionable. Their apprehension involves two main issues.

First, they consider it important to give children a broad base—emotionally, intellectually, and in the five senses—before introducing something as technical and one-dimensional as a computer. Second, they believe that the human and physical world holds greater learning potential.

The importance of a broad base for a child may be most apparent when it's missing. In *Endangered Minds,* Jane Healy wrote of an English teacher who could readily tell which of her students' essays were conceived on a computer. "They don't link ideas," the teacher says. "They just write one thing, and then they write another one, and they don't seem to see or develop the relationships between them." The problem, Healy argued, is that the pizzazz of computerized schoolwork may hide these analytical gaps, which "won't become apparent until [the student] can't organize herself around a homework assignment or a job that requires initiative. More commonplace activities, such as figuring out how to nail two boards together, organizing a game . . . may actually form a better basis for real-world intelligence."

Others believe they have seen computer games expand children's imaginations. High-tech children "think differently from the rest of us," William D. Winn, the director of the Learning Center at the University of Washington's Human Interface Technology Laboratory, told *Business Week* in a recent cover story on the benefits of computer games. "They develop hypertext minds. They leap around. It's as though their cognitive strategies were parallel, not sequential." Healy argues the opposite. She and other psychologists think that the computer screen flattens information into narrow, sequential data. This kind of material, they believe, exercises mostly one half of the brain—the left hemisphere, where primarily sequential thinking occurs. The "right brain" meanwhile gets short shrift—yet this is the hemisphere that works on different kinds of information simultaneously. It shapes our multifaceted impressions and serves as the engine of creative analysis.

Opinions diverge in part because research on the brain is still so sketchy, and computers are so new, that the effect of computers on the brain remains a great mystery. "I don't think we know anything about it," Harry Chugani, a pediatric neurobiologist at Wayne State University, told me. This very ignorance makes skeptics wary. "Nobody knows how kids' internal wiring works," Clifford Stoll wrote in *Silicon Snake Oil,* "but anyone who's directed away from social interactions has a head start on turning out weird. . . . No computer can teach what a walk through a pine forest feels like. Sensation has no substitute."

This points to the conservative developmentalists' second concern: the danger that even if hours in front of the screen are limited, unabashed enthusiasm for the computer sends the wrong message: that the mediated world is more significant than the real one. "It's like TV commercials," Barbara Scales, the head teacher at the Child Study Center at the University of California at Berkeley, told me. "Kids get so hyped up, it can change their expectations about stimulation, versus what they generate themselves." In *Silicon Snake Oil,* Michael Fellows, a computer scientist at the University of Victoria in British Columbia, was even blunter. "Most schools would probably be better off if they threw their computers into the Dumpster."

Faced with such sharply contrasting viewpoints, which are based on such uncertain ground, how is a responsible policymaker to proceed? "A prudent society controls its own infatuation with 'progress' when planning for its young," Healy argued in *Endangered Minds.*

> Unproven technologies . . . may offer lively visions, but they can also be detrimental to the development of the young plastic brain. The cerebral cortex is a wondrously well-buffered mechanism that can withstand a good bit of well-intentioned bungling. Yet there is a point at which fundamental neural substrates for reasoning may be jeopardized for children who lack proper physical, intellectual, or emotional nurturance. Childhood—and the brain—have their own imperatives. In development, missed opportunities may be difficult to recapture.

The problem is that technology leaders rarely include these or other warnings in their recommendations. When I asked Dyson why the Clinton task force proceeded with such fervor, despite the classroom computer's shortcomings, she said, "It's so clear the world is changing."

REAL JOB TRAINING

In the past decade, according to the presidential task force's report, the number of jobs requiring computer skills has increased from twenty-five percent of all jobs in 1983 to forty-seven percent in 1993. By 2000, the report estimates, sixty percent of the nation's jobs will demand these skills—and pay an average of ten to fifteen percent more than jobs involving no computer work. Although projections of this sort are far from reliable, it's a safe bet that computer skills will be needed for a growing proportion of tomorrow's work force. But what priority should these skills be given among other studies?

Listen to Tom Henning, a physics teacher at Thurgood Marshall, the San Francisco technology high school. Henning has a graduate degree in engineering, and helped to found a Silicon Valley company that manufactures electronic navigation equipment. "My bias is the physical reality," Henning told me as we sat outside a shop where he was helping students to rebuild an old motorcycle. "I'm no technophobe. I can program computers." What worries Henning is that computers at best engage only two senses, hearing and sight—and only two-dimensional sight at that. "Even if they're doing three-dimensional computer modeling, that's still a two-D replica of a three-D world. If you took a kid who grew up on Nintendo, he's not going to have the necessary skills. He needs to have done it first with Tinkertoys or clay, or carved it out of balsa wood." As David Elkind, a professor of child development at Tufts University, puts it, "A dean of the University of Iowa's school of engineering used to say the best engineers were the farm boys," because they knew how machinery really worked.

Surely many employers will disagree and welcome the commercially applicable computer skills that today's high-tech training can bring them. What's striking is how easy it is to find other employers who share Henning's and Elkind's concerns.

Kris Meisling, a senior geological-research adviser for Mobil Oil, told me that "people who use computers a lot slowly grow rusty in their ability to think." Meisling's group creates charts and maps—some computerized, some not—to plot where to drill for oil. In large one-dimensional analysis, such as sorting volumes of seismic data, the computer saves vast amounts of time, sometimes making previously impossible tasks easy. This lures people in his field, Meisling believes, into using computers as much as possible. But when geologists turn to computers for "interpretive" projects, he finds they often miss information, and their oversights are further obscured by the computer's captivating automatic design functions. This is why Meisling still works regularly with a pencil and paper—tools that, ironically, he considers more interactive than the computer, because they force him to think implications through.

"You can't simultaneously get an overview and detail with a computer," he says. "It's linear. It gives you tunnel vision. What computers can do well is what can be calculated over and over. What they can't do is innovation. If you think of some new way to do or look at things and the software can't do it, you're stuck. So a lot of people think, 'Well, I guess it's a dumb idea, or it's unnecessary.'"

I have heard similar warnings from people in other businesses, including high-tech enterprises. A spokeswoman for Hewlett-Packard, the giant California computer-products company, told me the company rarely hires people who are predominantly computer experts, favoring instead those who have a talent for teamwork and are flexible and innovative. Hewlett-Packard is such a believer in hands-on experience that since 1992 it has spent $2.6 million helping forty-five school districts build math and science skills the old-fashioned way—using real materials, such as dirt, seeds, water, glass vials, and magnets. Much the same perspective came from several recruiters in film and computer-game animation. In work by artists who have spent a lot of time on computers "you'll see a stiffness or a flatness, a lack of richness and depth," Karen Chelini, the director of human resources for Lucas/Arts Entertainment, George Lucas's interactive-games maker told me recently. "With traditional art training, you train the eye to pay attention to body movement. You learn attitude, feeling, expression. The ones who are good are those who as kids couldn't be without their sketchbook."

Many jobs obviously will demand basic computer skills if not sophisticated knowledge. But that doesn't mean that the parents or the teachers of young students need to panic. Joseph Weizenbaum, a professor emeritus of computer science at M.I.T., told the *San Jose Mercury News* that even at his technology-heavy institution new students can learn all the computer skills they need "in a summer." This seems to hold in the business world, too. Patrick MacLearny, an executive vice-president of Hellmuth Obata & Kassabaum, the country's largest architecture firm, recently gave me numerous examples to illustrate that computers pose no threat to his company's creative work. Although architecture professors are divided on the value of computerized design tools, in MacLearny's opinion they generally enhance the process. But he still considers "knowledge of the hands" to be valuable—today's architects just have to develop it in other ways. (His firm's answer is through building models.) Nonetheless, as positive as MacLearny is about computers, he has found the company's two-week computer training to be sufficient. In fact, when he's hiring, computer skills don't enter into his list of priorities. He looks for a strong character; an ability to speak, write, and comprehend; and a rich education in the history of architecture.

THE SCHOOLS THAT BUSINESS BUILT

Newspaper financial sections carry almost daily pronouncements from the computer industry and other businesses about their high-tech hopes for America's schoolchildren. Many of these are joined to philanthropic commitments to helping schools make curriculum changes. This sometimes gets businesspeople involved in schools, where they've begun to understand and work with the many daunting problems that are unrelated to technology. But if business gains too much influence over the curriculum, the schools can become a kind of corporate training center—largely at taxpayer expense.

For more than a decade scholars and government commissions have criticized the increasing professionalization of the college years—frowning at the way traditional liberal arts are being edged out by hot topics of the moment or strictly business-oriented studies. The schools' real job, the technology critic Neil Postman argued in his book *The End of Education* (1995), is to focus on "how to make a life, which is quite different from how to make a living." Some see the arrival of boxes of computer hardware and software in the schools as taking the commercial trend one step further, down into high school and elementary grades. "Should you be choosing a career in kindergarten?" asks Helen Sloss Luey, a social worker and a former president of San Francisco's Parent Teacher Association. "People need to be trained to learn and change, while education seems to be getting more specific."

Indeed it does. The New Technology High School in Napa (the school where a computer sits on every student's desk) was started by the school district and a consortium of more than forty businesses. "We want to be the school that business built," Robert Nolan, a founder of the school, told me last fall. "We wanted to create an environment that mimicked what exists in the high-tech business world." Increasingly, Nolan explained, business leaders want to hire people specifically trained in the skill they need. One of Nolan's partners, Ted Fujimoto, of the Landmark Consulting Group, told me that instead of just asking the business community for financial support, the school will now undertake a trade: in return for donating funds, businesses can specify what kinds of employees they want—"a two-way street." Sometimes the traffic is a bit heavy in one direction. In January, *The New York Times* published a lengthy education supplement describing numerous examples of how business is increasingly dominating school software and other curriculum materials, and not always toward purely educational goals.

People who like the idea that their taxes go to computer training might be surprised at what a poor investment it can be. Larry Cuban, the Stanford education professor, writes that changes in the classroom for which business lobbies rarely hold long-term value. Rather, they're often guided by labor-market needs that turn out to be transitory; when the economy shifts, workers are left unprepared for new jobs. In the economy as a whole, according to a recent story in *The New York Times*, performance trends in our schools have shown virtually no link to the rises and falls in the nation's measures of productivity and growth. This is one reason that school traditionalists push for broad liberal arts curricula, which they feel develop students' values and intellect, instead of focusing on today's idea about what tomorrow's jobs will be.

High-tech proponents argue that the best education software does develop flexible business intellects. In the *Business Week* story on computer games, for example, academics and professionals expressed amazement at the speed, savvy, and facility that young computer jocks sometimes demonstrate. Several pointed in particular to computer simulations, which some business leaders believe are becoming increasingly important in fields ranging from engineering, manufacturing, and troubleshooting to the tracking of economic activity and geopolitical risk. The best of these simulations may be valuable, albeit for strengthening one form of thinking. But the average simulation program may be of questionable relevance.

Sherry Turkle, the sociology professor at MIT, has studied youngsters using computers for more than twenty years. In her book *Life on the Screen: Identity in the Age of the Internet* (1995) she described a disturbing experience with a simulation game called SimLife. After she sat down with a thirteen-year-old named Tim, she was stunned at the way

Tim can keep playing even when he has no idea what is driving events. For example, when his sea urchins become extinct, I ask him why.

TIM: "I don't know, it's just something that happens."
ST: "Do you know how to find out why it happened?"
TIM: "No."
ST: "Do you mind that you can't tell why?"
TIM: "No. I don't let things like that bother me. It's not what's important."

Anecdotes like this lead some educators to worry that as children concentrate on how to manipulate software instead of on the subject at hand, learning can diminish rather than grow. Simulations, for example, are built on hidden assumptions, many of which are oversimplified if not highly questionable. All too often, Turkle wrote recently in *The American Prospect,* "experiences with simulations do not open up questions but close them down." Turkle's concern is that software of this sort fosters passivity, ultimately dulling people's sense of what they can change in the world. There's a tendency, Turkle told me, "to take things at 'interface' value." Indeed, after mastering SimCity, a popular game about urban planning, a tenth-grade girl boasted to Turkle that she'd learned the following rule: "Raising taxes always leads to riots."

The business community also offers tangible financial support, usually by donating equipment. Welcome as this is, it can foster a high-tech habit. Once a school's computer system is set up, the companies often drop their support. This saddles the school with heavy long-term responsibilities: maintenance of the computer network and the need for constant software upgrades and constant teacher training—the full burden of which can cost far more than the initial hardware and software combined. Schools must then look for handouts from other companies, enter the grant-seeking game, or delicately go begging in their own communities. "We can go to the well only so often," Toni-Sue Passantino, the principal of the Bayside Middle School, in San Mateo, California, told me recently. Last year Bayside let a group of seventh- and eighth-graders spend eighteen months and countless hours creating a rudimentary virtual-reality program, with the support of several high-tech firms. The companies' support ended after that period, however—creating a financial speed bump of a kind that the Rand Corporation noted in a report to the Clinton Administration as a common obstacle.

School administrators may be outwardly excited about computerized instruction, but they're also shrewdly aware of these financial challenges. In March of last year, for instance, when California launched its highly promoted "Net-Day '96" (a campaign to wire two thousand California schools to the Internet in one day), school participation was far below expectations, even in technology-conscious San Francisco. In the city papers school officials wondered how they were supposed to support an Internet program when they didn't even have the money to repair crumbling buildings, install electrical outlets, and hire the dozens of new teachers recently required so as to reduce class size.

One way around the donation maze is to simplify: use inexpensive basic software and hardware, much of which is available through recycling programs. Such frugality can offer real value in the elementary grades, especially since basic word-processing tools are most helpful to children just learning to write. Yet schools, like the rest of us, can't resist the latest toys. "A lot of people will spend all their money on fancy new equipment that can do great things, and sometimes it just gets used for typing classes," Ray Porter, a computer resource teacher for the San Francisco schools, told me recently. "Parents, school boards, and the reporters want to see only razzle-dazzle state-of-the-art."

INTERNET ISOLATION

It is hard to visit a high-tech school without being led by a teacher into a room where students are communicating with people hundreds or thousands of miles away—over the Internet or sometimes through video-conferencing systems (two-way TV sets that broadcast live from each room). Video conferences, although fun, are an expensive way to create classroom thrills. But the Internet, when used carefully, offers exciting academic prospects—most dependably, once again, for older students. In one case schools in different states have tracked bird migrations and then posted their findings on the World Wide Web, using it as their own national notebook. In San Francisco eighth-grade economics students have e-mailed Chinese and Japanese businessmen to fulfill an assignment on what it would take to build an industrial plant overseas. Schools frequently use the Web to publish student writing. While thousands of self-published materials like these have turned the Web into a worldwide vanity press, the network sometimes gives young writers their first real audience.

The free nature of Internet information also means that students are confronted with chaos, and real dangers. "The Net's beauty is that it's uncontrolled," Stephen Kerr, a professor at the College of Education at the University of Washington and the editor of *Technology in the Future of Schooling* (1996), told me. "It's information by anyone, for anyone. There's racist stuff, bigoted, hate-group stuff, filled with paranoia; bomb recipes; how to engage in various kinds of crimes, electronic and otherwise; scams and swindles. It's all there. It's all available." Older students may be sophisticated enough to separate the net's good food from its poisons, but even the savvy can be misled. On almost any subject the Net offers a plethora of seemingly sound "research." But under close inspection much of it proves to be ill informed, or just superficial. "That's the antithesis of what classroom kids should be exposed to," Kerr said.

This makes traditionalists emphasize the enduring value of printed books, vetted as most are by editing. In many schools, however, libraries are fairly limited. I now volunteer at a San Francisco high school where the library shelves are so bare that I can see how the Internet's ever-growing number of research documents, with all their shortcomings, can sometimes be a blessing.

Even computer enthusiasts give the Net tepid reviews. "Most of the content on the Net is total garbage," Esther Dyson acknowledges. "But if you find one good thing you can use it a million times." Kerr believes that Dyson is being unrealistic. "If you find a useful site one day, it may not be there the next day, or the information is different. Teachers are being asked to jump in and figure out if what they find on the Net is worthwhile. They don't have the skill or time to do that." Especially when students rely on the Internet's much-vaunted search software. Although these tools deliver hundreds or thousands of sources within seconds, students may not realize that search engines, and the Net itself, miss important information all the time.

"We need *less* surfing in the schools, not more," David Gelernter, a professor of computer science at Yale, wrote last year in *The Weekly Standard*.

"Couldn't we teach them to use what they've got before favoring them with three orders of magnitude *more?*" In my conversations with Larry Cuban, of Stanford, he argued, "Schooling is not about information. It's getting kids to think about information. It's about understanding and knowledge and wisdom."

It may be that youngsters' growing fascination with the Internet and other ways to use computers will distract from yet another of Clinton's education priorities: to build up the reading skills of American children. Sherry Dingman, an assistant professor of psychology at Marist College, in Poughkeepsie, New York, who is optimistic about many computer applications, believes that if children start using computers before they have a broad foundation in reading from books, they will be cheated out of opportunities to develop imagination. "If we think we're going to take kids who haven't been read to, and fix it by sitting them in front of a computer, we're fooling ourselves," Dingman told me not long ago. This doesn't mean that teachers or parents should resort to books on CD-ROM, which Dingman considers "a great waste of time," stuffing children's minds with "canned" images instead of stimulating youngsters to create their own. "Computers are lollipops that rot your teeth" is how Marilyn Darch, an English teacher at Poly High School, in Long Beach, California, put it in *Silicon Snake Oil.* "The kids love them. But once they get hooked. . . . It makes reading a book seem tedious. Books don't have sound effects, and their brains have to do all the work."

Computer advocates like to point out that the Internet allows for all kinds of intellectual challenges—especially when students use e-mail, or post notes in "newsgroup" discussions, to correspond with accomplished experts. Such experts, however, aren't consistently available. When they are, online "conversations" generally take place when correspondents are sitting alone, and the dialogue lacks the unpredictability and richness that occur in face-to-face discussions. In fact, when youngsters are put into groups for the "collaborative" learning that computer defenders celebrate, realistically only one child sits at the keyboard at a time. (During my school visits children tended to get quite possessive about the mouse and the keyboard, resulting in frustration and noisy disputes more often than collaboration.) In combination these constraints lead to yet another of the childhood developmentalists' concerns—that computers encourage social isolation.

JUST A GLAMOROUS TOOL

It would be easy to characterize the battle over computers as merely another chapter in the world's oldest story: humanity's natural resistance to change. But that does an injustice to the forces at work in this transformation. This is not just the future versus the past, uncertainty versus nostalgia: it is about encouraging a fundamental shift in personal priorities—a minimizing of the real, physical world in favor of an unreal "virtual" world. It is about teaching youngsters that exploring what's on a two-dimensional screen is more important than playing with real objects, or sitting down to an attentive conversation with a friend, a parent, or a teacher. By extension, it means downplaying the importance of conversation, of careful listening, and of expressing oneself in person with acuity and individuality. In the process, it may also limit the development of children's imaginations.

Perhaps this is why Steven Jobs, one of the founders of Apple Computer and a man who claims to have "spearheaded giving away more computer equipment to schools than anybody else on the planet," has come to a grim conclusion: "What's wrong with education cannot be fixed with technology," he told *Wired* magazine last year. "No amount of technology will make a dent. . . . You're not going to solve the problems by putting all knowledge onto CD-ROM. We can put a Web site in every school—none of this is bad. It's bad only if it lulls us into thinking we're doing something to solve the problem with education." Jane David, the consultant to Apple, concurs, with a commonly heard caveat. "There are real dangers," she told me, "in looking to technology to be the savior of education. But it won't survive without the technology."

Arguments like David's remind Clifford Stoll of yesteryear's promises about television. He wrote in *Silicon Snake Oil*,

> "Sesame Street" . . . has been around for twenty years. Indeed, its idea of making learning relevant to all was as widely promoted in the seventies as the Internet is today.
>
> So where's that demographic wave of creative and brilliant students now entering college? Did kids really need to learn how to watch television? Did we inflate their expectations that learning would always be colorful and fun?

Computer enthusiasts insist that the computer's "interactivity" and multimedia features make this machine far superior to television. Nonetheless, Stoll wrote,

> I see a parallel between the goals of "Sesame Street" and those of children's computing. Both are pervasive, expensive and encourage children to sit still. Both display animated cartoons, gaudy numbers and weird, random noises. . . . Both give the sensation that by merely watching a screen, you can acquire information without work and without discipline.

As the technology critic Neil Postman put it to a Harvard electronic-media conference, "I thought that television would be the last great technology that people would go into with their eyes closed. Now you have the computer."

The solution is not to ban computers from classrooms altogether. But it may be to ban federal spending on what is fast becoming an overheated campaign. After all, the private sector, with its constant supply of used computers and the computer industry's vigorous competition for new customers, seems well equipped to handle the situation. In fact, if schools can impose some limits—on technology donors and on themselves—rather than indulging in a consumer frenzy, most will probably find themselves with more electronic gear than they need. That could free the billions that Clinton wants to devote to technology and make it available for impoverished fundamentals: teaching solid skills in reading, thinking, listening, and talking; organizing inventive field trips and other rich hands-on experiences; and, of course, building up the nation's core of knowledgeable, inspiring teachers. These notions are considerably less glamorous than computers are, but their worth is firmly proved through a long history.

Last fall, after the school administrators in Mansfield, Massachusetts, had eliminated proposed art, music, and physical education positions in favor of buying computers, Michael Bellino, an electrical engineer at Boston University's Center for Space Physics, appeared before the Massachusetts Board of Education to protest. "The purpose of the schools [is] to, as one teacher argues, 'Teach carpentry, not hammer,'" he testified. "We need to teach the whys and ways of the world. Tools come and tools go. Teaching our children tools limits their knowledge to these tools and hence limits their futures."

QUESTIONS FOR REACTION AND DISCUSSION

1. In your own words, what is the thesis of Oppenheimer's essay?
2. At the end of the opening section of this essay, Oppenheimer outlines what he calls "five main arguments" that are a part of the movement to computerize schools. Which of these are familiar to you? Before you read this essay, would you have agreed with all these arguments?
3. One of the themes in this essay is the importance of "project-oriented learning." What does that mean? How does Oppenheimer suggest that computers support or alter such learning? What experiences have you had with project-oriented learning?
4. Oppenheimer uses catchy subtitles for the various sections of his essay. What does "hypertext minds" mean? Is that an effective title for this part of the essay? Why or why not?
5. According to Oppenheimer, many employers complain that employees who are too dependent on computers are less effective at developing innovative ideas, seeing relationships among information sets, and asking constructive questions. What are the implications for your own education and preparation for being an employee?

QUESTIONS FOR WRITING

1. Oppenheimer challenges the assumption that computers improve teaching and student achievement. What evidence, beyond what he suggests, can you find that supports or contradicts this assumption? Write an essay in which you counter Oppenheimer's argument or an essay in which you provide further evidence for his position.
2. Many commentators on technology have suggested that computer literacy should be taught early in a child's development. What evidence can you find that gives guidelines or support for such a position? Write an essay in which you explain recent studies that you have located and suggest a list of resources for parents and educators.

3. Interview three or four persons with full-time jobs in similar businesses or institutions about their positions on whether computer skills are a priority in a high-tech world. What do they think are the most important job skills for employees? Where do they rank computer skills? Write an account of your experience in interviewing these individuals and draw some conclusions that support or counter those of Oppenheimer.

4. Oppenheimer counters the notion that working with computers provides valuable connections for students. What evidence can you find that supports or contradicts Oppenheimer's views? Interview some of your classmates about their experiences in finding and using information on the Internet—and working with others on projects. Write your own feature article, arguing for or against the position that computers help students build collaborative work skills.

5. In this article, Oppenheimer chooses his examples and experts carefully to support his contention that there is little hard evidence to support the popular assumptions that computers improve education. To what extent does Oppenheimer share assumptions with other authors in this section (like Sven Birkerts and Gertrude Himmelfarb) about the intrinsic value of the printed book? How are his argument and evidence similar? How are they different? Write an essay in which you compare and contrast his views with others who are skeptical about the widespread use of computer technology in the schools.

QUESTIONS FOR FURTHER EXPLORATION

1. Oppenheimer refers to government reports, task forces, and studies throughout his essay. Access government Web sites to find out what resources are being spent on computers in the schools and what studies have been undertaken. Begin by accessing the White House <http://www.whitehouse.gov> and search the site for a record of the Clinton Administration's reports and initiatives on educational technology, many of which are used as background information in this article. Also check <http://ciir2.cs.umass.edu/Govbot/>, the Database of Government Web Sites, and search for sources on educational technology. Prepare a directory of resources on the state of educational technology in the schools for your classmates.

2. Oppenheimer refers to a number of recent books and studies on computer use in the school. Locate one, read it, and write a review of it for the members of your class.

3. Access the *Atlantic's* Web site <www.theatlantic.com> and read about the history of the magazine. Who is the audience for the magazine today? What other articles have been published in the last five years on computers? Read them and compare them with "The Computer Delusion." Is the *Atlantic* advocating a consistent position? Write a report for your class.

8

A NEO-LUDDITE REFLECTS
ON THE INTERNET

*Gertrude Himmelfarb is professor emeritus of British history at the
Graduate School and University Center of the City of New York.
During her career, she published a dozen books on Victorian history
and culture. Experts like Himmelfarb are often invited to write opinion pieces for "Point of View," the last essay in each issue of* The
Chronicle of Higher Education, *a weekly newspaper published in
printed form and on the Internet <http://chronicle.com>. The*
Chronicle *covers higher education in the United States and abroad
and is read by more than 400,000 college and university administrators and faculty members. Each issue includes new articles about
campuses in the United States and abroad, articles on developments
in scholarly research, features on professional issues, articles and reviews on information technology, reports on state and federal government actions that affect higher education, statistical reports on
varied topics like student enrollment and tuition figures, lists of new
scholarly books, job listings, and a calendar of events. The* Chronicle
*is an excellent source of information on all aspects of higher educa-
tion. In this essay, Professor Himmelfarb offers her views on the
value of the Internet as the "latest technological revolution" and
refers to herself as a "Neo-Luddite." As a scholar of nineteenth-
century British history, Professor Himmelfarb is alluding to the Luddites, a group of English workers who destroyed manufacturing
equipment designed to produce machine-made cloth and woolen
goods that had previously been made by hand. The Luddites feared
that the new technology would destroy their cottage industries,
which, in fact, it did. But Himmelfarb does not present herself as a
Luddite in the strictly historical sense; she refers to a more general
late-twentieth century definition of a Luddite as a person who is opposed to new technology in the workplace.*

QUESTIONS FOR READING

1. In this "Point of View" essay, Himmelfarb's task is to present an argument, based on her opinion, examples, and evidence. As you read, make notes about the details of her argument. What is her thesis? What are her primary examples?

2. Himmelfarb alludes to several texts and authors in this essay, using terms like "postmodern." Look up any references that are unfamiliar to you. Does the effectiveness of her argument depend upon familiarity with those terms and references?

GERTRUDE HIMMELFARB

A NEO-LUDDITE REFLECTS
ON THE INTERNET

The Chronicle of Higher Education *(November 1, 1996, p. A56)*

On the subject of our latest technological revolution, cyberspace, I am a neo-Luddite. Not a true Luddite; my Luddism is qualified, compromised. I revel in the word processor; I am grateful for computerized library catalogues; I appreciate the convenience of CD-ROMs; and I concede the usefulness of the Internet for retrieving information and conducting research. But I am disturbed by some aspects of the new technology—not merely by the moral problems raised by cybersex, which have occupied so much attention recently, but also by the new technology's impact on learning and scholarship.

Revolutions come fast and furious these days. No sooner do we adapt to one than we are confronted with another. For almost half a millennium, we lived with the product of the print revolution—the culture of the book. Then, a mere century ago, we were introduced to the motion picture; a couple of decades later, to radio and then to television. To a true Luddite, those inventions were the beginning of the rot, the decline of Western civilization as we have known it.

To a true revolutionary, such as Marshall McLuhan, they were giant steps toward a brave new world liberated from the stultifying rigidities of an obsolete literacy. To the rest of us, they were frivolities, diversions, often meretricious (as some popular culture has always been), but not threatening to the life of the mind, the culture associated with books.

Not that the book culture has been immune from corruption. When the printing press democratized literature, liberating it from the control of clerics and scribes, the effects were ambiguous. As the historian Elizabeth Eisenstein pointed out in her seminal 1979 work *The Printing Press as an Agent of Change,* the advent of printing facilitated not only the production of scientific works, but also of occult and devotional tracts. It helped create a cosmopolitan secular culture and, at the same time, distinctive national and sectarian cultures. It stimulated scholarship and high culture, as well as ephemera and popular culture. It subverted one intellectual elite, the clergy, only to elevate another, the "enlightened" class.

Yet for all of its ambiguities, printing celebrated the culture of the book—of bad books, to be sure, but also of good books and great books. Movies, radio, and television made the first inroads on the book, not only because they distracted us from reading, but also because they began to train our minds to respond to oral and visual sensations of brief duration rather than to the cadences, nuances, and lingering echoes of the written word. The movie critic Michael Medved has said that even more detrimental than the content of television is the way that it habituates children to an attention span measured in seconds rather than minutes. The combination of sound bites and striking visual effects shapes the young mind, incapacitating it for the longer, slower, less febrile tempo of the book.

And now we have the Internet to stimulate and quicken our senses still more. We channel-surf on television, but that is as naught compared with cyber-surfing. The obvious advantage of the new medium is that it provides access to an infinite quantity of information on an untold number and variety of subjects. How does one quarrel with such a plenitude of goods?

As an information-retrieval device, the Internet is unquestionably an asset, assuming that those using it understand that the information retrieved is only as sound as the original sources—an assumption that applies to all retrieval methods, but especially to one whose sources are so profuse and indiscriminate. Yet children and older students, encouraged to rely upon the Internet for information and research, may not be sophisticated enough to question the validity of the information or the reliability of the source. A child whom I saw interviewed on television said that it was wonderful to be able to ask a question on one's home page and have "lots of people answer it for you." Before the age of the Internet, the child would have had to look up the question in a textbook or encyclopedia, a source that he would have recognized as more authoritative than, say, his older brother or sister (or even his mother or father).

As a learning device, the new electronic technology is even more dubious—indeed, it may be more bad than good. And it is dubious at all levels of learning. Children who are told that they need not learn how to multiply and divide, spell, and write grammatical prose because the computer can do that for them, are being grossly miseducated. More important, young people constantly exposed to "multimedia" and "hypermedia" replete with sound and images often become unable to concentrate on mere "texts" (known as books), which have only words and ideas to commend them. Worse yet, the constant exposure to a myriad of texts, sounds, and images that often are only tangentially related to each other is hardly conducive to the cultivation of logical, rational, systematic habits of thought.

At the more advanced level of learning and scholarship, the situation is equally ambiguous. Let me illustrate this from my own experience. I used to give (in the preelectronic age) two sequences of courses: one on social history, the other on intellectual history. In a course on social history, a student might find electronic technology useful, for example, in inquiring about the standard of living of the working classes in the early period of industrialization, assuming that the relevant sources—statistical surveys, diaries, archival collections, newspapers, tracts, journals, books, and other relevant materials—were online (or at least that information about their location and content was available).

This kind of social history, which is built by marshaling social and economic data, is not only facilitated, but actually is stimulated, by the new technology. One might find oneself making connections among sources of information that would have had no apparent link had they not been so readily called up on the computer screen (on the other hand, now one might not make the effort to discover other kinds of sources that do not appear).

But what about intellectual history? It may be that the whole of Rousseau's *Social Contract* and Hegel's *Philosophy of History* are now online. Can one read such books on the screen as they should be read—slowly, carefully, patiently, dwelling upon a difficult passage, resisting the temptation to scroll down, thwarting the natural speed of the computer? What is important in the history of ideas is not retrieving and recombining material, but understanding it. And that requires a different relation to the text, a different tempo of reading and study.

One can still buy the book (or perhaps print out a "hard copy" from the computer), read it, mark it up, and take notes the old-fashioned way. The difficulty is that students habituated to surfing on the Internet, to getting their information in quick easy doses, to satisfying their curiosity with a minimum of effort (and with a maximum of sensory stimulation) often do not have the patience to think and study this old-fashioned way. They may even come to belittle the intellectual enterprise itself, the study of the kinds of books—"great books," as some say derisively—that require careful thought and study.

Perhaps I am exaggerating the effect of the electronic revolution, just as critics have said that Elizabeth Eisenstein has exaggerated the effect of the print one. She sometimes seems to suggest that printing was not only *an* agent of change, but *the* primary agent. Without the printing press, she has implied, the Renaissance might have petered out or the Reformation been suppressed as yet another medieval heresy. "The advent of printing," she notes, preceded "the Protestant revolt."

The electronic media cannot make that claim to priority. The intellectual revolution of our time, postmodernism, long antedated the Internet. Nonetheless, the Internet powerfully reinforces postmodernism: It is the postmodernist technology *par excellence*. It is as subversive of "linear," "logocentric," "essentialist" thinking, as committed to the "aporia," "indeterminacy," "fluidity," "intertextuality," and "contextuality" of discourse, as deconstruction itself. Like postmodernism, the Internet does not distinguish between the true and the false, the important and the trivial, the enduring and the ephemeral. The search for a name or phrase or subject will produce a comic strip or advertising slogan as readily as a quotation from the Bible or Shakespeare. Every source appearing on the screen has the same weight and credibility as every other; no authority is "privileged" over any other.

The Internet gives new meaning to the British expression describing intellectuals, "chattering classes." On their own home pages, subscribers can communicate to the world every passing reflection, impression, sensation, obsession, or perversion.

Michael Kinsley, editor of the new cyberspace journal *Slate*, defensively insists that his magazine will retain the "linear, rational thinking" of print journalism. To have to make that claim is itself testimony to the nonlinear, nonrational tendency of the new medium. Each article in *Slate* gives the date when it was "posted" and "composted" (archived). Composted! One recalls the computer-programming acronym a few years ago—"GIGO," for "garbage in, garbage out." (As it happens, the articles in *Slate* are not garbage, but much on the Internet is.)

One need not be a Luddite, or even a neo-Luddite, to be alarmed by this most useful, most potent, most seductive, and most equivocal invention.

QUESTIONS FOR REACTION AND DISCUSSION

1. What does Himmelfarb mean by casting herself as a "Neo-Luddite"? What do you understand her use of this term to imply?
2. Himmelfarb devotes much of her essay to praising the advantages of book culture. But she is also mindful of the disadvantages. What are they?
3. According to one expert that Himmelfarb quotes, television has altered the attention span of children. Is this true? How would one defend such a position?
4. Define "social history" and "intellectual history." What are the advantages and disadvantages for the study of both using electronic technology?

QUESTIONS FOR WRITING

1. One of the central points in Himmelfarb's argument is that "Like Postmodernism, the Internet does not distinguish between the true and the false, the important and the trivial, the enduring and the ephemeral." Similar criticisms were made in the nineteenth century,

when daily newspapers began to publish articles and advertisements on the same page. Imagine that you are on an orientation committee planing a program about the use of the Internet for new students at your college or university. What guidelines would you suggest for making judgments about what you access on the Internet? How would you encourage fellow students to distinguish between "the important and the trivial"? Work with another student and write a set of guidelines to present to your class.

2. Himmelfarb contends that "as a learning device, the new electronic technology is even more dubious." She further suggests that children are told that "they need not learn how to multiply and divide, spell, and write grammatical prose, because the computer can do that for them." Some might accuse Himmelfarb of overstatement here. What examples can you find of how children are being taught to use computers? Write your own opinion piece in which you agree or disagree with the proposition that computer technology is a dubious learning device.

3. Following the publication of Himmelfarb's essay, several letters to the editor appeared in the *Chronicle*, including the following by a professor of psychology. Read his letter and write your own letter to the editor, commenting on his view of Himmelfarb's essay.

THE RISKS AND REWARDS OF THE INTERNET AS A RESEARCH TOOL

To the Editor:

I agree wholeheartedly with Ms. Himmelfarb on the primacy of reading. I have long argued that students should be assigned more readings and be taught to reflect upon what they have read. However, I must disagree with her when she claims that "students . . . often do not have the patience to think and study this old-fashioned way." Instead, I would say that students are not *taught* to think in the old-fashioned way. Nor are many teachers ready to teach them to use the new tools at hand.

To me, the Internet is an ever-growing treasure trove of primary and secondary sources. The simple convenience of being able to sit anywhere and tap into that trove is the single greatest feature of the Internet. The Internet makes it easier to be a scholar now than at any time in history. As much as I love libraries, I find it much easier to travel virtually from my office to the sources I need than to even walk across the campus. When I need books and articles now, I usually get them by contacting the librarian via electronic mail.

Teaching students to do the same kind of "library research" that I do is an important part of our curriculum now. Not only do we teach our students to use the old-fashioned library, we also teach them to use the Web, FirstSearch, Uncover, File-Transfer Protocol, Gopher, and other similar tools.

Two issues predominate here. The first is that students must learn that using the Internet is more than just plain surfing. Learning how to find useful materials on the Internet for a class is not easy and can be time consuming. However, once the tools above are mastered, the Internet . . . becomes a place where students can find what they need quickly or quickly realize that they will have to look elsewhere.

The second issue is that the same kind of filters that students use to screen out useful information from garbage everywhere else must also be used when dealing with Internet-derived materials. . . .

I also agree with Ms. Himmelfarb that new media have made "inroads" on books. Again, however, I disagree as to whether that is necessarily a bad thing for teaching and scholarship. When used correctly, new media can be powerful tools in teaching. . . . I recall once seeing a computerized demonstration of how the neural groove becomes the neural tube in mammalian embryology. The teacher using that demonstration reported that it completely changed his students' understanding of the phenomenon.

I am no postmodernist and I cherish logical trains of thought. Still, I see virtue in hypermedia and nonlinear thought. The tools to express such modes of thinking are barely here. Wait until they are and teachers learn to use them. The classroom will become a very different place. Learning . . . will still be characterized by effort and thought, but the tools for learning will be different, and I, for one, look forward to using them and teaching them.

Edward P. Kardas
Professor of Psychology
Southern Arkansas University
Magnolia, Arkansas

QUESTIONS FOR FURTHER EXPLORATION

1. Himmelfarb specifically refers to *Slate,* an online magazine of news, political commentary, and features on contemporary culture edited by Michael Kinsley. Access *Slate* <http//www.slate.com> and read some of the articles. Is it true, as Himmelfarb suggests, that the magazine retains the linearity of print journalism? Is this an advantage for an online magazine? Why or why not?

2. Himmelfarb refers to Elizabeth Eisenstein's *The Printing Press as an Agent of Change,* a book that traces how the printing press forever altered both western culture and consciousness. Himmelfarb suggests that although there were negative effects, the printing press "celebrated the culture of the book." Many see the computer as significant a development as the printing press. Write an essay in which you relate the development of the computer with the printing press, focusing on either the negative or positive effects of both.

9

MEN, WOMEN, AND COMPUTERS

Barbara Kantrowitz is a senior editor at Newsweek, *which has been one of the top weekly news magazines in the United States since its founding in 1933. Geared toward a young and mostly liberal audience,* Newsweek *has won many awards for coverage of contemporary issues, like civil rights, space exploration, foreign affairs, and science and technology. A graduate of Cornell University, Kantrowitz has covered technology, education, and family issues since 1985 and helped create the popular "Cyberscope" section of the magazine. A distinguished journalist, Kantrowitz has also worked for a variety of other publications, including newspapers such as the* Philadelphia Inquirer *and* The New York Times. *"Men, Women, and Computers" was among the first essays to recognize and analyze the gender differences at work in cyberspace. Following the publication of this essay, Kantrowitz was the recipient of the Front Page Award from the Newswomen's Club of New York.*

QUESTIONS FOR READING

1. Kantrowitz takes the position that women are disadvantaged citizens in cyberspace, a position that has received a great deal of publicity in the last ten years. What is your sense of the differences between men and women as computer users?
2. Kantrowitz uses a variety of examples in this essay: quotations from experts, anecdotes, survey results, and statistics. What examples are most effective? Why?

BARBARA KANTROWITZ

MEN, WOMEN, AND COMPUTERS

Newsweek *(May 16, 1994, pp. 48–55)*

Cyberspace, it turns out, isn't much of an Eden after all. It's marred by just as many sexist ruts and gender conflicts as the Real World.

As a longtime *Star Trek* devotee, Janis Cortese was eager to be part of the Trekkie discussion group on the Internet. But when she first logged on, Cortese noticed that these fans of the final frontier devoted megabytes to such profound topics as whether Troi or Crusher had bigger breasts. In other words, the purveyors of this *Trek* dreck were all *guys.* Undeterred, Cortese, a physicist at California's Loma Linda University, figured she'd add perspective to the electronic gathering place with her own momentous questions. Why was the male cast racially diverse while almost all the females were young, white, and skinny? Then, she tossed in a few lustful thoughts about the male crew members.

After those seemingly innocuous observations, "I was chased off the net by rabid hounds," recalls Cortese. Before she could say "Fire phasers," the Trekkies had flooded her electronic mailbox with nasty messages—a practice called "flaming." Cortese retreated into her own galaxy by starting the all-female Starfleet Ladies Auxiliary and Embroidery/Baking Society. The private electronic forum, based in Houston, now has more than forty members, including psychologists, physicians, students, and secretaries. They started with Trek-talk, but often chose to beam down and go where no man had ever wandered before—into the personal mode. When Julia Kosatka, a Houston computer scientist, got pregnant last year, she shared her thoughts with the group on weight gain, sex while expecting, and everything else on her mind. Says Kosatka: "I'm part of one of the longest-running slumber parties in history."

From the Internet to Silicon Valley to the PC sitting in the family room, men and women often seem like two chips that pass in the night. Sure, there are women who spout techno-speak in their sleep and plenty of men who think a hard drive means four hours on the freeway. But in general, computer culture is created, defined, and controlled by men. Women often feel about as welcome as a system crash.

About a third of American families have at least one computer, but most of those are purchased and used by males. It may be new technology, but the old rules still apply. In part, it's that male-machine bonding thing, reincarnated in the digital age. "Men tend to be seduced by the technology itself," says Oliver Strimpel, executive director of The Computer Museum in Boston. "They tend to get into the faster-race-car syndrome," bragging about the size of their discs or the speed of their microprocessors. To the truly besotted, computers are a virtual religion, complete with icons (on-screen graphics), relics (obsolete programs and machines) and prophets (Microsoft's Bill Gates, outlaw hackers). This is not something to be trifled with by mere . . . females, who seem to think that machines were meant to be *used*, like the microwave oven or the dishwasher. Interesting and convenient on the job but not worthy of obsession. Esther Dyson, editor of *Release 1.0*, an influential software-industry newsletter, has been following the computer field for two decades. Yet when she looks at her own computer, Dyson says she still doesn't "really care about its innards. I just want it to work."

Blame (a) culture (b) family (c) schools (d) all of the above. Little boys are expected to roll around in the dirt and explore. Perfect training for learning to use computers, which often requires hours in front of the screen trying to figure out the messy arcanum of a particular program. Girls get subtle messages—from society if not from their parents—that they should keep their hands clean and play with their dolls. Too often, they're discouraged from taking science and math—not just by their schools but by parents as well (how many mothers have patted their daughters on the head and reassured them: "Oh, I wasn't good at math, either").

The gender gap is real and takes many forms.

BARBIE VS. NINTENDO

Girls' technophobia begins early. Last summer, Sarah Douglas, a University of Oregon computer-science professor, took part in a job fair for teenage girls that was supposed to introduce them to nontraditional occupations. With great expectations, she set up her computer and loaded it with interesting programs. Not a single girl stopped by. When she asked why, the girls "told me computers were something their dads and their brothers used," Douglas sadly recalls. "Computer science is a very male profession . . . When girls get involved in that male world, they are pushed away and belittled. Pretty soon, the girls get frustrated and drop out."

Computer games usually involve lots of shooting and dying. Boy stuff. What's out there for girls? "If you walk down the street and look in the computer store, you will see primarily male people as sales staff and as customers," says Jo Sanders, director of the gender-equity program at the Center for Advanced Study in Education at the City University of New York Graduate Center.

Boys and girls are equally interested in computers until about the fifth grade, says University of Minnesota sociologist Ronald Anderson, who coauthored the recent report "Computers in American Schools." At that point, boys' use rises significantly and girls' use drops, Anderson says, probably because sex-role identification really kicks in. Many girls quickly put computers on the list of not-quite-feminine topics, like car engines and baseball batting averages. It didn't have to be this way. The very first computer programmer was a woman, Ada Lovelace, who worked with Charles Babbage on his mechanical computing machines in the mid-1800s. If she had become a role model, maybe hundreds of thousands of girls would have spent their teenage years locked in their bedrooms staring at screens. Instead, too many are doing their nails or worrying about their hair, says Marcelline Barron, an administrator at the Illinois Mathematics and Science Academy, a publicly funded coed boarding school for gifted students. "You're not thinking about calculus or physics when you're thinking about that," says Barron. "We have these kinds of expectations for young girls. They must be neat, they must be clean, they must be quiet."

Despite great strides by women in other formerly male fields, such as law and medicine, women are turning away from the computer industry. Men earning computer-science degrees outnumber women three to one and the gap is growing, according to the National Science Foundation. Fifteen years ago, when computers were still new in schools, they hadn't yet been defined as so exclusively male. But now girls have gotten the message. It's not just the technical and cultural barrier. Sherry Turkle, a Massachusetts Institute of Technology sociologist who teaches a course on women and computers, says that computers have come to stand for "a world without emotion," an image that seems to scare off girls more than boys.

In the past decade, videogames have become a gateway to technology for many boys, but game manufacturers say few girls are attracted to these small-screen shoot-'em-ups. It's not surprising that the vast majority of videogame designers are men. They don't call it *Game Boy* for nothing. Now some manufacturers are trying to lure girls. In the next few months, Sega plans to introduce "Berenstein Bears," which will offer players a choice of boy or girl characters. A second game, "Crystal's Pony Tale," involves coloring (there's lots of pink in the background). Neither game requires players to "die," a common videogame device that researchers say girls dislike. Girls also tend to prefer nonlinear games, where there is more than one way to proceed. "There's a whole issue with speaking girls' language," says Michealene Cristini Risley, group director of licensing and character development for Sega. The company would like to hook girls at the age of four, before they've developed fears of technology.

Girls need freedom to explore and make mistakes. Betsy Zeller, a thirty-seven-year-old engineering manager at Silicon Graphics, says that when she discovered computers in college, "I swear I thought I'd seen the face of God." Yet she had to fend off guys who would come into the lab and want to help her work through problems or, worse yet, do them for her. "I would tell them to get lost," she says. "I wanted to do it myself." Most women either asked for or accepted proffered help, just as they are more likely to ask for directions when lost in a strange city. That may be the best way to avoid driving in circles for hours, but it's not the best way to learn technical subjects.

Schools are trying a number of approaches to interest girls in computers. Douglas and her colleagues are participating in a mentorship program where undergraduate girls spend a summer working with female computer scientists. Studies have shown that girls are more attracted to technology if they can work in groups: some schools are experimenting with team projects that require computers but are focused on putting out a product, like a newspaper or pamphlet. At the middle and high-school level, girls-only computer classes are increasingly popular. Two months ago Roosevelt Middle School in Eugene, Oregon, set up girls-only hours at the computer lab. Games were prohibited and artists were brought in to teach girls how to be more creative with the computer. Students are also learning to use e-mail, which many girls love. Says Debbie Nehl, the computer-lab supervisor: "They see it as high-tech note-passing."

POWER NETWORKS

As a relatively new industry, the leadership of computerdom might be expected to be more gender-diverse. Wrong: few women have advanced beyond middle-management ranks. According to a study conducted last year by the *San Jose Mercury News*, there are no women CEOs running major computer-manufacturing firms and only a handful running software companies. Even women who have succeeded say they are acutely conscious of the differences between them and their male coworkers. "I don't talk the same as men," says Paula Hawthorn, an executive at Montage Software, in Oakland, California. "I don't get the same credibility." The difference, she says, "is with you all the time."

Women who work in very technical areas, such as programming, are often the loneliest. Anita Borg, a computer-systems researcher, remembers attending a 1987 conference where there were so few women that the only time they ran into each other was in the restroom. Their main topic of discussion: why there were so few women at the conference. That bathroom cabal grew into Systers, an online network for women with technical careers. There are now 1,740 women members from 19 countries representing 200 colleges and universities and 150 companies. Systers is part mentoring and part consciousness-raising. One graduate student, for example, talked about how uncomfortable she felt sitting in her shared office when a male graduate student and a professor put a picture of a nude woman on a computer. The problem was resolved when a couple of female faculty members, also on the Systers network, told their offending colleagues that the image was not acceptable.

Women have been more successful in developing software, especially when their focus is products used by children. Jan Davidson, a former teacher, started Davidson & Associates, in Torrance, California, with three programs in 1982. Now it's one of the country's biggest developers for kids' software, with 350 employees and $58.6 million in revenues. Multimedia will bring new opportunities for women. The technology is so specialized that it requires a team—animators, producers, scriptwriters, 3-D modelers—to create state-of-the-art products. It's a far cry from the stereotype of the solitary male programmer, laboring long into the night with only takeout Chinese food for company. At Mary Cron's Rymel Design Group in Palos Verdes, California, most of the software artists and designers are women, Cron says. "It's like a giant puzzle," she adds. "We like stuff we can work on together."

As more women develop software, they may also help create products that will attract women consumers—a huge untapped market. Heidi Roizen, a college English major, cofounded T/Maker Co. in Mountain View, California, a decade ago. She says that because women are often in charge of the family's budget, they are potential consumers of personal-finance programs. Women are also the most likely buyers of education and family-entertainment products, a fast-growing segment of the industry. "Women are more typically the household shopper," Roizen says. "They have tremendous buying power."

WIRED WOMEN

The Infobahn—a.k.a. the Information Superhighway—may be the most hyped phenomenon in history—or it could be the road to the future. In any case, women want to get on. But the sign over the access road says CAUTION: MEN WORKING. WOMEN BEWARE. Despite hundreds of thousands of new users in the last year, men still dominate the Internet and commercial services such as Prodigy or CompuServe. The typical male conversation online turns off many women. "A lot of time, to be crude, it's a pissing contest," says Lisa Kimball, a partner in the Meta network, a Washington, D.C., online service that is forty percent female. Put-downs are an art form. When one woman complained recently in an Internet forum that she didn't like participating because she didn't have time to answer all her e-mail, she was swamped with angry responses, including this one (from a man): "Would you like some cheese with your whine?"

Some men say the online hostility comes from resentment over women's slowly entering what has been an almost exclusively male domain. Many male techno-jocks "feel women are intruding into their inner sanctum," says André Bacard, a Silicon Valley, California, technology writer. They're not out to win sensitivity contests. "In the computer world, it's 'Listen, baby, if you don't like it, drop dead'," says Bacard. "It's the way men talk to guys. Women aren't used to that."

Even under more civilized circumstances, men and women have different conversational styles, says Susan Herring, a University of Texas at Arlington professor who has studied women's participation on computer networks. Herring found that violations of long-established net etiquette—asking too many basic questions, for example—angered men. "The women were much more tolerant of people who didn't know what they were doing," Herring says.

"What really annoyed women was the flaming and people boasting. The things that annoy women are things men do all the time."

Like hitting on women. Women have learned to tread their keyboards carefully in chat forums because they often have to fend off sexual advances that would make Bob Packwood blush. When subscribers to America Online enter one of the service's forums, their computer names appear at the top of the screen as a kind of welcome. If they've chosen an obviously female name, chances are they'll soon be bombarded with private messages seeking detailed descriptions of their appearance or sexual preferences. "I couldn't believe it," recalls fifty-five-year-old Eva S. "I said, 'Come on, I'm a grandmother'."

More and more women are signing on to networks that are either coed and run by women, or are exclusively for women. Stacy Horn started ECHO (for East Coast Hang Out) four years ago because she was frustrated with the hostility online. About sixty percent of ECHO's two thousand subscribers are men; among ECHO 's fifty forums, only two are strictly for women. "Flaming is nonexistent on ECHO," Horn says. "New women get online and they see that. And then they're much more likely to jump in." Women's Wire in San Francisco, started in January, has 850 subscribers, only ten percent of them men—the reverse of most online services. "We wanted to design a system in which women would help shape the community from the floor up," says cofounder Ellen Pack. The official policy is that there is no such thing as a dumb question—and no flaming.

Male subscribers say Women's Wire has been a learning experience for them, too. Maxwell Hoffmann, a forty-one-year-old computer-company manager, says that many men think that only women are overly emotional. But men lose it, too. A typical online fight starts with two guys sending "emotionally charged flames going back and forth" through cyberspace (not on Women's Wire). Then it expands and "everybody starts flaming the guy. They scream at each other and they're not listening."

If only men weren't so *emotional,* so *irrational,* could we all get along on the net?

TOYS AND TOOLS

In one intriguing study by the Center for Children and Technology, a New York think tank, men and women in technical fields were asked to dream up machines of the future. Men typically imagined devices that could help them "conquer the universe," says Jan Hawkins, director of the center. She says women wanted machines that met people's needs, "the perfect mother."

Someday, gender-blind education and socialization may render those differences obsolete. But in the meantime, researchers say both visions are useful. If everyone approached technology the way women do now, "we wouldn't be pushing envelopes," says Cornelia Bruner, associate director of the center. "Most women, even those who are technologically sophisticated, think of machines as a means to an end." Men think of the machines as an extension of their own power, as a way to "transcend physical limitations." That may be why they are more likely to come up with great leaps in technology, researchers say. Without that vision, the computer and its attendant industry would not exist.

Ironically, gender differences could help women. "We're at a cultural turning point," says MIT's Turkle. "There's an opportunity to remake the culture around the machine." Practicality is now as valued as invention. If the computer industry wants to put machines in the hands of the masses, that means women—along with the great many men who have no interest in hot-rod computing. An ad campaign for Compaq's popular Presario line emphasizes the machine's utility. After kissing her child good night, the mother in the ad sits down at her Presario to work. As people start to view their machines as creative tools, some-day women may be just as comfortable with computers as men are.

QUESTIONS FOR REACTION AND DISCUSSION

1. Kantrowitz's position in this essay is that there is a real gender gap in cyberspace and that it takes many forms. What are the assumptions about male and female behavior that guide the author of this essay? What is your own experience—as a male or a female? In what ways can you relate to specific behaviors described in this essay?

2. Kantrowitz gives examples from several schools that have worked to involve girls in computers. What methods have they used? How effective have they been? In your own experience, how did your schooling influence your involvement and interest in computers? Can you detect gender differences as you think about your experience?

3. Organize a class discussion on gender differences for computer use. Begin by composing a series of issues for discussion, such as collaborative learning, e-mail use, and computer games, and divide your class into panels for the discussion of the different issues. Ask each panel to summarize their discussions for the entire class.

QUESTIONS FOR WRITING

1. Kantrowitz suggests schools and companies are working to make computers more attractive to women as students and as consumers. What is your college or university doing to interest students—both men and women—in computers? Are there specific programs for women? Collect some computer advertisements and brochures about new product lines. What evidence do you find that businesses are specifically trying to interest women in computers? Write an informative essay in which you discuss the specific strategies schools and/or companies are using to attract women.

2. Kantrowitz's essay was published in *Newsweek* in 1994. There is considerable evidence that the gender gap in cyberspace has grown smaller since that time. What information can you find to support such a position? Write an update on "Men, Women, and Computers" in which you present new information and evidence.

QUESTIONS FOR FURTHER EXPLORATION

1. Investigate some of the networks, chatrooms, and Web sites targeted specifically for women. What are common themes? Common mechanisms for creating interest? Write a report of your findings and present them to your class.
2. One of the more controversial topics among parents today is the amount of time children should be permitted to play computer games. Investigate the current computer game market and describe what games are available. Is there evidence that the developers of some games play to specific gendered behavior? What studies are available about the effect of computer games on a child's educational development? Write an investigative report about your findings.

10

WOMEN EASE INTO MASTERY OF CYBERSPACE

John Tierney writes "The Big City" column for The New York Times, *which was founded in 1851 and is among the nation's oldest daily newspapers. In this twice-weekly column, Tierney covers local issues in New York City, although the column reprinted below is a good example of the ways in which Tierney enlarges city issues into matters of national interest. A graduate of Yale University, Tierney was first a newspaper reporter and then a writer for a variety of magazines, including the* Atlantic Monthly, Discover, Esquire, Health, Rolling Stone, Vogue, *and the* Wall Street Journal. *He joined* The New York Times *in 1990 and, in addition to "The Big City," has also written on AIDS in Africa, the 1992 Presidential election, and information technology. In this column, Tierney counters the notion that the Internet is the province of men.*

QUESTIONS FOR READING

1. Tierney challenges the perception that Internet use is mainly by men. What changes does he suggest have occurred on the Internet that have made broader use possible?
2. Consider your own Internet use as you read this article. How much time do you spend on research for class work? Communication with friends, classmates, professors, family members?

JOHN TIERNEY

WOMEN EASE INTO MASTERY OF CYBERSPACE

The New York Times *(December 17, 1998, B1)*

A new chapter in the history of communications is unfolding in New York, and it looks pretty much like the previous ones. Women are yet again taking over a medium invented by men.

Until now, the computer revolution has been guided largely by male engineers scattered along the West Coast in isolated garages, basements, and suburban office parks. But the hot Internet companies this fall exploit one of Manhattan's greatest resources: a network of educated women.

Five years ago, it was estimated that only five percent of the Internet's users were women, but today the figure is nearly fifty percent, and women are projected to become a majority in the next several years. So investors and media executives have become enthralled with Internet companies in New York run by and for women.

Wall Street is eagerly anticipating a public stock offering by iVillage, the SoHo company that operates the Internet's most popular female-oriented sites and recently announced partnerships with NBC and AT&T. Meanwhile America Online and Oprah Winfrey have formed alliances with Oxygen Media, a new-media company in midtown started this year by Geraldine B. Laybourne, the former head of cable television operations at Disney/ABC.

"The Internet is a natural place for women," Ms. Laybourne said, "because they care so much about relationships and staying connected. New York is the place to find women who know how to reach that audience, because there are so many smart women here with experience in cable television, magazines, publishing, and advertising."

Men have long had a knack for inventing communication gadgets, from pen and paper to the printing press, the telephone and the computer. But it's women who master the media and spend more time using them. They write more personal letters, send more cards and spend more time on the phone than men do. They're more likely to become authors, and they read more books and magazines.

"The Internet lets women use words, which is their natural tool," said Helen Fisher, an anthropologist at Rutgers University who is working on a book on gender differences. "Little girls speak in more complex, grammatical sentences than little boys do, and women never lose that superiority in verbal ability. The Internet is also a wonderful outlet for women's talent at networking. Men tend to be hierarchical, but women are driven to make lateral connections so they can cooperate."

While men are busy blasting virtual rocket launchers at one another over the Internet, women are talking. A survey this fall by Jupiter Communications, a market research company in SoHo, found that women spend less time on the Internet playing games and more time participating in chat rooms and exchanging e-mail.

"When we started iVillage, fun and games and surfing were key activities on the Web," Nancy Evans, the editor-in-chief, explains in an open letter to her site's visitors. "Today, using the Internet to help with real life has taken over the number one spot. Not that we don't like fun; but let's face it, we women are practical."

The practical means Web sites that look more like products of the Hearst and Condé Nast buildings than of Silicon Valley. They're devoted to health care, parenting (Oxygen has a site called Moms OnLine), fitness, beauty, and fashion, with plenty of self-improvement quizzes and advice.

Click on iVillage's Relationships site, and you find links to Dating Dilemmas, Couples Clinic, How to Kiss Better, The Wedding Women, Ms. Demeanor, and a chat session for the Ex-Wives Club. The site is called a "circle of help and support" by its editor-in-chief, Ms. Evans.

"One iVillager tells how she reinvented herself after getting fired, and three of you, maybe a dozen, even a hundred get inspired," Ms. Evans writes in her open letter. "Another iVillager tells her story of getting over trying to be perfect—size six, good hair days—and now she's living, just living, happily. And we feel emboldened by her resolve."

This may not sound so emboldening to veterans who still think of the Internet as a place for e-mail flame wars, chat rooms about sex and politics, and Web pages filled with arcana on debugging software and scoring higher on Quake. But these males will have to get used to sharing their turf. They may be able to beat one another in rocket-launcher shootouts, but they can't resist an army of well-spoken, well-connected women.

QUESTIONS FOR REACTION AND DISCUSSION

1. What assumptions about women's behavior on the Internet does Tierney draw on in this article?
2. What are the assumptions about male computer users that govern this essay?

QUESTIONS FOR WRITING

1. Contrast this essay with the "Men, Women, and Computers." What have been the major changes since 1994 and 1998 on the Internet,

according to Tierney? Research Internet usage (remember that Tierney says that today fifty percent of Internet usage is by women) and consider how such usage figures will alter how educators and students use computers.

2. Crucial to discussions about male and female use of the Internet and technology in general is communication. Most writers suggest that women use computers as tools for discussion and connection while men use computers as tools for computation and contest. Conduct a survey of your classmates by devising a list of questions about their computer use. How are these assumptions enforced by the responses from your classmates? How are they countered? Write an essay in which you discuss the differences between male and female use of the Internet among your classmates. Draw conclusions based on your limited sample.

QUESTIONS FOR FURTHER EXPLORATION

1. Tierney discusses iVillage, a New York-based company that publishes a Web site on parenting, working, health, and lifestyles, mainly for women. Emphasizing communities for women, the site provides a series of links to information, advice, and opportunities for discussion. Visit the site <http://www.ivillage.com> and explore a variety of links. How is the site set up to appeal to women? How is revenue generated for the site? Evaluate this site in light of Tierney's thesis that sites such as this one provide new "mastery" of cyberspace for women.

2. What other sites can you find that perform similar functions for women? Create a current directory of sites with descriptions of each.

3. What sites can you locate that seem to appeal more to men than to women? For example, access <www.nfl.com>. Make a list of the characteristics of this site that seem to be directed more toward men than toward women. Write a report for your class.

11

CYBERCHEATS: TERM-PAPER SHOPPING ONLINE

While swift access to information is among the most useful tools of using a computer, network technology also introduces new ethical questions for students. Although the buying and selling of research papers has long been the bane of college and university faculty members and administrators, the advent of online term paper companies makes plagiarism all too simple for students who are pressed for time and ideas. John N. Hickman, a recent graduate of Yale University who now works as a journalist, writes about the ease with which students can access, pay for, and submit essays and term papers that they have not written. The article reprinted here is from The New Republic, *a weekly magazine of news and political commentary as well as articles on books and the arts. The editorial staff includes a number of well-respected journalists like Jeffrey Rosen and Margaret Talbot, but each week a variety of articles by famous writers and high-profile academics are also published. Some of the frequent contributors are John Updike, Naomi Wolf, Arthur Schlesinger, Henry Louis Gates, Jr., and C. Vann Woodward. The New Republic, among the most prestigious of the news journals, always includes provocative essays about timely topics. Hickman's essay covers the beginning of an ongoing story: the efforts of one university to control the business of term-paper mills, companies that sell completed research papers. In 1997, Boston University sued eight companies that provide these services, and Hickman's essay is at once an account of the suit and a warning to students and faculty members about what is at stake.*

QUESTIONS FOR READING

1. Hickman assumes that all his readers understand "plagiarism." What is plagiarism? Most colleges and universities have policy statements (in catalogues, student guides, or on Web sites) about plagiarism and

the penalties for submitting work that is not the student's own. Find and read your school's statement and consider it as you read this essay.

2. Consider your own attitude toward buying a term paper that you haven't written yourself. What is your position? Does reading this essay alter your thinking?

JOHN N. HICKMAN

CYBERCHEATS: TERM-PAPER SHOPPING ONLINE

The New Republic *(March 23, 1998, Vol. 218, No. 12, pp. 14–15)*

It's four o'clock in the morning, you're just one page into a fifteen-page term paper that's due at ten o'clock, and the teaching assistant isn't giving extensions. A few years ago, that would have been it: you would have passed in the paper late, if at all, and dealt with the consequences. But this is 1998, and so, in your most desperate hour, you try a desperate ploy. You log on to the World Wide Web (the university has very generously connected every dorm room to the Internet), enter "term papers" into an online search engine, and find your way to www.al-termpaper.com. There you scroll down past the big red disclaimer ("All work offered is for research purposes only"), find a paper that fits the assignment, enter your credit card number, and then wait until the file shows up in your college e-mail account. You feel a little ashamed, but, hey, the course was just a distribution requirement, anyway. You put your own name on the title page, print it out, and set the alarm for nine o'clock.

A few years ago, "Al Termpaper" would have been just another tiny ad in the classifieds of *Rolling Stone* or *National Lampoon*—hardly a temptation for most self-respecting students, and hardly a worry for any serious institution of higher learning. But the Web now features dozens of similar sites—from the "Evil House of Cheat" to "Research Papers Online"—which enable students to purchase ready-made term papers on a wide variety of subjects.

The companies, of course, maintain they are merely providing learning materials for inquisitive students. But there's good reason to think online plagiarism is becoming a real problem on college campuses. The Evil House of Cheat page now boasts over one million hits; Al Termpaper claims thousands. Although a "hit" is a visit, not a sale, it is hard to imagine that thousands of students—at least eight thousand a week—are visiting these sites, and no one is buying. A spokesman for "The Paper Store" told me that his company's yearly traffic in papers was "well in the thousands." The owner of Al Termpaper says that he has sold between one thousand and two thousand papers in his first year of operation. According to Anthony Krier, a research librarian at

Franklin Pierce College in Rindge, New Hampshire, and a widely quoted source of Internet plagiarism (he maintains a database of term-paper Web sites), the number of term-paper sites has swelled from twenty-eight in the beginning of 1997 to seventy-two today. "Does the increase in the number of sites translate into an increase in cheating? Certainly," says Krier. "There's no doubt about it. People have got to realize the problem is not going away until they start taking it seriously."

At least one school, Boston University, is. Last year, it became sufficiently worried about online plagiarism that it launched a sting operation, in which a law student posed as an undergraduate in search of a paper on Toni Morrison's *Beloved*. In October, the university—which has been dogging term-paper mills for twenty-five years—filed suit against eight of the companies it claims to have snagged in the ruse, charging them with mail and wire fraud, racketeering, and breaking a Massachusetts law against term-paper sales.

But B.U. is the exception. Harvard University's Thurston Smith, secretary to the administrative board, is serenely confident that Internet plagiarism is not a problem at Harvard. "I'm sure it's going on somewhere," he says. "I just have to believe Harvard students would have too much respect for the faculty." Just as sanguine are administrators at Bucknell, Dartmouth, and Yale. Terri Barbuto, secretary of the executive committee, Yale's disciplinary body, insists, "It really hasn't been a problem at Yale."

My own sampling of student opinion suggests otherwise. One Yale student, for example, told me that, while researching an essay on Shakespeare, he inadvertently stumbled upon a term-paper site and, after asking around, realized that he wasn't the only student tempted by the ease of Internet plagiarism: "Everyone was finding them and keeping their mouths shut. I mean, at Yale, who would admit to having to buy a paper?" A Princeton freshman admitted to me that he had passed in a pilfered English paper: "Come on," he said, "it's just so easy, and the class was a waste of time, anyway."

Just how easy is it? Punching in "term papers" to an Internet search engine like AltaVista yields more than five million matches. The vast majority of these sites are, ironically, administrative warnings about online plagiarism, but among the first one hundred listings are links to a handful of term-paper sites. If you click on the link to the Evil House of Cheat (www.cheathouse.com), a dark, fiery-fonted homepage will appear on the screen, featuring links to about forty other term-paper sites. Many of these linked sites are staggering, library-like catalogues of thousands of prewritten papers. At Al Termpaper's Web site, which claims to offer "approximately twenty-thousand prewritten term papers," you could, for example, purchase the twenty-page essay, "Hegel's Theory of Religion," for $179, or acquire ten pages on the IMF for a mere $89.50. Or, if that just-right paper isn't already available, The Paper Store will be happy to compose a special one that fits your needs, for about $15 a page.

The proprietors of these services claim that what they do is legal and honorable. "I help people," says Abe Korn, the man behind "The Term Paper,

School, and Business Help Line." Korn, who talks a mile a minute in thick Brooklynese and claims to have been a professor at "a very major university," explains that his clients say, "'Abe, help me; I don't know how to write a paper.' I write them one, as an example, and then they go and pass it in. Is that my fault? No. If I help you in physics and work one problem, and you turn that problem in, am I to blame? No. I'm just a tutor."

Of course, a 1973 Massachusetts law forbids the sale of a term paper by someone knowing or "having reason to know" that it will be submitted as somebody else's work. And Texas passed a similar law last year. But, even if selling term papers is potentially illegal, the law can't do much to shut down sites like "School Sucks"—sites where students generously make their own papers available to others for free. By one count, there are thirty-eight free term-paper sites like School Sucks, a page started in 1996 by a former Florida International University student, Kenny Sahr. By last July, School Sucks, which started with one English paper Sahr borrowed from a friend, had grown into a megasite with two thousand free term papers and a convenient search engine to locate essays by key words. As of January, according to Sahr, his site registered 1,140,690 hits and advertising revenues of $5,000 a month.

Some of these free papers are, by anyone's standards, awful. One paper on *Macbeth* begins: "*Macbeth* is primarily about villains. And the villainy that the play has knows no bounds." Yet other free-paper sites, such as the one designed by Harvard sophomore Dorian Berger, are gems. Dorian's swanky homepage posts about twenty of his generally quite good Harvard papers, free to download.

Even more helpful are pages like "1 Stop Research Paper Shop," which links to thirty-two scholarly sites, each with free papers posted by altruistically minded academics. Linked to the site: economics papers from the Federal Reserve Bank of Minneapolis, research works from the NASA Laboratories, papers from the Center of Cognitive Science, like "Mechanics of Sentence Processing," and a trove of essays from an assistant professor of economics at the University of Chicago, Casey Mulligan. The homepage of J. Michael Miller, a teacher at Virginia's Episcopal High School, who has a master's degree in history from Georgetown University and a Ph.D. in Russian History from George Washington University, features five of Miller's college papers, ripe for the picking. Miller is only slightly troubled by the prospects of plagiarism. "It's really up to the individual reader," he says, "to do with the information what they will, good or evil. I belong to the school that says teach people to do the right thing and then turn 'em loose."

Concern over Internet plagiarism has led at least a few educators to contemplate high-tech solutions. Two employees of the National Institutes of Health, Dr. Ned Feder and Walter Stewart, have designed a computer program to scan text and recognize word-for-word similarities as short as thirty-two characters long. Still, the programs have their limits, and, in the end, it's a losing battle. The whole point of the Internet is to share information. To get the benefits of online technology, universities have to cope with the costs. The only real solution to cyberplagiarism, then, is old-fashioned vigilance. Having spent millions of dollars wiring their students to the Internet, universities may have to invest in smaller classes and a better teacher-to-student ratio. A return to some good old analog, face-to-face teaching may be the only way to keep on-line plagiarism at the fringes, where it belongs.

QUESTIONS FOR REACTION AND DISCUSSION

1. How effective is the opening of this essay? How does Hickman seek to interest you in the topic of this essay? How effective is the title? Why?
2. According to Hickman, the online term paper companies he investigated all clearly label their sites with disclaimers such as "All work offered is for research purposes only," which clearly appears on the A1 Termpaper Web site. What is the effect of such a disclaimer?
3. Conduct a panel discussion in your classroom in which you debate the issue of whether companies that sell research papers online are protected by the First Amendment right to freedom of speech.

QUESTIONS FOR WRITING

1. In December 1998, a federal judge dismissed Boston University's lawsuit against the online term-paper companies. Citing problems with the grounds on which the university filed the suit, Judge Patti B. Saris did not express an opinion on the position that the term-paper companies have taken—that selling already written research papers is a form of protected speech. Research this lawsuit and write an informative essay in which you explain the terms of the suit and the basis for the judge's decision.
2. Investigate your university's policy on academic dishonesty and computer use. Is there a policy that specifically governs research papers bought online? Assume that you have been asked to serve on a student government committee to prepare a policy statement to assist students in making decisions about how they might use Internet resources fairly and honestly. Include a section for faculty members as well, outlining what guidelines faculty members might follow in helping students learn to avoid plagiarism.

QUESTIONS FOR FURTHER EXPLORATION

1. This essay touches on the complex issues of freedom of speech and censorship on the Internet. On many library Web sites, you might notice a link to the "Blue Ribbon Campaign," <http://www.eff.org/

blueribbon.html>, a project of the Electronic Frontier Foundation. This Foundation is dedicated to the rights of users of online technologies and is especially concerned with, as they say in their promotional literature, "promoting liberty and social responsibility in the information age." Investigate this site and others concerned with the issues of free speech and responsibility on the Internet.

2. Investigate some of the Web sites that Hickman mentions in his essay and locate others. How great is the potential for academic dishonesty by using Internet resources? Evaluate a dozen of the sites, question your fellow classmates, and write a response to Hickman's essay in which you support or reject the position of the secretary of the Yale University executive committee that Internet plagiarism is not a significant problem.

3. Access the Center for Academic Integrity at Duke University <http://www.academicintegrity.org/>, a forum specifically designed as a resource for faculty members and for students to participate in discussions about academic honesty. Investigate the services of the site and participate in the chat room for students. What is the mission statement of the organization? What is the current thinking of students about academic honesty and the Internet? What did you learn from participating in the chat sessions? Write an e-mail message to your classmates, in which you summarize your experiences and make a recommendation about using this site.

Suggestions for Further Reading, Thinking, and Writing

1. Several of the writers whose works are represented in this section take different positions on the future of printed texts in an electronic world: especially Janet Murray, Laura Miller, Kevin Hunt, Sven Birkerts, and Paul Roberts. Write an essay in which you compare and contrast the views of several writers about the effects of technology on books, being careful to provide a clear explanation for the differing views of each writer.

2. Many of the writers in this section assume that easy access to sophisticated technology is not an issue for college students. Yet it is clear that students come to colleges and universities with a variety of computer experiences and, at the same time, that not all institutions can afford the same level of computer support. How important is the issue of access to technology to college students? Write a report on the current state of computer access at American colleges and universities, explaining what institutions are doing to support their initiatives.

3. Virtually all of the writers in this section comment on the process of writing itself as part of their discussions of technology. Using these essays as a departure point, investigate how using computers has altered the process of writing for professionals. What suggestions or ideas about writing can you glean from these essays? What are the implications for students learning to write essays, reports, and papers for college classes?

4. In "The End of Serendipity," published in *The Chronicle of Higher Education* on November 21, 1997, writer Ted Gup observed that "Like other journalists, I have spent much of my life writing stories that I knew, even as I worked on them, would not be welcomed by my readers. Accounts of war, of hardship, or want seldom are. But those stories found their way first into readers' hands and then into their minds. They were read sometimes reluctantly, sometimes with resentment, and, most often, simply because they appeared on the printed page." Gup echoes the concerns of many writers, including some in this book, that electronic technology allows us to isolate only what we wish to read in a way that a printed newspaper or magazine does not. In fact, this essay can be called up on a screen on <http://chronicle.com>, and a reader can scroll through it without the distractions of any of the other works that appeared in that issue of the *Chronicle*. Is there a danger in our increasing ability to tailor

our computer screens so that we ignore all but what we wish to know? Write an essay in which you defend or reject the notion that computer technology supports isolation and ends what Gup calls "serendipity."

5. Although many other authors here discuss writing, even more of them discuss how electronic culture changes the ways in which we *read*, what Sven Birkert's calls the "fate of reading." Discuss some of the specific consequences that affect and will continue to affect the ways in which we *read* as our culture shifts from print to electronic screen. How are you being asked to read in the college courses you are taking now? How are these different from your secondary school experiences?

6. Many writers refer to a highly touted advantage of networked computers, the ability to communicate quickly and widely. Does the electronic/computer age bring us closer to other people? Does it isolate us from them? Will the electronic/computer age isolate us from our own sense of self? Discuss these questions in the context of the positions of some of the authors presented in this text. Survey your classmates to discover how much time they spend in using computers for communication as opposed to how much time they spend talking face-to-face with other students or professors.

7. Censorship, freedom of expression, and first amendment rights—these are all pressing issues on college campuses. Research a recent incident on a campus network at your own or another institution—e-mail abuse, dissemination of pornographic materials, or sexual harassment—and write a report about the current state of policy and law in relation to this incident.

8. The fair use of copyrighted material and images on the Internet has recently become the topic of considerable legal discussion, often under the rubric of "intellectual property." What is the current state of copyright laws for using material from the Internet? Does your college or university have a policy that informs computer users of these laws? What are the gray areas of the law? Write a report for your classmates in which you provide them the information you feel they should know.

9. Consider the ways in which computer technology has altered, or is in the process of altering, your college education. You might address such issues as instruction in disciplinary areas such as language, math, social or physical science; the roles of students and teachers; expectations for the use of the Internet; the campus library; and/or events on the campus itself. Write an article for the campus newspaper in which you discuss the role of electronic technology in a specific aspect of your life as a student at your institution.

10. The purpose of this chapter of the text, "Cyberliteracy," is to invite you to read and think about a variety of issues related to the Internet, computer technology, and your own education. What have you learned from your reading, thinking, and writing? What are the major issues for college students? What do you need to know more about? Send an e-mail message to your classmates, inviting them to participate in an electronic discussion with you about the issues most crucial to them. Summarize the results and post them to your class.

V

AN EDUCATION OF ONE'S OWN

INTRODUCTION

The nineteenth-century essayist, Ralph Waldo Emerson, frequently wrote about the difficulty that most people experience in determining an individual, independent course of action in the world. In "Experience," published in 1844, he said, "Where do we find ourselves? In a series of which we do not know the extremes, and believe that it has none. We wake and find ourselves on a stair; there are stairs below us, which we seem to have ascended; there are stairs above us, many a one, which go upward and out of sight." Many students can identify with that confused awakening on the stairs. Making a decision about going to college and getting into one are just the first steps toward getting an education. Students often feel bewildered and overwhelmed during their first experiences on a campus and struggle, in the way that Emerson suggests about life in general, to see the steps that come next. Knowing what to do once you're in college is neither easy nor obvious. The range of choices within a curriculum and the variety of extracurricular activities even on a small campus are inevitably greater than what most students experience even in large secondary schools.

Determining what you want from your own college education is the topic of this section of the book. The readings here provide a series of perspectives on the backgrounds of college students, the opportunities that institutions provide for students, how students learn and find their own identities, the distractions that students face, and how the classroom fosters or inhibits student learning.

Some of the questions that the writers explore in this section are:

+ What are the goals and aspirations of most college students?
+ What are the interests of most college students?
+ How do colleges and universities provide activities and programs for students of diverse interests, beliefs, and values?
+ How do extracurricular activities provide opportunities for students?
+ How does gender impact how students learn both inside and outside the classroom?
+ What is the role of student activism in a college or university?

- How do differences in race, gender, sexual orientation, and class within a student body provide challenges for all students?
- What is the relationship between a college major and a career choice?
- Are the goals of college sports programs for men and women compatible with the goals of higher education?
- How does contemporary music culture affect college students?
- What constitutes a "classroom" and what dynamics make for a successful learning experience for students?

In this section, a group of writers provide some answers to these questions and raise additional ones. "This Year's Freshmen: A Statistical Profile" provides a wealth of statistical information on current college students—their religious beliefs, the education of their parents, high school grades, career goals, and favorite leisure activities. A higher education reporter, Ben Gose, reports on the efforts of one campus to establish a richer social life for students—in the interests of ensuring that students learn about themselves and their interests as well as their academic subjects. A set of related readings on two controversial reports by the AAUW on the status of women in the classroom provides a perspective on how gender differences impact learning. A professor, Robert Rhoads, discusses the challenges presented for college students who are not heterosexuals and the ways students can organize to change a campus climate. D. Stanley Eitzen presents a strong case for how a university's emphasis on "big-time" sports affects student athletes. A lawyer, Kathleen Green, provides case studies of people who prepared for one career in college and ended up with entirely different jobs; the final essay in this section is written by a professor, Jane Tompkins, who questions how the traditional classroom provides an appropriate learning environment for all students. As you read the essays in this section, consider what you want from your own college education—and what suggestions offered here can help you define that education.

I

This Year's Freshmen:
A Statistical Profile

Since 1966, the Higher Education Research Institute at the University of California, Los Angeles, has conducted an annual survey of first-year students. The purpose of the survey is to provide information to colleges, universities, and organizations about the backgrounds, opinions, interests, activities, views, and goals of current first-year students. This survey, which was conducted in 1998, is based on the responses of 275,811 students at 469 two- and four-year institutions. The survey reprinted here was first published in The Chronicle of Higher Education, *a weekly newspaper published in printed form and on the Internet <http://chronicle.com>. The* Chronicle *covers higher education in the United States and abroad and is read by more than 400,000 college and university administrators and faculty members. Each issue includes news about campuses in the United States and abroad, articles on developments in scholarly research, features on professional issues, articles and reviews on information technology, reports on state and federal government actions that affect higher education, statistical reports on varied topics like student enrollment and tuition figures, lists of new scholarly books, job listings, and a calendar of events. The* Chronicle of Higher Education *is an excellent source of information on all aspects of higher education. As you read the survey of "This Year's Freshmen," consider how you might have responded to the questions if you had participated in the survey.*

QUESTIONS FOR READING

1. What do you know about how surveys are conducted? What information do you expect to learn from this survey?
2. How do you read the charts in the survey? What skills are necessary to understand the charts?
3. Have you participated in any surveys during your educational experience? For what purpose? How honestly did you respond to the questions you were asked?

THIS YEAR'S FRESHMEN:
A STATISTICAL PROFILE

The Chronicle of Higher Education *(January 29, 1999, A37–39)*

AGE ON DECEMBER 31, 1998

16 or younger	0.1%
17	1.9
18	66.9
19	26.3
20	2.0
21 to 24	1.4
25 to 29	0.6
30 to 39	0.6
40 to 54	0.2
55 or older	0.0

RACIAL AND ETHNIC BACKGROUND

American Indian	2.1%
Asian	4.0
Black	9.4
White	82.5
Mexican-American	2.1
Puerto Rican	1.0
Other Latino	1.4
Other	2.3

DISABILITY STATUS

Speech	0.5%
Orthopedic	0.8
Learning disability	3.5
Health-related	1.7
Partially sighted or blind	1.2
Other disability	1.9

AVERAGE GRADE IN HIGH SCHOOL

A or A+	15.5%
A–	16.9
B+	20.0
B	23.3
B–	10.9

C+	8.1
C	5.0
D	0.3

Year of high-school graduation

1998	94.5%
1997	2.2
1996	0.5
1995 or earlier	1.6
High-school equivalency (GED test)	1.1
Never completed high school	0.1

Type of high school attended

Public	85.7%
Private, denominational	11.0
Private, nonreligious	2.3
Other	1.0

High school required community service for graduation

Yes	21.3%
No	78.7

Met or exceeded recommended years of high-school study in these subjects*

English (4 years)	96.7%
Mathematics (3 years)	94.2
Foreign language (2 years)	84.2
Physical science (2 years)	47.0
Biological science (2 years)	38.1
History/American government (1 year)	98.3
Computer science (half year)	58.8
Arts and/or music (1 year)	75.6

Current religious preference

Baptist	16.8%
Buddhist	0.6
Eastern Orthodox	0.5
Episcopal	1.8
Islamic	0.5
Jewish	1.6

Latter-day Saints (Mormon)	1.1
Lutheran	4.3
Methodist	8.1
Presbyterian	3.9
Quaker	0.2
Roman Catholic	28.6
Seventh-Day Adventist	0.3
United Church of Christ	1.9
Other Christian	11.5
Other	4.0
None	14.5

RESIDENCE PLANNED DURING FALL TERM

With parents or relatives	30.9%
Other private home, apartment, or room	5.7
College dormitory	61.0
Fraternity or sorority house	0.4
Other campus student housing	1.3
Other	0.7

MILES FROM COLLEGE TO HOME

5 or less	8.5%
6 to 10	9.0
11 to 50	30.2
51 to 100	16.3
101 to 500	27.7
501 or more	8.3

FATHER'S OCCUPATION

Artist (including performer)	0.7%
Businessman	25.8
Member of clergy or religious worker	1.2
Clerical worker	0.9
Engineer	7.9
Farmer or forester	3.2
Homemaker (full-time)	0.2
Lawyer	1.6
Military (career)	1.4
Nurse	0.4
Physician or dentist	2.0

Other health professional	1.3
Research scientist	0.5
Social, welfare, or recreation worker	0.6
Teacher or administrator, college	0.6
Teacher or administrator, elementary school	1.0
Teacher or administrator, secondary school	3.1
Worker, skilled	9.6
Worker, semi-skilled	4.0
Worker, unskilled	3.3
Other occupation	27.7
Unemployed	3.0

FATHER'S EDUCATION (HIGHEST LEVEL)

Grammar school or less	2.6%
Some high school	6.6
High-school graduate	27.6
Postsecondary other than college	4.2
Some college	15.5
College degree	24.7
Some graduate school	2.0
Graduate degree	16.9

MOTHER'S OCCUPATION

Artist (including performer)	1.3%
Businesswoman	14.3
Member of clergy or religious worker	0.2
Clerical worker	7.6
Engineer	0.3
Farmer or forester	0.4
Homemaker (full-time)	10.7
Lawyer	0.4
Military (career)	0.1
Nurse	9.0
Physician or dentist	0.8
Other health professional	2.6
Research scientist	0.1
Social, welfare, or recreation worker	1.7
Teacher or administrator, college	0.5
Teacher or administrator, elementary school	9.8
Teacher or administrator, secondary school	4.9
Worker, skilled	1.9

Worker, semi-skilled	2.3
Worker, unskilled	1.9
Other occupation	24.1
Unemployed	5.3

MOTHER'S EDUCATION (HIGHEST LEVEL)

Grammar school or less	2.1%
Some high school	4.8
High-school graduate	29.6
Postsecondary other than college	5.5
Some college	17.5
College degree	25.8
Some graduate school	2.6
Graduate degree	12.2

STATUS OF PARENTS

Living with each other	70.2%
Divorced or living apart	25.5
One or both deceased	4.3

STUDENTS ESTIMATE CHANCES ARE VERY GOOD THAT THEY WILL:

Change major field	12.1%
Change career choice	11.4
Fail one or more courses	1.2
Graduate with honors	17.3
Be elected to student office	3.1
Get a job to help pay college expenses	39.3
Work full-time while attending college	6.7
Join a social fraternity, sorority, or club	14.4
Play varsity/intercollegiate athletics	15.5
Be elected to an academic honor society	8.6
Make at least a B average	48.4
Need extra time to complete degree	6.8
Get bachelor's degree	66.1
Participate in student protests or demonstrations	4.2
Drop out temporarily	1.1
Drop out permanently	0.7
Transfer to another college before graduating	12.2
Be satisfied with college	47.1
Get married while in college	5.7
Participate in volunteer or community service work	18.9
Seek personal counseling	4.5

Student rated self above average or in highest 10 percent in:

Academic ability	56.6%
Artistic ability	26.8
Competitiveness	53.5
Cooperativeness	68.3
Creativity	51.7
Drive to achieve	65.3
Emotional health	52.4
Leadership ability	54.6
Mathematical ability	39.0
Physical health	54.5
Popularity	37.5
Public-speaking ability	31.0
Self-confidence (intellectual)	54.1
Self-confidence (social)	48.6
Self-understanding	53.4
Spirituality	43.0
Understanding of others	61.7
Writing ability	41.0
Athletic ability	40.7

Number of other colleges applied to for admission this year

0	34.0%
1	14.2
2	15.2
3	14.5
4	8.9
5	5.4
6	3.3
7 to 10	3.8
11 or more	0.7

College attended is student's:

First choice	71.6%
Second choice	19.9
Third choice	5.1
Other	3.4

Reasons noted as very important in selecting college attended

Relatives' wishes	9.4%
Teachers' advice	4.2

College has a very good academic reputation	48.4
College has a good reputation for its social activities	23.5
Offered financial assistance	32.3
College offers special education programs	18.9
Low tuition	28.9
Advice of high-school counselor	7.6
Advice of private college counselor	2.0
Wanted to live near home	21.3
Information in a multicollege guidebook	6.1
Not offered aid by first choice	5.6
Graduates gain admission to top graduate/professional schools	27.4
Graduates get good jobs	45.4
Religious affiliation/orientation of college	6.2
Size of college	32.1
Not accepted anywhere else	3.0
Rankings in national magazines	7.4

HIGHEST ACADEMIC DEGREE PLANNED

None	1.0%
Vocational certificate	0.9
Associate (or equivalent)	5.5
Bachelor's	28.0
Master's	38.7
Ph.D. or Ed. D.	13.5
M.D., D.O., D.D.S., or D.V.M.	7.0
LL.B. or J.D.	3.0
B.D. or M. Div.	0.4
Other	2.0

PROBABLE CAREER OCCUPATION

Accountant or actuary	3.2%
Actor or entertainer	1.4
Architect or urban planner	1.5
Artist	1.7
Business (clerical)	1.1
Business executive	7.9
Business owner or proprietor	2.5
Business salesperson or buyer	1.1
Clergy (minister, priest)	0.3
Clergy (other)	0.1

Clinical psychologist	1.6
College administrator	0.1
Computer programmer or analyst	5.0
Conservationist or forester	0.5
Dentist	0.7
Dietitian or home economist	0.3
Engineer	7.2
Farmer or rancher	0.7
Foreign-service worker	0.4
Homemaker (full-time)	0.2
Interior decorator	0.4
Lab technician or hygienist	0.3
Law-enforcement officer	1.7
Lawyer or judge	3.0
Military service (career)	0.6
Musician	1.4
Nurse	3.4
Optometrist	0.2
Pharmacist	0.9
Physician	4.6
Policy maker/government	0.8
School counselor	0.3
Scientific researcher	1.5
Social, welfare, or recreation worker	1.4
Teacher or administrator (elementary)	6.3
Teacher or administrator (secondary)	4.0
Teacher (college)	0.5
Therapist (physical, occupational, speech)	3.9
Veterinarian	1.2
Writer or journalist	2.1
Skilled trades	1.9
Other occupation	10.4
Undecided	11.8

ESTIMATED PARENTAL INCOME

Less than $6,000	2.7%
$6,000–$9,999	2.4
$10,000–$14,999	3.8
$15,000–$19,999	3.8
$20,000–$24,999	5.3
$25,000–$29,999	5.7

$30,000–$39,999	11.4
$40,000–$49,999	11.5
$50,000–$59,999	12.0
$60,000–$74,999	13.3
$75,000–$99,999	12.3
$100,000–$149,999	9.1
$150,000–$199,999	3.0
$200,000 or more	3.6

RECEIVED ANY AID FROM:

Parents, relatives, or friends	76.6%
Spouse	1.2
Savings from summer work	47.9
Other savings	30.4
Part-time job on campus	21.4
Part-time job off campus	24.5
Full-time job while in college	4.3
Pell Grant	21.1
Supplemental Education Opportunity Grant	5.8
State scholarship	17.1
College Work-Study	11.6
Other college grant	28.9
Vocational rehabilitation funds	1.2
Other private grant	10.6
Other govt. aid (ROTC, GI, etc.)	2.6
Stafford/Guaranteed Loan	24.8
Perkins Loan	9.0
Other college loan	10.1
Other loan	7.1
Other source	5.0

RECEIVED $1,500 OR MORE FROM:

Parents, relatives, or friends	51.2%
Spouse	0.3
Savings from summer work	8.5
Other savings	7.3
Part-time job on campus	2.6
Part-time job off campus	2.7
Full-time job while in college	1.3
Pell Grant	7.0

Supplemental Education Opportunity Grant	1.2
State scholarship	4.6
College Work-Study	1.9
Other college grant	17.1
Vocational rehabilitation funds	0.5
Other private grant	3.4
Other govt. aid (ROTC, GI, etc.)	1.5
Stafford/Guaranteed Loan	12.8
Perkins Loan	2.9
Other college loan	6.1
Other loan	4.4
Other source	2.5

CONCERN ABOUT FINANCING COLLEGE

None	34.9%
Some (but I will probably have enough funds)	51.4
Major (not sure I will have enough funds to complete college)	13.7

NUMBER OF HOURS PER WEEK IN THE LAST YEAR SPENT ON THESE ACTIVITIES

NONE:

Studying or doing homework	2.8%
Socializing with friends	0.3
Talking with teachers outside of class	10.5
Exercising or sports	5.5
Partying	18.6
Working for pay	24.3
Volunteer work	36.9
Student clubs or groups	32.0
Watching television	5.4
Household or child-care duties	20.0
Reading for pleasure	28.1
Playing video games	52.8
Prayer or meditation	34.8

SIX OR MORE HOURS:

Studying or doing homework	32.9%
Socializing with friends	77.8
Talking with teachers outside of class	5.0
Exercising or sports	49.3
Partying	31.2

Working for pay	64.5
Volunteer work	8.6
Student clubs or groups	13.0
Watching television	29.4
Household or child-care duties	11.5
Reading for pleasure	8.7
Playing video games	6.6
Prayer or meditation	4.9

NOTE: The statistics are based on survey responses of 275,811 freshmen entering 469 two-year and four-year institutions in the fall of 1998. The figures were statistically adjusted to represent the total population of approximately 1.64 million first-time, full-time freshmen. Because of rounding or multiple responses, figures may add to more than one hundred percent.

*Based on curriculum recommendations of the National Commission of Excellence in Education.

SOURCE: "The American Freshman: National Norms for Fall 1998," published by American Council on Education and University of California at Los Angeles Higher Education Research Institute.

Average Grade in High School

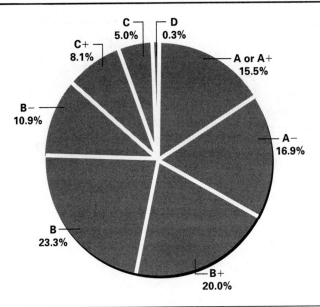

This Year's Freshmen: Their Opinions, Activities, and Goals

ACTIVITIES IN THE PAST YEAR	TOTAL	MEN	WOMEN
Attended a religious service	81.9%	78.7%	84.7%
Was bored in class*	37.7	39.5	36.2
Participated in organized demonstrations	45.9	44.0	47.6
Tutored another student	47.8	44.1	51.0
Studied with other students	83.5	79.7	86.8
Was a guest in a teacher's home	27.3	27.4	27.2
Smoked cigarettes*	15.8	14.9	16.6
Drank beer	51.6	57.8	46.3
Drank wine or liquor	54.9	55.2	54.8
Felt overwhelmed by all I had to do*	29.6	19.2	38.5
Felt depressed*	9.3	7.3	10.9
Performed volunteer work	74.2	70.3	77.5
Played a musical instrument	36.6	36.8	36.5
Asked a teacher for advice after class*	21.5	19.4	23.3
Overslept and missed class or appointment	34.5	35.8	33.5
Discussed politics*	14.0	16.3	12.0
Voted in a student election*	21.1	19.8	22.2
Socialized with someone of another racial or ethnic group*	61.6	58.1	64.4
Took a prescribed antidepressant	5.9	5.3	6.4
Came late to class	60.3	61.7	59.2
Attended a public concert or recital	73.5	70.5	76.0
Visited an art gallery or museum	53.1	50.0	55.7
Discussed religion*	26.0	24.0	27.8
Read the editorial page in the daily newspaper	62.9	61.4	64.2
Checked out a book or journal from school library*	18.7	14.4	22.4
Communicated via e-mail	65.9	68.0	64.2
Used the Internet for research or homework	82.9	84.4	81.6
Participated in Internet chat rooms	54.2	58.0	51.1
Played computer games	80.4	85.3	76.2
Had Internet use other than above	72.9	79.3	67.4

	Total	Men	Women
Reasons noted as very important in deciding to go to college			
My parents wanted me to go	39.5%	37.4%	41.3%
I could not find a job	7.3	6.8	7.7
Wanted to get away from home	17.2	17.9	16.6
To be able to get a better job	76.9	76.6	77.1
To gain a general education and appreciation of ideas	62.0	55.9	67.2
To improve my reading and study skills	41.5	37.5	44.9
Because my friends were going	4.5	5.9	3.3
To make me a more cultured person	45.1	39.4	50.0
To be able to make more money	74.6	78.5	71.3
To prepare myself for graduate or professional school	49.0	42.6	54.5
A mentor or role model encouraged me to go	15.5	15.0	15.9
To prove to others I could succeed	37.0	35.7	38.1

	Total	Men	Women
Agree strongly or somewhat that:			
There is too much concern in the courts for the rights of criminals	72.8%	74.3%	71.5%
Abortion should be legal	50.9	52.5	49.5
The death penalty should be abolished	22.8	19.5	25.6
If two people really like each other, it's all right for them to have sex even if they've known each other for only a very short time	39.6	53.6	27.7
Marijuana should be legalized	32.4	38.6	27.2
It is important to have laws prohibiting homosexual relationships	33.3	43.4	24.8
Employers should be allowed to require drug testing of employees or job applicants	78.5	74.6	81.8
Just because a man thinks that a woman has "led him on" does not entitle him to have sex with her	87.4	81.5	92.3
The federal government should do more to control the sale of handguns	82.5	72.7	90.8
Racial discrimination is no longer a major problem in America	21.1	25.2	17.6
Realistically, an individual can do little to bring about changes in our society	31.9	36.6	27.9
Wealthy people should pay a larger share of taxes than they do now	58.7	60.3	57.3
College should prohibit racist/sexist speech on campus	61.8	58.0	65.1

Same-sex couples should have the right to legal marital status	49.4	41.1	56.4
Material on the Internet should be regulated by the government	43.2	32.0	52.6

	TOTAL	MEN	WOMEN
OBJECTIVES CONSIDERED ESSENTIAL OR VERY IMPORTANT			
Becoming accomplished in one of the performing arts	12.7%	12.8%	12.7%
Becoming an authority in my field	60.2	61.8	58.8
Obtaining recognition from my colleagues for contributions to my special field	49.8	50.8	49.0
Influencing the political structure	16.0	18.5	13.9
Influencing social values	36.4	31.7	40.4
Raising a family	73.0	71.1	74.6
Having administrative responsibility for the work of others	36.9	38.1	35.9
Being very well-off financially	74.0	76.0	72.4
Helping others who are in difficulty	59.9	49.9	68.3
Making a theoretical contribution to science	15.3	17.8	13.2
Writing original works	13.5	14.0	13.1
Creating artistic work	13.8	14.0	13.6
Becoming successful in a business of my own	38.9	45.4	33.4
Becoming involved in programs to clean up the environment	18.8	18.4	19.1
Developing a meaningful philosophy of life	40.9	40.2	41.5
Participating in a community-action program	21.8	17.7	25.2
Helping to promote racial understanding	29.5	26.4	32.0
Keeping up-to-date with political affairs	25.9	29.1	23.3
Becoming a community leader	29.9	30.2	29.6

	TOTAL	MEN	WOMEN
POLITICAL ORIENTATION			
Far left	2.7%	3.5%	2.1%
Liberal	20.8	19.0	22.3
Middle of the road	56.5	55.2	57.6
Conservative	18.6	20.1	17.2
Far right	1.5	2.3	0.7

Note: The statistics are based on survey responses of 275,811 freshmen entering 469 two-year and four-year institutions in the fall of 1998. The figures were statistically adjusted to represent the total population of approximately 1.64 million first-time, full-time freshmen. Because of rounding or multiple responses, figures may add to more than one hundred percent.

*Frequently only; all other activities frequently or occasionally.

SOURCE: "The American Freshman: National Norms for Fall 1998," published by American Council on Education and University of California at Los Angeles Higher Education Research Institute.

This Year's Freshmen: What Students Expect to Major In

	TOTAL	MEN	WOMEN
ARTS AND HUMANITIES			
Art, fine and applied	2.2%	1.9%	2.5%
English	1.4	1.1	1.7
History	0.8	1.0	0.6
Journalism	1.3	1.0	1.6
Language and literature, except English	0.3	0.2	0.5
Music	1.3	1.5	1.1
Philosophy	0.2	0.3	0.1
Speech	0.1	0.1	0.2
Theater or drama	0.9	0.9	1.0
Theology or religion	0.4	0.5	0.3
Other	0.9	0.6	1.2

	TOTAL	MEN	WOMEN
BIOLOGICAL SCIENCES			
Biology (general)	2.8%	2.2%	3.3%
Biochemistry or biophysics	0.5	0.6	0.5
Botany	0.1	0.1	0.1
Environmental science	0.7	0.8	0.6
Marine science	0.4	0.3	0.5
Microbiology or bacteriology	0.2	0.2	0.3
Zoology	0.4	0.3	0.4
Other	0.5	0.5	0.6

	TOTAL	MEN	WOMEN
BUSINESS			
Accounting	3.2%	2.6%	3.7%
Business administration (general)	4.5	5.3	3.7
Finance	1.2	1.8	0.7
International business	1.2	1.1	1.2
Marketing	2.2	2.4	2.0
Management	2.8	3.9	1.9
Secretarial studies	0.4	0.1	0.7
Other	1.0	1.2	0.8

	TOTAL	MEN	WOMEN
EDUCATION			
Business education	0.2%	0.3%	0.2%
Elementary education	5.8	1.1	9.7
Music or art education	0.6	0.5	0.7
Physical education or recreation	1.2	1.7	0.8
Secondary education	2.1	2.0	2.2
Special education	0.7	0.1	1.2
Other	0.5	0.2	0.8

	TOTAL	MEN	WOMEN
ENGINEERING			
Aeronautical engineering	0.6%	1.1%	0.1%
Civil engineering	0.9	1.6	0.2
Chemical engineering	0.7	1.0	0.5
Electrical or electronic engineering	2.0	4.1	0.3
Industrial engineering	0.2	0.4	0.1
Mechanical engineering	1.9	3.9	0.3
Other	1.9	3.4	0.7

	TOTAL	MEN	WOMEN
PHYSICAL SCIENCES			
Astronomy	0.1%	0.1%	0.0%
Atmospheric science	0.1	0.2	0.1
Chemistry	0.6	0.6	0.5
Earth science	0.1	0.2	0.1
Marine science	0.2	0.2	0.2
Mathematics	0.5	0.6	0.5
Physics	0.3	0.5	0.1
Other	0.2	0.2	0.1

	TOTAL	MEN	WOMEN
PROFESSIONAL			
Architecture or urban planning	1.2%	1.8%	0.6%
Home economics	0.1	0.1	0.2
Health technology	1.0	0.5	1.4
Nursing	3.5	0.5	6.0
Pharmacy	0.8	0.5	1.2
Pre-dental, pre-medical, pre-veterinary	4.0	3.0	4.9
Therapy (occupational, physical, speech)	3.5	2.0	4.8
Other	1.1	0.7	1.4

	Total	Men	Women
SOCIAL SCIENCES			
Anthropology	0.2%	0.2%	0.3%
Economics	0.3	0.4	0.2
Geography	0.0	0.1	0.0
Political science	2.0	1.8	2.1
Psychology	4.1	2.0	5.7
Social work	1.1	0.2	1.9
Sociology	0.4	0.3	0.5
Other	0.3	0.2	0.3

	Total	Men	Women
TECHNICAL			
Building trades	0.7%	1.6%	0.0%
Data processing or computer programming	1.5	2.4	0.7
Drafting or design	0.7	1.1	0.4
Electronics	0.4	0.9	0.0
Mechanics	0.5	1.1	0.0
Other	0.6	1.2	0.1

	Total	Men	Women
OTHER FIELDS			
Agriculture	1.2%	1.6%	0.9%
Communications	1.8	1.6	1.9
Computer science	3.5	5.7	1.6
Forestry	0.2	0.4	0.1
Law enforcement	2.2	3.1	1.4
Military science	0.0	0.1	0.0
Other	1.9	1.8	1.9
Undecided	7.5	6.8	8.1

Note: The statistics are based on survey responses of 275,811 freshmen entering 469 two-year and four-year institutions in the fall of 1998. The figures were statistically adjusted to represent the total population of approximately 1.64 million first-time, full-time freshmen. Because of rounding or multiple responses, figures may add to more than one hundred percent.

SOURCE: "The American Freshman: National Norms for Fall 1998," published by American Council on Education and University of California at Los Angeles Higher Education Research Institute.

What Students Expect to Major In

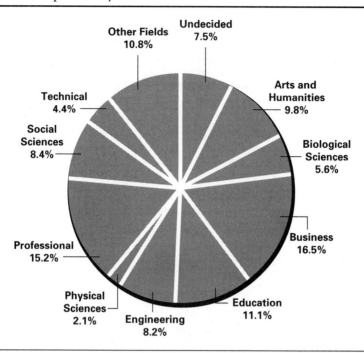

SOURCE: *Copyright* © 1999 by The Chronicle of Higher Education.

Freshman Views and Activities

Attitudes About Abortion and Casual Sex

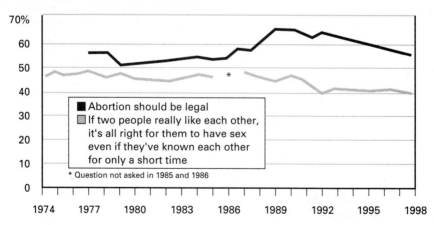

Political Views

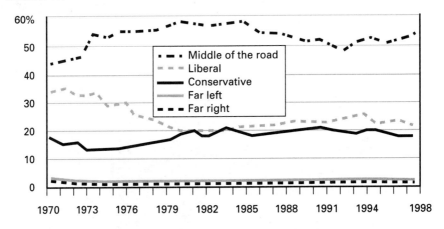

Proportion Using E-Mail During the Last Year, by Type of Institution

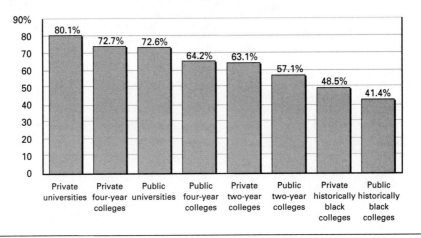

SOURCE: "The American Freshman: National Norms for Fall 1998."
Chronicle charts by Sherrie Good.

QUESTIONS FOR REACTION AND DISCUSSION

1. To your way of thinking, what is the most surprising piece of information you learned from the survey? Why? What is the most
   controversial? Why?
2. Examine the list of characteristics in "Student Rated Self Above Average or in Highest 10 percent In" and rate these characteristics for

yourself. Ask your classmates to rate the characteristics as well. How do you compare with the survey? With the members of your class? Is there any characteristic that you would have added to the list? Why?

3. Based on the survey, how are most students paying for their educations?

4. Study the average grades that students made in high school. What are the implications for how first-year students feel about college grades? Why?

5. What do most students expect to major in? Why is this important information for a college or university to know? What do you and your classmates expect to major in?

QUESTIONS FOR WRITING

1. Compare the education and background information on students' fathers and mothers. What does the survey suggest about the similarities and differences among parents? What is the background and educational experience of your own parents? What impact did your parents' backgrounds and educations have on your own decision to attend college? Write an essay in which you describe the general profiles of a student's father and mother and compare the profiles with those of your own parents or step-parents.

2. Based on the survey, students select a school for a variety of differing reasons. How do most college students select the school they attend? How did you? Write an essay in which you discuss the ways in which students can explore the colleges and universities they wish to attend and describe the process by which you selected the school you are currently attending.

3. Examine the statements that ask students to "agree strongly or somewhat that." Construct your own survey instrument based on these statements, take this survey yourself, and then ask ten of your classmates to rate the statements. How do you and your classmates compare with the survey participants? Are there any statements that you think should be added to the list? What generalizations can you make about the published survey of attitudes and those of your group of classmates? Write an essay in which you analyze the survey of attitudes, comparing and contrasting the results with those of your classmates.

4. Using the information from "This Year's Freshman Profile," define a typical college freshman. Then consider the information you have read about the core curriculum or general education program of your college or university. How do the goals of the general education program meet the expectations of the typical college freshman that you have defined? What are the strengths of the program likely to be? At what

points do you think the program will seem alien or strange to some students? What conclusions can you reach about your university's general education curriculum? Write an essay in which you analyze the points at which the typical freshman you have constructed is likely to be challenged or confused during his or her first year at your college.

Questions for Further Exploration

1. Assume that you have been asked to "cover" the "Survey of Freshmen" for your college newspaper. Write a feature story in which you explain the survey, highlight the most important facts and attitudes, and summarize the major findings of the report.
2. Consult past Freshman Surveys (covered in *The Chronicle of Higher Education* each January and elsewhere in magazines and newspapers) and compare the major findings of the survey printed here with ones five, ten, or fifteen years old. Write a report of your research for your class.
3. For the first time in its history, the "Survey of Freshmen" asked questions about the use of the Internet and e-mail. What do the responses suggest about computer use among first-year students? What are the primary uses of computers? What other information would you like to know about first-year students? Write an essay in which you explain what the survey does (and does not) suggest about computer usage among first-year students.

"U. OF CHICAGO SOCIAL LIFE" MAY NO LONGER BE AN OXYMORON

For most colleges and universities, facilitating an active and healthy social life for students is an important part of the overall mission of the institution. For students, a social life is an important way to feel integrated into the campus community and also to form enduring relationships; beyond that, a social life helps a student define his or her own goals. In this essay, Ben Gose, a senior editor of The Chronicle of Higher Education, *reports on the efforts of a large urban university to establish a more visible program of social functions for students. The article reprinted here was first published in the* Chronicle, *a weekly newspaper published in printed form and on the Internet <http://chronicle.com>. The* Chronicle *covers higher education in the United States and abroad and is read by more than 400,000 college and university administrators and faculty members. Each issue includes news about campuses in the United States and abroad, articles on developments in scholarly research, features on professional issues, articles and reviews on information technology, reports on state and federal government actions that affect higher education, statistical reports on varied topics like student enrollment and tuition figures, lists of new scholarly books, job listings, and a calendar of events. The* Chronicle *is an excellent source of information on all aspects of higher education; this essay first appeared in the section devoted exclusively to student issues, such as admissions, housing, tuition, race relations, and activities.*

QUESTIONS FOR READING

1. What is an "oxymoron" and what does the title of this essay suggest to you about the essay?
2. What are your expectations for a social life on your campus? Is having an active social life important to you as a college student? Why or why not?

BEN GOSE

"U. OF CHICAGO SOCIAL LIFE" MAY NO LONGER BE AN OXYMORON

The Chronicle of Higher Education (*November 15, 1996, A49–50*)

Chicago—Last fall, the University of Chicago sent out fliers with a slash through the words "The Reg," which is what students here call the Joseph Regenstein Library, a popular spot for studying.

Students at some colleges protest when administrators try to take away their beer kegs. Here, students erupted when the university suggested that they put down their Aeschylus and live a little.

"This is a place that has always been very proud of its nerdiness," says David Bird, a senior and managing editor of *The Chicago Maroon,* the student newspaper. "Some people were very much concerned that the administration was trying to steer us away from that."

The flier promoted changes that the administration hopes will improve social life on a campus where not having a social life can be a badge of pride. Chicago has renovated its student union, added several coffee shops to other buildings, and made plans to build a thirty million dollar athletics facility.

The additions are intended to attract more students. Hugo F. Sonnenschein, the university's president, announced last spring that Chicago planned to increase its undergraduate enrollment by one thousand students over the next decade, to four thousand five hundred.

The new emphasis on undergraduate education represents a major shift for Chicago, which is famous for its graduate programs. It has learned that having one of the most prestigious faculties in the world—six of its active professors and researchers have won Nobel Prizes—isn't enough to lure seventeen-year-olds to its campus here.

Chicago receives far fewer undergraduate applications than do the elite institutions to which it compares itself. Harvard, Princeton, and Stanford Universities each received more than fourteen thousand applications last year; Chicago got 5,470. (Each of the three competitors has more undergraduates than Chicago.)

"I take very seriously the fact that we don't get the same kind of applicant pool that universities with similar faculties do," says Dr. Sonnenschein. "We don't want students to run away from this place just because it is missing some of the things that they want."

He has appointed faculty committees to consider other changes, too. Among them: replacing the intense, eleven-week "quarters" with a more leisurely semester system; scaling back the "Common Core," the general education requirements that consume students' first two years; and modifying financial-aid policies to appeal more to middle-class and upper-middle-class students.

The changes are prompted in large part by concern about money. In a letter sent to professors last spring, Dr. Sonnenschein wrote that the university was on a financial course that "will not sustain excellence."

Chicago's ratio of undergraduates to graduate students—about one to one—is far lower than those of its competitors. Princeton, for example, has more than three undergraduates for every graduate student. This limits Chicago's tuition revenue, comparatively speaking, because many graduate students receive free tuition plus stipends. What's more, in the long term, fewer undergraduates mean fewer potential alumni donors.

"We have to create a university economy that invests in the future, one that builds buildings when they should be built, and puts the right faculty in those buildings," Dr. Sonnenschein says in an interview, explaining the need for change.

Columbia University—like Chicago, an urban institution best known for its graduate education—is also beginning an expansion. Columbia plans to add five hundred undergraduates by the year 2000, raising enrollment to four thousand students. "We want to bring the undergraduate experience into the center of the university," says Jonathan R. Cole, Columbia's provost.

Mr. Bird, the student editor here at Chicago, says the efforts to improve social life have been less odious than he expected: the "tower of fun" he feared amid the university's Gothic buildings didn't materialize. But he worries about the other proposals. Students who come to Chicago put a far higher premium on intellectual challenge than on fun, he says, and how many such students can there be?

He calls the expansion plans "a potentially horrible thing that could erode the quality of the university."

Sarah Rose, a senior, says Chicago offers such a rigorous curriculum that it will never be as popular with the masses as a Princeton or Stanford. "They're trying to attract students who would be better off at another school," she says of the administrators who have proposed the expansion.

Chicago students are smart—they average thirteen hundred on the Scholastic Assessment Test—but the applicant pool isn't deep. Two years ago, the university admitted seventy-one percent of those who applied; last year, it took fifty-eight percent. Fewer than one in three of the students it admits decide to enroll, a much lower proportion than at Ivy League colleges.

Why do applicants look past a place where famous professors teach classic texts in small classes?

For one thing, Chicago is difficult. Twenty-one courses are required, including two years of lab science. Such rigor has all but disappeared from academe; Stanford, for example, requires just eleven courses, and no lab science.

Another problem in recruiting is that, outside of academe, Chicago is not as well known as faculty members here think it should be. Many people—even local cabdrivers—confuse it with the University of Illinois at Chicago. Many students say they found their way here by themselves; their high-school counselors had tried to steer them toward the Ivy League or big-name public institutions.

And, despite the nerd bravado, the campus is not much fun. In a 1995 survey of more than seven hundred students, social life was cited most often as the aspect of the Chicago experience that had not met their expectations. Two years ago, Chicago ranked dead last in a decidedly unscientific survey on social life on three hundred campuses by the now-defunct magazine *Inside Edge*.

The university's sports teams are virtually unknown. Their nickname is the "Maroons," one joke goes, because the campus is hemmed in by Lake Michigan to the east and low-income, high-crime neighborhoods on all other sides.

"It's not in a beautiful town, like Columbia. It's not Stanford, with its climate. And it's not Princeton, with Nassau Street," says Marshall Sahlins, an anthropology professor who is cochairman of a panel that is looking at alternatives to expansion. "We've got 53rd Street."

Many here doubt that the university can add thousands to its applicant pool. And many are skeptical of Dr. Sonnenschein's pledge that Chicago will not increase enrollment before it gets a bigger and better pool.

Some professors and students say the president would prefer a campus more like that of his former employer, Princeton. One faculty member, who doesn't want his name used, says many of his colleagues feel that Dr. Sonnenschein wants to turn the university into an "undergraduate playground for the golden youth of white suburbia."

Robert B. Pippin, chairman of the Committee on Social Thought, an interdisciplinary social sciences program, says there is fear that what Dr. Sonnenschein has in mind is a "University of Chicago Lite."

"The impression some people have is that we're trying to find wealthy, private-school students to come here, then we'll make the curriculum easier for them so that they'll enjoy their experience here with the new swimming pool, and thus they'll give more money when they get out," says Dr. Pippin, a philosophy professor. He says he is taking a wait-and-see attitude on the changes.

Critics say an increase in class size—freshman humanities classes might rise to twenty-six students from twenty—would not in itself be a major problem. The fear is that the students would be unqualified, thus hampering the classroom discussions that are an essential part of the Common Core, says Dr. Sahlins. "If three or four of them are as bad as some who are getting in now, it changes the nature of the discussions."

The panel that he chairs has formed this summer after 116 professors signed a petition asking for a "year of reflection" on Dr. Sonnenschein's proposals.

The group is meeting with the university's chief financial officer to get a better grip on the long-term financial picture. In the meantime, it has suggested other ways to make money: create new master's programs in the humanities and social sciences; start a summer school for international students; tape a lecture series with high-profile faculty members and sell it over the Internet.

"There are many alternatives to just admitting a bunch of bodies," says Andrew Abbott, a sociology professor who wrote a twelve-page paper critical of the university's plans. He circulated it among faculty members last month.

Dr. Sonnenschein is confident that Chicago can snare more qualified applicants. The university, he says, has simply done a poor job of marketing itself.

Now, for the first time, Chicago has a brochure showing students off campus—playing guitar in the blues club, taking violin lessons from principals in the Chicago Symphony Orchestra, working as interns in the mayor's office.

"There are people who tell me that there aren't enough seventeen-year-olds in the country who want a serious education," says the president. "I just think that's crap."

Dr. Sonnenschein has his supporters here. Among them are several students who note that Chicago has lagged far behind other universities in providing services to its students.

Vasant Narasimhan, a junior and president of Chicago's Delta Kappa Epsilon fraternity, sits in the Reynolds Club, the renovated building that serves as the student union, and talks about the club's influence.

Nearby, students shoot pool and play Foosball in this central room, which housed the career center just over a year go. Others watch the TV that sits above a coffee bar.

"Without a central place where their energy can be focused, students here aren't going to find something to do," says Mr. Narasimhan. "This building has changed the mentality of the school right before my eyes, and that's very cool."

Chicago, he says, is "trying to catch up with what other universities realized ten years ago: If you don't have the best facilities, you're at a disadvantage in the whole recruiting game."

Other students, such as Kjersten Moody, don't care much about the new Reynolds Club or the other attempts to improve social life. What Ms. Moody, a junior, cares about is the intellectual atmosphere here. She has always taken four classes per quarter—one more than her friends at Dartmouth College, where the quarter system calls for three classes—and while she jokes that she envies them, she wouldn't trade places.

For fun, she eats in ethnic restaurants, goes downtown to see the Lyric Opera of Chicago, or stays up late for freewheeling discussions with friends about Plato's *Republic* or socialism in China.

She calls the University of Chicago "a great place" but says she's troubled by a decline in quality that she's witnessed in the last two classes. The sophomore class in particular, she says, doesn't have much to contribute. "They're the kind of people one would expect to find at a state school or your average private college," Ms. Moody says. "They're boring."

QUESTIONS FOR REACTION AND DISCUSSION

1. What are the special problems that the University of Chicago faces in cultivating more social experiences for its students? Are these similar or different to problems on your own campus?

2. How does the undergraduate enrollment of the University of Chicago compare to your campus? How does the graduate enrollment compare? Which program is emphasized on your campus? How do you know? What difference does it make to campus life?
3. Why are some students concerned about a new emphasis on social life?
4. What was the faculty reaction to the president's proposal to improve the social life?
5. What do you think colleges and universities should provide by way of social activities for students?

Questions for Writing

1. What are the major features of social life on your campus? What, in your opinion, are the most successful activities? The least successful? Write an essay in the form of a letter to a friend who is a student at another college and describe the activities and programs available to students at your school.
2. Is there a central office on your campus that coordinates social activities? Where is it and how is it organized? Prepare a set of questions about social activities on your campus and make an appointment with a student activities officer. Ask the officer about the number and variety of activities, what the officer's responsibilities are, and what he or she thinks of the quality of the social life on your campus. Write a report of your interview and the responses you receive.
3. On many campuses, fraternities, sororities, and/or selective social clubs provide the majority of social activities for some students. Is there such a system on your campus? Are you interested in becoming a member of a selective social organization? Why or why not? Write an essay in which you explain why you do or do not wish to join a fraternity, sorority, or a selective social club on your campus.
4. Study your campus calendar and attend an event on your campus that is a sponsored activity that you would not normally undertake—a reception for new students, an athletic event, a concert, a play, a poetry reading, or an organized outing. What did you learn? Did you meet new people? What efforts were made to encourage students to interact with faculty members and with one another? How would you rate the experience in terms of enhancing your social life or the general social life of the college? Write a report of your experience for your classmates.

QUESTIONS FOR FURTHER EXPLORATION

1. When you were considering where to apply for college, you may have used one of the dozens of guidebooks and handbooks for selecting colleges and universities. Some examples are: *Barron's Profiles of American Colleges;* James Cass and Max Birnbaum, *Comparative Guide to American Colleges; The College Blue Book;* Dale Parnell and John W. Peltason, eds., *American Community, Technical, and Junior Colleges: A Guide;* as well as many guides written from student perspectives, such as *The Insider's Guide to the Colleges.* Consult several of these guidebooks (widely available in college and public libraries), and collect information on what the books say about the social life at your college and two or three other schools where you have friends. Write a review of your findings and share them with your classmates.

2. What do college and university Web sites reveal about social activities on a campus? Select three or four colleges and universities that are similar to the one that you attend, and locate their main Web sites on the Internet (by using the Excite search engine, you can easily find a school by simply typing in the full name of the institution). Review the Web sites and write a report of what you can (and cannot) learn about the social life of a campus from the Web site.

3

THE ABSENCE OF GIRLS IN THE CURRENT DEBATE ON EDUCATION, ACHIEVEMENT AND PARTICIPATION: WHAT DO THE DATA SHOW?, AND COURSE-TAKING PATTERNS

How important is your gender in determining your preparedness for college and for your choice of college major or even your career? The American Association of University Women has a history of wanting to know the answers to these questions. The AAUW is a national organization of over 150,000 members committed to promoting education and equity for women and girls. Their research program began in 1885, when the AAUW funded a report that provided sufficient evidence to overturn the prevalent notion that higher education was damaging to a girl's health. Since then, the AAUW has sponsored a series of research reports; the controversial How Schools Shortchange Girls *was published in 1992. Based on the concerns of the AAUW membership that girls had not been adequately represented in several national educational reports that were published in the late 1980s, this report was designed to analyze the educational experience of girls in contrast to the experience of boys. Copies of the report were in such demand that a trade paperback of it was published in 1995. The president of AAUW at that time, Alice Ann Leidel explains that the report "is credited with drawing national attention to the disturbing evidence that girls are not receiving the same quality, or even quantity, of education as their brothers. By stereotyping women's roles, popular culture plays a role in shortchanging girls by limiting their horizons and expectations. Unintentionally, schools sometimes follow suit, depriving girls of classroom attention, ignoring the value of cooperative learning, and presenting texts and lessons in which female role models are conspicuously absent."* How Schools Shortchange Girls *made a set of recommendations to schools to ensure that both girls and boys are prepared for the future. These included suggestions to strengthen the enforcement of Title IX, strengthen gender equity in programs, include the experiences of women and men in the curriculum, promote mathematics and science programs to girls, revise testing procedures to accurately reflect the abilities of girls and boys, involve girls and women in educational reform, and increase education about sexuality and health for girls and boys.*

Six years after the publication of How Schools Shortchange Girls, *the AAUW decided to conduct a follow-up study to determine what progress had been made since the 1992 report and determine how the recommendations have been followed.* Gender Gaps: Where Schools Still Fail Our Children *is the result; the new report suggests what progress has been made in some areas and where new issues in gender equity have arisen. Maggie Ford, the president of the AAUW Educational Foundation in 1998, comments that "Our goal is to ensure equal chances for all public school students to learn, excel, and achieve educationally. As* Gender Gaps *makes clear, the goal of school excellence that drives the standards movement is one and the same goal behind educational equity. The ideas are irreparably linked. Equity without excellence would be a terrible waste of talent. Excellence without equity is a contradiction in terms." As you read the excerpts from the reports, consider your own educational experience as a male or a female and how these reports address your own concerns about educational excellence and equity.*

QUESTIONS FOR READING

1. What do you know about the American Association of University Women?
2. What is a research report? How do the titles of these reports shape your expectations of the nature of the reports?
3. What is gender equity? Why and how is it important in the public schools?
4. Do you think boys and girls have similar or different experiences in the public schools? Why?

AMERICAN ASSOCIATION OF
UNIVERSITY WOMEN

The Absence of Girls in the Current Debate on Education

How Schools Shortchange Girls: The AAUW Report: A Study of Major Findings on Girls and Education (Washington D.C.: American Association of University Women Educational Foundation and National Education Association, 1992)

In 1983, the U.S. Department of Education published *A Nation at Risk*, sparking school-reform efforts across the country. Educational commissions, committees, and special studies were quickly assembled and funded by a wide range of organizations, foundations, and government agencies. Many of their findings have since been published. Thirty-five reports issued by special task forces and commissions were reviewed for this study to assess the amount of attention given to gender and sex equity issues. The review addressed four questions:

- To what degree did women participate as members or hold leadership positions on the special task forces or commissions?
- Did the issues or concerns that prompted a particular report include gender or sex equity?
- Did the data, the rationale, or background information presented include sex or gender as a separate category?
- Did the recommendations specifically address gender issues?

Few women held leadership positions on the thirty-five commissions, task forces, or boards of directors studied.[1] Although women were members of all the groups except one, their percentage varied greatly; only two groups had at least fifty percent female representation.[2] Most of the reports do not define the educational issues under review in terms of gender, nor do they include sex as a separate category in their data analyses and background information. Few of the recommendations are framed with sex or gender in mind. The majority of the reports imply that the only significant problems girls may face are getting pregnant at an early age, dropping out of school, and thereby increasing the number of female-headed households living in poverty. While these are incontestable problems, the concentration on these issues to the exclusion of others leads to strategies directed toward individual rather than systemic change and programs focused on girls' personal decisions rather than policy initiatives to improve the educational system.

Four of the reports include gender as a category in defining the students seen at risk and/or the issues under consideration.[3] One of these reports was published by the National Board of Inquiry, convened by the National Coalition of Advocates for Students (NCAS); this board was one of the few cochaired by a woman. The NCAS report, *Barriers to Excellence: Our Children at Risk* (1985), defined its focus this way:

Who are the children at risk? They include a large proportion of young people from poor families of all races. They include minority and immigrant children who face discriminatory policies and practices, large numbers of girls and young women who miss out on education opportunities routinely afforded males, and children with special needs who are unserved, underserved, or improperly categorized because of handicap or learning difficulties.[4]

The NCAS rationale and background statement specifically mention race, class, culture, and sex. The report suggests that teen pregnancy may be directly linked to poor achievement and low educational aspirations. It is also the only report of the thirty-five reviewed to directly address Title IX of the Education Amendments of 1972, prohibiting sex discrimination in education programs receiving federal funds. The report urges, "Renew commitment to Title IX, thereby assuring that female students will have an opportunity to develop their talents and skills fully."[5]

TITLE IX

Under Title IX of the Education Amendments of 1972, discrimination on the basis of sex is illegal in any educational program receiving federal funding. Federal enforcement of Title IX is complaint driven, and over the past decade the U.S. Office of Civil Rights has not actively pursued Title IX enforcement. In 1990, researchers who spent six months visiting twenty-five rural school districts in twenty-one states reported that thirty-seven percent of the district administrators they interviewed saw no Title IX compliance issues in their districts. Some of these administrators expressed the view that it was "stupid" or "frivolous" to worry about equal opportunities for girls and boys. Furthermore, the research team reported that in some of the school districts where the administration perceived no problems, Title IX violations appeared to exist in terms of athletic opportunities and sex segregation in higher-level mathematics and science classes. An additional twenty-eight percent of the district administrators interviewed replied that they believed their districts were within the letter of the law but that they had not gone beyond equal access. A third group, thirty-five percent of the sample, reported that they were concerned that equal access in the narrow sense was not sufficient to provide genuine equal opportunity for girls and boys. Administrators in this latter group had been faced with sex discrimination suits and/or had attended equity workshops.[6]

This research indicates that sex and gender equity issues are still not well understood by many educators. The research also suggests that in-service training on equity issues can both increase awareness and provide specific tools for achieving a more equitable educational environment. Renewed attention to the vigorous enforcement of Title IX must be a top priority for everyone concerned with the quality of public education in the United States.

Needed: Women in the Leadership of Public Education

School Boards

In 1927, 10.2 percent of all local school board members were female. By 1990 that percentage had risen to only 33.7 Minority constituencies are even more severely underrepresented. Only 2.9 percent of school board members are black and only 1.3 percent are Hispanic. The data are not reported by sex within racial categories.

Teachers and Administrators

Policies of local boards of education are implemented by the superintendent of schools and central office staff. Despite the fact that public elementary and secondary education is still considered a "woman's field"—seventy-two percent of all elementary and secondary school teachers are female—women hold few of the upper-management positions in our public schools (see graph).

Chief State School Officers

The chief state school officer in each state provides leadership and direction for the state public school system. In 1991, only nine of the fifty chief state school officers were women—the largest number in recent years.

The method of selecting chief state school officers varies from state to state; in eighteen states they are elected by popular vote, in twenty-seven they are appointed by the state board of education, and in five they are appointed by the governor. Eight of the nine women heading state education agencies in 1991 were elected by popular vote; one was appointed by a governor.

Graph excludes states that do not report data by sex and race.

SOURCE: *Women and Minorities in School Administration: Facts and Figures 1989–90.* American Association of School Administrators, 4,5,8,9,14,20.

THE NATIONAL EDUCATION GOALS

Education has remained on the national agenda ever since the 1983 publication of *A Nation At Risk*. In February 1990, President Bush and the National Governors Association set a series of ambitious education goals to be met by the year 2000.[7] Setting goals is one thing; reaching them is another. Educators across the nation are faced with the task of developing programs that will remedy in a decade all that we have not managed to accomplish in the last century.

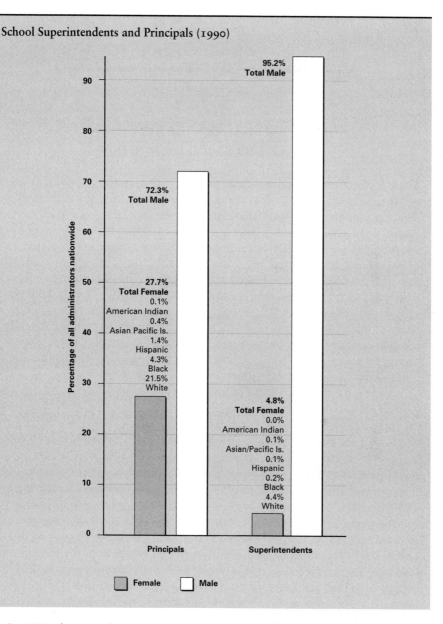

School Superintendents and Principals (1990)

In 1991 the President and the Department of Education presented *Amer-ica 2000* as a "plan to move every community in America toward these goals."[8] None of the strategies proposed in *America 2000* are gender specific. Girls are once again ignored in setting the national agenda.

The National Coalition for Women and Girls in Education has repeatedly noted that the National Education Goals cannot be met without specific atten-tion to girls.[9] Solutions designed to meet everyone's needs risk meeting no one's. Attention must be directed to those characteristics that differentiate girls from boys as well as to the differences found among girls to various racial, ethnic, socioeconomic, and cultural groups. Thus *The AAUW Report* focuses—to the extent the data allow—both on the things girls share as well as on their differences.

ACHIEVEMENT AND PARTICIPATION: WHAT DO THE DATA SHOW?

There is considerable evidence that girls earn higher grades than boys throughout their school careers.[10] Test scores, however, because they measure all students on exactly the same material and are available nationally, are the measures most often used to discuss sex differences in achievement. The latest work on achievement differences presents a rather different picture than much of what has been reported and accepted in the past. The traditional wisdom that girls are better in verbal areas while boys excel in quantitative skills is less true today. Data indicate a narrowing of sex differences in tested achievement on a variety of measures.[11] However, a narrowing of differences is not an absence of differences. Important insights can be gained by looking carefully at the continuing gender gaps in educational achievement and participation. Furthermore, research that looks at sex, race, ethnicity, and socioeconomic status reveals critical vulnerabilities among various groups of girls.

VERBAL SKILLS: LANGUAGE ARTS AND READING

Research does not entirely support the still-common assumption that girls do better in verbal areas than do boys. Almost twenty years ago Eleanor Maccoby and Carol Jacklin challenged the prevailing view that girls performed better than boys on verbal measures in their early years.[12] However, researchers continued to document that girls outscored boys on tests of verbal ability starting at grade five or six.[13] Recent work indicates that sex differences in verbal abilities have decreased markedly. Researchers completing a meta-analysis comparing earlier studies of verbal abilities with more recent research conclude: "There are not gender differences in verbal ability at least at this time, in American culture, in the standard ways that verbal ability has been measured."[14]

Some researchers argue that girls do have certain verbal advantages but that these are not adequately measured by most tests.[15] Furthermore, although boys have outscored girls on the verbal section of the Scholastic Achievement Test (SAT) since 1972, some suggest this may merely reflect the inclusion of more scientifically oriented items on which boys often perform better than do girls.[16] An additional difficulty with the SAT is that test-takers are not a nationally representative sample; they are a self-selected group.

READING

A review of three representative surveys of reading skills indicates a mixed picture. In two major surveys—the National Assessment of Educational Progress (NAEP) and the National Education Longitudinal Survey (NELS)—girls perform better than boys on reading tests. In the High School and Beyond Survey (HSB), boys perform better than girls on reading and vocabulary tests. In all three surveys, the sex differences are very small.

NAEP is the most comprehensive survey of achievement. A congressionally mandated project of the National Center for Education Statistics (NCES), it measures the proficiency of nine-year-olds, thirteen-year-olds, and seventeen-year-olds in a variety of disciplines. In all age groups, girls have consistently received higher test scores in reading and writing since the 1970s. Since 1971, however, boys have made gains relative to girls, particularly in the seventeen-year-old group.[17]

The NELS is a longitudinal survey of eighth graders also being conducted under the auspices of NCES. The first wave of eighth graders were interviewed and tested in 1988. Mean test scores for girls were higher than those for boys, although the difference was modest. Girls were less likely to score below "basic" and more likely to be rated as "advanced" when compared to boys.[18] This sex difference is found for all racial and ethnic groups.

The HSB, also sponsored by NCES, is a longitudinal study of high-school sophomores and seniors begun in 1980. Contrary to the other studies, boys consistently score better than girls on the HSB reading tests. This is true of sophomores and seniors, and for whites, blacks, and Hispanics.[19] One possible explanation for the differences in these surveys is that sex differences narrow as children grow older. This would be consistent with the very small difference found for seventeen-year-olds in the NAEP and the gains boys make relative to girls in the follow-up of the HSB cohort.[20]

Another explanation is that these differences may reflect differences in the tests given for each survey. The HSB tests were shorter and the NAEP tests much more comprehensive. This could prove to be another case where apparent sex differences may instead reflect test differences rather than differences in the test-takers' knowledge or ability.

Even within the NAEP reading test, the performance of boys relative to girls varied, depending on the type of reading exercise. Boys did as well as girls on the expository passages and were most disadvantaged relative to girls in the literary passages. This is consistent with the finding that boys read more nonfiction than girls, and girls read more fiction than boys.[21] This is also consistent with the finding that boys do slightly better than girls on other NAEP tests in subjects requiring good skills in expository reading and writing: civics, history, and geography.[22]

If, as some suggest, boys regard fiction as more "feminine," any advantage girls experience relative to boys in the NAEP may reflect culturally defined biases against boys' reading certain kinds of material.[23] It has been suggested that even if the small gender difference favoring girls is *statistically significant*, it may not be *educationally significant*.[24] Boys still do better than girls in almost every other subject tested by NAEP, and the difference in reading scores appears to narrow and possibly even favor boys in older age groups.

Finally, it has also been argued that gender differences in reading favoring girls may be more pronounced among low-achieving or low-income students.[25] This is particularly relevant given the recent heightening of concern about the education of low-income minority boys. An examination of achievement by race, sex, and social class is presented later in this section.

WRITING

Writing skills are tested less frequently. NAEP data do indicate that girls consistently outperform boys on writing-skills assessment.[26] Smaller studies of particular populations do not always support these national findings. A seven-year longitudinal study comparing the development of written language skills of boys and girls from kindergarten through grade six found that—at least in the population studied—neither sex had an advantage over the other.[27]

MATHEMATICS AND SCIENCE

The past fifteen years have seen an explosion of research on the relationship between gender and mathematics. While there has been less study on the linkage of gender and science, there still is sufficient information to draw preliminary conclusions. However, the usual cautions apply. Most of the research does not break down the data by both race/ethnicity and gender. Furthermore, the interactions of race ethnicity and gender are rarely studied, and most conclusions based on predominantly white respondents cannot be generalized to women and girls of color.[28]

Achievement in mathematics   Gender differences in mathematics achievement are small and declining. Recent meta-analyses have found only very small differences in female and male performance in mathematics. Furthermore, meta-analyses comparing recent research with studies done in 1974 indicate a significant decline in gender differences.[29] The High School and Beyond study of high-school sophomores and seniors also shows that gender differences favoring boys in mathematics are declining.[30]

Gender differences in mathematics do exist but are related to the age of the sample, how academically selective it is, and which cognitive level the test is tapping. Indeed these three variables were found to account for eighty-seven percent of the variance in one meta-analysis.[31] For example, no gender differences were found in the problem-solving ability of elementary- and middle-school girls and boys, but moderate to small differences favoring males emerged in high school.[32] Large research studies support these results, finding no gender differences in math performance at age nine, minimal differences at age thirteen, and a larger difference favoring males at age seventeen.[33] The most recent National Assessment of Educational Progress (NAEP) report finds few gender-related differences in math ability in grades four and eight other than a higher average proficiency in measurement and estimation for boys. However, by grade twelve males showed a small advantage in every content area except algebra.[34]

Larger differences are found at the higher academic and cognitive levels. For example, an earlier NAEP report stated that 8.2 percent of the males but only 4.5 percent of the females were at the highest math levels, while fifty-four percent of the males and forty-eight percent of the females could do moderately complex procedures and reasoning.[35] The College Board reports that males in 1988 scored an average of thirty-seven points higher than females on the Level I Math Achievement Test and thirty-eight points higher on the Level II Math Achievement Test.[36] Another study revealed that nearly all differences in math performance between girls and boys at ages eleven and fifteen could be accounted for by differences among those scoring in the top ten to twenty percent, with boys more often in the top-scoring groups. However, in classroom work, girls' math grades are as high or higher than boys'.[37]

Gender differences on the SAT-Math have decreased, although they are still large. Between 1978 and 1988 female scores increased by eleven points while male scores increased by four points. However, males still outscored females 498 to 455.[38] The Educational Testing Service does test a demographically matched sample of girls and boys on the Preliminary Scholastic Aptitude Test (PSAT) each year. From 1960 through 1983 gender differences in math from this group declined, although males still slightly outscored females.[39]

A smaller body of research tying both gender and ethnicity to math achievement indicates that the patterns may differ for various groups. A study in Hawaii found non-Caucasian girls outperforming boys in math and outnumbering boys in the highest-achieving groups.[40] Other studies have reported fewer gender differences in mathematics for minority students than for white students.[41]

Gender differences in tests of spatial skills are also declining.[42] For example, a large study found that girls and boys gained equally from instruction in spatial-visualization skills, despite initial differences.

The research results reported here must be examined in light of the achievement of all American students, female and male, in mathematics. An international assessment of the mathematics skills of thirteen-year-olds found U.S. students scoring below students in the other four countries and four Canadian provinces participating. Korean students had the highest average score (567.8), while the U.S. students scored 473.9.[43] In addition, the most recent National Assessment of Educational Progress reports that more than a quarter of fourth graders failed to demonstrate the ability to do arithmetical reasoning, and only five percent of high school seniors demonstrated the skills needed for high technology or college-level work.[44]

Achievement in science   Gender differences in science achievement are not decreasing and may be increasing. While no meta-analyses of studies linking gender and science achievement have been done, the National Assessment of Educational Progress does track science performance. Its results indicate that for nine- and thirteen-year-olds, gender differences in achievement increased between 1978 and 1986, due to the combination of a lag in performance for females and significant increases in the performance of males. According to the NAEP, gender differences in science achievement are largest for seventeen-year-olds, and these differences have not changed since 1978. The areas of largest male advantage are physics, chemistry, earth science, and space sciences.[45]

In addition, gender differences exist at various levels of achievement. NAEP found only five percent of seventeen-year-old girls as compared to ten percent of seventeen-year-old boys scoring at or above NAEP's "highest cognitive level," defined as students' ability to integrate specialized knowledge.[46] SAT achievement test scores show a similar pattern. The Educational Testing Service reports that in 1988, males scored on average 29 points higher than females on biology achievement tests. This, incidentally, was the only science area tested by ETS where gender differences declined; the spread between male and female test scores shrunk eleven points from the forty-point gap measured in 1981. Males also scored about fifty-six points higher than females on the 1988 physics achievement tests.[47] However, once again girls receive grades in science that are as high or higher than those of boys.[48]

As with gender differences in mathematics achievement, gender differences in science should be looked at in a large context. American students, both female and male, are not doing well in science. Their low levels of scientific knowledge, even at the factual level, have been documented in both national and international studies. One international assessment of the science skills of thirteen-year-olds found U.S. students placing ninth among the twelve nations and provinces participating.[49]

Mathematics participation   Gender differences in math-course participation are small, occur only in higher-level courses, and appear to be stable. In 1989 the National Science Board of the National Science Foundation reported that from 1982 to 1987, the average number of math credits that a male high school student received increased from 2.61 to 3.04. During the same time period, the average number of math credits that a female student received increased from 2.46 to 2.93. In 1982 males received .15 more math credits than females; in 1987, .11 more. The National Science Board found that approximately the same percentages of females and males took the same math courses up to calculus, which was taken by 7.6 percent of the boys but only 4.7 percent of the girls.[50] The 1991 NAEP reports that for the District of Columbia and the thirty-seven states participating in the study "Up to Algebra III/Pre-Calculus and Calculus," there were no gender differences in either course-taking or average proficiency."[51] These results are similar to the findings of a 1990 survey by the Council of Chief State School Officers.[52]

Career Plans of Students Taking the SAT

Women and Minorities in Science and Engineering (Washington D.C.: National Science Foundation [1990] 128)

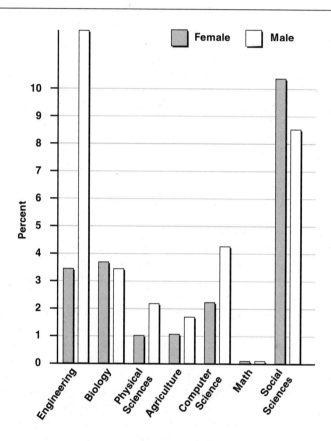

Science participation   Gender differences in the number of science courses students take are small. However, the pattern of course-taking differs, with girls being more apt to take advanced biology and boys being more apt to take physics and advanced chemistry. In 1989 the National Science Board of the National Science Foundation reported that from 1982 to 1987, the average number of science and computer-science credits a male high-school student received increased from 2.25 to 2.69. During the same time period the average number of science credits a female student received increased from 2.13 to 2.57. In both 1982 and 1987, males received .12 more science credits than did females.[53] Another study based on 1987 data reports young women taking .2 fewer science courses than young men (2.93 versus 3.13).[54] Using the 1988 data, the National Science Foundation reported girls taking an average of 3.1 science courses compared to boys' 3.3.[55]

All three studies found approximately the same numbers of females and males taking Biology I and Chemistry I but more males taking physics. In 1987 the National Science Board reported 25.3 percent of the males but only 15 percent of the females took physics. This is, however, an improvement. In 1982, 18.2 percent of the males but only 10 percent of the females enrolled in physics.[56]

These results are mirrored by a 1991 survey by the Council of Chief State School Officers. The survey reports that sixty percent of the students enrolled in first-year high-school physics are male and that seventy percent of second-year physics students are male.[57]

Career plans   Gender differences show up in career plans as well. The bar graph on page 569 shows large differences between young women and men in terms of future career plans, even within the math and science fields.

High-school girls, even those with exceptional academic preparation in math and science, are choosing math/science careers in disproportionately low numbers.[58] A study of Rhode Island seniors found that sixty-four percent of the male students who had taken physics and calculus were planning to major in science or engineering in college compared to only 18.6 percent of the female students who had taken these courses.[59]

Girls who do go on in scientific fields after high school report that the encouragement provided by their teachers is very important.[60] One study reports that girls who went on to study engineering felt that teachers encouraged them; unfortunately, they also felt that counselors discouraged them.[61] Clearly, differential treatment on the basis of sex contributes to the student choices reported here, but there are other factors as well.

Math and science influences   As they grow, girls and boys have difference science experiences. Girls are more apt to be exposed to biology-related activities and less apt to engage in mechanical and electrical activities.[62] One study found that by third grade, fifty-one percent of boys and thirty-seven percent of girls had used microscopes, while by eleventh grade forty-nine percent of males and seventeen percent of females had used an electricity meter.[63] Gender differences in science-related activities may be reinforced in schools if children are allowed always to select science topics based on familiarity or interest.

Eighth-grade boys have been found to use more science instruments in class, particularly physical-science tools such as power supplies.[64] Although nine-year-old girls express interest in many science activities, they do not *do* as many as boys. This gender difference continues through ages thirteen and seventeen and is paralleled by an increasingly negative view of science, science classes, and science careers on the part of girls.[65]

Gender differences in confidence are strongly correlated with continuation in math and science classes. Math confidence is the surety a student has of her or his ability to learn and perform well in mathematics.[66] Math confidence has been found to be more highly correlated with math performance than any other affective variable.[67]

Females, more than males, have been found to doubt their confidence in math.[68] The Educational Testing Service reports that gender differences in perceptions of being good at math increase with age. Third-grade girls and boys think they are good in math in about the same percentages (sixty-four percent versus sixty-six percent); by seventh grade, fifty-seven percent of the girls agree, compared to sixty-four percent of the boys; by eleventh grade the gap widens to forty-eight percent of girls versus sixty percent of boys.[69] In a classic study, researchers Elizabeth Fennema and Julia Sherman found a strong correlation between math achievement and confidence. Their research revealed a drop in both girls' math confidence and their achievement in the middle-school years.[70] The drop in confidence *preceded* a decline in achievement.

One result of this diminished confidence is a lowering of the role that competence plays in girls' decisions about continuing in math and science. Researchers have found that competence is a more important prerequisite for the attainment of male career ambitions than it is for females.[71] That is, females and males abandon math and science for different reasons. Males who drop out of math and science tend to do so because of a lack of competence—they cannot do the work; many females who drop out do so even though they can do the work.

Other researchers have also found that males are more apt than females to attribute their success to ability, while females are more apt to attribute failure to lack of ability.[72] As boys get older, those who do not like math are more likely to attribute this feeling to the subject itself: they don't like math, they say, because it is "not useful." Girls, instead interpret their problems with math as personal failures.[73]

Concern about the difficulty or competitiveness of the field can also be an issue. One study found that the perceived competitiveness of engineering was seen by girls as a major barrier to women entering the field.[74] This finding is supported by research that shows girls who see themselves as highly competitive to be more interested in taking math and science courses than other girls.[75] For boys, the degree of competitiveness is not related to interest in taking math and science.

While most students who dislike math do so because they consider it too hard, most students who dislike science say science is "not interesting." Adolescent girls are more likely than adolescent boys to find science uninteresting. Adolescent boys are more likely than girls to discount the importance of science itself.[76]

In general, students' interest in and enthusiasm for math and science decline the longer they are in school. The poll commissioned by the American Association of University Women in 1990 found that all students' enthusiasm for math and science was greatest in the elementary years and dropped as they got older. However, losses for girls were larger than were those for boys.[77]

In addition, males are more apt than females to envision themselves using math as adults.[78] In assessing what factors they used to decide whether or not to continue math study, students listed the usefulness of math, followed by their confidence in their ability and their enjoyment of the subject.[79]

Gender stereotyping also appears to influence whether girls persist in mathematics. Data from the National Assessment of Educational Progress indicate that girls who reject traditional gender roles have higher math achievement than girls who hold more stereotyped expectations. Moreover, girls in advanced math classes tend not to see math as a "male" subject.[80]

Meta-analysis of affective variables associated with taking math courses indicate that gender differences are all small with the exception of the view of math as "something men do." Boys see math as very "male."[81] A longitudinal study that tested students at sixth, eighth, tenth, and twelfth grades found that for girls a view of math as "male" was negatively correlated with math achievement at each grade level. This was the only affective variable for which consistent gender differences were found.[82]

IMPLICATIONS

It is important that equal attention be given to both girls and boys in teaching reading and writing skills. The assumption that boys are in greater need of instruction in these areas should not be made. Furthermore, girls need particular encouragement to read more broadly in nonfiction areas and boys should be encouraged to read more fiction.

The gender gap is closing in math achievement but not in science achievement. Issues of gender and math have received more attention than issues of gender and science. Much of the work that has been done in science—beyond counting who is taking what courses—has been done in biology, a field in which there are many women, as opposed to physics, a field with very few women.

Since the growing gender gap in science is clearly related to males' climbing test scores, we need to ask why reforms in science education are apparently working for males and not for females. Just as the SAT-Math has been studied and found to underpredict women's achievement, science tests need to be checked for bias as well.

Building on the work done in math, we need to study more fully the possible causes of the gender gap in the sciences. Particular emphasis should be placed on issues of confidence.

Once students satisfy math and science requirements for graduation and college admission, gender differences in science and math course-taking emerge. More students are taking more science and math, but at the advanced levels the gender gap remains constant. It appears that messages about math and science as critical assets for later employment have been somewhat successful, at least for middle-school students. However, while we have more girls taking more math and science, the numbers and percentages of girls interested in careers in math and science is increasing minimally, if at all. During senior high school and college, female students drop out of the math/science pipeline because they choose not to pursue scientific careers.[83]

Changing the public images of physics and chemistry to reflect the diversity of these fields and the way they tie in to our everyday lives can provide

There is no math gene

Despite the fact that the specter of a math gene favoring males is often in the news, there is strong evidence against arguments for biological/ genetic causes of gender differences in math. These include:

- The gender gap in mathematics is rapidly decreasing; genetic differences tend to remain stable.
- The gap can be reduced or eliminated by changing teaching practices and providing opportunities for both girls and boys to practice building math skills; biological differences are not so easily influenced.
- Gender differences in math achievement are not consistent across racial/ethnic groups. If there were a sex-linked math gene, differences would be consistent across all groups.

The findings that gifted seventh-grade boys are much more likely than girls to score well on the SAT-Math, often used to suggest a biological basis for math gender differences, are seriously flawed because the researchers

- Assume that because girls and boys have been in the same math classes, they have had the same experiences;
- Do not look at effects of differential treatment in and out of the classroom;
- Use the SAT in part because it finds larger gender differences than other standardized tests;
- Postulate a biological basis for differences in SAT scores, whereas ETS has reported that this test underpredicts girls' performance and overpredicts boys';
- Assume that gifted children whose parents pay more than thirty dollars for their children to take a test represent the population as a whole;
- Indicate in written materials sent to students before they take the SAT that girls do not do as well as boys.[1]

[1] P. Campbell, T. Kibler and K. Campbell-Kibler, "Taking the SAT at Twelve: One Family's View of Talent Search," *College Prep* 7 (1991): 8–10.

more girls with the "inside information" that daughters of scientists appear to get. Meeting, getting to know, and working with scientists also reduce negative and intimidating stereotypes about the field. Providing students, especially girls, with more real-life experiences with science and scientists may make a big difference.

Teaching methods to decrease or eliminate the gender gaps in math and science already exist. Having students read and try out math and science problems before they are covered in class appears to narrow the "experience" gap between girls and boys, thus helping to reduce gender differences in class performance.[84] Providing a structure in which all students answer questions, pose questions, and receive answers, rather than one that emphasizes target students or those who call out answers loudest, increases girls' opportunities and interest. Girls also respond well to special programs where they work co-operatively in a relaxed atmosphere where math is fun. Such programs significantly increase the number of math and science courses girls take. However, while hands-on experience is more successful than the lecture approach, such experiences must allow sufficient time and opportunities for girls to reach the same level of performance that teachers expect from boys.[85]

Schools can learn much from out-of-school programs that encourage girls in math and science. Girls are not required to take special out-of-school programs. Designers of successful out-of-school math and science programs have learned how to get girls to attend and, more important, how to keep them interested so that they will keep on attending. We need to continue and expand programs like those developed by Girls, Incorporated; the Girl Scouts; and several AAUW branches. These offer unique opportunities for girls to learn together to overcome stereotypes. What's more, such programs also act as laboratories for developing effective techniques to keep girls involved in math and science. We can't rely on these programs alone, however. Compared to the school system, they can reach only small numbers of girls for relatively short periods of time. Since all girls go to school and go for many years, we must focus most of our effort there, incorporating techniques that work for girls throughout our schools, and doing so in ways that continue to work for girls systemwide.

COURSE-TAKING PATTERNS

Gender Gaps: Where Schools Still Fail Our Children
(Washington, D.C.: American Association of University Women Educational
Foundation and National Education Association, 1998)

The courses students take in high school and the degree to which they master these subjects affect the choices open to them for years to come. College acceptances, scholarship offers, and employment opportunities can hinge on student course-taking decisions and subsequent performance. Understandably, this area has drawn researchers' attention over the past several years.

Much of this attention has focused on math and science courses, where boys have historically outnumbered and outperformed girls. This gap is a portent of the gender gap in college math and science programs and, later, in well-paying math and science careers. The rapid growth of technology has also fueled concern about girls' computer skills, which generally lag behind boys'. Boys significantly outnumber girls in higher-skill computer courses, while girls tend to cluster in lower-end data entry and word processing classes.

This chapter reviews girls' and boys' uneven participation across the entire curriculum. We review not just girls' much-researched and discussed participation rates in science, mathematics, and computer science, but also boys' participation in English, foreign language, social sciences, and the arts. Examining gender differences among boys and girls, across the curriculum, reflects the goals of educational equity research, which attempts to document different educational outcomes according to factors such as sex, race, or class, regardless of which group these differences favor.

As Valerie Lee explains, "reading, writing, social studies, and foreign language are seldom discussed in the [gender equity] venue, although gender differences exist in these areas . . . Why should we examine only curriculum areas where girls are disadvantaged?"[86]

SUBJECT ENROLLMENTS

Girls' participation is improving in some academic areas where it previously lagged, particularly in math and science. The number of courses taken in a discipline, however, doesn't tell the whole story; class-by-class comparisons show that girls are still less well represented in some higher-level courses in math, science, and computer science. Boys' participation, meanwhile, is lower in some of the humanities, including English, language, sociology, psychology, and the fine arts.

Girls' enrollments are up in mathematics and science courses, and the difference between girls' and boys' course patterns here appears to be narrowing. Girls still enroll in language arts courses (including foreign languages) with greater frequency than boys. In fact, course-taking patterns, when viewed as a whole, suggest that girls may be getting a broader education than boys by deepening their exposure to math and science and by enrolling in more courses in other subject areas.

MATHEMATICS

A much-discussed gap between girls and boys—average numbers of mathematics courses taken—appears to be diminishing. But gender differences remain in the kinds of courses taken. In an encouraging development, more girls are enrolling in algebra, geometry, precalculus, trigonometry, and calculus than in 1990. However, girls are more likely than boys to end their high school math careers with Algebra II.

TABLE 3-1   Percentage of 1990 and 1994 High-School Graduates Taking Specific Mathematics Courses by Gender

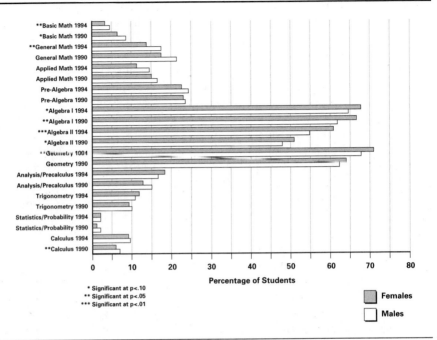

* Significant at p<.10
** Significant at p<.05
*** Significant at p<.01

☐ Females
☐ Males

SOURCE: U.S. Department of Education, National Center for Education Statistics, 1994 High School Transcript Study, Tabulations, 1997.

Both the Council of Chief State School Officers and the 1994 High-School Transcript Study found that males and females take comparable numbers of high-school mathematics courses.[87] In 1994—the most recent year for which data is available—both groups averaged nearly 3.5 credits of math courses.

Yet an examination of course-by-course enrollment figures for girls and boys reveals remaining gender divisions. A significantly larger proportion of male than female high-school graduates took the lowest-level high-school mathematics courses (basic mathematics and general mathematics), according to 1994 data from the High-School Transcript Study.[88] Girls outnumber boys in algebra and geometry. Roughly equal proportions of girls and boys take pre-calculus or calculus prior to leaving high school.

In another sign that the overall math gap is shrinking, more girls entered Algebra I, Algebra II, geometry, precalculus, trigonometry, and calculus in 1994 than in 1990. This finding is encouraging in light of research that cites taking Algebra I and geometry early in high school—generally in the ninth and tenth grades—as the major predictor of a student's continuing on to college.[89]

Additionally, in 1994, roughly equal numbers of girls and boys took precalculus, trigonometry, and statistics/probability enrollments.[90] (See Table 3-1.)

Among college-bound girls, enrollment in math courses has increased more over the past decade than it has for college-bound boys, according to ACT, Inc., a nonprofit organization best known for its college admissions testing program. In this population, more females than males now take geometry and second-year algebra. In addition, the proportion of girls taking trigonometry and calculus has increased by seven and nine percent respectively since 1987, while the percentage of boys taking trigonometry has held steady and the percentage enrolling in calculus has increased by only six percent. Between 1987 and 1997 college-bound girls' enrollment in geometry also increased by eight percent; in Algebra II it increased by fifteen percent. In contrast, college-bound boys' enrollment in those courses rose by five and ten percent.[91]

State-level data collected by the Council of Chief State School Officers indicate that slightly greater percentages of girls enrolled in Algebra II/Integrated Math in 1996 than in 1990. Seven of eighteen states reporting data by gender indicated increases, ranging from one to six percent, from 1990 to 1996. Twelve of the eighteen states reported an increase in girls' enrollments in trigonometry/precalculus (from two to six percent) over the same time period.[92]

However, girls are significantly more likely than boys to end their high-school mathematics careers with Algebra II. Fifty-three percent of girls versus forty-seven percent of boys end their high-school mathematics careers with the completion of this course. Stopping a math education at this level can close the door on future studies, scholarships, and careers.

SCIENCE

A greater percentage of female high-school graduates took science courses in 1994 than in 1990. Girls are more likely than their male counterparts to take both biology and chemistry. Roughly equal proportions of girls and boys enroll in engineering and geology. Physics, however, remains a largely male domain. While more girls enroll today than in 1990, the gender gap here is sizeable.

Even though male and female high-school students take a similar average number of science courses, males are more likely than females to have taken all three of the core science courses—biology, chemistry, and physics—by graduation. Girls' enrollment in physics has been increasing, but a significant gender gap persists. The science education community acknowledges the "physics problems" and has developed interventions to increase girls' participation.[93] Science reforms are more recent than those in mathematics, which may partly explain the lingering disparity between girls' and boys' participation in physics.[94] (See Table 3-2.)

TABLE 3-2   Percentage of 1990 and 1994 High-School Graduates Taking Specific
Science Courses by Gender

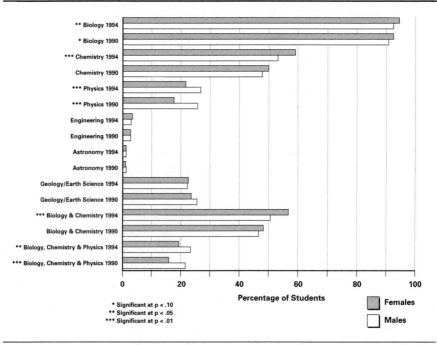

* Significant at p < .10
** Significant at p < .05
*** Significant at p < .01

Females

Males

SOURCE: U.S. Department of Education, National Center for Education Statistics, 1994 High
School Transcript Study, Tabulations, 1997.

COMPUTER-RELATED STUDIES

> *Enrollments in higher-skill computer courses show a puzzling
> drop for both boys and girls, although boys clearly outnumber
> girls. In comparison, girls tend to cluster in lower-end data-entry and
> word-processing classes that lead to less stimulating jobs.*

States' lavish investment in computers across K–12 education has visibly transformed the appearance and teaching philosophy of many public schools. Yet,
for reasons that are unclear, fewer boys and girls are enrolling in computer-
science classes that prepare students for careers in computer programming and
theory. The enrollment drop is puzzling in light of burgeoning industry needs
for technically skilled workers.

Computer application courses in graphic arts and computer-aided design,
while not especially common, attract very few girls. Girls are significantly more
likely than boys to enroll in clerical and data-entry classes, the 1990s version
of typing.[95] (See Table 3-3.)

TABLE 3-3   Percentage of 1990 and 1994 High-School Graduates Taking Specific Computer Courses by Gender

** Significant at p < .05
*** Significant at p < .01

SOURCE: U.S. Department of Education, National Center for Education Statistics, *Vocational Course Taking and Achievement: An Analysis of High School Transcripts and 1990 NAEP Assessment Scores* (Washington, DC: 1995).

ENGLISH

Girls outnumber boys in all English classes except remedial English, earning more credits here than boys.

No advocate of high educational standards and improved U.S. public education questions the need for literacy, reading, writing, and oral communications skills as prerequisites for success in all careers.[95] In the standards movement, literacy denotes not only reading comprehension and traditional courses in English literature, but also spoken language; technological communication; knowledge of written, spoken, and visual texts; and knowledge of the processes involved in creating, interpreting, and critiquing such texts.[96]

Despite the centrality of language arts to the criteria of excellent education, boys and girls do not pursue the language arts in equal proportion. In both 1990 and 1994, female high-school graduates were more likely than males to have enrolled in every type of English course except for remedial English.[97] Girls as a group earned more than four credits of English in 1994, a slight rise from 1990. Boys as a population also score lower than girls on verbal skills on most standardized tests.[98]

TABLE 3-4   Percentage of 1990 and 1994 High-School Graduates Taking Specific
English Courses by Gender

***Remedial English 1994
***Remedial English 1990
English as a Second Language 1994
English as a Second Language 1990
4 Years of English 1994
4 Years of English 1990
Literature 1994
Literature 1990
Composition 1994
** Composition 1990
Speech 1994
Speech 1990

Percentage of Students

** Significant at p < .05
*** Significant at p < .01

Females
Males

SOURCE: U.S. Department of Education, National Center for Education Statistics, 1994 High School Transcript Study, Tabulations, 1997.

Crucially, gender differences in language arts performance and course taking rarely are noted in discussions of equity or standards. According to Elisabeth Hayes, "one of the most striking findings" in a 1996 study of gender and literacy, in fact, "was the real lack of serious attention to gender issues in scholarship on reading education."[99] Yet equity means that an educational system does not produce uneven outcomes by any characteristic of social background—in this case, gender. The fact that boys do not perform to girls' level in certain subject areas therefore belongs in the gender equity discussion.

A few studies since 1992 have examined why girls excel in verbal, language, and writing skills, and how their strengths shape the school's overall approach to this important content area of the curriculum. (See Table 3-4.) A cross-national comparison in 1996 found that gender differences are more apparent for the language arts than for mathematics, and perhaps emerge out of a widespread cultural belief that language arts is a female domain. The perception of literacy, reading, writing, and verbal precocity as feminine characteristics shapes the way schools teach reading: they may cater to girls' interests and strengths, promoting "versions of literacy that appeal more to girls than boys."[100] Girls' acuity with language results in a deeper, more imaginative engagement with the writing process and with reading material. A 1992 study examined student journals of their reading experiences and reactions to a novel taught in school. Researchers discovered that "girls were much more apt to write their internal response as they read a novel than boys, and when the book had two strong main characters, girls made more entries about these characters [and identified them by name] than boys."[101]

Student acceptance of purportedly "natural" male and female strengths has undoubtedly fed the expectation that boys will lag behind in the language arts. When researchers in one study asked students why girls and boys differ in reading performance, the largest category of responses was, "It's the way things are."[102] By the time they leave school, students exhibit deeply entrenched ideas of male and female domains of competency. Yet boys and girls do not begin their formal education with these notions. Perceptions of girls as uniquely suited for the language arts appear to intensify after the fourth grade and are most dramatic in the last years of high school.[103]

SOCIAL STUDIES

In the social studies field, encompassing such courses as history, geography, anthropology, economics, sociology, and psychology, more girls than boys tend to enroll in sociology and psychology.

Enrollment differences for males and females in social studies courses are not statistically significant. The one exception, in both 1990 and 1994, is sociology/psychology, where females are more likely to enroll than males. The pattern continues in higher education, where females are more likely to pursue college majors in certain social sciences.[104] (See Table 3-5.)

FOREIGN LANGUAGES

Female high-school graduates were significantly more likely than male high-school graduates to have taken French or Spanish in both 1990 and 1994.

The percentages of students, both male and female, who took Spanish increased across the four-year time period, while the percentage of both male and female students who took French declined slightly. (See Table 3-6.) More girls than boys took French or Spanish in 1990 and 1994.

FINE ARTS

In both 1990 and 1994, female high-school graduates were significantly more likely than males to have taken courses in music, drama, and dance.

TABLE 3-5   Percentage of High-School Graduates Taking Specific Social Studies Courses in 1990 and 1994 by Gender

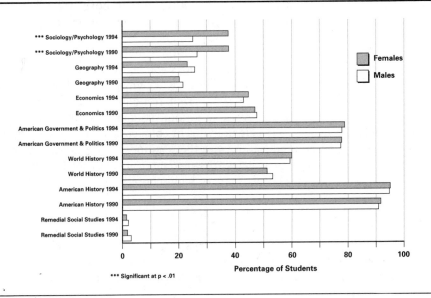

*** Significant at p < .01

Percentage of Students

SOURCE: U.S. Department of Education, National Center for Education Statistics, *Vocational Course Taking and Achievement: An Analysis of High School Transcripts and 1990 NAEP Assessment Scores* (Washington, DC: 1995).

Differences in both years were particularly large in music; in 1994, forty-four percent of girls and twenty-eight percent of boys had taken at least one semester of music, including participation in band or orchestra. Males and females enrolled in courses in art or music appreciation at fairly comparable rates in 1990, although relatively few students of either sex had taken courses of this type while in high school. (See Table 3-7.)

There is some evidence that girls' higher enrollments in fine arts and music may enhance their performance in other subject areas. The National Education Association noted in 1997 that students who took four years of high school art or music classes scored an average thirty-two points higher on the verbal section of the SAT and an average twenty-three points higher in math.[105]

HEALTH AND PHYSICAL EDUCATION

Fewer students are taking physical education now than in 1990, and the dropoff is steeper for girls than boys.

TABLE 3-6   Percentage of 1990 and 1994 High-School Graduates Taking Specific Foreign Language Courses by Gender

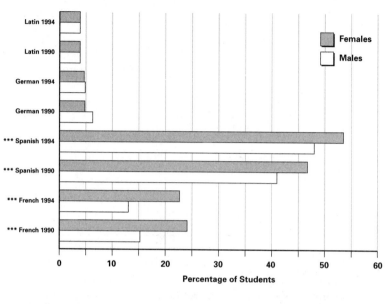

*** Significant at p < .01

SOURCE: U.S. Department of Education, National Center for Education Statistics, *Vocational Course Taking and Achievement: An Analysis of High School Transcripts and 1990 NAEP Assessment Scores* (Washington, DC: 1995).

> *Differences between males and females appear to have increased somewhat between 1990, when sixty-seven percent of females and seventy percent of males had taken a year of physical education, and 1994, when the respective percentages declined to sixty-one and sixty-seven percent.[106]*

Research links physical activity for girls to higher self-esteem, positive body image, and lifelong health. Young females are twice as likely to be inactive as young males.[107] Male high-school graduates were more likely than females to have taken at least one year of physical education. Although more girls now participate in a wider array of physical activities and sports than ever before, the decline in physical education is troubling, especially given the secondary academic benefits associated with girls' athletic participation.[108] (See Table 3-8.)

TABLE 3-7   Percentage of 1990 and 1994 High-School Graduates Taking Specific Fine Arts Courses by Gender

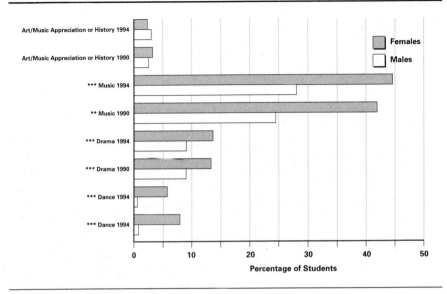

SOURCE: U.S. Department of Education, National Center for Education Statistics, *Vocational Course Taking and Achievement: An Analysis of High School Transcripts and 1990 NAEP Assessment Scores* (Washington, DC: 1995).

REMEDIAL AND SPECIAL EDUCATION

Girls are likelier than boys to have their abilities overlooked, particularly in math and science. Nonwhite and nonaffluent students— girls and boys—are more likely to be steered to remedial classes.

Schools play a pivotal role in allocating or withholding opportunities to students by identifying them as "regular," "college preparatory," "gifted and talented," or "learning disabled," or otherwise designating their ability level.[109] National data show that school policies of sorting or "tracking" students into lower-level classes result in less actual learning for both boys and girls overall. Maureen Hallinan asserts, "Empirical research provides considerable evidence that the quality and quantity of instruction increases with track level," and that "the higher the track level, the greater the students' academic status, self-esteem, and motivation to learn."[110] Jomills Braddock and Robert Slavin write that "being in the low track in eighth grade slams the gate on any possibility that a student can take the courses leading to college. The gate remained open for equally low-achieving eighth graders who had the good fortune to attend untracked schools."[111]

TABLE 3-8   Percentage of 1990 and 1994 High-School Graduates Taking Specific Health and Physical Education Courses by Gender

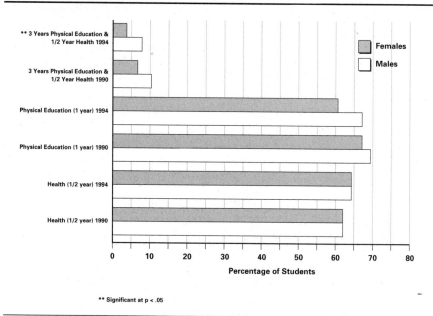

** Significant at p < .05

SOURCE: U.S. Department of Education, National Center for Education Statistics, *Vocational Course Taking and Achievement: An Analysis of High School Transcripts and 1990 NAEP Assessment Scores* (Washington, DC: 1995).

In theory, tracking might advance gender equity because it groups students according to their academic skills, rather than arbitrary variables such as race, socioeconomic status, or sex. However, some researchers have concluded that ratings of academic talents and skills are mediated by race, gender, and socioeconomic status, among other factors. Recognition of physical disabilities in schools are proportionate across the sexes, but recognition of more subjective disabilities such as learning disorders are not. This suggests that gender expectations bias tracking decisions.[112] Sally Reis and Carolyn Callahan found that male teachers, in particular, tend to stereotype girls and their talents.[113] Such critical judgments of their abilities deter many girls from persevering, particularly in mathematics and sciences.[114] Nonwhite and nonaffluent students—girls and boys—are especially likely to have their abilities overlooked.[115]

Significantly, placement into "remedial," special education, or lower academic tracks often occurs as students enter school in the fall—a difficult time for many students. Because tracking occurs so early in the school year, teachers and administrators may not have learned enough about individual students to challenge prior gender-stereotyped expectations. The earlier in the year a student is tracked, the more likely the decision is affected by stereotypes of performance and behavior rather than substantive knowledge—acquired only over time—of the student's abilities. Students who experience difficulties in the first few weeks of school often have trouble later with grades, behavior, grade retention, absenteeism, and dropping out of school.[116]

ADVANCED PLACEMENT, GIFTED, AND HONORS PROGRAMS

In 1992 enrollments in gifted programs favored girls. No new data contradict this finding.[117] However, girls drop out of high-school gifted tracks at a faster rate than boys.

Participation in top-level high school courses and in gifted and honors programs indicate, in large part, how teachers, parents, and students themselves perceive their academic abilities and interests. Participation in these courses also powerfully predicts enrollment in higher education.

Most schools identify children for gifted and talented programs at around third grade, on the basis of teacher recommendations and standardized tests.[118] Educators and administrators generally identify girls for gifted programs at equal or greater numbers than boys, yet students are identified for different kinds of programs, according to gender expectations. Schools do not identify girls for their mathematics and science talents in the same proportions as boys, who, likewise, are not identified for their English, language, or arts abilities in the same proportions as girls.[119]

Furthermore, girls are not retained in high-level gifted tracks to the same extent as boys. Despite the early identification of special talent in girls, Carolyn Read found that there is an abrupt reversal of this pattern around the tenth grade.[120] Something leads many girls not to enroll or to drop out of gifted and talented programs early in high school; others are not identified for these programs. What happens in middle school and early high school to discourage girls' identification with and participation in gifted programs? Read hypothesizes that, during elementary school, educators identify more girls for gifted and talented programs because girls are more likely to meet sex-role expectations.[121] However, as girls reach adolescence, their focus often shifts from being the "good girl" in school to fitting in with peer groups. For girls, fitting in often involves playing dumb, hiding their intelligence, and being quiet.

Sally Reis and M. Katherine Gavin also observed that although teachers in general did not engage in sex-role stereotyping, they did stereotype their best students in the area of mathematics, attributing characteristics such as volunteering answers, enjoying mathematics, and working independently to males.[122] Teachers rated females higher than males on the effort they put into schoolwork and on the quality of their work; however, teachers gave boys and girls the same grades, despite girls' higher ratings on effort and quality of work.[123] Perhaps this occurs because, as Pat Ross maintains, U.S. culture often equates higher expenditure of effort with lower ability.[124]

If educators and peers cast gifted white girls as quiet, good students, they sometimes cast gifted, academically successful black girls as troublemakers rather than as outspoken, independent leaders of tomorrow.[125] Signithia Fordham found "the most salient characteristic of the academically successful [black] females . . . is a deliberate silence, a controlled response to their evolving, ambiguous status as academically successful students."[126] Research on educational reform and gender has found that school response to girls' behavior plays a crucial role in recasting potentially "unfeminine" traits such as intellectual aggressiveness into positive and encouraged behavior. For example, one study notes, "girls who speak out may be treated as leaders or renegades," depending in some measure on the school's approach to the behaviors.[127]

AP AND HONORS ENROLLMENT

Girls' AP and honors course enrollments are comparable to or greater than those of boys, except in physics. In AP and honors calculus and chemistry, girls' course enrollments improved relative to boys' from 1990 to 1994.

Advanced placement (AP) and honors courses are generally the highest-level courses high schools offer. Both kinds of courses are taught at an accelerated pace. Honors courses offer students a deeper understanding of the subject matter and challenge them to produce a higher quality of work. AP courses cover material at college level and can earn college credit for students who score three or higher on a five-point voluntary course-end exam.

In 1997, fifty-eight percent of all public high schools offered AP courses. Today, roughly the same percentage of males and females enroll in AP or honors courses in Western civilization, calculus, or chemistry—an improvement over 1990. Overall, girls' enrollments in AP or honors courses are comparable to those of males across all subjects except for AP physics. Girls are significantly more likely than males to enroll in AP or honors courses in English, foreign language, and biology. Except in foreign languages, girls' and boys' participation in AP or honors courses increased between 1990 and 1994.[128] From 1983 to 1993 there was a substantial increase (from thirty-seven to forty-three percent) in the proportion of female AP test takers in math and natural science subject areas.[129] (See Table 3-9.)

SUMMARY

After lagging for years, girls' high-school course enrollment patterns are beginning to look more like boys'—an encouraging sign because course selections can open or close future opportunities to students. But progress is not uniform.

TABLE 3-9   AP Course Taking by Gender, Subject, Year

SOURCE: U.S. Department of Education, National Center for Education Statistics, 1994 High School Transcript Study, Tabulations, 1997.

In terms of *numbers* of courses taken, girls are closing the much-discussed gap in math and science. But important differences still rest in the specific courses taken. For example, more girls are taking Algebra I and geometry today than in 1990. The increase in girls' enrollments is welcome news: Taking Algebra I and geometry by the ninth and tenth grade is viewed as a major predictor of a student's continuing to college. But more girls than boys end their high-school math careers with Algebra II. Stopping a math education at this level is troubling because it can close the door on future studies, scholarships, and careers. Girls are also less likely than boys to take physics and high-level computer courses.

Girls' failure to take more top math and science courses remains an obstinate problem, with a long-term impact. Data on college majors and degrees earned indicate that girls may not make the transition from high-school math and science courses to advanced postsecondary courses in these fields. This failure threatens to make women bystanders in the burgeoning technology industry of the twenty-first century and keep women underrepresented in high-salaried, intellectually challenging engineering, biochemistry, and biotechnology careers.

However, to review girls' enrollments in the sciences only is to subscribe to an arbitrary hierarchy of subject areas, and to relegate areas in which girls excel to a lesser status than they deserve. English, foreign languages, the social sciences, and fine arts are all educational prerequisites for higher education and career, particularly in the information-driven economy of the twenty-first century. Equally important, they are prerequisites for personal expression, informed citizenship, an understanding of global trends, and an ability to analyze and interpret contemporary cultures. In these courses, girls outnumber boys. Boys' underenrollment in English, languages, and the arts warrants attention if public schools aspire to achieve high standards for all students.

Schools' practice of tracking students—formally or informally—affects girls' and boys' course-taking patterns differently. Girls are more likely than boys to have their abilities overlooked in math and science—a pattern that limits their future opportunities. On the other hand, girls are also more likely than boys to be identified at a young age for gifted programs. However, girls fall off this gifted track at a higher rate than boys, particularly once they reach high school. There, peer pressure tells many girls to hide their intelligence and be quiet.

The message is received differently by black and white girls, say some researchers. White girls are rewarded for fitting in, for meeting expectations of being the "good girl" in school. Those black girls who are outspoken and independent often find themselves cast as troublemakers rather than leaders. They may pay more of a social price for conforming to expectations of silence.

Roughly the same percentage of boys and girls enroll in the most challenging high school courses: AP and honors courses. Girls' and boys' enrollment in specific AP or honors courses reflects subject enrollment patterns elsewhere: Girls are more likely than boys to enroll in English, foreign language, and biology. Boys are more likely to enroll in physics.

RECOMMENDATIONS

In light of improving participation rates overall for girls in math and science, these recommendations focus on the types and timing of courses boys and girls take.

- In developing curriculum standards, states should make rigorous courses of Algebra I and geometry mandatory for all students, as the gatekeeper classes for college admissions and for advanced study in math, science, engineering, and computer science.
- Schools and school districts should concentrate on increasing the percentage of girls who take the trio of core science courses: physics, biology, and chemistry. In this trio, physics shows the most obstinate gender gap.
- Teachers and counselors should encourage talented girls to take math and science classes at the challenging AP or honors level.
- Educators need to develop interventions at the classroom, school, district, or state level to equalize enrollments in computer-science technology. Girls are dramatically underrepresented in regular and AP

computer science courses, with the exception of word processing, the 1990s version of typing. This has ramifications beyond the classroom. There already is a shortage of talent to fill high-skill, well-paying jobs in the field.

♦ Educators should develop curriculum and other incentives to encourage more boys to enroll in fine arts, foreign languages, advanced English electives, and AP languages and humanities courses. Areas such as these where boys underenroll or underperform girls are relevant to the equity agenda. Educators should ask: Why do these courses attract fewer boys? Are there curricular changes that might encourage their engagement in these crucial areas of the curriculum?

♦ States and schools should reassess tracking policies not only in light of racial and class equity concerns, but also in light of gender equity. Currently, educators identify more girls than boys for gifted programs in the elementary years, yet girls are not retained in high-level tracks to the same extent as boys once they reach middle school.

♦ State and federal data on participation in gifted and special education programs should be disaggregated by sex.

NOTES

1. The only women in leadership positions on the thirty-five commissions and task forces we reviewed were: Judith Lanier, President of the Holmes Group; Marian Wright Edelman, Cochair of the National Coalition of Advocates for Students National Board of Inquiry; Eleanor Holmes Norton, Cochair of the Joint Center for Political and Economic Studies' Committee on Policy for Racial Justice; Cecily Cannon Selby, Cochair of the National Science Board's Commission on Precollege Education and Mathematics, Science and Technology; Mari-Luci Jaramillo, Cochair of the Hispanic Policy Development Project; and Barbara Sizemore, Cochair on the National Alliance of Black School Educators' Task Force on Academic and Culture Excellence. Eleanor Farrar was Staff Coordinator for the report *Black Initiative and Government Responsibility*; Cheryl Hayes was Executive Director of the National Commission on Children; Shirley McBay directed the development of *Education That Works,* and Glenda Partee was the principal author for *Family Support, Education and Involvement*.

2. The only one of the thirty-five reports without women on the oversight group was *Three Realities: Minority Life in the United States,* sponsored by the Business–Higher Education forum in affiliation with the American Council of Education. See Appendix A for further information.

3. The four reports were: *A Common Destiny; Barriers to Excellence: Our Children at Risk; From Gatekeeper to Gateway: Transforming Testing in America; Turning Points: Preparing America's Youth for the 21st Century.*

4. National Coalition of Advocates for Students, *Barriers to Excellence: Our Children at Risk* (New York: National Board of Inquiry, 1985) 21.

5. National Coalition of Advocates for Students, 104.

6. R. Schmuck and P. Schmuck, *Small Schools, Big Problems* (Los Angeles, CA: Corwin Press, forthcoming, 1992).

7. National Governors Association, *National Educational Goals* (Washington, DC: 1990). See Appendix A for a list of the goals.

8. *America 2000: An Education Strategy* (Washington, DC: U.S. Department of Education, 1991) 1.

9. *Education for All: Women and Girls Speak Out on the National Education Goals* (Washington, DC: National Coalition for Women and Girls in Education, 1990); see also testimony submitted to the National Education Goals Panel by the National Coalition for Women and Girls in Education, May 1991.

10. See for example, D. Rock et al., *Study of Excellence in High School: Longitudinal Study* (Princeton, NJ: Educational Testing Service, 1986).

11. This survey of the current literature on girls' achievement is based on original research with a major exception. Results of a method called meta-analysis were used to explore gender differences in performance. Meta-analysis is the application of quantitative methods to combine evidence from different studies. In meta-analysis the effect size d is computed; d is the difference between the female mean score and the male mean score divided by the pooled within-group standard deviation. Because it looks at the relative size of gender differences, meta-analysis is considered a more valid way of summarizing the literature in a specific area than, for example, counting the studies that find gender differences and those that do not. When interpreting meta-analysis results, it is important to remember that effect sizes of .2 or less are considered small, while those close to .5 are considered of medium size, and effect sizes of .8 and higher are considered large.

12. E. Maccoby and C. Jacklin, *The Psychology of Sex Differences* (Stanford, CA: Stanford University Press, 1974) 84.

13. Maccoby and Jacklin; D. Denno, "Sex Differences in Cognition: A Review and Critique of the Longitudinal Evidence," *Adolescence* 17 (Winter 1982):779–88.

14. J. Hyde and M. Linn, "Gender Differences in Verbal Activity: A Meta-Analysis," *Psychological Bulletin* 104 (January 1988):53–69.

15. D. Halpern, "The Disappearance of Cognitive Gender Differences: What You See Depends on Where You Look," *American Psychologist* 44 (August 1989):1156–57.

16. Hyde and Linn, "Gender Differences" 63. *See* Appendix C for a more thorough discussion of this issue.

17. I. Mullis and L. Jenkins, *The Reading Report Card, 1971–88: Trends from the Nation's Report Card* (Princeton, NJ: Educational Testing Service, 1990); I. Mullis, E. Owens, and G. Phillips, *Accelerating Academic Achievement: A Summary of Findings from 20 Years of NAEP* (Washington, DC: U.S. Department of Education, 1990).

18. U.S. Department of Education, National Center for Education Statistics, *The Tested Achievement of the National Education Longitudinal Study of 1988 Eighth Grade Class,* December 1990.

19. M. Hogrebe, S. Nist, and I. Newman, "Are There Gender Differences in Reading Achievement? An Investigation Using the High School and Beyond Data," *Journal of Educational Psychology* 77 (1985):716–24; Rock et al., *Study of Excellence in High School Education: Longitudinal Study, 1980–82 Final Report* (Washington, DC: U.S. Department of Education Center for Statistics, 1986); L. Winfield and V.

Lee, "Gender Differences in Reading Proficiency: Are They Constant across Racial Groups?" presented at the Annual Meeting of the American Psychological Association, Washington, DC, August 26, 1986.

20. See Winfield and Lee, "Gender Differences in Reading Proficiency."

21. National Assessment of Education Progress, *Reading Comprehension of American Youth: Do They Understand What They Read?* (Princeton, NJ: Educational Testing Service, 1982).

22. Mullis, Owens, and Phillips, *Accelerating Academic Achievement.*

23. National Assessment of Educational Progress, *Reading Comprehension of American Youth.*

24. Hogrebe, Nist, and Newman, "Are There Gender Differences in Reading?" 721.

25. Hogrebe, Nist, and Newman; B. Hare, *Black Girls: A Comparative Analysis of Self-Perception and Achievement by Race, Sex, and Socioeconomic Background* (Baltimore, MD: The Johns Hopkins University Center for Social Organization of Schools, 1979).

26. Mullis, Owens, and Phillips, "Accelerating Academic Achievement" 52.

27. B. Arbrorough and R. Johnson, "Sex Differences in Written Language Among Elementary Pupils: A Seven Year Longitudinal Study," *Psychological Reports* 64 (1989):407–14.

28. A second caution concerns using the Scholastic Aptitude Test results as a measure of gender differences in math. While the sheer number of students taking the SAT makes it an attractive and frequently used basis of comparison, the gender differences that are found using the SAT are much larger than those found on comparable tests.

29. L. Friedman, "Mathematics and the Gender Cap: A Meta-Analysis of Recent Studies on Sex Differences in Mathematical Tasks," *Review of Educational Research* 59 (1989):185–213; J. Hyde, E. Fennema, and S. Lamon, "Gender Differences in Mathematics Performance: A Meta-Analysis," *Psychological Bulletin* 107 (1990): 139–55.

30. G. Wilder and K. Powell, *Sex Differences in Test Performance: A Survey of the Literature,* College Board Report 8903, ETS RR 89-4, (New York: College Board Publications, [1989]); A. Kolstad and J. Thorne, "Changes in High School Course Work from 1982 to 1987: Evidence from Two National Surveys," paper presented at the annual meeting of the American Educational Research Association, San Francisco, March 1989.

31. Hyde, Fennema, and Lamon, "Gender Differences."

32. Hyde, Fennema, and Lamon, "Gender Differences."

33. J. Dossey et al., *The Mathematic Report Card,* 17-M-01 (Princeton, NJ: Educational Testing Service, 1988), 54–55; *Women and Minorities in Science and Engineering* (Washington, DC: National Science Foundation, 1990) 14.

34. I. Mullis et al., *The State of Mathematics Achievement: NAEP's 1990 Assessment of the Nation and the Trial Assessment of the States* (Princeton, NJ: Educational Testing Service, 1991) 15.

35. Dossey et al., *The Mathematics Report Card* 54–55; "The Gender Gap in Education: How Early and How Large," *Educational Testing Service Policy Notes* 2 (October 1989).

36. *1988 Profiles of SAT and Achievement Test Takers* (Princeton, NJ: Educational Testing Service, 1988); *Women and Minorities.*

37. J. Stockard and J. Wood, "The Myth of Female Underachievement: A Reexamination of Sex Differences in Academic Underachievement," *American Education Research Journal* 21 (1984):825–38; T. Dick and S. Rallis, "Factors and Influences on High School Students' Career Choices," *Journal of Research in Math Teaching* (forthcoming).
38. *Women and Minorities* 15.
39. Friedman, "Mathematics and the Gender Gap."
40. P. Brandon, B. Newton, and O. Hammond, "Children's Mathematics Achievement in Hawaii: Sex Differences Favoring Girls," *American Educational Research Journal* 24 (1987):25–36.
41. Friedman, "Mathematics and the Gender Gap"; Hyde, Fennema, and Lamon, "Gender Differences"; E. Moore and A. Smith, "Sex and Ethnic Groups Differences in Mathematics Achievement: Results from the National Longitudinal Study," *Journal for Research in Mathematics Education* 18 (1987):25–36.
42. M. Linn and J. Hyde, "Gender, Mathematics and Science," *Educational Researcher* 18 (November 1989):17–27.
43. A. Lapointe, N. Mead, and G. Phillips, *World of Difference: An International Assessment of Mathematics and Science* (Princeton, NJ: Educational Testing Service, 1989).
44. Mullis et al., *The State of Mathematics Achievement* 6.
45. I. Mullis and L. Jenkins, *The Science Report Card,* report No. 17-S-01 (Princeton, NJ: Educational Testing Service, [1988]) 30–31; Lapointe, Mead, and Phillips, *World of Difference.*
46. Mullis and Jenkins, *The Science Report Card* 107–13; *Women and Minorities* 14.
47. Mullis and Jenkins, *The Science Report Card.*
48. Stockard and Wood, "The Myth"; S. Rallis and R. Ahern. "Math and Science Education in High Schools: A Question of Sex Equity," paper presented at the annual meeting of the American Educational Research Association, San Francisco (April 1986); Dick and Rallis, "Factors and Influences."
49. Lapointe, Mead, and Phillips, *World of Difference.*
50. National Science Board, *Science and Engineering Indicators—1989* (Washington, DC: National Science Foundation, 1990).
51. Mullis et al., *The State of Mathematics Achievement* 32.
52. R. Blank and M. Dalkilis, *State Indicators of Science and Mathematics Education, 1990* (Washington, DC: Council of Chief State Officers, State Education Assessment Center 1991).
53. National Science Board, *Indicators—1989.*
54. Kolstad and Thorne, "Changes in High School Course Work."
55. National Science Board, *Indicators—1989; Women and Minorities* 15.
56. National Science Board, *Indicators—1989.*
57. Blank and Dalkilis, *State Indicators of Science and Mathematics Education, 1990.*
58. Mullis et al., *Women and Minorities* 30.
59. Dick and Rallis, "Factors and Influences."
60. N. Hewitt and E. Seymour, "Factors Contributing to High Attrition Rates Among Science and Engineering Undergraduate Majors," report to the Alfred P. Sloan Foundation (April 26, 1991) 100.
61. P. Campbell and S. Metz, "What Does It Take to Increase the Number of Women

Majoring in Engineering?" conference proceedings of the American Society for Engineering Education (1987) 882–87.

62. J. Kahle and M. Lakes, "The Myth of Equality in Science Classrooms," *Journal of Research in Science Teaching* 20 (1983): 131–40.

63. Mullis and Jenkins, *The Science Report Card* 30–33.

64. L. Zimmer and S. Bennett, "Gender Differences on the California Statewide Assessment of Attitudes and Achievement in Science," paper presented at the annual meeting of the American Educational Research Association, Washington, DC, 1987. Unlike Mullis and Jenkins, authors of *The Science Report Card,* Zimmer and Bennett found girls using microscopes in numbers equal to boys.

65. Zimmer and Bennett.

66. L. Reyes and G. Stanic, "Race, Sex and Math," *Journal of Research in Math Education* 19 (1988):26–43.

67. E. Fennema and J. Sherman, "Sex-Related Differences in Math Achievement, Spatial Visualization and Affective Factors," *American Educational Research Journal* 14 (1977):51–71; L. Reyes, "Affective Variables and Mathematics Education," *The Elementary School Journal* 84 (1984):558–81.

68. Reyes, "Affective Variables."

69. Dossey et al., *The Mathematics Report Card,* 17-M-01 (Princeton, NJ: Educational Testing Service, 1988).

70. Fennema and Sherman, "Sex-Related Differences."

71. A. Kelly, "Does That Train Set Matter? Scientific Hobbies and Science Achievement and Choice," paper presented at the Girls and Technology Conference, Ann Arbor, July 1987; J. Eccles, "Bringing Young Women to Math and Science," in *Gender and Thought: Psychological Perspectives,* M. Crawford and M. Gentry, eds., (New York: Springer-Verlag, 1989) 36–58.

72. C. Leder, "Teacher Student Interactions in the Mathematics Classroom: A Different Perspective," in *Mathematics and Gender: Influences on Teachers and Students,* E. Fennema and C. Leder, eds. (New York: Teachers College, 1990) 149–68.

73. American Association of University Women, *Shortchanging Girls, Shortchanging America* (Washington, DC: American Association of University Women, 1990) 13.

74. Campbell and Metz, "The Number of Women Majoring in Engineering" 882–87.

75. P. MacCorquodale, "Self-Image Science and Math: Does the Image of 'Scientist' Keep Girls and Minorities from Pursuing Science and Math," paper presented at the American Sociological Association, San Antonio, 1984.

76. American Association of University Women, *Shortchanging Girls* 14.

77. *Shortchanging Girls.*

78. J. Armstrong, "A National Assessment of Participation and Achievement of Women in Mathematics," in *Women and Mathematics: Balancing the Equation,* C. Chipman, L. Brush, and D. Wilson, eds., (Hillsdale, NJ: Erlbaum, 1985) 56–94.

79. J. Armstrong.

80. J. Armstrong.

81. Hyde, Fennema, and Lamon, "Gender Differences."

82. L. Tartre and E. Fennema, "Mathematics Achievement and Gender: A Longitudinal Study of Selected Cognitive and Affective Factors (Grades 6–12)," paper

presented at the annual meeting of the American Educational Research Association, Chicago, April 1991.

83. J. Oakes, *Lost Talent: The Underparticipation of Women, Minorities and Disabled Persons in Science* (Santa Monica, CA: RAND Institute, 1990).

84. P. Flores, "How Dick and Jane Perform Differently in Geometry: Test Results on Reasoning, Visualization, Transformation, Applications and Coordinates," paper presented at the annual meeting of the American Educational Research Association, Boston, 1990.

85. J. Kahle, "Why Girls Don't Know," in *What Research Says to the Science Teacher: The Process of Knowing*, vol. 6, M. Rowe, ed., (Washington, DC: National Science Teachers' Association, 1990); P. Campbell, *Eureka! Participant Follow Up Analysis* (Groton, MA: Campbell-Kibler Associates, 1990).

86. Valerie Lee, "Is Single-Sex Secondary a Solution to the Problem of Gender Inequity?" in *Separated by Sex: A Critical Look at Single Sex-Education* (Washington, DC: American Association of Women Educational Foundation, Mary 1998): 42.

87. Rolf Blank and Doreen Gruebel, *State Indicators of Science and Mathematics Education: State by State Trends and New Indicators from the 1993 1994 School Year* (Washington, DC: Council of Chief State School Officers, 1995; U.S. Department of Education, Office of Educational Research and Improvement, National Center for Education Statistics, *Vocational Course Taking and Achievement: An Analysis of High School Transcripts and 1990 NAEP Assessment Scores* (Washington, DC, 1995).

88. Throughout this report, statistical significance is reported either when such tests were noted in the material reviewed for this report or when the appropriate information was provided allowing calculation of such tests. Several test procedures were used depending upon the nature of the data. Significance levels of .10, .05, and .01 are noted on the tables. A finding that is statistically significant at the .05 level, for example, means that there is less than five percent chance that the differences can be attributed to random variation.

89. Michael Kane and Sol Pelavin, *Changing the Odds: Factors Increasing Access to College* (New York: The College Board, 1990).

90. Attention to and concern for the underrepresentation of women in mathematics and science fields has resulted in numerous gender equity initiatives focusing on these two curriculum areas (for example, the National Science Foundation's Program for Women and Girls, the Women's Educational Equity Clearinghouse within the U.S. Department of Education; the Collaboration for Equity Among the American Association for the Advancement of Science; Girls, Inc; Educational Development Center, Inc.; and Campbell-Kibler Associates, Inc.).

91. "Females Taking More Math Courses Than Males," http://www.act.org, April 23, 1998.

92. Ruth K. Blank et al., *Mathematics and Science Content Standards and Curriculum Frameworks: State Progress on Development and Implementation* (Washington, DC: Council of Chief State School Officers, 1997).

93. Patricia B. Campbell and Karen Steinbrueck, *Striving for Gender Equity: National Programs to Increase Student Engagement with Math and Science* (Washington, DC: Collaboration for Equity, Fairness in Science and Mathematics Education, 1996); Cinda-Sue Davis et al., *The Equity Equation: Fostering the Advancement*

of Women in the Sciences, Mathematics, and Engineering (San Francisco: Jossey-Bass, 1996); Sue V. Rosser, *Re-Engineering Female Friendly Science* (New York: Teachers College Press, 1997).

94. Sue V. Rosser, *Female-Friendly Science* (Elmsford, NY: Pergamon P, 1990); Sue V. Rosser, *Re-Engineering Female Friendly Science* (New York: Teachers College P, 1997).

95. James Collins, "How Johnny Should Read," *Time* 150, no. 17 (October 27, 1997).

96. Arthur Halbrook and Katherine Woodward, *National and State Content Standards in English Language Arts* (Washington, DC: GED Testing Service, American Council on Education): 3.

97. With the exception of English composition in 1990, these differences are not statistically significant. We report these findings, however, because of the consistent direction of the differences and the importance of discussing and monitoring boys' participation in the English/language arts curriculum.

98. Nancy Cole and Warren W. Willingham, *Gender and Fair Assessment*, (Princeton: Educational Testing Service, Mahwah, NJ: Lawrence Erlbaum Associates, 1997): 122.

99. Elizabeth Hayes and Jennifer Hopkins, "Gender Literacy Learning: Implications for Research in Adult Literacy Education," paper presented at the annual meeting of the American Educational Research Association (New York: April 1995) 15.

100. Elaine Millard, "Differently Literate: Gender Identity and the Construction of the Developing Reader," *Gender and Education* 9, no. 1 (March 1997): 31–48.

101. Kathleen Gormley et al., "Gender Differences in Classroom Writing: An Analysis of Sixth Grade Students' Reader Response Entries," *ERIC Digests ED353578* (Washington, DC: ERIC Clearinghouse, 1992).

102. Rebecca Cummings, "11th Graders View Gender Differences in Reading and Math," *Journal of Reading* 38, no. 3 (November 1994): 196–99.

103. Eileen McKenna, "Gender Differences in Reading Attitudes," master's thesis, Kean College of New Jersey, May 1997.

104. *Women, Minorities, and Persons with Disabilities in Science and Engineering: 1996* (Washington, DC: National Science Foundation, 1996).

105. Elaine Woo, "Classroom Renaissance," *LA Times*, February 4, 1997.

106. Although not statistically significant, we note these findings because we believe the apparent widening gap between males and females deserves monitoring.

107. Linda K. Bunker et al., *The President's Council on Physical Fitness and Sports Report: Physical Activity and Sports in the Lives of Girls* (Washington, DC: President's Council on Physical Fitness and Sports, 1997).

108. U.S. Department of Education, Office of Educational Research and Improvement, National Center for Education Statistics, *Digest of Educational Statistics 1997* (Washington, DC, 1997).

109. Jeannie Oakes, "Can Tracking Inform Practice? Technical, Normative, and Political Considerations," *Educational Researcher* 21, no. 4 (1992a): 12–21; Jeannie Oakes, "Detracking Schools: Early Lessons from the Field," *Phi Delta Kappan* 73, no. 4 (1992b): 448–54; Relsa N. Page, *Lower Track Classrooms: A Curricular Perspective* (New York: Teachers College P. 1991).

110. Maureen T. Hallinan, "School Differences in Tracking Effects on Achievement," *Social Forces* 72, no. 3 (March 1994): 799–820.

111. Jomills Henry Braddock II and Robert E. Slavin, "Why Ability Grouping Must End: Achieving Excellence and Equity in American Education," *Beyond Tracking: Finding Success in Inclusive Schools,* eds., H. Pool and J. A. Page (Bloomington: Phi Delta Kappa Educational Foundation, 1995): 7–20.

112. M. L. Wehmeyer and M. Schwartz, "Disproportionate Representation of Males in Special Education Services: Biology, Behavior, or Bias," Gender Equity in Special Education, unpublished; M. Wagner, "Being Female—A Secondary Disability? Gender Differences in the Transition Experiences of Young People with Disabilities," prepared for presentation to the Special Education Special Interest Group of the American Education Research Association annual meeting, San Francisco, 1992; Wagner et al., "Youth with Disabilities: How Are They Doing? The First Comprehensive Report from the National Longitudinal Transition Study of Special Education Students," prepared for the Office of Special Education Programs and the U.S. Department of Education, SRI International, 1991; D. L. Caseau et al., "Special Education Services for Girls with Serious Emotional Disturbance: A Case of Gender Bias?," *Behavorial Disorders* 20, no. 1 (1994): 51–60.

113. Sally M. Reis and Carolyn M. Callahan, "My Boyfriend, My Girlfriend, or Me: The Dilemma of Talented Teenaged Girls," *The Journal of Secondary Gifted Education* 7, no. 4 (1996): 434–46.

114. Nancy Kreinberg and Ellen Wahl, eds. *Thoughts and Deeds: Equity in Mathematics and Science Education* (Washington, DC: American Association for the Advancement of Science, Collaboration for Equity, 1997); Jane B. Kahle, "Opportunities and Obstacles: Science Education in the Schools," in Cinda-Sue Davis et al., *The Equity Equation: Fostering the Advancement of Women in the Sciences, Mathematics, and Engineering* (San Francisco: Jossey-Bass, 1996): 57–95.

115. Peter M. Hall, ed. *Race, Ethnicity, and Multiculturalism: Policy and Practice,* Missouri Symposium on Research in Educational Policy, vol. 1 (New York: Garland Publishing, 1997); Barbara J. Bank and Peter M. Hall, eds., *Gender, Equity and Schooling: Policy and Practice,* Missouri Symposium on Research in Educational Policy, vol. 2 (New York: Garland Publishing, Inc., 1997).

116. Susan L. Dauber et al, "Tracking and Transition through the Middle Grades: Channeling Educational Trajectories," *Sociology of Education* 69, no. 4 (October 1996): 290–307.

117. Gail Crombie et al, "Gifted Programs: Gender Differences in Referral and Enrollment," *Gifted Child Quarterly* 36, no. 4 (1992): 212–213; Carolyn Reeves, "Read, Achievement, and Career Choices: Comparisons of Males and Females, Gender Distribution in Program for the Gifted," *Roeper Review* 13, no. 4 (1991), *Digest of Education Statistics* 1997.

118. Pat O'Connell Ross, *National Excellence: A Case for Developing America's Talent* (Washington DC: U.S. Department of Education, Office of Educational Research and Improvement, National Center for Educational Statistics, October 1993); Thomas J. Ward et al., "Examination of a New Protocol for the Identification of At-Risk Gifted Learners," paper presented at the annual meeting of the American Educational Research Association, San Francisco, April 1992.

119. Ross, *National Excellence.*

120. Carolyn Reeves Read, "Achievement, and Career Choices: Comparisons of Males and Females, Gender Distribution in Program for the Gifted," *Roper Review* 13, no. 4 (1991).

121. Read, "Achievement, and Career Choices."
122. Sally M. Reis and M. Katherine Gavin, *Why Jane Doesn't Think She Can Do Math: How Teachers Can Encourage Talented Girls in Mathematics* (Reston, VA: National Council of Teachers of Mathematics, in press).
123. Donna Siegel and Sally M. Reis, "Gender Differences in Teacher and Student Perceptions of Student Ability and Effort," *The Journal of Secondary Gifted Education* (Winter 1994/1995): 86–92.
124. Ross, *National Excellence.*
125. Signithia Fordham, "Those Loud Black Girls: (Black) Women, Silence, and Gender Passing in the Academy," *Anthropology and Education Quarterly* 24, no. 1 (1993): 3–32. Signithia Fordham, *Blacked Out: Dilemmas of Race, Identity, and Success at Capital High* (Chicago: The University of Chicago Press, 1996).
126. Fordham, "Those Loud Black Girls."
127. Research for Action, Inc., Jody Cohen and Sukey Blanc et al., *Girls in the Middle: Working to Succeed in School* (Washington, DC: American Association of University Women Educational Foundation, 1996).
128. Virginia B. Edwards et al., "The Urban Challenge," *Education Week* 17, no. 17 (January 8, 1998): 6.
129. Cole and Willingham, *Gender and Fair Assessment.*

QUESTIONS FOR REACTION AND DISCUSSION

1. How do the writers of these reports characterize the "absence of girls" in the debate on education? What facts and statistics do they use to support their claims? Are these convincing? Why or why not?
2. What is Title IX of the Education Amendments of 1972? What does it mean to say that federal enforcement of Title IX is "complaint driven"? What direct experience have you or your classmates had with the implications of Title IX?
3. To what do the writers of *How Schools Shortchange Girls* attribute the narrowing of the gender gaps in verbal and mathematical achievement?
4. Discuss the graph of "Career Plans of Students Taking the SAT." To what do the writers of the report attribute the large difference between males and females planning to major in engineering?
5. What is "math confidence" and why is this important to the writers of the report?
6. What roles can teachers and out-of-school programs play in increasing performance in math and science for girls?
7. What is educational equity and what issues do these reports raise?
8. How do the course-taking patterns of 1998 differ from the patterns of 1992? Where is the most significant difference—for girls and boys?

QUESTIONS FOR WRITING

1. Think carefully about your own educational experiences to this point—teachers, classes, counselors, test scores, extracurricular activities, and fellow students. In what ways do you think you have been encouraged or discouraged based strictly on your gender? Write an essay in which you describe how you have or have not been "short-changed," regardless of whether you are male or female.

2. The writers of the AAUW report place a great deal of emphasis on how teachers can make a significant difference to girls in a classroom. What can teachers do to encourage girls? What do the writers of the report suggest? Think of some examples from your own experience (or those of friends) and write an essay in which you explain how teachers can better facilitate the learning of girls.

3. The writers of both reports mention several standardized tests the children take on a regular basis in school. The National Assessment of Educational Progress (NAEP) is a test that assesses the academic performance of fourth, eighth, and twelfth graders in a range of subjects. Access the Web site for NAEP <http://nces.ed.gov/nationsreportcard/ site/home.asp> and investigate the nature of the tests. What can you learn from the Web site? What current reports are available? Is it still true that boys generally perform better on the tests as twelfth graders than girls do? In what areas are girls and boys excelling today? Write an essay in which you discuss the nature of the NAEP and comment on how the writers of the AAUW report use the findings of this test.

4. Interview several of your female classmates about their experiences in school. Ask them about their degree of "math confidence," their experiences in classrooms, and the degree of encouragement to do well in school that they received from fellow students and teachers. What similarities and differences do you find? What conclusions can you draw from your informal interviews? Write an essay in which you describe the experiences of this small group and explain what you learned about the experience of girls in schools.

5. What do we learn from these reports about the different experiences of girls and boys in math, computer, and science education? What gains have been made? What losses? How would you rate your own secondary school in these areas? What was your own experience—as a girl or a boy? Write an essay in which you summarize the reports and analyze the specific claims that the research reports make about the research. Conclude your essay with a recommendation to your secondary school about what they might need to know and do to improve math, computer, and science education.

6. One solution to equal treatment of girls and boys in schools is the establishment of single-sex schools. The AAUW has sponsored additional reports on these experiences, and there is a large body of information and research about the effects of same-sex schooling on children. Work with a group of your classmates to research the advantages and disadvantages of such schools. Prepare a committee report of your findings.

QUESTIONS FOR FURTHER EXPLORATION

1. The authors of the AAUW studies mention that their reports are in part a response to a major national report, *A Nation at Risk: The Imperative for Educational Reform,* undertaken by the National Commission on Excellence in Education and sponsored by the Department of Education in 1983. The first sentence of the report has become a famous statement: "Our nation is at risk." The report clearly outlined specific reasons for the declining state of the educational system in the United States and identified a number of problem areas. As a result of their assessment of the state of national education, the writers prepared recommendations that have had a significant impact on education ever since. Read this report (as a government document, copies are widely available in college and public libraries), and consider the reaction of the AAUW. In what ways are girls left out of the report? In a short essay, write a brief analysis of how the gender of students is addressed (or not addressed) in this report.

2. Access the American Association of University Women Web site <http://www.aauw.org> and study the programs they sponsor. What are their current research programs? What are the issues they plan to study in the future? What kinds of fellowships, grants, and awards does the organization sponsor? Write a report on the activities of the AAUW and e-mail it to your class.

3. Investigate the history of Title IX and its enforcement. What are some of the major changes that have come about because of this amendment? Choose one or two of interest to you and write a brief report for your class.

4. Access the National Center for Education Statistics Web site <http://nces.ed.gov> and investigate the current "Digest of Education Statistics." What can you learn there about the nature of American education today? Participate in an online discussion about an education topic of interest to you. Write a brief report for your classmates on what kind of information you can learn from this site.

5. The AAUW reports have attracted a great deal of attention in the popular press. Search the *Reader's Guide to Periodical Literature* for articles that review or describe either *How Schools Shortchange Girls* or *Gender Gaps: Where Schools Still Fail Our Children*. How would you describe the coverage of the AAUW reports? Write an annotated bibliography of the coverage for your classmates, carefully documenting the articles you find so that they may look them up easily.

6. An extensive and highly publicized study about undergraduate science education was published in 1997: *Talking about Leaving: Why Undergraduates Leave the Sciences* by Elaine Seymour and Nancy M. Hewitt. Locate a copy of this book and read some of the findings of Seymour and Hewitt. What do they have to say about the experiences of men and women undergraduates? How are they different from the experiences of secondary school girls and boys? Write a report of your reading for your classmates.

4

STUDENT PERFORMANCE: MALES VERSUS FEMALES

The AAUW Research Reports, How Schools Shortchange Girls *and* Gender Gaps: Where Schools Still Fail Our Children, *have prompted a considerable amount of public debate about the extent to which these reports accurately assess the state of public education for girls and boys. At times the debate has been shrill and heated; there are those who defend the reports, calling the critics conservative and reactionary, while some of those who question the findings and the conclusions often tend to view the authors of the reports as radicals. Name-calling and overblown rhetoric aside, the debate provides a good opportunity to study how research reports are sometimes used and discussed in the United States. Among the most articulate of the critics of the AAUW has been Judith Kleinfeld, a professor of psychology at the University of Alaska, Fairbanks. Kleinfeld, the director of the Northern Studies program at her institution, has written two books on fetal alcohol syndrome, as well as studies of the effects of sparsely populated areas on women. She also writes a syndicated column for major Alaskan newspapers on current research in psychology and education. At the suggestion of the Women's Freedom Network, which was founded in 1993, Kleinfeld embarked on her own analysis of the research reported by the AAUW and wrote a position paper, "The Myth That Schools Shortchange Girls: Social Science in the Service of Deception." A version of this analysis, and the one that is reprinted here, was later published in a journal devoted mainly to conservative interests,* The Public Interest. *Charging that the AAUW reports erroneously depict girls as victims in the schools, Kleinfeld's provocative commentary has ensured that a national debate on the question of gender equity continues.*

QUESTIONS FOR READING

1. What is your expectation about the subject of this article based on your reading of the title?

2. Based on your own educational experiences, do you think girls are generally well served by public schools? Why or why not?

JUDITH KLEINFELD

STUDENT PERFORMANCE: MALES VERSUS FEMALES

The Public Interest 134 (1999, pp 3–20)

Women's advocacy groups have waged an intense media campaign to promote the idea that "schools shortchange girls." Their goal has been to convince the public that women are "victims" of an unfair educational system and that they deserve special treatment, extra funding, and heightened policy attention. Their sophisticated public-relations campaign has succeeded. The idea that girls are shortchanged by schools has become the common wisdom—what people take for granted, without a thought concerning whether or not it is true.

This idea that girls are not well served by our schools—that gender differences in performance result from institutional unfairness—received its greatest boost from a highly publicized report, *How Schools Shortchange Girls: A Study of Major Findings on Girls and Education.* Published in 1992 by the respected organization, the American Association of University Women (AAUW), along with a survey of self-esteem and aspirations among boys and girls, the AAUW report quickly became the basis for countless newspaper articles, magazine features, books, and university courses on gender and education. While a few voices challenged the report's findings—notably Christina Hoff Sommers, in *Who Stole Feminism?*—the mainstream media for the most part ignored dissenting views.

The AAUW report makes three principal claims: First, girls fall behind boys in science and mathematics; second, girls participate less than boys in class or, as it is said, are "silenced" in the classroom; and third, girls suffer a major decline in self-esteem at adolescence while adolescent boys gain in self-esteem. As the AAUW Executive Summary declares:

> The educational system is not meeting girls' needs. Girls and boys enter school roughly equal in measured ability. Twelve years later, girls have fallen behind their male classmates in key areas such as higher-level mathematics and measures of self-esteem.

And, in the 1998 study *Gender Gaps: Where Schools Still Fail Our Children,* the AAUW claimed that a gender gap was opening up in the field of computer science. "The failure to include girls in advanced-level computer science courses threatens to make women bystanders in the technological twenty-first century." Again, the accusation received great attention while dissenting opinions were ignored.

Certainly, the AAUW has done women and the nation a service in drawing attention to the gender gap in science and mathematics and in encouraging an array of policies and programs designed to boost female performance in these fields. But most of the other findings of the AAUW are either misleading or false, and even its findings on the math and science gap need to be put into perspective. Indeed, the fact is that policy makers should be as concerned about the educational progress of boys as girls. For it is boys, not girls, who lag behind in verbal skills, who are falling behind in college attendance, and who believe that schools are hostile to them. As the eminent researcher Jere Brophy reminds us, in a chapter written for the classic study *Gender Influences in Classroom Interaction,* neither boys nor girls have a lock on school success (or failure):

> Claims that one sex or the other is not being taught effectively in our schools have been frequent and often impassioned. From early in the century, criticism was usually focused on the treatment of boys, especially at the elementary level. Critics noted that boys received lower grades in all subjects and lower achievement test scores in reading and language arts. They insisted that these sex differences occurred because the schools were "too feminine" or the "overwhelmingly female" teachers were unable to meet boys' learning needs effectively.

Not so long ago, it was boys who were viewed as victims of the school system; today, it is the girls. The remedy proposed then was to encourage adult males to go into elementary school teaching; the remedy proposed today is a plethora of special policies and programs designed to help girls succeed. But the truth is, then as now, that males and females bring different developmental patterns, strengths, weaknesses, and interests to school, not that schools engage in institutional discrimination requiring national policy attention.

WHO MAKES THE GRADES?

If schools were shortchanging females, such gender discrimination should be easy to spot. Schools give clear and measurable rewards: grades, class rank, and academic honors and prizes. And these rewards are not inconsequential. They help determine who gains admission to selective colleges and graduate schools and who lands the best jobs. Which group—males or females—receives a disproportionate share of the school's institutional rewards? The answer is undisputed: females.

From grade school through graduate school, females receive higher grades, even in mathematics and the sciences. They also receive more academic honors in every field except science and mathematics. The female advantage in grades appears in virtually every study. In their essay, "Grades, Accomplishments, and Correlates," which was published in *Gender and Fair Assessment,* Carol Dwyer and Linda Johnson put the matter clearly:

Data from a wide variety of sources and educational settings show that females in all ethnic groups tend to earn higher grades in school than do males, across different ages and eras, and across different subject matter disciplines. Many researchers in past times and today consider this to be such an obvious fact that they treat it as axiomatic . . . Modern reviews of the subject are unanimous in their finding of higher grades for females.

In a nationally representative longitudinal study of the high-school class of 1992, discussed by Dwyer and Johnson, it was found that high-school girls outdistanced boys in making the honor roll, in getting elected to a class office, and in receiving writing awards and other academic honors. In the academic arena, boys outdistanced girls only in awards in science and mathematics competitions.

More recently, a 1998 report sponsored by the Horatio Alger Association came up with the same female grade advantage—this time a gap far larger than reported in earlier studies. In a survey of 1,195 randomly selected high-school students, one-third of the girls said that they had gotten "mostly As on their last report card" compared to less than one-fifth of the boys. The students in the Horatio Alger study were divided into three groups: "Successful Students," who were doing well in school, "Strivers," who were working hard, and "Alienated Students," who were bitter and disillusioned. Of the successful students, two-thirds were girls; of the strivers, fifty-five percent were girls; of the alienated, seventy percent were boys.

Mathematics and science honors are the single area of male advantage, but females are catching up. Take performance on the Westinghouse Science Talent Search, a contest notable for producing winners who later receive the Nobel Prize. Westinghouse finalists used to be overwhelmingly male. From 1950 through 1959, for example, only twenty-two percent of the top forty finalists were female. In the late 1990s, in contrast, close to forty percent of the top forty finalists were female; in 1997, the proportion of female finalists was forty-five percent.

TESTING MALES AND FEMALES

Even though girls surpass boys in school grades, that does not necessarily mean they are learning more. Grades, after all, depend not only on how much students know but also on conformity to institutional demands, such as whether students follow the teacher's directions and turn in assignments on time. Scores on standardized tests provide a measure of school achievement less influenced by such subjective matters.

The research on gender differences in achievement test scores is complex and voluminous. But the Educational Testing Service recently consolidated numerous studies of nationally representative samples of twelfth graders on a variety of standardized tests, including the National Assessment of Educational

Progress and the Preliminary Scholastic Aptitude Test. The final report, *Gender and Fair Assessment,* published by Lawrence Erlbaum in 1997, shows a clear pattern. Neither males nor females emerge as victors or victims; each group has its own distinctive strengths and weaknesses.

In a nutshell: On standardized achievement tests of basic school skills, females surpass males in writing ability and reading achievement while males surpass females in science and mathematics. Generally, these gender differences are small. The one exception is the significant female advantage in writing skills. *Indeed, the female advantage on standardized tests of reading and writing achievement substantially outstrips the male advantage on standardized tests of science and mathematics.*

As for the male advantage in mathematics and science, it is shrinking. The National Assessment of Educational Progress has measured the knowledge of nine-, thirteen-, and seventeen-year-olds in mathematics and science for over twenty years. In mathematics, the gender gap among seventeen-year-olds has declined significantly since the 1970s and no longer reaches statistical significance. In science, the gender gap has also declined.

BELL CURVES

In the general population then the mathematics and science gap is small. Another way of measuring gender inequality, however, is to see whether males or females dominate the top of each field. Are the conspicuous achievers, who for better or worse contribute most to our images of success mostly male or female? Among students who take the Scholastic Assessment Test (SAT) and Advanced Placement (AP) Tests in mathematics and science, men do score substantially higher than women, especially in such areas as physics. Why?

The fundamental reason has less to do with bias than with a peculiarity of males as a group. On many human characteristics, not just math and physics, males display greater variability than females. This fact is well known to researchers, and it goes a long way toward explaining what many in the public find disturbing, the greater number of males who end up at the top in most fields.

Bell-shaped curves with the identical averages can take different forms— high and peaked (low variability) or broad and spreading (high variability). The greater variability of males means that males more often appear in the far right-hand tail of the curve, among the top talent. This occurs even when male and female averages in the general population are the same. (Where males score higher on the average, as they do in science and mathematics, the male advantage in the far right-hand tail becomes even more extreme.) The practical result is that, in fields with small numbers of people, such as physics, few women will appear in the far right-hand tail, with the Albert Einsteins, Richard Feynmans, or Stephen Hawkings. This is unfortunate for women. But, as we shall see, this pattern has an unfortunate result for men as well. The greater

Illustration: Bell-shaped curves with the same averages but different variability

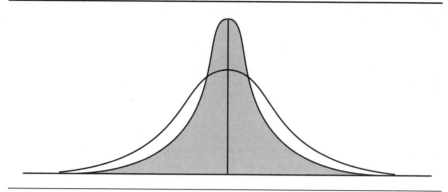

variability of males means that more males also end up at the extreme left of the normal curve—the failures.

DO SCHOOLS SHORTCHANGE BOYS?

In virtually every category of educational, emotional, behavioral, and neurological impairment, males are overrepresented. Reviewing the literature on this phenomenon, Diane Halpern points out, in "Sex Differences in Intelligence," published in the *American Psychologist,* that "males are overrepresented at the low-ability end of many distributions; including the following examples: mental retardation (some types), majority of attention deficit disorders, delayed speech, dyslexia (even allowing for possible referral bias), stuttering, and learning disabilities, and emotional disturbances." Even the AAUW report acknowledges that "boys outnumber girls in special educational programs by startling percentages." According to the National Center for Education Statistics, more than double the number of males compared to females are enrolled in special-education programs.

The AAUW report predictably attributes such gender differences to school discrimination: Teachers are biased against badly behaved boys. The mislabeling of active boys may be part of the explanation. It may be true that too many boys are prescribed drugs like Ritalin to make them easier to control in class. But biology is also part of the explanation.

Gender differences appear long before children enter school and even before birth. As the physician Ruth Nass points out, in "Sex Differences in Learning Abilities and Disabilities," published in *Annals of Dyslexia*, obstetrical complications such as toxemia are more common with male fetuses (1.7:1) as is abruptio (2:1), spontaneous abortion (1.4:1), and birth trauma (1.8:1). Dyslexia, a reading and language disorder that has enormous impact on school success, and autism are both four times more common among males. Males are more apt to display virtually every neuro-developmental and psychiatric disorder of childhood.

The point is this: Just as the greater number of males at the top in science and mathematics does not necessarily mean that the schools are shortchanging girls, so too the greater number of males at the bottom in special-education classes does not necessarily mean that the schools are shortchanging boys. The fact is that males are more variable than females on many neurological dimensions.

While schools may not cause such gender differences, they may still have a significant role to play in ensuring that both sexes have the opportunity to develop a broad range of intellectual skills. Schools need to be attentive to the problems of males and females. Teachers should make sure that boys in the early grades, who may lag developmentally in reading skills, are not stigmatized as "slow learners" and assigned to classes where they receive lower-quality instruction. Teachers should also avoid labeling unruly boys as suffering from "attention deficit disorder" and prescribing drugs that depress their nervous systems and ability to learn. By the same token, girls should be encouraged to take mathematics and science courses and to participate in these classes more.

Mathematics and science education for girls has indeed improved. The National Science Foundation and other government agencies, private foundations, and universities have developed and funded an array of gender-equity programs designed to encourage young women in mathematics and the sciences. The Program for Women and Girls at the National Science Foundation alone has an annual budget of nine million dollars a year for such efforts. No comparable programs have targeted boys' academic deficiencies in, for example, reading and writing. And no program has been created to boost college attendance among males.

The policy that does the most to boost female achievement in math and science was, in fact, not designed specifically for girls. That policy is stricter requirements for high-school graduation. In the 1980s, high-school girls were far less likely than boys to take science and mathematics classes. According to the National Center for Educational Statistics, this particular gender gap has closed. Female high-school students now take as many mathematics and science classes as males do. The exception is physics: In 1994, twenty-seven percent of males compared to twenty-two percent of females took a course in physics. But females surpassed males in taking courses in chemistry, algebra, geometry, precalculus, and biology. In trigonometry and calculus, the percentage of males and females are the same.

Increasing numbers of females are also enrolling in Advanced Placement (AP) courses in mathematics and science. We see again the familiar pattern of gender strengths and weaknesses. A greater proportion of the total number of students who take demanding AP examinations are female. More females take AP English and language tests while more males take AP mathematics and science tests. But since the proportion of females taking AP mathematics and science tests is increasing, we are also seeing an increase in the total number of talented, high-achieving women in mathematics and science.

HIGHER SEX-ED

Ignored by the AAUW is another gender gap—a very serious one in college attendance and graduation. But this gender gap favors females. And the biggest losers are African-American males. In 1995, women were the majority of college students (fifty-five percent), and women now earn the majority of both bachelor's and master's degrees. African-American college women (sixty-two percent) vastly outnumber African-American college males. In some colleges, as *The Chronicle of Higher Education* has reported, the gender imbalance in favor of females has become such a serious problem that administrators have quietly developed affirmative-action programs for males admitting them with lower grades and test scores.

Since the 1960s, women have made stunning progress in gaining professional and doctoral degrees too. In 1994, women attained over forty percent of all professional degrees, up from almost none in 1961. Minority women made especially large gains, with African-American women receiving fifty-seven percent of the professional degrees awarded to African-Americans.

The professional field that most attracts women is law, an occupation that tends to reward strong verbal skills. In law, the gender gap is decreasing rapidly: In 1994, forty-three percent of those receiving a law degree were female. In several professional fields, women now surpass men. More than sixty-five percent of degrees in veterinary medicine, for example, go to women. The number of MBAs awarded to women has increased more than a hundredfold. In 1965, women received only about three hundred MBAs; thirty years later, women received almost thirty-five thousand MBAs, almost forty percent of the total awarded to American citizens. Similar progress has been made in doctoral degrees. They received substantially more doctorates than men in such fields as health, psychology, English, and education.

Virtually unknown, given the continuing clamor over the gender gap in science and mathematics, is the great advance women have already made in these fields. In the biological and life sciences, women in 1994 received over forty percent of the doctoral degrees. Even in mathematics and the physical sciences, women received over twenty percent of the doctorates up from only four percent in 1961.

American women are actually making more progress in mathematics and the sciences than these historical analyses reveal. The reason is the increasing number of students from other countries, overwhelmingly male, who now receive doctorates from American universities. In 1994, more than one-third of all American doctorates and almost one-half of all mathematics and science doctorates went to students who were not American citizens. Among these foreign students, males outnumber females by more than three to one. By considering only the doctorates awarded to American citizens and resident aliens in recent years, we can see that the gender gap in doctoral degrees has almost closed. American women received forty-five percent of all doctoral degrees in 1994. In the biological sciences, American women received forty-three percent of the doctorates. Large gender gaps remain in mathematics, where American women received twenty-four percent of the doctorates, and in the physical sciences, where they received twenty-two percent of doctorates.

The federal government and private foundations have devoted considerable resources to closing the gender gap in mathematics and the physical sciences. What most people do not realize is just how few people this particular gender gap affects. In 1994, for example, only 450 American men received doctorates in mathematics compared to 146 American women. In the physical sciences, 2,335 American men received doctorates compared to 659 American women. The doctoral gender gap in mathematics and the physical sciences, in essence, affects the careers and prospects of fewer than two thousand women each year. In a country of more than 265 million people, the math and science gender gap is far from a monumental social problem.

What most women want are professional degrees, not doctoral degrees in mathematics and the physical sciences. A 1996 study of college freshmen, done by the Higher Education Institute, shows that twice as many women (more than twenty percent) sought professional occupations compared to men (less than ten percent). Almost the same proportion of men and women sought careers in the biological and natural sciences. A large gender gap did occur in engineering and the computer sciences, fast becoming the new frontier in gender-gap lobbying. But the significance of this new gap is hardly what the AAUW in its 1998 study *Gender Gaps* claims. That few women take advanced-level computer-science classes does not, as the report asserts, mean that women are not taking advantage of the new technologies in the work place. You don't need to take a computer-science course in order to work with computers any more than you need to be a car mechanic to drive a car. Besides, that more women prefer to be attorneys than cubicle-confined Dilberts hardly seems a social problem of great moment.

SILENCED GIRLS?

If girls make higher grades in school, get higher ranks in class, receive more academic honors, surpass boys on standardized tests in two subjects (reading and writing) and lag only a little behind in two other subjects (mathematics and science), enter and graduate from college in greater numbers than boys, attain more master's degrees, and are closing the gap in more advanced degrees, then what is the basis for the charge that schools shortchange girls? A fair judge might look at the evidence and call it a draw: Females do better in some academic areas and males do better in others.

Well, as it happens, the AAUW's charge that schools shortchange girls is based not on such objective and comprehensive measures of educational attainment but instead on soft criteria, like the supposed "silencing" of girls in the classroom. The AAUW report emphasizes dramatic, highly publicized findings by David and Myra Sadker who claim that "research spanning the past twenty years consistently reveals that males receive more teacher attention than do females." According to the AAUW report, the Sadkers "report that boys in one study of elementary and middle school students called out answers eight times more often than girls did." Even more inflammatory, the study supposedly found that when boys called out comments in class, the teacher usually listened; but when girls called out comments, the teacher socialized them into "good girl" behavior, making such comments as, "Please raise your hand if you want to speak."

The Sadkers' findings, if true, are indeed shocking, and the media have spread them with a vengeance. The problem is that the research on which these dramatic findings are based has strangely disappeared. When Christina Hoff Sommers pointed this out in *Who Stole Feminism?*, I was quite disturbed. Like many others, I had emphasized the Sadkers' work in my own university teaching. Is it possible for a study simply to disappear into thin air? Apparently it is: When I telephoned David Sadker to ask him for a copy of the research, he could not locate one.

Leaving aside the Sadkers' lost study, what other evidence do we have that teachers give more attention to boys or even that boys talk more in the classroom? This may seem like a straightforward question, but it actually contains a tangle of murky issues. First, the question carries a hidden assumption—that differences in teacher attention actually influence how much students learn. No study has shown that talking in class or getting attention from the teacher makes any difference in student achievement. Certainly, the objective criteria documenting the higher achievement of females (e.g., grades, test scores, college attendance) suggest otherwise.

Second, the meaning of "getting attention from the teacher" is unclear. Suppose, for example, that a teacher asks a fourth-grade boy a question in class. Is this a genuine academic question, which will help him learn the material? Or is the teacher's question actually a reprimand in disguise? The teacher may see that the boy is acting up and use the question to get him back on task.

Third, we do not have large, representative studies that objectively describe what goes on in different classrooms, different subject areas, and different locales. To get stable and reliable observational measures, a well-trained researcher must sit in the classroom for many hours and count who talks, who asks questions, and who answers questions. We have no such comprehensive studies. Most classroom-interaction studies, especially in recent years, have been conducted in classrooms where females are suspected to be, and may well be, at a disadvantage. These are high-school mathematics and science classrooms, subjects in which females do not do as well, and law-school classrooms, where aggressive classroom questioning, the "Socratic method," has been considered crucial to preparing students for combative legal discourse. The research on gender interaction in the classroom does not feature studies conducted in literature classes or in foreign language classes, areas of female strength. In these classrooms, girls may well participate more than boys.

What the research does show is that sex differences in classroom participation, as measured by observers, are small and inconsistent. Some studies show teachers favoring boys while others show teachers favoring girls. The classic study *Gender Influences in Classroom Interaction,* published in 1985 presents the results of the leading researchers who have examined patterns of classroom talk at a time when social expectations for girls were more stereotyped than they are today. In their "Overview," Janet Lindow, Cora Marrett, and Louise Cherry Wilkinson summarize the basic pattern. "Research conducted in elementary school classrooms shows rather consistently that teachers give more attention to boys than to girls although there is also research to the contrary. However, much of the contact with boys tends to be negative; it is managerial and disciplinary in nature." No consistent evidence was found that teachers give more *academic* attention to boys.

Observational studies of gender differences in classroom participation are difficult to conduct and interpret. But we have another valuable source of information on teacher favoritism—the perceptions of the students themselves. Research on student views of teacher bias—which AAUW commissioned but did not release[1]—yields clear and consistent findings. In the views of elementary- and high-school students, teachers do show favoritism. But they are biased against boys.

Boys and girls reported receiving virtually identical amounts of attention—fifty-nine percent of girls and fifty-seven percent of boys said that they "get called on often" in class. When asked specifically about teacher bias, boys and girls saw some bias, but the discrimination was directed against the boys: fifty-nine percent of boys and fifty-seven percent of girls said that teachers called more often on girls. When asked, "Who does the teacher pay more attention to?," sixty-four percent of boys and fifty-seven percent of girls again said the preferred group was girls.

In short, the research on classroom interaction does not show any pattern of consistent teacher favoritism toward either boys or girls. Boys do get more attention in elementary schools, usually for disciplinary reasons. But we have no clear evidence that boys get more academic attention, and we have no clear evidence that talking in class boosts academic achievement. A few areas, such as participation in mathematics and science classrooms and law-school classrooms, may be exceptions. The field of classroom-participation research has become so politicized, however, that any data must be scrutinized with great care.

SELF-ESTEEM: GIRLS VERSUS BOYS

Another highly publicized AAUW message—that adolescent girls have lower self-esteem than boys—rests on equally shaky grounds. But the commercial success of psychologist Mary Pipher's pop-feminist book, *Reviving Ophelia: Saving the Selves of Adolescent Girls,* fueled parents' worries about the self-esteem of their daughters, reinforcing the AAUW's message. (That Pipher's conclusions were based on her clinical practice with disturbed girls went unnoticed.) Now so often aired, on "Oprah" and the "Today" show, and in *Time* and *Newsweek,* this message has become the received wisdom. Everyone now knows that girls have lower self-esteem than boys. Everyone now knows that girls suffer a severe drop in self-esteem at adolescence, that boys gain in self-assurance as they age while girls lose the vitality and sense of self they displayed in childhood. But is it true?

A careful review of the literature on gender, adolescence, and self-esteem reveals a picture far different from the message of the AAUW report. First, self-esteem itself turns out to be a muddled concept. No study shows that adolescent self-esteem depends on success in school; rather, it is rooted in friendships and physical appearance. Second, boys and girls (and young people from different ethnic groups) turn out to have quite different areas of proficiency in mind when they respond to vague questions such as, "I like most things about myself" (an item in the AAUW study of self-esteem). For example, Avril Thorne and Qhyrrae Michaelieu reported in *Child Development* that high and rising self-esteem among adolescent females was linked to memories about attempting to help female friends. High and rising self-esteem among adolescent males, in contrast, was linked to success in asserting themselves with male friends. Low and decreasing self-esteem among adolescent females was rooted in failing to win approval from friends while decreasing self-esteem among adolescent males was rooted in romantic failures. Other research shows the same. For most adolescents, school success is hardly paramount in their sense of self-worth.

On the vague and general questions that many surveys use to measure self-esteem, boys indeed are apt to score higher than girls. But the differences tend to be quite small and can be explained, in part, by the tendency of boys to choose the extreme response categories on multiple-choice questions. The Commonwealth Fund Survey of the Health of Adolescent Girls released in 1997, and ballyhooed in the press as showing once again that adolescent girls lag behind adolescent boys in self-esteem, is a recent illustration.

What this survey actually shows is unreasonably high levels of self-confidence in both boys and girls, though boys are more apt to give extreme responses. But if the "strongly agree" and "somewhat agree" categories are added together, the much-lamented self-esteem gap disappears. As an example, on the question, "I feel that I have a number of good qualities" seventy percent of boys "strongly agree" and sixty-seven percent of girls "strongly agree." If we add the category "somewhat agree," we find that exactly eighty-seven percent of girls and eighty-seven percent of boys believe that they "have a number of good qualities." This is the stuff of which the self-esteem gap is made!

In fact, problems with the concept of self-esteem have become so obvious that even feminist researchers have quietly retracted the original charge of a gender gap. This is evident in the much-publicized study, *The Girls' Report: What We Know and Need to Know About Growing Up Female.* The report was published in 1998 by the National Council for Research on Women, a coalition of seventy-eight women's studies programs and women's research organizations, including the American Association of University Women Educational Foundation. *The Girls' Report* criticizes the very concept of self-esteem, though in prose so turgid that it is difficult to make out: "In popular discussion, as well as in much of the research literature, the complex and dynamic process of identity development is too often collapsed into an oversimplified concept of self-esteem, which is typically framed as an internal, psychological phenomenon or a static entity—someone has a lot or a little."

This psychobabble is obviously no more than a screen for the report's embarrassing failure to replicate earlier assertions of low self-confidence among teenage girls. The most careful research acknowledged in *The Girls' Report,* done by University of Denver psychologist Susan Harter, shows no gender differences in the self-esteem of adolescents. Harter examined "lack of voice" in approximately nine hundred boys and girls from grades six through twelve. Contrary to the feminist argument that "voice" declines for females as they enter adolescence, Harter finds that "there is no evidence in our data for loss of voice among adolescent females as a group . . . We have also found no evidence for *gender differences* favoring males." (emphasis in original)

Nor does Harter find that girls, any more than boys, are likely to suppress their opinions in school because they don't want to seem smart and aggressive. "Once again, we found no gender difference supporting the claims that this is merely a problem for girls," concludes Harter. "Anecdotal reports from within the high school suggest that certain boys are fearful of being considered 'nerds,' 'dorks,' or 'brains' if they are too smart, risking peer rejection." Some girls and some boys do lack self-confidence, Harter emphasizes, but this is an individual problem. "Reviving Ophelia is certainly a worthy goal," she tartly concludes; "however, Hamlet also displayed serious problems of indecision and lack of voice."

For many years, Metropolitan Life has supported studies of important issues facing the public schools. In 1997, their report focused on gender issues, based on a nationally representative sample of 1,306 students from grades seven through twelve and 1,035 teachers in grades six through twelve. The report concludes bluntly:

> •1) Contrary to the commonly held view that boys are at an advantage over girls in school, girls appear to have an advantage over boys in terms of their future plans, teachers' expectations, everyday experiences at school and interactions in the classroom.
> •2) Minority girls hold the most optimistic views of the future and are the group most likely to focus on educational goals.
> •3) Minority boys are the most likely to feel discouraged about the future and the least interested in getting a good education.
> •4) Teachers nationwide view girls as higher achievers and more likely to succeed than boys.

The report received no attention from the media.

WHAT'S THE HARM?

But so what, a sensible person might say. What harm has been done by emphasizing—or overemphasizing—the problems faced by females in education? After all, women have been at a historical disadvantage. Girls do lag behind in science and mathematics, at least at the top. All those federal programs for boosting female academic performance, such as summer programs that introduce minority girls to scientific fields can't be a bad thing.

The harm is this: In their zeal to advance the interests of women and their own organizational interests, the AAUW and other feminist advocacy groups have distorted the achievements of women and the experience of girls and boys in schools. True, many of these groups are retracting some of their previous positions, acknowledging that the gap in adolescent self-esteem may not exist and that the math gap is, in fact, closing. But they are searching for new areas of female victimization, such as the low numbers of females in engineering and computer sciences. Meanwhile, resources and attention are drawn away from the group that the schools truly fail, African-American males. Unfortunately, the feminist agenda, because it is pushed so strongly and receives so much attention from media elites, distracts us from the real problem of low educational achievement among African-American males and boys more generally.

Recently, I was on a panel with several school counselors. The first question to the panel was the AAUW chestnut, "What can we do to help girls, who suffer such a loss of self-esteem at adolescence?" The first speaker, a school counselor, launched into a fiery description of the emotional problems of teenage girls. Adolescents she knew had changed from vital children who spoke their minds to bored and passive teenagers. This counselor was not aware that she was repeating chapter and verse from the AAUW report. These ideas were just in the air, promoted for years in teacher education workshops and university courses (such as the courses I myself taught).

I came next on the panel. Should I flat out contradict this counselor and tell the teachers in the audience that the research actually shows no differences in adolescent boys and girls in self-esteem, that this research has been politicized to serve a feminist agenda? As diplomatically as I could, I did so. The school counselor's reaction astonished me.

"I'm so glad you said that!" she proclaimed with fervent relief. "I know that boys have problems, too. But we just don't give the boys much attention." Other teachers chimed in. "Come to think of it, I have four suicidal adolescents in my classes this year, and all four are boys," one teacher said. "Get the word out," said the sole male teacher at the workshop. "We're too busy to read the professional literature. We didn't know this."

Teachers have limited attention, time, and energy. Schools are hectic, crowded worlds. Teachers are honing in on the problems of girls—and they are overlooking the problems of boys.

Notes

1. I discovered that gaining access to the data is difficult. While the AAUW's *How Schools Shortchange Girls* can be easily ordered for $16.95 by dialing an 800 number, obtaining the unpublished research on student views takes weeks of telephoning and a payment of $85. In *Who Stole Feminism?*, Christina Hoff Sommers reports a similar experience. Even more shocking is that she was asked to sign the following statement before she could get the report: "Please send a statement outlining how you plan to use the survey instrument and results, along with your payment for the full research report. If your review and analysis of the data results in a possible publication or presentation, that use of data must receive advance approval from AAUW."

Questions for Reaction and Discussion

1. How effective is the introduction to this essay? Why? What provokes you or prompts you to read further?
2. Do you find yourself in agreement or disagreement with Kleinfeld's initial assessment that there is a false public perception that girls are shortchanged by schools? Why?
3. What do you know about reading research reports and conclusions based on reports? What cautions should readers consider as they study research findings and the conclusions of the researchers?
4. How does Kleinfeld establish authority and credibility in this essay? Discuss specific examples with your classmates.
5. Why do you think Kleinfeld chose to take on the AAUW reports? How does she counter the evidence that the AAUW provides? How do her conclusions differ from the AAUW?

Questions for Writing

1. One of Kleinfeld's major points is that the evidence of gender discrimination is easy to spot through indicators such as grades, class rank, and academic honors and prizes. The authors of the AAUW use different evidence. Using Kleinfeld's counter evidence as your departure point, write an essay in which you compare and contrast the evidence of gender discrimination used by AAUW and Kleinfeld.
2. Kleinfeld's research has led her to the conclusion that African-American males are the most disadvantaged group in American schools. Examine her evidence carefully. What are her principal sources of statistics? What can you find by accessing the National Center for Education Statistics Web site <http://nces.ed.gov> that

would update her findings or provide counter evidence? Write an essay in which you discuss the particular problems of African-American males as a group within the public school system.

3. The research on classroom interaction and gender, as Kleinfeld suggests, leads to mixed conclusions about what effect the behavior of teachers finally has on students. Consider your own experiences as a student in elementary and secondary school. What can you recall about your own level of classroom participation? Were you encouraged or discouraged to speak? Did you ever feel that you were being encouraged because you belonged to a particular group? Write an essay in which you describe your response to Kleinfeld's assessment of classroom interaction and gender and use your own experiences as evidence to support your response.

4. Kleinfeld's major point in this essay is that as teachers hone in on the problems of girls, they overlook the problems of boys. Is this true? Why or why not? Write an essay in which you defend or reject Kleinfeld's thesis.

5. Observe the classroom behaviors in one of your own classes. Consider how men and women students react with one another, the seating arrangements of the class, the level of interactions with the professor or instructor, frequency and nature of questions and answers, and the overall degree of participation by men and women. What conclusions can you draw from your own observations? Do you find any evidence to support or reject Kleinfeld's thesis? Write an essay in which you describe the classroom you observed and compare and contrast your findings with those of Kleinfeld.

QUESTIONS FOR FURTHER EXPLORATION

1. A number of educators and journalists have responded to the AAUW reports. The principal author of the original study, Susan McGee Bailey, defended her position in writing, and Kleinfeld's response to the AAUW reports was extensively covered in many magazines and newspapers, including U.S. *News and World Report, The New York Times,* and *The Wall Street Journal.* Research the reactions of the popular press to the AAUW reports and prepare an annotated bibliography of sources for your classmates.

2. Access the Web sites of some major women's organizations, such as the AAUW <http://www.aauw.org>, The Women's Freedom Network <http://www.womensfreedom.org>, and the National Organization for Women <http://www.now.org>. Study the services and programs that they provide for their members. What are the purposes of the organizations? How are they alike? How are they different? What political activities are they involved in? What can you learn about their

educational activities? Write a brief summary of your findings for the class.

3. Access Kleinfeld's original analysis of the AAUW reports, "The Myth That Schools Shortchange Girls: Social Science in the Service of Deception," from her Web site, <http://www.uaf.edu/northern/schools/myth.html>. Compare and contrast the original analysis with the version printed here. What additional information do you learn by examining the graphs and charts that Kleinfeld provides? Write a brief report on your findings for your classmates.

4. One of Kleinfeld's concerns is that the AAUW reports have placed undue evidence on the experience of girls in schools. Using the *Reader's Guide to Periodical Literature* and the *Education Index,* research what popular magazines and newspapers have had to say on this topic for the past five years. Are there more articles about the experiences of girls than boys? What about specific groups, such as African-American boys? Write a brief report for your class.

5

GAY LIBERATION AND THE PASSAGE OF THE SEXUAL ORIENTATION CLAUSE AT PENN STATE

Yet another aspect of determining the course of one's own education is participating in campus activities and organizations. In so doing, students have a chance to understand their own identities and learn ways of working with one another outside the classroom. This selection, taken from a book that provides several accounts of how student activities can influence and change campus life, is a case study of how a group of dedicated, organized students altered a campus climate and prompted the passage of a sexual orientation clause as an addition to the statement of nondiscrimination at the Pennsylvania State University main campus. It is at once a story of how students can successfully effect policy changes as well as a suggestive narrative about what it means to be a nonheterosexual on a college campus. Robert A. Rhoads is a professor in the Department of Educational Administration at Michigan State University, where he teaches courses in research methods and participates in the Center for the Study of Advanced Learning Systems. He is also the author of several books, including Coming Out in College *and* Democracy, Multiculturalism, and the Community College.

QUESTIONS FOR READING

1. What is homosexuality? What do you know about the history of homosexuality, especially in other cultures?
2. What do you know about sexual orientation clauses and nondiscrimination as a part of campus policy statements?

ROBERT A. RHOADS

GAY LIBERATION AND THE PASSAGE
OF THE SEXUAL ORIENTATION
CLAUSE AT PENN STATE

Freedom's Web: Student Activism in an Age of Cultural Diversity
(Baltimore: The Johns Hopkins University Press, 1998)

"We're Here. We're Queer.
Get Used to it."
Gay Liberation at Penn State

In March of 1993, a group of over a hundred students from Pennsylvania State University traveled to Washington, D.C., to join a march for lesbian, gay, and bisexual equal rights and liberation. They represented only a fraction of what amounted to somewhere in the neighborhood of two hundred thousand demonstrators. For many of the Penn State students, the trip was the culmination of several years of political and cultural work aimed at improving the campus climate for lesbian, gay, and bisexual people. These were the students who organized campus rallies, coming-out celebrations, teach-ins, and a variety of political and educational activities as part of their contribution to gay liberation. Several of them played major roles in what was perhaps the key struggle for equal rights when they challenged the administration to add a sexual orientation clause to its official statement of nondiscrimination. The effort these students put into creating campus change was draining at times, and a trip to Washington and a chance to participate in a national day of celebration was a much needed reprieve.[1]

The day was still young as the Penn State delegation relaxed on the mall across from the White House and awaited their turn to join the march. The students reflected on the positive changes they had achieved and the long struggle that lay before them. Timothy Jones,[2] a senior, talked about the hard work and energy he had given to winning the approval for the sexual orientation clause. He recalled the many meetings with members of the board of trustees and other key officials. The most draining thing for Jones had been all the time spent educating misinformed members of the academic community about "the gay lifestyle," as straights frequently described it. Those were painful words to Timothy. His identity as a gay man was not simply a matter of a choice of lifestyle. Being gay was a complex and central facet of his identity. "Why was it so difficult for them to understand that?"

Samuel Bennett, a junior, shared Timothy's frustrations. He too had been heavily involved in student activism as a means to transform the campus climate. He played a key role in the efforts to get the sexual orientation clause passed and more recently helped to form a new student organization committed to fighting discrimination within the Penn State ROTC program. With the passage of the clause, Samuel and others felt that the program was in violation because of its official stance toward "homosexual" students. He had planned a number of resistance activities, including an educational campaign to make people aware of ROTC's discriminatory practices. One of his ideas was the development of a poster encouraging Penn State students to violate campus policies—"just like ROTC." His recommendations on the banner included the following: ride bikes on the sidewalks, keep library books, pay someone to take your exams, smoke in your classes, drink beer in front of Old Main, have sex on the golf course, and plagiarize in papers. Although Samuel believed wholeheartedly in challenging ROTC, he also recognized that he was up against a powerful organization whose governmental connections made his provocative activities that much more serious. There was a touch of irony in Samuel's commitment, in that he had been raised in a military family and his dad was a high-ranking officer. Thus, for Samuel, the fight with ROTC was personal in many ways: "This issue is something that I felt I had to take on. It had to be addressed. I really feel that I am effective because of my family's background in the military. I feel that what I'm doing is the right thing."

The Penn State delegation was one of hundreds from their state scattered within a large section of the mall lawn. The march was organized by states, and Pennsylvania was not scheduled to join the procession until later in the day. Consequently, the students from Penn State had time to kill, and the sunny March day made for a warm and peaceful break from the hustle and bustle of a typical weekend spent catching up on school work.

Sitting on the grassy lawn, several students relaxed hand in hand. Some leaned their heads on the shoulders of the persons next to them, while others took turns rubbing one another's backs. A few couples shared a kiss from time to time, while new romances blossomed like the cherry trees they had passed along the Potomac. For some, it was the first time they had displayed affection in public. No wonder so many of the Penn State contingent described their day as empowering.

As the students waited their turn, many shared their thoughts, their emotions. The students sensed the contribution they were about to make to what many perceived as a momentous occasion. For Samuel, the march was a "moment in history" of which he could be a part. A second student offered a similar view but worried about the "conservative backlash" he believed the march would generate. The entire event was overwhelming for a third student: "It's almost beyond words. I have never seen this many queer people at one place in all my life. I just don't know what to say. When we came out of the subway it was like every single person was lesbian, gay, or bisexual. People were even cheering."

With his new boyfriend resting on the grass in front of him, Samuel took on a glow seldom seen back in State College. From time to time, his partner leaned back against Samuel's chest as Samuel draped his arms around him, as if holding on to time itself. The smiles they cast expressed their joy. "It's like a fantasy world where you don't have to be concerned about holding hands. It's like what the world should be like," commented Samuel. And his partner added, "I can be myself for a while. I can be who I am." Another student, who essentially was in the closet back at school, started to talk but then paused for a few seconds. He looked at the vastness of the crowd that surrounded him, and then simply said, "I feel proud here."

The atmosphere on the mall lawn was a stark contrast to earlier that same day when the students had gathered in front of the HUB (the student center) at Penn State for the trip to Washington. A defensive posture was the norm and they were careful about expressing open affection. Although Penn State was a great improvement from their high school days of near complete isolation and fear, the campus nonetheless had a conservative quality to it that made most gay students think twice about coming out. Once on the bus, however, students began to clasp hands and embrace one another. Kisses shared by a few couples might have given a casual observer the impression that this was a typical college field trip. The sense of relief revealed by their physical expressions was powerful.

The battle for gay liberation had been waged for years, and even the conservative campus of Penn State University had not been immune to student stirrings. The passengers on the bus knew the history of how lesbian, gay, and bisexual students had fought for acceptance within the university and the surrounding community of State College. There had been a long struggle simply to win approval for a gay student organization. And then came the fight to add the sexual orientation clause. For them it was difficult to imagine why others failed to see the need to protect the rights of lesbian, gay, and bisexual people. How could someone argue that such rights were "special rights" for gays? That kind of logic angered students like Samuel Bennett and Timothy Jones. They just wanted the same rights and protections enjoyed by others. They imagined walking out of a campus movie holding hands with their lovers without fear of getting harassed or beaten up. They dreamt of raising personal experiences in classes, like heterosexual students often did, without other students or the professor snickering. They envisioned going to college parties without fear for their lives. And they wondered what it would be like to sit on the HUB lawn on that first warm spring day and embrace like so many other Penn State lovers did. Why could they not share in these precious college experiences?

To achieve the equal rights they dreamt of having, many of the lesbian, gay, and bisexual students from Penn State knew they had to sacrifice. They had to work to transform the images people held of gay lives. This was the challenge they faced. From their perspective, participation in the march on Washington was one more step in the larger struggle to change people's views. Being out and proud, which is what the march symbolized to many, was part of an empowerment agenda that had become central to the movement at the university. Student leaders had given up on the quiet, less offensive strategies of the past that they believed had achieved limited success. Instead, a group of student leaders from the Lesbian, Gay, and Bisexual Student Alliance (LGBSA) had begun to embrace queer politics and were inspired to follow in the footsteps of their late 1980s predecessors, Queer Nation and ACT UP. Their efforts, however, remained forever linked to the legacy of an earlier generation when gay liberation had its first success at the university.

HOMOPHILES OF PENN STATE

Pennsylvania State University has a history of strained relationships with its lesbian, gay, and bisexual students. In 1972 Joseph Acanfora was removed from his student teaching assignment at Park Forest Junior High School in State College, Pennsylvania.[3] At the time it was not clear to Acanfora as to whether the university or the State College Area School District had made the decision. What was clear, however, was the motivation behind his removal: his involvement in the campus group Homophiles of Penn State (HOPS). Also clear was the fact that the university had found it necessary to inform the Park Forest school that Acanfora was a member of HOPS.[4] To understand the significance of Acanfora's relationship to HOPS, one must step back to one year earlier when the organization began its struggle for official recognition as a student group.

On April 21, 1971, a request from HOPS for a student charter was approved by Penn State's Undergraduate Student Government (USG) only to be suspended three weeks later by then acting vice-president for student affairs Raymond Murphy. In a letter addressed to HOPS Vice-President Diane Whitney, Murphy explained: "This is to notify you that the facilities of the University will not be available to your organization until such time as there has been a complete review of the legality of this organization by University Legal Counsel. Beyond legal matters, there may also be a question of educational policy with respect to this charter. At the time that a review has been made you will be notified of a final decision with respect to this matter." Some four months later, Murphy announced that the student charter for HOPS was denied on the grounds that it posed a threat to the educational policies of the university. Once again, in a letter addressed to HOPS, Murphy elaborated the university's position: "We are advised that based upon sound psychological and psychiatric opinion, the chartering of your organization would create a substantial conflict with the counseling and psychiatric services the University provides to its students and that such conflict would be harmful to the best interests of the students of the University."

After months of legal preparations, on February 11, 1972, HOPS filed a lawsuit against the university alleging that their First (right to free speech) and Fourteenth (right to equal protection) amendment rights had been violated. A student plaintiff named in the suit was one Joseph Acanfora.[5] Three days later, Acanfora was removed from his student teaching assignment.

Acanfora sought an injunction from Centre County Court Judge R. Paul Campbell, and on February 22 he was reinstated in his student teaching assignment at Park Forest Junior High. Following a very successful student teaching experience in which the vast majority of students rated his overall performance as "good" or "excellent," he faced another barrier: The university decided to hold a hearing as to whether or not Acanfora should get his Pennsylvania Teacher's Certificate. Traditionally, such hearings are held only when there is cause to deliberate on the moral character of a student. And typically, cause involves some kind of legal violation such as a student's being arrested for falsifying a driver's license (a common practice for students under twenty-one who seek to be served in local bars). Of course, in Acanfora's case, there was no cause except that he identified himself as a "homosexual." Among the questions he faced at the meeting of the six-member University Teacher Certification Council chaired by the dean of the college of education, Abram W. VanderMeer, were the following: "What homosexual acts do you prefer to engage in or are you willing to engage in?" and "Do you look for other males with which to have sex?" As Acanfora explained, "I [couldn't] believe they were serious. It was so insane. . . . You just can't put a person in a box and label it 'homosexual.' . . . Homosexuals are people, and you have to remember that."[6]

The council was split in its decision, with three supportive of Acanfora and three opposed. This meant that the case would be passed on to the state education secretary, John C. Pittenger, who ultimately approved the certification, stating, "There is no legal barrier to granting a certificate to Mr. Acanfora since he has not been convicted of any criminal violation."[7]

The fact that the University Teacher Certification Council was serious is what is so frightening about the whole Acanfora and HOPS episodes and what makes the efforts of contemporary lesbian, gay, and bisexual student activists at Penn State so important. Acanfora, who would face additional problems when hired as a teacher in the state of Maryland, eventually appeared on the CBS show "60 Minutes," where the problems he faced as a gay teacher were brought to the nation's attention. And HOPS, after an out-of-court settlement, received its charter as a student group and paved the way for the present-day Lesbian, Gay, and Bisexual Student Alliance.

But the Acanfora and HOPS episodes did not end discrimination and homophobia faced by students at the university, as separate studies conducted during the late 1980s and early 1990s revealed. In 1988 the Campus Environment Team examined acts of intolerance that had occurred during the spring semester 1988. In all, thirty acts of intolerance were reported with seventy percent directed against gay men or lesbians. In 1990, professor Anthony D'Augelli conducted a survey of 131 gay men, lesbians, and bisexuals and found that seventy-three percent had been verbally insulted because of their sexual orientation; thirty-one percent had been threatened with bodily injury, with actual physical violence occurring in at least fourteen cases. A 1991 committee on gay and lesbian concerns chaired by professor William Tierney took the preceding findings into account when they recommended to the university's president that a sexual orientation clause be added to the university's statement of nondiscrimination. Adding the clause was seen by the committee as a necessary step toward achieving equal rights and full protection for lesbian, gay, and bisexual students, faculty, and staff.

PASSAGE OF THE SEXUAL ORIENTATION CLAUSE

In 1991, Penn State's new president, Joab Thomas, inherited the controversy over the sexual orientation clause from his predecessor, the recently retired Bryce Jordan. As part of their effort to influence campus politics, students from LGBSA held teach-ins (often referred to as "straight talks"), candlelight vigils, demonstrations, marches, and coming-out rallies. Their goal was to raise the consciousness of the campus community by making their lives and struggles known to all. Although less prominent in their tactics, faculty and staff also played key roles, often organizing behind the scenes and offering their support and guidance to students.

In the process of building liberal and progressive support, gay activists also solidified the opposition; conservatives in the community were antagonized by what they saw as the dominance of gay issues at campus events and discussions. At many of the rallies, conservative students, led by religious organizations such as the Alliance for Christian Fellowship and Intervarsity Christian Fellowship, offered counterdemonstrations that often were equal or greater in student turnout. Clearly, the campus was divided on the issue. Divisiveness was most apparent by the many letters to the editor published on an almost daily basis in the school's student-run newspaper, the *Daily Collegian*. Gay students were described as "sick" or "perverted" by conservative students, who also complained that gays were corrupting the American family and that the country's demise was caused by gays and other liberals who were undermining traditional values. Religious students often resorted to biblical passages and described lesbian, gay, and bisexual students as "sinners" whose behavior was "abominable in the eyes of God." A frequently used line was "Love the sinner, but hate the sin." Such comments incensed gay students and allies, who responded with their own letters pointing out that being gay was about much more than simply sleeping with someone of the same sex. A liberal campus ministry supported lesbian, gay, and bisexual students by posting a pamphlet on its bulletin board that read: "Everything that Christ had to say about homosexuality." Upon opening the brochure one discovered a blank page, which was intended to reflect the teachings of Christ on the subject. As one minister affiliated with this ministry explained, "Why is there so much fuss about an issue that had little relevance to Christ?" The same minister practically was run out of town when she appeared at a local gay pride rally carrying the following sign: "If Christ returned today, she would be a bisexual woman of color."

In an effort to appease campus liberals, who supported adding a sexual orientation clause, and conservatives, led by several members of the board of trustees who opposed specific mention of "sexual orientation" in any official university document, President Thomas drafted the following nondiscrimination statement for approval by the faculty senate (the proposed amendment is in italics):

> The Pennsylvania State University, in compliance with federal and state laws, is committed to the policy that all persons shall have equal access to programs, admission, and employment without regard to race, religion, sex, national origin, handicap, age, or status as a disabled or Vietnam era veteran. *In addition, the Pennsylvania State University will take appropriate measures to protect all of its students and all of its employees from harassment, abuse, or assault; and bases all educational and employment decisions on an individual's abilities and qualifications without reference to personal characteristics that are not related to academic ability or job performance.*

In seeking guidance from the faculty, President Thomas hoped to achieve greater support before passing on the recommendation to the board of trustees, which, in the end, had to approve any changes to the official policy.

But the faculty were less than thrilled with Thomas's clever wording, which to them was designed to avoid the inclusion of "sexual orientation" and therefore compromised its intent. Consequently, the faculty found it insufficient for protecting members of the gay community. They called for the addition of "sexual orientation" as a protected class equivalent to other classes already mentioned within the nondiscrimination policy. The majority felt that anything less than the inclusion of the phrase "sexual orientation" was short of the university's professed commitment to diversity. They also made it clear that being added as a protected category in a statement of nondiscrimination was not the same as being included in affirmative action policies: Rights to equal protection are not the same as being identified as a group which historically has been denied equal employment or educational opportunity.

On February 7, 1991, the Special University Faculty Senate Committee held public hearings to solicit feedback on the president's addition as well as their own recommendation to add the phrase "sexual orientation" to the statement. Extended testimony was offered by many within the campus community. Most favored the addition of the phrase "sexual orientation." The University Student Advisory Board, representing some twenty student organizations including the Association of Residence Halls, the Black Caucus, the Graduate Student Association, and the Interfraternity Council, came out in support of the faculty senate's version. Other groups such as the Commission for Women and the Lesbian, Gay, and Bisexual Student Alliance also voiced their support. Faculty members spoke on behalf of adding "sexual orientation" and several gave impassioned testimony of evidence of discrimination that they either had experienced or had witnessed at the university.

Despite support for the clause, there was an equally impassioned (though not as large) oppositional voice. As expected, the Intervarsity Christian Fellowship offered its rationale for not supporting the addition of "sexual orientation."

It may surprise some people to learn that God does not accept all kinds of activities, either in this life or the next. He separates himself from those who do not conform to his will as expressed in his holy word. Some people think it doesn't matter what one believes, or does—that tolerance and acceptance is a virtue in and of itself. However, this is not what the scriptures teach. "Do you know that the wicked will not inherit the kingdom of God? Do not be deceived: Neither the sexually immoral nor idolaters nor adulterers nor male prostitutes nor homosexual offenders nor thieves nor the greedy nor drunkard nor slanderers nor swindlers will inherit the kingdom of God."

But another Christian perspective was offered by the Reverend Ann Ard of United Campus Ministry, an organization serving Penn State students that traditionally affiliated with seven liberal to moderate denominations including the local Quaker and Mennonite churches, the United Church of Christ, and the Church of the Brethren. She spoke to the different interpretations of scripture among Christians:

> The disagreement you may hear today between people representing Christian groups is based on differing interpretations of the Bible and Christian teaching. Our various doctrinal and theological disagreements ought not to influence the decision-making process at a public university. It is not the responsibility of the university to make decisions based on the religious feelings of some in the community. It is the responsibility of the university to protect the rights of members of its community, whether or not some might be offended by that protection. . . . I urge you to recommend to the President the inclusion of the words "sexual orientation" in the University's policy. It is the courageous and right thing to do.

Ard brought a voice of reason to the religious differences that had moved to the forefront of the controversy surrounding lesbian, gay, and bisexual rights. Her testimony served as a reminder not only of the diversity within the Penn State community but of the diversity within the Christian community as well.

Additional testimony was heard in the voice of Lori Ginzberg, an assistant professor of history and women's studies, who spoke on her own behalf. She alluded to comparisons between being Jewish and being gay and how historically both groups had faced widespread oppression, with the most obvious example being the reign of Nazi Germany and the Holocaust:

> There are many lessons which Jews and gay men and lesbians have learned from the Holocaust, not least of which is the urgency of defending the liberties of people other than one's own. These lessons relate directly to the question of including the words "sexual orientation" in Penn State's nondiscrimination policy. What we have learned, Jews and gay folks, is that our best defense against bigotry is visibility, our greatest hope for change is neither assimilation nor silence, but identifying ourselves as a people.

Ginzberg not only reminded those in attendance that silence and invisibility are indeed dangerous; she also provided some insight into why identity politics may be something far more significant than simply an effort to foster "self-esteem," as critics such as Dinesh D'Souza and Arthur Schlesinger sarcastically suggest.

Following the public hearing of February 7, the faculty senate passed a motion to recommend that President Thomas include "sexual orientation" in the statement of nondiscrimination. There was still, however, one more hurdle to overcome: Getting the conservative board of trustees to pass the measure would be difficult. Eventually, this too was accomplished, as a group of students from LGBSA threatened a takeover of the president's office. In a secret meeting with a key member of the board, several students detailed their plan of action in the event that the board were to fail to approve the rewritten Thomas amendment. The student sit-in would be carried out with one intent: to generate media attention and bring embarrassment to the university officials involved in rejecting equal protection for lesbian, gay, and bisexual people. In a university as image conscious as Penn State, a student takeover was not the kind of publicity deemed desirable. After all, the school was still recovering from a takeover at the hands of African-American students who in the spring of 1989 commandeered the university's communications center as part of their effort to boost Penn State's commitment to students of color. The board of trustees certainly did not want that kind of debacle on their hands again. With the possibility of an intense student demonstration hanging over their heads, the board voted to add the sexual orientation clause to the university's statement of nondiscrimination. The passage of the clause was seen as a giant step toward creating an affirmative campus climate for members of the Penn State lesbian, gay, and bisexual community.

The statement from professor Ginzberg provided important insight about the need for lesbian, gay, and bisexual people to be visible and to build upon a collective sense of identity. This was one of the primary objectives of LGBSA, which continued its activism in the aftermath of the passage of the clause.

Notes

1. The case study upon which this chapter is based is part of a larger ethnographic project focused primarily on gay and bisexual college males. For a more detailed analysis of the experiences of gay and bisexual college males, see Robert A. Rhoads, *Coming Out in College: The Struggle for a Queer Identity* (Westport, Conn.: Bergin & Garvey, 1994).
2. Throughout this chapter pseudonyms are used for the students who participated in the case study.
3. Barb Snyder, "HOPS Member Removed," *Daily Collegian* February 16, 1972: 1.
4. Barb Snyder, "HOPS: 1 Year Old, But Learning Life Fast," *Daily Collegian* April 27, 1972: 1.
5. Barb Snyder, "HOPS Sues University," *Daily Collegian* February 14, 1972: 1.

6. Jeff DeBray and Rick Nelson, "Acanfora: The Struggle Continues," *Daily Collegian* February 27, 1973: 1.
7. DeBray and Nelson.

Questions for Reaction and Discussion

1. How effective is the introductory description of the group of students traveling to Washington, D.C.? Why? What does the author do to overcome resistance that some students might have to reading this essay?
2. Have you ever participated in an organized march or demonstration? What were the circumstances? Under what circumstances would you participate in such an activity?
3. What is a homophile and how does the author demonstrate the tensions on the Penn State campus?
4. Why did so many students and faculty members object to the non-discrimination statement as originally proposed by President Joab Thomas? Why were the comments by Professor Lori Ginzberg so crucial to the success of the initiative?

Questions for Writing

1. What organizations and programs are available on your campus for gay and lesbian students? Access your college Web site and locate information you can find there; in addition, visit the office of student activities and inquire about organizations, programs, and discussion groups. Write a summary of the information you find in the form of a letter to a prospective student who has written you to ask about what programs are available for gay and lesbian students.
2. Assume that you are a student member on a task force to review the current state of nondiscrimination policies on your campus. Read the policy statements about nondiscrimination and any other materials you can find that deal with this issue. Does your campus have a sexual orientation clause? Why or why not? Interview campus leaders and student activity officers to find out more information about nondiscrimination policies on your campus. Write a summary of your findings and present any recommendations you have for future action.
3. Rhoads and the students he discusses throughout this essay are clearly concerned with establishing a presence for gay and lesbian students within a campus community. In her statement before the faculty committee, Professor Lori Ginzberg observed that "our best defense against bigotry is visibility, our greatest hope for change is neither assimilation nor silence, but identifying ourselves as a people." In what ways does assimilation and silence restrict the freedom of individuals

and what are the consequences for a community? Write an essay in which you explore the relationship between silence and oppression and use specific examples from your reading and educational experiences.

Questions for Further Exploration

1. Access the Web site of Michigan State University (where Robert Rhoads teaches) <http://www.msu.edu> and locate information about the Alliance of Lesbian-Bi-Gay and Transgendered Students. Access the Web site of Pennsylvania State University <http://www.psu.edu> and locate the Penn State Coalition of Lesbian, Gay, and Bisexual Students. Read through the organizational statements of purpose and calendar of activities. Check out the links to other resources and sites. Write a review of these two sites and present them to your classmates.
2. The Gay and Lesbian Alliance against Defamation (GLAAD) was founded in New York in 1985, primarily to "improve the public's attitudes toward homosexuality and put an end to violence and discrimination against lesbians and gay men." Today GLAAD maintains a national membership and sponsors a large number of projects and publications. Visit the Web site <http://www.glaad.org> and review the various services GLAAD provides. What programs and services might be especially useful to colleges and universities? Write a brief report of your findings and present them to your classmates.
3. Locate some books and articles on the experiences of gay and lesbian students in college; you might begin with Rhoads's own book, *Coming Out in College: The Struggle for a Queer Identity*. Prepare an annotated list of print resources for students and offer them for use by your campus organization for gay and lesbian students.
4. Access the Web sites of several colleges and universities and evaluate the resources they provide for gay and lesbian students. Check the links to other organizations, either on or off campus. Prepare an annotated list of electronic resources and offer them for use by your campus organization for gay and lesbian students.

6

BIG-TIME COLLEGE SPORTS

For colleges and universities, few activities unite the student body, divide the faculty, and provide more immediate institutional identification for everyone than do sports. The team mascot pops up as an instantaneous feature on virtually every college and university Web site; "Athletics" as a category is usually prominently displayed, often right next to "Academics." Over fifteen percent of all students expect to participate in varsity sports during their college years, and an overwhelming majority of students regularly attend sporting events on their campuses. Although college sports is amateur in status, the increasing professionalism of sports, especially men's basketball and football, has prompted considerable discussion on campuses about the role of college athletic programs within higher education. For student athletes, the stakes are very high; the long hours of practice and the pressures on teams to succeed have led to many suggestions about how colleges can handle highly competitive athletic programs while maintaining the integrity of the academic program. In recent years as violations and problems have emerged in many sports programs, calls for a variety of reforms have become numerous. Dean Smith, who coached Michael Jordan at the University of North Carolina, suggested in an interview in Sports Illustrated *in 1997 that while freshmen should be eligible for scholarships, they should get acclimated to college during their first year. They should "study first and play later." Coaches, professors, politicians, and alums have all contributed to the growing body of articles and position papers on how to reform college sports.*

D. Stanley Eitzen, a retired professor of sociology at Colorado State University, delivered the essay reprinted here as a speech to the Kansas Sociological Society on October 9, 1997. Eitzen concentrates on the tensions between ethics and economics in college sports programs.

Questions for Reading

1. What kinds of intercollegiate sports programs are on your campus? What information do you know about the numbers of students involved and the life of a student athlete?
2. What is the National Collegiate Athletic Association?
3. What is your view of athletics on your campus? Are you involved? Why or why not?
4. What is your experience of reading speeches? Are your expectations different for a speech that is meant to be heard rather than read? Why or why not?

D. STANLEY EITZEN

BIG-TIME COLLEGE SPORTS: CONTRADICTIONS, CRISES, AND CONSEQUENCES

Vital Speeches of the Day *Sixty-Four (December 1, 1997 pp.122-6)*

A few years ago, after Duke was eliminated from the NCAA Division I men's basketball tournament, its highly successful and respected coach, Mike Krzyzewski, made an emotional speech. Coach K, as he is affectionately known, extolled the virtues of big-time college sport—the camaraderie, the shared sacrifice, the commitment to excellence, collective responsibility, and integrity. He said: "All this stuff where people talk about college sports and things as bad, you have no idea. I want to whack everybody who says that. College sports are great."

I love sports. But while I love college sport and I am especially energized by the Division I men's basketball tournament, I believe that big-time college sport compromises the values of higher education. In short, I am one of those critics that Coach K "wants to whack." Coach K acknowledges that there are abuses in college sports—cheating and other unethical practices. In his view these are behaviors by bad people "who have lost sight of the true purpose of college sport and let the pursuit of winning override the pursuit of teaching." I do not question Coach K's genuine affection for his players or his sincerity about the glories of big-time college sport. I do question his perception and analysis. Coach K takes an individualistic perspective, which means that he does not see—and this is the crucial sociological point—the wrongs that occur because of the way big-time college sport is organized.

The overriding question that I address is this: Is big-time college sport compatible with higher education? We know it has entertainment value, that it unites supporters of a given school, that it provides free publicity for the schools, that it gives good athletes from economically disadvantaged backgrounds the chance for a college education, and that it is a training ground for the relatively few future professional athletes. But is big-time college sport— I'm referring exclusively to men's football in the 106 Division I-A schools and the 305 Division I schools in men's basketball—consistent with the educational mission of U.S. colleges and universities?

Scholarships. To answer this question, let's look at a number of problematic areas, beginning with scholarships. Isn't it ironic that many schools award more merit-based scholarship money to athletes than to all other scholarship students combined. Not only that, many of these athletic scholarships are given to athletes who have little chance of making it academically or even to those who do not care about receiving a college education. One egregious example from the past: North Carolina State, where the average SAT score for the student body was 1030 at the time, admitted a basketball player, Chris Washburn, who had an SAT of 470 and an IQ of 86. Especially telling about this example is that over one hundred universities offered Chris Washburn a full scholarship. A Chris Washburn cannot receive a scholarship or be eligible to play under current NCAA rules. There is a higher SAT requirement now (900 if a high school GPA of 2.0 in 13 core courses, 820 if the high school GPA is 2.5). Nevertheless, athletes who are marginal students continue to be admitted. Football and men's basketball players in big-time sports programs are more than six times as likely as other students to receive special treatment in the admissions process; that is, they are admitted below the standard requirements for their universities.

Many argue that special admissions criteria should be targeted to assist underprivileged minority students. This is a legitimate argument because many young people live in a Third World of grinding poverty, violent neighborhoods, inadequately financed schools, and few successful role models. However, I argue that these exceptions for admission should be granted to those who have the potential for academic success not, as is the case now, exclusively athletic success. What is troubling about this imbalance is not that athletes are undeserving or that helping them is wrong. The problem is that we miss the opportunity to provide an education of academically talented minorities. African-Americans, while constituting 12.6 percent of the population, account for only 3.7 percent of all physicians, 3.4 percent of all lawyers, and 6.9 percent of all managers and professionals in the United States. On the other hand, African-Americans are overrepresented as professional athletes—eighty percent in professional basketball, sixty percent in professional football, and twenty-two percent in professional baseball. Some argue that this disproportionate number of African-Americans in professional sports is an appropriate rationale for giving them scholarships to college where they can hone their skills for a professional sports career. This is fallacious reasoning, however, since only about one percent of college athletes make it at the professional level and many of them will not make it by the second year. When schools over-recruit minorities for their athletic skills and under-recruit minorities for their academic skills, they contradict the fundamental reason for their existence. Moreover, when the African-Americans on campus are there mostly for their physical skills, this reinforces the negative stereotype that African-Americans are endowed with special physical attributes but lack the necessary mental attributes.

Let's face the facts: college athletes in big-time programs are recruited to be part of a commercial entertainment organization that has nothing to do with the educational mission of schools. Murray Sperber presents the following apt analogy:

> If colleges searched for and gave scholarships to up-and-coming rock stars so that they could entertain the university community and earn money for their schools through concerts and tours, educational authorities and the public would call this "a perversion of academic values." Yet every year, American institutions of higher education hand out over a hundred thousand full or partial scholarships, worth at least $500 million, for reasons similar to the hypothetical grants to rock performers.

The Education of Athletes. The latest data show that athletes in big-time programs are more than two hundred points behind the average student on the SAT. How do the schools deal with this discrepancy? The athletic departments hire tutors for their athletes. Typically, they have mandatory study sessions for freshmen and for nonfreshmen whose grades are in jeopardy. That's the good news. The bad news is that academically challenged athletes are counseled to take easy courses, to choose easy majors, and to take courses from cooperative faculty members who will give athletes "special" considerations in the classroom. For many coaches, the point is to keep their athletes eligible, not their education.

Meanwhile, the athletes in these commercialized professionalized programs have trouble reconciling the roles associated with their dual statuses of athlete and student. A study of one basketball program by sociologists Patricia and Peter Adler found that the pressures of big-time sport and the academic demands resulted in the gradual disengagement of the athletes from their academic roles. They found that most athletes entered the university feeling idealistic about their impending academic performance. This idealism was soon replaced by disappointment and a growing cynicism as they realized how difficult it was to keep up with their schoolwork. The typical response to these athletes was role distancing: that is, they minimized the student role. The Adlers say that for these athletes, when it came to academics, "it was better not to try than to try and not succeed." This attitude was reinforced by the peer subculture. Thus, the structure of big-time programs often works to maximize the athlete role and minimize the academic role—clearly opposite the goals of higher education.

COLLEGE SPORT AS BIG BUSINESS

Big-time college sport is organized so that separating the business aspects from the play on the field is impossible. The intrusion of money into college sport is evident in the following representative examples:

- Some university athletic budgets are now as much as $33 million.

- Each school in the 1997 Rose Bowl received $8.25 million, which it divided with other schools in its conference.

- Coors Brewing Company paid $5 million to the University of Colorado when the university agreed to name the new field house "Coors Events Center."

- Notre Dame has a $38 million contract to televise its football games. The sale of Notre Dame merchandise brings the school another $1 million in royalties and an appearance in a bowl game raises another $3 to $6 million.

- The University of Colorado receives $5.6 million (in shoes, apparel, and cash) over six years from Nike. In addition, CU will receive a $100,000 bonus from Nike if its football team ends the season ranked number one. If CU wins the NCAA men's basketball tournament, it receives $200,000 in bonuses ($50,000 for a Final Four appearance).

- In 1994 CBS agreed to pay the NCAA $1.725 billion ($215.6 million a year) for the rights to televise the men's basketball tournament through 2002.

- When Kentucky basketball coach Rick Pitino was being sought by the pros in 1996, he was offered a $3 million deal to stay (three times more than any other college basketball coach at the time). He turned this down, and his replacement, Tubby Smith signed a deal worth $1.2 million. The highest paid college football coach is Steve Spurrier of Florida, who has a contract through the 2002 season that averages $2 million a season in salary, bonuses, and extras.

These illustrations have serious implications for institutions of higher education. First, the system creates economic imperatives that lead college administrators, athletic directors, and coaches to engage in an ever-spiraling athletic arms race. They believe that to make money an athletic department must spend money on such items as increasing the recruiting budget; hiring more fundraisers; improving practice facilities; adding new seating in the stadiums and arenas, especially the addition of "skyboxes"; purchasing the latest equipment; and building expensive new sports annexes with state-of-the-art locker rooms, weight rooms, training rooms, meeting rooms, and offices for the coaches and athletic administrators.

Second, except for a few schools, athletic programs lose money. It is commonly believed that men's basketball and especially football bring in the funds that pay for the rest of the athletic budget. But, for the most part, this is a fiction. The NCAA reported that a majority of Division I football programs reported a deficit and forty-five percent lost an average of $628,000 in 1995. And these deficits would be much greater if the accounting procedures were more appropriate. That is, teams play in stadiums and arenas that are paid for by taxpayers, contributors, and, more typically, bonds being paid off by students at no expense to the athletic departments. Moreover, a large proportion of student fees are automatically turned over to the athletic departments, as are subsidies from state legislatures and school administrators to pay for the athletes' scholarships. Using the University of Colorado as an example, the 1995 athletic budget included $900,000 in presidential support, $1,064,331 in chancellor's support, and $1,254,000 in support from mandatory student fees. These student fees and university subsidies artificially inflate athletic department income.

These subsidies also show how universities make business decisions concerning athletics that supersede educational considerations. In 1996, for example, Tulane's governing board announced that it would increase its subsidy to the athletic department six-fold, from $550,000 to $3.4 million. This action by the board occurred at the same time that it approved a plan to trim $8.5 million from the university's budget, while raising the tuition by four percent, freezing most faculty and staff salaries for one year, cutting fifty staff positions, and reducing funds for undergraduate student financial aid and graduate student stipends. This is clearly a situation where monies are transferred from the educational function of the universities to the entertainment function in a difficult economic climate—a questionable transfer of wealth, to say the least.

A third consequence of an athletic department's quest for money is that decision making tends to leave the university and flow toward the sources of revenue. Television money dictates schedules, for example. At the University of Colorado, for instance, twenty-five boosters pledged forty thousand dollars each toward the purchase of a new house for football coach Rick Neuheisel. What kind of power will these twenty-five big spenders have over the University of Colorado's athletic program? Similarly, who has the power when a football coach makes more than eight times the money as the university's president (which is the case at the University of Florida) and who has a powerful constituency outside the university?

Corporate sponsors may intrude in various ways as they give or withhold their monies.

The point, as Murray Sperber says, is that these practices "undermine one of the fundamental tenets of colleges and universities—their independence." Ironically, students who typically help the athletic department through their fees, which total more than a million dollars annually at most big-time programs, have no influence over how their money is spent. Of all the categories of contributors to athletics, students are the only ones left out of the power equation.

Students are also left out in the distribution of the relatively scarce seats available in the arenas of successful teams. These seats tend to go to big-spending boosters, depriving many students of the chance to watch their teams play. The University of Louisville, for example, allots ten percent of its seats for basketball games to students. The University of Arizona holds a lottery to choose the students who may attend basketball games. The situation worsens during tournament time when each school is allotted relatively few tickets. This common practice raises the serious question: Shouldn't school sports primarily be for the enjoyment of students?

Winning begets money. This increases the pressure to win, which, when the pressure becomes too great, may result in cheating. Cheating takes several forms. Most common is the offer of special inducements outside the rules by coaches and/or boosters to lure athletes to the school and to keep them there. Cheating may also involve unethical means to ensure the scholastic eligibility of the athletes. According to a recent expose by *Sports Illustrated*, test fraud on the SAT examination is common, promoted by recruiters, high-school coaches, middlemen, agents, and college coaches. Scandals also involve the altering of transcripts, fraudulent courses from diploma mills, the use of surrogate test takers, and bogus credit for taking phantom courses.

In most instances school administrators, students, and supporters do not demand that guilty coaches be fired for their transgressions—if they win. As *Sports Illustrated* writer John Underwood has characterized the situation: "We've told them that it doesn't matter how clean they keep their programs. It doesn't matter what percentage of their athletes graduate or take a useful place in society. It doesn't even matter how well the coaches teach their sports. All that matters are the flashing scoreboard lights."

One final point concerning money. Despite the problems associated with big-time college sports, including the long odds against financial success, there are always schools that seek to move into the big-time category. This creates major fiscal problems for them. They must upgrade their facilities. They have to launch special fund-raising campaigns that may siphon monies that might otherwise be donated to the academic side of the university. They need increased subsidies from the university and they require more money from student fees. These schools, typically, schedule away games with established powers for big payouts. On the surface, this is a win-win situation for the two schools. The big-time school adds a win to its record, fills the arena, and keeps its place in the polls while the school-on-the-make gets money to float its program. The downside for the would-be big-time school is that it might be humiliated on the field and some of its players might be injured by the superior team. Surely this practice of scheduling mismatches for money is a form of prostitution.

THE DOMINANCE OF MALE ELITE SPORT

Title IX, passed by Congress in 1972, mandated, among other things, gender equity in school sports programs. Women's intercollegiate sports programs have made tremendous strides toward that goal in the intervening years. Participation in intercollegiate sports has risen from thirty thousand women in 1971 to more than 116,272 in 1996. Athletic scholarships for women were virtually unknown in 1972; now women athletes receive thirty-five percent of the athletic scholarship money that is distributed. These increases in a generation represent the good news concerning gender equity in collegiate sport. The bad news, however, is quite significant. Assessing the situation at big-time schools for 1995–96, we find the following disparities by gender: (1) head coaches of women's teams were paid sixty-three cents for every dollar earned by coaches of men's teams and this inequity does not include the many more extras that the coaches of men's teams receive; (2) only seven schools met proportionality tests for equity (i.e., the percentage of women athletes in a school was within five percent of the proportion of women undergraduates enrolled); (3) the athletes in the average athletic department were sixty-five percent male and thirty-five percent female, with a similar disproportionate distribution of scholarships; (4) spending for recruiting was skewed in favor of males with a seventy-six percent/twenty-four percent ratio; (5) operational expenditures were distributed more unevenly at seventy-eight percent/twenty-two percent. And, most telling, it was not uncommon for a school with a big-time football program to spend twice as much on its football team as it spent on all women's sports.

Clearly, gender equity is not part of big-time college sports programs. To move toward gender balance, athletic administrations have three choices: they can either spend more on women's sports, reduce or eliminate nonrevenue men's sports, or constrict football. Typically, athletic departments add low-cost women's sports such as soccer and crew and cut low-profile men's sports such as wrestling, gymnastics, and baseball. Adding women's sports increases their participation but it does not move much closer to gender parity in scholarships or in other forms of economic assistance. Cutting men's programs is unfair to them because it reduces their participation and opportunities in the so-called minor sports. College sport, it seems to me, should enhance opportunities for participation, not limit them. Athletic departments have high male participation, but they do this with disproportionate participation opportunities for men in football where Division I-A programs may have squads as large as 130 players. Thus, football is a huge drain on the athletic budget and the basis for gender inequality in college athletics.

The rationale for this unequal largesse to one sport is that football underwrites women's sport. This is a myth. Only about one-third of Division I-A football programs make a profit and one-third of them run an annual deficit that averages more than $1 million.

Another myth is that football has already been cut to the bone. The NCAA a few years back did institute some cost-cutting reforms for football, such as reducing scholarships to eighty-five and limiting the number of coaches. But there remain some incredibly extravagant practices such as quartering entire squads in off-campus hotels on the nights before home games, buying out the lucrative contracts for coaches no longer in favor and replacing them with even more expensive coaches, and building ever more palatial football annexes and arenas.

One possible solution to the gender equity bind is for women's sports to generate more revenue. In 1995–96 men's sports teams generated thirteen dollars for every one dollar from women's sports at the Division I level. Women's sports programs are at a disadvantage in producing significant revenues for several reasons: (1) men's intercollegiate sport had a one hundred-year head start in building tradition and fan support; (2) it takes money to make money and, as we have seen, women's sports programs have not been given anything approaching parity in resource allocation; (3) women's sports are relatively ignored by the sports publicity and promotions staffs of the universities, local and national newspapers, magazines, and television; and (4) women's sports continue to be trivialized and deathleticized by the schools in the naming of their teams (e.g., "Wildkittens," "Pink Panthers," "Teddy Bears," and "Lady Rams").

Granted, some of these obstacles to gender equity are changing slowly with more television time devoted to women's play, better promotions by the athletic departments, and the success of U.S. women athletes in international competition. Some women's basketball programs are profitable. But with success, women's budgets and expenses increase just as what has occurred with successful men's programs. The problem with women's programs focusing on revenue is that in time they will likely replicate all of the problems that money has brought to men's collegiate programs. Women's programs need more money, but at what point will money taint the women's game?

Finally, with regard to gender, universities must address this question: Is it appropriate for a college or university to deny women the same opportunities that it provides men? Shouldn't our daughters have the same possibilities as our sons in all aspects of higher education? Should women be second-class in any aspect of the university's activities? The present unequal state of affairs in sport is not inevitable. Choices have been made in the past that have given men advantage in university sports. University administrators could implement true gender equity if they wished. Why do they continue to drag their collective feet on gender equity?

SHAMATEURISM

Although many athletic programs lose money, they nevertheless are involved in a commercial activity. Some coaches, as we have seen, make millions. Universities invite corporations to advertise in their arenas for large sums. The schools sell sweatshirts, beer mugs, sculpture, and other memorabilia with university sport logos for profit. Clearly, big-time college sport is market driven. Ironically, though, athletic departments engage in these money-making activities while exploiting their labor under the guise of amateurism. In other words, athletes generate millions, yet they receive only room, board, tuition, and books. As "amateurs," athletes cannot use their celebrity for income although their employers can use the players' celebrity for commercial purposes. They cannot sell tickets allotted to them. They cannot be reimbursed for trips home. Nor can their parents be compensated with a complimentary trip to a game, although university administrators, coaches, and their spouses can attend with all expenses paid.

The definition of the labor force as amateurs serves at least four purposes. First, it maximizes profits for the schools, the leagues, and the NCAA. Second, as "amateurs," the athletes are not considered employees and therefore not subject to "workmen's compensation," and other employee benefits. Third, by clinging to the myth that athletes are amateurs, the activity is viewed as part of the educational program of the universities. This means that none of the money generated by the athletic departments and the NCAA is taxable and that all taxpayers help pay for sports because colleges and universities are tax-exempt and every booster gets a tax deduction for their donation. And, fourth, if the athletes were considered employees, then the NCAA would likely come under federal scrutiny as an illegal business cartel.

In effect, the university administrators are using the ideal of amateurism as an exploitive ideology. This clearly is hypocritical, to say the least.

Deviant Athletes. A final and especially disturbing issue concerning big-time college sport is that the athletes in these programs are disproportionately involved in assaults, rapes, robberies, and other crimes. In the late 1980s, for example, over a thirty-two-month interval, there were twenty incidents among University of Colorado athletes that resulted in criminal charges. Arizona State in one year had fourteen of its football and men's basketball players involved in arrests, charges, plea bargains, probations, or jail terms. *The Los Angeles Times* reported that in 1995, some 220 college athletes were the subject of criminal proceedings. Also in 1995 *Sports Illustrated* noted that no fewer than one of every seven scholarship players on the 1994 University of Miami foot-balls team had been arrested while enrolled at that university.

Two large studies reveal that these examples are not anomalies. A study of reported violence against women (battering and sexual assaults) at ten Division I schools over a three-year period found that while male student-athletes comprised three percent of the total male population, they represented thirty-five percent of the reported perpetrators. A 1990 national survey of thirteen thousand students found that male athletes were three and a half times more likely than the nonathlete males to admit to having committed date rape.

Keeping in mind that an extremely small percentage of student athletes actually engage in criminal acts, we must ask why college athletes are, nevertheless, disproportionately involved in deviance. There are a number of reasons, but I'll focus on two that have special relevance for this evening's discussion. First, many big-time programs recruit players who were in trouble before college. For example, five big-time college programs tried to recruit New York City high school star Richie Parker despite his felony conviction for sexual abuse. Cleveland State gave a scholarship to basketball player Roy Williams, even though he had been convicted of murder as a teenager in California. While at Cleveland State he was arrested for rape. The University of Cincinnati basketball program offered scholarships to three athletes who had criminal problems before college. The point is clear: some coaches are willing to add a criminal element to their player mix if they believe that it will increase their chances of success on the field. While providing second chances and redemption have their place, should a university's scarce scholarship dollars go to convicted felons just because they are big, strong, and fast?

Second, many athletes come from deprived economic backgrounds. They are on scholarship but this does not give them money for clothes, food, and entertainment. These athletes are well aware that the school, the administrators, the coaches, and seemingly everyone else connected to the athletic program make money off their athletic performance. Logically, it seems to many of them, they deserve a piece of the action, so they take money from an agent, or use the athletic department's long distance telephone credit card, or they accept money under the table from a booster or assistant coach, or they shoplift or steal a stereo from a dorm room.

Whatever the reason for the disproportionate criminality by college athletes, universities have to do some soul searching regarding their possible complicity in such deviance. The evidence is that the problem athletes are male and from the revenue-producing sports of football and basketball. This clearly raises serious questions about the extra subsidies that are given these programs, the evaluation of athletes that might receive scholarships, and the monitoring of athletes when they are on campus.

Big-time college sport confronts us with a fundamental dilemma. Positively, college football and basketball offer entertainment, spectacle, excitement, festival, and excellence. Negatively, the commercial entertainment function of big-time college sport has severely compromised academia. Educational goals have been superseded by the quest for big money. And, since winning programs receive huge revenues from television, gate receipts, bowl and tournament appearances, boosters, and even legislatures, many sports programs are guided by a win-at-any cost philosophy.

The enormous pressures to win result sometimes in scandalous behaviors. Sometimes there are illegal payments to athletes. Education is mocked by recruiting athletes unprepared for college studies, by altering transcripts, by having surrogate test-takers, by providing phantom courses, and by not moving the athletes toward graduation. Add to this ugly mix the problems associated with the exploitation of athletes, gender inequality, and the maintenance of a male-segregated athletic subculture that, when compared to its nonathletic peers, tends to be more antiintellectual, sexist, aggressive, and criminal. One can only wonder how any university can defend and promote this hypocritical, scandal-laden activity.

Let me further summarize the dilemma that big-time college sports presents by delineating several contradictions. The overarching contradiction is that we have organized a commercial entertainment activity within an educational environment. And, in the process, educational goals are compromised.

A fundamental contradiction is that athletes are recruited also as students. Not only do demanding coaches work against the student role, but so does the athletic subculture. At the heart of this contradiction is that institutions of higher learning allow the enrollment and subsidization of ill-prepared and un-interested students solely for the purpose of winning games, enhancing the vis-ibility of the university, and producing revenue. Sometimes these universities recruit known thugs for the same purposes.

The third contradiction is that while big-time sports produce revenue, they also drain money away from academics.

The fourth contradiction is that while the marketing/sales side of big-time sport is big business, the production side is an amateur extracurricular activity in which athletes are "paid" only with an "education."

A final contradiction involves the issue of whether participation in sport is educational or not. University administrators often give this as the rationale for college sport. If so, then these administrators are caught in a contradiction be-cause most of them willingly accept the present maldistribution of resources, scholarships, and opportunities for women's sport. As sociologist Allen Sack has asked: "If sport is educational, what possible academic justification can there be for denying this aspect of education for women? Wouldn't the denial of equal athletic opportunities be tantamount to saying that men should have more microscopes, laboratory facilities, and library privileges than women?"

What are we to do about these contradictions? Do we ignore them and maintain the shame and the sham of the status quo or do we seek true reform? The question: Can the corporate and corrupted sports programs at our major universities be changed to redress the wrongs that make a mockery of aca-deme's educational goals? I believe that we can but that we won't. The presi-dents of the universities involved in big-time sport are too weak or too meek or too unwilling to change. If history is a guide, the presidents will push the NCAA to make cosmetic changes, but they will balk at meaningful structural changes and continue to look the other way while athletic programs do what they have to do to win. Too many want the present system despite its faults. Too many benefit from it.

What I foresee is a further bifurcation of college sport. The money from television and bowl/tournament appearances, the media exposure, and the best athletes will gravitate to a relatively small number of schools. This elite will be composed of, say, sixty-four premier schools, divided into eight conferences and an overarching administrative organization. These schools will have sport programs explicitly designed and packaged commercially as part of a mega-entertainment industry. Eventually, players will be paid professionals, recruited as entertainers, with contracts, salaries, bonuses, and insurance. They will not be required to register as students, although this would be an option. No more rules concerning academic eligibility. No more empty rhetoric about the ideals of amateurism. No more talk of making big-time sport compatible with the ed-ucational mission of universities. This plan removes the hypocrisy in current programs but, of course, if implemented it mocks the purpose of the university.

This is the dilemma. We like—I like—big-time college sport—the festival, the pageantry, the exuberance, the excitement, and the excellence. But are we then willing to accept the hypocrisy that goes with it. I, for one, wish for a more pristine sports system for our schools, such as found at the Division III level or among the NAIA level schools. Academic institutions should leave the professional level to the professional leagues and to an established minor league system funded by professional teams that is outside of the school system.

QUESTIONS FOR REACTION AND DISCUSSION

1. How important are sports on your campus? With the members of your class, discuss the level of involvement by students on your campus and the role of sports within the institution.
2. Eitzen began his speech with a provocative statement: "I believe that big-time college sport compromises the values of higher education." Ask the members of your class to divide themselves into two groups— one that supports Eitzen's statement and another that rejects it. Why did students choose the sides they did? What evidence, perceptions, and/or experiences were students using to determine their responses? Conduct a discussion in which you and your classmates analyze the reasons for the responses.
3. Eitzen expresses significant concern for the education of athletes on campuses generally. What services and tutorial programs are in place in your campus for athletes who must miss classes and tests? How do student athletes feel about the effectiveness of these programs? What support services are in place for student athletes who become overwhelmed with their workloads and schedules?
4. What does Eitzen mean by saying that "university administrators are using the ideal of amateurism as an exploitive ideology"? Discuss with your classmates the definition of an amateur and how that notion is reflected in the sports program on your campus.

QUESTIONS FOR WRITING

1. Interview three or four men and women student athletes who are involved in an intercollegiate sport on your campus. Begin with questions such as: How much time is spent in practice each week? How much time is spent studying and attending classes? What services are provided for student athletes who must miss classes and tests? What major is the student pursuing? What are the career plans? How does the student feel about his or her experience as an athlete? As a student? Write an essay in which you summarize the results of your interviews, using the information you learn from the students you

interviewed to make some statements about the climate for student athletes on your campus.

2. William Schughart, a professor in the Economics Department at the University of Mississippi, wrote a provocative opinion essay, "Protect College Athletes, Not Athletics," in *The Wall Street Journal,* on December 26, 1990. In this essay, Schughart suggested three reform measures that would protect college athletes: (1) colleges should create four-year degree programs in football and basketball (similar to programs in art, music, and drama); (2) colleges should extend the time limit on athletic scholarships by two years in order to compensate athletes for the extraordinary amount of extracurricular time athletic programs demand; and (3) the NCAA should allow institutions to offer wages to athletes and not limit compensation strictly to tuition, books, room, board, and nominal expenses. Select one of these reform measures and write an essay in which you defend or reject it; use examples from your reading and your observation of athletics on your campus.

3. One of the many compelling statistics that Eitzen uses effectively in his speech is that only one percent of college athletes are sufficiently talented to become professional athletes. What are the career expectations for student athletes on your campus? Interview several men and women athletes and ask them what their career aspirations are. How many intend to become professional athletes? How many of them want a career in a sports-related field? Research the career of a former professional athlete. How long did the athlete play his or her sport? What happened to him or her after the career was over? Write an essay in which you compare and contrast the expectations of student athletes with the realities of a career in professional sports.

4. While over fifteen percent of college students participate in an intercollegiate sport, many more participate in physical education courses; enjoy recreational games such as golf, tennis, and squash; and use the increasingly sophisticated sports facilities that colleges and universities offer. What facilities are available on your campus for students who are not participating in intercollegiate sports? Write a report on sports programs on your campus in the form of a letter to a prospective student who isn't an athlete but who is interested in physical fitness.

5. Eitzen ends his essay by suggesting several contradictions that he sees between college sports and higher education. Select one of the contradictions, such as the presence of a "commercial entertainment activity within an educational environment," and write your own speech defending or rejecting Eitzen's contradictions. Use examples from your reading and your experiences as an observer or a participant of sports on your campus.

QUESTIONS FOR FURTHER EXPLORATION

1. The National Collegiate Athletic Association (NCAA) is a voluntary organization of more than one thousand two hundred colleges and universities. The NCAA serves as an accrediting agency for college athletic programs, publishes rules and regulations, and offers a variety of services to member institutions. Access the NCAA Web site <www.ncaa.org> and read some of the position papers on topics like gambling in college sports, the financing of college sports, or a topic of interest to you. Write a report of your findings for your classmates.

2. Because of Title IX of the Education Act, colleges and universities must provide equal opportunities for men and women in sports programs. From 1978 through 1996, the Women's Sports Foundation Gender Equity Report Card study showed that women gained 1,658 sports programs at 767 colleges and universities. Eitzen suggests that the picture for women's sports is considerably less positive than these figures would suggest. Investigate the extent to which gender equity in college sports has contributed to the continuing rise of women's sports on campuses. What can you learn about the success of these programs? Have they affected men's sports programs? Write a report of your findings for your classmates.

3. There are a large number of recent essays, articles, reviews, and opinion pieces about reform of college sports. Use the *Reader's Guide to Periodical Literature* and search for articles written within the last two years. Read what you find and determine what you think are the current issues for reform. Write a report of your findings and share them with your classmates.

4. A number of handbooks are in print that are designed to help student athletes succeed both in sports and in the classroom. One example is *Going the Distance: The College Athlete's Guide to Excellence on the Field and in the Classroom* by Stephen Figler and Howard Figler. Locate a copy of this guide and find others that offer advice to student athletes. What are the most important suggestions that guidebooks make? Is the advice realistic? Prepare an annotated list of guidebooks and share it with student athletes that you know.

7

TRADITIONAL DEGREES, NONTRADITIONAL JOBS: A DEGREE IS NOT A LIFE SENTENCE

The process of determining an education of one's own always involves choosing a major field of study, with the expectation that the choice of a major will be, at least at some level, a preparation for a career directly related to it. Students are often under pressure to make decisions about college majors; most institutions require students to register a major by the end of their second year. While this is an easy task for some, many students find it difficult to select a major because they are uncertain about what careers they wish to pursue. In this essay, Kathleen Green discusses the large number of people who prepare for one occupation and end up pursuing a different career. Green, a lawyer, is also the managing editor for the Occupational Outlook Quarterly, *where this article was originally published. The* Occupational Outlook Quarterly *is published by the Bureau of Labor Statistics of the United States Department of Labor and provides a number of regular features of interest to college students, such as statistics on occupational projections and the outlook in occupations requiring a college education, as well as feature articles on how to seek summer employment, college activities that provide good work experiences, and opportunities in information technology.*

QUESTIONS FOR READING

1. Have you decided on your major field of study? Why or why not?
2. What are your career goals? What are the main influences on your current thinking?
3. Do you expect to change careers? Why or why not?

KATHLEEN GREEN

TRADITIONAL DEGREES, NONTRADITIONAL JOBS: A DEGREE IS NOT A LIFE SENTENCE

Occupational Outlook Quarterly 41 (Spring 1997, pp.12–19)

If it walks like a duckling, quacks like a duckling, and looks like a duckling, it will become a duck. And most workers with specialized job preparation establish a career in their field. Those who study dental hygiene become dental hygienists, education majors become teachers, and medical students become doctors. Most—but not all.

In every field of study, at least some people who prepare for a specific occupation end up working in another. A 1993 National Science Foundation survey of 200,000 college graduates showed that even in a field as specialized as nursing, as many as twenty percent of the male degree holders were employed in other fields. Many, of course, were likely to be in a closely related field or managerial position. But others were doing something completely different.

Their reasons vary. Some people have difficulty finding a good-paying job in their bailiwick and take an unrelated position to pay the bills. Others get sidetracked in their career search but wind up doing something else they enjoy. Still others lose their jobs or become discouraged in their field. But some people, after working in their field for a few months or for many years, decide they want to pursue another career. These workers, found at all educational levels, eschew a traditional job in their field but still make their training work for them. By following their interests, they often progress on career paths much different from the ones they expected to be on. "I love the outdoors, I love backpacking, and I was an engineer," says Ted Ganio, a buyer for an outdoors equipment company who uses his civil engineering background in his work. "I never would've thought I could combine all these things. I didn't even know this job existed." But it did, and he found it.

Focusing on three specialized occupations—nurse, engineer, and lawyer—this article looks at how some people have transferred their specialized skills and knowledge from one field to another. It also discusses some of the options and obstacles you might face if you decide to move your career in a different direction. And to help you with your decisions, additional sources of information are suggested at the end.

A NICHE IS NICE, BUT ZEST IS BEST

Before you start a new job, you probably have ideas about what you want your work life to be like. Your expectations might concern the amount of responsibility you will have, how much say you'll have in major decisions involving your efforts, the number of hours you'll be expected to work, and so forth. You may also have, in the back of your mind, a personal deadline for moving on if reality clashes with your hopes.

At some point in your career, though, you might decide to choose between staying in a job that is secure but unsatisfying or taking a risk on something else that is more closely aligned with your passions. It may take a while for your dream job to become a reality; after all, rookies are expected to pay their dues. But as the following examples illustrate, staying focused on an ideal can lead to rewarding results.

ONCE A NURSE, ALWAYS A NURSE

"Ever since I was a little girl, I've always been fascinated by other cultures," says nurse entrepreneur Dotti Dasher-Riddle. "And I've always been very committed to continuing education, even though it's not required by many states for nursing."

So, after earning a diploma in nursing and working as an emergency room nurse and developing college continuing education programs, Dasher-Riddle had an idea for something new. "I took all of my passions in life—my vocation and my avocations—and rolled them into one," she says. "I asked myself, 'What do I want to do? Where do I want to go?'" The answers to those questions convinced her to start her own company, HealthCare GLOBE, Inc. (Global Learning Opportunities for Broadening Education), which provides international continuing education experiences for health-care professionals. In March, Dasher-Riddle traveled to Australia, where she led a group of fifteen health-care professionals in studying that country's approach to community health.

"I came from a career where working together as part of a team was imperative. It was a matter of life and death," she says. "What I'm doing now is very exciting. I still have the adventure, the excitement, of bringing people, concepts, and ideas together. But the neat thing about my job now is nobody dies."

Generally, registered nurses and licensed practical nurses care for the sick and injured. Their specific duties vary, based on factors such as level of education, specialty, and work setting. Registered nurses must complete a two- or four-year educational program and pass a licensing exam; licensed practical nurses complete a one-year program and pass an exam. Nursing qualities—which include being caring, sympathetic, attentive to detail, and able to accept responsibility and give direction to others—have far-reaching applicability to other occupations both within and outside health care.

But nurses' health-care knowledge is itself an asset. Nurse entrepreneur Diane Pabilonia created her own interior design company, Medical Interiors, after working as an operating-room, intensive-care, missionary, and private-duty nurse. "I never found an office that was really designed right for the nurses and doctors," she says. "Now, I put myself in the position of someone working there and ask myself, 'How would I want to work?'" Pabilonia is also executive director of planning and business development for a managed health-care services organization, tapping her nursing background and a network of health-care professionals.

Credentials and contacts are invaluable for nurses working outside direct patient care in positions such as health-insurance fraud investigator, political activist, expert witness, administrator, educator, and, like Dasher-Riddle and Pabilonia, entrepreneur within the health-care industry. "One thing nursing has taught me is to be inventive. We always had to explore different ways of doing things," says Dasher-Riddle. "But it's also very important to realize you don't have all the answers. I'm not an expert on anything, but I have an extensive network available to me."

On their own, nursing knowledge and contacts in the field are rarely adequate preparation for the business world. Although most nurses are accustomed to learning by doing, would-be entrepreneurs may have to take additional classes. Dasher-Riddle says she wishes she had taken education and business courses while she was in school. Pabilonia agrees some business background would have helped prime her for at least one concern nurses do not have to think about: profits. "In private industry, you have to really target your financial goals," she says. "Nurses are never trained to think that way. I was happy doing missionary nursing for no money."

Job satisfaction is one of the benefits of the nurse entrepreneurial life—especially since entrepreneurism provides an escape from the administrative delays and lack of independence nurses often face in patient care. "I like the freedom of developing things and having them done quickly," says Pabilonia. Adds Dasher-Riddle: "When you work for someone else, somebody other than you always has the last say. But now I have the final call."

There were 1,977,000 registered nurses and 399,000 licensed practical nurses employed in 1995. According to the American Nurses' Association, however, there are no data available on how many nurses do something other than directly care for patients. "Some people have the sense that nurses get burned out and leave the profession, but that's not the case; it's not supported by data," says the Association's Joan Meehan, director of media relations and community affairs. "They may switch to some other occupation, but they are still nurses."

REDESIGNING AN ENGINEER

Paul Floreck knew at an early age what he wanted to be when he grew up. "I wanted to be an engineer," he says, "and I was always fascinated by airplanes." Earning a bachelor's degree in aerospace engineering followed by a master's in mechanical engineering were educational steps to fulfilling that flight of fancy.

Floreck worked for about a decade in the aerospace industry, primarily on the West Coast, holding engineering jobs as a designer and analyst. But he wanted to live closer to family on the East Coast, so he took a position in New Jersey as a consultant in the rail transportation industry. Eighteen months later, about the time he realized the rail industry was not his forte, he noticed a *New York Times* want ad for a person who could provide sales staff with technical information on an aircraft company's products. "I really wanted the job, and I knew the competition would be tough," says Floreck. "I took the ad apart and made sure my resume showed every bit of my experience directly relevant to the position." His strategy worked; he got the job.

"My background is pretty conventional for what I do now," says Floreck. "I have had so many opportunities along the way, but I was never quite sure where they would lead. As I got further into my career, especially working for a big company, I got a taste of which things I liked and didn't like to do. I was very, very fortunate that I found a position in which I could do what I like doing."

An engineer typically uses science and math to find innovative, cost-effective solutions to technical problems. Job duties may include design, planning, supervision, development, evaluation, and cost estimating. A bachelor's degree in engineering is the minimum educational requirement for most engineering jobs. There are more than twenty-five major specialties, plus numerous subdivisions, within engineering.

Engineers should be creative, detail-oriented, and analytical; they also need to communicate well and be able work as part of a team. Those skills, coupled with their technical understanding, give engineers multifaceted work options. Ted Ganio worked in a backpacking shop while earning a degree in civil engineering, then spent two years as an engineer with the Peace Corps in Nepal. He now blends his knowledge of both areas in a job as buyer of outdoors equipment. "All the backpack manufacturers are trying to do the same thing: design a product that carries the most weight with the least amount of stress," he says. "Because of my engineering background, I understand what they're trying to accomplish and how they're trying to accomplish it."

Technical expertise benefits engineers employed in nonengineering business jobs. "In business, marketing is huge, and a lot of it is voodoo science," says Ganio. "As a buyer, being able to see through the voodoo science is very useful." Engineers in other occupations include accountant, financial analyst, financial planner, and computer professions. Some engineers work in engineering management or sales and, like Floreck, use their engineering background to provide technical information.

Both Ganio and Floreck agree that business courses would have helped them prepare for the work they do now. Because engineering education is highly structured, however, there isn't much room for electives. Engineering study does include some business foundation, says Ganio: "Financing a project (in engineering) is not unlike financing a product. The bottom line is to try to make money for the company by investing in products." But Floreck says, "Engineering as a raw discipline is interesting, but you're really not prepared for much else when you get out of school." And, he adds, many skills engineers need cannot be taught in college. "You can bury your head in a book, but it won't help with your ability to interact with others or to understand the 'big picture' elements of your business."

Floreck and Ganio find themselves willingly working overtime, due, in part, to their enthusiasm for their work. "As a consultant in a field that was new to me, I felt a lot of frustration in coming up with ideas that no one seemed interested in. And I was frustrated putting in a lot of overtime because I didn't like what I was doing," says Floreck. "My current job requires a lot of overtime, too, but I don't mind it because I enjoy the work." Ganio says the same is true for him. "I love what I'm doing—that's what I like about my job," he says. "I like it so much I get in trouble for working too much. But I'm working hard because I choose to do it."

There were 1,934,000 engineers employed in 1995. The American Association of Engineering Societies has no data on the number of engineers working in nonengineering jobs.

PRACTICE NOT PERFECT FOR ALL LAWYERS

Like many people who become lawyers, Jim Doerfler had thought about it long before college and started honing his skills to prepare for it. "I had always considered law school," he says. "My high school had a strong speech and debate program, and I took part in that and competed at the state and national levels." He also did some debating in college. After graduating from law school, he worked for a judge and then for a law firm, where he defended large corporate clients in civil lawsuits.

Meanwhile, Doerfler's father and his father's business partner in an electrical subcontracting business started talking about retirement. And Doerfler started thinking about taking over their business. "I was assessing my career options," he says, "and the idea of having my own business, especially continuing into the future something that had already been established, was very appealing to me." He quit his job at the law firm and began working at the family business as a project manager and cost estimator. Now, the owner-partners are negotiating a deal to turn the business over to their sons.

"I didn't think about going into the family business until I was out in the working world, where I was faced with issues like downsizing and job security," says Doerfler. "I started thinking that the best of all possible worlds is the family business. It allows you to do as much as you're capable of. I wanted to do something different and continue what's been done before."

In law practice, lawyers advise clients about their legal rights and obligations and suggest courses of action; they also represent parties in court by submitting evidence that best supports their client's position. Depending on the area of expertise, lawyers' specific responsibilities and tasks vary. Preparation for becoming a licensed lawyer generally requires three years of full-time study after earning a bachelor's degree and admission to the state bar, usually by passing an exam upon completion of law school.

Their understanding of the law, along with the ability to analyze complex documents and situations, gives lawyers skills applicable to many fields. Doerfler expects his legal training to be useful in business for everything from ensuring compliance with equal employment laws to understanding contracts. "My law degree in the short run is not as much a benefit as it will be in the long run," he says. "Now, it tends to put people off a bit. But in the long run, a law degree is potentially very beneficial in the construction industry."

Lawyers also should enjoy working with people and be responsible, honest, creative, and attentive to detail. Thuy Tran uses her legal training and people skills as a senior benefits specialist for Fairfax County, Virginia, reviewing documents from applicants who need long-term, residential care. "When I saw the announcement, I thought the job would be perfect for me. I'd be working with people, and, at the same time, it would allow me to use my legal background," she says. "What I'm doing now is part social worker, part coordinator—there are a lot of different things involved. But I'm not allowed to give advice. That's the most difficult change that's different from law."

A law degree's versatility results in lawyers working outside the law in a wide range of fields, including counseling, teaching, administration, management, politics and government, communications, and business and entrepreneurial ventures. "A good friend of mine, a law professor in Baltimore, told me that no matter what you want to do, a law degree is good to have," says Tran. "The people who interviewed me for my current job said my law degree is what they found most attractive about my qualifications."

As broad as a legal education can be, however, law students preparing for the bar exam usually enroll primarily in bar-related courses. Doerfler says he might have taken courses such as tax, labor, and employment law if he had foreseen a future in business ownership. But he backs up a step further, to his undergraduate studies. "My father was always urging me to get some accounting and engineering background, and I probably should've heeded his advice," says Doerfler, whose undergraduate degree is in economics and who now takes courses to beef up his understanding of business. "I'm not so arrogant to think I can come in and tell everyone how things should be done. I view this as being a long-term process."

Especially compared with the work they did in their law practices, Doerfler and Tran say they are much happier in their jobs now. Doerfler prefers the strategic planning required in business to the battle perspective lawyers take in their work; he also likes having a productive business rather than feeling he is simply redistributing wealth. And the new hours mean an improved quality of life for him and his family. "I found that the demands of legal practice resulted in an inability to balance corporate expectations with family life," he says. "Now, I'm able to take more time off for my family."

For Tran, the rewards of her work are greatly satisfying. "After I finished law school, I worked for six months in a private law firm and hated it," she says. "But now I really enjoy what I'm doing. I have yet to have a boring day."

Both Tran and Doerfler acknowledge there are things they dislike about their new positions, however. Tran has discovered she does not like dealing with lawyers in her job: "There are some who are good, but others are just taking advantage of their clients' fear and ignorance of the law." Doerfler, coming from a prestigious position with an estimable law firm, has noticed a lack of respect for workers in the construction industry—as well as a focus on cost over caliber. "In law, the emphasis is on quality," he says. "But in business, price pretty much rules and quality is sometimes sacrificed."

There were 894,000 lawyers employed in 1995. A National Association for Law Placement survey of the class of 1995 found over ten percent of the graduates were employed in nonlegal full- and part-time jobs six months after graduation. A survey conducted by the American Bar Foundation in 1991, the most recent year the survey was conducted, found that of 744,000 employed attorneys 76,857 were employed in occupations not related to the legal field.

NOT JUST A JOB:
CHANGING CAREERS FOR LOVE OF WORK

Don't despair if you feel you have made a wrong career move. But instead of simply staying put and being miserable, take steps to move your career in the right direction. Floreck advises, "The first ten years of your career, you should plan to move around if you're not doing what you want to be doing." After all, says Dasher-Riddle, "It's absolutely imperative that people like what they do."

Knowing what your skills and interests are will help you determine which jobs you would like to do. (Self-assessment exercises are found in many job-hunting guides.) Once you identify your skills and interests, figure out how they help you become marketable in the workforce. "If you can combine several interests, it will make you very valuable in the job market," says Pabilonia. "Be creative in inventing your own job; think about dual interests." Prepare to use that creativity to show potential employers how your specialized skills can be applied to other areas as well.

Anyone thinking about making a career change should plan on doing a lot of exercises in areas like self-assessment, ranking priorities, and setting goals. But people with specialized skills have additional considerations. Your training might be narrowly tailored; as discussed previously, education for occupations such as nurse, engineer, and lawyer does not always leave room for broad-based electives. Careful assessment of your skills and knowledge will help you determine what courses, if any, you need to take before embarking on a new career.

Even if you take a few classes leading toward a new career, try to ensure that the direction you plan to take is one you really want to pursue. Volunteering or working part-time provides a test run for finding out how well the expertise you have combines with your craving to do something else. It's better to discover that you lack acting ability when you are in community theater than after you've quit your job. Volunteer and part-time jobs, like internships, can also help prepare you for your new career. "When I was in college, I didn't think internships were really important," says Doerfler. "But internships provide opportunities for networking and getting hands-on experience, which are the most important tools you can develop."

Convincing an employer that you have what it takes to do a job always requires preparation. But when it comes to pursuing a new career field, you may have some additional explaining to do. When Pabilonia was asked in an interview how a nurse could be prepared for the business world, she focused on her ability to get things accomplished: "I told them I've always been successful at whatever I've done." Demonstrate to potential employers your enthusiasm, self-confidence, resourcefulness, flexibility, perseverance, and commitment to a new career direction. "Go into every interview like you really want the job," says Floreck. "You have to do your research and be prepared. But also try to prepare yourself to find alternatives."

The better you ready yourself to move into a new field, the more sure you will be of your decision to change careers. Self-doubt might be one of the biggest hurdles you have to overcome, especially since there are no guarantees the doubt will evaporate when you embark on your new career. Feeling confident about your calling, however, makes it easier to be comfortable that the decision is right for you. "I see a dam or a structure and think, 'I could've done this,'" Ganio says. "But when I think a step beyond, to the work environment, I know I wouldn't be happy doing that."

If you've spent two or five or seven years training for a specific occupation, you're bound to encounter bewilderment from others when you decide to pursue something else. Pabilonia still gets surprised reactions when she attends nursing reunions and reports what she's doing now. "I loved being a nurse; I loved every specialty. And although I have many other interests, I always thought I would stay in nursing," she says. "Most of my classmates have stayed with nursing, so they're really surprised to hear I've gotten away from patient care because they know how much I like nursing."

Some reactions span both ends of the spectrum. "People who knew I was an engineer—it's almost like they're disappointed to hear what I'm doing now," says Ganio. "But people who've known me all along know I'm in my element." Doerfler encounters different reactions from those in his former profession and the ones he works with now. "Lawyers I talk to generally understand what's going on. Some even ask, 'Can I have a job, too?'" he says. "But a carpenter who was in one of my classes used to say, 'I'm a doctor, but I do carpentry on the side.' He didn't really understand. I think sometimes people have an idyllic view of the legal profession."

But responding to others' reactions, both positive and negative, is elementary once you incorporate your training into your new career. "People say to me, 'You go to all this trouble to get your law degree, and you're not using it?'" says Tran. "But I'm glad I had the experience with law. I tend to ask 'What-if' questions, more contingency questions, in my work now. Because of my legal background, I do have a different perspective that I bring to my job."

FINDING MORE INFORMATION

Being informed is one of the best things you can do to sort your way through the job maze. To learn about specific occupations—job duties, working conditions, education and training required, earnings, employment prospects, and more—consult the *Occupational Outlook Handbook* (OOH). Find out which occupations would allow you to use your talents and interests, and then learn as much as you can about those jobs. Most occupational entries in the OOH also include associations to contact for more information.

The OOH is in the career reference section of many libraries. Bring your library card when you go because you'll want to investigate the rest of the career and employment section, too. Look for resources on topics such as choosing and changing careers, job-hunting strategy, work options, and resume writing. Don't overlook tomes that could be packed with useful tips but are written about another field; much of the information in books about lawyers changing careers, for example, is adaptable to job changes in general. Plan to spend a few hours of reading to find the ones you like best. You may settle on a source or two worth perusing, or you might elect to pluck bits of wisdom from sages old and new to the career information field.

Career counseling is another plan worth following. Whether you're still in school or have been out many years, career counselors often have a wealth of information at their fingertips. In addition to any resources and online services they may have, they often also have a network of contacts available for you to explore your prospective field. If you're a college graduate, check with your alma mater to find out if career counseling services are still available to you.

Questions for Reaction and Discussion

1. How many of your classmates have selected a major? How many have a specific career goal in mind? In a group discussion, poll the members of the class and determine the range of majors and career goals. What have been the major influences on the members of the class in determining these choices?

2. What are the similarities and differences among the people Green mentions in her article? What characteristics do people seem to share who change careers?

3. Many students enter college with the goal of becoming a lawyer; in recent years, the legal field in all areas has become crowded. What other opportunities are suggested in this article for a person with a legal background?

4. What are the most useful suggestions in this article about making a good career choice? Make a list with your classmates.

QUESTIONS FOR WRITING

1. What services does your college or university provide to assist students in determining majors and career options? Research what is available on your campus, prepare a list of resources, and write a report for your classmates on the services that can help them choose a major and a career.

2. Investigate information resources available to students about the department or program in which you intend to pursue a major. Interview people who majored in the field you are considering and ask them about how they determined a career path for themselves. Locate print and electronic resources on such topics as what one can do with an English major or a history major or your particular interest. Write a report for your class on what career possibilities there are for a person who graduates with a major in the field you are considering.

3. Using the information resources that Green suggests at the end of her article, investigate a career you are thinking of pursuing. What training will you need? What should your college major be? What is the current outlook for employment? How competitive is the field? Will you need training beyond an undergraduate degree? Write a report, including information resources, about the career you want to pursue.

QUESTIONS FOR FURTHER EXPLORATION

1. Check your library holdings for the *Occupational Outlook Quarterly* and other print publications sponsored by the U.S. Department of Labor. Prepare an annotated list of current articles and information sources on making career decisions, published within the last two years, that would be of interest to your classmates. If your library subscribes to O*NET, the Occupational Information Network, explore this database and include information on using it for your classmates.

2. The United States Department of Labor is specifically charged with "preparing the American workforce for new and better jobs and ensuring the adequacy of America's workplaces." As an information agency, the Department of Labor provides a wealth of information to citizens. Visit the Web site <http://www.dol.gov> and explore the resources and general information about occupations that you find there. Write a report of your findings and share them with your classmates.

3. In his book, *What's College For?*, Zachary Karabell suggests that "A college degree has always been perceived as a ticket to a better life, but never before has it been so perceived as a ticket to a career." As he also notes, however, a lively debate exists about whether or not a college education is actually necessary for a successful career. Search the *Reader's Guide to Periodical Literature* for recent articles about the relationship between higher education and jobs. Write a brief report about recent opinions about the necessity of a college education for job-seekers.

8

THE CLOISTER AND THE HEART

Early in her career, Jane Tompkins established herself as a major scholar in American literature. The author of several books on literary and cultural criticism, she has taught at numerous colleges and universities, including Connecticut College, Temple University, and Duke University. In recent years, however, her interests have centered on pedagogy, the study of teaching practices. In her current position at the University of Illinois, Chicago, Tompkins teaches courses in the Department of Education. In A Life in School: What the Teacher Learned, *Tompkins writes an account of her own experiences as a student—from her elementary school days through her life as a university professor. The book is partly a memoir and partly a critique of contemporary higher education, especially of college classrooms themselves. Tompkins fears that universities have become assembly lines. Concerned that too many students passively accept information provided by a central authority—the professor— Tompkins suggests alternative ways of learning and knowing. She is also deeply troubled by the emphasis on professional training by colleges and universities and argues that college should be an "introduction to life" and not merely preparation for a career. In this essay, which is the final chapter of her book, Tompkins meditates on the idea of a college as a "cloister" and the implications for students, educators, and parents.*

QUESTIONS FOR READING

1. What is a "cloister"?
2. What do you think the title suggests about the essay you are about to read?
3. Are you considering a career in education? Why or why not?

JANE TOMPKINS

THE CLOISTER AND THE HEART

A Life in School: What the Teacher Learned *(New York: Addison-Wesley, 1996)*

I've been struggling with the concept of college as a cloister. I know not every university enjoys this privileged seclusion. I went to a college that did—Bryn Mawr—and taught for many years at one that didn't—Temple University. What I have to say applies more to the first kind of school than to the second, but it's relevant to most institutions of higher learning because most of them emulate what the cloister stands for: a place hallowed and set apart. It was the experimental courses I taught at Duke, courses in which I got to know the students much better than I did when I taught in the normal way, that led me to question the usefulness of college as a cloister and also to see the cloister as a missed opportunity. It was those courses that let me see how cut off from life the students were, how cut off from the world they were about to enter, and at the same time, how cut off from themselves. It was also those courses that re-called to me the tremendous passion that the quest for knowledge had aroused in me when I was an undergraduate.

When I was in college, I didn't worry much about what would happen af-terward; and as far as I know, neither did my friends. Either you got married, or you got a job, or you went to graduate school, in which case you had a scholarship or your parents paid. The issue seemed straightforward and not a problem. Besides, what happened after college had very little reality while I was still in school.

The opposite is true for undergraduates today. They seem tasked and shad-owed by the future. My student, Shannon, who confessed that she hated to read, but had come to Duke because if she hadn't, she thought she'd end up at McDonald's, is not the exception but the norm. Students who go to schools like Duke are afraid that if they don't get an expensive, high-status liberal arts degree, they'll end up in a low-level job, usually conceived as working for a fast-food chain. And even if they complete the four years successfully, they're afraid of not finding a job when they leave. The other day, crossing the quad, I heard one female undergraduate say to another, in a wail: "I'll be unemployed, have no place to live, and be a hundred thousand dollars in debt!"

Many students, driven by the fear of not getting a good enough job after they graduate, make choices that go against the grain of their personalities. One student I had who was an actor and loved the theater was majoring in economics. When I questioned him about it briefly, he seemed not to have con-sidered a career that would make use of his talents. It was as if his love of the theater and his career plans were on two separate tracks. Over and over I've been surprised to learn that a student in one of my classes was planning to at-tend law school or medical school—vocations that seemed to bear no relation to his or her aptitudes or interests.

Over time I've come to think about my undergraduate students, whom I treasure and admire and have tremendous affection for, under the metaphor of a train journey. Someone, a parent or other influential adult in their lives, has given them a ticket. On it is stamped medical school, or law school, or business school, or in rarer cases, graduate school. They're on the train and holding this ticket, the countryside is going by very fast, and they're not getting to see much of it. All they know is that when the train arrives at their stop, they'll be getting off.

My experimental courses were about helping students to discover who was holding the ticket so that they could make up their own minds about whether the destination was right for them. More than once, a student would explain why it wasn't right and then turn around and hotly defend the choice anyway. What my experiments revealed was how pressured the students felt to perform in a way that would get them approval from their parents and their peers. They seemed to have little knowledge of themselves, little knowledge of what possibilities the world had to offer, and little sense that they really could choose on their own behalf.

This last point, the students' sense of not being agents on their own behalf, troubles me the most. I think it's the result of an educational process that infantilizes students, takes away their initiative, and teaches them to be sophisticated rule followers. Of course, as professors, we don't see the ways in which what we do as teachers narrows and limits our students: for we ourselves have been narrowed and limited by the same process.

From the teacher's point of view, the classroom is a place of opportunity. Here students can enrich themselves, are inspired, motivated, made curious, enlightened by the professor. Here students participate in producing knowledge themselves, since most professors nowadays would agree that students need to be active learners. The great example of student participation in the learning process is class discussion. From the teacher's perspective, class discussion constitutes freedom. It gives students a chance to express themselves. Instead of the teacher talking, the students talk. They air their opinions, exchange ideas; they disagree with one another, and sometimes they even disagree with the instructor. They raise their hands, they speak, their voices are heard.

But one day my cousin, Jane Dibbell, and I were talking about teaching—she is both a lifelong teacher and an actress, whose view of the classroom is sensitive to its theatricality. She started to mimic what happens when students talk in class, and a new vision of classroom dynamics opened up for me. She raised her hand and began to wave it, her voice filled with anxiety: "Am I smart?" she said. "Am I really smart? Am I the smartest?"

In class discussion, students compete with one another for the teacher's approval. They seek reassurance, and they want to be rewarded with praise. It's a performance they're engaged in, not a spontaneous utterance, and a performance on which a lot depends: their own self-esteem, the regard of their fellow students, the good opinion of the teacher, and ultimately their grade and their grade point average. There are many ways to fail.

You can go wrong by parroting what the teacher has already said, or by *not* repeating what she's said. You can use the wrong vocabulary or misunderstand the question. You can appear so knowledgeable that the teacher becomes uncomfortable and the other students jealous. You can find out to your surprise that nobody agrees with you. You can say something inadvertently funny, and everyone will laugh. You can come across as naive and dorky, a nerd. . . .

Practically everything about you is open to inspection and speculation when you talk in class, since, in speaking, your accent, your vocabulary, the intonations of your voice, your display of feeling or lack of it, the knowledge you can call on, or not, all contain clues about who you are—your social class, ethnic background, sense of yourself as a gendered being, degree of self-knowledge, the way you relate to other people. You can seem aggressive, defensive, shy, manipulative, exhibitionistic.

My cousin was right in intuiting the theatrical nature of the college classroom. People who take the classroom seriously have invested themselves in perfecting a certain kind of performance. Knowing just how to answer the question, performing exactly right for the teacher, learning how not to offend the other students become the guidelines for success in life. Slowly, with practice, the classroom self becomes the only self. At preprofessional colleges where students (largely as a result of parental influence) are headed for law school, medical school, business school, graduate school, the performance mentality intensifies; people are so grade conscious and worried about doing well on their LSATs, MCATs, or GREs, that how they do on tests and papers becomes the measure of their worth as human beings.

My point is that classroom learning can constrict a person's horizons even as it broadens them. Learning too well the lessons of the classroom exacts a price. Its exclusive emphasis on the purely intellectual and informational aspects of learning, on learning as individualistic and competitive, can create a lopsided person: a person who can process information efficiently, summarize accurately, articulate ideas, and make telling points; a person who is hard-working, knows how to please those in authority, and who values high performance on the job above all things.

Everything I have learned in the last ten years has shown me that this is not the sort of person to become. But the educational deck is stacked against becoming anything different. Keith Johnstone, the British playwright, director, and teacher of actors writes of the destructive effects of schooling:

> I tried to resist my schooling, but I accepted the idea that my intelligence was the most important part of me. I tried to be *clever* in everything I did. The damage was greatest in areas where my interests and the school's seemed to coincide: in writing, for example (I wrote and rewrote, and lost all fluency). I forgot that inspiration isn't intellectual, that you don't have to be perfect. In the end I was reluctant to attempt anything for fear of failure, and my first thoughts never seemed good enough. Everything had to be corrected and brought into line.

It's the people who are most susceptible to authority who suffer the most from their schooling, and who must liberate themselves later on from its effects. Many of those who do not wake up to their condition remain in school as teachers, pleased with the rewards of having performed well, so the codes of the classroom are passed on.

The *format* of higher education, its mode of delivery, contains within itself the most powerful teachings students receive during their college years. But most college professors, being products of the system, have given little thought to the ways in which the conventions of classroom teaching stunt and warp students as well as enabling them to expand their horizons. Johnstone writes,

> One day, when I was eighteen, I was reading a book and I began to weep. I was astounded. I'd had no idea that literature could affect me in such a way. If I'd have wept over a poem in class the teacher would have been appalled. I realised that my school had been teaching me *not* to respond.

When I look back at my schooling today, I see what Johnstone sees—a person who was taught not to feel. The long process of coming back into possession of my feelings, learning to recognize their presence, then learning to express them in safe situations, allowing them to be there instead of pushing them down as I had always done—*this* education has dominated the last several years of my life. When I look at my undergraduate students, I see how their schooling is forcing them into the same patterns I have struggled to overcome: a divided state of consciousness, a hypertrophy of the intellect and will, an undernourished heart. I see how compartmentalized the university is, with the philosophy department at one end of the campus, the gymnasium at the other. I see how conditioned the students are—though not terminally so—to keeping their own experience out of the learning process. And I am filled with an inchoate yearning for integration.

But I hear these voices of my friends and colleagues saying, *Aren't you forgetting how much you wanted to become an intellectual? Aren't you forgetting your old love of knowledge? of books and ideas? Aren't you turning your back on something precious? And aren't you forgetting how hard it was to enter the gates of academe, to become an initiate, to learn the trade so that you could take part in the central activities of your profession?*

What about all the people who are eager to have even a glimpse of the life you seem so willfully to throw away?

Isn't your discontent the result of too much privilege?

I listen to the voices and I want to say, Of course, of course; each person's situation is different. Many people did not suffer what I suffered, or enjoy the advantages I enjoyed. My critique of school comes from my experience of it, which is limited, as all experience is. Yet I believe that the lesson I learned holds good for many people other than myself. Human beings, no matter what their background, need to feel that they are safe in order to open themselves to transformation. They need to feel a connection between a given subject matter and who they are in order for knowledge to take root. That security and that connectedness are seldom present in a classroom that recognizes the students' cognitive capacities alone. People often assume that attention to the emotional lives of students, to their spiritual yearnings and their imaginative energies, will somehow inhibit the intellect's free play, drown it in a wash of sentiment, or deflect it into the realms of fantasy and escape, that the critical and analytical faculties will be muffled, reined in, or blunted as a result. I believe the reverse is true. The initiative, creativity, energy, and dedication that are released when students know they can express themselves freely show, by contrast, how accustomed they are to holding back, playing it safe, avoiding real engagement, or just going through the motions. Besides, it's not a question of repressing or cutting back on intellectual inquiry in school, but rather of acknowledging and cultivating wholeness. As Maria Montessori wrote in *The Absorbent Mind*, education is not just "of the mind," nor should it be thought of as "the mere transmission of knowledge. . . . For what is the use of transmitting knowledge if the individual's total development lags behind?"

The real objection to a more holistic approach to education lies in a fear of emotion, of the imagination, of dreams and intuitions and spiritual experience that funds commonly received conceptions of reality in this culture. And no wonder, for it is school, in part, that controls reality's shape. The fear of these faculties, at base a fear of chaos and loss of control, is abetted by ignorance. For how can we be on friendly terms with those parts of ourselves to which we have never received a formal introduction, and for which we have no maps or guides? The strength of the taboo can be gauged by the academician's inevitable recourse to name-calling when emotion, spirituality, and imagination are brought into the curricular conversation: "touchy-feely," "soft," "unrigorous," "mystical," "therapeutic," and "Mickey Mouse" are the all-time favorites, with "psychobabble" and "bullshit" not far behind. The implication is always that something mindless, dirty, and infantile is being recommended, which in a certain sense is true, since the faculties in question have not been allowed to mature and remain in an unregulated state. The concern that things will fall apart and no one will learn anything if these unruly elements are allowed into the picture stems precisely from their historic exclusion from our system of education. The less we know about these unpredictable domains, the less we want to know.

Throughout this discussion of the compartmentalization of learning, two themes have been running parallel to each other. One concerns the intense focus on performance, geared to the perceived necessity of gaining a foothold in a fiercely competitive marketplace; the other concerns higher education's exclusive emphasis on intellectual development. As things stand now, these two emphases reinforce one another; there are very few ways to excel academically, and thus to become marketable, that include attention to creativity, selfknowledge, and compassion for oneself and others.

I became so interested in this problem, which I called the problem of preprofessionalism, that I came back from leave and created a temporary job in order to study it and report on it to the deans of liberal arts at my university.

The process of gathering information was revealing in itself. Like an animal loose in the forest for the first time, I roved at will and discovered how little I had learned, in the course of my academic life, about what goes on in a university. I talked to people who, as a full-time professor, I'd never gotten to know before: the dean and assistant dean of academic advising, the head of the Career Development Center, the head of Counselling and Psychological services, the vice provost for student affairs, the deans of residential life, the university chaplain, the resident advisors in the dorms. I found that these people did essential, life-sustaining work, that they gave of themselves generously, that they had been thinking for some time about issues that were new to me, and that they were generally underrecognized and underpaid.

Professors, I realized, are the Chinese emperors of the institution—with students as the crown princes. Without knowing it, I had occupied an isolated, privileged space, unaware of what kept the institution running day to day, ignorant of the lives my students led outside the classroom, of the people who helped them when they needed help. I had been generally uninterested in these matters, which, I tacitly assumed, were being taken care of by people with intellects and qualifications vaguely inferior to my own—for if not, wouldn't they have Ph.D.s and tenure-track positions?

This hierarchical structure, which places people who take care of students' emotional, physical, and spiritual lives lower on the ladder than people who deal only with their minds, kept troubling me as I went about my business. I didn't know what it had to do with the problem of preprofessionalism, but it wouldn't go away. Finally, some months later, it dawned on me that the hierarchy reflected exactly what I felt was wrong with undergraduate education. It depreciates those aspects of being human that are missing from the curriculum and from our pedagogy. The way we perceive the process of schooling—the mastering of skills and the ingesting of information by disembodied minds—is reflected in the way we organize the institution.

This is not lost on the students themselves.

Not surprisingly, the students I talked to in my researches had by far the most trenchant critiques of the university, since they are less invested in it than faculty and staff, whose income and sense of identity largely depend on the institution. I met with various student groups and talked with individual students and soon formed a picture of the problem as they see it. The students complained of the tremendous pressure they were under to get good grades in order to be competitive in the rush to professional school and on the job market. They were headed in this direction so that they could find work, work that would pay back their loans or satisfy their parents, who wanted to see some financial return on their $100,000 investment. So much in the students' experience seemed constrained by this motive: they chose majors that would satisfy the requirements of professional school and took electives that would not spoil their grade point averages.

At the same time, students wanted to explore; they wanted to study marine botany, take a course in twentieth-century religious cults, learn Russian, and write short stories. Their advisors told them: "Take what you love." Meanwhile, their parents pressured them to major in economics. One student summed it up dramatically by saying that he felt caught in a kind of schizophrenia. "Duke wants to produce competitive students, and it wants to encourage self-exploration. Sure, students want to 'take what they love,' but people don't want to be beachcombers."

The most ringing critique I heard came from two students I'd taught two years before. I'd called up the students I'd had in Reading for Yourself, who were about to graduate. I wanted to find out what the Duke experience had been like for them, and to see them one more time before they left, for I loved them. I asked: What did you like best about your education, and what would you change if you could?

One of the students had been premed and had gotten into a prestigious medical school; he was planning to go the following fall. His was a success story, but not to hear him tell it. I took notes on our conversation because I was stunned by the harshness of his views.

He began by citing statistics: the university had a ninety percent rate of acceptance to medical school, a ninety-five percent rate of acceptance to law school, and was, in his words, "a preprofessional warehouse, an expensive stepping-stone." "I used Duke," he said, "and Duke used me. . . . It's like Monopoly, a money mill. . . . Learning is second. Achievement is first."

The bitterness in his tone struck me. "What would help?" I asked. "Someone like me saying the things I'm saying to you," he replied.

At freshman orientation for premed and prelaw students, he said that he had been told what grades he needed to make. The message freshmen ought to get, he said, was "Learn for learning's sake, not just to get a grade."

The other student whose reactions impressed me, an English major, who in the flush of graduation week said that everything about her Duke experience had been perfect, later wrote a long reflective letter in a darkened tone. She, too, began by citing statistics. "Of the one thousand four hundred people in my class, six hundred are going to law school in the fall, and three hundred are going to medical school." Of the remainder, she said, some would go to graduate school. "I guess most everybody got what they came for—a ticket to some other place."

She continued: "Why aren't we ever encouraged to believe that a liberal arts education is enough? . . . Does my Duke degree lose its lustre if it's not joined by another? The practices of medicine and law and the academy do not need one thousand Duke students, but the world does." Like the medical student, she felt keenly that her education had had too little application to the world.

The end product of an educational system that fails to help its students find out who they are and where in the world their talents might best be employed is not difficult to foresee. One day I was telling a friend who is a senior partner at a premier Washington law firm about how career driven my students were. He said he couldn't count the number of younger colleagues who ended up in his office saying that they were miserable but didn't know what to do. They'd gone to the best colleges, had gotten the highest grades, gone to the best law schools, made law review, been hired by a top firm and then—it turned out they hated the work. *Hated* it. But they'd never made any independent decisions, had never stepped off the track; they didn't dare leave for fear of being seen as failures. They felt trapped.

I understand the argument that the university can't do everything. Academic courses, it goes, *are* for the mind. Let the home and the church and the psychotherapist and the athletic program attend to the spirit and the body and the rest. We professors have our hands full already trying to get across the riches of our subject matter in fourteen weeks. We can't be therapists and doctors and spiritual directors, too.

What I am asking for is a more holistic approach to learning, a disciplinary training for people who teach in college that takes into account the fact that we are educators of whole human beings, a form of higher education that would take responsibility for the emergence of an integrated person.

I'll never forget an incident told to me by a professor of Portuguese language and literature from UMass Amherst, a dedicated teacher who had been teaching for a long time. One day, she said, she was walking down the street in Amherst when she saw this striking woman crossing the street—the woman seemed powerful and fearless as well as beautiful. Then the professor did a double take. This was the same undergraduate who had huddled in a seat at the back of her language class all semester, never opening her mouth. My friend said she never forgot that moment—how strong and free, full of life and energy the student seemed, compared to the weak, mousy person the professor had imagined her to be, because she wasn't very good at Portuguese.

One way of making education more holistic is to get outside the classroom and off the campus. It interrupts the programming twelve years of classroom conditioning automatically call up; the change in environment changes everything. The class becomes a social unit; students become more fully rounded human beings—not just people who either know the answer or don't know it. Inside the classroom, it's one kind of student that dominates; outside, it's another. Qualities besides critical thinking can come to light: generosity, steadfastness, determination, practical competence, humor, ingenuity, imagination. Tying course content to the world outside offers a real-world site for asking theoretical questions; it answers students' need to feel that their education is good for something other than a grade point average. And it begins to address the problem of the student who has no conception of what is possible after graduation.

The head of Duke's Career Development Center told me: There are two things students trust, their parents and their own experience. If their parents are pressuring them to attend professional school, then the only thing they have to place in the balance against that is some firsthand experience of the world. Staying inside the classroom won't provide them with that. As Montessori wrote in *The Absorbent Mind* in 1915: "The world of education is like an island where people, cut off from the world, are prepared for life by exclusion from it."

All the same, while speaking about the advantages of moving the classroom off-campus, I'm troubled by the memory of my own college days. I loved college, and the main reason I loved it had to do with being in a cloistered atmosphere. Without knowing it, I chose a small liberal arts college for women located in an affluent suburb because it did not ask me to cope with too many new things at once.

It was intellectual achievement above everything at Bryn Mawr, and I identified with that. It was bliss to be in a place where if you scored one hundred on your tests, it didn't mean people wouldn't like you. It was bracing to be indoctrinated by Bryn Mawr's ethos: that women not only could but should be intellectuals, could and should compete successfully with men in the world of mind, where, presumably there was no marrying or giving in marriage. So saturated was I in the values emanating from Bryn Mawr's unofficial motto—Only our failures marry (though I didn't take it literally; I knew you could get married and not be a failure as long as you also got your Ph.D.)—that I went to the best graduate school in my field and became a professor.

I realize as I write that one can never second-guess reality, that it's folly to look back and say I should have done this or not done that. Bryn Mawr's seclusion was probably right for me at the time, all I could have understood and coped with, given who I was. Though who knows? Perhaps if the college had offered a carefully crafted apprenticeship program or the chance to sample a variety of work situations, I might have sprung for the experience and ended up as a social worker or an editor or a journalist. Whatever the case may be, it was a different kind of omission that my education really suffered from, a more intrinsic lack. I wish that the college I bound my identity over to had introduced me to my heart. I wish it had set mercy and compassion before me as idols, instead of Athena's cold brow. I wish I had been encouraged to look inward, been guided on a quest for understanding my own turmoil, self-doubts, fears. How much pain it might have saved me later on.

This was a use for the cloister: to screen out the world and enable the gaze to turn inward in contemplation. For the growth of human beings an environment set apart and protected from the world is essential. But the cloister needs to be used for the purposes for which it was originally intended: quiet reflection, self-observation, meditative awareness. These are the gifts of the cloister that allow the heart to open without fear.

Most institutions of higher learning in our country do not address the inner lives of their students, except as a therapeutic stopgap. To get help with yourself, you have to go to a clinic and be assigned a psychiatric counsellor to help you with your problem, or, if you are a member of a mainstream religious denomination, you can go to its representative in the campus ministries. As far as the university is concerned, the core of the human being, his or her emotional and spiritual life, is dealt with as a necessary evil, on the sidelines, and the less heard about it the better. We don't want people to think of our students as having problems. But having a problem with your self is the existential dilemma, the human condition. Learning to deal with our own suffering is the beginning of wisdom. I didn't learn this—that is, that I had to start with myself—until I was in my late forties. I could have begun sooner.

The curriculum of American education, kindergarten through graduate school, is externally oriented. Even psychology and religion are externalized bodies of knowledge, with terminologies and methodologies and histories to be mastered like anything else. Every freshman can tell you that Socrates said, "Know thyself," but is she or he then given any way to carry out the charge? Undergraduates, you may say, are preoccupied with nothing but themselves. They are self-absorbed to a fault. Perhaps, but their self-preoccupation is a function of the stage of life they're at; they want to ask the big existential questions, and they want to know themselves in the Socratic sense. But instead of giving them the means, or the incentive, our present system sidelines this hugely important phase of human development and relegates it to the dormitory. Whoever wants to know herself is strictly on her own.

Occasionally in a literature class, or a women's studies class, undergraduates will be asked to write or speak from their own experience. Often they do so passionately, eloquently. But this is a kind of exception practiced in the corners of humanities departments and is widely regarded as "soft," unrigorous, not a substitute for history, methodology, theory, terminology, information. And of course it's not a substitute; it's simply knowledge of a different kind, but of a kind that, although essential to the conduct of every single human life, has practically no standing in our curricula.

I am not advocating a curriculum devoted exclusively to the pursuit of self-knowledge. I too well remember the rapture of my undergraduate days in the east wing of the Bryn Mawr library reading the thirteenth-century Italian poets. I loved the voyage out. It was full of wonder and excitement. But in order to have a balanced, nonobsessive relation to the world outside yourself, some inner balance and self-understanding are needed. Otherwise, your engagement with the world sooner or later becomes captive to the claims of obscure actors to whom you are paying hush money behind your own back. The old unmet demons—anger, fear, self-hatred, envy, you name it—end up running the show, under the guise of doing sociolinguistics, or molecular biology, or tax litigation, or child advocacy, or ikebana, or whatever it happens to be.

Inside and outside, the cloister and the world. We need both. But somehow higher learning has evolved to a point where it offers neither. Neither contact with the world nor contact with ourselves. This has come about because the university has relinquished responsibility for envisioning life as a whole. Instead, it has become an umbrella organization under which a variety of activities go on, but one that has no center and no soul. Correspondingly, the university doesn't see the student as a whole person but only as a kind of cutout part of a person, the intellect—a segment that it services diligently.

I don't know how to bring into being the world I'm trying to imagine here. I can't imagine it, really. All *I* can imagine are the kinds of adjustments I suggested in my report to the deans, such as: educating parents about the purpose of a liberal arts education, expanding and deepening the role of advisors, introducing more experience-based courses into the curriculum, finding ways to deemphasize grades. In fact, I'm *afraid* to envision the kind of world my experience has taught me to reach for because I fear it would seem too outlandish, too impossible. I don't think most of us ever try to imagine our ideal world as educators. We're not encouraged to, certainly. I have taught in colleges and universities for thirty years, but no one has ever said to me: "Tompkins, have your vision of an ideal university on my desk by tomorrow morning." When did anybody ever say that?

The university has come to resemble an assembly line, a mode of production that it professes to disdain. Each professor gets to turn one little screw—his specialty—and the student comes to him to get that little screw turned. Then on to the next. The integrating function is left entirely to the student. The advising system, which could be of great help, seems to exist primarily to make sure people don't bollix up their graduation requirements.

Higher education, in order to produce the knowledge and skills students need to enter certain lucrative professions, cuts students off from both their inner selves and the world around them. By not offering them a chance to know themselves and come into contact with the actual social environment, it prepares them to enter professional school but not to develop as whole human beings. Although parents might object—what, all that tuition and no ticket to financial security and social success?—it would be more helpful to students if, as a starting point, universities conceived education less as training for a career than as the introduction to a life.

QUESTIONS FOR REACTION AND DISCUSSION

1. How does Tompkins emerge as a person in this essay? What do you learn about her personal life and interests? What is the effect of this information on you as a reader?
2. Tompkins suggests that "classroom learning can constrict a person's horizons even as it broadens them." How? In what ways? Can you think of some specific examples? In a class discussion, exchange your responses to this statement.
3. How many students in your class are planning to be educators? Ask the students who are planning such a career to prepare a panel discussion about their reactions to Tompkins's criticisms about traditional teaching methods.
4. What does Tompkins mean by a "holistic" approach to education?
5. What does Tompkins finally assess as the value of the "cloister"? Would a better title for this essay have been "The Cloister and the World"? Why or why not?

QUESTIONS FOR WRITING

1. The subtitle of Tompkins's book is *What the Teacher Learned in School.* What have you as a student learned in school so far? Tompkins says that, as a teacher, she has come to see the classroom as a "place of opportunity." What is your view of the classroom as a student? Using your own educational experiences as the basis, write an essay entitled, "What the Student Learned in School."
2. Tompkins makes a number of observations about how classrooms restrict or dictate student responses. Conduct a study of one of the courses you are now taking and observe the "climate" of the classroom. How do the students and professors interact? What kinds of questions are asked and answered? Do students compete with one another? How? In what ways are the students and the professor performing? Write an analysis of the classroom you observe and discuss your opinion about what Tompkins calls "learning too well the lessons of the classroom."
3. Although Tompkins says that she is not finally advocating a college curriculum devoted "exclusively to the pursuit of self-knowledge," she strongly encourages colleges and universities to find ways to help students learn about themselves through more experienced-based courses and classrooms that are focused less on the teacher and more on the student. What ways are there on your campus for you to learn more about yourself? Have you participated in any classes or activities that promote self-knowledge? Write an essay in which you discuss the opportunities you have had to develop your own identity and speculate on additional ways in which your college or university could foster these experiences.

QUESTIONS FOR FURTHER EXPLORATION

1. Reaction to Tompkins's book, *A Life in School: What the Teacher Learned,* has been mixed. Called "controversial" by many, it was reviewed in a variety of magazines, newspapers, and academic journals. Locate three or four of the reviews and read them carefully. What criticisms did reviewers make? What praise did reviewers offer? Why do you think some reviewers felt so positively or negatively about the book? Write a report of the reviews you read, indicating the similarities and differences you found among the reviewers.
2. Access the University of Illinois, Chicago Web site <http://www.uic.edu> and investigate the programs that are offered through the Department of Education, where Tompkins teaches a course each year. What is the mission of the department? What special programs does the department offer? Write a summary of the department's activities that are of interest to you.

3. Tompkins begins this essay with a contrast between Bryn Mawr College, a small, private liberal arts college in suburban Philadelphia, and Temple University, a large, public university in the city of Philadelphia. Visit the Web sites <http://www.brynmawr.edu> and <http://www.temple.edu> and contrast the two institutions. How are they alike? How are they different? Why are these two schools effective in demonstrating Tompkins's concern that a cloister is both useful and a missed opportunity?

4. One of the educators quoted in this essay is Maria Montessori, author of *The Absorbent Mind,* whose ideas led to the development of Montessori Schools. Access the Montessori Web site <http://www.montessori.org> and investigate the mission of the Montessori Foundation and its programs and services. Why do you think the ideas of Montessori would appeal to Tompkins? Write a report of what you learn about Montessori schools for your classmates.

Suggestions for Further Reading, Thinking, and Writing

1. A number of writers in this section speculate about the nature of the contemporary college student—what major interests students have, how they should be educated, and even what kinds of social opportunities should be made available. How close are any of these writers' assessments of students to your own experience as a student now? Which writers seem out of touch with student interests? Why? Write an essay in which you defend or reject the portrayal of students offered by one or more of the writers in this section.

2. Some of the writers in this section, such as Kleinfield and Tompkins, discuss the everyday activities of the classroom—how students are treated, how professors conduct classes, and how students interact with one another. What does the college classroom reveal about the priorities of a college or university? How are most college classrooms arranged? Write an essay in which you analyze the classroom as a physical space, noting the features that suggest how colleges and universities think students learn.

3. In this section, Eitzen and Gose discuss at least some of the extracurricular activities that are available to students on a campus. What is the role of extracurricular activities at your school? What are the most popular activities? Who is involved? Conduct a survey of a dozen of your classmates and ask them to rate and comment on their favorite activities. Write a report of your finding.

4. As the AAUW Report and the essay by Kleinfield suggest, there is a considerable controversy about the extent to which gender differences are handled in school. How important do you think this topic is for the college classroom? What issues are apparent in the classes you have taken on your campus? Write an essay in which you explore the extent to which gender differences and student learning are acknowledged on your campus.

5. In this section, Rhoads discusses one group of students—gays and lesbians at Penn State—who were able to work together to change a

policy on their campus. On any campus, there are groups of students who, because of age, gender, sexual orientation, race, and ethnicity, share similar interests and goals. Select one of these categories and investigate the services available to a particular group on your campus. For example, what services are available to assist the particular needs of older students? What organizations serve the interests of African-American students? Write a report of the services available for one particular group.

6. According to the statistical profile of freshmen included in this section, college students represent a broad spectrum of religious beliefs. What activities are available on your campus for various religious groups? Are there specific centers for religious groups? How are they organized? Who directs them and what is their relationship to the college or university administration? What is the degree of student involvement? Select a religious group on your campus and write a profile of its activities and programs.

7. In her essay, Green profiles the ways in which a college degree does not necessarily determine a lifetime career. According to the statistical profile of freshmen, 12.1 percent of students expect to change their majors and 11.4 percent expect to change careers. Interview three or four working adults and ask them about their original major and career choices. Did they change their minds? Under what circumstances? How did they get the jobs they now hold? Write an essay in which you narrate the career paths of the people you interviewed.

8. Review the section of the statistical profile of freshman that is devoted to opinions, activities, and goals. To what extent does the extracurricular program on your campus "match" the opinion, activities, and goals of most freshmen? For example, 73.5 percent of the students surveyed attended a public concert or recital in the past year; 38.9 percent of the students surveyed indicated that an important objective was to become successful in their own business. Take some related opinions, activities, or goals used in the survey and study the extent to which the student ratings are reflected in your campus curriculum and extracurricular programs.

9. The extracurricular programs of colleges and universities have received increasing attention in recent years by students, faculty members, and administrators, especially because students and their parents have become more selective in the schools to which they apply. By using databases through your college or university library (such as ERIC), search for recent articles about extracurricular activities in higher education. What are the most important issues? How are colleges dealing with the high cost of sports and other facilities?

10. The purpose of this section of the text, "An Education of One's Own," is to invite you to read and think about the variety of ways in

which you can derive the most from your own college education. What have you learned from your reading, thinking, and writing? What are the major issues about your own education for you right now? What activities and programs on your campus do you need to know more about? Write an essay in the form of a letter to a close friend or to your parents assessing how you feel about your own education to this point.

FOR FURTHER READING
AND EXPLORATION

LITERACY NARRATIVES

Print

Andrews, William L., Ed. *Classic American Autobiographies*. New York: Penguin, 1992.

Antin, Mary. *The Promised Land*. New York: Houghton Mifflin, 1912.

Azoulay, Katya Gibel. *Black, Jewish, and Interracial: It's Not the Color of Your Skin, but the Race of Your Kin, and Other Myths of Identity*. Durham: Duke University Press, 1997.

Dyson, Michael Eric. *Making Malcolm: The Myth and Meaning of Malcolm X*. New York: Oxford University Press, 1995.

Eldred, Janet Carey, and Peter Mortensen. "Reading Literacy Narratives," *College English* 54 (1992): 512-39.

Erdoes, Richard. *Crying for a Dream: The World through Native American Eyes*. Santa Fe: Bear and Co., 1989.

Ewen, Elizabeth. *Immigrant Women in the Land of Dollars: Life and Culture on the Lower East Side, 1890-1925*. New York: Monthly Review Press, 1985.

Fishman, Andrea, and Glenda L. Bissex. *Amish Literacy: What and How it Means*. New York: Heinemann, 1992.

Haley, Alex, and Malcolm X. *The Autobiography of Malcolm X*. New York: Ballantine Books, 1964.

Keller, Helen. *The Story of My Life*. New York: Doubleday, 1907.

Merrifield, Juliet, Mary Beth Bingham, David Hemphill, and Kathleen P. Bennett deMarrais. *Life at the Margins: Literacy, Language, and Technology in Everyday Life*. New York: Teachers College Press, 1997.

Minatoya, Lydia. *Talking to High Monks in the Snow: An Asian-American Odyssey*. Harper Collins, 1992.

Rodriguez, Richard. *Days of Obligation: An Argument with My Mexican Father*. New York: Viking, 1992.

———. *Hunger of Memory: The Education of Richard Rodriguez*. Boston: Godine, 1981.

Rose, Mike. *Lives on the Boundary*. New York: Penguin, 1989.

Steiner, George. *Errata: An Examined Life*. New Haven: Yale University Press, 1998.

Sone, Monica. *Nisei Daughter*. Boston: Little, Brown, 1953.

Zaborowska, Magdalena. *How We Found America: Reading Gender through East European Immigrant Narratives*. Chapel Hill: University of North Carolina Press, 1995.

Electronic

American Memory, The Library of Congress <http://rs6.loc.gov/>

National Association for Bilingual Education <http://www.nabe.org>

674

The National Writing Project <http://www-gse.berkeley.edu/Research/NWP/nwp.html>
United States Department of Education <http://www.ed.gov>
The United States Holocaust Memorial Museum <http://www.ushmm.org>

THE PURPOSE OF A COLLEGE EDUCATION

Print

Bloom, Allan. *The Closing of the American Mind: How Higher Education Has Failed Democracy and Impoverished the Souls of Today's Students*. New York: Simon and Schuster, 1987.

Booth, Wayne. *The Knowledge Most Worth Having*. Chicago: University of Chicago Press, 1967.

———. *The Vocation of a Teacher*. Chicago: University of Chicago Press, 1988.

Cabranes, José a. "Our Common Ground." *The Wall Street Journal*. 9 June 1995.

Carnochan. W. B. *The Battleground of the Curriculum: Liberal Education and American Experience*. Stanford, CA: Stanford University Press, 1993.

Eliot, Charles W. "What Is a Liberal Education?" in Eliot, *Educational Reform: Essays and Addresses*. New York: Century Co., 1898.

Gless, Darryl J., and Barbara Herrnstein Smith, eds. *The Politics of Liberal Education*. Durham: Duke University Press, 1992.

Katz, Michael B. *The Irony of Early School Reform: Educational Innovation in Mid-Nineteenth Century Massachusetts*. Cambridge, MA: Harvard University Press, 1968.

Newman, John Henry. "The Idea of a University. In Discourses on the Scope and Nature of University Education." Dubuque, IA: Wm. C. Brown Reprint Library, 1967.

Nussbaum, Martha C. *Cultivating Humanity: A Classical Defense of Reform in Liberal Education*. Cambridge, MA: Harvard University Press, 1997.

Rudolph, Frederick. *Curriculum: A History of the American Undergraduate Course of Study Since 1636*. San Francisco: Jossey-Bass, 1977.

Schor, Ira, and Paulo Freire. *A Pedagogy for Liberation: Dialogues on Transforming Education*. South Hadley, MA: Bergin and Garvey, 1987.

Whitehead, Alfred North. *The Aims of Education and Other Essays*. New York: Macmillan, 1929.

Veysey, Laurence R. *The Emergence of the American University*. Chicago: University of Chicago Press, 1965.

Weingartner, Rudolph H. *Undergraduate Education: Goals and Means*. New York: American Council on Education, 1992.

Electronic

The American Association for Higher Education <http://www.aahe.org>
The American Council on Education <http://www.acenet.edu>
The Chronicle of Higher Education <http://chronicle.com>
College View <http://www.collegeview.com>

LITERACIES FOR A DIVERSE WORLD

Print

Bennet, William J. *To Reclaim a Legacy: A Report on the Humanities in Higher Education*. Washington, D.C.: National Endowment for the Humanities, 1984.

Cheney, Lynn V. *Telling the Truth: A Report on the State of the Humanities in Higher Education*. Washington, D.C.: National Endowment for the Humanities, 1992.

Cohen, Mark Nathan. *Culture of Intolerance: Chauvinism, Class, and Racism in the United States.* New Haven: Yale University Press, 1998.

Hirsch, E. D. *Cultural Literacy: What Every American Needs to Know.* Boston: Houghton Mifflin, 1987.

hooks, bell. *Talking Back: Thinking Feminist, Thinking Black.* Boston: South End Press, 1989.

Levine, Lawrence W. *The Opening of the American Mind: Canons, Culture, and History.* Boston: Beacon Press, 1996.

Morrison, Toni. "Black Matter(s)." *Grand Street* 40 (1991): 205-25.

Moffett, James. *The Universal Schoolhouse: Spiritual Awakening through Education.* New York: Calendar Islands, 1998.

Ravitch, Diane, and Chester E. Finn, Jr. *What Do Our 17-Year-Olds Know?* New York: Harper & Row, 1987.

Reed, Ishmael. "American: The Multinational Society," in *Multicultural Literacy.* Rick Simonson, Scott Walker, eds. St. Paul: Graywolf Press, 1988.

Takaki, Ronald. *A Different Mirror: A History of Multicultural America.* Boston: Little Brown, 1993.

U.S. Senate. *Indian Education: A National Tragedy—A National Challenge.* 91st Congress, 1st Session, 1969. Report #91-501.

Walzer, Michael. *On Toleration.* New Haven: Yale University Press, 1997.

Electronic

César E. Chávez Instructional Center in Interdisciplinary Chicana and Chicano Studies <http://www.sscnet.ucla.edu/chavez>

Core Knowledge Foundation <http://www.coreknowledge.org>

W.E.B. DuBois Institute for Afro-American Research <http://web-dubois.fas.harvard.edu>

CYBERLITERACY

Print

Birkerts, Sven. *The Gutenberg Elegies: The Fate of Reading in an Electronic Age.* Boston: Faber and Faber, 1994.

Bolter, Jay David. *Writing Space: The Computer, Hypertext, and the History of Writing.* Hillsdale, NY: Lawrence Erlbaum, 1991.

Hafner, Katie, and Matthew Lyon. *Where Wizards Stay Up Late: The Origins of the Internet.* New York: Simon and Schuster, 1996.

Hudson, David. *Rewired.* New York: Macmillan, 1997.

Landow, George P. *Hypertext 2.0: The Convergence of Contemporary Critical Theory and Technology.* Baltimore: Johns Hopkins University Press, 1997.

Lanham, Richard. *The Electronic Word: Democracy, Technology, and the Arts.* Chicago: University of Chicago Press, 1993.

Murray, Janet H. *Hamlet on the Holodeck: The Future of Narrative in Cyberspace.* New York: The Free Press, 1997.

Petersen, Rodney J., and Marjorie W. Hodges. "Legal, Ethical, and Policy Issues." *New Directions for Student Services* 78 (Summer 1997): 45-58.

Purves, Alan C. *The Web of Text and the Web of God: An Essay on the Third Information Transformation.* New York: The Guilford Press, 1998.

Electronic

Amerika, Mark: "Grammatron" <http://www.grammatron.com>

Blue Ribbon Campaign <http://www.eff.org/blueribbon.html>
Calliau, Robert. "A Little History of the World Wide Web." <http://www.w3.org/ History.html>
Center for Academic Integrity at Duke University <http://www.academicintegrity.org/>
Database of Government Web Sites <http://ciir2.cs.umass.edu/Govbot/>
Eastgate Systems, Inc. <http://www.eastgate.com>
Educational Technology Homepage, The White House <http://www.whitehouse.gov>
Molnar, Andrew R. "Computers in Education: A Brief History." *T.H.E. Journal Online,* June 1997. <http://www.thejournal.com/magazine/vault/A1681.cfm>
Salon Magazine <http://www.salonmagazine.com>
Slate <http//www.slate.com>

AN EDUCATION OF ONE'S OWN

Print

Bloom, Allan, trans. *The Republic of Plato.* 2nd ed. New York: Basic Books, 1991.

Figler, Stephen, and Howard Figler. *Going the Distance: The College Athlete's Guide to Excellence on the Field and in the Classroom.* Princeton, NJ: Peterson's Guides, 1991.

Fordahm, Signithia, and John U. Ogbu. "Black Students' School Success: Coping with the 'Burden of Acting White.'" *The Urban Review* 18 (1986): 176-206

Gardner, David P., et al. *A Nation at Risk: The Imperative for Educational Reform.* Washington, D.C.: Department of Education, 1983.

Gender Gaps: Where Schools Still Fail Our Children. Washington, D.C.: American Association of University Women Educational Foundation and National Education Association, 1998.

How Schools Shortchange Girls: The AAUW Report: A Study of Major Findings on Girls and Education. Washington, D.C.: American Association of University Women Educational Foundation and National Education Association, 1992.

Karabell, Zaccary. *What's College For? The Struggle to Define American Higher Education.* New York: Basic Books, 1998.

Loeb, Paul Rogat. *Generation at the Crossroads: Apathy and Action on the American Campus.* New Brunswick, NJ: Rutgers University Press, 1994.

Montessori, Marie. *The Absorbent Mind.* New York: Bantam, 1984.

Rhoads, Robert A. *Coming Out in College: The Struggle for a Queer Identity.* Westport, CT: Bergin & Garvey, 1994.

————. *Freedom's Web: Student Activism in an Age of Cultural Diversity.* Baltimore: Johns Hopkins University Press, 1998.

Schughart, William. "Protect College Athletes, Not Athletics." *The Wall Street Journal* 26 December 1990.

Seymour, Elaine and Nancy M. Hewitt. *Talking about Leaving: Why Undergraduates Leave the Sciences.* New York: Westview Press, 1997.

Tompkins, Jane. *A Life in School: What the Teacher Learned.* New York: Addison-Wesley, 1996.

Electronic

American Association of University Women Web Site <http://www.aauw.org>
The Gay and Lesbian Alliance against Defamation (GLAAD) <http://www.glaad.org>
National Assessment of Educational Progress <http://nces.ed.gov/nationsreportcard/site/home.asp>
National Collegiate Athletic Association (NCAA) <http://www.ncaa.org>
The National Organization for Women <http://www.now.org>
The United States Department of Labor <http://www.dol.gov>
The Women's Freedom Network <http://www.womensfreedom.org>

Guides to Conducting Research

Print

The American Psychological Association Publication Manual
The MLA Handbook
Munger, David, Daniel Anderson, Bret Benjamin, Christopher Busiel, and Bill Parades-Holt.
Researching Online. Second Edition. New York: Longman, 1999
The Turabian Guide
University of Chicago Style Publication Manual

Electronic

The Committee on Computers and Emerging Technologies in Teaching and Research of the MLA
   <http://www.mla.org/reports/ccet/ccet_index.htm>
"Information Literacy: The Web Is not an Encyclopedia." The University of Maryland.
   <http://www.inform.umd.edu/LibInfo/literacy>

CREDITS

INDEX